T&T Clark
Reader in Theological
Anthropology

T&T Clark Reader in Theological Anthropology

Edited by

Marc Cortez and Michael P. Jensen

Bloomsbury T&T Clark
An imprint of Bloomsbury Publishing Plc

B L O O M S B U R Y
LONDON · OXFORD · NEW YORK · NEW DELHI · SYDNEY

Bloomsbury T&T Clark

An imprint of Bloomsbury Publishing Plc

Imprint previously known as T&T Clark

50 Bedford Square	1385 Broadway
London	New York
WC1B 3DP	NY 10018
UK	USA

www.bloomsbury.com

BLOOMSBURY, T&T CLARK and the Diana logo are trademarks of Bloomsbury Publishing Plc

First published 2018

© Marc Cortez and Michael P. Jensen, 2018

Marc Cortez and Michael P. Jensen have asserted their right under the Copyright, Designs and Patents Act, 1988, to be identified as Author of this work.

British Library Cataloguing-in-Publication Data
A catalogue record for this book is available from the British Library.

ISBN: HB: 978-0-5676-5556-1
PB: 978-0-5676-5557-8
ePDF: 978-0-5676-5554-7
ePub: 978-0-5676-5555-4

Library of Congress Cataloging-in-Publication Data
Names: Cortez, Marc (Marc Allen), 1972- editor. | Jensen, Michael P. (Michael Peter), 1970- editor.
Title: T&T Clark reader in theological anthropology/edited by Marc Cortez and Michael P. Jensen.
Description: New York: Bloomsbury T&T Clark, An imprint of Bloomsbury Publishing Plc, 2017. | Includes bibliographical references and index.
Identifiers: LCCN 2017036094 (print) | LCCN 2017037339 (ebook) | ISBN 9780567655547 (ePDF) | ISBN 9780567655554 (ePUB) | ISBN 9780567655561 (hpod: alk. paper) | ISBN 9780567655578 (pbk.: alk. paper)
Subjects: LCSH: Theological anthropology.
Classification: LCC BL256 (ebook) | LCC BL256 .T29 2017 (print) | DDC 233–dc23
LC record available at https://lccn.loc.gov/2017036094

Cover image: Urban Rythms: Leicester Square Series (6x9'); oil on canvas, © Oona Hassim

Typeset by Deanta Global Publishing Services, Chennai, India
Printed and bound in Great Britain

CONTENTS

Introduction 1

1   Sources and Methods 7

    TEXT 1: Claus Westermann, *The Human in the Old Testament* 9

    TEXT 2: Werner Georg Kümmel, Man in the New Testament 20

    TEXT 3: J. Patout Burns, Theological Anthropology 25

    TEXT 4: Karl Barth, *Church Dogmatics* 33

    TEXT 5: Kathryn Tanner, "On the Difference Theological Anthropology Makes" 50

    TEXT 6: Ada María Isasi-Díaz, "Elements of a *Mujerista* Anthropology" 61

2   The Image of God 73

    TEXT 1: Augustine of Hippo, *The Literal Meaning of Genesis* 75

    TEXT 2: Thomas Aquinas *Summa Theologiae* 80

    TEXT 3 John Calvin, "Commentary Upon Gen. 1:26-28" 90

    TEXT 4: Karl Barth, *Church Dogmatics* 93

    TEXT 5: Mary McClintock Fulkerson "The Imago Dei and a Reformed Logic for a Feminist/Womanist Critique" 100

    TEXT 6: Colin Gunton "The Human Creation: Towards a Renewal of the Doctrine of the Imago Dei" 107

    TEXT 7: Michael S. Horton, "Image and Office Human Personhood and the Covenant" 117

3   Human Ontology 129

    TEXT 1: Tertullian, *A Treatise on the Soul* 131

    TEXT 2: Gregory of Nyssa, *On the Making of Humanity* 138

    TEXT 3: Thomas Aquinas, *Summa Theologica* 145

    TEXT 4: Hans Walter Wolff, "Nephesh" in *Anthropology of the Old Testament* 150

TEXT 5: Wolfhart Pannenberg, *Systematic Theology* 157

TEXT 6: Nancey C. Murphy, "Nonreductive Physicalism: Philosophical Issues" 170

TEXT 7: Alvin Plantinga, *Against Materialism* 180

4   Free Will 199

TEXT 1: Gregory of Nyssa "Sixth Sermon on the Beatitudes" 201

TEXT 2: Augustine, *On Grace and Free Will?* 207

TEXT 3: Anselm: *On Free Will* 213

TEXT 4: Desiderius Erasmus, On the Freedom of the Will, & Martin Luther "On the Bondage of the Will" 226

TEXT 5: William GT Shedd, *Dogmatic Theology* 234

TEXT 6: Peter G.H. Clarke, "Determinism, Brain Function and Free Will" 246

5   Gender and Sexuality 261

TEXT 1: Gregory of Nyssa, *On Virginity* 263

TEXT 2: Augustine, *Of the Good of Marriage* 269

TEXT 3: Thomas Aquinas, *Summa Theologiae* 273

TEXT 4: Martin Luther, *The Estate of Marriage* 277

TEXT 5: John Paul II, *Man and Woman He Created Them: A Theology of the Body* 285

TEXT 6: Rosemary Radford Ruether, "Can a Male Saviour Save Women?" 291

TEXT 7: Sarah Coakley, "The Eschatological Body: Gender, Transformation, and God" 300

6   Human Personhood 311

TEXT 1: John Zizioulas, "Human Capacity and Human Incapacity: A Theological Exploration of Personhood" 312

TEXT 2: Harriet A. Harris, "Should we say that personhood is relational?" 330

TEXT 3: Robert Spaemann, *Persons: The Difference between "Someone" and "Something"* 342

TEXT 4: Robert Jenson, *Systematic Theology* 350

TEXT 5: David H. Kelsey, *Eccentric Existence: A Theological Anthropology* 361

7 Worship and Desire 371

TEXT 1 Bernard of Clairvaux *On Loving God* 373

TEXT 2: John Calvin, *Institutes of the Christian Religion* 379

TEXT 3 William James *The Varieties of Religious Experience* 381

TEXT 4: Fergus Kerr, *Immortal Longings* 390

TEXT 5: Uffe Schjoedt, "The Religious Brain: A General
       Introduction to the Experimental Neuroscience of Religion" 395

Author Index 415

Subject Index 418

Introduction

In many ways, theological anthropology has become one of the most pressing areas of inquiry in theology today. Its primary topics are areas of intense debate: the nature of gender and sexuality, the ethics of sexual behavior, the difficulty of maintaining the freedom of the will or the existence of the "soul" in an increasingly materialist universe, and the pervasive challenges of various anthropological "isms" (e.g. racism, sexism, classism, and ageism). To such challenging debates we can add the rapid growth of information about the human person generated by such disparate disciplines as biology, the neurosciences, philosophy, sociology, and psychology, to name just a few. Thus, theological anthropology today stands at the juncture of rapidly expanding knowledge and intense debates about the proper ways in which to interpret that information and relate it to a theological understanding of the human person. Consequently, the modern era witnessed an unparalleled explosion of publications devoted specifically to theological anthropology as a distinct locus of theological reflection, as theologians from every tradition wrestle with this daunting task.

Despite the unrivaled attention that theological anthropology has received in the modern period, however, it would be a mistake to conclude that earlier theologians neglected the doctrine of humanity. It is true that few patristic theologians approached theological anthropology as a distinct focus of theological reflection. This stems partially from the fact that theologians devoted the majority of their efforts to issues surrounding the triune nature of God, the incarnation, salvation, and the church—which were the primary foci of the debates that these early theologians had to negotiate. With the exception of the free will debate that raged in the West around the theology of Pelagius, anthropological issues were rarely at the center of these controversies. Consequently, their creedal affirmations rarely addressed specifically anthropological concerns,[1] and few early theologians devoted entire works to the doctrine of humanity.[2] Another reason for the scarcity of explicitly anthropological

---

[1] However, the creeds do occasionally make anthropologically significant statements in the context of wrestling with other theological issues. For example, after affirming that Jesus was "truly man," the Chalcedonian definition indicates that this requires affirming that he had "a rational soul and body." Thus, it would not be true to say that the creeds have nothing to say about anthropology, only that this was not their primary focus.

[2] Among the important exceptions to this, see Basil, *On the Human Condition*, trans. Verna E. F. Harrison (Crestwood, N.Y: St. Vladimir's Seminary Press, 2005); Gregory of Nyssa, "On the Making of Man," in *A Select Library of the Nicene and Post-Nicene Fathers*, ed. Philip Schaff, vol. 5, Series 2 (Grand Rapids: Eerdmans, 1978); Nemesius, *On the Nature of Man*, trans. Philip Van Der Eijk and R. W. Sharples (Liverpool: Liverpool University Press, 2008).

works, however, is the fact that these theologians seem to have viewed *theology itself* as inherently anthropological.[3] The drama of redemption necessarily involves sustained reflection on the redeemed. Thus, rather than writing *separate* theological treatises on anthropology, they typically engaged anthropological concerns in the context of other theological issues because they did not think it necessary—maybe not even *possible*—to address those other doctrines apart from some understanding of the human person. How does one talk about the Creator without the creature? The incarnation apart from some concept of the human nature? Salvation apart from who is being saved? The church apart from those who comprise the church and the purpose for which they are gathered? Eschatology apart from some vision of true human flourishing? And so on. Viewed from this perspective, the lack of separate treatises on anthropology suggests the *centrality* of theological anthropology, not its neglect.

Although the essentially integrative nature of theological anthropology remained true in later periods as well, with the rise of more systematic approaches to theology in the medieval period, theologians began to devote more attention to anthropology as a distinct locus of theological reflection.[4] Anthropology thus developed into an identifiable "doctrine" with its own set of traditional questions and concerns: most often the origin of humanity and the relationship between humans and other creatures, the image of God, the body-soul relationship, the freedom of the will, the impact of sin, and the ultimate destiny of humanity. The idea that anthropology is an identifiable doctrine that warrants consideration alongside the other major doctrinal loci has characterized Christian theology ever since. Indeed, although an early theologian like Augustine could produce his immense corpus without ever devoting a single treatise to anthropology in its own right,[5] it is now rather standard to devote a chapter, or even an entire book, to the doctrine of humanity when writing in systematic theology.[6]

These historical developments create real challenges for producing a reader in theological anthropology. First, any reader like this faces the challenge of selecting

---

[3]For an excellent study of this, see M. C. Steenberg, *Of God and Man: Theology as Anthropology from Irenaeus to Athanasius* (London: T & T Clark, 2009).

[4]In Lombard's *Sentences*, for example, the doctrine of humanity comprises well over half of Book II, which focuses on the theology of creation and the fall. Similarly, Thomas Aquinas offers extended treatments of anthropology in his *Summa Theologica* (esp. I.Q75-102 and I-II.Q.1-70).

[5]Augustine did produce several works that focused on particular issues within anthropology. For example, he wrote treatises on the nature of the soul, the significance of marriage, and even the proper care of the dead. And, of course, he wrote extensively on the issue of the "will," especially through the course of his debate with Pelagius. Unlike some of his contemporaries (e.g. Gregory of Nyssa), however, Augustine did not focus any of his writings on the doctrine of humanity as a whole.

[6]Karl Barth, for example, devoted an entire part-volume of the *Church Dogmatics* to theological anthropology (III/2). The doctrine receives similar attention in other modern systematic theologies like Hans Urs von Balthasar, *Theo-Drama: Theological Dramatic Theory: The Dramatis Personae: Man in God, Vol. 2*, trans. Graham Harrison (San Francisco: Ignatius Press, 1990); Louis Berkhof, *Systematic Theology* (London: Banner of Truth, 1984); Millard J. Erickson, *Christian Theology* (Grand Rapids: Baker, 1998); Stanley J. Grenz, *Theology for the Community of God* (Grand Rapids: Eerdmans, 2000); Robert W. Jenson, *Systematic Theology* (New York: Oxford University Press, 1997); Anthony C. Thiselton, *Systematic Theology* (Grand Rapids, MI: Eerdmans, 2015); Karl Rahner, *Foundations of Christian Faith: An Introduction to the Idea of Christianity*, trans. William V. Dych (New York: Crossroad, 1982).

the authors it will highlight in the readings. How do you determine which voices to privilege? One of the primary goals of this reader in particular is to help students of theological anthropology develop an awareness of how theologians have addressed key anthropological issues throughout history. Yet the very centrality of anthropology means that no single set of readings could possibly represent all the diverse perspectives on humanity that have been offered by Christian theologians. Given the lack of creedal affirmations about key anthropological issues, it is not even possible to orient the selected readings around "orthodox" perspectives on anthropology. Nonetheless, you have to begin somewhere. So we have chosen to highlight those thinkers whose perspectives have had the greatest impact on theological anthropology. This necessarily requires us to downplay more "marginal" perspectives, some of which might offer even more interesting insights into human nature, but which have not shaped subsequent reflection to the same degree. This is particularly the case in the readings from the earlier periods, where it is a matter of historical judgment which voices have had the greatest impact on subsequent developments. For those readings that we have selected from the modern period, of course, such historical judgments are far more difficult to make. Consequently, those readings reflect more of a judgment about perspectives that are having the greatest impact on contemporary discussions. Given modern theology's appreciation of both the value and the necessity of diverse theological expressions, then, it is in these more recent readings that we will see the greatest emphasis on perspectives that may have been viewed as more marginal in earlier periods.

The challenge of selectivity arises in a second area as well. A reader like this must not only select particular voices, but it must also privilege certain topics to the exclusion of others. To adequately represent how theologians have approached anthropology throughout history, some of those choices have virtually been made for us. Issues like the *Imago Dei*, the constitution of the human person, free will, and sexuality have dominated Christian reflection on the human person from the beginning. Other topics, however, may not have received as much attention throughout history, but they are still important for understanding theological anthropology today. Thus, for example, the readings in Chapter 1 focus on some of the issues surrounding the proper method of theological anthropology. As many have noted, modern theology evidences a particular preoccupation with methodological questions. Rather than simply assuming a particular way of addressing theological issues, as earlier theologians tended to do, modern theologians often reflect at some length on the proper way to engage a theological issue. Thus, the readings in this chapter wrestle with a number of questions that rarely troubled earlier theologians: What is theological anthropology? What is the proper starting point for understanding the human person? How does a *theological* perspective on anthropology relate to other anthropological disciplines like biology or sociology? What topics should theological anthropology address? Such questions are now characteristic of modern theological approaches, making it important to devote at least some space to such considerations in this reader. We could say the same about the chapters on personhood and race. Although the tradition has not been entirely silent on these issues, they certainly have not dominated to the extent that they do in modern theological anthropology. Consequently, each of these chapters will differ somewhat from the other chapters in this reader in that they will not evidence the same degree of historical diversity as the others, necessarily privileging modern perspectives on the issues. Nonetheless, it seemed to us that they were simply too important to theological anthropology to exclude them.

This last comment leads to a final challenge created by the historical development of theological anthropology. As mentioned earlier, theological anthropology tended not to be a distinct theological locus in the patristic period. Instead, patristic theologians integrated their anthropological discussions into their discussions of other theological loci. That often makes it difficult to find discrete anthropological discussions for a reader like this. To include those insights, we often faced the difficulty of either including short excerpts that would have been isolated from their original theological context or including more of that original context at the risk of having readings that were not clearly focused on theological anthropology. To appreciate the complexity of the arguments developed by each of our authors, we determined that it would be most helpful if we retained as much of the original context as possible, thus avoiding the "short excerpt" approach, but we also chose to avoid readings in which anthropology was merely an embedded issue in a larger theological discussion. Although we were able to identify good patristic readings for each chapter, this necessarily means that these readings may not reflect the full diversity and creativity of patristic reflection on the human person. For that we apologize. We can only hope that the readings we have included will spark interest in these early perspectives on the human person, motivating people to dive into those early sources for themselves so they too can appreciate the breadth of insight they offer.

Before moving on to the content of the readings, we should also make a few comments about the style and format of these excerpts. Although we have chosen to utilize longer excerpts than you will find in many readers, we still found it necessary to trim those readings for the sake of space. In cases where we have omitted material that is relatively short and falls under the same heading in the original text, we have used ellipses. Where it became necessary to omit larger blocks of text, particularly any text that contained headings or subheadings, we indicated these omissions with a series of asterisks. Another formatting decision arose with the question of footnotes. In order to retain as much of the main body of the text as possible, we chose to eliminate footnotes unless they were necessary to support a direct quotation in the text. Consequently, the numbering of the footnotes in these excerpts will not necessarily match the numeration of the original text. Finally, we have chosen to retain the language of the original texts, even where such texts use gendered language in ways that would be considered inappropriate in academic discourse today (e.g. using "man" as a generic term for all humanity).

With these three challenges in mind, you will hopefully appreciate the reasons behind how we selected the particular topics and readings for this project. Chapter 1 reflects some of our modern preoccupations by starting the project with questions of the proper methods and content of theological anthropology. The overarching question in this chapter is what makes an anthropology properly *theological*. Many modern disciplines are hard at work answering the question "What does it mean to be human?" What does it look like to offer a distinctively *theological* answer to this question? And how does such an answer relate to those other perspectives? Should theological anthropology participate in this broader dialog about humanity? If so, what are the rules by which this anthropological conversation should conduct itself?

Chapter 2 shifts its attention to the topic that has long served as the central issue in theological anthropology: the *Imago Dei*. This topic radiates out from a specific biblical passage: Gen. 1:26-8; but the exegetical and theological debate doesn't stop there, because of the Christological use that the New Testament makes of this motif. What does it mean to image God? How has this been affected by the impact of sin? To what extent should our view of the image shape our understanding of what it means to live fully human lives today? Embedded in this last question is an ongoing concern that definitions of the *Imago* have been driven by cultural conceptions that privilege certain kinds of humanity (esp. conceptions of the "ideal male") to the denigration of other forms of humanity.

Chapter 3 dives into another of the perennial topics in anthropology: the constitution of the human person. Theologians have long recognized the Bible's emphasis on the physicality of the human person. We are embodied beings at creation, we long for the eschatological consummation of our physicality in the resurrection, and the incarnation itself exemplifies the intrinsic importance of the body. Thus, the earliest theologians wrestled with and rejected the temptation toward a gnostic rejection of the body's intrinsic goodness. At the same time, though, they also had to deal with biblical language about the eternal value of the human soul or spirit, and many passages that suggested a more reserved attitude toward human physicality, at least in its fallen condition (e.g. Paul's warnings about the "flesh"). From its earliest period, then, theologians wrestled with the relationship between two forms of biblical discourse: that which appears to value the intrinsic goodness "material" realities like the body and that which seems to privilege "immaterial" realities like the human soul or spirit. Do these two ways of speaking refer to discrete parts of the human person (e.g., dualism) or are they just ways of speaking about complex aspects of human life (e.g., nonreductive physicalism)? Although earlier theologians may not have used the more precise labels of modern anthropology, we will see that they nevertheless wrestled with many of the same questions.

In Chapter 4 we engage the freedom of the will, a topic that has generated perhaps the most heated debates in theological anthropology. The readings in this chapter focus on demonstrating why theologians have found this to be a vital issue to address in a Christian understanding of the human person and why well-respected theologians from various traditions have landed on different sides of this perennial debate. It is intriguing that though this debate has taken different forms down the centuries, it is still reappearing. In what sense is the human will "free," if at all? Is that the right adjective to use for a creature who is so embedded in creation? But if the human will is not in some sense "free," can there be any meaningful discussion of morality?

Chapter 5 turns to the issues surrounding human sexuality. Although this has become a dominant topic in modern theological anthropology, we will see that theologians throughout history have reflected on what it means that God created us "male and female," and how this shapes our understanding of humanity. A key question in this section is whether we should view sexuality as essential to being human or whether we should emphasize our common humanity and present sexuality as an important but secondary anthropological reality. This will also lead us into some of the questions about the relationship between culture and sexuality, or to the extent to which culture shapes how we understand and express our sexuality.

In Chapter 6, we raise the notion of human "personhood." The idea of a "person" is a curious one, since it emerges from the vocabulary of the Trinitarian debates of the third and fourth centuries as a way of describing the different members of the Trinity in their distinctness. Human beings share this "personhood" with the divine persons. But what exactly distinguishes a person from any other sort of being? Are the nonhuman creatures persons—and if not, then in what sense not? The term has been both helpful and unhelpful in discussions of theological (and general) anthropology well into the modern era. The readings in this chapter are all very recent, but reference the long theological debates about idea of personhood.

Chapter 7 is concerned with the question of to what degree and in what way human beings are made as worshipping creatures. The phenomena of human religiosity is extraordinarily diverse, and deeply persistent. The readings in this section take both theological and 'scientific' perspectives—especially given the recent interest from neuroscientists in human religious feelings. But the discussion of the human longing for God also has a theological dimension: Is our sense of the transcendent indicative of God, and of the nature of God, or is it a idolatrous distraction? And in the allegedly secular age in which we now live, is there any apologetic value in this endemic sense that there is something beyond us?

Despite the breadth and diversity of the following readings, we cannot lose sight of the fact that these readings offer no more than a glimpse of the manifold ways that Christians through the ages have sought to understand the complexity of the human person. Rather than offering a comprehensive summary of Christian theological anthropology, we hope that these readings will serve as more of an entry point, illuminating some of the key questions and highlighting some of the more significant perspectives. As such, they should help spark meaningful reflection and conversation about the perennial question of the human, captured by the psalmist with his query, "What is mankind that you are mindful of them, human beings that you care for them?" (Ps. 8:4).

1

Sources and Methods

One of the great challenges in theological anthropology comes from the diversity of its sources and the challenging methodological questions that arise from navigating that complexity. If we define theological anthropology as the discipline that reflects theologically on what it means to be human, we immediately encounter the question of where we derive the data upon which we are to reflect.

One possibility, of course, is that theological anthropology should focus primarily on the ways in which the human person is presented in the biblical texts. Indeed, it is difficult to see how any anthropology could be considered adequately theological unless it engaged seriously with the anthropological insights of the biblical authors. In this chapter, then, the readings from Westermann and Kümmel introduce the reader to the many perspectives on the human person offered in both the Old and New Testaments.

As important as the biblical texts are as sources for theological anthropology, though, most theologians have recognized the importance of engaging with other sources as well. And here the task becomes truly daunting. Nearly every field of human activity offers some anthropological data, some perspective on what it means to be human. The theologian, for example, faces an overwhelming amount of information from the sciences, disciplines like biology, chemistry, the neurosciences, psychology, and sociology, each offering an ever-growing mountain of data about different aspects of human existence. The arts present a similarly diverse array of perspectives, every author, poet, artist, and musician saying something about the human condition. We could continue this list almost indefinitely: philosophy, economics, religious studies, politics, law, history medicine, and more. Indeed, we can understand entire cultures as complex presentations of some view of human flourishing along with the manifold ways in which societies seek to implement and sustain their vision of humanity, all of which requires theological anthropology to be aware of the importance of historical and cultural location. Engaging anthropological insights from other times and places broadens and deepens each of these sources, helping us see the ways in which society itself shapes, and often limits, our vision of what it means to be human.

Needless to say, finding data upon which to reflect has never been a challenge for theological anthropology. Instead, the difficulty has always come from understanding the relationship between these non-theological approaches to studying humanity and a properly theological account of what it means to be human. As we will see in the reading from J. Patout Burns, this is not a new challenge. From the beginning, the theologians of the church utilized resources from their cultural context to develop their vision of humanity, a pattern that continued throughout the history of theological anthropology. With the rise of modernity's preoccupation with methodological issues, though, we find a growing desire to address more explicitly anthropology's interdisciplinary nature. Should the theologian seek to integrate these various insights into her theological account of humanity? If so, how? These questions are the focus of the readings from Barth, Van Huyssteen, Isasi-Diaz, and Tanner. Each offers a slightly different perspective from which to address the questions that surround the sources and methods of a properly theological approach to anthropology.

TEXT 1: CLAUS WESTERMANN,
THE HUMAN IN THE OLD TESTAMENT[1]

Claus Westermann (1909–2000), a professor of Old Testament at the University of Heidelberg, was one of the most prominent Old Testament scholars of the twentieth century, writing prolifically on Genesis, Psalms, and Old Testament theology. The Old Testament offers a diverse array of perspectives on the nature of human existence. From the narratives of creation in Genesis—with their emphasis on the human person as the divine image bearer who stands as a creature before the sovereign Creator and called to a particular vocation in the created world—to the wisdom books with their emphasis on the quotidian realities of everyday human living, the Old Testament presents human persons as complex beings who struggle to live faithfully before God and each other.

Although no single article could possibly do justice to the diverse anthropological perspectives we find in the Old Testament, this reading highlights a number of important themes that Westermann sees as central to the Old Testament's vision of humanity. He thus begins with the fact of creation, which he contends is a fundamental assumption about humanity that pervades the entire Old Testament. However, his emphasis throughout is that although the authors of the Old Testament occasionally reflected in more abstract terms on the origin and destiny of humanity, they primarily focused on stories about everyday human experience. He thus highlights how the Old Testament reflects on the significance of such common human experiences as birth, death, and work, as well as the fundamental importance of the human community we experience in the family and society. Old Testament anthropology, for Westermann, is really about understanding human persons who stand before God as both individuals and communities seeking to live out this calling in their everyday realities.

In a little known story at the end of the book of Judges, we are told about a man taking a journey with his concubine and his servant. Arriving at Gibeah, they meet an old man.

> And the old man said, "Where are you going? and whence do you come?" And he said to him, "We are passing from Bethlehem in Judah to the remote parts of the hill country of Ephraim, from which I come. I went to Bethlehem in Judah; and I am going to my home; and nobody takes me into his house. We have straw and provender for our asses, with bread and wine for me and your maidservant and the young man with your servants; there is no lack of anything." And the old man said, "Peace be to you; I will care for all your wants; only, do not spend the night in the square." So he brought him into his house, and gave the asses provender; and they washed their feet, and ate and drank. (Judges 19:17b–21)

---

[1]Claus Westermann, "The Human in the Old Testament," *Word & World* 9, no. 4 (1989): 318–27. Originally published as *Der Mensch im Alten Testament,* Schriften des Evangelischen Arbeitskreises für kulterelle Fragen (Bremen: B. C. Heye, n. d.). Translated and edited by Frederick J. Gaiser.

That is the human in the Old Testament—someone we meet in a story like this one, with its everyday atmosphere. We can only understand this Old Testament picture of humanity if we are prepared to enter its simple everyday world, to affirm that world and participate in it.

What is fascinating about this brief segment of the Judges story, despite its distance from us, is the peculiar and finely nuanced dignity given simple events and conversations. The traveler seeking shelter does not go door to door, but waits for someone to speak to him and offer an invitation. The old man coming home from work addresses the stranger and inquires about him, taking him in with no thought of remuneration. We are quietly introduced to the order of an intact community, where each person has a clearly determined place and where the common life, down to the smallest detail, is carefully structured.

This story brings to mind other, better known stories from the Old and New Testaments: Mary and Joseph on the way to Bethlehem or fleeing to Egypt, the visit of the divine messengers to Abraham, the wooing of Rebekah by Abraham's servant. Considering these together helps us see something about the Bible that we must learn anew, namely, that its stories take place in our own world, between ordinary people like ourselves, in the various forms and relationships of life which belong—also for us—to human existence.

I The human as creature

The human is a creature among creatures. We probably no longer perceive that so directly as did the people of the Old Testament. In the course of the development of western culture the simple juxtaposition of creator and creature has gradually been replaced by that of humanity and nature. As the human began to be seen as the center of all things, God was removed to a distant transcendence; humanity's opposite number became nature—something to be comprehended and ruled. Then as the technical consequences of scientific development eroded a unified concept of nature and produced a humanity which in its everyday life had to do with technical production and with things that were technically produced, the biblical notion of creature and creator was pushed even farther into the background. The basic question today is not at all whether or not one believes in a creator—this question is much too abstractly formulated for the present situation; the basic question is much more whether or not we can find any clear and genuine way to relate our technicalized existence—as we now have to live it, with its machines, its nuclear physics, and its modern genetics—to what the Bible says about God the creator.

It is important, therefore, to listen anew to the biblical witness, asking what it has to say to today's changed world that we cannot hear elsewhere.

The human is a creature among creatures. In the Old Testament that is not something people must be taught or which must be revealed to them. It is taken for granted, completely natural; it encompasses all human thought and life. The world around us cannot be understood as anything but creation, a creation which participates fully in the worshipful joy humans direct to God. Sun and moon, fire and hail, snow and frost join in praising the creator (Psalm 148).

Israel in exile, trapped in weary mourning, is reminded of the "creator of the ends of the earth," who "does not faint or grow weary" (Isa 40:28). When people in such situations realize that they themselves are creatures of God, the questions that plague us—like whether or not it is possible to harmonize creation and evolution— become irrelevant. They have nothing to do with this joy in being creature, this respectful astonishment over the miracle of being human—made "little less than God" and crowned with "glory and honor" (Ps 8:5). The people of the Old Testament were amazingly aware of what it meant to be creatures of God:

> O Lord, thou has searched me and known me!
> Thou knowest when I sit down and when I rise up;
> thou discernest my thoughts from afar. (Psalm 139:1–2)

Words like these speak to us directly across the intervening millenia; but what we do not hear, what we must learn again from the Bible, is that this knowledge— that as creatures we always stand before God—is accompanied by a full and complete affirmation of this creatureliness. When the singer of Psalm 139 says, You are "acquainted with all my ways" (v. 3), he means the daily ways on this earth—his everyday concerns in all their variety. The Old Testament makes no attempt to present us with a doctrine or abstract portrayal of "the human." It speaks about a general humanity only rarely and peripherally. Normally, its human is a man or a woman or a child, someone with a name who appears on a rather small stage at a particular time and place. It is important for the Old Testament to tell us who the father and mother were of the person under consideration; hunger and thirst play a significant role as do the variety of physical movements and gestures—like a greeting or a shining face.

Great attention is paid to the basic phenomena of human need: hunger and thirst, exhaustion and illness. The Bible knows that a healthy person is not the same as a sick one. It knows that a person dying of lack of water can no longer think beyond the reality of thirst; that one who is totally exhausted needs compassion rather than moral admonition. Only one who has personally known a similar situation can comprehend why Israel held on to the memory of its years of famine and thirst up to the end and why it never forgot that the one who is thirsty experiences God's miraculous power in a drink of fresh water.

Consider two passages which seem to stand in marked contrast to one another. First, there is the drastic description of the murmuring of the people in the wilderness with its detailed list of the things for which they hunger: fish, cucumbers, melons, leeks, onions, and garlic (Num 11:5). The particularity is an indication that the memory is real—as anyone who has ever been in a similar situation can confirm. On the other hand, in apparent contrast to this, a sermon reflecting on the same period announces:

> And he humbled you and let you hunger and fed you with manna, which you did not know, nor did your fathers know; that he might make you know that man does not live by bread alone, but by everything that proceeds out of the mouth of the Lord. (Deut 8:2–3)

Actually, the two things belong together: the realism of hard experience and the proclamation as a present reality of the help once experienced.

II The human between birth and death

In the creation faith of the Old Testament, the individual human is always seen in the context of an existence that spans birth and death. Every age group has its particular and necessary function, and only a community which includes both children and elderly can be called intact.

One must realize, of course, that in the Old Testament period the family had a different structure than today. Because of early marriage, successive generations were much closer to each other. Further, the still purely agrarian economy made possible a closely shared life in an extended family. Even more important, the relationship between old and young was not primarily a matter of authority (as is usually surmised from our present distance); authority arose as a consequence of the blessing; it was the blessing which finally held young and old together in the family. We can only comprehend this with great difficulty. The old, even the very old, had something to pass on to the young which the young could get nowhere else than in the blessing received from their elders. The actual content of that blessing cannot be described or explained. It is that which has matured—that which God has made mature—in a person's life. And the elderly could pass this on, at least in part, to the young. That was the basis for the respect shown to elders (which is nicely described in Job's reflection on his previous good fortune [Job 29:7–111]). This is also why wisdom has its place in the Bible. For it is in the realm of wisdom that the blessing is effective; wisdom is something which can only grow and mature.

At the same time, the young have their own distinct voice in the Old Testament. Being human includes exuberance and enthusiasm. Judges is a decidedly youthful book, marked by the exuberance of youthful enthusiasm. The history of the monarchy is also largely the story of the deeds and decisions of quite young persons.

It is important to all the narratives that the human be taken seriously in the whole course of life. As a touching feature of the laws of war, we learn that a young man who is newly married is relieved of military duty so that he can participate in the blessing meant for him.

In the Old Testament, death is also understood in its relationship to the whole course of life. The extermination of a young person who is in the midst of life, whose powers are just developing, is not the same as the death of one who, as the texts often say, is "old and full of years." Death is not merely the cessation of life; it is a power breaking into the midst of life.

> Man that is born of a woman
>   is of few days, and full of trouble.
> He comes forth like a flower, and withers;
>   he flees like a shadow, and continues not. (Job 14:1–2)

But over against this knowledge of death and its power stands a radiant joy of life, as shown, for example, by the psalm of Hezekiah:

For Sheol cannot thank thee, death cannot praise thee ...
The living, the living, he thanks thee, as I do this day. (Isa 38:18–19)

That this joy in life breaks out in praise of God—indeed, that it is virtually identified with the praise of God—is particularly characteristic of the Old Testament's understanding of existence. It corresponds exactly to Psalm 139's amazed consciousness that being creature is what it means to exist before God.

III Human work

Work is included without question as part of human existence—the work of the peasant, the shepherd, the handworker, in a poor land and on stony ground. With a contrast that is difficult for us to explain, two passages describing the work of the peasant stand at the beginning of the Old Testament. In the story of the exodus, Canaan is called the land flowing with milk and honey; yet in one of the creation narratives the ground is cursed: "Thorns and thistles it shall bring forth to you ... In the sweat of your face you shall eat bread" (Gen 3:18–19). Both passages can only be understood in their contexts. To the Israelites wandering in the desert, the cultivated land which was their goal seemed a land of milk and honey. Even when they had long since discovered how poor and meager it was, they never forgot how they had once longed for it; it remained for them the gift of God they had once seen from the desert. That is precisely why it was so hard for them to deal with the experience of thorns and thistles. Their struggle with difficult experience is reflected in the story of the cursing of the ground. It would be a crude misunderstanding to say that in this curse work itself is cursed. Rather, this text is based on the deep realization that all human work has to come to terms with thorns and thistles, that there is no such thing as ideal work, and that no one can become happy through work alone. But this realization does not alter the fact that, before their disobedience to God, human beings were given the commission to till and to keep the garden. This commission includes all work worthy of humanity—even up to the present day. Every human work, insofar as it understands itself to be involved with tilling and keeping the ground (of whatever kind), takes place as a divine commission.

But the Old Testament does not include only this general word upon which all human work is based; it also considers the differences in work that arise in the course of social development. Traces of such thought occur already in the story of Jacob and Esau. One can clearly recognize an older form of the narrative, behind the present one, in which the vocations of peasant farmer and nomadic shepherd are played against one another. In a later text, the differentiation of human work, with all its problematic, comes right to the surface. Along with Israel's monarchy, there arose a group of people who were opposed to it. Their polemic against the innovation of the monarchy included the Jotham fable (Judges 9:8–15), which views the rule of the king with contempt compared to the work of those who produce something useful. It is a protest of the free farmer against this new form of permanent sovereignty.

What has been scarcely noticed is that the Old Testament already displays early traces of a more decisive development in human work, whose full effects have been seen only in the last two centuries, namely, technological inventions. I will not dwell on the fact that the transition from the Bronze Age to the Iron Age can be seen in several Old Testament passages (part of the reason for the rule of the Philistines over the Israelites is their privileged access to the production of iron; at that time a revolutionary new weapon arose: the war chariot). More important for us is the passage which reflects one of the greatest technological discoveries of human history: the fathoming of the earth itself in mining. Excavations in Palestine have found beginnings of mining and of metallurgy already in the time of Solomon. Such mining is described in the book of Job in such a way that one can sense the joy of astonishment over this human invention (Job 28:1–11). This is one of the very few passages in the Bible that talks about what we would call human technical progress. It is important that such work is here affirmed; the text's joyful sympathy with this new human possibility cannot be overlooked.

The Old Testament knows the work of the mind as well and regards it highly. Early on, the wisdom teacher already belonged in a leadership role, alongside the prince, the priest, and the prophet. Wisdom had so much significance that collections of proverbs and wisdom songs found their way into Holy Scripture, even though they deal essentially with matters that are fully profane. We can observe here how the first traces of scientific thought grow out of the process of observation, comparison, and abstraction seen in the simple popular maxims (found among all peoples of the earth). An example would be the observations of nature found in Proverbs 30:24–28.

The book of Ecclesiastes, at the very periphery of the Old Testament, looks at the theme of human investigation, an investigation that wants to explore everything—but it is seen there with deep skepticism:

All this I have tested by wisdom; I said, "I will be wise"; but it was far from me. That which is, is far off, and deep, very deep; who can find it out? (Eccl 7:23–24; cf. also 8:16–17)

IV Human community

Today we are in the midst of a transformation of human community whose radicality is comparable only to that of the period which saw the beginnings of human agriculture and permanent settlement. The proclamation and counsel of the Christian church in this revolution dare not exhaust itself with a call to hold on to the old forms. On the other hand, neither is it helpful for some to try frantically to be as modern as possible and to be involved in everything. What we need is thorough and fundamental deliberation over the relationship of the church to the other elements of society that are undergoing change. Up to now, the Old Testament has not been sufficiently employed in such deliberation; in my opinion, it has more to say about the basic relationships of human community than has previously been recognized. Such an area of inquiry is, of course, so broad that here I can make only a few suggestions.

A Community and individual

It is fundamental to the Old Testament understanding of human beings that the human is not seen first as an individual—who then goes on to build communities— but as one who is from the beginning part of a larger pre-existing entity. The human is not the tree, but the branch; not an organism, but an organ; the human is a member of a body. The traditional order of the biblical narrative makes it appear that the human was first created as an individual, with family and nation following thereafter. But as it actually arose, the Old Testament begins with the journey of a group, as reported in the book of Exodus. The foundational experience of Israel's history is the experience of a group, not that of an individual. The individual participates in this history only as he or she participates in the whole.

The cycle of stories that begins with the exodus and runs to the conquest of the promised land contains not one single episode that revolves around the destiny of an individual. (The only exception is Moses, the group leader; but even then we are told only that which belongs unavoidably to his office.) Only in one other epoch of Israel's history do stories about individuals fully disappear behind the story of the group: the time of the exile. The prophet of the exile, Second Isaiah, is the only one of the prophets whose words always address only the whole community, never a single individual.

These two epochs—exodus and exile—are the two periods of most intensive waiting and hoping, waiting and hoping for a home or for a return home. In other words, there are in God's history with his people times when the destiny of the individual must give way completely to the destiny of the whole group. But it is not God's will that such periods should endure. The Bible can never be used to affirm a theory of human society which sees as the desired goal the dissolution of the individual—of personal relationships and personal destiny—into the communal or the collective.

On the other hand, the history of the people of God does inevitably include those moments when the individual and individual destiny recede in the face of an elemental threat to the whole. During the forty years in the wilderness Israel had to face the ongoing threat of death with no other security than trust in the one who alone could help. This endurance—persevering when the fulfillment of the promise always slipped away into a more distant future—was made possible only by following the way God showed to Israel. During this period, to obey meant to follow. Even when the Israelites murmured, protesting the never relenting trials, the continuation of the journey was what mattered. Notwithstanding the recurrent murmuring, this period is seen favorably in the later tradition, because despite everything the people continued on the way in which God was leading.

B The family

The family is the basic form of human community in the Old Testament. As we said before, it is impossible to equate the family of that time with the family of today; nevertheless, I think the texts say something here which speaks to us directly. The ancestral history in Genesis, from Abraham to Joseph, depicts the primary relationships of human community—as seen first in the family—from the perspective of a tradition which encompasses several centuries. Additional centuries of experience and reflection stand behind the present portrayal. In no other human religion or holy writings is the family given such great and far-reaching importance in defining communal life and the human relationship to God. A different basic familial relationship is used as the characteristic motif in each of the three cycles of the ancestral history: in the Abraham stories, the relationship of parents to children; in the Jacob–Esau stories, the relationship of sibling to sibling; in the Joseph story, the relationship among the parent, the child, and the other siblings.

An abundance of simple human relationships is presented in these three cycles of the ancestral history—all anchored in the work of God. Placing the ancestral history in front of the history of the nation shows that a person's nature and character come from the family, with all its diverse connections. What is said about people in the ancestral history continues implicitly to hold true for all the people who appear later in the history of the nation. All of them are first son and brother, husband and father, sister or mother. Whatever happens in the larger movements of history—in economics and politics, in social and cultural affairs—has its origins and its roots in the small circle of the family—the source of the first human impressions.

A few examples best illustrate how people are understood in this material. In Abraham, we meet a father who has been placed by God in the middle of a most extreme and overwhelming trial. The conversation between the father and the son, in its moving restraint, lets us sense something of the hardship:

> And Isaac said to his father Abraham, "My father!" And he said, "Here am I, my son." He said, "Behold, the fire and the wood; but where is the lamb for a burnt offering?" Abraham said, "God will provide himself the lamb for a burnt offering, my son." So they went both of them together. (Gen 22:7–8)

The execution of the sons of Saul, demanded by the Gibeonites as an expiation for Saul's transgression against their city, is a terrifying episode in the David story. The punishment is intensified because with the death penalty comes the refusal to permit the burial of the bodies. But the mother, one of Saul's concubines, acts in opposition to the royal command and performs her maternal duty, protecting the bodies (2 Sam 21:9–10). In this way the mother forces the king finally to permit the burial of the bones of the dead sons.

The elder brother plays a special role in the Joseph story. In the absence of the father, he is responsible for the other brothers. Toward the end of the story, the elder brother motif reaches its climax in Judah's speech before Joseph. He asks to take upon himself the punishment intended for the youngest brother who had been arrested for theft (Gen 44:30–34).

One more thing: in the Old Testament the passing on of tradition has its primary and most important place in the family; it occurs in the parents' answers to the children's questions. One sees this especially in the many Deuteronomy texts which begin, "When your son asks you." This is the most important way for the faith to be transmitted from one generation to the next; it happens chiefly in simple stories.

Israel's unique historical consciousness is also grounded in this transmission of the great acts of God from the parents to the children.

C Social structures

This brings us to the question of the affiliation of the individual Israelite to the larger society. One needs to realize that for centuries in Israel to belong to the nation meant to belong to the people of God. Church and community were identical.

We just referred to the amazing historical consciousness found everywhere in the Old Testament. For example, the portrayals of the beginnings of the monarchy under Saul and David are of rare historical value. Other such portrayals—also of outstanding significance—have undoubtedly been lost. But all such stories were made possible only because the entire people had such a remarkable historical consciousness, which itself is based in Israel's faith in God. For Israel experienced God's wonders in its history; history is the proper field of divine action.

The great drama of this history arises with the office of king. There a political, social, and religious activity begins which endangers the basic convictions about God's action in history. This is the reason for the cool, clear objectivity in the portrayal of David's monarchy—for the description of David, with all his success and all his splendor, as a simple, fallible human being. It is deeply moving that flaws and blemishes are never removed from the picture of this greatest of Israel's kings, who remained honored even after centuries; here we see quite emphatically the Old Testament's understanding of the human.

This is also the place for the beginning of prophecy. The threat of the monarchy required that through its entire history the prophet was needed to raise objection when the king overstepped the boundaries. In contrast to the kind of nationalism that looks to the people's own achievements, the individual Israelite is told to remember that he or she has been brought into a land filled with good things, cisterns, vineyards, and olive trees, which came not from Israel's hand, but from God's (Deut 6:10–12).

To complete this picture we would have to discuss the social expressions of the people and those who held office within them—the kings, the court and the officials, the legal system and laws, the masters and slaves, the priests and the prophets. Only then would we be able to see the Old Testament person as part of his or her people in the full panoply and variety of possible relationships. The importance of many of these social structures is poignantly seen in their loss at the time of the destruction of Jerusalem (cf. Lam 5:1–16).

V The human before God

In conclusion, think once more about Psalm 139. In the Old Testament people know they are creatures of God; that means, in all situations and relationships of life they see themselves before God. It goes without saying that this relationship, in all its aspects, would find expression in words. The Psalter, Israel's prayer book, is nothing other than the verbal record of this regular and self-evident relationship. Like the rhythm of breathing, the ups and downs of human existence—the joys and the pains—find words in lament and praise. That people pour out their troubled hearts before God, that they rejoice before God when their hearts are filled with joy—that is as natural for these people as inhaling and exhaling. When we hear or repeat the Psalms today, we can still perceive how directly and how spontaneously they speak to God.

The royal history reports how King Hezekiah once received a letter from the Assyrian commander during the siege of Jerusalem. Jerusalem was in a hopeless situation and was commanded to surrender. "And Hezekiah went up to the house of the Lord, and spread (the letter) before the Lord. And Hezekiah prayed to the Lord" (Isa 37:14–15). This almost childlike, simple gesture—spreading the threatening letter before God in the temple, and praying to him—is characteristic of human speech in the Old Testament. The people perceived themselves to be quite genuinely in relationship to God, and they spoke to him. Recall once more the prayer of this same King Hezekiah at the time of his illness, when it became clear that God had healed him. The prayer of thanksgiving is simply the joyful sigh of relief of the one who has been rescued. The Psalter is full of both kinds of prayers— lament and praise.

Yet the Old Testament also recognizes a deep break in the relationship between God and human beings. Alongside the creation narrative, the primeval history contains several stories which deal with the break between the world as created and the reality of the present. The Yahwist writes a quite dramatic account of the ever growing deterioration of the humanity God created. The Priestly document confirms the world's corruption without offering an explanation. None of this is uniquely biblical. Other peoples and other religions have similar stories. What is uniquely biblical is the way the Yahwist places the history of blessing, beginning with Abraham, over against the dark background of this serious deterioration of the human race.

The story of the fall into sin is so full of significant insights into human life that no generation can exhaust its meaning. Let me lift up just one thing. This story asserts that no human being can stand before God without trespass and disobedience. But then the trespass and disobedience take on their own weight and push and pull the person where he or she does not want to go. The trespass has its own power which the human cannot master. Therefore, God's reaction to this trespass has two parts. On the one hand, God exposes the trespass and punishes the person. But, in order to expose the sin, God pursues the human; and to ensure that those whose trespass has been exposed can continue to live, God clothes them. This clothing is a quiet sign of forgiveness—but a forgiveness that works in and with the punishment. The punishment leads to death, but forgiveness gives the human time—time to enjoy life before death occurs.

All of this applies to human existence in general, not only to the people of God. It is pre-theological, something like a biblical philosophy of existence. Therefore it is not appropriate to base fundamental theological doctrines on these stories. The Old Testament never uses Genesis 1–11 to draw out general teachings about the original state, the fall, and death as its punishment. What we have here rather is the furthest extension of a line which begins in the middle, with the story of Israel's rescue. The more naturally we hear these stories, the more they will have to say to us. Their purpose is to provide us a way—by hearing about the primeval history—to understand the essential features of contemporary history better and more profoundly. These stories arose out of a burning interest in the broad directions and the moving forces of human history and were then affixed to the history of God with his people.

In this connection there is a relationship between the book of Job and the primeval history. Job is a non-Israelite; he does not belong to the people of God. Nevertheless, a powerful drama runs its course involving the God of Israel and Job, the non-Israelite. Job's speeches always go beyond his own situation to include the incomprehensible fate of all suffering people in the world. As in the primeval history, the perspective of the writer of the book of Job goes beyond the people of God to include all humanity and its fate—the puzzles and the precipices of suffering and guilt that are common to all humanity. And just as the primeval history asserts that God's work has to do with all humanity and implies that the history of redemption that commences with Abraham means to lead to the blessing in Abraham of all the families of the earth, so also the writer of Job lays out the great human questions, with the hopeful prospect of a transformation that will include not only Israel, but everyone.

> On one occasion Job declares how he sees this transformation:
> Oh that thou wouldest hide me in Sheol,
> that thou wouldest conceal me until thy wrath be past ...
> Thou wouldest call, and I would answer thee;
> thou wouldest long for the work of thy hands. (Job 14:13,15)

That would be the end of the story that began when God called to Adam, "Where are you?" A powerful dialogue! One that encompasses the whole of human history. Only in the span of this dialogue is it possible to understand what the Bible says about God and about humanity.

Questions

1 When it comes to understanding humanity today, what are the "big questions" that we typically focus on? How are those similar to or different from the issues Westermann highlights from the Old Testament?

2 What do you think about the Old Testament emphasis on "everyday" humanity rather than focusing on more "abstract" issues? In what ways might that be helpful? Are there ways in which that might also be limiting?

3 Which of the particular issues Westermann highlights do you think are most important for theologians to focus on today? Why?

4 What does Westermann think about the role of Genesis 1–11 in understanding humanity? How would you assess that approach?

TEXT 2: WERNER GEORG KÜMMEL, MAN IN THE NEW TESTAMENT[2]

Werner Georg Kümmel (1905–95) was professor of New Testament at the University of Marburg. Having succeeded Rudolf Bultmann in that post, he was an influential figure in New Testament studies, and his Man in the New Testament stood for many years as one of the few summaries of perspectives on humanity in the New Testament as a whole. Given the extented diversity of the New Testament material about the human person, most scholars have chosen to focus more specifically on particular biblical authors, with Pauline anthropology undoubtedly receiving the most extensive treatments. Without intending to downplay the significance of other biblical authors, the reading included in this section follows that model by offering Kümmel's treatment of Paul's anthropology. This allows us to see how Kümmel addresses key anthropological terms (e.g. *sarx, soma, pneuma, psuche*) and how these relate to Paul's emphasis on the "whole man." Kümmel also introduces us to the impact of sin on Paul's view of humanity and how this shapes Paul's anthropology around decidedly soteriological issues.

The question now arises how the Pauline view stands in relation to that of Jesus. Paul is, indeed, particularly important, for he is the only New Testament writer who to any great extent offers us direct statements about man's nature, and uses extensively the anthropological terminology of his time. Paul's anthropological statements have, therefore, always determined quite decisively the whole picture of man which Christian doctrine has extracted from the new Testament. It is to be questions, furthermore, whether the Pauline picture of man differs essentially from Jesus' conception.

It is extremely difficult to describe Paul's anthropology, both because he uses a series of anthropological terms in his description of human existence which are not clearly defined one from the other, and also because he uses these terms in a quite careless way. Ever since H. Lüdemann's basic work, the attempt has been made to read a metaphysical dualism in the Pauline view of man. The 'history of religions school' has thus further explained Paul's anthropology as founded upon ecstatic experience, and therefore most closely related to Hellenistic mysticism. Both explanations are false, as has been already emphasized many times ... Here, we shall only attempt to place Paul's anthropological views within the collective framework of his whole preaching of salvation.

Paul sees man as a member of the *kosmos* (Rom. 1:8; 3:19; 11:12, 15; 1 Cor. 1:20-21, 27–28; 4:13; 6:2; 2 Cor. 1:12; 5:17; Col. 1:6) and therewith as a created being (1 Cor. 11:9; cf. Rom. 9:20ff; Col. 1:23). As a creature of God, man must recognize himself as standing over against God, and give honour to God as God (*hōs Theon doxazein*) (Rom. 1:21). His attitude, however, is the opposite of this; man refuses to acknowledge God and allows himself to be determined by the powers of

---

[2]Werner Georg Kümmel, *Man in the New Testament* (London: Epworth, 1963), 38–71.

the kosmos and by human traditions (Rom. 1:21; 1 Cor. 1:21; 2:12; Col. 2:8). Like Jesus, Paul sees man exclusively as a being standing over against God, a being whose real vocation of service to God is opposed to his actual slavery to the creation (*ktisis*) (Rom. 1:25), a slavery which shows itself in 'boasting' (*kauchasthai*) (1 Cor. 1:27ff). Paul sees man trapped by the *kosmos*, standing distinct from God, set in the midst of the great antithesis of *sarx* and *pneuma*.

What does Paul mean by *sarx*? First, he can use the word quite unemphatically, as an indication of the natural man and his corporeality, and thus simply denoting his earthly origin (1 Cor. 1:29; Rom. 3:20; Gal. 1:16; Rom. 1:3). But '*sarx*' is more frequently used to indicate the opposite of God or '*pneuma*', and it then denotes the whole man, who faces the Creator as a sinner. So Romans 7:14; 8:4; 1 Corinthians 3:8: Are you not still fleshly (*sarkikoi*), and walking according to man? Man as *sarx* is therefore a sinner. So Romans 7:14: I am fleshly, 'the purchased slave of sin' (NEB).

This connexion of *sarx* with sin has often been understood as if Paul regarded man as sinful simply because of his attachment to material things. That is undoubtedly wrong. Paul does not think that sin is naturally bound up with *sarx*. One can live 'in the flesh' (*en sarki*), without fighting 'according to the flesh' (*kata sarka*) (2 Cor. 10:3). The sinfulness of the *sarx* does not belong to it simply because it is bodily, earthly existence. That Paul does not refer the connexion between *sarx* and sin back to *sarx* as material body is shown especially in the fact that he does not see any dualism inside man with a higher inner man related to God. It has often been pointed out that Paul knew the Greek dualism of outer and inner man. Indeed, the whole Pauline anthropology has been seen as founded on this antithesis. However, by 'the inner man', Paul means (2 Cor. 4:16) the renewed being of the Christian. Romans 7:22 deals with the natural man who agrees to God's will according to his inner man, but there is no thought here, as we shall show, of any antithesis between the inner man which is peculiarly near to God on the one hand, and the earthly body on the other. Only an examination of the terms Paul uses for the spiritual man could show whether Paul thinks of a dualism of this kind in the inner man.

Unfortunately, accurate and relative definitions of the different terms for the inner man as used by Paul (*psuche, nous, noema, kardia, pneuma, suneidesis, dianoia, splagchna, phrenes*) are a priori impossible, for the terms do not denote psychologically different functions, but are used promiscuously. Psuche, 'soul', is already clearly placed on the side of sarx, as Paul denotes the earthly man separate from God, unable to understand the divine pneuma, with psuchikos as well as with sarkikos (1 Cor. 2:13–14; 15:44–45). The nous, 'mind', of man, again, is called 'fleshly' (*nous tes sarkos*) and 'reprobate' (*adokimos nous*) (Col. 2:18; Rom. 1:28), and Paul demands its regeneration. However, Paul speaks of the fact that man can with his *nous* perceive the eternal power of God and His divinity (Rom. 1:20), and insists that man with his *nous* confirms the law of God, even while his members are at the service of sin (Rom. 7:23, 25b). It will immediately be asked if Paul does not assume thereby a higher side in man which is related to God.

It is even more difficult to answer the question of *pneuma*, 'spirit', as an indication of the inner man. That Paul can use *pneuma* as an anthropological term is shown when he expresses his distress at Titus' absence once with *pneuma* ('I still found no relief for my spirit', 2 Cor. 2:13) and once with *sarx* ('our flesh had no relief',

2 Cor. 7:5). Moreover, Paul also speaks of a 'spirit (*pneuma*) of the man which is in him' (1 Cor. 2:11). But these places in which *pneuma* denotes the inner man are few and unterminological and the context shows that this human *pneuma* stands in no way particularly close to God, but rather belongs entirely to the side of *sarx*.

* * * * *

Thus we must conclude that the three texts under discussion (Rom. 1:20; 2:15; 7:14ff) confirm our argument that Paul sees the whole man as *sarx* and consequently as sinner.

If we have been correct in seeing man as essentially a sinner because of his nature as *sarx*, and in claiming that his sinfulness cannot be attributed simply to his fleshly and material existence, then one important question remains: How are we to understand the connexion between *sarx* and sin? In many instances, *sarx* appears in Paul as a great power opposing man. Man is 'in the flesh' (*en sarki*, Gal. 2:20; 2 Cor. 10:3), as if he were not himself identical with the *sarx*. The *sarx* has thoughts (*phronema*, Rom. 8:6–7), desires (*epithumia*, Gal. 5:16), mind (*nous*, Col. 2:18), and the Christian is seen between the two conflicting powers *sarx* and *pneuma* (Gal. 5:17). Consequently, it has often been said that for Paul *sarx* is a principle or power governing human kind.

But against this it must be insisted that Paul employs *sarx* and *soma* in the same way for mankind and his actual, human, fleshly existence (cf. 1 Cor. 5:3 with Col. 2:5; also Rom. 8:13; 2 Cor. 4:10–11; 7:5). It is the man who is in the body, it is fleshly, *en sarki* mankind which is governed by sin. The sinfulness of mankind characterized as *sarx* appears in open rebellion against God's will (Rom. 8:7), in acting according to one's desire (Gal. 5:16), in 'boasting' (*kauchasthai*, 1 Cor. 1:29; 2 Cor. 11:18), and in adherence to human and worldly traditions (Col. 2:18, 23). The man characterized by *sarx* is under the *kosmos* and its powers. Thus, Galatians 3:3, 'Are you now perfected in the flesh (*sarki*)?', corresponds to 4:9, 'How can you turn back to the mean and beggarly spirits of the elements?' (NEB). *Sarx* denotes the man who lets himself be determined by his actual historical existence in the world; it does not describe man in his fundamental nature, but rather in his membership in this passing evil age (Gal. 1:4). In so far as man lets himself be determined by the reality of 'this age' (aoin houtos), and thereby denotes that he is yet *sarx*, so far is he 'a slave of sin and death' (Rom. 6:16).

This connexion of *sarx* and sin, shown in man's historical behavior, has no exceptions (Rom. 3:9, 23; 8:7ff). Moreover, this judgement is not the result of Christian experience, as Paul insists upon the possibility that heathens also can be obedient to the commands of the Law. So Romans 2:14–15, 26. This whole point of view is to be seen as Paul's post-conversion judgement upon his own former life as a Torah-righteous Pharisee who since his conversion has learnt to regard his Jewish adherence to the Law as the wrong way to salvation, as indeed, a 'loss' (*zemia*) (Rom. 3:20; 9:31; 10:3; Phil. 3:7). The common and unavoidable sinfulness of all mankind is not deduced by Paul from his nature as *sarx*, but is, indeed, the necessary consequence of the certainty that only 'in Christ' can God's approval be gained (Rom. 3:21ff; 8:7–10; Gal. 5:5-6). Moreover, this sinfulness involving all mankind is something which is only clear to the eyes of faith, looking back upon the past. Only from the Christian point of view is it clear that man is *sarx* in his very existence, and is determined by *sarx* (Rom. 7:14; 8:6–7).

Paul does not anywhere explain the source of this connexion between man's fleshly and sinful existence. On one occasion only he says that sin began with Adam: 'It was through one man that sin entered the world, and through sin death, and thus death pervaded the whole human race, inasmuch as all men have sinned' (Rom. 5:12, NEB). The exact meaning of this text is still debated, but it is scarcely debatable that Paul here expresses two views side by side which cannot immediately be reconciled: 'Through the sin of the first man, sin and its consequence death, entered the world' and 'death has come to all men, because all have sinned.' Paul does not here maintain that each man has by his birth inherited Adam's sin, but only that it is since Adam's sin to be found in every man, and that in consequence of the sin of each man, all men die. But he puts beside that the statement that each man merits his own death because of his own sin—death which since Adam has been the punishment for sin. This thought about each individual's responsibility for his own death cannot be described or dismissed as an unfortunate notion of secondary importance. On the contrary, for Paul it is not important, because only by retaining this idea of personal responsibility does man appear as guilty of his own death (cf. Rom. 6:20–21, 23). Moreover, Paul is only following Jewish tradition in placing side by side inherited death as a result of common sinfulness and man's own responsibility for his death as a result of his sin. From the fact that Paul has not tried to find any logical compromise between these two important claims about the universality of sin and therefore of death on the one hand and the individual's responsibility for his death by reason of his sin on the other hand, it can be concluded that in Romans 5:12 Paul speaks about the beginning of sin and hence of death, but is not particularly interested in this beginning; rather it is the universality of sin and death which interests him and which he wants to contrast with the universality of the life given in Christ. The reference to Adam is not intended to explain the origin of sin or pardon man for his sinfulness, but only to emphasize, by referring to its historical beginnings, the universality of sin and, with it, death which Christian faith substantiates.

Paul, therefore, does not intend to derive man's common sinfulness and hence his liability to death from his life in the flesh, or from his descendance from a common father of the race, but rather, is merely concerned to establish this universality of sin and death as a historical fact. Much more, he sets its source in the actual behavior of the individual who violates God's will and therefore is liable to death. And so, like Jesus, Paul sees man exclusively from the point of view of his relation to God and therefore judges man as being hostile to Him and lost in the *kosmos*. Paul connects this fact of man's remoteness from God with his existence as *sarx*. This is a use of terms, capable of misunderstanding, which can at best be explained with A. Schlatter by saying that Paul contrasts man with God as the bearer of the Spirit: 'the Spirit is the mark of God and the Agent of His activity. Flesh, on the other hand, is the mark of man in all his dissimilarity from God.' Nevertheless, in whatever way the origin of this terminology is to be explained, it is clear that man, for Paul, is a historical being who derives his nature from his existence as a member of the present evil age, and from his living in accordance with this historical existence.

Paul thus differs from Jesus in his view of man inasmuch as his use of Rabbinical and Hellenistic terminology often leads him into a word-usage which is not always unambiguous. However, the main lines of Paul's picture are in accord with that of Jesus. Consequently, for Paul also salvation is not a natural or human solution to man's problems, but a historical action of God, involving the beginning of the new age and empowering man to a new way of life by transferring him 'into the Kingdom of His beloved Son' (Col. 1:13). The picture of man in the teaching of Paul is like that of Jesus not an a priori presupposition, but has been formed retrospectively, out of his own experience of present salvation, but using concepts and doctrines which he brought with him from his own background as a Hellenistic Jew. Thus, Paul's view of man distinguishes itself completely from every purely humanistic or descriptive view of man, as much as from every idealistic or dualistic conception.

Questions

1. Why does Kümmel think that Paul is particularly important for theological anthropology?

2. According to Kümmel, why is Paul's anthropology so difficult to describe? Why might this be important to keep in mind as we read Paul's statements about humanity?

3. What is the fundamental misunderstanding that most people have when it comes to Paul's use of the term *sarx*?

4. Kümmel argues that we have a similarly difficult time understanding Paul's use of *pneuma*. What is our mistake here and why is it significant?

5. What is the main point Kümmel wants to make about what Paul means by the "inner man"? Do you think this is an important point? Why or why not?

6. What are the two irreconcilable perspectives that Kümmel finds in Paul's discussion of the relationship between our sin and Adam's sin? Why is this an important issue for Christian anthropology?

7. Why does Kümmel think Paul is more interested in the universality of sin than its beginning? What do you think about this argument?

TEXT 3: J. PATOUT BURNS, THEOLOGICAL ANTHROPOLOGY[3]

J. Patout Burns is the Edward A. Malloy Professor Emeritus of Catholic Studies at Vanderbilt Divinity School. He is a prominent patristic scholar with particular expertise in the Christianity of North Africa and the theologies of Cyprian and Augustine. This reading illustrates two important aspects of the sources for theological anthropology. First, theological anthropology needs to be aware of and operate in dialog with the theological perspectives of the past. Burns' reading thus offers a useful overview of several important themes in the first few centuries of Christian theology, serving as an exemplar of using historical theology as a resource for understanding the human person. Second, the reading illustrates the many ways in which those early theologians used the thoughts and ideas of their surrounding cultures as resources for reflecting on anthropology. The reading from Ada Maria Isasi-Diaz later in this chapter offers a more contemporary illustration of the significance of social location for theological anthropology. This reading thus offers some needed historical perspective to establish that theologians have always developed their visions of humanity in critical and constructive dialog with their cultural context.

Theological anthropology investigates the resources, the limitations, and the destiny of the human person. The authors represented in this anthology share the conviction that humanity's present condition does not correspond to God's ultimate purpose and original intention in its creation. Common to all as well is the assurance that human beings are themselves responsible for this disparity. They also demonstrate that the human capacity for failure was either inevitable or the necessary consequence of the perfection God intended humanity to attain. Finally, all firmly believe that, in Christ, God reverses the consequences of the Fall and moves human beings to a beatitude from which they will not again fall. Although they agree in all of these assumptions and assertions, the authors differ significantly in explaining the initial state and vocation of humanity, in estimating the damage done in the Fall, and in describing the resources for recover provided in Christ.

This introduction presents an overview of a variety of theological anthropologies which enjoyed fairly broad acceptance in early Christianity ...

The Gnostic movement

By the middle of the second century, a Christian form of the already widespread Gnostic religious movement had emerged. Although it was ultimately judged deviant and heterodox, the Gnostic interpretation of Christ's work gained long-

---

[3]J. Patout Burns, *Theological Anthropology*, Sources of Early Christian Thought (Philadelphia: Fortress Press, 1981), 1–22.

lasting support and influenced the other Christian anthropologies. The Gnostics (e.g., Valentinus, Basilides) identified the material world and the flesh as the source of humanity's difficulties. The human person was characterized as a spirit whose presence in this alien world resulted when God purified the heavenly realm of the consequences of a sin among angelic beings. The human spirit longs to be liberated from matter and to attain a spiritual existence characterized by knowledge of God. The spirit's natural kinship with the divine grounds this desire and provides the principal resource for its fulfillment. God aids this liberation through Jesus Christ, who reminds human beings of their true destiny and shows them the way of life which will liberate the spirit form a dissipating and enslaving concern with material pursuits and then develop its spiritual potential. Its separation from the flesh in death enables the mature spirit to enter into the heavenly realm. Thus the Gnostic anthropology regards the material condition of humanity as a tragic accident for which human beings do not bear primary responsibility. Existence in this world makes no contribution to the eventual salvation of the human person.

Toward the end of the second century Irenaeus of Lyon (d. ca. A.D. 200) composed the most extensive surviving report and refutation of Gnostic doctrines, his *Detection and Overthrow of the Pretended But False Gnosis,* or more popularly, *Against Heresies.* He rejected both the denigration of the flesh and the absolution of humanity from responsibility for the problems of its actual condition. Human beings were originally created in a bodily condition and will attain the perfection of that condition in the eschatological restoration and renewal of the whole creation in Christ. The imperfection of the present condition indicates neither a failure of divine power over matter nor a lack of divine love for humanity. Divine wisdom actually arranged the creation of humanity in an immature state and its gradual growth into perfect happiness.

To be truly good, Irenaeus reasoned, human beings must be free; the love of good has value only when a choice of the contrary evil has been rejected. Instead of giving humanity immortality and beatitude at the outset and risking their loss through free choice, therefore, God devised a strategy to foster a firm commitment to good which would then treasure and preserve full goodness once he had finally bestowed it. First he made human beings immature, capable of learning and development through enjoying the fruits of good choices and suffering the consequences of evil ones. By experiencing the contrast between virtue and sin, human beings can come to appreciate, prefer, and preserve the good; they can build a strong commitment which stabilizes them in the preference of good. God then gives immortality and beatitude to such a mature person, who will not neglect and lose his perfection. Although the sufferings of the present age actually result from sinful choices which should be avoided, God uses them as an educational instrument to move human beings to a full and stable happiness.

Some aspects of Irenaeus' theological anthropology are almost commonplaces in the ancient church, such as the assertion that the possibility of sin is essential to the practice of true virtue. He was singular, however, in claiming that humanity was actually created in an immature condition and has progressed through the experience of good and evil. This aspect of his theory was, of course, directed against the Gnostic evaluation of the present human condition as contrary to the divine will, a situation to be escaped rather than accepted and lived as the way to perfection.

The ascetic movement

By the middle of the third century, the two movements which produced the dominant anthropologies of the ancient church had begun to flourish: asceticism and Christian Platonism. Although these two tendencies were sometimes integrated both in practice and in theory, they actually involved significantly different perspectives on the human situation before God and on the nature of salvation and the means to attain it.

The beginnings of the ascetic movement can be traced back to the practice of fasting, almsgiving, continence, and even virginity within local Christian communities. In the third century the tendency toward a life of fuller self-denial and a withdrawal from the temptations of urban and village life quickened. Chaotic social conditions, the instability of the imperial government, an increasing burden of taxation, and the systematic persecution of Christians all contributed to the retreat. While emphasizing the evils of the social environment, which could be escaped by solitude or life in an isolated Christian fraternity, the movement rested on an optimistic estimate of the resources of human nature itself for maintaining a commitment to good through obedience to God's commands. In this sense, the ascetics (e.g., Antony of Egypt, Martin of Tours) were heirs to the spirituality of the confessors and martyrs: they trusted that God would reward their fidelity unto death by raising them from the dead and granting them unending happiness in a paradise which was occasionally described in sensual terms.

The differences between the condition of Adam and that of his offspring are, in the ascetic theory, largely environmental. Adam was placed in pleasant surroundings conducive to his appreciation of God's goodness and there given a clear command which he could obey without difficulty. He had that freedom of choice or self-determination which made him deserving of reward for fidelity and of punishment for disobedience. God intended that Adam do the good; he allowed the capacity for evil only to make his preference of good free, virtuous, and worthy of reward. Contemporary human beings are born with this same capacity to choose between good and evil and are given the opportunity to earn an eternal reward. Like Adam, the individual person can squander his resources by turning to evil. Sinful choices establish customs within a person, patterns of response to the enticements of evil or addictions to forbidden pleasures which make good choice and action increasingly difficult and improbable. The evil customs of a group in a society can establish a whole culture oriented to sin which then undermines an individual's efforts for good. Thus Adam's sin began a process which has made the environment more conducive to sin than to obedience. Sin is everywhere presented for imitation, and true good is hard to discern and accomplish. Custom, in its individual or social forms, cannot deprive a person of his freedom of choice between good and evil. Cultural orientations actually gain power over a person only through his free consent, which appropriates and internalizes them. As free choices have built evil customs and conceded them power over the person, so his free choices can reverse these patterns and supplant them with good customs which facilitate obedience and virtue.

The Christian life can be described as a struggle to serve God in a hostile environment. The person retains the internal resources of human nature: the light of reason to recognize the good, and the freedom to choose it. Like the obstacles, the aids to using these resources are largely environmental. As sinful acts establish an external and even internal environment that promotes evil, so the collaboration of committed Christians can build a community which helps the individual to choose the good, and his own virtuous actions develop customs which stabilize him in fidelity to God. God's grace also intervenes to change the environment. The patriarchs lived well by the resources of human nature alone and maintained their fidelity to God in the most difficult circumstances. When the assimilation of sinful customs had obscured the true good, God clarified his commands in the Mosaic Law, particularly the Decalogue. Prophets and philosophers continued this work, and Christ finally perfected the law in his own teaching. Similarly, the example of virtuous living set by the saints demonstrates the true capacity of human nature and draws others to imitate them. Christ himself provided the supreme exhortation both by the example of his life and death and by his exhibition of the promised rewards in his resurrection. The only other, nonenvironmental form of grace generally recognized in this tradition was the forgiveness of the sins of those who heed the call to conversion.

God makes his grace generally available and holds each individual responsible for responding and using it effectively. He gives special assistance only to those who deserve it. Thus differences in individual situations are earned by good or evil merits.

The freedom of self-determination to good or evil, which is the inalienable divine image implanted in humanity at its creation, stands as the foundation of this anthropology. The exercise of this autonomy for good may be enhanced or encumbered by environmental factors whose actual influence, however, depends upon the individual's own prior consent. Through repeated choices a person will orient himself to either good or evil. In the resurrection God will stabilize the just in good as a reward for fidelity and fix the sinner in the evil he has consistently preferred.

The ascetic movement produced a literature which ranges from pastoral treatises on specific practices and virtues to collections of wise observations by desert monks and the popular biographies of such heroes as Antony of Egypt and Martin of Tours. It is here prepresented by a section of Pelagius' (fl. Early fifth century) hortatory Letter to Demetrias.

Christian Platonism

A second tendency in Christian anthropology, Christian Platonism, in the third and fourth centuries shared some of the assumptions and recommended many of the practices grounding the ascetic perspective just considered. It was specifically different, however, in its attempt to assimilate the resources of non-Christian religious philosophy, especially the current forms of the Platonic tradition. In the second century, Justin Martyr (d. ca. 165) had interpreted Christ as the ordering principle in the universe who manifests himself in the natural light of human moral reasoning as well as in the history of Israel. Origen, the third-century Alexandrian theologian (d. ca. 254), elaborated a Christian understanding of the universe which charted the fall of the human spirit into the flesh and its journey of return to God through Christ. His thought dominated Greek Christianity, particularly in the fourth century, and found adherents on both sides of the major dogmatic controversies. Origen's appropriation and development of the allegorical interpretation used by exegetes of the Homeric writings and the Hebrew scriptures provided a method for the prayer and speculation of Christian mysticism.

Christian Platonism identifies the divine image in humanity not as the autonomy of self-determination but as rationality, the human capacity for knowledge of God. It finds a connaturality between the human spirit and the divine Spirit which manifests itself in a desire for union with God in knowledge and love, an innate and inalienable drive of the human toward the divine.

This desire was implanted in a spirit which was brought into existence from nonbeing through change and therefore always remains subject to change. A certain instability afflicts all created beings; they are always either advancing or retreating in goodness and being. A creature can attain stability and fulfillment only by participating in the unchangeable goodness of uncreated being. Thus the human spirit's natural capacity and desire for union with God provides the basic resource for salvation. The material creation, being irrational and thus incapable of union with God, remains subject to a meaningless repetition of growth and decay which is opposed and inimical to the spirit's development into God. In this understanding of the diversity between the nature and destiny of matter and spirit, the divine purpose in joining them to form humanity becomes puzzling and mysterious. Origen himself seems to have considered in the consequence of a prior sin, though many of his disciples attempted less radical solutions.

Those Christian Platonists who affirmed that God originally created human beings as a union of body and spirit also asserted that God subjected the appetites and desires of the body to the governance of the spirit and ordered them to its fulfillment. In its sin and fall the human spirit turned away from God to itself, lost its dominion over the desires of the flesh, and then fell under the spell of sensual satisfactions. The proper order within the human person was reversed: the dynamism of the spirit became the passion which serves bodily appetites. Although he retains a capacity and desire for God, each human being inherits concupiscence, the independence of bodily appetite and the passion which draws spiritual energy to temporal and temporary satisfactions. The conflict can be fully healed only through the dissolution of the flesh in death and its reconstitution in a spiritualized form. During this life, concupiscence can be aggravated by free consent to bodily desires, which adds the power of custom and deepens the person's servitude. Alternately, the spirit can direct itself to God, subdue fleshly desires by ascetical practices, and thereby begin to recover its proper liberty. In fact, the inheritance of concupiscence permits fleshly desire to seduce the spirit and sensitize it to bodily pleasure and pain before a person reflects upon the true destiny of his nature. Thus the spirit regularly forgets itself and falls under the influence of passion.

The Christian life, according to its Platonic interpretation, begins with the revelation of God in Christ; the divine goodness manifests itself in a sensible form to the spirit immersed in matter. Christ arouses the desire for God and teaches the way of life through which the spirit can reestablish its governance over the flesh and pursue its proper finality. The gradual purification of the spirit liberates its desire and clarifies the divine image imprinted in that natural dynamic. The Christian whose heart becomes pure notices the revelation of God in the creation, contemplates his manifestation in the earthly works of Christ, and, through the deeper figurative understanding of the scriptural record of the economy of salvation, moves to an ever-fuller awareness and appreciation of God's goodness.

The human spirit does not attain stability and beatitude by being fixed in a good state it has maintained until death; rather, the constant change to which it is subject as a creature is focused into a steady growth into union with God. God is inexhaustible, and the human desire for God is insatiable. Once the human spirit is freed from the distractions of the flesh and centered on God, the development process accelerates. The more a person knows and loves God, the more he hungers for God. As the desire grows, a relapse into sensual pursuits becomes increasingly improbable. The created spirit can never stop changing; hence its beatitude consists in an unceasing and ever-increasing development in the knowledge and love which unites it to the divine Spirit. This union with God may begin during earthly life, and its joys may be anticipated in mystical prayer.

Platonic Christianity differs significantly from the anthropology of the ascetic tradition. It describes the Christian life as the growth of a spiritual desire for God rather than as the faithful obedience to the divine commands through which one earns a reward in the next life. It conceives of grace as God's operation which revives and nourishes, which removes the obstacles to the development of the desire God created in humanity. The primary grace is God's self-revelation in the economy of creation and salvation which culminates in the incarnation of the Word. Participation in the death and resurrection of Christ, either in baptism or through physical death and resurrection, heals the concupiscence of the flesh and gives it a new, spiritual life. The commandments of God, along with the teaching and example of Christ and his saints, inspire and guide the Christian's purification and development.

Autonomy and self-determination have a more limited significance in this anthropology than in that of the ascetical tradition, because the liberation and development of the spiritual desire displace the earning of a reward as the basic way to salvation. The power of passion can reduce the liberty of the human spirit. The beginning Christian must oppose the force of concupiscence which has afflicted him from birth and for whose power in him he bears a limited personal responsibility. The more adept have not established virtuous customs by which they commit themselves to good; they have liberated and given free rein to a dynamism which God himself planted and nourished in them. Despite this divine initiative, however, free choice retains its significance in the observance of the commandments and in the exercise of asceticism through which the Christian cooperates with the divine action and labors to free the gift of God within him.

This Platonic movement produced an extensive literature in a variety of forms. It ranges from the scriptural commentaries of Origen through the ascetical treatises of Evagrius of Pontus to the sermons of Ambrose of Milan and the early philosophical treatises of Augustine. It is here represented by a sermon of Gregory of Nyssa (d. ca. 395) on the purity of heart which prepares a person to see God.

Fourth-century developments

The social factors which encouraged the emergence and development of these two traditions within the Christian movement during the second and third centuries were intensified in the fourth. The century began with a violent and sustained persecution named for its instigator, the Emperor Diocletian (reigned 284–305), in which the imperial government attempted to suppress Christianity. The same century ended with the establishment of the Christian church, the destruction of pagan temples, and the enactment of laws against the traditional Roman religion.

The toleration promised Christianity in A.D. 313, when Emperor Constantine brought Licinius to terms at Milan, developed into a collaboration between church and empire. Constantine and his successors actively sought the unification of the church and the solution of divisive doctrinal disputes, often as a means to secure their internal political control and strengthen the defense of the empire. Some Christians reacted to the new situation by withdrawing from secular involvement; others actively took up the challenge of adapting their faith and converting the empire.

The ascetical movement flourished not only in the wilderness of Egypt and Palestine, but also in the west and even in the major cities. Some continued the martyrs' opposition to all compromise with the power of this world. They led simple lives of prayer, manual labor, and asceticism alone or in communities organized to train and sustain them in these exercises. Many Christians of the upper classes were captivated by the lives and practices of these simple monks. Some abandoned their positions and responsibilities, choosing to found or enter monasteries in the Holy Land; others remained in their mansions, dedicating themselves to self-denial and the study of the Scriptures. Teachers and guides such as Jerome (d. 420) and Pelagius developed a following among these aristocrats. Pelagius, for example, was an ascetic of British or Irish origin who came to Rome near the end of the fourth century and became a popular exegete and spiritual director. He composed a commentary on the Epistles of St. Paul and treatises on the virtuous life. Joining the exodus of wealthy Romans after the sack of the city in A.D. 410, he went first to Africa and then to Palestine. There, in 413, he composed his letter of exhortation to Demetrias, the daughter of a wealthy widow who had just refused an advantageous marriage in order to consecrate herself to virginity. Other Roman friends, Melania the Younger and her husband Pinianus, later attempted to mediate his dispute with Augustine (354–430).

The growth of this fairly straightforward ascetical spirituality was more than matched by the assimilation of Neoplatonic philosophy and its elaboration into a specifically Christian anthropology and spiritual theology. The toleration and eventual establishment of the Christian church brought significant numbers of well-educated men into its service as bishops and theologians. Cultured laymen involved themselves in religious discussions. Dogmatic questions such as those of the Trinity and the constitution of Christ were debated not only by reference to Scripture but also with the best instruments of philosophical analysis available. These doctrinal disputes all involved questions of salvation: the human condition and the means of overcoming sin. Origen's earlier formulations were developed and perfected first by Athanasius (d. 373) and then by the Cappadocian theologians. Origen also provided the foundation for the mystical theology developed by Gregory of Nyssa and Evagrius of Pontus (d. 399) to guide Christians beyond the practical wisdom and ascetical practices of the Egyptian monks.

Questions

1   What are the fundamental assumptions that Burns says are shared by these early theologians? Do you agree that these should constitute the basic starting point of Christian anthropology?

2   Which features of a "gnostic" anthropology did Burns identify that would have been problematic for a Christian view of the human person? Do you see any of those same features in modern anthropologies?

3   What was unique about Irenaeus' theological anthropology? How would you assess this contribution?

4   What is "asceticism" and why do you think it was such an influential aspect of early anthropologies? Is there anything we should learn from asceticism for anthropology today?

5   According to Burns, Christian Platonism was an attempt to utilize non-Christian philosophy as a resource for theological anthropology. What do you think about this move? To what extent should philosophy inform our understanding of humanity?

6   What aspects of Christian Platonism would you affirm? Which do you find problematic?

TEXT 4: KARL BARTH,
CHURCH DOGMATICS[4]

Karl Barth (1886–1968) was the most prominent Swiss theologian of the twentieth century. After teaching in Germany for ten years, he became professor of systematic theology at the University of Basel. In this excerpt, Barth wrestles with the question of what it means to have a truly theological approach to anthropology. Although he recognizes the existence of other approaches to anthropology, which he categorizes as either speculative or scientific, even acknowledging the value of the latter, he contends that we can only see true humanity as it is revealed to us in Christ. Every other approach to anthropology sees only humanity as it has been polluted by sin. Barth thus wrestles with how the doctrines of revelation and sin impact the way in which theological anthropology should relate to other anthropological disciplines. And, by arguing for a strongly christological approach to anthropology, he also raises important questions about what it means to say that Jesus somehow reveals true humanity and how we should thus understand the relationship between Christology and anthropology.

Man is made an object of theological knowledge by the fact that his relationship to God is revealed to us in the Word of God. We have seen it is this which distinguishes man from the rest of the cosmos. Of all other creatures the Word of God tells us only that they are the creatures of God, subject to His sovereignty, intended for His praise, and the heralds of His glory. How and why this is so is hidden from us. But how and why man is the creature of God is not hidden from us; it is revealed by the Word of God. As God speaks His Word, He not only establishes the fact but reveals the truth of His relationship to this, the human creature. The description of this relationship, or the account of its history, forms the content of Holy Scripture. This does not give us any description or recount any history of the relationship between God and the rest of the cosmos. God alone and man alone are its theme. This is the distinction of man which makes him the object of theological anthropology.

But anthropology has a special task. It is the task of dogmatics generally to present the revelation of the truth of the relationship between God and man in the light of the biblical witness to its history as a whole. Anthropology confines its enquiry to the human creatureliness presupposed in this relationship and made known by it, i.e., by its revelation and biblical attestation. It asks what kind of a being it is which stands in this relationship with God. Its attention is wholly concentrated on the relationship. Thus it does not try to look beyond it or behind it. It knows that its insights would at once be lost, and the ground cut from beneath it, if it were to turn its attention elsewhere, abstracting from this relationship. Solely in the latter as illuminated by the Word of God is light shed on the creatureliness of man. Thus theological anthropology cleaves to the Word of God and its biblical attestation. But in the revealed relationship

---

[4]Karl Barth, *Church Dogmatics* III/2 (London: T&T Clark, 1960), 19–54.

between God and man genuine light is thrown, not only on God, but also on man, on the essence of the creature to whom God has turned in this relationship.

* * * * *

Theological anthropology expounds the knowledge of man which is made possible and needful by the fact that man stands in the light of the Word of God. The Word of God is thus its foundation. We hasten to add that for this very reason it expounds the truth about man. As man becomes the object of its knowledge in this way, it does not apprehend or explain an appearance of human essence, but the reality; not its outward features, but its most inward; not a part but the whole. It is another matter whether and to what extent, as it uses the material offered, it will do justice to it in concreto. Not merely in the doctrine of God, but here too in the doctrine of man, we have always to reckon with the possibility that theology as a human work may and will seriously fail to do justice in concreto to its object. The light which falls on this object, and in which it first becomes an object of knowledge, is the divine light. Inevitably, then, theology can give only a dim and blurred reflection. But this does not affect in the least the uniqueness, the height and depth, the richness of the material which it tries to use for better or for worse. As it understands the creatureliness of man from the Word of God addressed to him and illuminating him as no other creature, it draws from the fountain of all truth, and it is enabled to see the depths of the being of man and summoned to utter the true and final word concerning him. This special origin and this special claim mark it off from all the very different attempts at self-knowledge which seem to be its competitors.

Apart from the theological, there are of course other types of anthropology, and a passing glimpse at their very different character and method is indispensable. It might even appear at first as if the field which we now enter as we take up the doctrine of man is one which has been long since occupied, so that what the dogmatics of the Church has to do in this respect is simply to discuss the very different attempts which have always been made. Comprehensively defined, the problem of man is in fact a problem of the universal understanding of being to which, in addition to all kinds of primitive intuitive convictions many serious hypotheses have been given in answer, together with the supposed axioms of generally human, non-theological knowledge, old and new. Indeed, we are forced to say that directly or indirectly, openly or latently, explicitly or implicitly, the problem of man has always been acknowledged as the key-problem of all human reflection.

* * * * *

In the non-theological anthropology which apparently dominates the field we do not have a sporadic but a very persistent rival with intentions which are implicitly or explicitly extremely comprehensive. Anthropology, which in the sphere of dogmatics is only one chapter among others, is in non-theological belief, myth, philosophy and science a kind of basic discipline which imposes its criterion on all other knowledge and perhaps claims to embrace it. The question which we have now to decide is whether we can at least orientate ourselves by this anthropology which is independent of theology, i.e., by one of its concrete expressions. In relation to man, can we profit by its methods and results? An even more radical question is whether we ought deliberately to regard theological anthropology merely as a species, placing it within the framework of a general non-theological anthropology, and establishing and securing it on the basis of the latter. To answer these questions we may recall the two types of non-theological anthropology which usually merge *in concreto*, but which are basically quite distinct, and therefore demand a different attitude in each case.

The first of these types is that of the speculative theory of man. Although there is no compulsion, it may proceed from certain hypotheses put forward by exact science. Alternatively, although there is again no compulsion, it may rest upon a pure self-intuition purporting to be axiomatic. In any event, it goes beyond the hypotheses of exact science, either depriving them of their hypothetical character and treating them as axiomatic principles, or discovering such principles and freely opposing them to the former. Either way, it belongs to the context of a world-view. *De facto*, and probably quite perceptibly, it forms the basic element in such a view, providing the framework which supports and maintains the whole. This speculative theory of man arises in the wide area between myth on the one hand and philosophy on the other. Hence what we have said about world-views as such is applicable to it. It arises in the arid place–unspiritual in the biblical sense of "spirit"–where man has not yet heard the Word of God or hears it no longer. In this place man supposes that he can begin absolutely with himself, i.e., his own judgment, and then legitimately and necessarily push forward until he finally reaches an absolute synthesis, a system of truth exhaustive of reality as a whole. On this assumption he also and primarily thinks that he can know and analyse himself. On this assumption he speculates: whether with or without regard to the hypotheses of exact science; whether with or without the intuitive discovery of a free basic principle. He thinks that in some way he can know himself. Anthropology on this basis is the doctrine of man in which man is confident that he can be both the teacher and the pupil of truth. Whether teaching of this kind includes or excludes the idea of God, and in what form it may perhaps include it, is unessential. It may well include it, and perhaps even in such a way as to make it of decisive and central importance in the foundation and development of the idea of man. Again, it may develop atheistically, or perhaps sceptically as regards the idea of God. The essential point, however, is not its attitude to this idea, but the fact that this teaching has its origin in that arid corner; that here at the start of human self-knowledge stands man himself in his unlimited self-confidence either with or without the thought of God, or with this thought or that. It might even assume the form of pure questioning, of the absolute renunciation of all positive theses. The self-confidence characteristic of this speculative type of anthropology then expresses itself in the confidence with which man confines himself to the investigation of himself, thinking it his duty to honour the truth by a perpetual seeking after truth.

This is not the place to grapple with an anthropology of this type. It is obviously an enemy which we can meet only by opposing to it the Christian confession. We need only say that the field which we are entering with our enquiry about man cannot possibly be occupied by an anthropology of this type. What is supposedly or actually achieved by this speculative anthropology is not in any case what we have to achieve. Nor can we achieve what is thought and declared to be achieved by these means. We cannot allow human self-knowledge to begin where this anthropology begins, with that unlimited self-confidence: not primarily because in view of our different understanding of man we consider that self-confidence out of place; but primarily because—and on this our different understanding of man rests—we are not able to see the essence and nature of man apart from the Word of God. Hence we cannot enter that sterile corner, nor can we argue from it. The Christian Church does not belong to that corner. It would cease to be itself if it wished to do so. This means that we cannot accept the presupposition of all speculative theories about man. Beyond the ground occupied by them we see open territory into which these theorists cannot move because they are not able to make use of our own presuppositions. Legitimately or illegitimately, they are otherwise engaged than we. They are just as incapable of fulfilling our task as we theirs. We cannot orientate ourselves by their attempts. And there can certainly be no question of theological anthropology being constrained or even able to enter the framework of an anthropology which has such a different basis. The different origin of theological anthropology is its frontier against all speculative anthropology. And it goes without saying that it must always guard this frontier.

The second type of non-theological anthropology is that of the exact science of man. Man, too, is an object—one among many, but nevertheless the nearest object— of the physiological and biological, psychological and sociological sciences. With more or less consensus of opinion, these sciences have at their disposal in every period temporarily authoritative formulæ which sum up the results of previous research, and which indicate hypotheses and pointers for future research. It is not difficult in any period to combine and co-ordinate these formulæ to form a picture or system which with due relativity may be advanced as, and may even claim to be, the authoritative doctrine of exact science in the period concerned. A sense of relativity will always be maintained. To the extent that science is exact, it will refrain from consolidating its formulae and hypotheses as axioms and therefore treating them as revealed dogmas. It will always be conscious that its concern is not with the being of man but the appearance; not with the inner but the outer; not with the totality but with the sum of specific and partial phenomena. It will realise that its temporarily valid picture or system can be only a momentary view for to-day which it may have to replace by another to-morrow, for the flux of phenomena is reflected also in the conclusions of science. Its exponents will either abstain from claiming, or will claim only with extreme reserve and with a warning against over-estimation and dogmatism, that their system constitutes the basis and criterion for all other investigation and knowledge. In this their attitude will contrast with that of speculative theorists. To the extent that science is exact its anthropology will necessarily and formally have this very different character. And what it can and will actually achieve corresponds to this character. Strictly speaking, what physiology and biology, psychology and sociology can offer, will not be statements to the effect that man in his physical, psychological and sociological existence is or is not this or that, but statements to the effect that man as a phenomenon is to be seen and understood by man according to this or that standpoint and in this or that aspect of his constitution and development, as determined by current knowledge of these facts accessible to human enquiry. Scientific anthropology gives us precise information and relevant data which can be of service in the wider investigation of the nature of man, and can help to build up a technique for dealing with these questions. Since it is itself a human activity, it presupposes that man is, and what he is, and on this basis shows him as to how he is, in what limits and under what conditions he can exist as the being he is. It is not concerned with his reality, let alone with its philosophical foundation and explanation. But it reveals the plenitude of his possibilities.

This second type obviously requires a different attitude from the first. As such, the exact science of man cannot be the enemy of the Christian confession. It becomes this only when it dogmatises on the basis of its formulæ and hypotheses, becoming the exponent of a philosophy and world-view, and thus ceasing to be exact science. As long as it maintains restraint and openness in face of the reality of man, it belongs, like eating, drinking, sleeping and all other human activities, techniques and achievements, to the range of human actions which in themselves do not prejudice in any way the hearing or non-hearing of the Word of God, which become acts of obedience or disobedience only in so far as they belong to individuals with their special tendencies and purposes, and which even as acts of a disobedient man, and in the context of a wrong purpose, are still good in themselves in so far as they correspond to the creaturehood of man, which as such cannot be changed by his disobedience. Hence the anthropology of science does not necessarily derive from the arid place in which the Word of God has not yet or is no longer heard.

It is not necessarily an unspiritual work, as is unfortunately true of the works of speculative anthropology which as such are to be explained only by the perverse intention of man. To the extent that it remains within its limits, and does not attempt to be more or less than exact science, it is a good work; as good as man himself as God created him. Hence our differentiation from it need not imply opposition. Opposition is required only if it becomes axiomatic, dogmatic and speculative.

If this is not the case, the differentiation consists simply in the fact that theological anthropology has not to do merely with man as a phenomenon but with man himself; not merely with his possibilities, but with his reality. It is in this way, in the light of God's Word and therefore in the light of truth, that he is known by it. Hence it may not frame its principles merely as temporarily and relatively valid hypotheses; as contributions to the wider investigation of the nature of man and the development of a technique for dealing with these questions. It has a responsibility to make the claim of truth. We repeat that this does not mean that it cannot err, that it does not need continually to correct and improve itself. But in virtue of its basis and origin it concerns itself with the real man. It not only comments on him, but denotes and describes him. It gives him his name. Interpreting him, it is concerned with the relation of this creature to God, and therefore with his inner reality and wholeness. This is something which the anthropology of exact science cannot do. How can it understand man as the creature of God? The fact that he is this does not belong to what is seen of man by exact science, to the external features which it can investigate and present, or to the sum of the parts in which he is present to it. Even the fact that man is the creation of God, standing as such in a special relation to God, is a fact that is not accessible to human thought and perception otherwise than through the Word of God. And this is even more true of the inner essence and character of this relation. It is from within this context that theological anthropology must interpret man. But in so doing it interprets man himself in his inner reality. For what he is as the creature of God, and in his relation to God, is his very being and reality. As theological anthropology concerns itself with this reality, it is fully aware of its own shortcomings, but it raises the claim to truth. Scientific anthropology cannot do this, even when its exponents have occasionally (or not just occasionally) to be taken seriously as obedient hearers of the Word of God; more seriously perhaps than theologians occupied on the other side. For if they are to fulfil the function of theological anthropology, they must look beyond the phenomenal man who is the object of exact science to the real man perceptible in the light of God's Word. In other words, they must become seekers asking and answering theological questions. And if there is no reason why the scientist who is obedient to God's Word should not look beyond the phenomenon of man to his inner reality, if it is self-evident that this should be the case and that to this extent he should become more or less basically a theologian, it is still true that what he does as a scientist, a physiologist, psychologist etc., can be no substitute for what theology has to do at this point. Where it is simply a question of man as a phenomenon—and exact science as such can go no further-there can be no perception of man as the creature and covenant—partner of God, and therefore of his true reality and essence, and the task of theological anthropology is thus untouched. Hence we cannot admit that scientific anthropology has already occupied the ground we propose to cover. On this side, too, the way is clear for the enquiry which we must undertake from our own particular standpoint.

But the differentiation of theological anthropology from other types of enquiry into the being of man is simple compared with the problem which now faces us. On our own assumption, what is in fact the theological standpoint from which we are to understand and describe the being and nature of man as created by God? For the presupposition that man may be known in the light of the Word of God, that in God's revelation man is disclosed as well as God, at once presents a difficulty the overcoming of which will be decisive for the whole course of our further enquiry.

The point is that the revelation of God does not show us man as we wish to see him, in the wholeness of his created being, but in its perversion and corruption. The truth of man's being as revealed in the Word of God and attested generally by Holy Scripture shows us man as a betrayer of himself and a sinner against his creaturely existence. It accuses him of standing in contradiction to God his Creator, but also to himself and the end for which he was created. It presents him as the corrupter of his own nature. It is no doubt true that this does not mean that God ceases to be God for him or that he ceases to stand before God. But his real situation in the sight of God is that he is the one who contradicts the purpose of God and therefore himself, distorting and corrupting his own being. What is sinful and strives against God and himself is not just something in him, qualities or achievements or defects, but his very being. And when he sins, entering into conflict with God and making himself impossible, it is not in virtue of his creation by God, but by his rebellion against it, by his own decisive deed, with which he takes up the history commenced with his creation. This history begins with the fact that at the very moment when God acts with the greatest faithfulness towards man His creature, man in supreme unfaithfulness takes sides against God his Creator. Whatever happens later in the history happens on this presupposition and with the determination that man is in contradiction with himself, thus making himself impossible. Because from the beginning of the history man is at war with himself, in its further course he can be helped only by the fact that God still takes his part, irrespective of the attitude of man. For this reason the grace of God alone can be his salvation.

* * * * *

When man is truly and seriously viewed in the light of the Word of God, he can be understood only as the sinner who has covered his own creaturely being with shame, and who cannot therefore stand before God even though he is the creature of God. And the difficulty which confronts us is this. In these circumstances how can we possibly reach a doctrine of man in the sense of a doctrine of his creaturely essence, of his human nature as such? For what we recognise to be human nature is nothing other than the disgrace which covers his nature; his inhumanity, perversion and corruption. If we try to deny this or to tone it down, we have not yet understood the full import of the truth that for the reconciliation of man with God nothing more nor less was needed than the death of the Son of God, and for the manifestation of this reconciliation nothing more nor less than the resurrection of the Son of Man, Jesus Christ. But if we know man only in the corruption and distortion of his being, how can we even begin to answer the question about his creaturely nature?

We do not forget, of course, that even as the sinner that he is man is still the creature of God. If his nature is wholly controlled by the fact that he has fallen away from God and can only be at odds with himself, yet this nature is not effaced, and he cannot succeed in destroying it and making himself unreal. The distortion or corruption of his being is not the same thing as its annihilation. Death itself does not spell annihilation. We cannot say, therefore, that he has ceased to exist as the one whom God created. That he still exists as such is implied in the fact that God still speaks to him. Thus he is still before God. Even as a sinner he is still real; he is still the creature of God. And therefore the question of his creaturely being, of the nature of man, is still meaningful and necessary in spite of his degeneracy.

* * * * *

But the knowledge of sin and the knowledge of the nature of man are possible both individually and in their inter-connexion within the comprehensive knowledge of the Word of God, i.e., of man as the partner in the covenant which God has made with him, of man as the object of the eternal grace of his Creator and Lord. On the one side, this embracing perception shows us that man is sinful, and indeed totally and radically sinful. But on the other hand the same perception forbids us to stop at this understanding of man and invites and commands us to look further and deeper. If man is the object of divine grace, his self-contradiction may be radical and total, but it is not the last word that has been spoken about him. For with God and from God he has a future which has not been decided by his self-contradiction or the divine judgment which as the sinner guilty of this self-contradiction he must inevitably incur, but which by the faithfulness and mercy of God is definitely decided in a very different way from what he deserves. If he is the object of God's favour, his self-contradiction may be radical and total, but it cannot even be the first word about him. The fact that he became a sinner cannot mean that he has spoken an originally valid word about himself, even in respect of his own origin and beginning.

For the fact that he covered his creaturely being with infamy cannot mean that he has annulled or destroyed it. The fact of his fall cannot mean that what he is eternally before God and from God, His Creator and Lord, has been changed. If, as a result of his self-contradiction, he had really ceased to be God's creature and to stand as such before God, how could this very different future, beyond his present contradiction, be disclosed to him by the faithfulness and goodness of God?

* * * * *

For all its newness the behaviour of God to sinful man as revealed in His Word is in continuity with His purpose in creation to the extent that it takes place on the presupposition and in the framework of certain relationships of the being of man which are influenced by sin but not structurally modified by it. His attitude reveals and confirms these relationships in their unchanged and unchangeable character. And the sum of these relationships is what we here understand by the creaturely essence and nature of man. Rightly this has always been taken to mean the invariable being of man as this persists through the antitheses of sin, reconciliation and redemption. It is that which always and in all circumstances belongs to the basic concept and view of man, no less in relation to his status in sin than to his status in the newly demonstrated grace of God and the final status of his eternal perfection. It is the being which according to the biblical witness is common to Jew and Gentile, to the obedient and disobedient, to apostles and Pharisees, to Peter and Judas. The Word of God instructs us concerning it to the extent that God's attitude to man as revealed and knowable in it always refers to and counts on this creaturely essence of man, so that we cannot hear this Word without being instructed concerning this creaturely essence of man as we are instructed concerning the deeds and commands of God, His threats and promises, His judgments and favours. This instruction is formally indirect because it is only incidental, because it is given us only in connexion with a very different instruction. But materially it is very direct because we cannot really receive the true and decisive instruction of the Word of God if we do not accept what it tells us incidentally about our human nature.

We have now reached the point where good reason can be seen for the most important thesis of this section: "As the man Jesus is Himself the revealing Word of God, He is the source of our knowledge of the nature of man as created by God." The attitude of God in which the faithfulness of the Creator and therefore the unchanging relationships of the human being created by Him are revealed and knowable, is quite simply His attitude and relation to the man Jesus: His election of this man; His becoming and remaining one with Him; His self-revelation, action and glorification in Him and through Him; His love addressed to Him and through Him to those who believe in Him and to the whole of creation; His freedom and sovereignty which in this man find their creaturely dwelling and form, their Bearer and Representative. He is God as even in His eternal Godhead He became this man in His human creatureliness. This is God's attitude towards sinful man. He answers or reacts to the sin of man by this relation to the man Jesus. Everything else that the biblical testimony to this divine answer and reaction discloses has at this point its beginning, centre and goal, and receives from it its light and explanation. And our hearing and reception of this testimony are true and right and clear and effective when we allow ourselves to be enlightened and instructed at this point. The Word of God is the Gospel of Jesus Christ. That is, it is the revelation of God's attitude to this man. As it reveals this, it reveals sin in its terrible gravity and judges it with supreme force, showing man that he cannot atone for it, and delivering him by assuring him in his heart that God Himself atones for it, and showing how He does this. In God's attitude to this man the decision is made that the divine grace is primary and the sin of man secondary, and that the primary factor is more powerful than the secondary. Recognising that it is made at this point, we cannot contradict the order which it establishes. We are forbidden to take sin more seriously than grace, or even as seriously as grace. At this point there is disclosed the merciful will of God, who chides and judges but cannot forget man because of his sin, who even in His wrathful judgment on his sin has not ceased to be his Creator, or to be free to justify His creature, knowing him as the being whom He created out of nothing according to His wisdom. At this point it may be seen how God sees man in spite of and through his sin, and therefore how we ourselves are incapable of seeing him. What is impossible with man but possible with God emerges at this point, namely, the vision of nature and essence which can be distorted by sin but not destroyed or transmuted into something different, because even in its sinful distortion it is held in the hand of God, and in spite of its corruption is not allowed to fall.

It would be foolish to expect this vision to be attained in any other way or to be generally accessible.

The attitude of God to sinful man, in which the order of grace and sin is present and revealed, is primarily and originally His attitude to the man Jesus alone. If God has elected any other man to Himself in spite of his sin, He has done so because primarily and originally He eternally elected this man, and in and with Him this other as a member of the body of which Jesus is the Head. If He calls others who are His enemies to fellowship, it is because He does not see and treat their sin as their own but as that of His beloved Son, whose obedience He sees and treats as theirs. If he reveals Himself to these others who have finally forfeited the possibility of knowing Him, it is because He confronts them in this man as the eternal light whose force is more than a match for their blindness. If He acts to and for others, it is in the work of this man which takes place absolutely in their place and favour. If He glorifies Himself in others, it is as this man gives them a part in His own glory. If He loves them, it is in the fact that He loves Him, and them through Him. If the freedom and lordship of His grace, which as sinners they have despised and affronted, is the kingdom in which they too may live, it is because this man, and in and with Him He Himself and therefore His kingdom, are radiantly present in their midst. Always and in every respect it is primarily and originally in this man that we see God's attitude to sinful man to be of such a kind that it maintains and discloses the interrelation of sin and grace. It would be unwise to look elsewhere to discover the interrelation of sin and grace and to become originally and basically certain of it. And it would be unwise not to look back to it continually even though subsequently and by deduction we have become aware and assured of it elsewhere as well. Nowhere but in this man is it primarily and properly established and revealed. In all other connexions, even as a general truth, it can be recognised afresh only on the basis of the special recognition of the attitude of God to this man. He is its disclosure. All other disclosures of it go back to the disclosure in Him. We must look and keep to the man Jesus when we think we can know and assert that man, even in his sinful corruption, is held in the hand of God and in spite of that corruption is not allowed to fall. Otherwise we do not know what we are saying when we make this statement. We can make it only with a final uncertainty, threatened by the possibility that it might be quite otherwise, or that this perception might again slip from our grasp. It is by faith, and indeed by faith in the Word of God which is the Gospel of Jesus Christ, that we have to say that God is gracious to man and that man is the creature to whom God is gracious. Otherwise this is a mere religious phrase, the sound of which may perhaps for a time refresh us, but by which we cannot live.

The same applies to the view given by this perception of human nature corrupted by sin, but not destroyed nor transmuted into something different. The nature of the man Jesus alone is the key to the problem of human nature. This man is man. As certainly as God's relation to sinful man is properly and primarily His relation to this man alone, and a relation to the rest of mankind only in Him and through Him, He alone is primarily and properly man. If we were referred to a picture of human nature attained or attainable in any other way, we should always have to face the question whether what we think we see and know concerning it is not a delusion, because with our sinful eyes we cannot detect even the corruption of our nature, let alone its intrinsic character, and are therefore condemned to an unceasing confusion of the natural with the unnatural, and vice versa. We do not have to rely on these vague ideas, and we are not therefore condemned to this confusion, because true man, the true nature behind our corrupted nature, is not concealed but revealed in the person of Jesus, and in His nature we recognise our own, and that of every man.

But we must really keep to the human nature of Jesus. Thus we may not deviate from it, nor may we on any account rely upon, nor take for granted, what we think we know about man from other sources. We must form and maintain the conviction that the presupposition given us in and with the human nature of Jesus is exhaustive and superior to all other presuppositions, and that all other presuppositions can become possible and useful only in connexion with it.

We have thus to formulate the theological enquiry into the nature of man in the following terms. What is the creaturely nature of man to the extent that, looking to the revealed grace of God and concretely to the man Jesus, we can see in it a continuum unbroken by sin, an essence which even sin does not and cannot change? It is the special and characteristic task of theological anthropology to consider this question. In so doing, it does not prevent other anthropological discussion. But it cannot be blocked or diverted by any other. Here lies its freedom and objectivity. Even in its investigation of human nature, its enquiries are not based on any creaturely insight into the creature. It places the contemplative and reflective reason of the creature in the service of the Creator's knowledge of the creature revealed by God's own Word. We have seen what this means. Here, too, it asks concerning the revealed grace of God, Jesus Christ, and the treasures of wisdom and knowledge concealed in Him.

But it is as well not to take this as our point of departure without a preliminary understanding of what we are undertaking and not undertaking, and within what limits we have to move as we start from this point. If we rightly consider the special difficulty of a theological anthropology, there can be no question of any other point of departure. But the choice of this point of departure means nothing more nor less than the founding of anthropology on Christology.

* * * * *

In conclusion, we have to consider the problems involved in grounding anthropology on Christology and to give a first basic and general indication of the way to their solution.

For one thing, it is clear that there can be no question of a direct equation of human nature as we know it in ourselves with the human nature of Jesus, and therefore of a simple deduction of anthropology from Christology. The analysis of individual man, even and especially when undertaken in the light of God's Word, leads us to very different and indeed opposed conclusions. At this point, we can indicate these only in general outline. Human nature as it is and in ourselves is always a debatable quantity; the human situation as we know and experience it is dialectical. We exist in antitheses which we cannot escape or see beyond. We bear various aspects none of which can be disowned. Our life has no unity. We seek it, as the various theories of man bear witness. But we only seek it. All theories of man are one-sided, and must contradict other theories and be contradicted by them. There is no undisputed and ultimately certain theory of man. At bottom there is only a theoretical search for the real man, as in practice there is only a striving to attain real humanity. The final thing is always unrest: not a genuine, pure and open unrest; but an unrest which is obscured by a forceful interpretation or dogmatic view of man, by an exculpation and justification of his existence on the basis of this dogma; or even more simply, an unrest which is made innocuous by conscious resignation or lack of thought. The ultimate fact about our human nature, as we shall constantly see in detail, is the self-contradiction of man, and the conscious or unconscious self-deception in which he refuses to recognise this truth. But the first thing which has to be said about human nature in Jesus is that in Him an effective protest is lodged against our self-contradiction and all the self-deception in which we try to conceal it. It is a protest because the antitheses in which we live are no antitheses in Him, and therefore do not require any attempted solution, so that in Him all illusions about the success of these attempts are quite irrelevant. And it is effective because His human nature shows us the dialectic of our situation and the hopelessness of our illusions by showing them to be the sin which in Him is no longer imputed to us but forgiven, being taken from us and removed and eliminated, like a vicious circle which is ended by Him, so that by right we can no longer move in it. The human nature of Jesus spares and forbids us our own. Thus it is our justification. And because it is this, it is the judgment on our own humanity. It is the revelation of the complete impossibility of explaining, exculpating or justifying it of ourselves, and therefore the revelation of the end of the illusion or the lack of thought in which we might hope to affirm our humanity, and the beginning of the genuine, pure and open unrest about our nature. It is clear from these considerations that when we look in these different directions, at Jesus on the one hand and ourselves and man in general on the other, we at once find ourselves in very different spheres. But that they are different is not the final thing which is to be said about them. We cannot really look at Jesus without—in a certain sense through Him—seeing ourselves also. In Him are the peace and clarity which are not in ourselves. In Him is the human nature created by God without the self-contradiction which afflicts us and without the self-deception by which we seek to escape from this our shame. In Him is human nature without human sin. For as He the Son of God becomes man, and therefore our nature becomes His, the rent is healed, the impure becomes pure and the enslaved is freed. For although He becomes what we are, He does not do what we do, and so He is not what we are. He is man like ourselves, yet He is not a sinner, but the man who honours His creation and election by God, not breaking but keeping the covenant of grace. The good pleasure of God rests on Him. And because of this He has power to forgive sin. What God does not find in us He finds abundantly in Him—with sufficient wealth to make up for all that lacks in us. Thus human nature in Jesus is the reason and the just foundation for the mercy in which God has turned to our human nature. Even in His mercy God is not capricious. His holiness, His faithfulness to Himself, to His Creator-will and to the obligations of the covenant of grace, suffer no disruption in the fact that He is gracious to us. He is justified in His own eyes when He justifies us sinful men. For He does this for the sake of Jesus, i.e., in view of human nature as it is in Him. Here God finds human nature blameless. This is the basis of our pardon and of the continuance of the covenant which we have broken. God does not have regard to the fact that we have broken it, but to the fact that Jesus keeps it. And His judgment on us is determined by this. And because it is determined by it, He is to us a gracious—and in His very grace a supremely just—Judge. This does not mean that our sin is overlooked, or unremoved, or unexpiated. The sinlessness, purity and freedom of human nature in Jesus consists precisely in the fact that, laden with the sin which is alien to His own nature, He causes Himself to be condemned and rejected with us. Thus the sin of our human nature is not only covered by Him but rightfully removed and destroyed. But this means that it is truly buried and covered, so that before God and in truth there now remains only the pure and free humanity of Jesus as our own humanity. This is the connexion between those very different and separated spheres. The purity, freedom, peace and clarity of the human nature of Jesus do not remain His privilege alone, but for His sake this privilege becomes ours as well. As God knows Him, He also knows us. As He knows Jesus, He also knows our nature, against which no accusation can stand because He has created it. In virtue of the exoneration from sin validly effected in Jesus, we may count on this nature of ours and its innocence as we could not otherwise do. This judicial pardon gives us the courage and shows us the way to think about man as God created him. It is the true ground of theological anthropology.

There does, of course, remain a true and abiding privilege of Jesus which is exclusive to Him in spite of our justification. We do well not to forget this. It reminds us of the reserve which is incumbent upon us if we are really to venture, on the basis of that judicial pardon, to think about man as created by God. For if our acquittal allows and commands us to recognise in human nature as it is in Jesus our own, we must not fail to appreciate how different are His nature and ours. Human nature in Him is determined by a relation between God and Himself such as has never existed between God and us, and never will exist. He alone is the Son of Man and the Son of God. Our fellowship with God rests upon the fact that He and He alone is one with God. He Himself is the living God. He in His own person is the kingdom of God. He alone is primarily and truly elected as the Head and the Lord of all the elect.

If we too are elected, we are only the members of His body. He alone gives grace as well as receives it. We can only receive it. He alone can forgive sins. We can only ask for forgiveness, receiving it as grounded in Him, and imparting it as received from Him. He alone has the Spirit of God directly, as the source of His holy Spirit. We can have it only from His fullness. Thus He alone is in the true sense of the word the Representative, Instrument, Ambassador and Plenipotentiary of God in the creaturely world. He alone is the Revealer, Reconciler and Lord, the Prophet, Priest and King. In these capacities, which devolve on Him alone, we can only follow and serve Him, with no dignity or power which are not His and do not redound to His glory. Hence He alone is the Word of God. We can only hear it. What we say cannot be more than a promise and warning based on this Word. He alone can represent God before men and men before God. We can represent God and men only in so far as He is the true Mediator. It is because He is the foundation that we can build. It is because He has come and died and is risen from the dead and will come again that there is Israel and the Church, and hope for all men and all creation. These are irreversible relationships. In all these things He goes before us once for all; not in His humanity as such, for in this respect He makes us like unto Himself; but in the way in which He is a man, i.e., in virtue of His unique relation to God; and in the fact that we need His humanity in order to be like Him as men. He has it immediately from God to be man in that purity and freedom and peace and clarity. We have it immediately from Him, on the ground of the judicial pardon under which we are placed for His sake. If we may use this privilege and be the servants, friends and children of God, it is for His sake, as His younger brethren, and therefore on the basis of the inequality between Him and us, in the possession and enjoyment of a gift. Without Him we would not be what we are. What we are we must always seek in Him and receive from Him. Our human nature rests upon His grace; on the divine grace addressed to us in His human nature. It is both His and ours, but it is His in a wholly different way from that in which it is ours.

Our primary emphasis must be upon the fact that on the ground of His unique relation to God it is first His and then and only for this reason ours. It is actualised in Him as the original and in us only as the copy. Jesus is man as God willed and created him. What constitutes true human nature in us depends upon what it is in Him. The fact that natural humanity as God created it was subsequently concealed by our sinful corruption is a lesser mystery than the fact that humanity is originally hidden in Jesus, so that primarily it is His and not ours. What man is, is determined by God's immediate presence and action in this man, by His eternal election and the mighty work of His life and death and resurrection corresponding to this election. There in the eternity of the divine counsel which is the meaning and basis of all creation, and in the work of His life accomplished at the heart of time, the decision was made who and what true man is. There his constitution was fixed and sealed once and for all. For this reason it cannot be different in any other man. No man can elude this prototype. We derive wholly from Jesus not merely our potential and actual relation to God, but even our human nature as such. For it is He who, as the ground and goal of the covenant of grace planned for man, is also the ground and goal of man's creation: man as God willed him to be when He became his Creator; and as He wills him to be when as the Creator He does not cease to be actively concerned for him. We are partakers of human nature as and because Jesus is first partaker of it. It is for this reason that it is our nature; that it is ours unchangeably and inalienably; that while it may be distorted and corrupted by sin, in all its degradation and corruption it cannot be cancelled or annihilated; that in spite of sin and through the cloak of sin it can and must be recognised as ours. In Jesus both the first and the last word is spoken about us, and the last with all the power of the first. In his relation to God a man may become a sinner and thus distort and corrupt his own nature, but he cannot revoke what was decided in Jesus apart from him concerning the true nature of man. By his fall he can deny his Creator and his own creaturely nature. But he cannot make it a lie. What he is, is decided elsewhere in such a way that he cannot affect the decision. And if Jesus forgives his sins and restores his spoiled relation to God, this means that Jesus again controls what originally belongs to Him; that again He takes to Himself what was never lost to Him. In so doing. He merely restores in human nature that which originally corresponds to Him, is like Him, and is constituted in Him. He has the freedom and power to do this. He has only to apply them. And He does just that by making Himself our Saviour. It is with the freedom and power of the Creator that He is also our Saviour. It is His own property. His own house, which He sets in order as such. But to say this is to say that we participate in the true nature of man only because He does so first and that our recognition of this true nature can be effective only in so far as we recognise it in Him, not hearing or accepting as the first word in this matter any other logos of supposed humanity, but only Him.

That human nature is one thing in Him and another in us means secondly that in Him it is not distorted by sin and therefore concealed in its reality, but maintained and preserved in its original essence. The second difference to be noted at this point consists, therefore, in the sinlessness of Jesus. This again can be understood only in the light of the unique relationship to God which was His by right. It does not consist, therefore, in any special quality of His humanity by which He is as it were physically incapable of sin. If His relation to God is originally and utterly different from our own, His human nature as such is not different from our own, and does not simply exclude the possibility of the corruption to which it has fallen victim in us. He, too, was tempted as we are. What protects Him and His human nature from temptation is not a particularity of His creatureliness but the particularity of the way in which He is creature. He is so as the Son of God, and therefore as the Creator and Lord. It is the eternal mercy of God which is a human person in Him; the mercy with which God is so far from abandoning creation to itself that He wills to impart to it nothing less than His own immediate personal presence and action, nothing less than Himself. Again, we are confronted by the basis and goal of the divine covenant of grace which is also the basis and goal of creation. What protects Him from sin, and keeps His human nature from corruption, is the eternal mercy of God which refuses to be limited and suspended, but wills to maintain itself in vulnerable human nature. It is the fact that "God so loved the world, that he gave his only begotten Son," and that Jesus is this Son. Even in Him human nature would not have been capable of this of itself. Even in the person of Jesus it might have become a prey to the corruption which was its fate in us. For even in Him it is still creaturely, not creative and divine, and therefore not precluded from sin, as we should have to say of the creative nature of God itself. It is for this reason that in various places the New Testament speaks very plainly of the liability of Jesus to temptation, and of the temptation which He had actually to face. But He could not succumb, and therefore could not sin, because as the Bearer of humanity He was Himself its Lord, the Creator God active within it. He asserted Himself against temptation with the freedom and power with which God as Creator confronted chaos, separating light from darkness and uttering His Yes to the real and His definitive No to the unreal. The fact that even and precisely in becoming man God remained true to Himself, true to His mercy to creation, is the secret of the sinlessness of Jesus and therefore of the maintenance of human nature in Him. He delivered it when it could not save itself. There is therefore a deliverance and preservation of human nature as created by God. Hence we cannot in any circumstances understand its distortion and corruption as a natural necessity. Sin is powerless against the faithfulness with which God the Creator is merciful to us. By the fact that He Himself came amongst us, this impossibility was made impossible, as is only right. The same human nature as ours can be sinless on the assumption that God takes up its case. This assumption was realised in the human nature of Jesus. We cannot consider Him without accepting this. Nor, of course, can we accept the assumption without considering Jesus. In our own humanity as such we cannot find any evidence for it. Of this nature we cannot say either that in some hidden depths it is sinless or that it has in some way the power to be sinless. Sinlessness and the power to be sinless are divine qualities. In the creaturely world they are to be seen only in the work which was accomplished in Jesus, and which could be accomplished only in Him, because that assumption was fulfilled in Him, and only in Him.

The third point in which Jesus is the same as us, but very differently in virtue of His unique relationship to God, is simply that in Him human nature is not concealed but revealed in its original and basic form. It is not intrinsic to it to be hidden from us, just as it is not intrinsic to God to be hidden from us. What is real requires no secrecy, and is incapable of it. Essentially, neither the Creator nor the creature is absolutely hidden from us, but strictly speaking only evil, only the darkness which was rejected by God and separated from the light. Divinely created human nature as such is not evil, and therefore essentially it cannot be completely hidden from us. It is the good creature of God, and as such can only be manifest to us. The creature becomes unknowable and unrecognisable only when it is distorted and ruined by sin. In us the real creature is of course unknowable. In us it cannot express itself. Thus of ourselves we do not know what we really are. In respect of self-knowledge we grope no less blindly in the dark than in respect of our knowledge of God. But it is not necessarily so. When God Himself takes the initiative in the creature—and this is what has taken place in Jesus—then the creature also begins to speak; it becomes manifest to us; it becomes itself a word. Then the Creator who has become one with His creature speaks of it as well as Himself, and He speaks the truth in both respects. Thus the incarnate Word of God, Jesus Christ, is really the true Word about man as well as God, and about the nature of man. It needed Jesus, for the latter to become knowable and known. As it is real in Him first and only then and for this reason in us, it can only become true for us, i.e., revealed and manifest, through Him. Through Him! It is not that we interpret Him, but that He discloses and explains Himself to us, that through and in Himself He manifests His nature to us as our own true nature. Hence there is revelation in this respect also; the revelation of God which as such is also the revelation of true man. It is also as such God's own irreplaceable action. This action was performed in Jesus. Here again we cannot try to stand by His side, nor to anticipate Him, nor to compete with Him. It is either through Him that we know what we truly are as men, or we do not know it at all. Our self-knowledge can only be an act of discipleship. But as an act of discipleship it can be a true and established and certain knowledge.

These are the limits which theological anthropology cannot exceed. In its investigation of the nature of man in general, it must first look away from man in general and concentrate on the one man Jesus, and only then look back from Him to man in general. If it keeps within these limits, but also makes use of the possibilities offered within these limits, it is differentiated from all other forms of human self-knowledge. In spite of every difference—and this point must be emphasised again and no less strongly—we share the same nature with Jesus. If His relation to God is other than our own, and if as a result human nature is His in a different way from that in which it is ours, yet it is the same both in Him and us. The threefold fact that it is first in Him, that in Him it is kept and maintained in its purity, and that it is manifest in Him, implies a different status but not a different constitution of His human nature from ours. All the otherness to be noted here is rooted in the fact that as man He is also God, and as creature Creator. But this does not mean an intrinsic otherness of His humanity and creatureliness. Jesus is not an angel. He is not an intermediate being, a third entity between God and man. He is both true God and true man. And "true" does not mean only that He is man as God created him, but also that He is this as we all are, and that He is therefore accessible and knowable to us as man, with no special capacities or potentialities, with no admixture of a quality alien to us, with no supernatural endowment such as must make Him a totally different being from us. He is man in such a way that He can be the natural Brother of any other man. And this likeness between Him and us is the other presupposition which is as much actualised and noteworthy in Him as the presupposition which we have expressed as a threefold dissimilarity. That Jesus is utterly unlike us as God and utterly like us as man is the twofold fact which constitutes the whole secret of His person. If in one respect there were not complete and strict likeness, all that which on the other side stands only in virtue of His unlikeness to us would collapse. If the election of Jesus were not the election of true man even in this sense, how could others realise that they were elected in Him? How could He be the goal and the fulfilment of the covenant of God with men, the Messiah of a human Israel, the Lord of a human Church? How could the good-pleasure of God for His sake rest on other men too? How could He represent us to God and God to us? How could the forgiveness of sins take place in Him and the promise and law of a new life be established by Him? How could men come to believe in Him, and through belief in Him come to know themselves as the children of God and fellow-recipients of the grace of God disclosed in Him? In this event we could not be the body of which He is the Head. We would be creatures of a very different order, and there could be no communion between Him and us. It would be quite impossible to recognise in Him the reality of human nature. There would be no theological knowledge in this matter—and of course no knowledge of the relation of God to man—because the relation between God and man would remain hidden from us, and therefore finally there would be no theological knowledge at all. But there is no foundation for this hypothesis.

We should be thinking on Manichean or Marcionite lines in respect of sin, and docetically in Christology, if we proposed to ascribe to human nature as it exists in us and in Jesus a difference of constitution. And perhaps it is because of a remaining trace of Docetism, which the Church has failed to eliminate in spite of its formal rejection, that our appreciation of the bearing of the divine election effected in Jesus Christ, the institution of the covenant fulfilled in Him, and the reconciliation accomplished in Him, has been so small that it still strikes us as strange that in Jesus Christ we should have to do not only with the order and the revelation of the redeeming grace of God the Creator, but also with the order and revelation of the creature, and therefore of the truth of man.

In this regard the one presupposition is as firm as the other. The man Jesus is one nature with us, and we unreservedly with Him. But this means that we are invited to infer from His human nature the character of our own, to know ourselves in Him, but in Him really to know ourselves. When the New Testament speaks of the Son of God it speaks without any kind of qualification of One who is a man as we are. All the extraordinary things that it says of this man are just as radically meant as said against this background, and they resist any dilution or distortion into more innocuous statements. It declares His likeness to all other men no less precisely than it declares His unlikeness to them all. Not for a moment shall we lose sight of His unlikeness to them all. But this is the very reason why His likeness to them all is so real, the light in which this likeness is disclosed. And we take seriously the likeness between Jesus and ourselves as grounded and revealed in this way if we now attempt to press on to an understanding of human nature as such on the presupposition of the validity of the humanity of Jesus for the question which mainly concerns us.

Questions

1 According to Barth, what is the "special task" of theological anthropology?

2 Why does Barth think that speculative approaches to anthropology have no place in theological anthropology? What approaches to anthropology today would qualify as speculative?

3 Why does Barth think we should have a different attitude toward scientific approaches? When can these become problematic as well?

4 How would you describe Barth's position on the relationship between theological anthropology and other anthropological approaches?

5 What is the significance of sin for theological anthropology? How does this impact the role of non-theological disciplines in anthropology?

6 Why does Barth think that anthropology needs to be grounded in Christology?

7 What problems does Barth identify when it comes to grounding anthropology in Christology and how does he address them?

TEXT 5: KATHRYN TANNER, "ON THE DIFFERENCE THEOLOGICAL ANTHROPOLOGY MAKES"[5]

Kathryn Tanner (b. 1957) is the Frederick Marquand Professor of Systematic Theology at Yale Divinity School. A prolific author, Tanner has written on a wide range of theological issues, focusing primarily on Christology, Trinity, salvation, creation, culture, and justice. She is particularly well known for drawing on a range of classic and contemporary voices, weaving insights from both ancient and modern theologians together with resources from social, cultural, and feminist theorists. Tanner's own theology thus exemplifies a pervasive interdisciplinarity. In this article, Tanner reflects on how this interdisciplinarity affects theological anthropology, offering a robust account of how theology can and should affirm the importance of its distinct contribution to anthropology even while embracing the importance of other anthropological perspectives.

A theologian discusses human beings in relation to God. Discussion of this relationship to God is the theologian's contribution to the understanding of human life, his or her pride and joy. But such a focus for discussing human life also marks the theologian's humility, signaling the limits of the theological enterprise and the dependence of the theologian upon other forms of inquiry and other contexts of investigation. I hope to offer here an account of humanity in relation to God that highlights the distinctive contribution of theological anthropology. First, however, I want to clarify, more generally, how the contribution of theology to the understanding of human life is both exalted and, at the same time, lowly.

I

Theology intends to be comprehensive. No element or aspect of the universe is really independent of a relation to God, since God is the Lord of all creation: "The earth is the Lord's and all that is in it, the world, and those who live in it" (Ps. 24). Thus, the theologian wishing to do justice to this relevance of God to the whole should exempt no element or aspect of the universe from theological comment. Within the purview of the eye trained on God come the stars in the sky, the trees and the oceans, wild beasts, creeping things of the earth, and certainly human beings, with whom God covenants, human beings with whom God chooses to be intimate in Jesus Christ. Because God's reach is universal, discussion about God is relevant, moreover, to more than the religious aspects of human life. God is a matter for concern not just in times of private prayer or within the walls of church, not just in ritual contexts when

---

[5]Kathryn Tanner, "The Difference Theological Anthropology Makes," *Theology Today* 50, no. 4 (1994): 567.

calling upon and praising God or bringing the bread and wine to one's lips, but in every affair of human life, no matter how mundane and trivial or seemingly profane, in one's workplace, on the street, in the home.

Theology does not try to insure this comprehensiveness by generating out of its own resources all there is to say on these matters. A theological discourse designed to cover the whole world is not entirely self-generated. It does not come forth from the theologian's mind in the way the world in itself comes to be from God's Word out of nothing. The theologian, as a theologian, is not an expert on plant growth, ocean tides, the molecular structure of biological compounds, human physiology and psychology, or group dynamics. Such topics, though included within the theologian's purview, are beyond theology's specific competence. The theologian does not have the resources—say, in biblical texts or church teachings—to render adequately informed judgments concerning them. The theologian depends upon other habits of inquiry and upon other disciplines for knowledge concerning such matters.

The theologian's specific concern is not so much to determine what is related to God—the height of the skies, the extent of the universe, the make-up of its inhabitants, their essential natures, accidental features or functionings—but how all things are related to God, a relation the theologian feels competent to discuss in light of the biblical witness, doctrinal pronouncements, church teachings, and the religious practices of Christians. Of course, if theology hopes to be comprehensive, the theologian's concern is not limited to this question of how God is related, bare and unadorned. Theologians make discussion of this question relevant to the whole world by taking up the best thought about the cosmos and its inhabitants and subjecting it to their particular angle of vision, by investigating how all this appears when one understands the world in its relation to the God of all.

The theologian who produces a comprehensive commentary is, therefore, not like a self-determined creator of cultural artifacts—say, a writer of a novel or a composer of a symphony. He or she is, instead, like an active reader or an orchestra conductor metaphorizing the artistic creation of others, diverting it from its intended course, transposing it into a new register or key. When producing a comprehensive commentary, the theologian does not provide his or her own place of habitation. The theologian engaged in such an enterprise is, instead, a perpetual renter, making do, making use of, working over the property of other disciplines, in the service of theology's own interests and purposes. The theologian producing a comprehensive commentary is, poor and incapacitated, a poacher or a parasite. Like those birds that lay their eggs only in other birds' nests, theologians bring their hope for a comprehensive commentary to fruition only by interjecting their own distinctive viewpoint within the spaces of other disciplines.

Ironically, this lowly dependence on forms of knowledge not its own allows theology to intimate the way in which God's own Word is a word not simply for one time and one place, but for all. Theology has no special stake in any particular account of the natural world or of the human beings in it. Theology does not become irrelevant, therefore, when its accounts of such things become obsolete. Claims made about the natural world and its inhabitants may come and go, influencing the theologian's commentary on them in this or that way. Unlike God's Word, every theological commentary on the world is transitory and fleeting; it shows its humanity by perishing, replaced by other human words for another time and place. Yet in and through this changing variety of theological production, there may continue to appear a distinctive theological modus operandi, particular patterns of poaching or styles of deflective transposition.

I intend to uncover a few of these patterns or styles of use in theological discussions of humanity. I do not provide a full-fledged theological commentary on human life, informed as it would need to be by the best natural and physical science, sociology, and psychology of the day. Restrictions of space alone prohibit the attempt. Indeed, I try to minimize the degree of this dependence on other disciplines and sources of knowledge, focusing instead on the relation to God that is the basis for the distinctiveness of a theological viewpoint, merely indicating those places where the conclusions of other forms of knowledge might make an appropriate entrance. Even so, the account I offer is clearly influenced by a contemporary outlook on humanity—in its respect for human powers of self-determination, for example, and its sense of human life as inextricably embedded in wider worldly spheres, both ecological and socio-political. Moreover, the very stress in this account on the relation of human beings to God reflects a contemporary interest. This stress is the result of my judgment that, in an age of highly refined and well-respected sciences, theological anthropology needs to show not so much that it approves of their conclusions but that it has something of its own to say.

II

At the most fundamental level, the human being is one creature among others. The relation that human beings enjoy with God, therefore, is one they share with all God's creatures. God's creatures are related to God as the recipients of God's good gifts or blessings. "The Lord is good to all, and his compassion is over all that he has made" (Ps. 145:9). God holds creatures up in the palm of God's hand, bestowing upon them their existence in space and time, their living vitality and productive powers, their growth, increase, and capacities for communal fellowship in harmony with one another. God acts bountifully in wonderful works; God expresses God's power in gifts of abundance: "You visit the earth and water it, you greatly enrich it; the river of God is full of water; you provide the people with grain…You water its furrows abundantly, settling its ridges, softening it with showers and blessing its growth. You crown the year with your bounty; your wagon tracks overflow with richness. The pastures of the wilderness overflow,…the meadows clothe themselves with flocks, the valleys deck themselves with grain, they shout and sing together for joy" (Ps. 65:9–13). God's solicitude and care extend to all God's creatures; God intends their well-being by seeing to their needs and satisfying their hungers. "O Lord, how manifold are your works! In wisdom you have made them all; the earth is full of your creatures…These all look to you, to give them their food in due season; when you give to them, they gather it up; when you open your hand, they are filled with good things" (Ps. 104:24–28). "Satisfying the desire of every living thing" (Ps. 145:16), "you save humans and animals alike, O Lord" (Ps. 36:6).

Faithful to this intention to bring about the creature's good, God works to uphold "all who are falling" (Ps. 145:14), healing the sick, bringing captives out from their bondage, protecting the weak, easing the plight of the poor and the downtrodden. God's blessings continue even under the disrupted conditions of sin:

> There is the beauty and utility of the natural creation, which the divine generosity has bestowed on man, for him to behold and to take into use, even though mankind has been condemned and cast out from paradise into the hardships and miseries of this life. How could any description do justice to all these blessings? ... Think ... of the abundant supply of food everywhere to satisfy our hunger, the variety of flavours to suit our pampered taste, lavishly distributed by the riches of nature, not produced by the skill and labour of cooks! Think, too, of all the resources for the preservation of health, or for its restoration, the welcome alternation of day and night, the soothing coolness of the breezes.[6]

Moreover, God's blessings to sinful humanity are not limited to those of the natural world: God sends God's own Word among us, to be born, to suffer, and to die for our sakes. And more, Christ's coming is a prelude to even greater gifts of the kingdom: "He who did not withhold his own Son, but gave him up for all of us, will he not with him also give us everything else?" (Rom. 8:32). "What blessings are we to receive in that Kingdom, seeing that in Christ's death for us we have already received such a pledge!"[7] "What blessings in that life of happiness will [God] provide for those for whom in this life of wretchedness he willed that his only-begotten Son should endure such sufferings, even unto death?" In some future time, Christ's compassion for the suffering, Christ's miraculous healings, Christ's feeding of the multitudes, will be brought to fulfillment in the well-being of a universal community in which the world and all its inhabitants will be reconciled for their harmony, peace, and security. Enjoying in coming ages "the immeasurable riches of [God's] grace in kindness towards us in Christ Jesus" (Eph. 2:7), we humans, along with the rest of God's creatures, will suffer no wants, becoming peaceful and harmonious with one another at a table set in glorious abundance by God.

Human beings should rejoice in these gifts of God, given for themselves and for others, and esteem their goodness. Whatever a good God brings forth must be good in its own being. "God saw everything that he had made, and indeed, it was very good" (Gen. 1:31). This gift-giving, value-producing, creative working of God cannot be limited, moreover, to some places or some times. "My Father is still working, and I also am working" (John 5:17). "God works ceaselessly in the creatures He has made....This work is that by which He holds all things and by which his Wisdom 'reaches from end to end mightily and governs all graciously.' It is by this divine governance that 'we live and move and have our being in Him'."[8] Nothing of the creature's good is therefore exempt from the obligation to praise God for gifts bestowed. Everything that creatures have for the good, every precondition and means to their well-being, is to be attributed to God's giving: "You are my Lord; I have no good apart from you" (Ps. 16:2).

---

[6]Augustine, *City of God* (New York: Penguin, 1972), xxii.2
[7]Ibid., xxii.24.
[8]Augustine, *The Literal Meaning of Genesis* (New York: Newman Press, 1982), 4:12.23.

This relationship between creatures and a gift-giving God suggests a first, rather complex formality or pattern in theology's use of the sciences. The sciences may tell us about the creatures the earth contains, about their number and differences, about their natures, powers, and interrelations, about their inclinations, tendencies, and desires, and the manner in which they may or may not be satisfied in the present course of the world's compass. The theologian tells us, on the one hand, that those creatures are to be esteemed and their well-being valued. Creatures may be praised and respected without offense to God's glory, since this world and its inhabitants are the beauty with which God's glory clothes itself. Praise for creatures does not detract from praise for the Creator, since all that is to be valued in the one is the gift of the other. On the other hand, the theologian admonishes us that value is not to be ascribed to creatures apart from the continuous working of God in and for them. Esteem for the creature apart from the God who makes it is idolatrous, a vain and empty esteem, since the good that is the creature's own remains dependent on God's giving. Dependent indeed, since, without God, the goods of created beings—their existence, nature, powers, perfections—cease to be. Should God withhold God's gifts and "take back his spirit to himself and gather to himself his breath, all flesh would perish together and all mortals would return to dust" (Job 34:14–15).

According to this first, complex formality, human beings must, therefore, be humble before God, even and especially for that of which they are most proud. Human achievements, for instance, come to pass only when God hears the plea that "the favor of the Lord our God be upon us, and prosper for us the work of our hands" (Ps. 90:17). "Unless the Lord builds the house, those who build it labor in vain" (Ps. 127:1). In adversity and opposition, it is not one's own arm alone, but one's own arm backed by the Lord's gracious giving that gives one the victory: "I worked harder than any of them—though it was not I [who achieved the success], but the grace of God that is with me" (1 Cor. 15:10). Joy in one's accomplishments is appropriate, then, only to the extent one continually boasts in the Lord's gracious help. "Neither the one who plants nor the one who waters is anything, but only God who gives the growth ... For we are God's fellow workers ... God's field" (1 Cor. 3:7,9).

III

Even though the human being is one creature among others, human beings are not merely one aspect of the created world; their relationship with God is not just that of any other creature. They have some special standing as the focus of God's concern. God may covenant with all the earth and its inhabitants (Gen. 9:10–17), but God makes a special covenant with a particular people and, despite their continual failings, remains faithful to them with a steadfast love. God's Word may come into the world in order to bring about the eventual consummation of all things in a loving and just community, every one with every other and with God. God's Word nevertheless takes up humanity by becoming incarnate in Jesus Christ. Jesus Christ suffers and dies, first of all, for human sin and, by his death and resurrection, exalts human beings, first of all, to a new life in God in and through the Holy Spirit.

The creation of human beings in God's image (Gen. 1:26) may sum up this distinction. The biblical narrative remains silent, however, about any qualities of human nature that might account for their special standing. Creation in God's image is not a way of saying something about human beings as such; it is a way of pointing out a special relation between them and God. Human beings gain their unique dignity not by virtue of anything they possess in and of themselves but by being God's image—by reflecting, corresponding to, following obediently after, making an appropriate response to, the God who has created them for such a relationship.

To be created in the image of God means, in other words, to have a particular vocation, one of fellowship and communion with God in which one uses all one's powers to glorify God and carry out God's purposes. Human beings may be alone among God's creatures in rendering conscious praise in word and deed for God's blessings in their own lives and throughout creation. Unlike other inhabitants of the earth who are merely charged with furthering their own fecundity and prosperity, human beings reflect God by adopting God's own project of universal well-being. Like the shepherd kings of antiquity, they mediate God's blessings, as best they are able, to both their own kind and the rest of creation—for example, replenishing the earth and helping it to body forth bountifully, furthering the prospects for human community by protecting and caring for the weak, the infirm, and the oppressed.

As a second formality or pattern of use, then, the theologian takes up all that the sciences teach about human qualities and capacities in order to consider the manner and extent to which they may hinder or help human beings to fulfill their vocation of community and fellowship in relation to God. Thus, certain prerequisites might exist for that fulfillment: Human beings might need to possess intelligence and will, powers of judgment and inner determination. They might require both spiritual and bodily aspects, self-consciousness and capacities for communication. Influenced by their varying cultural milieus, theologians over the centuries have offered these and any number of other characterizations of what makes human beings the image of God. Indeed, they have often simply identified one or another such characterization with that image. The biblical text, however, simply talks of human beings without any distinction of aspects; God creates in God's image the whole of the human in its entirety, and the special relations that hold between God and human beings bear not on some aspect of humanity but on human beings as such, in and through all that they are.

IV

This second formality specific to human life, which I have developed with reference to the creation of human beings in God's image, does not take away, however, from the first formality that concerned creatures as such. This second formality presupposes the first: Creation in God's image is just a further explication of what being created means for human beings.

Bringing that first formality back into the discussion now produces a third formality: The distinction of being human, its special value and goodness, can be affirmed appropriately only against the backdrop of human unworthiness for it.

Say what one will in praise of human beings—their special place in creation, their marvelous and unique qualities and capacities, the glorious nature of their partnership with God in the covenant and of their fellowship with God in Jesus Christ—none of it is appropriate apart from the affirmation of God's utter graciousness as the provider of such gifts. The general fact that the creature is not to be esteemed apart from a reference to God returns here in a new, more specific register.

First of all, the sheer extent of God's wondrous working, the universal scope of God's concern as the creator of all, puts human distinction in perspective. God's hand is behind the course of the sun, moon, and stars, behind the grass that grows on the hills and the majestic rains that nourish them, behind the wild and fierce beasts of the seas, forests, and sky. "Although heaven and the heaven of heavens belong to the Lord your God, the earth with all that is in it, yet [something wonderfully strange!] the Lord set his heart in love on your ancestors alone and chose you, their descendants after them, out of all the peoples" (Deut. 10:14–15). Considered within the context of creation as a whole, the exaltation of the human in general is an unexpected grace: "When I look at your heavens, the work of your fingers, the moon and the stars that you have established; what are human beings that you are mindful of them, mortals that you care for them?" (Ps. 8:3–4). Far from a matter of confident presumption, any special standing of humanity in relation to God requires the universal solicitude of God for its reassurance: "Are not five sparrows sold for two pennies? Yet not one of them is forgotten in God's sight ... Do not be afraid; you are of more value than many sparrows" (Lk. 12:6–7). The favors God bestows on human beings appear undeserved, in the second place, when considered in light of God's majesty. Who are human beings to be exalted by God, when, before God, "even the nations are like a drop from a bucket," "inhabitants [of the earth] are like grasshoppers" (Is. 40:15, 22), "the whole world before you is like a speck that tips the scales, and like a drop of morning dew that falls upon the ground" (Wisd. 11:22)? "Who can search out [God's] mighty deeds? Who can measure his majestic power? ... When human beings have finished, they are just beginning, and when they stop, they are still perplexed. What are human beings, and of what use are they?" (Ecclus. 18:4–8). The fleeting insignificance of humanity compared with God's eternity and everlasting might is the backdrop against which God's elevation of humanity is to be measured: "O Lord, what are human beings that you regard them, or mortals that you think of them? They are like a breath; their days are like a passing shadow" (Ps.144:3–4).

God's special gifts to human beings are discussed in biblical imagery of condescension. Insofar as they are mere creatures of this world, human beings clearly have no capacity to storm heaven with a demand for God's favor. In bestowing blessings on human beings, "the Lord our God, who is seated on high,...looks far down on the heavens and the earth" (Ps. 113:5–6). God reaches down from the heights to care for us in the depths.

Although all human beings are lowly in this way before God in the heights, it is especially for the "lowly" among human beings, those human beings with no status in the eyes of the world, that God comes down. The very ones with no claim to favor in human estimation—the sick, the despised, and the weak—receive God's special blessings. "I am poor and needy, but the Lord takes thought for me" (Ps. 40:17). The Lord who is seated on high looks down upon the earth specifically to raise the poor from the dust, the sick from death, and the needy from the ash heap (Ps. 113:5–9). Those who boast before God of their health, prosperity, might, or social standing, considering all these the secure possessions of their own hands, fail to find such favor. God scatters them and exalts, instead, those of low degree with no illusions about the ultimate source of their favor in God's gracious giving. "Heaven is my throne and the earth is my footstool ... All these things my hand has made, and so all these things are mine, says the Lord. But this is the one to whom I will look, to the humble and contrite in spirit" (Isa. 66:1–2).

The special favors human beings get from God, moreover, can never be counted on as theirs by rights. God will remain faithful to God's loving intentions for us, but the gifts God bestows out of love remain just that—gifts. God is, therefore, never required to bless those that God does bless. God has, in fact, done otherwise on occasion, bringing affliction instead of blessings even to those people with whom God covenants. God could yet do otherwise, tearing down in an instant the goods enjoyed by those who fail to see God as their refuge and source of strength. "So if you think you are standing," Paul counsels, "watch out that you do not fall" (1 Cor. 10:12) and lose God's benefits. Finally, the special favors granted to human beings by God are undeserved in a more strictly juridical sense: They have not been earned. No one can stand before the God who made him or her and claim to be blameless, spotless and pure (Job 4:17). But much more than this, human beings have proven their unworthiness of special favor by piling up their sins. No one, therefore, has a valid claim on God's partnership and fellowship. Human beings cannot be said to deserve the love and concern displayed by God in becoming incarnate and living among us or the intimacy with God achieved through the workings of the Holy Spirit. God's special favors to human beings are, instead, the result of God's mercy and continued faithfulness to a partnership broken by its human participants. "Since all have sinned and fall short of the glory of God, they are now justified by his grace as a gift" (Rom. 3:23–4). In acts of generous, unmerited invitation, God spreads out God's hands all the day to a rebellious people (Isa. 65:2). God "does not deal with us according to our sins, nor repay us according to our iniquities" (Ps. 103:10); though our misdeeds multi- ply, God still considers our distress, hears our cries (Ps. 106), and returns good for evil. Dead through our trespasses, we are nevertheless made alive with Christ and exalted through him to sit with God in the heavenly places, only because of God's rich mercy and great love for us (Eph. 2:4–6).

Our infirmity and sin prove the graciousness of God's benefits to remedy our plight. We are all like Jonah in the belly of the whale—enjoying a deliverance from God that desperate straits make an unexpected and unhoped for surprise. We should therefore "repeat that word which was uttered ...by Jonah: 'I cried by reason of my affliction to the Lord my God and He heard me out of the belly of hell' (Jn. 2:2);...[so] that he [and we also] might always continue glorifying God, and giving thanks without ceasing for that salvation which he has derived from Him, 'that no flesh should glory in the Lord's presence' (1 Cor. 1:29)."[9]

---

[9]Irenaeus, *Against Heresies*, edited by A. Roberts and J. Donaldson, vol. 1, *Ante-Nicene Fathers* (Edinburgh: T&T Clark, 1989), 111:20.

V

I hope what I have said sufficiently demonstrates that a theological perspective on humanity exists that is not reducible to the conclusions of other habits of inquiry. There is something to a theological account of humanity even apart from its fleshing out by way of other modes of investigation. This kind of independence of other disciplines takes the shape of formalities or patterns for their use, and, therefore, it does not imply that a theological commentary on human life proceeds in isolation from other forms of inquiry. Theology has something of its own to say, which it does not need to prove by a procedure of that sort. A theological perspective on humanity has its distinctiveness, but it is not one that must be bought at the price of vain attempts at self-sufficient insularity. The other disciplines that discuss human beings are not foreign to a theological commentary on human life, since that commentary does not proceed independently of them. But neither does a theological commentary simply conform to those disciplines, since it does not receive its identity as a theological commentary from them.

What may not yet be clear is the manner in which conclusions of other disciplines are altered when brought within a theological purview. Are they, for example, altered at all? Perhaps a theological formality merely leaves the conclusions of other disciplines alone, assimilating them as is within its own perspective. In that case, theological anthropology would assure its distinctiveness by leaving most of the field of inquiry about human life to entirely secular disciplines. Other disciplines would not encroach on theology's territory, but neither would theology encroach on theirs. Theology could provide a comprehensive commentary on human life, but people with no prior theological interest in life would have no reason to listen to it. They might know something more should they view what they know under a theological formality—something about God and the nature of our relations with God. In that sense, theological anthropology might make a difference to their understanding of human life, but a theological formality could neither challenge nor correct what they thought they knew before. Theological anthropology in this respect would make very little difference indeed.

The impropriety of such conclusions is hard to show on the basis of what I have provided here—a bare bones sketch of a few theological formalities themselves. The difference theology makes to the conclusions of disciplines it incorporates would certainly be easier to see if I had incorporated many such conclusions myself in order to produce a more fully-fledged theological commentary on human life. A few rejoinders are, nevertheless, possible on the grounds of the theological formalities I have discussed.

At a minimum, one can say that the relation between theology's contribution to an understanding of human life and that of other disciplines is more than merely additive. When incorporated in a theological commentary, the conclusions of other disciplines at least undergo transposition into a religious key. We know we are not alone in the universe as self-sufficient masters of ourselves. All that we are for the good is a gracious gift, for which we should render praise and thanks to God. Such a change in register marks more than simply a change in the way one maintains or holds the conclusions of other disciplines, that is, more than a change in one's subjective disposition or attitude with respect to what one knows on other grounds to be true of human beings. Thus, the first formality of creaturehood suggests human beings are properly understood only within the widest possible purview of the universe as a whole. Isolated investigation of the human makes little sense if human beings are part of a universal society of creatures held together by God's loving intentions. The second formality of human distinction implies, moreover, that human beings are made for a destiny of which the human and natural sciences may know nothing. The clearer that destiny in relation to God, the more theological anthropology will have to say of itself about human prerequisites for it. And the closer human beings are to fulfilling such a destiny, the more the qualities human beings display may require a reference to God in order to make sense. Finally, the third formality of human unworthiness for God's favors saves scientific investigation of the human from self-interested conclusions. A theological anthropology that knows that human beings owe such favors to God's grace contests any effort by the human or natural sciences to glorify humanity by exaggerating our differences from, and superiority to, other beings within the world.

The implications of theological anthropology for secular ethics are certainly material and more than merely formal. Insofar as it follows the three formalities discussed above, theological anthropology lodges an attack on both over- and under-valuations of human life, fostering instead a humble but healthy self-respect. Human life is genuinely valuable but not absolutely or unquestionably so in a way that would make all other beings of the universe mere means to human well- being. A theological contribution like this to ethics cannot be restricted, furthermore, to a counsel about proper individual attitudes, a restriction that would leave conclusions about politics and society to secular spheres. Theology, on the basis of its understanding of God, proclaims the objective value of God's creatures, a value that must, therefore, be respected in the relations human beings establish with one another and with other kinds of beings in the world. A whole socio-political and ecological ethics can be developed from this starting point, one that might differ substantially from any offered by non-theological disciplines. At its most general, such an ethic would maintain that, since all human beings have been created in the image of God, the propriety of human behaviors is to be assessed within the widest possible frame of a universal human society. It would maintain, moreover, that, since the special standing of human beings is a mere modification of what it means to be a creature of God, the good of humanity cannot be furthered without attention to the good of all God's creatures—the whole world and all its inhabitants. In this way, the theological formalities I have discussed erase customary boundaries of moral concern. Even without contributing new ethical recommendations, theology, at a minimum, extends the application of those recommendations that exist so as to fall into conflict with every provincial and parochial ethic: "Sparrows and sheep and lilies belong within the network of moral relations The line cannot even be drawn at the boundaries of life; the culture of the earth as a garden of the Lord and reverence for the stars as creatures of his intelligence belong to the demands of [God's] universal will."[10]

---

[10]Niebuhr, *Meaning of Revelation*, 122. See also the still helpful essay by Robert King, "The 'Ecological Motif' in the Theology of H. Richard Niebuhr," *JAAR*, 42/2 (June 1974): 339–43.

Questions

1 What does Tanner mean when she says that theology strives to be "comprehensive"? How does that relate to the necessary limitations of theology?

2 Tanner claims that the theologian should not be primarily concerned with "what is related to God ... but how things are related to God." What does she mean by this and what do you think about it?

3 What does it mean to say that theology is a "perpetual renter"?

4 Tanner argues that one of the real challenges of theology today is to demonstrate that it has something meaningful of its own to say. How do you think this relates specifically to theological anthropology?

5 How does the fact that humans are both part of creation and yet unique within creation relate to the interdisciplinary nature of theological anthropology?

6 According to Tanner, how should we treat the conclusions of the non-theological disciplines? What role do they play in theology?

TEXT 6: ADA MARÍA ISASI-DÍAZ, "ELEMENTS OF A *MUJERISTA* ANTHROPOLOGY"[11]

Ada María Isasi-Díaz (1943–2012) was professor of ethics and theology at Drew University. One of the leading U.S. Hispanic theologians of the twentieth century, Isasi-Díaz specialized in understanding feminist theology from a distinctively Latina perspective, which she terms "mujerista" theology. Isasi-Díaz's anthropology thus pays close attention to the ways in which our understanding of the human person is shaped by culture and experience, especially those that involve gender and ethnicity. In this reading, Isasi-Díaz highlights several key aspects of a specifically mujerista anthropology, demonstrating how her experience as a Latina theologian contributes to her vision of what it means to be human. At the same time, then, this reading invites us to consider the role that our own cultures and experiences have played in shaping our anthropologies.

There are three Spanish phrases that I have come to recognize as critical to the self-understanding of Hispanic Women: *la lucha* (the struggle), *permítanme hablar* (allow me to speak), *la comunidad/la familia* (the community/the family). These phrases are repeated with such frequency that they seem to express essential elements of who Latinas are, of how we see ourselves, understand ourselves, value ourselves, construct ourselves, describe ourselves. These phrases that are so common and at the same time so precious for Hispanic Women seem to be, therefore, a key to the elaboration of a *mujerista* anthropology. I will explore their meaning in this article, offering them—that is, the phrases and my explorations of their meanings—as elements that need to be considered when elaborating a *mujerista* anthropology, which must have as its source the lived-experience of Latinas and as its goal our liberation.

I am not claiming that these phrases constitute the only elements to be elaborated in a *mujerista* anthropology. Nor am I saying that the understandings they illumine are uniquely ours. But I am saying that they are central and specifically that they come out of our experience as Latinas living in the United States. Furthermore, I am saying that these phrases offer a valid starting point for an anthropological exploration of Latinas. A more complete anthropological elaboration from a *mujerista* perspective will, we may hope, critique and amplify this initial attempt.

La Lucha

The daily ordinary struggle of Hispanic Women to survive and to live fully has been the central element of *mujerista* theology from the very start because it is, I believe, the main experience in the lives of the majority of Latinas. Ever since I learned how

[11]Ada Maria Isasi-Diaz, "Elements of a Mujerista Anthropology," in Ann Elizabeth O'Hara Graff, ed., *In the Embrace of God: Feminist Approaches to Theological Anthropology*, (Maryknoll, NY: Orbis, 1995), 90–104.

hard and difficult life is for grass-root Hispanic Women, I have wondered how they manage to live in the midst of such arduous, demanding, rough and trying reality, in the midst of great suffering. One of my earliest insights, which becomes deeper and clearer with the passing of time, has to do with Hispanic Women's ability to deal with suffering without being determined by it. It is an indication that we are unwilling to allow ourselves to be defined by others or by the circumstances over which we have no control. Thus, I have come to see that the insistence on the value of suffering for Christians and its placement as a central element of the Christian message is questionable. I believe, applying a hermeneutics of suspicion, that it has become an ideological tool, a control mechanism used by dominant groups over the poor and the oppressed.

Allow me to make clear what I am saying, using the *via negativa*. I do not negate the reality of suffering in our lives, but I refuse to romanticize it, which I believe is what happens when one ascribes value to suffering in itself. I do not negate the connection between suffering and evil, nor do I dismiss or ignore either of them. I do not negate that Jesus suffered while he walked in "this valley of tears" but I cannot accept that his suffering was greater than all other human suffering or that the God whom Jesus called Father demanded, even required, Jesus to suffer in order to fulfill his mission on earth.

La lucha and not suffering is central to Hispanic Women's self-understanding. I have gotten the best clues for understanding how Latinas understand and deal with suffering by looking at Latinas' capacity to celebrate, at our ability to organize a fiesta in the midst of the most difficult circumstances and in spite of deep pain. The fiestas are, of course, not celebrations of suffering but of the struggle against suffering. The fiestas are, very often, a way of encouraging one another not to let the difficulties that are part of Hispanic Women's daily life overcome us. They are opportunities to distance ourselves from the rough and arduous reality of everyday life, at times mere escapism, but often a way of getting different perspectives on how to carry on *la lucha*. Listening to the conversations that go on at the fiestas and participating in them makes this evident. What one hears is talk about the harshness of life. Of course at times it is a matter of simply complaining. But often it is a matter of sharing with others in order to convince oneself of what one knows: that one is not alone; that what each Hispanic Woman is going through is not necessarily, or at least mainly, her fault but is due to oppressive structures. We also hope, by talking about it, to get the support of others, to get advice and help on how to deal with the situation. Fiestas are a very important way for Latinas not to allow only the suffering in our lives to determine how we perceive life, how we know, how we understand and deal with reality.

An old Latina song says *la vida buena, es la que se goza*, the good life is the one that one enjoys. This points to the fact that living is, among other things and maybe predominantly, a search for the good life. The struggle for survival, then, is not only a struggle not to die; it is a struggle to live, but not just barely. It is a struggle to live fully.[12] The struggle for survival is a search for pleasure among

---

[12] Ada Maria Isasi-Diaz and Yolanda Tarango, *Hispanic Women: Prophetic Voice in the Church* (San Francisco: Harper and Row, 1988; reprint Minneapolis: Fortress Press, 1993), 4.

those who think of themselves as *familia/comunidad*, "a search for lasting joy, deep delight, gratuitous enjoyment, contagious good fortune."[13] The good life does not ignore suffering. It struggles to go beyond it, to transcend it. As a matter of fact, what our fiestas suggest is that Latinas need parties and celebrations to deal in a creative way with the suffering that surrounds us instead of allowing it to define us. The celebrations that we so easily pull together and enjoy so very much often are opportunities for Hispanic Women to "appreciate and accompany the affliction of others with solidarity and tenderness"[14] in *lo cotidiano*—the the everyday life—for us.

By *lo cotidiano* we mean

> The structured patterns of action, discourse, norms, and established social roles ... considered "from below." A partial list includes particular forms of speech, the experience of class and gender distinctions, the impact of work and poverty on routines and expectations, relations within families and among friends and neighbors in a community, the experience of authority, and central expressions of faith such as prayer, religious celebrations, and conceptions of key religious figures like the saints, or Jesus and Mary.[15]

Lo cotidiano provides a needed framework for explaining *la lucha* as an important element of *mujerista* anthropology. A *mujerista* description of *lo cotidiano* would add to the perspective "from below" the consideration of "from within," and "of our own selves." In other words, *lo cotidiano* for us has to do with the way that we Latinas ourselves consider action, discourse, norms, established social roles, and our own selves.

It is precisely when Hispanic Women's perspective of reality—including ourselves—is the lens used that *la lucha*, not suffering, is seen as central to Latinas' humanity. Even in the moments of greatest suffering in our lives, if looked at from below and from within, the suffering is not what is most influential in determining how we act, talk, make decisions. Though Hispanic Women suffer racial/ethnic and sexist oppression and most of us also suffer poverty, we do not go about our *vida cotidiana*—our everyday life—thinking that we suffer but rather thinking how to struggle to survive, to live fully. We do not go around saying to ourselves or to others, "I am suffering." Instead we go around saying, "*asi es la vida* (such is life)." Many think that this denotes a certain fatalism. But the "*asi es la vida*" of Latinas goes hand in hand with our *lucha diaria*— the daily struggle which is the stuff out of which our lives are made.

It could be argued that *la lucha* and suffering are two sides of the same coin. But for *mujerista* anthropology there is a great difference between these two perspectives. Those who use suffering as their lens and see it as central to Hispanic Women's

---

[13]Otto Maduro, *Mapas Para La Fiesta* (Buenos Aires: Centro Nueva Tierra para la Promoción Social y Pastoral, 1992), 25–27.

[14]Ibid.

[15]Daniel H. Levine, *Popular Voices in Latin American Catholicism* (Princeton, NJ: Princeton University Press, 1992), 317.

lives historically have idealized suffering in a way that results in a certain fatalism. I believe Christianity has much to do with this focus. Christianity has tended to endorse and encourage a certain masochism that has influenced to a great extent the discourse about suffering and its role in the lives of Latinas. On the other hand, from the inside, from the perspective of Hispanic Women, it is the struggle against oppression and poverty and for liberation that is central to who we are.

Permítanme Hablar

A *mujerista* anthropology is about Latinas as human beings, not in the abstract but within the context of our given reality. It takes into consideration what we understand our task in history to be. Each and every Hispanic Woman as a "human being is not primarily a definition but rather a history within space and time."[16] Latinas are makers of history. A *mujerista* anthropology insists on the need to denounce the way that Hispanic Women have been erased from the histories of our communities and our countries of origin and from the history of the U.S.A. This is what the phrase *permítanme* hablar indicates. We have never been absent from history, but we have been ignored by historical accounts. Therefore, our insistence on speaking, on making known our histories,

> is not a matter of reassuring nostalgia and pleasant reveries. It is a subversive memory, and it lends force and sustenance to our positions, refuses to compromise or equivocate, learns from failures, and knows (by experience) that it has the capability of overcoming every obstacle, even repression itself.[17]

Our insistence on speaking is not only a matter of making known our past; it is also a matter of participating in making present and future history, of being protagonists, of being agents of our own history. If when we speak we are not listened to, if Latinas continue to be spoken to, spoken about, or simply—supposedly—included what is said about Hispanics in general, our humanity will continue to be diminished not only in the eyes of the dominant group but also, unfortunately, in our own eyes as we internalize such objectification of ourselves. As long as our voices are not heard, as long as the role we play in history is not recognized and its specificity is not appreciated, we will not be able to become full moral agents, full persons in our own right. This is why we insist that a *mujerista* anthropology has to center on Hispanic Women as human beings in time and history; it is an anthropology "from within" and "from below." It recognizes that anthropology is not about an idealized type of humanity or an abstract understanding of humanity, but that anthropology rises out of a context. Since Latinas are an intrinsic part of that context, our self-understanding cannot be ignored.

---

[16]Ivone Gebara and Maria Clara Bingemer, *Mary: Mother of God, Mother of the Poor* (Maryknoll, NY: Orbis Books, 1989), 11.
[17]Gustavo Gutierrez, *The Power of the Poor in History* (Maryknoll, NY: Orbis Books, 1983), 80.

There are several difficulties in recognizing and affirming the perspective of Hispanic Women about our humanity as a necessary element of all anthropologies. First, when it comes to women, the well-known split of the private and the public sphere continues to exist. History is about the public sphere, and since women are given a role and some authority—though little power—only in the private sphere, women are mostly absent from written history, from what is recognized as the official (the "true" version) of what has happened. Much can be said about this false dichotomy, but we will limit our comments here to two. First, what is called history deals mostly with political and military events. Yet this history does not exist apart from social history: history of the family, history of ideas, history of social and religious movements, history of the churches and religions. Social history is not mere secondary history.

Social history deals with that same *lo cotidiano* in which Latinas are key players. It is important to point out that *lo cotidiano*, as defined above, does not have to do only with what Hispanic Women do in our homes, within our communities, in the activities that one classifies as "Hispanic." *Lo cotidiano* also refers to what Latinas think about the patterns of action, discourse, norms, and established social roles of "institutional formations like church, state, or major economic groups major economic groups ... [that] control real resources, both symbolic and material, which they use to project messages and power over time, space, and social boundaries."[18] In other words, Hispanic Women are very conscious of how the world we live in is defined for us without taking us into consideration. It is precisely this omission that a *mujerista* anthropology seeks to denounce and correct.

Another important consideration is this: the history of social movements is about movements that have been and are populated and carried out by the common folk, with women playing a very important role in them. In Hispanic communities, religion often plays a key role in many of these social movements. Though unrecognized by many of the churches' institutions, Latinas are indeed most of the leaders and workers in our communities. Therefore, though receiving very little credit, Hispanic Women play an important role within social movements and thus in a true understanding of history.

For example, without in any way diminishing the work and leadership provided by Cesar Chavez to the United Farm Workers, it is critical to study, know, and publicly acknowledge the role Dolores Huerta has played and continues to play in the struggle of the UFW as its vice-president. Another example is that of COPS, a Mexican-American community organization in San Antonio, Texas, that had several women presidents. The organization usually has depended on more women than men to carry out its programs and make effective demands upon the city, state, and industries on behalf of the Latina community.

Besides the desire and capacity of Latinas to have a protagonistic role in history, permítanme hablar indicates a second difficulty in asserting the role of Latinas' self-understanding and our view of reality as intrinsic to a *mujerista* anthropology. It has to do with the fact that women in general and Hispanic Women in particular are considered incapable of reflecting, of thinking, of conceptualizing. As we have always

---

[18]Levine, *Popular Voices*, p. 317.

insisted, Hispanic Women are not only doers; we are thinkers also. We do engage each other and the society of the U.S.A—our reality—in a critical way. We analyze and we understand. Latinas reflect, and that is a way of making a real contribution to history, to the transformation of history. This is why as *mujeristas* we have always insisted that we must not separate action from reflection. We have always insisted that praxis is reflective action. Since the dominant culture and even our own Latino brothers often do not recognize Latinas' capacity to think, this is precisely why we have insisted on identifying grass-root Hispanic Women as organic intellectuals.

We have been told that to highlight the phrase *permítanme hablar*—allow me to speak—would take power from Latinas, would seem to recognize that others have to give us permission to talk. This act common expression might be construed that way if one were to start from the position that Hispanic Women have not spoken. But the fact is that we have repeatedly spoken throughout history, that we speak daily, constantly. In highlighting this phrase, I am insisting that people pay attention to us, to what we say about ourselves and the reality we and our communities live.

When Latinas use the phrase *permítanme hablar*, we are not merely asking to be taken into consideration. When we use this phrase we are asking for a respectful silence from all those who have the power to set up definitions of what it is to be human, a respectful silence so others can indeed hear our cries denouncing oppression and injustice, so others can understand our vision of a just society. We know that if those with power, within as well as outside the Hispanic communities, do not hear us, they will continue to give no credence to the full humanity of Latinas. That is why we insist on the capacity of Hispanic Women to speak our own word. For Latinas to speak and to be heard is fundamental in the elaboration of a *mujerista* anthropology, for it makes it possible for us to attest to our humanity.

For many Hispanic Women who have seldom found anyone to listen to them listen to them—to hear them—their *permítanme hablar* is a way of insisting on recognition of our right to think, to defend our rights, to participate in setting what is normative of and for humanity. To demand that we be listened to is a way for us to assert our own identity, to demand that our understanding of our own humanity has to be taken into consideration in the understanding of all humanity. And, given all that we have said, our self-understanding is not divorced from our daily struggle, from our *lucha* to live fully and to bring lo cotidiano into the full view of society at large.

La familia, la comunidad

Recently several Latinas were sharing our reaction to the often heard comment that Hispanic families are "being destroyed," or "are falling apart." Though some of us agreed somewhat with these statements, all of us disagreed with this negative view of the status of Latina families. What we all did agree with is that, for us, *la familia* "is the central and most important institution in life."[19] Whether our family situation is

---

[19] Roberto R. Alvarez, Jr., "The Family," in Nicolas Kanellos, ed., *The Hispanic American Almanac* (Washington, DC: Gale Research, Inc., 1993), 155.

positive or negative, still the ideology of family as central to our lives, to who we are, is primary. This is why it has to be an intrinsic element of a *mujerista* anthropology. But it is important that we understand what kind of familia are we talking about. We need to look at how *la familia* has changed, and we must evaluate those changes not by comparing them with the way family has been in our culture, but in view of the role it has today.

It is my contention that the often familiar comment about how poorly the Hispanic family is faring in today's society is a veiled but nonetheless direct accusation of the change in the role of Latinas in, our families. I believe, however, that women continue to be the mainstay of our families and that what we are no longer willing to do—in part because more and more of us are gainfully employed outside the home—is to remain married or living with men who oppress us and, yes, even mistreat us. Careful observation of Hispanic Women who are single mothers is what led me initially to suspect that cries about the demise of Latina families are unfounded. What is really behind such cries is fear of the demise of the patriarchal family, not the destruction of Hispanic families as ethnic families.

First of all, we need to question seriously the conclusion that sees Latina families as they move from one generation to another and become acculturated as reaching a point where they stop being ethnic families and become "modern American families."[20] Neither modernization nor acculturation are the major reasons for the changes one can observe in our families, changes that are not anti-Hispanic. Instead it seems that the changes reflect the decreasing need for sex role differentiation because of technological innovations that make it unnecessary to "reward males with the myth of male superiority."[21] As women acquired more resources and skills through education and paid employment, "they achieved greater equality in conjugal decision making without sacrificing ethnicity in other realms of family life."[22] The changes have to do mainly with the way we Latinas look upon *machismo* and *hembrismo*. But there is very little credence given, even within our communities, to the reasons for these changes in behavioral attitudes because the dominant culture has successfully projected Latinas and Latinos as primary examples of male chauvinism and female inferiority.

Both *machismo* and *hembrismo* have become concepts that use Spanish nouns as their names. Though indeed both concepts are based on Hispanic ideologies and behaviors, nowadays they are pancultural and refer to "forms of individual deviancy ... rarely normative in any culture."[23] What has happened to Latina communities is that the word *machismo* has been adopted in the U.S.A. as the accepted terme when speaking in English—to connote the idea of extreme male chauvinism. Though the word hembrismo is not used, what it—traditional feminine roles characterized by weakness, passivity, and inertia—is considered by the dominant culture to be exemplified by Hispanic. In other words, Latinas are the best examples of such

---

[20]Oscar Ramirez and Carlos H. Arce, "The Contemporary Chicano Family: An Empirically Based Review," in Agustine Baron, Jr., ed., *Explorations in Chicano Psychology* (New York: Praeger Publishers, 1981), 19.

[21]Melba J. T. Vazquez and Anna M. Gonzalez, "Sex Roles among Chicanes: Stereotypes, Challenges, and Changes," in Baron, *Explorations*, 63.

[22]Ibid.

[23]Ramirez and Arce, "The Contemporary Chicano Family" 63.

female characteristics. Holding Latina Women and men as exemplars when it comes to behavioral and ideological deviance is a useful and efficient way for people of the dominant culture, both men and women, to consider themselves in a superior position to us.

This does not take away from the fact that as Latinas we have much struggling to do within our families. But in many ways, family has been Latinas' domain through the ages. It is in la familia that we are agents of our own history, that we can claim a historical role within space and time, that we make our mark—so to speak—by making viable and by influencing future generations. Though our realm has been a small one compared to the one commanded by Hispanic men, it certainly goes way beyond the small, nuclear family characteristic of the dominant culture. Our domain, la familia, is an amplified family that includes the nuclear family members, particularly the mother and children, plus the extended family—grandparents, cousins two and three times removed, aunts and uncles, in-laws—plus comadres and compadres, godparents brought into the family for a variety of reasons. Family for us is a vast network of relationships and resources in which Hispanic Women play a key role. I believe this is why Latinas want to preserve our families while ridding ourselves of oppressive elements and understandings about the family and about our role in it.

Instead of devaluing and rejecting our traditional roles in our families, what Latinas want is the opposite: we want the value of those roles to be recognized and their status to be enhanced. Once this happens we believe Hispanic men might have an easier time in accepting their responsibilities as sons, brothers and fathers, as nurturers and transmitters of family values and ideology. This is of utmost importance if we are to change the terrifying picture of Hispanic children today, 38.4 percent of whom live in poverty.

To understand better the kind of familia that is Hispanic Women's realm, we need to see how in Latina culture the community is an extension, a continuation of the family. As a matter of fact, the importance community has for us follows on the heels of the great significance of family in our culture. To understand the connection between family and community we need to look at compadrazgo, the middle point between family and community. Compadrazgo extends family, embraces neighbors, and through it Latinas extend our domain to include important members of the community. Compadrazgo refers to the system of relationships that are established between godparents and godchildren and between the godparents and the parents of godchildren. Comadres and compadres—co-mothers and co-fathers are additional sets of parents who act as guardians or sponsors, caring for the godchildren and providing for them when needed. But the system of compadrazgo is extended beyond religious occasions such as baptism and confirmation to secular activities and enterprises. Dances have madrinas (godmothers) or padrinos (godfathers); so do businesses, sports teams, religious processions.

The system of compadrazgo works because of the significance of "personalism" in our culture. Personalism is "an orientation toward people and persons over concepts and ideas."[24] Therefore, the connections among people are very important. Our

---

[24]Guillenno Bernal, "Cuban Families," in Monica McGoldrick, John K. Pearce, and Joseph Giordano, eds., Ethnicity and Family Therapy (New York: The Guilford Press, 1982), 192.

amplified families function in many ways because of personal contacts. The more numerous the family, the more widespread the network of "intimate" connections. So the *compadrazgo* system creates an effective infrastructure of interdependence, with Latinas most of the time being at its center. Through *compadrazgo*, family ideology and family values of unity, welfare and honor reach into the community. It is this amplified family, in many ways a community, that guarantees protection and caretaking for its members as long as we remain faithful to it. It is not hard to see that, given the importance Hispanic Women have within our *familias*, rather than giving up or diminishing the role we have within them, we seek to enhance that role.

One very important area of Hispanic Women's self-understanding and self-worth that has not found a positive ambience in *la familia* is that of embodiment. On the contrary, most of the time, it is precisely because of the role we play in our families that we do not have control over our bodies, that our sexuality is restricted and negated, that our bodies are used against ourselves. *Familia/comunidad*, unfortunately, is not a safe place for women when it comes to considerations of Latinas' bodies. The aspects of sexuality that have to do with pleasure, communication, and affection are negated, and only procreation is valued. As a matter of fact, it is precisely because procreation is given such a high value that other aspects of sexuality are denied to us. Our procreative role and the functions connected with it—nurturing and responsibility for the children—most of the time work against us.

Latinas' bodies continue to be objectified. Hispanic men as well as other men and women of the dominant culture objectify Hispanic Women's bodies. Rape and all forms of irresponsible sex are perhaps the clearest examples of such objectification. Here I am not talking only about the begetting of children but also about the psychological and emotional trauma that sexuality outside of a committed relationship causes many of us.

Still another significant form of objectification of Latinas' bodies is exploitation of our physical labor. Many Hispanic Women endure sleep deprivation because of the double and triple work burden they bear. Luisa is up by five in the morning and never goes to bed before midnight. She is a single mother with two children. She keeps house, makes a living by working (a bus plus a subway ride away from home) and is trying to finish high school. Maria is a middle class woman who has to work outside the home. Her husband helps her with their child and the house. But, that is precisely it: he helps; it is her responsibility to bring up their son, to tend to the house even if she works many more hours than he does and earns more than double the amount of money he does.

Exploitation of the labor of Latinas is clear in the lack of available household conveniences that could ease the physical work we have to do to survive. And here I remember my own grandmother, who suffered from a very young age of a heart condition brought on by arthritis, caused in part by her exhausting work as a washerwoman. But then, as a single mother of two girls, and without much schooling, what else could she do to survive? Disregard for our bodies continues the custom among Hispanics for women to be served food last, for Latinas to consider it their obligation to give their food to the children and men and, if necessary, go hungry themselves. I have seen this happen many times, including yesterday, when I went to visit a friend in *el barrio*, East Harlem. This is not something that happens only among poor Latinas. For example, in my middle class family, my mother insists on serving my father, brothers, and brothers-in-law better and bigger portions of food. All of this, I believe, is grounded in the objectification of Latinas' bodies, in the exploitation of our bodies.

Again, what is most worrisome about this is that Hispanic Women have internalized—and continue to internalize—such negativity about our bodies. The negation of sexuality as a key element of our humanity, lack of understanding that our bodies are ourselves, is one of the main reasons, I believe, for the self-loathing of our teenagers, for the irresponsible way in which they "use" their bodies. We lack an understanding of the intrinsic-ness of our bodies to who we are, of the fact that we are at all times embodied beings, and that every human being is one single entity body-spirit. Unfortunately, *familia/comunidad* is a negative factor in this area by insisting on and supporting oppressive sexual relationships, with both Hispanic men and Hispanic Women being victims.

Yet *familia/comunidad* is women's domain because it is a distinct arena where we are historical protagonists. It is also what provides Latinas repeatedly with a sense of unity and cohesiveness, with a sense of self-identity and self-worth. *Familia/comunidad* relies on interdependence, and this allows some space for Hispanic Women to be counted, to be considered important and, therefore, to be dealt with in a respectful way, to be valued as a person and not just because of what we do. *Familia/comunidad* for Latinas/os does not subsume the person but rather emphasizes that the person is constituted by this entity and that the individual person and the community have a dialogic relationship through which the person reflects the *familia/comunidad* "out of which it was born, yet, as in a prism, that reflection is also a refraction .... In an authentic [family/]community, the identity of the 'we' does not extinguish the 'I'; the Spanish word for we' is Inosotros, which literally means 'we others,' a community of *otros*, or others."[25] In *familia/comunidad* the "I" of Hispanic Women is heard and embraced without fear, for it does not in any way threaten the "we."

This is not in any way an attempt to romanticize Latina families and communities or downplay conflicts and the oppression we suffer even within what I claim to be "our domain." There is strife in our families and communities, and unity of interests often does not exist there. But the fact is that *familia/comunidad* is a cultural value. Often it is the first and last recourse for survival for Hispanics. *Familia/comunidad* is the grounding element for Latinas, for our self-understanding, and, therefore, must be a central element in a *mujerista* anthropology.

Conclusion

Since the goal of all *mujerista* enterprise is the liberation of Latinas, a *mujerista* anthropology seeks to illumine how we understand ourselves, how we perceive and construct ourselves as human beings with a history and within a time-frame

---

[25]"*Nosotros*: Toward a U.S. Hispanic Anthropology," *Listening—Journal of Religion and Culture* 27 (1992): 57.

of existence, how we live our women-selves, which is the only way we can live our human-selves. No narrative, no discourse can capture the richness of our own experience, of our searching for opportunities to be more than we are, of our amazement when we discover how roles have defined us and limited us while at the same time realizing the potential richness of such roles.

A *mujerista* anthropology is definitely framed by *la lucha*, not a struggle against anyone or anything but/or recognition of the fullness of our humanity as women-selves, and on behalf of all persons. To do this we have to repeat constantly, *permítanme hablar*, because as Latinas we are about begetting new realities for ourselves and for our *familias/comunidades*. We are about giving birth to a new understanding of humanity that starts by insisting on a protagonistic role for all persons and a society based on understandings of interdependence, while embracing differences that are at the heart of what it means for us to be familia.

Questions

1   In what ways do culture and/or experience shape Isasi-Díaz's theological anthropology? In what ways have culture and experience shaped your own understanding of what it means to be human?

2   What is *la lucha* and how does it relate to theological anthropology?

3   What is the difference between *la lucha* and suffering? Why is this difference important?

4   What does *permítanme hablar* mean and what significance does it have for Isasi-Díaz's anthropology?

5   What are the main difficulties involved in understanding the experience of Latinas in this area?

6   What is *lo cotidiano* and why is it significant for Isasi-Díaz's anthropology? What role do you think it should play in your own understanding of humanity?

7   Why is *la familia* important for Isasi-Díaz?

2

The Image of God

Any authentically Christian theological anthropology must of course reckon with the biblical testimony that human beings were created "in the image of God." The striking power of this phrase is evidenced by its pervasive influence on political and ethical thinking even down to the present day. As is well known, the classic text is from Gen. 1:26-8:

> Then God said, "Let us make mankind in our image, in our likeness, so that they may rule over the fish in the sea and the birds in the sky, over the livestock and all the wild animals, and over all the creatures that move along the ground."
>
> So God created mankind in his own image, in the image of God he created them; male and female he created them.
>
> God blessed them and said to them, "Be fruitful and increase in number; fill the earth and subdue it. Rule over the fish in the sea and the birds in the sky and over every living creature that moves on the ground."

And yet, despite the considerable impact of this text, its meaning has been the subject of a great deal of debate—a debate which has, if anything, intensified in the last century or so. It has proved to be something of a test case for the relationship between biblical exegesis and systematic theology. Exegetes and theologians have agreed that the phrase "the image (*selem*) of God" indicates that humankind is to be the reflection of God to the creation. Unlike the other creatures, the human has the capacity to be the conduit for the divine being in the world he made. The question is: In what exactly do human beings reflect the deity? The assumption of many writers has been that the image must refer to a particular capacity or ability given to humankind. That is, there is some capacity or function that is integral to God that is also fundamental for human beings.

If it is the case that the image of God is found in some capacity that human beings possess, it is not surprising that the *Imago Dei* has been understood over the course of Christian history as the capacity for rational thought. The argument comes from two directions. On the one hand, it is rational thought that most obviously separates us from the beasts and the birds. Human beings could be said to be unique because of this capacity. As fallen creatures, we lapse when we give over ourselves to our passions and instincts, as the animals do. On the other hand, it would seem that God is distinguished as a being by his supreme capacity for rational thought, in knowledge and in wisdom. Human beings are not by being in his image in any sense equivalent to him in rational capacity, but it would make sense to see them as analogous to him in it.

This position is well attested—even dominant—from the early church onwards. The church's first major theologian, Irenaeus, bishop of Lyons wrote of the human being as a being "endowed with reason, and in this respect like God." Gregory of Nyssa wrote of man as the "rational animal." In this way, the image of God concept functioned as a kind of mediating principle for an analogy of being between humankind and the divine. The interpretation of the *Imago Dei* in terms of rationality was then given further impetus by reference to the depiction of Jesus in the New Testament as the *logos* of God. This position is reflected in the following sections by two of the greatest theologians of the Church, Augustine of Hippo, and Thomas Aquinas.

But in the writings of Augustine we see another strand of interpretation of the *Imago* emerge. Noting that the voice of God speaks in the plural in Gen. 1:26 ("Let *us* . . ."), some Christian exegetes insisted that the human creature must reflect the unity in plurality of the Holy Trinity. The *Imago Dei* does not then refer to some capacity that humans possess that separates them from the other creatures, but instead to the *relational* nature of human being—with regard to each other and to God. Man and woman are made, like God, as beings-in-relation, and to live out this relational ontology in love. This theme was picked up in the Reformation, and later found an advocate in the writings of Karl Barth.

However, the work of expositors in the nineteenth and twentieth centuries on the Ancient Near Eastern background material pointed to the *vocation of dominion* given to humankind in the act of their creation—that they were to "rule over the fish in the sea and the birds in the sky and over every living creature that moves on the ground." The vocabulary of "image" was used by Ancient Near Eastern rulers to describe the enormous statues that they used to represent them in the far-flung corners of their lands. Man and woman as equipping them for that task are thus called to *represent* the Creator to his creation, ruling it as his vice-gerents; and we can understand the many extraordinary capacities that they have, in mind and body, as equipping for that task.

The history of humankind traces a tragic decline from this original calling to be the image. But the notion of the image is not simply a piece of datum given to describe the creation of human beings. The striking way in which the New Testament speaks about Jesus Christ as "the image of the invisible God" (Col 1:15) and "the exact representation of his being" (Heb 1:1-3) shows that the "image" needs to be understood in the light of the redemption of humanity proclaimed in him.

TEXT 1: AUGUSTINE OF HIPPO,
THE LITERAL MEANING OF GENESIS.[1]

By the time of Augustine of Hippo (354–430), commentary on the book of Genesis had become something of a theologian's set piece: Basil of Caesarea, Gregory of Nyssa, John Chrysostom and Lactantius are only some of the writers who composed commentaries of one sort or another. But more than any writer before him (with the possible exception of Origen of Alexandria), Augustine felt compelled to wrestle with the creation narratives. In all, he attempted some five separate commentaries on Genesis, including an extensive commentary in his autobiographical confessions. The intensive scrutiny of these texts in no small way stems from the alternative accounts of creation and the origin of humanity on offer—among them Neoplatonism and Manicheeism. The extract that follows comes from his fourth commentary, *De Genesi ad litteram* (The Literal Meaning of Genesis). The title indicates not a little about Augustine's exegetical method. He avoids allegorizing the text, and insists on the historical reality of the events described in the opening chapters of Scripture. At the same time, he is very alert to the literary features of the text—for example, Augustine interprets the six days of the creation story as a literary device intended by the ancient author to unfold a single, instantaneous act of creation.

19, 29. There will be more fruitful passages time and again later on for a more thorough reflection on the nature of man. Now however, to conclude our examination and discussion of the works of the six days, I must briefly insist in the first place that the following point is not to be passed over lightly: that while with the other works it says, *God said: Let it be made,* here on the other hand we have *God said: Let us make man to our image and likeness,* to insinuate, that is, a plurality of persons, if I may so put it, on account of Father and Son and Holy Spirit. He immediately advises us, however, of the unity to be understood in the godhead by saying, *and God made man to the image of God;* not as though Father made to the image of the Son, or the Son to the image of the Father—otherwise it would not be true to say "to our image," if man were made to the image of the Father alone or of the Son alone—but it is put like this: "God made to the image of God," as much as to say, "God made to his image."

When it now says *to the image of God,* after saying above *to our image;* it is giving a clear signal that that plurality of persons is not leading us to say or to believe or to understand gods in the plural, but to take Father and Son and Holy Spirit—the trinity on whose account it says *to our image*—as being one God in whose account it says, *to the image of God.*

In what respect man was made to the image of God; and why it does not say: after the creation of man, "And thus it was made."

20, 30. Here we must not neglect that other point either, that after saying, *to our image,* he immediately added, *and let him have authority over the fishes of the sea*

---

[1]Augustine. "The Literal Meaning of Genesis." In *On Genesis,* (Hyde Park, NY: New City Press, 2002), 232–40.

and the flying things of heaven and of the other animals which lack reason, giving us to understand, evidently, that it was in the very factor in which he surpasses non-rational animate beings that man was made to God's image. That of course, is reason itself, or mind or intelligence or whatever other word it may more suitably be named by. That is why the apostle too says: *Be renewed* in *the spirit of your minds and put on the new man, who is being renewed for the recognition of God according to the image of him who created him* (Eph 4:23–24; Col 3:10), where he makes it plain enough just in what part man was created to God's image—that it was not in the features of the body but in a certain form of the illuminated mind.

31. Now with that light of the first day, if by that name is rightly to be understood the created intellectual light which shares in the eternal and unchangeable Wisdom of God, it did not say, "and thus it was made" and then repeat with *and God made,* because as I have already argued to the best of my ability there was no being made in that first of creatures some knowledge of the Word of God, so that after that knowledge something lower down the scale would be made which was already being created in that Word; but that very light was being made first, in which knowledge would be made of the Word of God by whom it was being created; and this knowledge would itself be the light's conversion from its formlessness to the God forming it, would be its being created and formed. Later on, however, with the rest of creation it says and thus it was made, which signifies 'edge of the Word first being made in that light, that is in the intellectual creature; and next, when it says, and God made, it indicates the actual making of that kind of creature, of which it had been said in and by the Word of God that it should be made?'

Well, it is this principle that is being kept to in the making of man. God, you see, has just said, *Let us make man to our image and likeness* etc.; and then it does not say, *and thus it was made,* but leads straight into, *and God made man to the image of God,* precisely because human nature too is intellectual like that light, and that is why being made is the same thing for it as recognizing the Word of God by whom it is being made.

32. I mean, if it said *and thus it was made,* and after that led into and God rite, it would be understood as being first made in the knowledge of the rational creation, and then being made in some actual creature which was not rational. But because here too we have a rational creature, it too was perfected by the same recognition. Just as after man's fall into sin *he is being renewed in the recognition of God according to the image of him who created him* (Col 3:10), so it was in that recognition that he was created, before he grew old in crime, so he might again be renewed, rejuvenated, in the same recognition.

As for things however that were not created in that knowledge, because they were being created either as bodies or as non-rational souls, knowledge of them was first of all made in the intellectual creation by the Word, by whom it was said that they should be made, and on account of that knowledge it said, *and thus it was made,* to indicate that the knowledge of them was now made in that nature which was able to know this in the Word of God beforehand; and then the actual lies and non-rational creatures were made, on account of which it next added, *and God made.*

* * * *

The opinion that Genesis 1:27 refers to the creation of the human spirit, 2:7 to the creation of the body

22, 34. There are some people, however, who have even put forward this conjecture that at this time it was the interior man who was made, while the body of the man was made later on, when scripture says, *And God fashioned the en from the slime of the earth* (Gn 2:7); so that the word used here, *made,* applies to the spirit, the word *fashioned* to the body. They have disregarded the fact that man can only have been made male and female with respect to the body. There may be the most subtle arguments, to be sure, about the actual mind of man, in which he was made to the image of God, that its activity as a kind of rational life is divided between the contemplation of eternal truth and the management of temporal affairs; and that in this way it was made, as it were, male and female, with the former function directing, the latter conforming? With this division of roles however, that part alone is rightly said to be the image of God which clings in contemplation to the unchangeable Truth. It was as symbolically representing this that the apostle Paul says the man alone *is the image and glory of God, while the woman,* he goes on, *is the glory of the man* (1 Cor 11:7).

And so, although this external diversity of sex in the bodies of two human beings symbolizes what is to be understood internally in the one mind of a single human being, still the female too, because it is simply in the body that she is female, is also being renewed in the spirit of her mind in the recognition of God according to the image of him who created that in which there is no male and female. Now just as women are not cut off from this grace of the renewal and reshaping of the image of God, although their bodily sex has a different symbolic signification, according to which the man alone *is* called "the image and glory of God;" by the same token too in that original creation of man in terms of which "man" included woman as well, the woman of course also had her mind, a mind endowed with reason, with respect to which she too was made the image of God.

But on account of their being joined in one, *God made,* it says, man *to image of God.* And in case anyone should think it was only the spirit of man; was made, although it was only in the spirit that he was made to the to the image God, *he made him,* it says, *male and female* (Gn 1:27), to give us to understand that the body was also being made now. Again, in case anyone should suppose that it was made in such a way as to represent each sex in a single person, like those called hermaphrodites who are born occasionally, he shows that he put it in the singular on account of their being joined in one, and because the woman was made from the man, as will become clear later on when he begins to unfold more thoroughly what is said here in a nutshell; and that too is why he immediately continues in the plural, saying *he made them and blessed them* (Gn 1:27–28). But as I have already said, we shall be inquiring more thoroughly about the creation of man in the passage of scripture that follows on this.

What "And thus it was made" refers to here

22, 35. Now we have to note the fact that after saying, *And thus it was made,* he added straightaway, *And God saw all the things that he had made, and behold they were very good.* What is meant here is the actual right and provision given to the human species to take for food the fodder of the field and the fruits of trees. He referred *and thus it was made,* you see, to what started from the place where he says, *and God said: Behold, I have given you seed-bearing fodder, etc.* The fact is, if we refer his saying *and thus it was made* to everything that has been said earlier, the consequence will be that we will have to admit that they had already increased and multiplied and filled the earth on the sixth day, though we find scripture itself testifying that this only happened after many years.

For this reason, after the man had been given this right to eat, and had come to know it when God told him, it says *and thus it was made—in* the very fact, of course that the man came to know it when God told him. I mean, if he had already done it then, that is, had taken the things that had been given him for food and eaten them, scripture would have followed its established pattern, and after saying *and thus it was made,* which serves to express prior knowledge, would next have introduced the activity itself as well, and said, *and they took and ate.* It could have been said like that, you *see,* even if God were not mentioned, as in the passage where it says: *Let the water which is under the heavens be collected together into one collection, and let the dry land appear;* it then adds, *and thus it was made,* and does not say next, *and God made,* but still makes the usual repetition like this: *and the water was collected together into its collection, etc.*

Why does it does not say individually about the human creature "And God saw it was good."

24, 36. Now he did not say individually about the human creature, as in the then cases, *And God saw that it was good,* but after the man was made and given rights whether to rule or to eat, he concluded about them all: *And God saw all the things that he had made, and behold they were very good.* This is certainly a point that deserves investigation. The man could, after all, have been paid individually the same respect as had been paid individually to the other things that had been made before, and then finally it could have been said of all the things God made, *behold they were very good.* Perhaps because all the works were completed on the sixth day, is that the reason why it had to be said about them all, *And God saw all the things that he had made, and behold they were very good?* But then why *was* it said about the cattle and the beasts and the reptiles of the earth, which also belong to the same sixth day? Unless, of course, they were entitled to be called good both individually in their own kind and generally with all the other things, while the man, made to the image of God, was only entitled to be called this generally with the rest! Or was it because he was not yet completed, because not yet established in paradise—as if this that was left out here was said later on after he had been put there!

37. So what are we to say then? Was it that God foreknew the man was going to sin, and not to remain in the perfection of his image, and so did not wish to call him good individually, but only together with the rest, as though hinting at what was going to happen? Because when the things that have been made remain as what they were made, to the extent they received it, like those things that have not sinned or those that cannot sin, they are both good individually, and in the totality they are all very good. It was not for nothing, you see, that "very" was added, because the parts of the body too, if they are beautiful even by themselves, are all still much more beautiful in the total structure of the body. Thus the eye, for example causes pleasure and admiration; but still, if we saw one separate from the body, we would not call it as beautiful as *we* do when we observe it fitted into its proper place, in relation with the other parts, in the whole body.

Those things, however, which lose their proper comeliness by sinning, do not in the least for all that bring it about that they too are not good when rightly coordinated with the whole, with the universe. The man therefore before sin and in his own kind was of course good; but scripture forbore to say this, in order to say instead something that would foreshadow something yet to come. What was said about him, you see, was not untrue, because while someone who is good as an individual is clearly better when taken together with all the others, it does not follow that when he is good taken together with all the others he must also be good as an individual. And so it was arranged that something should be said which would be both true in the present and would signify foreknowledge of the future. God, after all, while being the best creator of natural things, is also the most just co-ordinator of sinners; so that even if things individually become deformed by transgressing, nonetheless the totality together with them in it remains beautiful. But now let us leave what follows to be dealt with in the next volume.

Questions

1 Augustine famously was a poor student of the biblical languages. Does it show in this commentary? Would it have made a difference to his exegesis?

2 How does Augustine introduce the Trinity in relation to the image of God?

3 In what aspect was man created "to God's image" in particular, according to Augustine? What is problematic about this analysis?

4 How does Augustine relate New Testament texts to his reading of Genesis?

5 According to Augustine, do women share in the image of God? How so?

TEXT 2: THOMAS AQUINAS
SUMMA THEOLOGIAE[2]

Thomas Aquinas (1225–74) was arguably the supreme theologian of the Middle Ages. He is certainly the one with the greatest ongoing impact on theology, philosophy, and ethics—even some seven centuries after his death. His *Summa Theologiae* is an extraordinary achievement in reasoned theological thinking. Incorporating the thought and methods of Aristotle (which Christendom had relearnt from its sometimes violent contact with Islam), Aquinas became known—and was sometimes criticized—as the exemplar of scholasticism. In this extract, Aquinas probes the concept of the *Imago Dei* by deploying his method of listing objections and answering them in turn by means of a combination of natural reason and scriptural proofs. He is clearly indebted to Augustine and cites him frequently as an authority.

Article 1. Whether the image of God is in man?

Objection 1. It would seem that the image of God is not in man. For it is written (Isaiah 40:18): "To whom have you likened God? or what image will you make for Him?"

Objection 2. Further, to be the image of God is the property of the First-Begotten, of Whom the Apostle says (Colossians 1:15): "Who is the image of the invisible God, the First-Born of every creature." Therefore the image of God is not to be found in man.

Objection 3. Further, Hilary says (*De Synod, Super i can. Synod. Ancyr.*) that "an image is of the same species as that which it represents"; and he also says that "an image is the undivided and united likeness of one thing adequately representing another." But there is no species common to both God and man; nor can there be a comparison of equality between God and man. Therefore there can be no image of God in man.

On the contrary, It is written (Genesis 1:26): "Let Us make man to Our own image and likeness."

I answer that, As Augustine says (*QQ.* 83, *qu.* 74): "Where an image exists, there forthwith is likeness; but where there is likeness, there is not necessarily an image." Hence it is clear that likeness is essential to an image; and that an image adds something to likeness—namely, that it is copied from something else. For an "image" is so called because it is produced as an imitation of something else; wherefore, for instance, an egg, however much like and equal to another egg, is not called an image of the other egg, because it is not copied from it.

But equality does not belong to the essence of an image; for as Augustine says (*QQ.* 83, *qu.* 74): "Where there is an image there is not necessarily equality," as we see in a person's image reflected in a glass. Yet this is of the essence of a perfect image; for in a perfect image nothing is wanting that is to be found in that of which

---

[2]Thomas Aquinas, *Summa Theologiae*, (New Advent), Ia. 93, I., 49–85

it is a copy. Now it is manifest that in man there is some likeness to God, copied from God as from an exemplar; yet this likeness is not one of equality, for such an exemplar infinitely excels its copy. Therefore there is in man a likeness to God; not, indeed, a perfect likeness, but imperfect. And Scripture implies the same when it says that man was made "to" God's likeness; for the preposition "to" signifies a certain approach, as of something at a distance.

Reply to Objection 1. The Prophet speaks of bodily images made by man. Therefore he says pointedly: "What image will you make for Him?" But God made a spiritual image to Himself in man.

Reply to Objection 2. The First-Born of creatures is the perfect Image of God, reflecting perfectly that of which He is the Image, and so He is said to be the "Image," and never "to the image." But man is said to be both "image" by reason of the likeness; and "to the image" by reason of the imperfect likeness. And since the perfect likeness to God cannot be except in an identical nature, the Image of God exists in His first-born Son; as the image of the king is in his son, who is of the same nature as himself: whereas it exists in man as in an alien nature, as the image of the king is in a silver coin, as Augustine says explains in *De decem Chordis* (*Serm.* ix, al, xcvi, *De Tempore*).

Reply to Objection 3. As unity means absence of division, a species is said to be the same as far as it is one. Now a thing is said to be one not only numerically, specifically, or generically, but also according to a certain analogy or proportion. In this sense a creature is one with God, or like to Him; but when Hilary says "of a thing which adequately represents another," this is to be understood of a perfect image.

Article 2. Whether the image of God is to be found in irrational creatures?

Objection 1. It would seem that the image of God is to be found in irrational creatures. For Dionysius says (*Div. Nom.* ii): "Effects are contingent images of their causes." But God is the cause not only of rational, but also of irrational creatures. Therefore the image of God is to be found in irrational creatures.

Objection 2. Further, the more distinct a likeness is, the nearer it approaches to the nature of an image. But Dionysius says (*Div. Nom.* iv) that "the solar ray has a very great similitude to the Divine goodness." Therefore it is made to the image of God.

Objection 3. Further, the more perfect anything is in goodness, the more it is like God. But the whole universe is more perfect in goodness than man; for though each individual thing is good, all things together are called "very good" (Genesis 1:31). Therefore the whole universe is to the image of God, and not only man.

Objection 4. Further, Boethius (*De Consol.* iii) says of God: "Holding the world in His mind, and forming it into His image." Therefore the whole world is to the image of God, and not only the rational creature.

On the contrary, Augustine says (*Gen. ad lit.* vi, 12): "Man's excellence consists in the fact that God made him to His own image by giving him an intellectual soul, which raises him above the beasts of the field." Therefore things without intellect are not made to God's image.

I answer that, Not every likeness, not even what is copied from something else, is sufficient to make an image; for if the likeness be only generic, or existing by virtue of some common accident, this does not suffice for one thing to be the image of another. For instance, a worm, though from man it may originate, cannot be called man's image, merely because of the generic likeness. Nor, if anything is made white like something else, can we say that it is the image of that thing; for whiteness is an accident belonging to many species. But the nature of an image requires likeness in species; thus the image of the king exists in his son: or, at least, in some specific accident, and chiefly in the shape; thus, we speak of a man's image in copper. Whence Hilary says pointedly that "an image is of the same species."

Now it is manifest that specific likeness follows the ultimate difference. But some things are like to God first and most commonly because they exist; secondly, because they live; and thirdly because they know or understand; and these last, as Augustine says (QQ. 83, qu. 51) "approach so near to God in likeness, that among all creatures nothing comes nearer to Him." It is clear, therefore, that intellectual creatures alone, properly speaking, are made to God's image.

Reply to Objection 1. Everything imperfect is a participation of what is perfect. Therefore even what falls short of the nature of an image, so far as it possesses any sort of likeness to God, participates in some degree the nature of an image. So Dionysius says that effects are "contingent images of their causes"; that is, as much as they happen to be so, but not absolutely.

Reply to Objection 2. Dionysius compares the solar ray to Divine goodness, as regards its causality; not as regards its natural dignity which is involved in the idea of an image.

Reply to Objection 3. The universe is more perfect in goodness than the intellectual creature as regards extension and diffusion; but intensively and collectively the likeness to the Divine goodness is found rather in the intellectual creature, which has a capacity for the highest good. Or else we may say that a part is not rightly divided against the whole, but only against another part. Wherefore, when we say that the intellectual nature alone is to the image of God, we do not mean that the universe in any part is not to God's image, but that the other parts are excluded.

Reply to Objection 4. Boethius here uses the word "image" to express the likeness which the product of an art bears to the artistic species in the mind of the artist. Thus every creature is an image of the exemplar type thereof in the Divine mind. We are not, however, using the word "image" in this sense; but as it implies a likeness in nature, that is, inasmuch as all things, as being, are like to the First Being; as living, like to the First Life; and as intelligent, like to the Supreme Wisdom.

* * *

Article 4. Whether the image of God is found in every man?

Objection 1. It would seem that the image of God is not found in every man. For the Apostle says that "man is the image of God, but woman is the image [*Vulg.* glory] of man" (1 Corinthians 11:7).

Therefore, as woman is an individual of the human species, it is clear that every individual is not an image of God.

Objection 2. Further, the Apostle says (Romans 8:29): "Whom God foreknew, He also predestined to be made conformable to the image of His Son." But all men are not predestined. Therefore all men have not the conformity of image.

Objection 3. Further, likeness belongs to the nature of the image, as above explained (1). But by sin man becomes unlike God. Therefore he loses the image of God.

On the contrary, It is written (Psalm 38:7): "Surely man passeth as an image."

I answer that, Since man is said to be the image of God by reason of his intellectual nature, he is the most perfectly like God according to that in which he can best imitate God in his intellectual nature. Now the intellectual nature imitates God chiefly in this, that God understands and loves Himself. Wherefore we see that the image of God is in man in three ways.

First, inasmuch as man possesses a natural aptitude for understanding and loving God; and this aptitude consists in the very nature of the mind, which is common to all men.

Secondly, inasmuch as man actually and habitually knows and loves God, though imperfectly; and this image consists in the conformity of grace.

Thirdly, inasmuch as man knows and loves God perfectly; and this image consists in the likeness of glory. Wherefore on the words, "The light of Thy countenance, O Lord, is signed upon us" (Psalm 4:7), the gloss distinguishes a threefold image of "creation," of "re-creation," and of "likeness." The first is found in all men, the second only in the just, the third only in the blessed.

Reply to Objection 1. The image of God, in its principal signification, namely the intellectual nature, is found both in man and in woman. Hence after the words, "To the image of God He created him," it is added, "Male and female He created them" (Genesis 1:27). Moreover it is said "them" in the plural, as Augustine (*Gen. ad lit.* iii, 22) remarks, lest it should be thought that both sexes were united in one individual. But in a secondary sense the image of God is found in man, and not in woman: for man is the beginning and end of woman; as God is the beginning and end of every creature. So when the Apostle had said that "man is the image and glory of God, but woman is the glory of man," he adds his reason for saying this: "For man is not of woman, but woman of man; and man was not created for woman, but woman for man."

Reply to Objections 2 and 3. These reasons refer to the image consisting in the conformity of grace and glory.

Article 5. Whether the image of God is in man according to the Trinity of Persons?

Objection 1. It would seem that the image of God does not exist in man as to the Trinity of Persons. For Augustine says (*Fulgentius De Fide ad Petrum* i): "One in essence is the Godhead of the Holy Trinity; and one is the image to which man was made." And Hilary (*De Trin.* v) says: "Man is made to the image of that which is common in the Trinity." Therefore the image of God in man is of the Divine Essence, and not of the Trinity of Persons.

Objection 2. Further, it is said (*De Eccl. Dogmat.*) that the image of God in man is to be referred to eternity. Damascene also says (*De Fide Orth.* ii, 12) that the image of God in man belongs to him as "an intelligent being endowed with free-will and self-movement." Gregory of Nyssa (*De Homin. Opificio* xvi) also asserts that, when Scripture says that "man was made to the image of God, it means that human nature was made a participator of all good: for the Godhead is the fulness of goodness." Now all these things belong more to the unity of the Essence than to the distinction of the Persons. Therefore the image of God in man regards, not the Trinity of Persons, but the unity of the Essence.

Objection 3. Further, an image leads to the knowledge of that of which it is the image. Therefore, if there is in man the image of God as to the Trinity of Persons; since man can know himself by his natural reason, it follows that by his natural knowledge man could know the Trinity of the Divine Persons; which is untrue, as was shown above (Question 32, Article 1).

Objection 4. Further, the name of Image is not applicable to any of the Three Persons, but only to the Son; for Augustine says (*De Trin.* vi, 2) that "the Son alone is the image of the Father." Therefore, if in man there were an image of God as regards the Person, this would not be an image of the Trinity, but only of the Son.

On the contrary, Hilary says (*De Trin.* iv): "The plurality of the Divine Persons is proved from the fact that man is said to have been made to the image of God."

I answer that, as we have seen (40, 2), the distinction of the Divine Persons is only according to origin, or, rather, relations of origin. Now the mode of origin is not the same in all things, but in each thing is adapted to the nature thereof; animated things being produced in one way, and inanimate in another; animals in one way, and plants in another. Wherefore it is manifest that the distinction of the Divine Persons is suitable to the Divine Nature; and therefore to be to the image of God by imitation of the Divine Nature does not exclude being to the same image by the representation of the Divine Persons: but rather one follows from the other. We must, therefore, say that in man there exists the image of God, both as regards the Divine Nature and as regards the Trinity of Persons; for also in God Himself there is one Nature in Three Persons.

Thus it is clear how to solve the first two objections.

Reply to Objection 3. This argument would avail if the image of God in man represented God in a perfect manner. But, as Augustine says (*De Trin.* xv, 6), there is a great difference between the trinity within ourselves and the Divine Trinity. Therefore, as he there says: "We see, rather than believe, the trinity which is in ourselves; whereas we believe rather than see that God is Trinity."

Reply to Objection 4. Some have said that in man there is an image of the Son only. Augustine rejects this opinion (*De Trin.* xii, 5, 6).

First, because as the Son is like to the Father by a likeness of essence, it would follow of necessity if man were made in likeness to the Son, that he is made to the likeness of the Father.

Secondly, because if man were made only to the image of the Son, the Father would not have said, "Let Us make man to Our own image and likeness"; but "to Thy image." When, therefore, it is written, "He made him to the image of God," the sense is not that the Father made man to the image of the Son only, Who is God, as some explained it, but that the Divine Trinity made man to Its image, that is, of the whole Trinity. When it is said that God "made man to His image," this can be understood in two ways: first, so that this preposition "to" points to the term of the making, and then the sense is, "Let Us make man in such a way that Our image may be in him."

Secondly, this preposition 'to' may point to the exemplar cause, as when we say, "This book is made (like) to that one." Thus the image of God is the very Essence of God, Which is incorrectly called an image forasmuch as image is put for the exemplar. Or, as some say, the Divine Essence is called an image because thereby one Person imitates another.

Article 6. Whether the image of God is in man as regards the mind only?

Objection 1. It would seem that the image of God is not only in man's mind. For the Apostle says (1 Corinthians 11:7) that "the man is the image . . . of God." But man is not only mind. Therefore the image of God is to be observed not only in his mind.

Objection 2. Further, it is written (Genesis 1:27): "God created man to His own image; to the image of God He created him; male and female He created them." But the distinction of male and female is in the body. Therefore the image of God is also in the body, and not only in the mind.

Objection 3. Further, an image seems to apply principally to the shape of a thing. But shape belongs to the body. Therefore the image of God is to be seen in man's body also, and not in his mind.

Objection 4. Further, according to Augustine (*Gen. ad lit.* xii, 7,24) there is a threefold vision in us, "corporeal," "spiritual," or imaginary, and "intellectual." Therefore, if in the intellectual vision that belongs to the mind there exists in us a trinity by reason of which we are made to the image of God, for the like reason there must be another trinity in the others.

On the contrary, The Apostle says (Ephesians 4:23–24): "Be renewed in the spirit of your mind, and put on the new man." Whence we are given to understand that our renewal which consists in putting on the new man, belongs to the mind. Now, he says (Colossians 3:10): "Putting on the new" man; "him who is renewed unto knowledge" of God, "according to the image of Him that created him," where the renewal which consists in putting on the new man is ascribed to the image of God. Therefore to be to the image of God belongs to the mind only.

I answer that, While in all creatures there is some kind of likeness to God, in the rational creature alone we find a likeness of "image" as we have explained above (1, 2); whereas in other creatures we find a likeness by way of a "trace." Now the intellect or mind is that whereby the rational creature excels other creatures; wherefore this image of God is not found even in the rational creature except in the mind; while in the other parts, which the rational creature may happen to possess, we find the likeness of a "trace," as in other creatures to which, in reference to such parts, the rational creature can be likened. We may easily understand the reason of this if we consider the way in which a "trace," and the way in which an "image," represents anything. An "image" represents something by likeness in species, as we have said; while a "trace" represents something by way of an effect, which represents the cause in such a way as not to attain to the likeness of species. For imprints which are left by the movements of animals are called "traces": so also ashes are a trace of fire, and desolation of the land a trace of a hostile army.

Therefore we may observe this difference between rational creatures and others, both as to the representation of the likeness of the Divine Nature in creatures, and as to the representation in them of the uncreated Trinity. For as to the likeness of the Divine Nature, rational creatures seem to attain, after a fashion, to the representation of the species, inasmuch as they imitate God, not only in being and life, but also in intelligence, as above explained (2); whereas other creatures do not understand, although we observe in them a certain trace of the Intellect that created them, if we consider their disposition. Likewise as the uncreated Trinity is distinguished by the procession of the Word from the Speaker, and of Love from both of these, as we have seen (28, 3); so we may say that in rational creatures wherein we find a procession of the word in the intellect, and a procession of the love in the will, there exists an image of the uncreated Trinity, by a certain representation of the species. In other creatures, however, we do not find the principle of the word, and the word and love; but we do see in them a certain trace of the existence of these in the Cause that produced them. For in the fact that a creature has a modified and finite nature, proves that it proceeds from a principle; while its species points to the (mental) word of the maker, just as the shape of a house points to the idea of the architect; and order points to the maker's love by reason of which he directs the effect to a good end; as also the use of the house points to the will of the architect. So we find in man a likeness to God by way of an "image" in his mind; but in the other parts of his being by way of a "trace."

Reply to Objection 1. Man is called to the image of God; not that he is essentially an image; but that the image of God is impressed on his mind; as a coin is an image of the king, as having the image of the king. Wherefore there is no need to consider the image of God as existing in every part of man.

Reply to Objection 2. As Augustine says (*De Trin.* xii, 5), some have thought that the image of God was not in man individually, but severally. They held that "the man represents the Person of the Father; those born of man denote the person of the Son; and that the woman is a third person in likeness to the Holy Ghost, since she so proceeded from man as not to be his son or daughter." All of this is manifestly absurd; first, because it would follow that the Holy Ghost is the principle of the Son, as the woman is the principle of the man's offspring; secondly, because one man would be only the image of one Person; thirdly, because in that case Scripture should not have mentioned the image of God in man until after the birth of the offspring. Therefore we must understand that when Scripture had said, "to the image of God He created him," it added, "male and female He created them," not to imply that the image of God came through the distinction of sex, but that the image of God belongs to both sexes, since it is in the mind, wherein there is no sexual distinction of sex, but that the image of God belongs to both sexes, since it is in the mind, wherein there is no sexual distinction. Wherefore the Apostle (Colossians 3:10), after saying, "According to the image of Him that created him," added, "Where there is neither male nor female" [these words are in reality from Galatians 3:28 (*Vulg.* "neither Gentile nor Jew").

Reply to Objection 3. Although the image of God in man is not to be found in his bodily shape, yet because "the body of man alone among terrestrial animals is not inclined prone to the ground, but is adapted to look upward to heaven, for this reason we may rightly say that it is made to God's image and likeness, rather than the bodies of other animals," as Augustine remarks (*QQ.* 83, *qu.* 51). But this is not to be understood as though the image of God were in man's body; but in the sense that the very shape of the human body represents the image of God in the soul by way of a trace.

Reply to Objection 4. Both in the corporeal and in the imaginary vision we may find a trinity, as Augustine says (*De Trin.* xi, 2). For in corporeal vision there is first the species of the exterior body; secondly, the act of vision, which occurs by the impression on the sight of a certain likeness of the said species; thirdly, the intention of the will applying the sight to see, and to rest on what is seen.

Likewise, in the imaginary vision we find first the species kept in the memory; secondly, the vision itself, which is caused by the penetrative power of the soul, that is, the faculty of imagination, informed by the species; and thirdly, we find the intention of the will joining both together. But each of these trinities falls short of the Divine image. For the species of the external body is extrinsic to the essence of the soul; while the species in the memory, though not extrinsic to the soul, is adventitious to it; and thus in both cases the species falls short of representing the connaturality and co-eternity of the Divine Persons. The corporeal vision, too, does not proceed only from the species of the external body, but from this, and at the same time from the sense of the seer; in like manner imaginary vision is not from the species only which is preserved in the memory, but also from the imagination. For these reasons the procession of the Son from the Father alone is not suitably represented. Lastly the intention of the will joining the two together, does not proceed from them either in corporeal or spiritual vision. Wherefore the procession of the Holy Ghost from the Father and the Son is not thus properly represented.

Article 7. Whether the image of God is to be found in the acts of the soul?

Objection 1. It would seem that the image of God is not found in the acts of the soul. For Augustine says (*De Civ. Dei* xi, 26), that "man was made to God's image, inasmuch as we exist and know that we exist, and love this existence and knowledge." But to exist does not signify an act. Therefore the image of God is not to be found in the soul's acts.

Objection 2. Further, Augustine (*De Trin.* ix, 4) assigns God's image in the soul to these three things—mind, knowledge, and love. But mind does not signify an act, but rather the power or the essence of the intellectual soul. Therefore the image of God does not extend to the acts of the soul.

Objection 3. Further, Augustine (*De Trin.* x, 11) assigns the image of the Trinity in the soul to "memory, understanding, and will." But these three are "natural powers of the soul," as the Master of the Sentences says (1 *Sent.* D iii). Therefore the image of God is in the powers, and does not extend to the acts of the soul.

Objection 4. Further, the image of the Trinity always remains in the soul. But an act does not always remain. Therefore the image of God does not extend to the acts.

On the contrary, Augustine (*De Trin.* xi, 2 *seqq.*) assigns the trinity in the lower part of the soul, in relation to the actual vision, whether sensible or imaginative. Therefore, also, the trinity in the mind, by reason of which man is like to God's image, must be referred to actual vision.

I answer that, As above explained (2), a certain representation of the species belongs to the nature of an image. Hence, if the image of the Divine Trinity is to be found in the soul, we must look for it where the soul approaches the nearest to a representation of the species of the Divine Persons. Now the Divine Persons are distinct from each other by reason of the procession of the Word from the Speaker, and the procession of Love connecting Both. But in our soul word "cannot exist without actual thought," as Augustine says (*De Trin.* xiv, 7). Therefore, first and chiefly, the image of the Trinity is to be found in the acts of the soul, that is, inasmuch as from the knowledge which we possess, by actual thought we form an internal word; and thence break forth into love. But, since the principles of acts are the habits and powers, and everything exists virtually in its principle, therefore, secondarily and consequently, the image of the Trinity may be considered as existing in the powers, and still more in the habits, forasmuch as the acts virtually exist therein.

Reply to Objection 1. Our being bears the image of God so far as if is proper to us, and excels that of the other animals, that is to say, in so far as we are endowed with a mind. Therefore, this trinity is the same as that which Augustine mentions (*De Trin*. ix, 4), and which consists in mind, knowledge, and love.

Reply to Objection 2. Augustine observed this trinity, first, as existing in the mind. But because the mind, though it knows itself entirely in a certain degree, yet also in a way does not know itself-namely, as being distinct from others (and thus also it searches itself, as Augustine subsequently proves—*De Trin*. x, 3, 4); therefore, as though knowledge were not in equal proportion to mind, he takes three things in the soul which are proper to the mind, namely, memory, understanding, and will; which everyone is conscious of possessing; and assigns the image of the Trinity pre-eminently to these three, as though the first assignation were in part deficient.

Reply to Objection 3. As Augustine proves (*De Trin*. xiv, 7), we may be said to understand, will, and to love certain things, both when we actually consider them, and when we do not thing of them. When they are not under our actual consideration, they are objects of our memory only, which, in his opinion, is nothing else than habitual retention of knowledge and love [Cf. 79, 7, *ad* 1]. "But since," as he says, "a word cannot be there without actual thought (for we think everything that we say, even if we speak with that interior word belonging to no nation's tongue), this image chiefly consists in these three things, memory, understanding, and will. And by understanding I mean here that whereby we understand with actual thought; and by will, love, or dilection I mean that which unites this child with its parent." From which it is clear that he places the image of the Divine Trinity more in actual understanding and will, than in these as existing in the habitual retention of the memory; although even thus the image of the Trinity exists in the soul in a certain degree, as he says in the same place. Thus it is clear that memory, understanding, and will are not three powers as stated in the Sentences.

Reply to Objection 4. Someone might answer by referring to Augustine's statement (*De Trin*. xiv, 6), that "the mind ever remembers itself, ever understands itself, ever loves itself"; which some take to mean that the soul ever actually understands, and loves itself. But he excludes this interpretation by adding that "it does not always think of itself as actually distinct from other things." Thus it is clear that the soul always understands and loves itself, not actually but habitually; though we might say that by perceiving its own act, it understands itself whenever it understands anything. But since it is not always actually understanding, as in the case of sleep, we must say that these acts, although not always actually existing, yet ever exist in their principles, the habits and powers. Wherefore, Augustine says (*De Trin*. xiv, 4): "If the rational soul is made to the image of God in the sense that it can make use of reason and intellect to understand and consider God, then the image of God was in the soul from the beginning of its existence."

Questions

1 How would you describe Aquinas' use of Scripture here? What use does he make of Christology in interpreting the image?

2 Why does the difference between "likeness" and "image" matter for Aquinas?

3 "Intellectual creatures alone, properly speaking, are made to God's image." True or false?

4 In what sense is the image of God found in man in a way in which it is not found in woman (for Aquinas)?

5 What is the difference between "image" and "trace"? What is the significance of this distinction?

6 Why does Aquinas seek to discern "trinities" in the soul?

TEXT 3 JOHN CALVIN, "COMMENTARY UPON GEN. 1:26-28."[3]

The French-Swiss reformer John Calvin (1509–64) is best known for his *Institutes of the Christian Religion*. He begins these by showing that proper theology and proper anthropology are inextricably linked. However, he saw the *Institutes* as only a supplement to his commentaries on the text of Scripture. Unlike Augustine and Aquinas, Calvin worked from the original languages which he accessed via printed editions. Like Aquinas, Calvin saw himself as writing in the tradition of Augustine—although he does not employ the "trinitarian" psychological analysis of the latter's *de Trinitate*.

Let us make man. Although the tense here used is the future, all must acknowledge that this is the language of one apparently deliberating. Hitherto God has been introduced simply as *commanding*; now, when he approaches the most excellent of all his works, he enters into *consultation*. God certainly might here command by his bare word what he wished to be done: but he chose to give this tribute to the excellency of man, that he would, in a manner, enter into consultation concerning his creation. This is the highest honour with which he has dignified us; to a due regard the *likeness*, and contents himself with mentioning the image. Should any one take the exception, that he was merely studying brevity; I answer, that where he twice uses the word image, he makes no mention of the likeness. We also know that it was customary with the Hebrews to repeat the same thing in different words. Besides, the phrase itself shows that the second term was added for the sake of explanation, 'Let us make,' he says, 'man in our image, according to our likeness,' that is, that he may be like God, or may represent the image of God. Lastly, in the fifth chapter, without making any mention of *image*, he puts likeness in its place, (verse 1). Although we have set aside all difference between the two words, we have not yet ascertained what this image or likeness is. The *Anthropomorphites* were too gross in seeking this resemblance in the human body; let that reverie therefore remain entombed. Others proceed with a little more subtlety, who, though they do not imagine God to be corporeal, yet maintain that the image of God is in the body of man, because his admirable workmanship there shines brightly; but this opinion, as we shall see, is by no means consonant with Scripture. The exposition of Chrysostom is not more correct, who refers to the dominion which was given to man in order that he might, in a certain sense, act as God's vicegerent in the government of the world. This truly is some portion, though very small, of the image of God. Since the image of God has been destroyed in us by the fall, we may judge from its restoration what it originally had been. Paul says that we are transformed into the image of God by the gospel. And, according to him, spiritual regeneration is nothing else than the restoration of the same image. (Col. iii. 10, and Eph. iv. 23.) That he made this image to consist in "righteousness and true holiness," is by the figure *synecdoche*; for though this is the

---

[3]John Calvin, *Commentaries on the First Book of Moses, Called Genesis* (Edinburgh: Printed for the Calvin Translation Society, 1847), 90–100.

chief part, it is not the whole of God's image. Therefore by this word the perfection of our whole nature is designated, as it appeared when Adam was endued with a right judgment, had affections in harmony with reason, had all his senses sound and well regulated, and truly excelled in everything good. Thus the chief seat of the Divine image was in his mind and heart, where it was eminent yet was there no part of him in which some scintillations of it did not shine forth. For there was an attempering in the several parts of the soul, which corresponded with their various offices. In the mind perfect intelligence flourished and reigned, uprightness attended as its companion, and all the senses were prepared and moulded for due obedience to reason; and in the body there was a suitable correspondence with this internal order. But now, although some obscure lineaments of that image are found remaining in us; yet are they so vitiated and maimed, that they may truly be said to be destroyed. For besides the deformity which everywhere appears unsightly, this evil also is added, that no part is free from the infection of sin.

In our image, after our likeness. I do not scrupulously insist upon the particles b (*beth,*) and k (*caph.*) I know not whether there is anything solid in the opinion of some who hold that this is said, because the image of God was only shadowed forth in man till he should arrive at his perfection. The thing indeed is true; but I do not think that anything of the kind entered the mind of Moses. It is also truly said that Christ is the only image of the Father, but yet the words of Moses do not bear the interpretation that "in the image" means "in Christ." It may also be added, that even man, though in a different respect, is called the image of God. In which thing some of the Fathers are deceived who thought that they could defeat the Arians with this weapon that Christ alone is God's image. This further difficulty is also to be encountered, namely, why Paul should deny the woman to be the image of God, when Moses honours both, indiscriminately, with this title. The solution is short; Paul there alludes only to the domestic relation. He therefore restricts the image of God to *government*, in which the man has superiority over the wife, and certainly he means nothing more than that man is superior in the degree of honour. But here the question is respecting that glory of God which peculiarly shines forth in human nature, where the mind, the will, and all the senses, represent the Divine order.

And let them have dominion. Here he commemorates that part of dignity with which he decreed to honour man, namely, that he should have authority over all living creatures. He appointed man, it is true, lord of the world; but he expressly subjects the animals to him, because they, having an inclination or instinct of their own, seem to be less under authority from without. The use of the plural number intimates that this authority was not given to Adam only, but to all his posterity as well as to him. And hence we infer what was the end for which all things were created; namely, that none of the conveniences and necessaries of life might be wanting to men. In the very order of the creation the paternal solicitude of God for man is conspicuous, because he furnished the world with all things needful, and even with an immense profusion of wealth, before he formed man. Thus man was rich before he was born. But if God had such care for us before we existed, he will by no means leave us destitute of food and of other necessaries of life, now that we are placed in the world. Yet, that he often keeps his hand as if closed is to be imputed to our sins

26. *So God created man.* The reiterated mention of the image of God is not a vain repetition. For it is a remarkable instance of the Divine goodness which can

never be sufficiently proclaimed. And, at the same time, he admonishes us from what excellence we have fallen, that he may excite in us the desire of its recovery. When he soon afterwards adds, that God created them male and female he commends to us that conjugal bond by which the society of mankind is cherished. For this form of speaking, "God created man, male and female created he them? Is of the same force as if he had said, that the man himself was incomplete.' Under these circumstances, the woman was added to him as a companion that they both might be one, as he more clearly expresses it in the second chapter. Malachi also means the same thing when he relates, (ii. 15) that one man was created by God, whilst, nevertheless, he possessed the fulness of the Spirit? For he there treats of conjugal fidelity, which the Jews were violating by their polygamy. For the purpose of correcting this fault, he calls that pair, consisting of man and woman, which God in the beginning had joined together, one man, in order that every one might learn to be content with his own wife.

Questions

1   A long debate has raged since patristic era about the difference (if any) between "image" and "likeness" in the text of Gen. 1:26-28. What is Calvin's reading?

2   "Since the image of God has been destroyed in us by the fall, we may judge from its restoration what it originally had been." What does Calvin mean?

3   Does Calvin modify the assertion of Aquinas and Augustine that the image is to be found in the intellect? How so?

4   In what respect are women created in the image of God (for Calvin)?

5   How (if at all) does Calvin link the notion of dominion to the *Imago Dei*?

TEXT 4: KARL BARTH, *CHURCH DOGMATICS*[4]

Karl Barth (1886–1968) was one of the most prodigious and original of twentieth century theologians. He left almost no area of theological reasoning undiscussed in his voluminous writings. When it came to the *Imago Dei*, Barth discarded the traditional ascription of the image to some capacity or attribute of the human creature (usually reason), and instead expounded the theme in terms of the human capacity for relationships—with God, and with other human beings. In particular Barth noted that the phrase "male and female he created them" exists in close proximity to the announcement of the image in both Gen. 1:26-7 and in Gen. 5:1-2. While the relational theme, based on the triune nature of God, had long been a part of the discussion of the image (as we have seen), the link to the gendered nature of humanity was a fresh—and to some later feminist critics, somewhat disturbing—perspective. The extract is from the pages just before Barth's lengthy (and controversial) exegesis of the text of Gen. 1:26-28—a passage which would itself repay close study.

... this brings us to the concept which is used by the first creation saga to denote the purpose and fulfilment of the divine creative will. The summons is as follows: "Let us make man in our image, after our likeness." "In our image" means to be created as a being which has its ground and possibility in the fact that in "us," i.e., in God's own sphere and being, there exists a divine and therefore self-grounded prototype to which this being can correspond; which can therefore legitimate it for all that it is a heterogeneous imitation; which can justify its existence; and by which, when existence is given to it, it will in fact be legitimated and justified. That it is created in this image proves that it has in it its ground of justification. The phrase "in our image" is obviously the decisive insight of the saga, for it is repeated twice. The other phrase: "In our likeness," means to be created as a being whose nature is decisively characterised by the fact that although it is created by God it is not a new nature to the extent that it has a pattern in the nature of God Himself; to the extent that it is created as a likeness of this divine image, i.e., in the likeness of this image. The being created in the likeness of this image is man. The rest of creation has this character of a copy or image only in so far as it has found its conclusion and climax in the creation and existence of man. We can thus see that the witness had a reason for keeping back this "Let us" until now, and for producing it only at this point. It is in the co-existence of God and man on the one hand, and man's independent existence on the other, that the real and yet not discordant counterpart in God Himself finds creaturely form and is revealed to the creature.

If we think of the rest of creation without man, we can think in terms of something other than God, but only in the sense of something distinct from God and not of a counterpart. Only with the first creatures with independent life do we begin to glimpse a true counterpart alongside and before God in the sphere of the rest of creation. But

---

[4]Karl Barth, *Church Dogmatics*, edited by Geoffrey William Bromiley and Thomas F. Torrance, III/1 (London: T&T Clark, 2004), 183–92.

not until the creation of man does it find a genuine and clearly visible form. Only in him does a real other, a true counterpart to God, enter the creaturely sphere.

This innovation is repeated in the distinctive existence of man as such. What is created without and alongside man exists in juxtaposition and even in a certain full-scale co-existence, but not in the true confrontation and reciprocity which are actualised in the reality of an "I" and a "Thou." Neither heaven nor earth, water nor land, nor living creatures from plants upward to land animals, are a "Thou" whom God can confront as an "I," nor do they stand in an "I-Thou" relationship to one another, nor can they enter into such a relationship. According to the first creation saga, however, man as such exists in this relationship from the very outset.

"He created them male and female." This is the interpretation immediately given to the sentence "God created man." As in this sense man is the first and only one to be created in genuine confrontation with God and as a genuine counterpart to his fellows, it is he first and alone who is created "in the image" and "after the likeness" of God. For an understanding of the general biblical use of this concept, it is advisable to keep as close as possible to the simple sense of "God-likeness" given in this passage. It is not a quality of man. Hence there is no point in asking in which of man's peculiar attributes and attitudes it consists. It does not consist in anything that man is or does. It consists as man himself consists as the creature of God. He would not be man if he were not the image of God. He is the image of God in the fact that he is man. For the meaning and purpose of God at his creation were as follows. He willed the existence of a being which in all its non-deity and therefore its differentiation can be a real partner; which is capable of action and responsibility in relation to Him; to which His own divine form of life is not alien; which in a creaturely repetition, as a copy and imitation, can be a bearer of this form of life. Man was created as this being. But the divine form of life, repeated in the man created by Him, consists in that which is the obvious aim of the "Let us." In God's own being and sphere there is a counterpart: a genuine but harmonious self-encounter and self-discovery; a free co-existence and co-operation; an open confrontation and reciprocity. Man is the repetition of this divine form of life; its copy and reflection. He is this first in the fact that he is the counterpart of God, the encounter and discovery in God Himself being copied and imitated in God's relation to man. But he is it also in the fact that he is himself the counterpart of his fellows and has in them a counterpart, the co-existence and co-operation in God Himself being repeated in the relation of man to man. Thus the *tertium comparationis*, the analogy between God and man, is simply the existence of the I and the Thou in confrontation. This is first constitutive for God, and then for man created by God. To remove it is tantamount to removing the divine from God as well as the human from man. On neither side can it be thought away. That it is God's divine and man's human form of life is revealed in the creation of man. God wills and creates man when He wills and creates the being between which and Himself there exists this *tertium comparationis,* this analogy; the analogy of free differentiation and relation. In this way He wills and creates man as a partner who is capable of entering into covenant-relationship with Himself-for all the disparity in and therefore the differentiation between man as a creature and his Creator. The grace of man's creation—in which all creation is now revealed as an act of God's creation—consists not only in the fact that He sets man in fellowship with Himself as a being existing in free differentiation and relationship, but in the fact that He has actually created him in fellowship with Himself in order that in this natural fellowship He may further speak and act with him.

It is striking, but incontestable, that in his description of the grace of God in this final and supreme act of creation, the biblical witness makes no reference at all to the peculiar intellectual and moral talents and possibilities of man, to his reason and its determination and exercise. It is not in something which distinguishes him from the beasts, but in that which formally he has in common with them, viz. that God has created him male and female, that he is this being in differentiation and relationship, and therefore in natural fellowship with God. The only thing that we are told about the creation of man, apart from the fact that it was accomplished by the Word of God in and after the image of God, is that "God created them male and female." Everything else that is said about man, namely, that he is to have dominion over the animal kingdom and the earth, that he is blessed in the exercise of the powers of his species and the exercise of his lordship, and that he is to draw nourishment from the plants and trees, has reference to this plural: he is male and female. And this plurality, the differentiation of sex, is something which formally he has in common with the beasts. What distinguishes him from the beasts? According to Gen. 1, it is the fact that in the case of man the differentiation of sex is the only differentiation. Man is not said to be created or to exist in groups and species, in races and peoples, etc. The only real differentiation and relationship is that of man to man, and in its original and most concrete form of man to woman and woman to man. Man is no more solitary than God. But as God is One, and He alone is God, so man as man is one and alone, and two only in the duality of his kind, i.e., in the duality of man and woman. In this way he is a copy and imitation of God. In this way he repeats in his confrontation of God and himself the confrontation in God. In this way he is the special creature of God's special grace. It is obviously the incomprehensible special grace of God that His singularity finds correspondence in a, created singularity. That the grace of God has this particular form; that it is in the differentiation and relationship of man and woman, the relation of sex, that there is this repetition, is an indication of the creatureliness of man—for this is something which he has in common with the beasts. But this creaturely differentiation and relationship is shown to be distinct and free, to reflect God's image and to prove His special grace, by the fact that in this particular duality (i.e., to the exclusion of all others) he is alone among the beasts and in the rest of creation, and that it is in this form of life and this alone, as man and woman, that he will continually stand before God, and in the form of his fellow that he will continually stand before himself. Men are simply male and female. Whatever else they may be, it is only in this differentiation and relationship. This is the particular dignity ascribed to the sex relationship. It is wholly creaturely, and common to man and beast. But as the only real principle of differentiation and relationship, as the original form not only of man's confrontation of God but also of all intercourse between man and man, it is the true *humanum* and therefore the true creaturely image of God. Man can and will always be man before God and among his fellows only as he is man in relationship to woman and woman in relationship to man. And as he is one or the other he is man. And since it is this and nothing else that makes him man, he is distinguished from the beast and every other creature, existing in the free differentiation and relationship in which God has chosen, willed and created him as His partner. The fact that he was created man and woman will be the great paradigm of everything that is to take place between him and God, and also of everything that is to take place between him and his fellows. The fact that he was created and exists as male and female will also prove to be not only a copy and imitation of his Creator as such, but at the same time a type of the history of the covenant and salvation which will take place between him and his Creator. In all His future utterances and actions God will acknowledge that He has created man male and female, and in this way in His own image and likeness. But these are matters which are more explicitly treated by the second biblical witness, and we will not anticipate their development at this point. The first witness, in the obvious context of his account of the divine likeness of man, is simply content to mention the fact and to give it a central position. God created them male and female, in this true plurality but in this alone. All else refers to men in this plurality. Men are all that this differentiation and relationship includes in its whole dialectic (not developed in this context) of gift and task, of need and satisfaction, of lack and fulfilment, of antithesis and union, of superiority and subjection. In every other differentiation and agreement they will always be male and female. Every other differentiation and agreement will continually prove to be preliminary or supplementary as compared with the fact that they are male and female. And this strictly natural and creaturely factor, which is held in common with the beasts, is not in any sense an animal element in man but the distinctively human element-not in itself but because it has pleased God to make man in this form of life an image and likeness, a witness, of His own form of life.

Of men who repeat the divine form of life in their creaturely being it is now said that God has assigned to them an exalted position of lordship within the surrounding animal kingdom of land, air and water. But it is not in this that the divine likeness consists. It is in consequence of their divine likeness that men are distinguished from all other creatures, and in the first instance from all other creatures with autonomous life, by a superior position, by a higher dignity and might, by a greater power of disposal and control. It is only in this relationship, in dependent connexion with man, that the animal kingdom can and will participate in the mystery of all creation as it is revealed in man, and in the promise of this mystery. The ascription of this position and function to man does not mean that the rest of creation is excluded from this mystery; it describes the manner of its inclusion. In this way, in basic subordination to man, and as his comradely followers and environment, they too are witnesses and to that extent partakers of the divine image and the history promised to him with his special creation. More than this must not be read into man's dominion over the beasts. Man is not their Creator; hence he cannot be their absolute lord, a second God. In his dignity and position he can only be God's creaturely witness and representative to them. He can be a *primus inter pares* among those over whom he rules. He can carry out a commission. But he does not possess the power of life and death; the right of capital punishment. Man's lordship over the animals is a lordship with internal and external limitations. His dignity and power over them is accompanied by a natural inferiority in the things which he has in common with them. Nor is any mention made in this connexion of his rationality as a feature which distinguishes him from them. As the Creator God is no less over him than He is over the animals. What distinguishes him and gives him authority and power is the fact that, although he is not radically different from the other creatures with independent life, he has been honoured by the grace of God to be the image of God in the uniqueness of his plurality as male and female. The animals in their multiplicity are not confronted by different groups and species of men, but, for all the provisional and subsequent differentiations in every individual, by the one man-male and female. This is what gives and maintains his superiority. But this, of course, is grace, and it can be brought out and asserted only as the superiority of grace. In the last analysis, therefore, it cannot be an end in itself. The distinction, responsibility and promise ascribed to man in the biblical witness which follows are undeniably more and other than the possession and exercise of this lordship. This is not the essence but the accessory of his true determination. The latter will include-but properly only as a negative determination-the fact that within the animal world of land, air and water he is distinct and superior, and that it has been placed under his control. His divine likeness does not depend upon this, but his power and position depend on his divine likeness.

That the saga has to be understood in this way may be proved by the fact that even after his creation man needs the special blessing of God for the exercise of his lordship. Like the procreation of his kind, his multiplication and expansion, this lordship is a matter of his own activity as this special creature with independent life. Like them, it takes place in spontaneous acts for whose legitimate and successful execution he has as much need of the Creator's authorisation, enabling and promise as he has of His creative Word for his existence. As God's image and likeness man exists as male and female, and no further blessing is needed for this presupposition of all his actions. This is not in any sense a matter of his spontaneous action. It is given and assured by the fact that in virtue of the divine creation man can actually be what he is. It consists in the fact that God chose and willed man in the utterance of that "Let us" and in the fact that it was actualised. But man needs God's blessing when (animal-like in this respect) he moves forward as male and female to the procreation of new individuals, to the multiplication and expansion of his kind; and when (God-like in this respect) he again moves forward as male and female to the exercise of this lordship. At the latter point his activity—in clear differentiation from that of the beast—assumes a dangerous proximity to God's activity as Creator in which it may be both supremely insolent and wholly ineffective. Here there commences the post-creation history in which not only the beast but also man would be lost if creation had not been accompanied at once by God's permission and promise for his activity, and if God had not stood behind him from the very first with His blessing. It is, therefore, still an element in the history of creation and already an element in the history of the covenant that man, male and female, created as God's reflection and image, needed and was actually granted the divine blessing for his future activity. From this we learn that the divine likeness of man does not affect in the slightest the creatureliness which he has in common with all other beings and in which, with all other beings, he is dependent on God's aid. In itself it would have preserved his actions neither from insolence nor ineffectiveness. It is a copy and not an original; a reflection and not a prototype. In virtue of the divine likeness, man-even more than the beast over whom he is given dominion-is directed in all his acts to hear this friendly Word of God. Furthermore, and supremely, we learn that he does actually hear this friendly Word of God; that he does actually receive the blessing of God for his propagation as well as for his actualisation as a being in the divine image. When his propagation takes place, and his power and position are actualised, his actions will take place under the blessing of God and therefore with His permission and promise. And when the first man and the first woman continue to live in their children and therefore in new individuals; when they multiply and populate the earth and have dominion over it, these new individuals will also be blessed with the blessing addressed to the first man in and with his creation. God will acknowledge them as He acknowledged the creaturely partner whom He chose and willed, and created at the very outset in His image and after His likeness. God will not retract His permission and promise either from the first man or his posterity, just as He will not cease to be their Creator, or to govern and sustain them as their Creator. Whatever the threats and dangers that may arise, they can only be temporary breaks in the line which commenced with God's blessing. Everything that takes place on this line must and will essentially and properly be salvation history. Only incidentally—even in its most dreadful form will it be the reverse. Because it rests on this divine blessing, at bottom it must always be a history of peace and covenant, not of enmity, conflict and wrath. The blessing may well be turned into a curse (i.e., the permission may take on the character of an abandonment and the promise of a burden), but the curse can only be a reversal of the blessing. Even the wrath and judgment of God which may overtake man do not indicate any retraction, but only a special form, and in the last analysis the most glorious confirmation, of the permission and promise given to him. It will indeed be shown that man, male and female, created in the image and likeness of God, does not owe his divine likeness to himself, and that he is unable of himself to maintain his existence. It will be shown that the repetition of his being in this image and after this likeness cannot be his own concern, but only that of a divine restoration and renewal. It will be shown that the divine likeness cannot actually exist for him in the continuance or even the progressive development of a deposited quality, but can only be the object of his hope in God his Creator; that as man he can look only for the man who is not only created in this image and after this likeness, but in accordance with it will actually be God's image. There will be the episode of the fall of man and woman—an arresting and disturbing intervention between their creation and corresponding being. And this will entail also the wrath and judgment of God, the turning of the blessing into a curse. It will be plainly revealed that the man who does not accomplish or merit either his creation or his blessing, but has brought this perversion upon himself, is in no position to endure, let alone to reverse it. And it will then be seen that, as God's image and likeness, he is wholly directed to set all his hope on God. But it will also be made plain that he may grasp and hold this hope because he is God's image and likeness, and because he was originally blessed, and is still blessed in spite of the fact that the blessing has been turned into a curse. It will be revealed also that God is faithful to Himself and work and Word; that the creation of man as male and female, and therefore in the image and likeness of God, is not overthrown by the episode of the fall, but remains even in face of the total contradiction between it and the being of man. It will be shown that man has reason to look for the man who will be different from him, but who for this reason will be real man for him, in the image and likeness of God male and female in his place and on his behalf, namely, Jesus Christ and His community. The history of the covenant whose beginning, centre and goal will be this man-this man and this woman- will confirm the history of creation, and thus confirm and fulfil the blessing given to man in relation to the act of his propagation and in relation to the assumption of his position of power and dignity as compared with other creatures. For both these he has the divine permission and promise, and these will not be abrogated by any episode or fall for the simple reason that they have reference to the man who will be the open mystery of the covenant history which begins after the completion of the history of creation. He has the divine permission and promise just because his own existence, willed and created by God, is only the external basis of the existence of this other man, but as the external basis of the existence of this other man may really be an existence in genuine hope on God which cannot be affected even by his own sin, even by the whole conflict between God and himself, even by all the menace of God's wrath and judgment. When man and woman beget and bear children by the divine permission and promise; when in the indestructible unity of the human race they are more than all the beasts and the rightful lords of the earth, they continually realise in themselves the sign of this hope. This human activity is the sign of the genuine creaturely confrontation in open differentiation and joyful relationship which is the image and likeness of the divine form of life. In itself and as such their activity is no doubt a denial of their divine image and likeness, and laden with all the mortal sickness which is a consequence of this denial, but this does not in any way alter the fact that this activity as such is the sign of the hope given to man; the sign of the Son of Man and of His community. And if man, if male and female necessarily point beyond themselves in this activity; if their activity has meaning only in the fact that it is the realisation of this sign, this again does not alter in the very least the fact that in realising this sign they participate in that to which they themselves point—in Jesus Christ and His Church, in the being of this man corresponding to His creation—even before they know Him, even before they believe in Jesus Christ, even before they are called to His Church. It does not alter the fact that in all their humanity, willingly and wittingly or not, they may have their hope in the divine will and plan which has this man as its goal, and may live in the strength of the truth and certainty of this hope. This is what has to be said of the power of the blessing given to man; of the range of the friendly Word of God which is spoken to him at the beginning of his way as the special creature with independent life that he is. This friendly Word affirms that the natural being and activity of man, irrespective of individual vagaries, is fundamentally and finally destined to be a sign of the fact that the One of whom he is the image and likeness, God Himself, has in and with his creation constituted Himself his pledge and hope.

Questions

1   The image is 'not a quality of man." What is it then, according to Barth, and what's wrong with this view?

2   What is the "analogy between God and man" that Barth describes here?

3   How does Barth argue for the prominence of "male and female" in explaining the image of God?

4   How does he relate the notion of dominion to gender?

5   How does "male and female" point to Jesus and His church?

TEXT 5: MARY MCCLINTOCK FULKERSON "THE IMAGO DEI AND A REFORMED LOGIC FOR A FEMINIST/WOMANIST CRITIQUE"

Given what we have seen in the previous texts about the place of women in the theological reading of the *Imago Dei*, it is not surprising that feminist theologians should have something to say in response. Mary McClintock Fulkerson (b. 1950), who has taught at Duke Divinity School in North Carolina since 1983, has returned several times in her work to the *Imago Dei* and its significance for women in their discipleship. She claims that it is "at the heart of feminist theology." Writing from within the Reformed tradition, Fulkerson asks whether there is a way to apply the *Imago Dei* ("the compliment of the *Imago Dei*") to all human beings without qualification.

The topic of the *Imago Dei* is in many respects at the heart of feminist theology. It refers to the claim that however different and alienated from God we are, human beings bear some likeness to the divine. Indeed, to say we are created in the image of God is to identify the human capacity to be in relationship with God, or, better, to claim that relationship with God is the human vocation. Thus, the image is a symbolic condensation of what in the Christian tradition it means to be fully human. Its significance increases further upon recognition that the *Imago Dei* has the double function of referring both to human beings and to God. It thereby directs us to ask not only about the way in which God is imaged and what that communicates, but about how such imaging contributes to the valuing and devaluing of human beings as well. In important respects the *Imago Dei* can serve as an index of whom the tradition has seen as fully human.

Given such complex potential, it is not surprising that feminist theology has contributed much to theological conversations about the way human beings image God, most particularly by foregrounding issues of representation in relation to the question of whom the tradition sees as fully human. Mary Daly's famous comment that "if God in 'his' heaven is a father ruling 'his' people, then it is in the 'nature', of things and according to divine plan and the order of the universe that society be male-dominated" is, in this sense, an example of theological reflection upon the *Imago Dei*.

The resources of Reformed traditions also provide insights into what it means to be fully human, insights that can be productive for feminist theology. Conversely, Reformed theological commitments are capable of further development in light of feminist theological explorations. For mutual enrichment both conversations will have to expand.

The compliment of the *Imago Dei*

Scripture is a prime source for thinking about the image of God. The opening chapters of Genesis tell of God's gracious creation—from light, the earth, vegetation, and animals to the human being—attesting to God's pronouncement that this plurivocity of being is good. The creature called *'adam* gets special notice when God says, "Let us make humankind in our image, according to our likeness" (Gen. 1:26). From

Scripture the theme of the *Imago Dei* enters the theological tradition of the church, where for centuries it had no particular doctrinal locus. The variety of claims about anthropology—human being as created, as distorted by sin, and as redeemed—are all within the purview of the *Imago Dei*, wherever they appear. Thus, for a classical theologian relevant discussions of the image can occur anywhere, from discussion of the knowledge of God to the doctrine of the church. Indeed, before the modern turn to the subject, anthropology was not a separate doctrinal locus or topic of theological consideration. Its various dimensions typically appeared in sections on God as creator, in the form of reference to the nature of creatureliness; in doctrines of salvation, in discussions about the nature of sin and its transformation; and in Christologies, as accounts of the implications of the iconic character of this ideal form of humanity.

John Calvin, for example, could discuss the *Imago Dei* in relation to knowledge of God, the end of human being, the distorting effect of sin, or the restoration of the image through Jesus Christ. Indeed, for Calvin and many other Reformed theologians, Jesus Christ is the paradigmatic image of God. Most important, the image functioned historically as a way to signal the finite goodness of human being. Even though in need of restoration through Jesus Christ, the human creature is thereby marked for a relation to God. This marking of the image has been identified with different features of human being over the ages. In addition to an implied physical resemblance (Gen. 3:8ff.) and stewardship over creation, premodern accounts have typically identified the image with rationality or the rational soul' (Thomas Aquinas), a reflecting mirror of God's reality (Calvin), and the conformity of the human will with the divine (Calvin and other Reformed thinkers).

Given the profound compliment paid to human being by this notion, creation in the image of God, the important question is whether it has be, a compliment paid in equal measure to all From a feminist perspective historically this has not been the case. While not refused the fruits the *Imago Dei*, namely, salvation, women have been viewed by much of, Christian tradition, Reformed and otherwise, as lesser bearers of the image. Indeed, the first topics of concern for feminist and womanist theologians have been those associated with representations of women and the human in the tradition. For example, accounts of creation that cite from Genesis have produced quite a number of problematic vie women's nature in the history of Christian biblical interpretation. Stories of Eve's so-called secondary creation after Adam have served to warrant women's subordination, just as her encounter with the serpent and the expulsion from the garden have grounded arguments for her less rational nature and her suffering in reproduction. The Bible is then read to portray woman as a dimmer creature than man, divinely ordained to be his submissive helpmeet. A further exacerbation of that kind of insult occurs in another topic where women come off badly—associations of women with in. The exploitation of Eve's encounter with the serpent for theories of female carnality and weak, temptation-susceptible nature has a long history. These are easily developed in the direction of the sexualization of women's bodies and the association of female flesh with danger and evil, as well as the racialization of this flesh?

While a full account of the Reformed tradition's participation in such denigrations is too long to give here, suffice it to say that the general belief of the church fathers from Calvin through the formative period of American Presbyterianism was that women's nature and place excluded her from positions of authority. Heavily shaped by surrounding cultural assumptions, this view was thought to be clearly authorized by Scripture. While asserting women's spiritual equality with men, male church leaders were fond of quoting 1 Timothy 2:12: "I permit no woman to teach or to have authority over a man; she is to keep silent" as justification for the exclusion of women from ordained leadership. In the face of the explosion of women's participation in voluntary societies and missions in American Presbyterianism in the early nineteenth century, this exclusion was codified into a constitutional prohibition against women's ordained leadership. Given this contradictory history of affirmation and denigration of women, the challenge is to take this rich tradition of the image of God and extend it most fully to all human beings. How might the resources of the Reformed tradition be appropriated by feminist thinking to pay all human beings the compliment of the *Imago Dei*?

Developing a reformed theological logic

As already suggested, the resources of Reformed theology for the task of extending the *Imago Dei* are not to be found by attending to what is said explicitly about women. Indeed, formative events of the Reformed tradition—the policies of Geneva, the tirades of John Knox, Calvinist scholasticism, the North American modernist controversies at the turn of the century, and the long-standing refusal to ordain women—render women invisible when they are not offering denigrating images of them. The resources of Reformed theology most useful for the challenge raised by feminist and womanist thinking have little to do with what has been said explicitly by the classic Reformers about "femaleness" or "race," except as reminders of the fallibility of even the best of the fathers. Rather, it is the resources of a theocentric tradition about idolatry that are most promising in relation to freeing the doctrine of *Imago Dei* from its entanglement with various kinds of practical injustice. Particularly by attending to contemporary Reformed thinkers who have developed understandings of the social cost of idolatry, we find theological clues for attending to the problematic accounts of subjects identified by feminists and womanists. Let us look at these themes and then consider them in relation to the critical issues raised by feminist and womanist thought.

A most obvious Reformed resource for the dilemmas of feminist and womanist thinking about the *Imago Dei* comes from the Reformed commitment to the redemption of a good creation distorted by sin. This, indeed, is the larger theological framework within which feminist theology has and will continue to work. The Reformed tradition's commitment to the goodness of creation in its finitude is a bedrock theological conviction that funds joy in and celebration of the creation as God's good work The Second Helvetic Confession of 1566 reminds us, "As the Scripture says, everything that God had made was very good, and was made for the profit and use of man." The tradition has always identified humanity as such as at least theoretically created in God's image and thereby potentially in relation to God; it thus grounds women's existence in God's gracious economy and allows us to expand what counts as good creation in the public consciousness. It also, crucially, fuels resistance to the deformation of this good work and provides the theological rationale for insisting that redemption is not the complete reinvention of human being—a denial of finitely good bodies and desire and will.

However, some adjustments are needed if this logic of redemption is to be made good for the groups that have been only "theoretically" included. For starters, the Reformed notion of sin centered most clearly on idolatry, which John Calvin took to be the basic sin of the medieval church. Indeed, the primary way to define idolatry for Calvin was pride, the desire to be like God. As we know from feminist responses to one of the modern expositors of a doctrine of sin, Reinhold Niebuhr, this continued focus on human pridefulness is most likely to capture the experience of white males rather than that of women of any race or class. Sin looks different for populations that lack the social space and power to indulge in self-promotion. The crucial connection of idolatry to social sin needs expansion as well. There are indications that the sin of idolatry was understood as something that entailed the oppression of marginalized communities; for example, Calvin and other sixteenth-century Reformers connected the Catholic Church's idolatries the oppression of minority religious communities such as their own.

However, contemporary understandings of identities as socially constructed, that is, as defined by social conventions, will require much more complicated ways to connect idolatry to social brokenness, raising issues of gender, race, and sexual orientation that were foreign to Calvin's frame of reference. Thus, a first adjustment to this expansion requires attention to the forms of human sin that are not adequately represented in such notions as pride.

A second adjustment, about which I will say more later, requires that we think about more than simply adding marginalized groups to what counts as good creation. Simply to add new subjects to that honored status would ignore insight yielded by feminist attention to representation, namely, that reigning frameworks are not neutral; they are liable to be marked by interests that screen out marginalized populations. It will be better, as I will show, to speak of destabilizing accounts of subjects than of additive ones. Three elements of the notion of the *Imago Dei* as good creation will help us think about extending that destabilizing.

First is the affirmation of the *theocentric* or God-centered nature of human beings. Human beings are incomplete, are unfulfilled, except in relation to the true God. As Calvinists insist, human life is to be lived to the glory of mod alone, *soli Deo Gloria*. This is to say that no worldly entity can finally satisfy human longing; it is a longing for the eternal—for God. Importantly, this view of a theocentric creature does not draw us away from the world. Rather, to describe human being as theocentric or theonomous is to describe the creature's distinctive posture of *engagement with* the creation.

Indeed, the second crucial point in this theological anthropology is that cur relation to God is inextricably connected to our relation to the neighbor, a unique manifestation of the creation. A God-centered posture toward the world is one that honors the worldly entity in its finitude and particularity, a finitude not hierarchically valued (maleness over femaleness, whiteness over blackness, hetero-desire over homosociality), but valued in its magnificent plurality.

Third, Calvin understood the *Imago Dei* as a task—the display of gratitude for God's gifts—and not simply a feature of the human soul. The relation to the neighbor is the place for just such a display, and it is that relation to the neighbor that signals whether the finite creation is honored in all its plurality. As Calvin puts it in the *Institutes*,

> We are not to consider that men merit of themselves but to look upon the image of God in all men, to which we owe all honor and love . . . therefore, whatever man you meet who needs your aid, you have no reason to refuse to help him. Say,

"He is a stranger"; but the Lord has given him a mark that ought to be familiar to you, by virtue of the fact that he forbids you to despise your own flesh. Say, "He is contemptible and worthless"; but the Lord shows him to be one to whom he has deigned to give the beauty of his image. Say that you owe nothing for any service of his; but God, as it were, has put him in his own place in order that you may recognize toward him the many and great benefits with which God has bound you to himself. Say that he does not deserve even your least effort for his sake; but the image of God, which recommends him to you, is worthy of your giving yourself and all your possessions.

As a Calvinist theologian attempting to develop Reformed thinking in a liberationist direction, John de Gruchy is quite instructive as we attempt to develop these themes. Arguing that the *Imago Dei* is fundamental to Calvin's ethics, he points out that damage to the image is inevitably damage to the relation to the neighbor.' De Gruchy takes this mutual connection with utmost seriousness: When the glorification of God comes "at the expense of humanity," even an account of God is "an idol that needs to be smashed in the service of human and social liberation." The Reformed conviction that God is at work reforming all reality sets up a logic that requires us to ask new questions about previously accepted social arrangements, always alert to human deformations of the *Imago Dei*. This Reformed logic does not simply add outsiders to our institutions, but moves to destabilize existing arrangements that have been falsely secured with idols. In that destabilizing, the logic thereby expands gracious, God-sustained neighbor relations.

Using a reformed logic: Starting out

How might this Reformed theological logic help in addressing feminist and womanist concerns? Let us take up these concerns by noting several developments in their very definition. By doing so, we begin to see a variety of forms of what we will later understand theologically as "damage to the image," as de Gruchy puts it. A first level of concern typical of Second Wave feminism—the period of emerging U.S. feminist consciousness in the early 1960s—deals with explicit exclusion of women from the opportunities afforded men. In the wider society these concerns included political representation, equal treatment under the law, and access to education and career; in the church, concerns focused on access to leadership, ordained and otherwise, and the full power to speak and to represent Christ. This level of concern and its typical response can be generally identified as the concern with inclusion. It is about adding women to the current structure of church or society.

This first problematic of the exclusion of women is typically focused the harm of images that denigrate and subordinate women. Thus it requires generation of counter images that confirm and celebrate the goodness woman as finite creation. Such work has been done by feminists and womanists for some time now in the form of creative imaging of the goodness female bodies, the honoring of female agents, and the refusal of stereotypical attributions of maleness and femaleness and their racializations. Insofar as the Reformed tradition's understanding of the goodness of finite creation can be galvanized to celebrate the fuller texture of finite creatureliness, it is an important resource that, not incidentally, continues the project of modern Reformed theology. Calvin's idea that the *Imago Dei* is a *task* characterized by the display of gratitude is quite useful in this regard, for it aids in disengaging the human "likeness" to God from narrow identification with such historically male-associated features as reason. To enact the *Imago Dei* is not to have a particular (gendered, racialized, etc.) identity, but to live in a mode of thankfulness and dependence on God.

Similarly for the early feminist criticism of categories of sin marked by male experience, we can appeal to the crucial Reformed linkage of sin against God with sin against the neighbor. This can move us away from the reed to think of idolatry only as the assertive ego with its male associations. De Gruchy's warning that an account of God can function as an idol when it comes "at the expense of humanity" is a Reformed version of feminist and womanist concerns about use of the historical tradition to denigrate human identities. As de Gruchy insists, such idols must be smashed in the service of human and social liberation."

As we think of application of this logic to broader examples of instances of exclusion/inclusion, we might begin with the public visibility of a group, which includes recognition of the group by those who draft laws, write theology, create culture, and attend to all forms of producing public reality. According to this criterion, illustrated by such issues as including women in leadership, we would say that at various points women as a group have historically been prevented from access to full citizenship, property rights, economic resources, forms of education, and political and cultural leadership—including ordination, among other things. For such in account of representation (or lack thereof), the Reformed theological logic is useful to fund arguments for the *inclusion* of women as a group historically rendered invisible. By showing that harm results from such exclusions and their associated confinements (to the domestic sphere or to worse depredations for those not historically put on domestic pedestals), the Reformed logic sets in motion the "always being reformed" imperative. The proper (just) relation to the other—women—is more important than my reading of Christian tradition that supports asymmetrical relations.

In this use of the Reformed logic, iconoclasm is directed toward any tradition, biblical or otherwise, that contributes to these exclusions, because human traditions are finite and created and not eternal or absolute. With such a challenge, the sin is identified as the placing of false qualifications on full participation in the church and God's good creation. The church is judged to diminish the *Imago Dei* of women by its assimilation of various cultural constructions about what women can properly do. Gender conventions cannot be made into idols; or, more subtly put, hierarchical anthropologies contravene the Reformed belief that God alone, not maleness (or any gendered or racial identity), is the grounding source of well-being for human creatures. The claim would be, then, that women as well as men are created in the image of God, and denigration of their bodies, sexuality, or female natures is a sinful denial of the goodness of a finite creation . . .

****

While we cannot avoid defining people—there is no other way to be determinate, finite creatures—these definitions and the power regimes that support them must always be subject to criticism. Reformed logic that is able to criticize the function of hierarchical notions of masculinity and femininity to keep women "down" is important, but it cannot be the only way to employ the logic of continual reformation. That logic of God's redeeming of a good creation must extend to the ways that systems of language and meaning are deployed. Thus this logic must include a destabilization that does not come to a halt with the identification of sin with current deformations around race, gender, and sexuality. That destabilization must be propelled by a posture of worship, and as such it can never be allowed to freeze. Reformed feminism can continue to honor God by exposing new idolatries. And it can take up the task of the *Imago Dei* by displaying gratefulness to God that (literally) in Christ, there is neither male nor female.

If I am right in saying that to be created in the image of God is a symbolic condensation of what in the Christian tradition it means to be fully human and who the tradition has seen as fully human, then these seemingly radical explorations of our language and frames of meaning are theologically justified. Calling for such a reform of feminist and womanist theological reflections can be taken as a healthy sign of our Reformed status. Occlusion is always operative in our theologizing, and feminist thinking is as likely to be guilty as any other form. Fortunately our symbols and narratives and traditions sometimes outrun our consciousness and reflective understanding. The United States Constitution, for example, could state that "all men are created equal" when it in fact only meant whit propertied men. And the excluded communities could (sometimes) hear themselves in the discourse and then go on to use it against its authors to expand the community of the legally enfranchised. In some analogous fashion, the reality of the God that we glorify, as well as the function of our traditions about Her, may well be trusted to continue to outrun our limited theological sense, calling us on to God's future.[5]

Questions

1 "In important respects the *Imago Dei* can serve as an index of whom the tradition has seen as fully human." In what ways has this been confirmed in the readings thus far?

2 Which themes from the Reformed tradition does Fulkerson find most promising for her argument here?

3 "To enact the *Imago Dei* is not to have a particular (gendered, racialized, etc.) identity, but to live in a mode of thankfulness and dependence on God." What do you think about this reading of the *Imago* exegetically and theologically?

[5]Mary McClintock Fulkerson, "The Imago Dei and a Reformed Logic for Feminist/Womanist Critique." In *Feminist and Womanist Essays in Reformed Dogmatics* (Louisville, KY: Westminster John Knox, 2006), 95–106

TEXT 6: COLIN GUNTON "THE HUMAN CREATION: TOWARDS A RENEWAL OF THE DOCTRINE OF THE IMAGO DEI"[6]

The British theologian Colin Gunton (1941–2003) was at the center of the renaissance in Trinitarian thought in the discipline of systematic theology that took place from the end of the 1980s onwards. His work is variously influenced by Karl Barth, Samuel Taylor Coleridge, and Basil of Caesarea; and was a strong critic of Augustine's influence on the theological tradition of the Western church. This excerpt, from his highly influential collection of essays *The Promise of Trinitarian Theology*, displays the elegance that is characteristic of his writing style and his attentiveness to the wider cultural and philosophical influences that have had a bearing on theological thought.

I Some problems of theological anthropology

Two interrelated questions face the enquirer after a theological anthropology: the ontological and what can for want of a better term be called the comparative. The ontological question is the question about what kind of entity is the human, and has: traditionally been answered in terms of a duality: of matter and spirit, body and soul, or the like; most radically perhaps Descartes' famous dualism of intellectual mind and mechanical body. In Descartes, the ontological dimension is apparent: the human constitution reflects the dual structure of the universe a matter and (divine) idea. Mind, the godlike part of the person is able by virtue of its equipment with innate ideas to comprehend by the use of pure reason the rational structure of the machine In terms of anthropology, the outcome is that despite Descartes attempts to show that his mind is more intimately related to body than is a pilot to a ship, we are inescapably presented the image of a mind pushing around a mechanical body. Ryle's characterisation of this as the 'ghost in the machine' is not so from the mark.

The comparative enquiry concerns the way in which the human being is and is not like other entities, supposed to people the universe: God on the one hand and, on the other, the non-human creation in all its various forms. The two questions sometimes conflated, if not confused, by supposing that argument for the distinctive ontology of the human might derived from a comparison and contrast: by means of a quest for ways in which the human is different from other entitle. Thus it might be held that God is infinite reason and the n human creation is without reason, so that, on the one hand, human is different from the divine by virtue of its finitude, and on the other, from the non-human by virtue of its possession of reason. We are here very near to the traditional form of the doctrine of the image of God, which by being

[6]Colin E. Gunton, 'The Human Creation: Towards a Renewal of the Doctrine of the Imago Dei,' in Colin E. Gunton, ed., *The Promise of Trinitarian Theology* (Edinburgh, T&T Clark, 1993), 104–21.

located in reason provides an answer to both of the questions with which we began. It is the possession of the image as reason which at once determines being and makes possible a comparative judgement both 'above' and below. Again, Descartes provides a fairly extreme example. The human mind, by virtue of its rationality, provides evidence both of a kind of image of God and at the same time a criterion of radical discontinuity from the rest of creation. The animals are merely machines, and it is said that some of the enlightened believed that their cries of pain were no more than the squeaks of unlubricated machinery.

But it is important to realise that the two questions do not have to be conflated. There are other ways of doing ontology than a process of speculative comparison and contrast: what Barth would call natural theology. Perhaps, as I shall argue, it is better to root contrast in ontology, and not the other way round. Moreover, it is in the long-lived tradition of rooting the image of God in reason that we see the deficiencies endemic in the tradition, deficiencies of which Descartes' anthropology provides but an example. A stress on reason elevates one characteristic of the human above others which have equal claim to consideration as part of our being. In particular, it encourages the belief that we are more minds than we are bodies, with all the consequences that that has: for example, in creating a non-relational ontology, so that we are cut off from each other and from the world by a tendency to see ourselves as imprisoned in matter. (Spelled out, the two dimensions would lead us into the problems' of individualism and ecology.)

The weakness in theological anthropology which is now so often observed can, accordingly, be seen to derive from errors of both method and content. Historically, the roots of the syndrome can be found in Irenaeus, whose anthropology in other dimensions takes so different a direction. In his famous distinction between image and likeness there began the process of making reason both a chief ontological characteristic and a criterion of difference between human and non-human. By the time of Aquinas the tendency had hardened into a dogma. Perhaps most revealing is his citation of John of Damascus: 'being after God's image signifies his capacity for understanding, and for making free decisions and his mastery of himself.' While that definition has the merit of not limiting the image to reason, it is to be noted that all of the characteristics are static possessions of the human as individual, rather than (say) characteristics implying relation. There remains, too, the problematic nature of the human relation to the rest of creation.

The theological dimension of the problems can be discerned in Augustine. From the outset, there is in Augustine a tendency to develop anthropology in terms of neoplatonic categories. For him the human likeness to God must be in the mind or soul, so that other possibilities are excluded from the outset. One implication is that our embodiedness cannot be the place where the image, and hence our true humanity, is found. That is a foreclosing of the ontological question which has a number of consequences. The first is a tendency to overstress the inner dimensions of the person. (I avoid here the words intellectual and psychological because their employment would prejudge questions about Augustine's meaning). The second is equally important Augustine's quest for the Trinity within the soul, the inner Trinity risks reducing the Trinity to theological irrelevance, for it becomes difficult to ask in what way the doctrine of the Trinity may in other ways throw light on the human condition. The heart of the matter is perhaps in the doctrine of relations. Since relations are qualifications of the inner Trinity, and not relations between persons, it becomes difficult to see how the triune relatedness can be brought to bear on the central question of human relatedness. God's relatedness is construed in terms of self-relatedness, with the result that it is as an individual that the human being is in the image of God, and therefore truly human The outcome is another, theologically legitimated, version of the tendency to individualism which arises in every dimension of what has been said so far.

II Cosmologies and anthropologies

It is considerations such as those outlined in the previous section that give credence to Barth's critique of the theological respectability of natural theology. Certain approaches to theological anthropology have as a matter of fact been foreclosed because of a priori philosophical decisions. The difficulty with Barth's approach, however, is that it leaves out certain stages of argument which seem to be advisable the modern context if an appearance of authoritarianism is to be avoided. The time has therefore come to ask whether an approach that is different from either the traditional or the straightforwardly 'Barthian' can be attempted. The question can be approached indirectly, with the observation that different theories about, the kind of entity that the world is bring in their train different conceptions of what it is to be human. That is to say, we can observe the way in which as a matter of fact cosmologies have been correlative with anthropologies. At its most simple level, the matter can be illustrated with the help of the distinction often made between Old Testament cosmologies and others of the Ancient Near East. While the latter tended to conceive the world as born from the womb of deity or developed from deity's defeated body—thus suggesting the at least potential deity of aspects of the world— the former, by distinguishing more definitely between God and what he had made, suggested a different view of the place of the human creature: more unified, and with fewer pretensions to deity. In later thought, a similar distinction emerges between broadly Greek and Hebrew views of the person.

    While not wishing to give simplistic views of their distinction, I want to begin with an account of a general difference. In *The Greeks and the Irrational*, E.R. Dodds traces the origins of Greek cosmological anthropology to the myth of the Titans. These were the giants who slew, cooked and ate the body of the infant Dionysus. In revenge, Zeus slew the Titans, from whose smoking ruins there derived the human race. Underlying that legend are the roots of an essentially dualistic ontology, which can be said to be almost universal in Greek thought and, through Augustine, though with qualifications, highly influential for Christian anthropology. The duality suggested is to be found on the one hand in the evil matter from which the human race arises; and from the fragment of deity deriving from the ingested divinity ('the horrid tendencies of the Titans, tempered by a tiny portion of divine soul-stuff'). Therein, undoubtedly is to be found the basis of the doctrine that the defining characteristic of humanity or the place of the image of God is reason.

    A more developed philosophical treatment of the dualism is to be found in Plato. In the *Republic*'s discussion of the tripartite soul, Plato is not far from suggesting that embodiment is in itself a form of fallenness. Physical desires and appetites are for the most part a bad thing, to be sternly controlled by reason. But for our purposes, the interesting discussion comes in the *Phaedo*. There we find the repeated assertion that the body is a prison, and death the liberation from it. The true philosopher abstains from pleasures and pains, each of which fastens the soul to the body with a kind of rivet, contaminating the soul in the process. Similarly, the soul is naturally immortal, because it resembles the divine, while the body resembles mortal things. Overall, the message is clear: with a dualistic cosmology, a dualistic anthropology is likely to be correlative.

But it is a mistake simply to contrast a Greek dualism with a more Hebrew or unitary approach. Monism is a problem, too. Something more sophisticated and complex than a simple opposition is required, and that is why Carver Yu, whose recent diagnosis of Western individualism is so good, cannot solve the problem by simply opposing to it a biblical and relational ontology, as he tends to do in the final chapter of his book. For a more subtle diagnosis of the possibilities we turn to Coleridge. In *On the Prometheus of Aeschylus* he offers an immensely valuable threefold typology of world-views. There are, he says, three available cosmologies, not just two (That is to say, he will not simply oppose 'Greek' and 'Hebrew', monist and dualist.) The first he calls the Phoenecian'. According to this, 'the cosmogony was their theogony and *vice versa*'. That is to say, the origin of the cosmos and the origin of the divine are one and the same process. What emerges is a conception of the world as a kind of undifferentiated unity. We have an equation containing only two terms: 'a selforganising chaos' and '. . . nature as the result'.

Moving on from Coleridge, or rather moving on to concern's he expressed in other writings than this, we might see in pantheism the typical modern version of this form of cosmology. According to Spinoza, for example, the coming to be of God and of the world are one and the same thing, except of course that in Spinoza's timeless system to speak of a cosmogony is perhaps not easy: nonetheless, his cosmogony is his theogony. The Coleridgean objection to such cosmologies can be seen in Spinoza's view that we can no more do other than we in fact do than the angles of a triangle can choose to be less or more than 180°. The outcome is the absolute necessitarian determinism that Coleridge saw to be enemy of human personality and freedom. Similarly, if we consider the description of the chaos as `self-organising' we may think of the implications for anthropology of an effective divinisation of the process of evolution. The authoritarian tendency of some of Teilhard de Chardin's work has sometimes been suggested, and in this context we can see why. In a 'Phoenician' cosmology, the person is not separable from the world, and so lacks the space to be free.

Coleridge's second cosmology, which he names the Greek, differs in that it has three rather than two terms. It is midway between the Phoenician, and the Hebrew. It does assume a divinity 'antecedent to the matter of the world. But on the other hand it coincides with the Phoenician in considering this antecedent ground . . . not so properly the cause of (corporeal natter), as the occasion and the still continuing substance. . . . The corporeal was supposed co-essential with the antecedent of is corporeity.' That is where Prometheus comes into Coleridge's conception of things. The 'fire' Prometheus steals from heaven s mind, the 'form', the incipient or potential divinity, which shapes human nature. (A modernised equivalent, we might say, of the fragment of divinity remaining in the immolated Titans). There are important and positive anthropological implications, of which Coleridge is aware: mind, being stolen from heaven, is no mere evolution of the animal basis', and reveals the distinction between the human and the other creation. But that, as we have seen, is also the beginning of danger. In some respects, as Coleridge points out 'the Greek philosopheme does not differ essentially from the cosmotheism, or identification of God with the universe. . .'

In general, the Greek cosmology has a number of problems. John Zizioulas has pointed one. 'In platonic thought the person is a concept which is ontologically impossible, because the soul, which ensures man's continuity, is not united permanently with the concrete "individual" man. . ." Platonic thought cannot handle concrete relatedness: the godlike part of us excludes relations with others through the medium of our embodiedness, because our bodies separate what is really ourselves—the 'inner'—from others of us. (The concept of love in the Symposium is the logical outcome). Similarly, the continuity with the divine that is implied brings problems for the divine-human relationship. As relations with other finite creatures are too distant through lack of relationship, here there is a danger that the relation will be too close. To be godlike in the wrong sense is a great burden, and the nature of the human image of the divine has to be handled very carefully if the burden is to be avoided. We require space as well as relation: to be both related to and other than those and that on which we depend.

III Space to be human: The Trinity

Coleridge believes the Hebrew view of things to be related to the Greek, which, as we have seen, he regards as a mid-point between the Phoenician and Hebrew, but superior. It is, first of all, mathematically superior, in that it has four terms in contrast to the preceding two and three. (Coleridge was perhaps too enamoured of mathematics, but at least the point can be taken that the greater possibilities of the four term conceptuality allows for greater ontological richness and openness). The four are as follows: the self-sufficient immutable creator; the antecedent night; the chaos; the material world resulting from the divine fiat. It is not very clear what is meant by all this, but some light can be shed by moving from the *Prometheus* to a consideration of Coleridge's theology of the Trinity in general. That is to say, we reach the place where we must go beyond the general matter of celebrating the Hebrew over against other cosmologies, and ask more particularly about the doctrine of God.

The idea of the Trinity was for Coleridge the transcendental of transcendentals, that which served as the supreme mark, determinant perhaps, of being. The Trinity is 'that Idea Idearum, the one substrative truth which is the form, manner and involvement of all truths. . ." Nor by 'idea' did he simply mean, as so many of his British predecessors had done, simply a mental construct or concept. As he shows in *On the Constitution of the Church and State*, an idea is antecedent to a conception, and has an (almost?) ontological status. It is, indeed, a kind of conception, but one 'which is not abstracted from any particular state, form, or mode, in which the thing may happen to exist at this or at that time; nor yet generalized from any number or succession of such forms or modes; but which is given by the knowledge of *its ultimate aim*. Interestingly for our purpose, Coleridge, in discussing one instance of idea, that 'of an ever-originating social contract', argues that it is dependent on 'the yet higher idea of person, in contra-distinction from *thing*. . .'. Person is somewhere near the top of the hierarchy of ideas. Yet, remarkably, all such ideas are in some way or other subordinate to the transcendental of transcendentals, the Trinity.

In his paper 'Coleridge on the Trinity', Daniel Hardy has spelled out some of the developments in Coleridge's doctrine of the Trinity after the *Prometheus* essay. Attempting to free himself from the 'restrictive notion of space-like being' to be found in that essay, Coleridge turned to the will as the clue to the Trinity. What he was seeking was a ground for reality without any of the anti-personal implications that follow from the rejected alternatives. Hardy quotes from the *Opus Maximum*: 'If then personeity, by which term I mean the source of personality, be, necessarily contained in the idea of the perfect will, how is it possible that personality should not be an essential attribute of this will, contemplated as self-realized.' The Augustinian and individualistic form of that formulation is manifest, but so also is its instinctive feeling for the right questions. Coleridge knew that if there was to be personality, there had to be both relatedness and space at once between God and the world and within the world between finite persons. He was not here concerned with narrowly pragmatic matters, but with the real, which 'had to be seen in its connection to its foundation.' His quest for the idea of the Trinity was a quest for that which would enable him both to think the real and to show the bearing of that reality on life into the world. At the very least, there is a concern for conceptualizing a kind of space between God and the world, a space in which personal freedom operates.

I have suggested by frequent use of the concept that underlying Coleridge's schematism is a concern for space in which the human can be human. According to the Phoenician scheme, there is no space between God and the world, and so no human freedom. According to the kind of Hellenism we have viewed, the space is placed in the wrong place: between mind and matter, so that there is too little space between the human mind and God, too much between one person and another: space is here at the expense of relation. In the third, Hebrew, scheme, there is space, because of the freedom of the immutable God to create *ex nihilo*. But we need more than space; Indeed, from one point of view, space is the problem individualism is the view of the human person which holds that there is so much space between people that they can in no sense participate in each other's being. There is clearly space and space, and our requirement now to find a conception which is correlative with that of relation.

IV In the image of God

On a more articulated account of the Trinity than Coleridge in practice allowed, we shall give prominence to the concept of the person rather than personeity. Only thus shall we avoid the monism that Coleridge so rightly feared, but risked by his emphasis on the will. *Person* is here difficult to define: if it is indeed one of those *ideas* which are logically primitive because they reflect what is ontologically primitive, that is what we should expect. Such concepts cannot be defined in other terms, because they are the *ideas*, and I continue to use the italics to indicate Coleridge's technical sense, in terms of which other, concepts can and must be understood. But that is not to say that they can in no way be *thought*. They can, for example, be thought when they are found to be concretely instantiated in particular forms of life. Classically, they came to be thought theologically under the impact of the Christian gospel. As a result the Greek theologians came to understand God as a communion of persons, each distinct but inseparable from the others, whose being consists in their relations with one another. As Barth said, but in a rather different way, person means primarily what it means when it is used of God. But before we take up this suggestion, asking what the theological concept of person contributes to the understanding of the finite person, we must first ask a preliminary question: how, in the light of Coleridge's third possibility, the trinitarian, are we enabled to see the world and human life within it? Is there here too a kind of cosmology within which anthropological possibilities may be articulated?

What flows from the conception of God as three persons in communion, related but distinct? First, there is something of the space we have been seeking. We have a conception of *personal* space: the space in which three persons are for and from each other in their otherness. They thus confer particularity upon and receive it from one another. That giving of particularity is very important: it is a matter of space to be. Father, Son and Spirit through the shape—the *taxis*—of their inseparable relatedness confer particularity and freedom on each other. That is their personal being.

* * * *

What in all this are we to make of the doctrine of the image of God? Given the rejection of the view that the image is to be found in reason, or any merely internal characterisation of the individual, there seem to be two recent contenders for the title, both dependent upon readings of the first two chapters of Genesis. The first locates it in the human stewardship of the creation. There is much to be said for this approach, especially in view of the close relationship in Genesis between the creation of humankind and the command to shepherd the earth. Such a theology is, however, too literalistic and too restricted, especially in the light of the New Testament re-orienting of the doctrine to Christ. Is the image of God as realised in Christ to be expressed in terms of his stewardship of the creation—indeed, part of the matter—or must other things also be said? We must here remember that the concept of image has in this respect very little biblical employment, and if it is to be used theologically must draw upon a wider -range of biblical background than such explicit talk of image as there is in scripture.

The second candidate for the interpretation of image interprets it with Genesis' 'male and female created he them.' Barth, famously, creatively and controversially pursued this approach, which was developed in somewhat less literalistic style by Derrick Sherwin Bailey. The weaknesses of this approach, Barth's particularly, have often been pointed. Two should be rehearsed. The first is its tendency to be binitarian: the anthropology reflects a Father-Son duality reflected in that of male and female, rather than expressing a theology of communion. That is not to say that there is nothing of anthropology of communion in Barth. The anthropology of mutuality in *Church Dogmatics* III/2 is immensely illuminating, as are many of the things he says about man woman relations, despite their unpalatability to a certain kind of feminism. The second weakness is a tendency to anthropocentrism in Barth. Andrew Linzey's analysis of Barth's treatment of the creation sagas has shown that Barth underplays the way in which Genesis brings the non-human creation into the covenant. We need more than an extended exegesis of Gen. 1.26f, and in particular a broader treatment of the topic, if we are really to make more satisfactory use of the concept of the *Imago Dei*.

Where, then, is the image of God to be found? Interesting about the two alternatives we have reviewed is that while one of them relates humankind to the cosmos, the other is chiefly concerned with relations within the human species. It is an unsatisfactory theological anthropology which requires a choice between the two, which are both right insofar as they discern in relatedness a clue to the solution of the problem. The weakness of both approaches can be obviated by finding a concept which bases them—and any other dimensions—in a theological ontology. Insofar as we are concerned with human being and not particular qualities or tasks there is a missing conceptual link to be found: it is, of course, that of the person. To be made in the image of God is to be endowed with a particular kind of personal reality. To be a person is to be made in the image of God: that is the heart of the matter. If God is a communion of persons inseparably related, then surely Barth is thus far correct in saying that it is in our relatedness to others that our being human consists.

That relatedness takes shape in a double orientation. In the first place, we are persons insofar as, we are in right relationship to God. Under the conditions of sin, that means, of course-, insofar as the image is reshaped, realised, in Christ. But since we are here enquiring about human createdness, we shall leave that in the background, as a very real background, nevertheless. The relation to God takes shape through the Son and the Spirit. To be in the image of God is to be created through the Son, who is the archetypal bearer of the image. To be in the image of God therefore means to be conformed to the person of Christ. The agent of this conformity is God the Holy Spirit, the creator of community. The image of God is then that being human which takes shape by virtue of the creating and redeeming agency of the triune God. The second orientation is the 'horizontal' one, and is the outcome of the work of the first. What is the shape that the image of God takes in time? The human person is one who is created to find his or her being in relation, first with other like persons but second, as a function of the first, with the rest of the creation. This means, first, that we are in the image of God when, like God but in dependence on his giving, .we find our reality in what we give to and receive from others in human community. One way into the content of the image, its concrete realisation, is through the concept of love. It seems likely that we shall be content here neither with the unitive concept of love which has tended to reign in the West, nor with the strong reaction signalled in Nygren's one-sided assertion of agape against eros. While it seems to me that agape does indeed reflect the 'biblical expression of the divine self-giving in Christ, to stress that alone can lead to an almost individualistic unrelatedness. Barth here is better when he sees our humanity as realised in the mutual giving and receiving of assistance with gladness.

But if we are to speak of realising our being in relations, something more than that has to be said. Of crucial importance is the matter of the way in which the structure—the taxis—of human community constitutes the particularity, uniqueness and distinctness of persons: their free otherness in relation. To be a person is to be constituted in particularity and freedom—to be given space to be—by others in community. *Otherness* and *relation* continue to be the two central and polar concepts here. Only where both are given due stress is personhood fully enabled. Their co-presence will rule out both the kind of egalitarianism which is the denial of particularity, and leads to collectivism, and forms of individualism which in effect deny humanity to those unable to 'stand on their own feet.'

It is important also to realise that this being in the image of God will embrace both what we have been used to call spiritual and our bodiliness. The merit of the approach to anthropology by means of the concept of person is that it relativizes so many inherited dualisms. Relations are of the whole person, not of minds or bodies alone, so that from all those created in that image of God there is something to be received, and to them something to be given. When the image is located in reason, or for that matter in any internal qualification like consciousness, problems like those of 'other minds' are unavoidable. The person as a being in relation is one whose materiality is in no way *ontologically* problematic, whatever problems derive from the way in which we relate in actual fact to others.

The contention that our realising of the image of God embraces our embodiedness as much as our intellect and `spirituality' leads into the further point that we are not human apart from our relation with the non-personal world. Much current misuse of the creation, with its attendant ecological disasters, derives from a lack of realisation of human community with the world. It is not the same kind of community, that of equals, as that with which we were concerned when speaking of the community of persons. But it is a fact that we receive much of what we are from the world in which we are set and from whose dust we come. It is the context within which we become persons, and it, too, is in a kind of community with us, being promised a share in the final reconciliation of all things. Although it is not itself personal, the non-human creation is bound up with that of the human, and depends upon us for its destiny. It is not something we stand over against in the sense that it is at our arbitrary disposal, as 'technocracy' assumes. It is rather, to use Polanyi's metaphor, the reality which we indwell bodily, intellectually and spiritually. Here, being in the image of God has something to do with the human responsibility to offer the creation, perfected, back to its creator as a perfect sacrifice of praise. It is here that are to be found the elements of truth in the claims that the image of God is to be found in the human stewardship of the creation.

In all of this, John Zizioulas' point that *person* is an eschatological concept constantly be borne in mind. To say that is to say that personhood is being that is to be realised, and whose final realisation will come only when God is all in all. And as Graham McFarlane has argued, that need not be taken to ermine the fact that it is also, and without inconsistency, a protological concept. It is a way of conceptualizing the origins of human being in the creating goodness of God, though without prejudice to the dynamic orientation of this being to a purposed end. Irenaeus' theory that Adam and Eve were created childlike of in every way satisfactory, but it does suggest that human in the image of God is human life directed to an end. The image is not a static possession, but comes to be realised in the various relationships in which human life is set. The New Testament's reorientation of the concept to Jesus makes the point. It is because Jesus is 'the image of the invisible God' that is 'through him to reconcile all things, whether on earth or heaven...'(Co1. 1:15,20). The one through whom all was created is also the means of the re-establishment of the image in humanity. The image, therefore, created through the Word and in the it, has in like manner to be realised through them, between resurrection of Jesus and his return in glory.

V Conclusion

The paper began with the linking of two questions: the ontological and the comparative. What kind of being is the human? In what ways is the human species like and unlike God? We have come to answers rather unlike those of much of the tradition. *Ontologically*, it has been argued that where the latter led to stress the non-bodily, a trinitarian theology will stress relations width involve all dimensions of our reality. Where the tradition tended to see our imagedness to consist in the session of certain faculties, here the stress is on the ontology of personhood. To be in the image of God is at once to be created as a particular kind of being—a person—and to be called to realise a certain destiny. The shape of that destiny is to mind in God-given forms of human community and of human responsibility to the universe.

The *comparative* question also finds a different kind of answer. Human difference from the rest of the creation does not lie in some absolute ontological distinction, but in an asymmetry of relation, and therefore a relative difference. As created beings, human persons are bound up closely with the fate of the rest of the material universe, as stewards rather than absolute lords. And the difference between God and those made in his image? The interesting point now is that the question of our difference from and likeness to God becomes less pressing. It is not found in some structural difference, but in the most basic one of all: God is the creator, we are of his creation. The triune God has created humankind as finite persons-in-relation who are called to acknowledge his creation by becoming the persons they are and by enabling the rest of the creation to make its due response of praise.

Questions

1   What is the difference between the ontological and the comparative questions that face theological anthropology? How are these related?

2   What is the substance of Gunton's critique of Augustine's anthropology?

3   Why do we "require space as well as relation"? What does Gunton mean by "personal space"?

4   Where is the image of God to be found? How does Gunton critique the successive options for understanding the *Imago* found in the Christian tradition?

5   What place does the body have in Gunton's account of anthropology?

6   In what sense is "person" an eschatological concept?

TEXT 7: MICHAEL S. HORTON, "IMAGE AND OFFICE HUMAN PERSONHOOD AND THE COVENANT"[7]

Michael Horton (b. 1964) is the J. Gresham Machen Professor of Theology and Apologetics at Westminster Seminary, California, and one of the leading advocates for a recent revival of Reformed orthodoxy. This movement owes a great deal to the Protestant theologians of the seventeenth century. Nevertheless, Horton also interacts with contemporary philosophy and theology at a very sophisticated level. Horton's piece is an attempt to revive the concept of Covenant as a way of encapsulating many of the themes of theological anthropology raised in conjunction with the *Imago Dei* down the centuries.

As is well known, modernity after Descartes was dominated by a notion of the self that was constrained by substance metaphysics. And yet, a line is often (and not entirely without warrant) drawn from Augustine to Descartes in this respect. Among others, Charles Taylor provides a reliable summary of this complex relationship.[8] If I were to attempt such an ambitious argument here, it would go something like this: Somewhat overdetermined by questions more germane to neoplatonic speculation, traditional Christian anthropologies have too often sought to ground human selfhood on the *Imago Dei*, the latter understood in quite essentialist terms. So whether one was an intellectualist or a voluntarist, the self was usually understood as the soul or mind. Returning more directly to classical rather than biblical categories, modernity radicalized and secularized this essentialist enterprise, especially with the addition of a sharp emphasis on autonomy. Personhood thus became reduced to knowing, duty, feeling, striving, overcoming, authenticity, and so on.

In all of its modern forms, it includes the crucial element of disengagement, to borrow Taylor's term, despite attempts to resituate the self in "lived experience," through language, culture, and history. What we often fail to see is a corresponding biblical-theological effort to resituate selfhood in the "lived experience" of the covenant and eschatology. Wilhelm Dilthey correctly discerned that in the empiricism and idealism of the Enlightenment period, "No real blood runs in the veins of the knowing subject that Locke, Hume and Kant constructed." Regardless of the classical and modern roots of this approach to our question, it is hoped that this proposal will provide an alternative paradigm for anthropology over against the more neoplatonic rivals and their secularized successors, without running into

---

[7]Michael S. Horton, "Image and Office: Human Personhood and the Covenant," in Richard Lints, Michael S. Horton, and Mark R. Talbot, eds,, *Personal Identity in Theological Perspective* (Grand Rapids, MI: Eerdmans, 2006), 178–203.

[8]Charles Taylor, *Sources of the Self The Making of the Modern Identity* (Cambridge, MA: Harvard University Press, 1989). This trajectory undoubtedly provided a basis for grounding selfhood in an inward quest, although for Augustine this was meant to lead through the noumenal self to God, while for Descartes it was meant to underwrite what has come to be known as modern autonomy (albeit, in his case, with an apologetic for God's existence added on).

the arms of a reactionary reductionism (namely, selfhood reduced to relations or language). Post-structuralist anthropologies, for very different reasons, bear some ironic similarities with a number of recent theological proposals. Space does not permit us here to raise the question as to just how far John Zizioulas and, in his own way, Karl Barth approximate Michel Foucault's prediction that "man" is about to be "erased like a face drawn in the sand at the edge of the sea."[9]

I will approach our topic in terms of two concentric circles: humanness more generally and the *Imago* specifically. In this way, I hope to steer a course between the more traditional essentialist approaches and the denial of a genuine human subject. I will aim at identifying the character of the *Imago Dei* in its context of covenant and eschatology and then suggest some ways in which this perspective might interact fruitfully with some recent approaches to the problematic status of the "postmodern self." Covenant and eschatology do not exhaust the meaning of the human but do significantly contextualize and orient it.

Covenant

The mature federal theology typically advanced three covenants: an eternal, intratrinitarian covenant of redemption, with the Son as mediator, and two covenants made between God and human beings, executed in time. The covenant of works (also designated covenant of "creation," "nature," or "law") was the natural state in which Adam and Eve were created and under which humanity "in Adam" stands condemned under the original covenant curses.

The *protoeuangelion*, however, announces a gracious covenant. Without setting aside the original covenant, God promulgates a covenant of grace in anticipation of the second Adam whom he will send. As the tree of life was the sacrament of the covenant of works, Adam and Eve are clothed sacramentally in animal skins by God to prefigure "the Lamb of God who takes away the sin of the world" (John 1:29). Through Abraham, God gives greater clarity to this gracious covenant by swearing unconditional loyalty to Abraham for the sake of his seed, identified by the apostle Paul as Jesus Christ (Gal. 3:16), and ordains circumcision as the sign and seal of the old covenant administration, with baptism as the new covenant sacrament of incorporation (Matt. 28:18-20; Mark 16:15-16; Col. 2a1-12).[10]

Thus, even after the fall, human existence remains intrinsically covenantal, even though it is divided between Cain's proud city (Gen. 4:17-24) and the City of God represented by Seth, whose descendants are distinguished by their invocation of the Great King for their salvation: "At that time people began to invoke the name of

---

[9]Michel Foucault, The Order of Things: An Archaeology of the Human Sciences (New York: Random House, 1970), 387. Let's not forget that modernity was never wholly individualistic Remember Spinoza? Hegel? Fichte? Marx? Freud? Not to mention the philosophy of history from Dilthey to the present. Furthermore, postmodernity celebrates atomistic individualism as often as Communitarianism. In both modernity and postmodernity are many mansions.

[10]Of course, Passover and the Lord's Supper are added to the old and new covenant administrations, respectively, but here we are indicating the sacrament of incorporation.

the LORD" (v. 26). Those who do not acknowledge God or embrace his covenant of grace are nevertheless included "in Adam" under the *original* covenant. Intrinsic to humanness, particularly the imago, is a covenantal office or commission into which every person is born; it is, therefore, as an equally universal phenomenon, the basis for God's righteous judgment of humankind even apart from special revelation (Rom. 1 and 2). This is to say that "law"—in particular, the divine covenant-law—is natural, a *verbum internum* identified with the conscience. Hardwired for obedience, human beings fell from this state of rectitude through no ontological weakness (such as finitude or concupiscence) but through an inexplicable rejection of the reign of God. The gospel, by contrast, is entirely foreign to the human person in this natural state. It comes as a free decision on God's part in view of the fall and can be known only by a *verbum externum*.

We will therefore look for an answer to the question, "What is it to be human?" not in ontological definitions of inner states or essences, much less in terms of contrasts with the nonhuman creation, but in terms of the unique *commission* given to human beings in the biblical narrative. For the biblical writers at least, "What is it to be human?" is ultimately a narrative-ethical rather than a metaphysical-ontological question. It cannot be named apart from the drama of creation, fall, redemption, and consummation. As covenant theology argues, then, the satisfactory answer to that question of human identity is to point to Jesus Christ—not because anthropology is subsumed under christology (pace Barth, Jungel, and others), but because it was he alone who fulfilled the covenant of works and did so not merely for himself but representatively (that is, federally) for his new humanity: "For their sakes I sanctify myself, that they may be truly sanctified" (John 17:19).

Eschatology

The notions of covenant and eschatology are closely intertwined in biblical theology. Both are oriented toward promise and fulfillment. Furthermore, both eschew any ontological dualism. As the covenant idea in Scripture excludes a nature-grace antithesis by emphasizing the ethical dimension (sin-and-grace), biblical eschatology similarly concentrates its antithesis between "flesh" and "Spirit" in terms of "this present aeon" and "the aeon to come," respectively. It is this world in its ethical rebellion that is under divine judgment, and it is this same world—"far as the curse is found"—that will be finally liberated when the work of the second Adam has resulted in the Spirit's consummation of all things in him. Thus, both body and soul are included in this image-bearing task and only in a psychosomatic unity enjoy the consummation in Jesus Christ.

According to this eschatological perspective I am proposing, which builds on the older Reformed theologians, creation was not the goal, but the beginning, of God's purpose for humankind specifically and the natural world generally. As Geerhardus Vos reminds us, the particular covenantal and eschatological orientation found in Scripture is thoroughly concerned with the ethical and personal sphere, not with abstract metaphysics and ontology. "The universe, as created, was only a beginning, the meaning of which was not perpetuation, but attainment." Thus, eschatology is prior to soteriology: creation began with a greater destiny lying before it. (Affinities with Irenaeus, particularly with the doctrine of recapitulation, may be recognized here as elsewhere.)

This has obvious implications for the concept of human immortality. While death should not, without qualification, be regarded as "a characteristic of frail, temporal creation," Jurgen Moltmann is nevertheless right to point out, on the basis of God's command to be fruitful and multiply, "that human beings were mortal from the beginning." Miroslav Volf correctly sees in Moltmann's construction a classic debate between Eastern and Western approaches, the former in-dwelling categories of corruption and completion, while the latter in-habits the paradigm of sin and redemption. By recognizing that creation even before the fall was awaiting its completion under Adamic dominion, however, and that this consummation included the conferral of immortality as well as indefectibility, covenant theology is able to integrate both of these strands—the eschatological and the soteriological, immorality and redemption. Thus conceived, death did not come as a consequence of mere human finitude (*pace* Barth, Moltmann, and others), nor was immortality a human possession from the beginning (especially not in virtue of an immortal soul). Immortality was a goal, not an origin; the Tree of Life was a prospect, not a presupposition, of human existence. Prior to the fall, Adam and Eve lived between the two trees: "You shall be confirmed in righteousness and immortality" and "You shall surely die."

As human beings are by nature covenantal, they are also constitutionally prospective—even utopian, despite the distorted ways in which fallen humanity seeks to win its glorification apart from and even against God. The fact that Adam and Eve were representatively created in God's image and yet were to attain the perfection and con-summation of that image in the future gives to human personhood both a retrospective and an anticipatory eschatological identity. This fact becomes crucial to the account of personhood that I will elaborate below in terms of *dramatic narrative emplotment*.

Person and image

As we gesture our way through a covenantal-eschatological approach to the vexing question of human personhood by specifying within that larger question the character of the *Imago Dei*, we might begin by distinguishing between what we may call prerequisites for image-bearing and the imago proper. The prerequisites are the broader concentric circle en-compassing the narrower circle of the image proper.

Prerequisite Characteristics for Human Image-Bearing

The Platonic rooting of the imago in reason has had disastrous effects, as recent criticisms have highlighted.[11] Furthermore, there is not a hint in Scripture of the oft-repeated theological axiom that human likeness to God has to do with a shared

---

[11]The mind-body dualism leads us "into the problems of individualism and ecology," as Colin E. Gunton warns in *The One, the Three and the Many: God Creation and the Culture of Modernity* (Cambridge: Cambridge University Press, 1993). The contrast between the biblical creation narrative and modernity's antithesis of the human and nonhuman spheres could not be greater. In the former, humans are dearly represented as belonging to the natural world, serving it as stewards of fellow-creatures.

"spirituality," since the concept of *ex nihilo* creation blocks any emanationist scheme with its chain of being. The human soul is no more to be identified with God than the human body.

While my proposal rejects any identification of the image of God with any faculty or substance, mental or physical, can there be any doubt that human beings are uniquely suited among the creation to be covenant partners with God? And can we not point out fairly obvious prerequisites such as certain natural capacities for deliberative reason, intentional relationality, moral agency, and linguisticality? Without identifying the image of God with any or all of these distinguishing traits, we can nevertheless affirm that they are endowments that render humankind uniquely suited to the commission that will constitute the image proper. Due to space, we cannot pursue a treatment of each of these prerequisite characteristics. Suffice it to say that human personhood requires these characteristics if it is to be construed as covenantal personhood, and yet the *Imago*, properly considered, cannot be identified with these. Rather, the image is to be understood in this account as an office or embassy, a covenantal commission with an eschatological orientation.

Further, this approach necessarily directs our attention away from the inner quest, out toward a conception of the self that is inseparable from though not reduced to its external relations in a specific "form of life" defined by mutual obligations. Although Calvin himself did not sufficiently develop this aspect of his thought, covenant theology is unthinkable apart from a basic commitment to relational categories. In fact, Stanley Grenz cites a number of representative sources for his claim that the Reformation in general and Calvin's theology in particular led to "the birth of the relational self." A. N. Whitehead's famous quip, "Religion is what the individual does with his own solitariness," may fit well with rationalism, idealism, and romanticism, but it is at far remove from any view of the self that is oriented covenantally.

****

The image of God (properly considered)

So far I have outlined essential features of a covenantal anthropology as touching the subject of human personhood generally. We now turn to what I regard as "the image proper." I will argue that the image, properly speaking, is constituted by the following four characteristics: sonship/royal dominion, representation, glory, and prophetic witness.

Sonship/Royal Dominion Concurring with Calvin's exegesis, accepted by a consensus of contemporary Hebrew scholars, I regard *selem* ("image") and *demut* ("likeness") as synonyms. And at least part of the significance of the *Imago Dei* is that it is the royal investiture of a servant-son. In his person and work, Jesus Christ receives in the place of fallen Adam his royal investiture in the Seventh Day as the image-son of God. Despite superficial similarities, the royal sonship motif in Genesis 1:26-28 differs significantly from ancient Egyptian and Mesopotamian myths. For instance, while the king in these myths is represented as the royal son of the chief deity—an incarnation, in fact, of the deity the creation of Adam and Eve was never regarded by the Jews as a divine incarnation. Furthermore, this royal investiture in Genesis included all human beings, "male and female," and not just a single ruler.

As Meredith Kline notes, the three principal elements of likeness that appear in all their redolence when the royal son appears are the following: temple (dominion, kingship); the ethical dimension (the foundations of the temple are justice, equity, truth, righteousness, holiness, goodness); and glory—physical beauty. "To be the image of God is to be the son of God." Similarly, Phyllis Bird observes that while *selem* by it-self tells us nothing, "The scion *elohim* in Genesis I is, accordingly, a royal designation, the precondition or prerequisite for rule." This interpretation, Bird argues, fits well with the parallel passage in Psalm 8, where coronation language and dominion language once more converge.

This sonship-likeness is seen most dearly, of course, in Jesus Christ, of whom Adam was himself a proleptic reflection. It is essential to recognize that in this sense the incarnate Lord of the Covenant is its servant, and that as the new Adam his royal sonship-likeness is not the same as his eternal sonship. In his humiliation, he must attain this sonship-likeness—this royal image—on behalf of his brothers and sisters. This is how we might understand a reference such as that in Psalms 27 and 89:26, repeated in Hebrews 1:5: "To which of the angels did God say, 'You are my Son. Today I have begotten you'?" In John's Gospel especially, Jesus' fulfillment of this destiny of royal sonship is repeatedly underscored (cf. John 5:17-21). Without separating the two natures of Christ, we must nevertheless distinguish between the everlasting sonship of Christ as a possession and his fulfillment of this human, Adamic sonship as a commission, Jesus is not only the Son of God but is also the Son of Adam, Seed of Abraham, Son of David, and Son of Mary who fulfills the human destiny of becoming the royal son of God.

Representation

* * * *

To speak of the image of God as representation is to place it in the realm of judicial commission rather than, as in the more traditional understanding, considering it a mirror of the divine essence. It refers not so much to a correspondence in attributes (even the so-called communicable ones), but to an official embassy. In the ascension, the royal repatriation and acceptance of reward are accomplished by Je-sus acting not as a private person but as a federal representative of his covenant people. Thus, just as was the case in connection with the royal sonship theme, a robust emphasis on the humanity of Christ is essential.

While there has been a widespread tendency throughout church history to treat the victory of Christ almost exclusively as the victory of God, covenant theology— particularly in its insistence on the necessity of the original covenant being perfectly fulfilled—has underscored its significance as the victory of a human person. To be sure, this person is the God-Man, but as the second Adam he is entrusted with a thoroughly human task.

* * * *

Jesus is, therefore, according to Calvin and the confessions and consensus of Reformed scholasticism, not merely the Son of God as to his divinity, but the true and faithful Son of Man who always obeys his Father's will in the power of the Holy Spirit.

This meritorious human life lived in full dependence on the Spirit (recapitulation) is not extrinsic but intrinsic to redemption; it is not merely a necessary prerequisite of a sacrificial offering, but part and parcel of that offering. Thus the Son of Man claims victory for himself by right and not merely by gift, nor indeed by virtue of his deity:

> *Very truly, I tell you, the Son can do nothing on his own, but only what he sees the Father doing; for whatever the Father does, the Son does likewise. . . . For just as the Father has life in himself, so he has granted the Son also to have life in himself; and he has given him authority to execute judgment, because he is the Son of Man. . . . I can do nothing on my own. As I hear, I judge; and my judgment is just, because I seek to do not my own will but the will of him who sent me. . . The works that the Father has given me to complete, the very works that I am doing, testify on my behalf that the Father has sent me.* (John 5:19, 26-27, 30, 36)

And later in John Christ says, "I glorified you on earth by finishing the work that you gave me to do. So now, Father, glorify me in your own presence with the glory that I had in your presence before the world existed" (John 17:4-5). So from the cross, it is not only his suffering on be-half of sinners but his completion of the Father's commission that he has in mind when he cries out, "It is finished" (John 19:30).

Because of this human achievement, Paul can say concerning Jesus, "being found in *human* form, he humbled himself and became obedient to the point of death— even death on a cross. *Therefore* God also highly exalted him and gave him the name that is above every name . ." (Phil. 2:7-9). Taking his cue from Daniel's vision of the four empires, Moltmann duly notes, "In the kingdom of the Son of Man, man's likeness to God is fulfilled. *Through this human man* God finally asserts his rights over his creation."

Essential, then, to the representation that marks Jesus Christ's office is its reciprocity. The Father's approval of the Son is not a question of grace but of being rewarded for a commission fulfilled. This underscores the notion of mutuality, which is involved in all covenants of the suzerainty-type. The creation covenant is not set aside or subsumed under grace, but is fulfilled representatively on our behalf, and the Covenant Servant dispenses the fruit of his victory under the terms of a covenant of grace.

This approach emphasizes for Oliver O'Donovan that Christ's resurrection is representative not in a symbolic way of independent and prior truths, but inasmuch as it effects its concrete results representatively for a people. It is "Not that the created order has changed, or was ever anything other than what God made it," O'Donovan writes, "but that in Christ man was able for the first time to assume his proper place within it, the place of dominion which God assigned to Adam." To be sure, there is an already-not yet character to this, as Hebrews re-minds us, after quoting Psalm 8:

> *Now in subjecting all things to them [humans], God left nothing outside their control. As it is, we do not yet see everything in subjection to them, but we do see Jesus, who for a little while was made lower than the angels, now crowned with glory and honor because of the suffering of death, so that by the grace of God he might taste death for everyone.* (Heb. 2:8-9).

Glory

While royal sonship and representation find ample support in Scripture, perhaps the theme most closely attached to the relevant pas-sages is that of "glory" (*kavod*).[12] It is this notion that best ties together both testaments and indicates the closest connection between covenant and eschatology. Furthermore, once we recognize its central importance to the concept of the *Imago Dei*, the latter's significance in even the Old Testament is capable of being recognized as well.

Pillaging the ancient cosmogenic myths, the creation narrative re-counts the Great King's completion of his cosmic house, then his filling of it with his Glory-Spirit as his own holy dwelling. One of the gains in this account is a greater integration of christology and pneumatology, as the Glory of God is identified directly with both the Spirit and the Son, and indirectly/reflectively with those whom the Spirit "fathers" by breathing into them the breath of life, rendering human beings prophetic witnesses to the Glory they reflect. Adam and Eve were created as temples of the same Glory-Spirit identified in Genesis 1:2. As Adam is represented as having been created by a "divine inbreathing" of the Spirit, Mary was told, "The Holy Spirit will come upon you and the Power of the Highest will overshadow you; therefore also that holy thing which shall be born of you shall be called the Son of God" (Luke 1:35). And in inaugurating his new creation, Jesus breathed on the disciples, saying, "Receive the Holy Spirit" (John 20:22). Individual believers and the corporate church are therefore re-creations in the image of Christ, the true temple filled with the Glory-Spirit.

All of this serves, retrospectively, of course, to illuminate the Gene-sis narrative. "As Genesis 2:7 pictures it," writes Ricoeur, "the Spirit-Archetype actively fathered his human ectype," showing that "image of God and son of God are thus twin concepts," as the birth of Seth in Adam's image seems to confirm (Gen. 5:I-3). It is "a making of man in the likeness of the Glory-Spirit." It is no wonder, then, that the Son sends the Spirit to inaugurate a new creation on the pattern of his own glory both as God and as the glorified new Adam.

---

[12]Ricoeur observes that Paul's development of the *Imago Dei* theme (for instance, in 2 Cor. 3:58) anchors itself not in the Old Testament notion of creation in the image of God (Gen. 1:26) but in the Old Testament motif of glory. There is a lot of exegetical support for such a view, and this underscores how the importance of the *Imago Dei* concept in Scripture will be determined by corollaries or constituent aspects of the image rather than direct statements concerning the image as such.

The eschatological and the protological are thus coordinated with each other, as when Paul states, "Thus it is written, 'The first man, Adam, became a living being'; the last Adam became a life-giving Spirit. . . . Just as we have borne the image of the man of dust, we will also bear the image of the man of heaven" (r Cor. 15:45, 49). In 1 Corinthians 11:7, as Stanley Grenz notes, "the apostle connects the *Imago Dei* with the concept of the divine glory (doxa). The way was paved by the Old Testament, most directly by the declaration in Psalm 8:5 that God has crowned humankind with 'glory and honor.'" This eschatological image, though effaced and marred by human sin, will be fulfilled in the new creation: the one who created us in his image by his Spirit in the beginning will re-create us in the same image by the same Spirit in the end. Thus, Christ identifies himself as no less than the Creator and Consummator, "the Alpha and Omega, the beginning and ending, the first and the last" (Rev. 1:8), "the faithful witness" to God's covenant (Rev. 1:5). The church is then the temple built according to the likeness of the heavenly city. The church therefore witnesses to Christ: that is its glory-image, and in its glorified state this witness is vindicated.

All of this serves to show the inextricable link between covenant, eschatology, and the judicial-official character of the divine image. Again, this glory is ethical-official, rather than corresponding to a particular essence in the human constitution. "As image of God," Kline writes, "man is a royal son with the judicial function appertaining to kingly office. The renewal of the divine image in men is an impartation to them of the likeness of the archetypal glory of Christ."

In drawing together these various strands, we can say that the creation of humankind represents the appearance of the image-bearing son, although the investiture of that son in the royal office is in a sense already eschatologically oriented at creation. In other words, 'Adam has not yet assumed the throne under God in the Sabbath glory. (See 2 Cor. 3:7-18; 4:4-6, with "the investiture figure" of "putting on Christ" in Eph. 4:24; Rom. 13:14; I Con 15:53; 2 Cor. 5:2ff.; Gal. 3:27; Col. 3:10.) Now those who even after the fall still bear an official glory are re-created to reflect the ethical glory of the Son in the power of the Spirit. Ricoeur therefore is justified in seeing union with Christ and not the imitation of Christ as the New Testament successor to the Old Testament prophetic idea: the summoned subject of the prophetic narratives is "the christomorphic self"

Related also to this covenant-bearing glory-image is the concept of "name." Adam and Eve are both named by God (a dear indication of their equality in creation and as image-bearing officers), while Adam is given the prior task of naming the animals. Similarly, notes Ricoeur, believers are "named 'sons of God,' just as people customarily are surnamed after the name of their forebears." This "naming" practice is also a treaty-making practice. "The name 'Christian' is a covenantal identification for the servant-son people of the new covenant." That we are not only created but created-in-covenant—and that we are named, both in creation (Adam) and then in redemption (Christ)—undermines all notions of autonomous self-creation. The federal or covenantal nature of this redemption undermines all anthropological individualism. Anthony Thiselton also indicates the significance of this naming in determining the biblical concept of selfhood: "In a distinctively theological sense the biblical text ... may be said to address the selfhood of the reader with transforming effects. It thereby gives the self an identity and significance as the recipient of loving and transforming address. In this sense, it 'names' the self." In baptism, Christ claims believers and their children, writing his name on their foreheads, setting them apart for himself as images of his glory. To bear the name of God is to bear the glory of God.

The creature thus named is a prophetic witness, authorized to declare God's word of command and promise. It is important to recognize that in Adam, humankind, like Moses with his disobedient fellow-travelers on the verge of the Jordan, never entered the Sabbath consummation and therefore does not yet possess the glorification that royal investiture indicates. "As originally created, man was not yet endowed with this [physical] form of Glory-likeness. Physical glorification might only be contemplated in eschatological hope." Adoption is finally and fully realized for us only in our bodily resurrection and glorification (Rom. 8:23).

Prophetic witness

Although something of the witnessing character of the image has been mentioned, we should add a bit more to this important aspect.

* * * *

Pentecost then, as a new creation, is nothing less than "a redemptive recapitulation of Genesis 1:2 and 27." "In the command of the voice from heaven, 'Hear him,' Peter perceived [Acts 3:22] the ultimate application of the Deuteronomic requirement that Israel obey God's prophet (Deut. 18:18). That was God's own identification of Jesus as the prophet like unto Moses." The preincarnate Son, as "Angel of the Covenant" (Mal. 3:1; Zech. 3), "was that archetypal prophet behind the human prophet paradigm." Through the descent of the Glory-Spirit at Easter and Pentecost, the "new creation" has dawned, equipping those once "dead in trespasses and sins" (Eph. 2:1) to be witnesses to the ends of the earth. The Son witnesses to the Father, and both the Father and the Spirit witness to the Son, as the Spirit sent by the Son makes of fallen office-bearers a resurrected prophetic priesthood. Kline observes, "In 2 Corinthians 3 and 4, Paul describes the Christian's transformation into the image of the glory of the Lord in terms of Moses' transfiguration.... According to 2 Corinthians 3 and 4, for Christ to re-create the church in his divine likeness is to create a prophet-church." "Christ is the original light; the church which he creates in his likeness is a reflective light," a "prophetic witness." The Son has witnessed to what he has seen and heard in the heavenly council, and now his disciples are to witness to what they have seen and heard as they have stood for these three years in that same council with the incarnate Lord himself among them.

In Revelation 11, "The figures in whom the likeness of Christ is re-produced are expressly denoted as witnesses (v. 3) and prophets (vv. 10, 18) and their mission is described as one of prophesying (v. 3), prophecy (v. 6), and testimony (v. 7)." Now all believers enter the holy of holies (as priests) and are prophets in the Spirit, wearing the garments of the Spirit as a bride adorned for her husband. And yet, the church is the bride of Christ, not yet the spouse. The confirmation in righteousness and the consummation of the glory-image that constitute royal investiture await believers in hope.

That the image necessarily involves—even centrally—the ethical dimension is evident in the close connection it bears with the repetition of God's work and rest in the seven-day pattern. Yet this is true only in the liminal state of the already-not yet, as believers—together with the whole creation—await their own resurrection from the dead and royal entrance into confirmed righteousness. The Glorification, already semi-realized in the possession of the Holy Spirit as a down payment, will be the full psychosomatic investiture of each believer as a royal son. This may be why Paul (Rom. 8:1825) puts an eschatological spin on adoption, deferring its full accomplishment until the whole creation is able to participate with redeemed humanity in the Sabbath enthronement of God. Although the whole earth will be full of the glory of God, human beings are central in this construction for theological reasons.

****

I hope to have shown also in the preceding section how christology informs our understanding of these themes without collapsing proctology into soteriology. Having allowed a space for the essential constitution of human beings as prerequisite conditions for a covenantal relationship, our conclusion is that the image of God in humankind is itself official rather than essential; ethical rather than ontological; eschatological rather than metaphysical.

Conclusion

****

Against essentialism I have argued that the image of God is chiefly an office, but that it is an office for which human beings are suited by specific capacities as agents directed toward ends. Without surrendering the inalienable status of all human persons as divine image-bearers, I have nevertheless indicated the eschatological, soteriological, and therefore christological character of this imagebearing in its proper operation. Neither creation nor redemption is assimilated into the other; each retains its distinctive character and space.

Questions

1   What are the "traditional essentialist" approaches with which Horton is unhappy, and why is he critical of them? Why is "covenant" to be preferred as a category for understanding the human?

2   What is the difference (for Horton) between "prerequisites for image-bearing" and "the *Imago* proper"? Why does this matter?

3   In what sense does Horton argue that the image involves "the ethical dimension"?

4   What does he mean by asserting that the image is "official rather than essential; ethical rather than ontological; eschatological rather than metaphysical"? Is he convincing on this score?

5   How does Horton integrate Christology into his consideration of the *Imago Dei*?

3

Human Ontology

Some of the more challenging questions in theological anthropology revolve around understanding the component "parts" of the human person. The discussion arises at least partly from the complex terminology the Bible uses to describe the human person. Terms like soul (*nephesh*, *psyche*) and spirit (*ruach*, *pneuma*) suggest to many an immaterial aspect, while terms like body (various terms in Hebrew, *soma*) and flesh *(basar*, *sarx)* suggest a material component. And some biblical passages combine the terms in ways that suggest they are closely related without explaining the precise nature of that relationship (e.g. Gen. 2.7; Mt. 10.28; 1 Thess. 5.23). Are we essentially immortal souls temporarily residing in physical bodies? Swinging to another extreme, maybe we are just physical bodies, our apparently robust "inner" lives being merely the result of random physical processes? Or are we some combination of the two, the interdependent interaction of body and soul producing the human person? Although the vast majority of Christian theologians have rejected the two extremes, there is still tremendous diversity and disagreement in understanding precisely what terms like "body" and "soul" mean, how they relate to one another, and what role each plays in the life of a human person.

According to one prominent tradition, *substance dualism*, the body and the soul are fundamentally different substances with radically different attributes. The body is a physical substance with characteristics like location and extension. The soul, on the other hand, is simple, immaterial, and often viewed as immortal. Although God created the human person to comprise a union of these two substances, having breathed into the physical body the "breath of life" (Gen. 2:7), one of the consequences of sin is the death of the physical body and the temporary separation of the two substances in the intermediate state (2 Cor. 5:1–10). The human person continues to exist in this intermediate state as a disembodied soul, as seen in the parable of the rich man and Lazarus (Lk. 16:19–31), and will return to its embodied state in the resurrection. According to substance dualism, then, the body is an important part of God's plan for the human person, as seen in both creation and resurrection, but the personhood of the human individual is grounded primarily in the soul, which is why the human person can continue to exist in the intermediate state.

Substance dualism has a long history of support in Christian theology, with many early theologians arguing for some form of this view. Indeed, some have worried that the dualism of the early church was so extreme that it undermined any real appreciation for the value of the body, resulting in extreme forms of asceticism and an overly spiritualized understanding of the Christian life. Nonetheless, theologians like Tertullian and Gregory of Nyssa clearly represent a dualistic tradition that maintained a high view of the body even as they insisted on the primacy of the soul in the human person. More recently, Alvin Plantinga has resisted the modern move toward materialistic view of the human person, offering an array of philosophical arguments in favor of substance dualism.

A slightly different understanding of the body/soul relation arises with the blend of Christian theology and Aristotelian philosophy that stems from the work of Thomas Aquinas. Aristotelian *hylomorphism* maintains that all things have both a "formal" cause (that which makes it the kind of thing that it is) and a "material" cause (the stuff from which something is made). In the human person, then, the body is the material cause (the "stuff" of the human) and the soul is the formal cause (what makes that stuff into a human rather than some other kind of creature). Rather than seeing the soul and the body as distinct substances, then, hylomorphism presents the soul and the body as distinguishable but equally necessary aspects of a human person. Thus, the person is not identical with the soul but only with the body/soul composite. Thomas Aquinas famously used Aristotelian hylomorphism to understand human ontology, resulting in a view commonly referred to as *Thomistic dualism*, in which the hylomorphic unity of the human person is retained but in a way that affirms the soul's ability to survive in a highly truncated state after the death of the body.

Throughout history, various forms of either substance dualism or Thomistic dualism were the dominant approaches to understanding human ontology in the Christian world. As a result of modern developments in biblical studies and science, however, many theologians shifted to viewing the human person as a purely physical being, albeit one with a complex mental, emotional, and spiritual life. In biblical studies, scholars began pointing out that the biblical words used to describe the various aspects of the human person all emphasize primarily the entire person as a holistic individual rather than various separable "parts" of the person. Thus, for example, Hans Walter Wolff's article on the use of *nephesh* (soul) in the Old Testament demonstrates that it has a wide range of meanings that are difficult to align with the traditional notion of an immaterial soul. Similarly, modern science demonstrated that many of the functions traditionally associated with the soul (reason, volition, love, etc.) are inseparably linked to states and functions of the body, raising questions about whether the soul has any real role to play in human life.

Based on such developments, many modern theologians argue for some form of *physicalism* (i.e. the human person as a wholly physical being). Although some secular thinkers have concluded that physicalism entails the complete rejection of such things as free will, mental causation, and consciousness, most theologians argue against such reductionist conclusions. For these theologians, then, we can maintain the essentially physical nature of the human person without losing any of the values and functions traditionally associated with the soul.

TEXT 1: TERTULLIAN,
A TREATISE ON THE SOUL[1]

One of the most significant theologians of the early church, particularly in the Latin-speaking West, Tertullian's *A Treatise on the Soul* (*De Anima*) stands as an early example of a theologian who wrestled extensively with the reality of the "soul" in a material world. For Tertullian (160–220), even though he maintains a form of substance dualism, he continues to argue for the real significance of the physical body. And he does so in critical dialog with non-Christian philosophers and scientists who also strive to understand human nature. Often referred to as one of the earliest studies of Christian "psychology," *De Anima* wrestles with the relationship between the body, the soul, the spirit, and the mind, all pertinent issues for contemporary anthropology.

One aspect of Tertullian's presentation warrants some explanation. Tertullian routinely refers to the "corporality" of the soul, a conception that raises difficulties for modern readers unaccustomed to thinking about the soul as having a body of any kind. For many Greek thinkers, though, creaturely realities must be embodied in at least some sense, otherwise they would not really exist in the world. For these thinkers, then, the spiritual entities differ from material ones in that they are made from spiritual stuff rather than physical stuff. Thus, they have a kind of embodiment (corporality) but in a markedly different way.

Chapter II.—The Christian Has Sure and Simple Knowledge Concerning the Subject Before Us.

Now I am not unaware what a vast mass of literature the philosophers have accumulated concerning the subject before us, in their own commentaries thereon— what various schools of principles there are, what conflicts of opinion, what prolific sources of questions, what perplexing methods of solution. Moreover, I have looked into Medical Science also, the sister (as they say) of Philosophy, which claims as her function to cure the body, and thereby to have a special acquaintance with the soul. From this circumstance she has great differences with her sister, pretending as the latter does to know more about the soul, through the more obvious treatment, as it were, of her in her domicile *of the body*. But never mind all this contention between them for preeminence! For extending their several researches on the soul, Philosophy, on the one hand, has enjoyed the full scope of her genius; while Medicine, on the other hand, has possessed the stringent demands of her art and practice. Wide are men's inquiries into uncertainties; wider still are their disputes about conjectures. However great the difficulty of adducing proofs, the labour of producing conviction is not one whit less; so that the gloomy Heraclitus was quite right, when, observing the thick darkness which obscured the researches of the inquirers about the soul, and wearied with their interminable questions, he declared that he had certainly not

---

[1]*ANF*, 2:183–229

explored the limits of the soul, although he had traversed every road *in her domains*. To the Christian, however, but few words are necessary for the clear understanding of the whole subject. But in the few words there always arises certainty to him; nor is he permitted to give his inquiries a wider range than is compatible with their solution; for "endless questions" the apostle forbids. It must, however, be added, that no solution may be found by any man, but such as is learned from God; and that which is learned of God is the sum and substance of the whole thing.

Chapter III.—*The Soul's Origin Defined Out of the Simple Words of Scripture.*

Would to God that no "heresies had been ever necessary, in order that they which are approved may be made manifest!" We should then be never required to try our strength in contests about the soul with philosophers, those patriarchs of heretics, as they may be fairly called. The apostle, so far back as his own time, foresaw, indeed, that philosophy would do violent injury to the truth. This admonition *about false philosophy* he was induced to offer after he had been at Athens, had become acquainted with that *loquacious* city, and had there had a taste of its huckstering wiseacres and talkers. In like manner is the treatment of the soul according to the sophistical doctrines of men which "mix their wine with water." Some of them deny the immortality of the soul; others affirm that it is immortal, and something more. Some raise disputes about its substance; others about its form; others, again, respecting each of its several faculties. One school of philosophers derives its state from various sources, while another ascribes its departure to different destinations. *The various schools reflect the character of their masters*, according as they have received their impressions from the dignity of Plato, or the vigour of Zeno, or the equanimity of Aristotle, or the stupidity of Epicurus, or the sadness of Heraclitus, or the madness of Empedocles. The fault, I suppose, of the divine doctrine lies in its springing from Judæa rather than from Greece. Christ made a mistake, too, in sending forth fishermen to preach, rather than the sophist. Whatever noxious vapours, accordingly, exhaled from philosophy, obscure the clear and wholesome atmosphere of truth, it will be for Christians to clear away, both by shattering to pieces the arguments which are drawn from the principles of things—I mean those of the philosophers—and by opposing to them the maxims of heavenly wisdom— that is, such as are revealed by the Lord; in order that both the pitfalls wherewith philosophy captivates the heathen may be removed, and the means employed by heresy to shake the faith of Christians may be repressed.

Chapter IV.—*In Opposition to Plato, the Soul Was Created and Originated at Birth.*

After settling the origin of the soul, its condition or state comes up next. For when we acknowledge that the soul originates in the breath of God, it follows that we attribute a beginning to it. This Plato, indeed, refuses to assign to it, for he will have the soul to be unborn and unmade. We, however, from the very fact of its having had a beginning, as well as from the nature thereof, teach that it had both birth and creation. And when we ascribe both birth and creation to it, we have made no mistake: for being *born*, indeed, is one thing, and being *made* is another,—the former being the term which is best suited to living beings. When distinctions, however, have places and times of their own, they occasionally possess also reciprocity of application among themselves. Thus, the being made admits of being taken in the sense of being brought forth; inasmuch as everything which receives *being* or *existence*, in any way whatever, is in fact generated. For the maker may really be called the parent of the thing that is made: in this sense Plato also uses the phraseology. So far, therefore, as concerns our belief in the souls being made or born, the opinion of the philosopher is overthrown by the authority of prophecy even.

Chapter VII.—The Soul's Corporeality Demonstrated Out of the Gospels.

So far as the philosophers are concerned, we have said enough. As for our own teachers, indeed, our reference to them is *ex abundanti*—a surplusage of authority: in the Gospel itself they will be found to have the clearest evidence for the corporeal nature of the soul. In hell the soul of a certain man is in torment, punished in flames, suffering excruciating thirst, and imploring from the finger of a happier soul, for his tongue, the solace of a drop of water. Do you suppose that this end of the blessed poor man and the miserable rich man is only imaginary? Then why the name of Lazarus in this narrative, if the circumstance is not in (the category of) a real occurrence? But even if it is to be regarded as imaginary, it will still be a testimony to truth and reality. For unless the soul possessed corporeality, the image of a soul could not possibly contain a finger of a bodily substance; nor would the Scripture feign a statement about the limbs of a body, if these had no existence. But what is that which is removed to Hades after the separation of the body; which is there detained; which is reserved until the day of judgment; to which Christ also, on dying, descended? I imagine it is the souls of the patriarchs. But wherefore (all this), if the soul is nothing in its subterranean abode? For *nothing* it certainly is, if it is not a bodily substance. For whatever is incorporeal is incapable of being kept and guarded in any way; it is also exempt from either punishment or refreshment. That must be a body, by which punishment and refreshment can be experienced. Of this I shall treat more fully in a more fitting place. Therefore, whatever amount of punishment or refreshment the soul tastes in Hades, in its prison or lodging, in the fire or in Abraham's bosom, it gives proof thereby of its own corporeality. For an incorporeal thing suffers nothing, not having that which makes it capable of suffering; else, if it has such capacity, it must be a bodily substance. For in *as* far as every corporeal thing is capable of suffering, in *so* far is that which is capable of suffering also corporeal.

Chapter X.—The Simple Nature of the Soul is Asserted with Plato. The Identity of Spirit and Soul.

It is essential to a firm faith to declare with Plato that the soul is simple; in other words uniform and uncompounded; simply that is to say in respect of its substance. Never mind men's artificial views and theories, and away with the fabrications of heresy! Some maintain that there is within the soul a natural substance—the spirit— which is different from it: as if to have life—the function of the soul—were one thing; and to emit breath—the alleged function of the spirit—were another thing. Now it is not in all animals that these two functions are found; for there are many which only live but do not breathe in that they do not possess the organs of respiration—lungs and windpipes. But of what use is it, in an examination of the soul of man, to borrow proofs from a gnat or an ant, when the great Creator in His divine arrangements has allotted to every animal organs of vitality suited to its own disposition and nature, so that we ought not to catch at any conjectures from comparisons of this sort? Man, indeed, although organically furnished with lungs and windpipes, will not on that account be proved to *breathe* by one process, and to *live* by another; nor can the ant, although defective in these organs, be on that account said to be without respiration, as if it lived and that was all. . . . Well, then, since you separate the spirit (or breath) and the soul, separate their operations also. Let both of them accomplish some act apart from one another—the soul apart, the spirit apart. Let the soul live without the spirit; let the spirit breathe without the soul. Let one of them quit men's bodies, let the other remain; let death and life meet and agree. If indeed the soul and the spirit are two, they may be divided; and thus, by the separation of the one which departs from the one which remains, there would accrue the union and meeting together of life and of death. But such a union never will accrue: therefore they are not two, and they cannot be divided; but divided they might have been, if they had been (two). Still two things may surely coalesce in growth. But the two in question never will coalesce, since to live is one thing, and to breathe is another. Substances are distinguished by their operations. How much firmer ground have you for believing that the soul and the spirit are but one, since you assign to them no difference; so that the soul is itself the spirit, respiration being the function of that of which life also is.

Chapter XI.—Spirit—A Term Expressive of an Operation of the Soul, Not of Its Nature. To Be Carefully Distinguished from the Spirit of God.

But (Holy) Scripture, which has a better knowledge of the soul's Maker, or rather God, has told us nothing more than that God breathed on man's face the breath of life, and that man became a living soul, by means of which he was both to live and breathe; at the same time making a sufficiently clear distinction between the spirit and the soul, in such passages as the following, wherein God Himself declares: "My Spirit went forth from me, and I made the breath of each. And the breath of my Spirit became soul." And again: "He giveth breath unto the people that are on the earth, and Spirit to them that walk thereon." First of all there comes the (natural) soul, that is to say, the breath, to the people that are on the earth,—in other words, to those who act carnally in the flesh; then afterwards comes the Spirit to those who walk thereon,—that is, who subdue the works of the flesh; because the apostle also says, that "that is not first which is spiritual, but that which is natural, (or in possession of the natural soul,) and afterward that which is spiritual." For, inasmuch as Adam straightway predicted that "great mystery of Christ and the church," when he said, "This now is bone of my bones, and flesh of my flesh; therefore shall a man leave his father and his mother, and shall cleave unto his wife, and they two shall become one flesh," he experienced the influence of the Spirit. For there fell upon him that ecstasy, which is the Holy Ghost's operative virtue of prophecy. And even the evil spirit too is an influence which comes upon a man. Indeed, the Spirit of God not more really "turned Saul into another man," that is to say, into a prophet, when "people said one to another, What is this which is come to the son of Kish? Is Saul also among the prophets?" than did the evil spirit afterwards turn him into another man—in other words, into an apostate. Judas likewise was for a long time reckoned among the elect (apostles), and was even appointed to the office of their treasurer; he was not yet the traitor, although he was become fraudulent; but afterwards the devil entered into him. Consequently, as the spirit neither of God nor of the devil is naturally planted with a man's soul at his birth, this soul must evidently exist apart and alone, previous to the accession to it of either spirit: if thus apart and alone, it must also be simple and uncompounded as regards its substance; and therefore it cannot respire from any other cause than from the actual condition of its own substance.

Chapter XII.—Difference Between the Mind and the Soul, and the Relation Between Them.

In like manner the mind also, or *animus*, which the Greeks designate ΝΟΥΣ (*nous*), is taken by us in no other sense than as indicating that faculty or apparatus which is inherent and implanted in the soul, and naturally proper to it, whereby it acts, whereby it acquires knowledge, and by the possession of which it is capable of a spontaneity of motion within itself, and of thus appearing to be impelled by the mind, as if it were another substance, as is maintained by those who determine the soul to be the moving principle of the universe—the god of Socrates, Valentinus' "only-begotten" of his father *Bythus*, and his mother *Sige*....As for [Aristotle], indeed, although he postpones his definition of the mind, yet he begins by mentioning, as one of the two natural constituents of the mind, that divine principle which he conjectures to be impassible, or incapable of emotion, and thereby removes from all association with the soul. For whereas it is evident that the soul is susceptible of those emotions which it falls to it naturally to suffer, it must needs suffer either by the mind or with the mind. Now if the soul is by nature associated with the mind, it is impossible to draw the conclusion that the mind is impassible; or again, if the soul suffers not either by the mind or with the mind, it cannot possibly have a natural association with the mind, with which it suffers nothing, and which suffers nothing itself. Moreover, if the soul suffers nothing by the mind and with the mind, it will experience no sensation, nor will it acquire any knowledge, nor will it undergo any emotion through the agency of the mind, as they maintain it will. For Aristotle makes even the senses passions, or states of emotion. And rightly too. For to exercise the senses is to suffer emotion, because to suffer is to feel. In like manner, to acquire knowledge is to exercise the senses; and to undergo emotion is to exercise the senses; and the whole of this is a state of suffering. But we see that the soul experiences nothing of these things, in such a manner as that the mind also is affected by the emotion, by which, indeed, and with which, all is effected. It follows, therefore, that the mind is capable of admixture, in opposition to Anaxagoras; and passible or susceptible of emotion, contrary to the opinion of Aristotle....We, however, affirm that the mind coalesces with the soul,—not indeed as being distinct from it in substance, but as being its natural function and agent.

Chapter XXVII.—Soul and Body Conceived, Formed and Perfected in Element Simultaneously.

How, then, is a living being conceived? Is the substance of both body and soul formed together at one and the same time? Or does one of them precede the other in natural formation? We indeed maintain that both are conceived, and formed, and perfectly simultaneously, as well as born together; and that not a moment's interval occurs in their conception, so that, a prior place can be assigned to either. Judge, in fact, of the incidents of man's earliest existence by those which occur to him at the very last. As death is defined to be nothing else than the separation of body and soul, life, which is the opposite of death, is susceptible of no other definition than the conjunction of body and soul. If the severance happens at one and the same time to both substances by means of death, so the law of their combination ought to assure us that it occurs simultaneously to the two substances by means of life. Now we allow that life begins with conception, because we contend that the soul also begins from conception; life taking its commencement at the same moment and place that the soul does. Thus, then, the processes which act together to produce separation by death, also combine in a simultaneous action to produce life. If we assign priority to (the formation of) one of the natures, and a subsequent time to the other, we shall have further to determine the precise times of the semination, according to the condition and rank of each. And that being so, what time shall we give to the seed of the body, and what to the seed of the soul? Besides, if different periods are to be assigned to the seminations then arising out of this difference in time, we shall also have different substances. For although we shall allow that there are two kinds of seed—that of the body and that of the soul—we still declare that they are inseparable, and therefore contemporaneous and simultaneous in origin....

Chapter LI.—Death Entirely Separates the Soul from the Body.

But the operation of death is plain and obvious: it is the separation of body and soul. Some, however, in reference to the soul's immortality, on which they have so feeble a hold through not being taught of God, maintain it with such beggarly arguments, that they would fain have it supposed that certain souls cleave to the body even after death. It is indeed in this sense that Plato, although he despatches at once to heaven such souls as he pleases, yet in his *Republic* exhibits to us the corpse of an unburied person, which was preserved a long time without corruption, by reason of the soul remaining, as he says, unseparated from the body. ... But not a particle of the soul can possibly remain in the body, which is itself destined to disappear when time shall have abolished the entire scene on which the body has played its part. And yet even this partial survival of the soul finds a place in the opinions of some men; and on this account they will not have the body consumed at its funeral by fire, because they would spare the small residue of the soul. There is, however, another way of accounting for this pious treatment, not as if it meant to favour the relics of the soul, but as if it would avert a cruel custom in the interest even of the body; since, being human, it is itself undeserving of an end which is also inflicted upon murderers. The truth is, the soul is indivisible, because it is immortal; (and this fact) compels us to believe that death itself is an indivisible process, accruing indivisibly to the soul, not indeed because it is immortal, but because it is indivisible. Death, however, would have to be divided in its operation, if the soul were divisible into particles, any one of which has to be reserved for a later stage of death. At this rate, a part of death will have to stay behind for a portion of the soul. . . . Death, if it once falls short of totality in operation, is not death. If any fraction of the soul remain, it makes a living state. Death will no more mix with life, than will night with day.

Questions

1   How does Tertullian describe the relationship between non-Christian
    philosophy/science and Christian theology in understanding the human
    person? What do you think about this?

2   What is the relationship between the soul, the spirit, and the mind, according
    to Tertullian? Why does he think this is important?

3   How does Tertullian describe the relationship between the soul and the
    body? Do you see any potential problems with this way of understanding
    human ontology?

4   How does death affect the body/soul union? What light does this shed on
    Tertullian's understanding of the human person?

TEXT 2: GREGORY OF NYSSA, *ON THE MAKING OF MAN*[2]

Gregory of Nyssa (335–94) wrote his *On the Making of Man* (*De Hominis Opificio*) as a supplement to his brother Basil of Caesarea's *Hexaemeron*, a study of Genesis 1 that dealt with the doctrine of Creation in general, but not the creation of humanity in particular. For Gregory, since the human person is the climax of the creation narrative, our understanding of creation is not really complete until we have wrestled with the nature and significance of the human person. So Gregory proceeds to do the impossible: to study the human person, that which is "second to none of the wonders of the world" (*preface*).

Gregory's discussion of human ontology is particularly interesting in the high value he places on the human body. People often view Gregory as operating out of a neoplatonic framework that was deeply suspicious of physicality and tended to prioritize mystical experience and aesthetic rigor in a way that downplayed the fundamental importance of embodied life. Although you will see that Gregory affirmed a dualist understanding of humanity in which the spiritual has a kind of primacy, he does so in a way that at least tries to affirm the full value and dignity of the human body.

IV. *That the construction of man throughout signifies his ruling power*

1. For as in our own life artificers fashion a tool in the way suitable to its use, so the best Artificer made our nature as it were a formation fit for the exercise of royalty, preparing it at once by superior advantages of soul, and by the very form of the body, to be such as to be adapted for royalty: for the soul immediately shows its royal and exalted character, far removed as it is from the lowliness of private station, in that it owns no lord, and is self- governed, swayed autocratically by its own will; for to whom else does this belong than to a king? And further, besides these facts, the fact that it is the image of that Nature which rules over all means nothing else than this, that our nature was created to be royal from the first. For as, in men's ordinary use, those who make images of princes both mould the figure of their form, and represent along with this the royal rank by the vesture of purple, and even the likeness is commonly spoken of as "a king," so the human nature also, as it was made to rule the rest, was, by its likeness to the King of all, made as it were a living image, partaking with the archetype both in rank and in name, not vested in purple, nor giving indication of its rank by sceptre and diadem (for the archetype itself is not arrayed with these), but instead of the purple robe, clothed in virtue, which is in truth the most royal of all raiment, and in place of the sceptre, leaning on the bliss of immortality, and instead of the royal diadem, decked with the crown of righteousness; so that it is shown to be perfectly like to the beauty of its archetype in all that belongs to the dignity of royalty.

---

[2]Gregory of Nyssa, "On the Making of Man," in *NPNF*, 2.5, 389–419.

VII. *Why man is destitute of natural weapons and covering*

1. But what means the uprightness of his figure? and why is it that those powers which aid life do not naturally belong to his body? but man is brought into life bare of natural covering, an unarmed and poor being, destitute of all things useful, worthy, according to appearances, of pity rather than of admiration, not armed with prominent horns or sharp claws, nor with hoofs nor with teeth, nor possessing by nature any deadly venom in a sting,—things such as most animals have in their own power for defence against those who do them harm: his body is not protected with a covering of hair: and yet possibly it was to be expected that he who was promoted to rule over the rest of the creatures should be defended by nature with arms of his own so that he might not need assistance from others for his own security.

2. Well, I think it would not be at all hard to show that what seems to be a deficiency of our nature is a means for our obtaining dominion over the subject creatures. For if man had had such power as to be able to outrun the horse in swiftness, and to have a foot that, from its solidity, could not be worn out, but was strengthened by hoofs or claws of some kind, and to carry upon him horns and stings and claws, he would be, to begin with, a wild-looking and formidable creature, if such things grew with his body: and moreover he would have neglected his rule over the other creatures if he had no need of the cooperation of his subjects; whereas now, the needful services of our life are divided among the individual animals that are under our sway, for this reason—to make our dominion over them necessary.

VIII. *Why man's form is upright; and that hands were given him because of reason; wherein also is a speculation on the difference of souls.*

1. But man's form is upright, and extends aloft towards heaven, and looks upwards: and these are marks of sovereignty which show his royal dignity. For the fact that man alone among existing things is such as this, while all others bow their bodies downwards, clearly points to the difference of dignity between those which stoop beneath his sway and that power which rises above them: for all the rest have the foremost limbs of their bodies in the form of feet, because that which stoops needs something to support it: but in the formation of man these limbs were made hands, for the upright body found one base, supporting its position securely on two feet, sufficient for its needs.

2. Especially do these ministering hands adapt themselves to the requirements of the reason: indeed if one were to say that the ministration of hands is a special property of the rational nature, he would not be entirely wrong; and that not only because his thought turns to the common and obvious fact that we signify our reasoning by means of the natural employment of our hands in written characters. It is true that this fact, that we speak by writing, and, in a certain way, converse by the aid of our hands, preserving sounds by the forms of the alphabet, is not unconnected with the endowment of reason; but I am referring to something else when I say that the hands co-operate with the bidding of reason.

4. But it seems to me that by these facts Moses reveals a hidden doctrine, and secretly delivers that wisdom concerning the soul, of which the learning that is without had indeed some imagination, but no clear comprehension. His discourse then hereby teaches us that the power of life and soul may be considered in three

divisions. For one is only a power of growth and nutrition supplying what is suitable for the support of the bodies that are nourished, which is called the vegetative soul, and is to be seen in plants; for we may perceive in growing plants a certain vital power destitute of sense; and there is another form of life besides this, which, while it includes the form above mentioned, is also possessed in addition of the power of management according to sense; and this is to be found in the nature of the irrational animals: for they are not only the subjects of nourishment and growth, but also have the activity of sense and perception. But perfect bodily life is seen in the rational (I mean the human) nature, which both is nourished and endowed with sense, and also partakes of reason and is ordered by mind.

5. We might make a division of our subject in some such way as this. Of things existing, part are intellectual, part corporeal. Let us leave alone for the present the division of the intellectual according to its properties, for our argument is not concerned with these. Of the corporeal, part is entirely devoid of life, and part shares in vital energy. Of a living body, again, part has sense conjoined with life, and part is without sense: lastly, that which has sense is again divided into rational and irrational. For this reason the lawgiver says that after inanimate matter (as a sort of foundation for the form of animate things), this vegetative life was made, and had earlier existence in the growth of plants: then he proceeds to introduce the genesis of those creatures which are regulated by sense: and since, following the same order, of those things which have obtained life in the flesh, those which have sense can exist by themselves even apart from the intellectual nature, while the rational principle could not be embodied save as blended with the sensitive,—for this reason man was made last after the animals, as nature advanced in an orderly course to perfection. For this rational animal, man, is blended of every form of soul; he is nourished by the vegetative kind of soul, and to the faculty of growth was added that of sense, which stands midway, if we regard its peculiar nature, between the intellectual and the more material essence being as much coarser than the one as it is more refined than the other: then takes place a certain alliance and commixture of the intellectual essence with the subtle and enlightened element of the sensitive nature: so that man consists of these three: as we are taught the like thing by the apostle in what he says to the Ephesians, praying for them that the complete grace of their "body and soul and spirit" may be preserved at the coming of the Lord; using, the word "body" for the nutritive part, and denoting the sensitive by the word "soul," and the intellectual by "spirit." Likewise too the Lord instructs the scribe in the Gospel that he should set before every commandment that love to God which is exercised with all the heart and soul and mind: for here also it seems to me that the phrase indicates the same difference, naming the more corporeal existence "heart," the intermediate "soul," and the higher nature, the intellectual and mental faculty, "mind."

XI. *That the nature of mind is invisible.*

2. "Who hath known the mind of the Lord?" the apostle asks; and I ask further, who has understood his own mind? Let those tell us who consider the nature of God to be within their comprehension, whether they understand themselves—if they know the nature of their own mind. "It is manifold and much compounded." How then

can that which is intelligible be composite? or what is the mode of mixture of things that differ in kind? Or, "It is simple, and incomposite." How then is it dispersed into the manifold divisions of the senses? How is there diversity in unity? How is unity maintained in diversity?

3. But I find the solution of these difficulties by recourse to the very utterance of God; for He says, "Let us make man in our image, after our likeness." The image is properly an image so long as it fails in none of those attributes which we perceive in the archetype; but where it falls from its resemblance to the prototype it ceases in that respect to be an image; therefore, since one of the attributes we contemplate in the Divine nature is incomprehensibility of essence, it is clearly necessary that in this point the image should be able to show its imitation of the archetype.

4. For if, while the archetype transcends comprehension, the nature of the image were comprehended, the contrary character of the attributes we behold in them would prove the defect of the image; but since the nature of our mind, which is the likeness of the Creator evades our knowledge, it has an accurate resemblance to the superior nature, figuring by its own unknowableness the incomprehensible Nature.

XII. *An examination of the question where the ruling principle is to be considered to reside; wherein also is a discussion of tears and laughter, and a physiological speculation as to the inter-relation of matter, nature, and mind.*

1. Let there be an end, then, of all the vain and conjectural discussion of those who confine the intelligible energy to certain bodily organs; of whom some lay it down that the ruling principle is in the heart, while others say that the mind resides in the brain, strengthening such opinions by some plausible superficialities. For he who ascribes the principal authority to the heart makes its local position evidence of his argument (because it seems that it somehow occupies the middle position in the body), on the ground that the motion of the will is easily distributed from the centre to the whole body, and so proceeds to operation; and he makes the troublesome and passionate disposition of man a testimony for his argument, because such affections seem to move this part sympathetically. Those, on the other hand, who consecrate the brain to reasoning, say that the head has been built by nature as a kind of citadel of the whole body, and that in it the mind dwells like a king, with a bodyguard of senses surrounding it like messengers and shield-bearers. And these find a sign of their opinion in the fact that the reasoning of those who have suffered some injury to the membrane of the brain is abnormally distorted, and that those whose heads are heavy with intoxication ignore what is seemly.

3. I admit it to be true that the intellectual part of the soul is often disturbed by prevalence of passions; and that the reason is blunted by some bodily accident so as to hinder its natural operation; and that the heart is a sort of source of the fiery element in the body, and is moved in correspondence with the impulses of passion; and moreover, in addition to this, I do not reject (as I hear very much the same account from those who spend their time on anatomical researches) the statement that the cerebral membrane (according to the theory of those who take such a physiological view), enfolding in itself the brain, and steeped in the vapours that issue from it, forms a foundation for the senses; yet I do not hold this for a proof that the incorporeal nature is bounded by any limits of place.

8. And although I am aware that the intellectual energies are blunted, or even made altogether ineffective in a certain condition of the body, I do not hold this a sufficient evidence for limiting the faculty of the mind by any particular place, so that it should be forced out of its proper amount of free space by any inflammations that may arise in the neighbouring parts of the body (for such an opinion is a corporeal one, that when the receptacle is already occupied by something placed in it, nothing else can find place there); for the intelligible nature neither dwells in the empty spaces of bodies, nor is extruded by encroachments of the flesh; but since the whole body is made like some musical instrument, just as it often happens in the case of those who know how to play, but are unable, because the unfitness of the instrument does not admit of their art, to show their skill (for that which is destroyed by time, or broken by a fall, or rendered useless by rust or decay, is mute and inefficient, even if it be breathed upon by one who may be an excellent artist in flute-playing); so too the mind, passing over the whole instrument, and touching each of the parts in a mode corresponding to its intellectual activities, according to its nature, produces its proper effect on those parts which are in a natural condition, but remains inoperative and ineffective upon those which are unable to admit the movement of its art; for the mind is somehow naturally adapted to be in close relation with that which is in a natural condition, but to be alien from that which is removed from nature.

XXVII. *That it is possible, when the human body is dissolved into the elements of the universe, that each should have his own body restored from the common source.*

1. Yet it may be thou thinkest, having regard to the elements of the universe, that it is a hard thing when the air in us has been resolved into its kindred element, and the warmth, and moisture, and the earthy nature have likewise been mingled with their own kind, that from the common source there should return to the individual what belongs to itself.

2. Dost thou not then judge by human examples that even this does not surpass the limits of the Divine power? Thou hast seen surely somewhere among the habitations of men a common herd of some kind of animals collected from every quarter: yet when it is again divided among its owners, acquaintance with their homes and the marks put upon the cattle serve to restore to each his own. If thou conceivest of thyself also something like to this, thou wilt not be far from the right way: for as the soul is disposed to cling to and long for the body that has been wedded to it, there also attaches to it in secret a certain close relationship and power of recognition, in virtue of their commixture, as though some marks had been imprinted by nature, by the aid of which the community remains unconfused, separated by the distinctive signs. Now as the soul attracts again to itself that which is its own and properly belongs to it, what labour, I pray you, that is involved for the Divine power, could be a hindrance to concourse of kindred things when they are urged to their own place by the unspeakable attraction of nature, whatever it may be? For that some signs of our compound nature remain in the soul even after dissolution is shown by the dialogue in Hades, where the bodies had been conveyed to the tomb, but some bodily token still remained in the souls by which both Lazarus was recognized and the rich man was not unknown.

5. Now to the element of our soul which is in the likeness of God it is not that which is subject to flux and change by way of alteration, but this stable and

unalterable element in our composition that is allied: and since various differences of combination produce varieties of forms (and combination is nothing else than the mixture of the elements—by elements we mean those which furnish the substratum for the making of the universe, of which the human body also is composed), while the form necessarily remains in the soul as in the impression of a seal, those things which have received from the seal the impression of its stamp do not fail to be recognized by the soul, but at the time of the World-Reformation, it receives back to itself all those things which correspond to the stamp of the form: and surely all those things would so correspond which in the beginning were stamped by the form; thus it is not beyond probability that what properly belongs to the individual should once more return to it from the common source.

XXVIII. *To those who say that souls existed before bodies, or that bodies were formed before souls; wherein there is also a refutation of the fables concerning transmigration of souls.*

1. For it is perhaps not beyond our present subject to discuss the question which has been raised in the churches touching soul and body. Some of those before our time who have dealt with the question of "principles" think it right to say that souls have a previous existence as a people in a society of their own, and that among them also there are standards of vice and of virtue, and that the soul there, which abides in goodness, remains without experience of conjunction with the body; but if it does depart from its communion with good, it falls down to this lower life, and so comes to be in a body. Others, on the contrary, marking the order of the making of man as stated by Moses, say, that the soul is second to the body in order of time, since God first took dust from the earth and formed man, and then animated the being thus formed by His breath: and by this argument they prove that the flesh is more noble than the soul; that which was previously formed than that which was afterwards infused into it: for they say that the soul was made for the body, that the thing formed might not be without breath and motion; and that everything that is made for something else is surely less precious than that for which it is made, as the Gospel tells us that "the soul is more than meat and the body than raiment," because the latter things exist for the sake of the former—for the soul was not made for meat nor our bodies for raiment, but when the former things were already in being the latter were provided for their needs.

3. Those who stand by the former doctrine, and assert that the state of souls is prior to their life in the flesh, do not seem to me to be clear from the fabulous doctrines of the heathen which they hold on the subject of successive incorporation: for if one should search carefully, he will find that their doctrine is of necessity brought down to this. They tell us that one of their sages said that he, being one and the same person, was born a man, and afterwards assumed the form of a woman, and flew about with the birds, and grew as a bush, and obtained the life of an aquatic creature;—and he who said these things of himself did not, so far as I can judge, go far from the truth: for such doctrines as this of saying that one soul passed through so many changes are really fitting for the chatter of frogs or jackdaws, or the stupidity of fishes, or the insensibility of trees.

4. And of such absurdity the cause is this—the supposition of the pre-existence of souls for the first principle of such doctrine leads on the argument by consequence

to the next and adjacent stage, until it astonishes us by reaching this point. For if the soul, being severed from the more exalted state by some wickedness after having once, as they say, tasted corporeal life, again becomes a man, and if the life in the flesh is, as may be presumed, acknowledged to be, in comparison with the eternal and incorporeal life, more subject to passion, it naturally follows that that which comes to be in a life such as to contain more occasions of sin, is both placed in a region of greater wickedness and rendered more subject to passion than before (now passion in the human soul is a conformity to the likeness of the irrational); and that being brought into close connection with this, it descends to the brute nature: and that when it has once set out on its way through wickedness, it does not cease its advance towards evil even when found in an irrational condition: for a halt in evil is the beginning of the impulse towards virtue, and in irrational creatures virtue does not exist. Thus it will of necessity be continually changed for the worse, always proceeding to what is more de-graded and always finding out what is worse than the nature in which it is: and just as the sensible nature is lower than the rational, so too there is a descent from this to the insensible.

5. Now so far in its course their doctrine, even if it does overstep the bounds of truth, at all events derives one absurdity from another by a kind of logical sequence: but from this point onwards their teaching takes the form of incoherent fable. Strict inference points to the complete destruction of the soul; for that which has once fallen from the exalted state will be unable to halt at any measure of wickedness, but will pass by means of its relation with the passions from rational to irrational, and from the latter state will be transferred to the insensibility of plants; and on the insensible there borders, so to say, the inanimate; and on this again follows the non-existent, so that absolutely by this train of reasoning they will have the soul to pass into nothing: thus a return once more to the better state is impossible for it: and yet they make the soul return from a bush to the man: they therefore prove that the life in a bush is more precious than an incorporeal state.

Questions

1   Gregory thinks that the very structure of the human body signifies royalty. How does it do this? What do you think about this way of talking about the body?

2   Gregory describes the human person as a "rational animal." What does he mean by this? How does he describe the relation between rationality and the body? Why is this important?

3   How is the soul different from the body? What is the relationship between them?

4   What is the "transmigration of souls"? How does it relate to substance dualism? Why does Gregory reject it?

TEXT 3: THOMAS AQUINAS,
SUMMA THEOLOGICA[3]

This reading from the medieval theologian Thomas Aquinas (1225–74) offers an important perspective on a different kind of dualism, though some dispute whether it should even be considered a kind of dualism, and it is one that remains prominent among Catholic and some Protestant theologians. Following Aristotle, Aquinas argued that material objects are composites of form and matter. The matter is the stuff from which an object is made, while the form provides the essential nature of the object: what makes it the kind of thing that it is. For a human person, then, the body is the matter out of which we are made, while the soul provides our form, that which makes us *human* things. Thus, the soul and the body both have their own kind of existence, and the soul does survive after the death of the body. But the human *person* only exists in the union of the two.

Article 1: Whether the Soul Is a Body?

Objection 1: It would seem that the soul is a body. For the soul is the moving principle of the body. Nor does it move unless moved. First, because seemingly nothing can move unless it is itself moved, since nothing gives what it has not; for instance, what is not hot does not give heat. Secondly, because if there be anything that moves and is not moved, it must be the cause of eternal, unchanging movement, as we find proved *Phys.* viii, 6; and this does not appear to be the case in the movement of an animal, which is caused by the soul. Therefore the soul is a mover moved. But every mover moved is a body. Therefore the soul is a body.

Objection 2: Further, all knowledge is caused by means of a likeness. But there can be no likeness of a body to an incorporeal thing. If, therefore, the soul were not a body, it could not have knowledge of corporeal things.

Objection 3: Further, between the mover and the moved there must be contact. But contact is only between bodies. Since, therefore, the soul moves the body, it seems that the soul must be a body.

On the contrary, Augustine says (*De Trin.* vi, 6) that the soul "is simple in comparison with the body, inasmuch as it does not occupy space by its bulk."

I answer that, To seek the nature of the soul, we must premise that the soul is defined as the first principle of life of those things which live: for we call living things "animate," [*i.e. having a soul], and those things which have no life, "inanimate." Now life is shown principally by two actions, knowledge and movement. The philosophers of old, not being able to rise above their imagination, supposed that the principle of these actions was something corporeal: for they asserted that only bodies were real things; and that what is not corporeal is nothing: hence they maintained that the soul is something corporeal. This opinion can be proved to be false in many ways; but we shall make use of only one proof, based on universal and certain principles, which shows clearly that the soul is not a body.

---

[3]Thomas Aquinas, *ST* Ia, Q75, A1-4.

It is manifest that not every principle of vital action is a soul, for then the eye would be a soul, as it is a principle of vision; and the same might be applied to the other instruments of the soul: but it is the "first" principle of life, which we call the soul. Now, though a body may be a principle of life, or to be a living thing, as the heart is a principle of life in an animal, yet nothing corporeal can be the first principle of life. For it is clear that to be a principle of life, or to be a living thing, does not belong to a body as such; since, if that were the case, every body would be a living thing, or a principle of life. Therefore a body is competent to be a living thing or even a principle of life, as "such" a body. Now that it is actually such a body, it owes to some principle which is called its act. Therefore the soul, which is the first principle of life, is not a body, but the act of a body; thus heat, which is the principle of calefaction, is not a body, but an act of a body.

Reply to Objection 1: As everything which is in motion must be moved by something else, a process which cannot be prolonged indefinitely, we must allow that not every mover is moved. For, since to be moved is to pass from potentiality to actuality, the mover gives what it has to the thing moved, inasmuch as it causes it to be in act. But, as is shown in Phys. viii, 6, there is a mover which is altogether immovable, and not moved either essentially, or accidentally; and such a mover can cause an invariable movement. There is, however, another kind of mover, which, though not moved essentially, is moved accidentally; and for this reason it does not cause an invariable movement; such a mover, is the soul. There is, again, another mover, which is moved essentially—namely, the body. And because the philosophers of old believed that nothing existed but bodies, they maintained that every mover is moved; and that the soul is moved directly, and is a body.

Reply to Objection 2: The likeness of a thing known is not of necessity actually in the nature of the knower; but given a thing which knows potentially, and afterwards knows actually, the likeness of the thing known must be in the nature of the knower, not actually, but only potentially; thus color is not actually in the pupil of the eye, but only potentially. Hence it is necessary, not that the likeness of corporeal things should be actually in the nature of the soul, but that there be a potentiality in the soul for such a likeness. But the ancient philosophers omitted to distinguish between actuality and potentiality; and so they held that the soul must be a body in order to have knowledge of a body; and that it must be composed of the principles of which all bodies are formed in order to know all bodies.

Reply to Objection 3: There are two kinds of contact; of "quantity," and of "power." By the former a body can be touched only by a body; by the latter a body can be touched by an incorporeal thing, which moves that body.

Article 2: Whether the human soul is something subsistent?

Objection 1: It would seem that the human soul is not something subsistent. For that which subsists is said to be "this particular thing." Now "this particular thing" is said not of the soul, but of that which is composed of soul and body. Therefore the soul is not something subsistent.

Objection 2: Further, everything subsistent operates. But the soul does not operate; for, as the Philosopher says (*De Anima* i, 4), "to say that the soul feels or understands is like saying that the soul weaves or builds." Therefore the soul is not subsistent.

Objection 3: Further, if the soul were subsistent, it would have some operation apart from the body. But it has no operation apart from the body, not even that of understanding: for the act of understanding does not take place without a phantasm, which cannot exist apart from the body. Therefore the human soul is not something subsistent.

On the contrary, Augustine says (*De Trin.* x, 7): "Who understands that the nature of the soul is that of a substance and not that of a body, will see that those who maintain the corporeal nature of the soul, are led astray through associating with the soul those things without which they are unable to think of any nature—i.e. imaginary pictures of corporeal things." Therefore the nature of the human intellect is not only incorporeal, but it is also a substance, that is, something subsistent.

I answer that, It must necessarily be allowed that the principle of intellectual operation which we call the soul, is a principle both incorporeal and subsistent. For it is clear that by means of the intellect man can have knowledge of all corporeal things. Now whatever knows certain things cannot have any of them in its own nature; because that which is in it naturally would impede the knowledge of anything else. Thus we observe that a sick man's tongue being vitiated by a feverish and bitter humor, is insensible to anything sweet, and everything seems bitter to it. Therefore, if the intellectual principle contained the nature of a body it would be unable to know all bodies. Now every body has its own determinate nature. Therefore it is impossible for the intellectual principle to be a body. It is likewise impossible for it to understand by means of a bodily organ; since the determinate nature of that organ would impede knowledge of all bodies; as when a certain determinate color is not only in the pupil of the eye, but also in a glass vase, the liquid in the vase seems to be of that same color.

Therefore the intellectual principle which we call the mind or the intellect has an operation "per se" apart from the body. Now only that which subsists can have an operation "per se." For nothing can operate but what is actual: for which reason we do not say that heat imparts heat, but that what is hot gives heat. We must conclude, therefore, that the human soul, which is called the intellect or the mind, is something incorporeal and subsistent.

Reply to Objection 1: "This particular thing" can be taken in two senses. Firstly, for anything subsistent; secondly, for that which subsists, and is complete in a specific nature. The former sense excludes the inherence of an accident or of a material form; the latter excludes also the imperfection of the part, so that a hand can be called "this particular thing" in the first sense, but not in the second. Therefore, as the human soul is a part of human nature, it can indeed be called "this particular thing," in the first sense, as being something subsistent; but not in the second, for in this sense, what is composed of body and soul is said to be "this particular thing."

Reply to Objection 2: Aristotle wrote those words as expressing not his own opinion, but the opinion of those who said that to understand is to be moved, as is clear from the context. Or we may reply that to operate "per se" belongs to what exists "per se." But for a thing to exist "per se," it suffices sometimes that it be not inherent, as an accident or a material form; even though it be part of something. Nevertheless, that is rightly said to subsist "per se," which is neither inherent in the above sense, nor part of anything else. In this sense, the eye or the hand cannot be said to subsist "per se"; nor can it for that reason be said to operate "per se." Hence the operation of the parts is through each part attributed to the whole. For we say that man sees with the eye, and feels with the hand, and not in the same sense as when we say that what is hot gives heat by its heat; for heat, strictly speaking, does not give heat. We may therefore say that the soul understands, as the eye sees; but it is more correct to say that man understands through the soul.

Reply to Objection 3: The body is necessary for the action of the intellect, not as its origin of action, but on the part of the object; for the phantasm is to the intellect what color is to the sight. Neither does such a dependence on the body prove the intellect to be non-subsistent; otherwise it would follow that an animal is non-subsistent, since it requires external objects of the senses in order to perform its act of perception.

Article 4: Whether the soul is man?

Objection 1: It would seem that the soul is man. For it is written (2 Cor. 4:16): "Though our outward man is corrupted, yet the inward man is renewed day by day." But that which is within man is the soul. Therefore the soul is the inward man.

Objection 2: Further, the human soul is a substance. But it is not a universal substance. Therefore it is a particular substance. Therefore it is a "hypostasis" or a person; and it can only be a human person. Therefore the soul is man; for a human person is a man.

On the contrary, Augustine (*De Civ. Dei* xix, 3) commends Varro as holding "that man is not a mere soul, nor a mere body; but both soul and body."

I answer that, The assertion "the soul is man," can be taken in two senses. First, that man is a soul; though this particular man, Socrates, for instance, is not a soul, but composed of soul and body. I say this, forasmuch as some held that the form alone belongs to the species; while matter is part of the individual, and not the species. This cannot be true; for to the nature of the species belongs what the definition signifies; and in natural things the definition does not signify the form only, but the form and the matter. Hence in natural things the matter is part of the species; not, indeed, signate matter, which is the principle of individuality; but the common matter. For as it belongs to the notion of this particular man to be composed of this soul, of this flesh, and of these bones; so it belongs to the notion of man to be composed of soul, flesh, and bones; for whatever belongs in common to the substance of all the individuals contained under a given species, must belong to the substance of the species.

It may also be understood in this sense, that this soul is this man; and this could be held if it were supposed that the operation of the sensitive soul were proper to it, apart from the body; because in that case all the operations which are attributed to man would belong to the soul only; and whatever performs the operations proper to a thing, is that thing; wherefore that which performs the operations of a man is man. But it has been shown above (A[3]) that sensation is not the operation of the soul only. Since, then, sensation is an operation of man, but not proper to him, it is clear that man is not a soul only, but something composed of soul and body. Plato, through supposing that sensation was proper to the soul, could maintain man to be a soul making use of the body.

Reply to Objection 1: According to the Philosopher (*Ethic.* ix, 8), a thing seems to be chiefly what is principle in it; thus what the governor of a state does, the state is said to do. In this way sometimes what is principle in man is said to be man; sometimes, indeed, the intellectual part which, in accordance with truth, is called the "inward" man; and sometimes the sensitive part with the body is called man in the opinion of those whose observation does not go beyond the senses. And this is called the "outward" man.

Reply to Objection 2: Not every particular substance is a hypostasis or a person, but that which has the complete nature of its species. Hence a hand, or a foot, is not called a hypostasis, or a person; nor, likewise, is the soul alone so called, since it is a part of the human species.

Questions

1   Aquinas begins by arguing that the soul should not be thought of as a body. How is this different from Tertullian's position? Why does Aquinas think Tertullian's approach is mistaken?

2   What does Aquinas mean when he says that the soul is "subsistent"? What does this tell you about the nature of the soul and its relationship to the body?

3   Does Aquinas think that the soul is identical to the human person? Why or why not?

TEXT 4: HANS WALTER WOLFF, "NEPHESH" IN *ANTHROPOLOGY OF THE OLD TESTAMENT*[4]

Hans Walter Wolff (1911–93) was an Old Testament scholar who taught in Germany during the middle part of the twentieth century. His *Anthropology of the Old Testament* was pivotal in reorienting people's understanding of biblical terms like "soul" (*nephesh*) and "spirit" (*ruach*), demonstrating that these terms have a far more diverse range of meaning than their English counterparts suggest. Rather than simply denoting some immaterial component of the human person, such terms can be used to designate a broad range of human realities, but they primarily emphasize simply that humans are living creatures, distinguishing them from inanimate objects but not necessarily from other living animals. Rather than emphasizing human uniqueness, then, all living creatures have *nephesh*. Arguments like this also helped scholars appreciate the essentially holistic picture of the human person presented in the Old Testament. If terms like *nephesh* do not denote some kind of immaterial substance, instead emphasizing the principles of life that animate physical bodies, then we begin to see that the Old Testament presents humans as essentially holistic beings.

The traditional English Bible generally translates *nepeš*, one of the basic words of Old Testament anthropology, as 'soul'. In so doing it goes back, like the French *âme* and the German *Seele*, to the Greek Bible's most frequent translation of *nepeš*, *psyche*, and to the Latin Bible's rendering, *anima*. *nepeš* occurs 755 times in the Old Testament and on 600 occasions the Septuagint translates it by *psyche*. This statistical difference shows that even the ancient writers noticed that the word bore another meaning in not a few places. Today we are coming to the conclusion that it is only in a very few passages that the translation 'soul' corresponds to the meaning of *nepeš*.

Notwithstanding, an almost definitory use of the Hebrew word to signify human existence cannot be from the outset denied. The Yahwist's account of the creation uses it in this way (Gen 2.7): "Yahweh God formed man of dust from the ground, and breathed into his nostrils the breath of life; and man became a living *nepeš*."

What does *nepeš* (which we shall from now on be referring to as *n.*) mean here? Certainly not soul. *n.* is designed to be seen together with the whole form of man, and especially with his breath; moreover man does not *have n.*, he *is n.*, he lives as *n.* Which aspect of human existence is being viewed in this way? For the moment the text we are using for our definition can only invite us to pace out the whole human area that *n.* encompasses. Access to the fullness of meaning lent by the synthetic way of thinking may be opened up for our analytical understanding when we ask: what part of the human body can be identified with the being and behaviour designated

---

[4]Hans Walter Wolff, *Anthropology of the Old Testament*, trans. Margaret Kohl (London: SCM, 1974), 10–25.

as *n.*? Methodologically we shall have to ask, in looking at the text, whether the context really allows us to deduce from it a particular physical organ. We shall then have to go on to enquire where the argument picks out particular functions and characteristics of that part of the body, and how the word finally brings out, more or less clearly, a particular aspect of human existence in general. We must always bear in mind that this is an outline of our method of arriving at an understanding, and is certainly not the pattern of a historical semasiology. The history of meaning can only bring out particular changes for a limited linguistic phase. In general stereometric-synthetic thinking sees a part of the body together with its particular activities and capacities, and these in their turn are conceived as being the distinguishing marks of the whole man. We must therefore always remember that the Hebrew uses one and the same word where we need widely differing ones. In each case the textual context of the instance decides.

1 Throat

We shall start from the image in Isa 5.14:

> The underworld wrenches wide its *nepeš*,
> and opens its mouth beyond measure.

The synonymous parallel talks about the mouth. As far as the *n.* itself is concerned, we are told that it is wide open. This is a clear indication that *n.* here means the gullet, the jaws, or the throat. In the same way Hab 2.5 can say about the rapacious man:

> He opens his *nepeš* wide as the underworld
> and is like death and has never enough.

According to this, *n.* is a term for the organ that takes in food and satisfies hunger. ... In his *n.* man realizes that he cannot live of himself (Prov 10.3):

> Yahweh does not let the righteous *n.* go hungry,
> but he repulses the craving of the wicked.

Again the argument shows clearly that the throat is meant, but at the same time it also shows that the word stands for the needy man *per se*.

But the *n.* does not only count as the organ for taking in nourishment; also the organ of breathing. This is quite clear in the case of the female in Jer. 2.24: 'In the lust of "her" *n.* she pants for breath.' Again and again we are told that the action of the *n.* is *nph*=to blow, breathe or pant. Thus the throat of a fainting mother pants heavily (Jer. 15.9); the hope of godless 'is to breathe out their *n.*' (Job 11.20), where the organ of breathing and the breath itself are viewed together; as they are in Job 41.21, the crocodile's *n.* kindles coals.

When we are told that the *n.* of the dying Rachel 'departed' (Gen. 35.18), it can only be the breath that the writer is thinking of. In I Kings 17.21f. *n.* returns to the child of the widow of Zarephath, of whom v.17 had reported that there was no breath (*nᵉsama*) left in him. In this archaic anatomy, therefore, the throat stands without terminological distinction for both the windpipe and the oesophagus. When 'the floods rise to the *n.*, there is danger of drowning (Jonah 2.5; Ps 69.1; cf. Ps 124.4f. and *sawwa'r* in Isa 8.8; 30.28).

2 Neck

Over against the copious evidence for the inside of the neck and the vital functions which take place there, the rarer use of *n.* for the external neck could be secondary. We see how easy the transition is for Hebrew thinking alone through the parallel use of *sawwa'r* (neck) and *n.* in the phrases about the threateningly rising floods. Ps. 105.18 is thinking solely of the outer neck:

> They forced his feet into fetters,
> his *n.* was put into iron.

* * * *

3 Desire

When, therefore, the throat or neck are mentioned, there is frequently an echo of the view of man as needy and in danger, who therefore yearns with his *n.* for food and the preservation of his life; and this vital *longing, desiring, striving or yearning* can, even when the *n.* is mentioned, dominate the concept by itself. This is clearly the case where a man's *n.* lies outside his own person. In the lament in Ps 35.25 the petitioner quotes his enemies, who are already saying about him: 'Aha, our *n!*' and who would like soon to be able to say, 'We have swallowed him up.' If a man has here become the *n.* of his opponent, he cannot be his throat or neck; he can only be his longing or desire, and here his positive 'enjoyment', whereby we ought also to think back to the *n.* as the organ of taste. When 13.2b defines the *n.* of the treacherous as 'violence', *n.* means there too only their striving and desire.

  n. is as a rule the still unslaked desire, which urges action. It is this that makes possible the remarkable maxim (Prov 16.26):

> A worker's *n.* works for him;
> his mouth urges him on.

n., parallel to mouth, is the throat in action, the hunger that urges a man to work. Deut 23.24: 'When you go into your neighbour's vineyard, you may eat your fill of grapes according to your *n.*' When the man has eaten his fill, *n.* as the unsated desire has reached the limits set for it. The *n.* as such stands for unlimited desire....

But still more frequently *n.* means man in his ardent desire, which is like the parched longing of the man who is dying of thirst. This is how the *n.* thirsts in Ps 42.1f.4, that is to say the longing desire for the living God felt by the author of the lament. And so, according to I Sam 1.15, does the childless Hannah pour out her *n.*—that is, her unsatisfied desire—to Yahweh. The Deuteronomic command to love Yahweh with the whole of the *n.* (Deut 6.5 and passim) means accordingly that man should carry the whole living force of his wishes and all his longing desire into his love for the one God of Israel. Cf. Mark 12.30. 'To fight with one *psyche* for the faith of the gospel' (Phil 1.27) means: striving in common.

4 Soul

It is only a short step from the *n.* as specific organ and act of desire to the extended meaning, whereby the *n.* is the seat and action of other spiritual experiences and emotions as well. Ex 23.9 exhorts Israel:

> You shall not oppress a stranger;
> You know the *n.* of a stranger,
> for you were strangers in the land of Egypt.

This is the place where we could translate *n.* by 'soul' for the first time. For the writer is thinking not only of the stranger's needs and desires but of the whole range of his feelings, arising from the alien land and the danger of oppression in his state of dependence. Job is also thinking of the soul as the central organ of suffering man when he asks his 'friends' (Job 19.2): 'How long will you torment my *n.*?' According to this, the *n.* is the typical organ of sympathy with the needy (Job 30.25). As the suffering soul especially, and as the tortured mind, the *n.* is the precise subject of the psalms of lamentation; it is frightened (6.3), it despairs and is disquieted (42.5f., 11; 43.5), it feels itself weak and despondent (Jonah 2.7), it is exhausted and feels defenceless (Jer 4.31), it is afflicted (Ps 31.7; cf. Gen 42.21) and suffers misery (Isa 53.11). The *n.* is often described as being bitter (*mar*), that is to say embittered through childlessness (I Sam. 1.10), troubled because of illness (II Kings 4.27), enraged because it has been injured (Judg 18.25; II Sam 17.8) or distressed in some other way (Prov 31.6); choice of the word 'bitter' certainly reminds us of *n.* as the organ of (Prov 27.7, see pp. 12f. above), but the context in the cases just quoted and in many similar ones shows clearly that here it is the state of that is being thought of....

With this the *n.*'s content of meaning has been considerably extended; but it does not go beyond the sphere marked out by the stirrings of the mind and the emotions; and here it is not uncommon for there to be a reminiscence of the physical organ and its particular functions.

5 Life

This reminiscence becomes still clearer in a highly extensive sector of the *n.* occurrences. If *n.* designates the organ of vital needs, which have to be satisfied if man is to go on living, the *n.* it is easy for synthetic thinking to see that *n.* further means 'life' itself. In Prov 8.35f. the argument enforces this translation: wisdom says:

> He who finds me has found life (*ḥayyim*)
> and has obtained favour from Yahweh.
> But he who misses me violates his *n.*;
> all who hate me love death (*mawet*).

In the antithesis to the preceding sentence, *n.* appears as an exact synonym for 'life', and in the parallel to the following stichos, *n.* forms the contrasting word to 'death'. In Ps 30.3 we read: 'O Yahweh, thou hast brought up my *n.* from the underworld.' The synonymous continuation goes on: 'thou hast called me into life (*ḥiyyitani*)', thus confirming that in what has gone before *n.* means nothing less than the life of the worshipper himself. In Prov 19.8, too, none of the meanings we mentioned earlier will fit:

> He who gets wisdom loves his *n.*
> he who keeps understanding 'finds' good things.

As in Prov 8.35f., wisdom is related to life itself as the good *per se*. In Prov 7.23 too:

> as a bird rushes into a snare
> without knowing that his *n.* is at stake,

n. no longer means the neck (cf. I Sam 28.9; Ps 124.7; Prov 18.7), but the life, since this simile in the great warning discourse also serves only as a guide to 'life' (7.2a) and as a guard against death (v. 27).

That the meaning 'life' can, in distinction from the last example, be separated entirely from the idea of 'neck' or 'throat' is proved surprisingly by the definition in Deut 12.23: 'The blood is the *n.*' With this the complete identification of blood and life has taken place, as justification for the precept that the blood—namely the life—is not to be eaten with the flesh. Lev. 17.11 puts it almost more clearly still: 'The *n.* of the flesh is in the blood.' The Priestly document also associates the *n.* as the life with the blood, as in Gen 94f.

The definition of blood is already evidence that *n.* means the life *per se*, animal and human (Deut 12.23; Gen 9.4f.). It is clearly in this context that Lev 24.17f. declares:

> He who kills the *n.* of a man
> shall be put to death.
> He who kills the *n.* of a beast
> shall make it good.

Both follow from the basic rule 'a *n.* for a *n.*' (v. 18b.). Here that can only mean, one life substitutes for another, one's own when a man has been killed, a living animal for a dead one. The older administration of justice is already familiar with this meaning of life for *n.* in the *lex talionis*, as the Book of the Covenant demonstrates (Ex 21.23f.): 'If an accident occurs, shall give life for life, eye for eye, tooth for tooth, hand foe hand, foot for foot.' In military life too the man on guard is responsible with his life foe the man whom he has to watch: 'your *n*. shall be for his *n*.', I Kings 20.39 (cf. v.42). Deut 24.6 commands: 'No man shall take a mill or an upper in pledge; for he would be taking the *n*. in pledge.' Anyone who takes away from a man the tools that are essential to support everyday life is taking away the life itself.

Rich and abundant though this use of *n*. for life is, we must not fail to observe that the *n*. is never given the meaning of an indestructible core of being, in contradistinction to the physical life, and even capable of living when cut off from that life. When there is a mention of the 'departing' (Gen 35.18) of the *n*. from a man, or of its 'return' (Lam 1.11), the basic idea, as we saw on p. 13 above, is the concrete notion of the ceasing and restoration of the breathing. When Yahweh leads up the *n*. from the underworld (Ps 30.3; 86.13), the idea is the return to healthy life of the whole man who has, through his illness, already been exposed to the power of death. Though much is said about *n*. as the life, any cult of life or death is lacking, and with it also every speculation about the fate of the 'soul' beyond the borders of death.

6 Person

We came across yet another new sense of *n*. when it is presupposed that man *is* *n*. and not, as up to now, that he possesses *n*. We see the differences most clearly in those texts which have something to say about the relation between *n*. and life (*ḥayyim*). We have just met sayings where *ḥayyim* and *n*. are treated as synonyms (e.g., Prov 8.35f. and see pp. 18f. above); but in Prov 3.22 we have:

> [Discretion and wisdom] will be life (*ḥayyim*) for your *n*.
> and adornment for your neck.

The translation 'life' for *n*. is impossible here, since life is only promised to it. *n*. therefore does not say what a man has, but who the person is who receives life (*ḥayyim*): 'person', 'individual', 'being'. Legal texts from the Law of Holiness make this interpretation clear. Lev 17.10: 'Every man . . . who eats any blood (of him it is true that) I will set my face against the *n*. that eats blood.' Here *n*. has to be translated as person, even though we should note that the person here is called *n*. in his function who eats (cf. 17.15). But this association is quite frequently missing. Lev 20.6 talks about the *n*. as the person who turns to the spirits of the dead, and 22.4 about an unclean person. In Lev. 23.30 we read: 'Every *n*. who does any work on this same day, that *n*. I will destroy from his people.' In this general sense *n*. means the single person, the individual as distinct from the ethnic unit; cf. also Lev 19.8; 22.3; Num. 13; and frequently elsewhere. It is not by chance that the Israelite would have seen *n*.—as the throat which by eating and breathing satisfies the vital needs of every individual—as being simply the appropriate term for the individual person as well....

It is this possibility of using n. that first shows us that the phrase *nepeš ḥayya* contains no superfluous epithet. This is what the Priestly document calls aquatic creatures (Gen. 1.20f.; also Lev. 11.10, 46; Ezek. 47:9), land animals (1.24), animals in general (Gen, 9.10, 12, 15) and men and animals together (Gen. 9.16), as living creatures. (According to Gen 1.30 the *n. ḥayya* is 'in' the animals, so that here we ought to think of the 'breath of life'.)

In the Yahwist's account of the creation (Gen. 2.7) we saw man expressly defined as *n. ḥayya*; he is so not simply on the basis of his creation out of the dust of the earth; he only becomes so because the God Yahweh breathes the breath of life into his nostrils. It is only the breath produced by the Creator that makes him a living *n.*, which is to say, therefore, a living being, a living person, a living individual. It is under this aspect, then, that man is here more closely defined. According to the tendency of the statements in Gen. 2.7, *n. ḥayya* introduces no *differentia specifica* for animal life; then the subsequent definition in 2.19 of animal life as being *n. ḥayya* as well would hardly be possible. But at the same time man is, through God's endowment with the breath of life, distinguished as living individual from the *n. met*, as a lifeless structure or corpse.

7 Pronouns

If in the contexts mentioned *n.* without any additional epithet simply means the individual person, it can easily come about that *n.* now merely the place of the personal or reflexive pronoun. The transitions are fluid. The modern reader will be inclined to see the pronominal character as being already present even in places where for the ancients the nominal content was still clearly to be heard. Consequently, even according to today's interpretation, instances of the pronominal meaning vary between 123 and 223. Here too it seems to me less important to draw an exact borderline than to observe the particular character of the synthetic-stereometric way of thinking, which permits different nuances of meaning in hand to a great extent.

Questions

1   Of the different meanings of *nepeš* that Wolff treats here, which surprises you the most? Why?

2   Do you think that there is an underlying common meaning that ties all these categories together?

3   If Wolff is right that *nepeš* rarely means "soul" in the Old Testament, what implications might that have for the theological anthropology of the Old Testament?

4   Assuming that the New Testament authors were well-versed in the Old Testament and its perspective on human persons, how might Wolff's argument impact the way we understand NT terms like *psyche*?

TEXT 5: WOLFHART PANNENBERG, *SYSTEMATIC THEOLOGY*[5]

One of the most influential theologians of the twentieth century, Wolfhart Pannenberg (1928–2014), a German Protestant theologian at the University of Munich, wrote extensively on theological anthropology. Though his most important works on the subject were *What Is Man?* (1970) and *Anthropology in Theological Perspective* (1985), he also dealt with issues relevant to understanding the human person in many of his other works including *Jesus: God and Man* (1968), *Faith and Reality* (1977), and his three-volume *Systematic Theology* (1988–1994), from which we have drawn the reading for this section.

This reading offers an excellent example of a theologian attempting to navigate the tension between two views of the human person deemed equally unacceptable: substance dualism and reductive physicalism. Although Pannenberg is well aware that substance dualism has been the preferred option for Christian theologians throughout history, he offers several reasons for thinking that we can no longer sustain this dualistic view of the human person in the modern world. At the same time, though, he also rejects any reductionistic account of humanity, one that presents us as nothing more than the sum of our material parts. For Pannenberg, the truth of human constitution lies between these two extremes.

Any interpretation of human reality must take into account the fact that we live and lead our lives consciously. One may try, as in radical behaviorism, to reduce all conscious experience to outwardly observable conduct and try to explain it as an epiphenomenon of brain functions. One may also view it as the expression of a soul that is different in principle from the body. At all events the fact of consciousness is a basic one in human life for which any anthropology must find a suitable interpretation. At the same time no one can deny that we know conscious and self-conscious life only as bodily life. Modern science also argues that bodily functions condition all psychological experience. This is true even of self-consciousness. Yet this fact has not always been evident to us. Many earlier cultures gave the self-conscious human soul a greater measure of independence vis-à-vis the body than our modern knowledge of the close mutual interrelations of physical and psychological occurrence will permit.

In the history of modern thought, advances in nuanced knowledge of these interrelations have robbed of their credibility the traditional ideas of the soul as a substance that is distinct from the body and that is detached from it in death. When the life of the soul is conditioned in every detail by bodily organs and processes, how can it be detached from the body and survive without it? Prevailing trends in modern anthropology see the soul and body as constitutive elements of the unity of human life that belong together and cannot be reduced to one another. The soul and

---

[5]Wolfhart Pannenberg, *Systematic Theology*, trans. Geoffrey W. Bromiley (Grand Rapids: Eerdmans, 1991), 2.181–201.

consciousness are deeply rooted in our corporeality. Conversely, the body is not a corpse. It is an ensouled body in all its expressions in life.

We may view this modern understanding as in line with the intentions of the earliest Christian anthropology. Over against Platonism, which was becoming the dominant philosophy of late antiquity by the middle of the 2nd century, the early fathers defended our psychosomatic unity as a basic principle of Christian anthropology. They did, of course, accept the view of the soul as an independent entity, which they corrected only to the extent of regarding both soul and body as partial principles of human reality, so that only the two together constitute the one human person. In spite of this emphasis on psychosomatic unity, however, the dualism of soul and body invaded Christian anthropology. This process illustrates the acceptance by early Christian thinking of ideas that the Hellenistic culture of the age took for granted; it is not an interpretation that has any essential place in Christian anthropology.

Tertullian already was referring to body and soul as two separate if related substances (De an. 27.1f. [CChrSL, 2, 1954, 822f.]). Like Tatian before him, he understood their relation along Stoic lines. The soul is the breath of the body, which manifests itself in the body (cf. Gerc 2:7). Like Irenaeus (Adv. haer. 2.34), Tertullian also regarded the soul as immortal (De an. 22.2 [CChrSL, 2, 814]) in contrast to Tatian's acceptance of its mortality (Ad Graec. 13.1). In support of this view Irenaeus appealed to the parable of Dives and Lazarus (Luke 16:19–31), whose fates after death presuppose their souls' immortality.

In early Christian theologians the interrelation of body and soul in the unity of the person received emphasis especially in apologetic arguments for the Christian hope of resurrection. Athenagoras claimed that the Creator purposed eternal life for the whole person. Hence a resurrection of the body is necessary, for the soul alone is not the whole person (De res. 15). With its doctrine of psychosomatic unity Christian theology at many points had to oppose Platonism, which had a very similar doctrine of God. First, except in Gnostic trends, it could not follow the Orphic teaching that Plato adopted, which viewed the body as the prison or grave of the soul (Gorg. 493a; Crat. 400b–c) and death as the liberation of the soul (Phaed. 64e; Gorg. 524b). In opposition Christian doctrine argued that the body as well as the soul is God's good creation and that the union of the two expresses his creative will.

Second, the soul is not divine, as in Plato (Rep. 611e). Rather, it is part of our created human nature. Already in Justin's Dialogue with Trypho the old man on the shore at Ephesus was stressing that the soul is created and therefore that it is corruptible like everything except God (Dial. 5). Although it is the vital principle of the body, it neither lives nor moves of itself (Dial. 6), as against Plato's view (Phaed. 245e). Later Christian theology certainly took over the doctrine of the soul's immortality but made it dependent on the will of the Creator and thus rejected its supposed inherent divinity. For the soul to attain to divine likeness, and therewith to participate in the immortal life of God, it needed gracious illuminating and elevating by the divine Spirit.

A third difference between Christian and Platonic anthropology was closely related to the first two. Christians rejected the preexistence of souls and the connected Platonic doctrine of their transmigration and reincorporation (cf. Phaed. 76e–77d, also 80c ff.). Irenaeus expressly opposed Plato on this issue, contesting both memory of life before birth and the related preexistence of the soul (*Adv. haer.* 2.33.2 and 5). Origen, however, took over the idea of preexistence; along the lines of Plato (*Phaed.* 248c–d) he understood the linking of souls to bodies as a consequence of earlier defects (*De princ.* 2.9.6f.; 1.7.4f.). But Origen soon ran into opposition, and in the 6th century the church condemned him for this view. In contrast, the church's own teaching maintained that the soul is created with the body. Two variations of this position are Tertullian's traducianism, which teaches that the individual soul is created with the body through conception, and creationism, which argues that each soul is directly created by God. Clement of Alexandria paved the way for the latter view, and Lactantius upheld it more decisively, while to the very end Augustine remained undecided on the question.

Though correcting Hellenistic and especially Platonic views, patristic anthropology did not attain fully to the biblical idea of psychosomatic unity, for it was limited by its model of a linking of two substances. Of all the philosophical positions held in antiquity, only the Aristotelian approach could lead to the right conclusion. This took place with the Christian Aristotelianism of High Scholasticism, when Aquinas advanced the thesis that the soul is the essential form of the body, a position that the Council of Vienna (1312) affirmed to be the church's teaching....On this view, the soul is not just a partial principle but that which makes us human in our bodily reality. Conversely, the body is the concrete form in which our humanity, the soul, finds appropriate expression.

For all the closeness to the biblical view of our bodily reality, there is still a shift of accent in Aquinas. It is not so much that he interprets the totality of this reality in terms of the soul. The second creation story could use "living soul" (*nephesh hayya*) for this reality (Gen. 2:7). The real difference lies in the understanding of the soul, and especially its spiritual or intellectual character (*anima intellectiva*). The biblical account certainly relates the soul to spirit, but in a very different sense. In Gen. 2:7 the soul is not merely the vital principle of the body but the ensouled body itself, the living being as a whole. Hence it does not have the autonomy expressed by the Aristotelian-Thomistic concept of substance. The description of Adam as *nephesh hayya* represents him as needy and therefore desirous; his life has the form of need and desire. The basic meaning of *nephesh* as throat, gullet, or larynx has in view the dry throat or hungry gullet. "Like cold water to a thirsty *nephesh*, so is good news from a far country" (Prov. 25:25). "A sated *nephesh* loathes honey, but to one who is hungry, everything bitter is sweet" (27:7). A human being as *nephesh* is a being of desires oriented to things that might meet the desires, and one that is searching for them. Hence an ensouled body does not live of itself but by the Spirit of God who breathes life into it.

In many ways the description of life as need and desire corresponds to the teleological description of living creatures in Aristotelian philosophy. Yet we must not link it to the idea of an organic development of living things in the sense of the Aristotelian concept of entelechy. A point of contact with the Christian Aristotelianism of Aquinas is that God alone can satisfy the desire for life that constitutes the life of the soul (Ps. 107:9; cf. 42:1f.). From the biblical standpoint to desire God is of the very nature of creaturely life as such, transcendent and unattainable though the divine reality may be to living creatures unless it addresses them itself with creative power.

In the biblical sense "spirit" does not mean intellect but vital creative force. Its nature is that of the wind. This is the obvious point of Gen. 2:7. God blows into Adam the breath of life, and this gives life to what he has formed (Job 33:4). "Only the Creator's breathing makes him . . . a living being, a living person, a living individual."[6] The wind of the Spirit or the breath of God is something that the creature always needs. It does not control the blowing of this wind. If the wind stops, death follows. If God "should take back his spirit to himself, and gather to himself his breath, all flesh would perish together, and man would return to dust" (Job 34:14f.). This does in fact happen when we die. "The dust returns to the earth as it was, and the spirit [*ruah*] returns to God who gave it" (Eccl. 12:7).

The texts just quoted show that the breath of life (*nishmat hayyim*) to which Gen. 2:7 refers cannot be separated from the Spirit (*ruah*). The two terms describe the same reality (cf. Gen. 6:17). The mortality of human life results from the fact that the Spirit of God is not always at work in it (Gen. 6:3). As "flesh," we are perishable like all other living creatures. Conversely, as long as human life lasts, it is due to the continued activity of the breath of life that comes from the Spirit of God.

The working of the Spirit in living creatures does not mean that he is a constituent part of the creature. Rather, it means that creaturely life has an eccentric character, that it is referred to the divine power of the Spirit that works upon it. Living creatures have the breath of life in them, but it is not at their disposal. God is always the Lord of creaturely life....

There is, of course, a group of OT sayings that depicts the special measure of the divine Spirit in some people as a charisma conferred upon them and as having some degree of independence vis-à-vis the transcendence of the Spirit of God. This independence is particularly noticeable in the case of what we might call a negative charisma, e.g., the evil *ruah* sent by God to King Saul (1 Sam. 16:14; cf. 1 Kgs. 22:20ff.; Isa. 19:14). In a broader generalization the Spirit that works for a limited time in us might also be called "our" spirit. But nowhere does the OT make any basic distinction between the divine *ruah* and the independent creaturely *ruah* as an essential constituent of living things. It was Hellenism that first brought into Jewish thinking the idea of vital processes as functions of essential constituents of human beings and their souls. The pneuma that works in us could then be regarded either as an essential creaturely element or as an essential divine part of the creaturely soul.

We find the first of these views in rabbinic writings as well as in the apostle Paul. Paul could describe human beings comprehensively as spirit, soul, and body (1 Thess. 5:23) and contrast the divine Spirit with the human spirit (Rom. 8:16ff.), even setting the two in opposition (1 Cor. 2:10f.). Did he see in the latter a divinely given pneuma that is finally alien to us? Did he make his statements on the self-evident but unexpressed presupposition that the pneuma at work in creatures derives totally from the Creator Spirit of God? If so, we would expect this presupposition to be stated at least in connection with the appeal to Gen. 2:7 in 1 Cor. 15:45. But that is not the case. Paul did not say that the living soul was breathed into the first Adam by the Spirit of God. He mentioned the life-giving Spirit (*pneuma zōopoioun*), not at the

---

[6]H. W. Wolff, *Anthropology of the OT* (Philadelphia, 1974), 22.

creation of the first man, but as a distinctive feature of the eschatological man. But how is it that the natural man, who is after the manner of the first Adam, can be or have pneuma (1 Cor. 2:11) if he was created only as a living soul without the Spirit, the Spirit being reserved for the eschatological man? At this point we obviously need an interpretation that goes beyond the express statements of the apostle. Only thus can we reconstruct their material unity.

We can hardly seek this material unity in Paul's use of the term "spirit" along the lines of the second interpretation above, namely, the idea that the spirit is an essential part of human beings or human souls. This was the understanding of Gen. 2:7 that Hellenistic Judaism developed, seeing in the inbreathing of the breath of life into Adam an imparting of the divine Spirit. Typical of this line of interpretation is the linking of the imparting of the Spirit to the knowledge of God. We find this in the Qumran texts. Behind it lies the understanding of wisdom as a charisma that the Spirit of God imparts to us. The number of years does not impart wisdom. "The Spirit enlightens men, the breath of the Almighty makes them understand" (Job 32:8; cf. Deut. 34:9). The Wisdom of Solomon even equates wisdom with the Pneuma. Hence humans having received the breath of life, ought to know God instead of worshiping idols (Wis. 15:11). Linking Spirit and wisdom according to a Hellenizing interpretation suggests that reason should be viewed as the divine Pneuma that is breathed into us at creation. Philo either made or came close to this momentous linking.

The interpreting of Gen. 2:7 as an imparting of reason by the Creator was the basis of equating the human spirit and reason, which led Christian theology to see in the spirit-soul a higher part of our human constitution. But this theology rejected the idea that the spirit-soul is divine. Christian Gnosticism might have played an important role in this regard.

For Gnostics the spirit imparted at creation (Gen. 2:7) could not be the true divine Pneuma because they ascribed creation to the demiurge and not to the Redeemer God. Only unnoticed by the demiurge could a true divine Spirit have also slipped in. Clement of Alexandria then distinguished between the breath of life in Gen. 2:7 and the imparting of the divine Spirit, viewing the former, like Philo, as an inbreathing of *nous* and reserving the latter for redemption. Similarly Tertullian in his work on the soul stressed against Hermogenes the origin of the soul in the breath of God (Gen. 2:7) but distinguishes between Spirit (*spiritus*) and breath (*flatus*) as between cause and effect, equating breath with the soul. Augustine took much the same view (*Civ. Dei* 13.24.2ff.). In Origen, however, Gen. 2:7 was no longer normative for anthropology because Origen taught the preexistence of souls. He thus based our spiritual nature on our creation in the divine rational image according to Gen. 1:26. Later theology followed the same line of argument (e.g., Gregory of Nyssa), although rejecting preexistence.

Under the influence of Augustine, Latin Scholasticism rejected the understanding of Gen. 2:7 along the lines of an imparting of the divine Spirit (Aquinas *ST* 1.91.4 ad 3) on the ground that the apostle differentiated the result of this inbreathing by the Creator (a living soul) from the life of the new Adam that is permeated by the Spirit (1 Cor. 15:45; cf. Augustine *Civ. Dei* 13.24.4 n. 6). It needed a return to the Hebrew wording and the uninhibited exegesis of Luther to find the Spirit of God again in the breathing in of the breath of life in Gen. 2:7, though still, of course, with a distinction between this work in creation and the eschatological work in the new

Adam. Even Luther failed to see, however, that the life-giving work of the divine Spirit in creation extends to all living things.

The profound difference between the patristic idea of a human spirit-soul and the biblical view of the relation between soul and spirit may be seen in the fact that neither the description of Adam as a living soul in Gen. 2:7 nor the view that life is a work of the divine breath of life gives humans any uniqueness as compared with other living creatures. Animals, too, rank as *nephesh hayya* (Gen. 2:19) and have the spirit of life in them (1:20; cf. 6:17; 7:22). In this regard humans simply share in what distinguishes all living things from the rest of creation. According to the first creation story, it is the divine likeness and the associated dominion over all other earthly creatures that distinguishes humans from animals. We find a similar view in Ps. 8:6ff. Similarly, in the second story the man has the privilege of being allowed to name the animals (Gen. 2:19). In view here is the distinctive faculty of speech and the related knowledge. Elsewhere, too, the OT finds a place for the significance of knowing and planning reason in human life, even though it is located in the heart and not the head.

But when it is a matter of the advantage of humans over all other creatures, the emphasis is not on intellectual ability but on the destiny of fellowship with God and the position of rule associated with closeness to God. Materially, of course, the latter is connected, as we see it, to the work of reason. But there can be no question of an autonomy of reason. Like all other expressions of human life, the work of reason is referred to the life-giving working of the divine Spirit. Even the Wisdom literature, which regards understanding as a particularly valuable gift of the Spirit (cf. Job 32:8; 33:4; Prov. 2:6; also the Wisdom of Solomon), does not equate this with our intellectual capacity but sees in it a gift that is not native to us. The biblical data thus differentiate between spirit and reason. But they give us little help in working out the distinction. Though what they say about the human heart gives evidence of its ability to know and judge, clarification of these points was to a much higher degree a concern of Greek thinking. Rightly, then, patristic theology gave a bigger place in their anthropology to Greek ideas of nous and its relevance. In so doing they linked the faculty of knowledge to the concept of the specifically human soul. They found a basis for this in the use of the term "reason" in Paul (Rom. 7:23; cf. 1:20; 12:2, etc.).

The Johannine doctrine of the Logos also suggested that along the lines of Greek ideas of the relation between *logos* and *nous*, they might view human reason as a sharing in the *logos* that comes to fulfillment in one man with the incarnation of the Logos. In this light it seemed to be plausible to see in the divine likeness an expression of the sharing of the *nous* in the Logos. What they had to avoid, however, was identifying reason and spirit. The life-giving working of the divine Spirit in us is not the same as our reason. Like all other living functions, our reason, too, needs to be actualized by the Creator Spirit of God. This fact does not rule out, however, a natural disposition of reason for such actualization nor a leading role for it, as the dominant function of the human soul, in the relation of the whole person to the Spirit.

Materially, though with no link to Gen. 2:7 or distinction between spirit and reason, we find the first of these two thoughts expressed in Augustine's doctrine that reason has an aptitude for enlightenment by the divine light of truth. On the basis of Plato's view of enlightenment Augustine developed here a conception analogous in many respects to what we find in the Bible (cf. John 1:9). As a theological interpretation of human reason, it was much superior to the view of knowledge in Christian Aristotelianism worked out by Latin High Scholasticism. On that view reason is an independent entity, though secondarily referred to God as its supernatural goal. Albert the Great and Aquinas, however, viewed the active intellect, which alone is immortal according to Aristotle, as part of the human soul and not as a superhuman power working on the soul from without. They thus laid the foundation for an understanding along Christian lines of our subjective freedom in acts of knowing, in contrast to the views of knowledge in antiquity, which regarded it as in some way the reception of a given truth of things.

Later, in Nicholas of Cusa, even sharper emphasis fell on the activity of reason in thinking knowledge as spontaneous productivity reflecting the creative freedom of the divine Spirit. Cusa's developed conception of a freedom of rational knowledge that approximates to the thoughts of the Creator with its conjectures on the reality of created things offered the model of an understanding that merely applied given, a priori forms of thought to the material of the senses. The argument has in its favor that it better took into account the freedom and historicity of rational activity. In the process the imagination became the true creative principle in intellectual activity. The understanding simply provided it with logical rules. But the activity of the imagination rested on a higher form of receptivity, not just on receptivity to sense impressions, nor on their reproduction by the memory in a free recombining of their contents, but on an openness that relates the infinite ground of subjectivity to finite data of the consciousness. This line of thinking could see itself as true to the theological intentions of Augustine's doctrine of enlightenment.

The crucial role of the life of the imagination, which unites receptivity and freedom, in the activity of reason and understanding, helps to elucidate the dependence of reason on the working of the Spirit as the basis of our subjective freedom. For a more precise understanding, however, it is necessary to attain some clarity on the relation of the Spirit to the general functions of the consciousness.

The basic relation of the consciousness to the infinite basis of life may well lie in the sense of life that in adult experience grasps the distinction between the self and the world, while in the symbiotic sphere of early childhood no clear distinction is yet made between the objective and the subjective aspects of the relation to the world. Feelings of pleasure and pain very early provide a self-reference, of course, which serves as a starting point for the later development of a sense of the self as distinct from an awareness of the world. This self-acquaintance, which is implicitly given in feeling, is something that we share with animal life and perhaps with all living things, for all living things, as autocatalysts, are processes of self-organization that are characterized as such by a relation to the totality of their own existence. To form an explicit self-consciousness, however, a link seems to be needed to a nonimpulsive objectivity of object-consciousness that is typical of humans and may be seen in children at play. Being with others as others makes possible the distinction and relation of different objects and also their distinction from one's own body as signified by the proper name and the use of "I," along with the placing of this body in the world of objects.

The being with others as others mediated by perception awareness thus seems to include, along with the distinction of objects from one another and from the I of one's own body, a field of consciousness in which the basic relation of I and world takes on its contours. The feeling for life as an expression of the presence of spirit with that of the indefinite totality of life that precedes and overarches the subject-object distinction underlies, then, the formation of the field of consciousness within which a survey of different contents is possible. In the experience of encounter with others, this world of consciousness is ascribed to one's own ego and is thus relativized as the world of this ego as distinct from others. The I-relativity of the world of consciousness and its difference from the real world are not constitutive of the consciousness of objects as such but become thematic only in the light of the different worldviews bound up with intersubjectivity. The presence of the infinite ground of being, the Spirit, which declares itself in the feeling for life, transcends, however, the difference of subjects; nor is this true only of one's own I, since awareness of this I is itself a product of the differentiating of the unity of the feeling for life in the process of experience.

Only in the field of intersubjectivity and in consequence of the awareness of the I-relativity of one's own self-consciousness can a distinction be made between body and soul. Over against the soul as the inner world of the consciousness stands the body, which, like the things of the world and in distinction from the inner world of my consciousness, is there for others as well as myself. It is tempting to regard the inner world of the consciousness as the true I in distinction from the body. But this is unduly to restrict the concept of the soul as well as that of the ego. In pointing to the speaker, the word "I" always indicates the physical individuality of the speaker. If we are to view the living body as ensouled inasmuch as it is living, then the term "soul" must cover more than the inner world of the consciousness. It must include also the unconscious, which is related to one's own corporeality and its history. It is possible here to relate the idea of the soul that is oriented to experience of an inner world of consciousness with the concept of the soul as the vital principle of the body. Yet the impression that the soul confronts the body as something independent might well derive from treating the inner world of consciousness as independently related to the I.

The inner world of consciousness is ascribed to the I as its own. In the tradition of Kantian transcendental philosophy the I (as in "I think") even rates as the basis of its unity, the unity of experience. But is this really true? Does not the world of the consciousness in some sense have its unity in itself, in its contents and its basic thoughts? Is not the consciousness of the I that thinks the thoughts actually the ground of the conscious experience of these contents and thus responsible for the way in which their apprehension deviates from their objective truth? In fact differentiation always implies a unity of that which is differentiated. This is not the external addition of the consciousness in its synthetic function. Naturally we do not self-evidently become aware of this unity. As the young Hegel would put it, we need perception, or specific perceptions. From the infinity of feeling these come through the imagination, which according to Fichte hovers between that infinity and the finite data that the consciousness distinguishes. But in the process, as Hegel emphasized, the perceptions generated by the imagination need disciplining by the differentiating work of reflection. Only thus do they take on content as a grasping of the unity of what is differentiated.

Since the exact determining of what is distinct itself depends on an awareness of the unity, the perceptions of the imagination must relate both to the different members in their particularity and to the unity that binds them together for all their distinctiveness. The unity is thus something other than the distinction. Grasping the unity in distinction is a function of the ability to keep one's distance in an awareness of otherness. The unity of what is distinct is thus a different thing from the consciousness. It is not owed to the unity of the ego. This unity, as the basis of all experience that underlies the unity of its contents subjectively and gives them unity in the course of life, is correlative to the objective unity of the "concept" that comprehends in its unity what is objectively distinct. There is thus formed an awareness of the unity of all that which is specific and distinct, of the "world" as the epitome of everything finite and limited, in contrast to which we can think of the infinite as something distinct from it. A further step in reflection then leads us to the insight that we can distinguish the infinite from the finite (and thus from every "something" as opposed to something else) only on the condition that it is not just something other than the finite, in which case it would itself be finite, but that it also comprehends everything finite. This thought of the infinite One gives expression to that which is always present to the consciousness as the indefinite Infinite. It thus forms the mental space in which there can be distance from the other and definition of its otherness and relationship, of the space that is opened thereby for the consciousness.

We can hardly regard the authority of the ego as a precondition of every form of objective awareness. It is developed in the process of objective experience and by distinction from everything else. In individual experience the social nexus precedes the use of the term "I," though an implicit self-reference such as we have in the feeling for life is a condition of learning to use this word. With the use of the word the self-reference becomes an explicit theme for the individual, and secondarily the I becomes the soil of all the contents of the consciousness. But first the multiplicity of the world and the living reality of the individual in distinction therefrom are opened up to the consciousness by the infinity of the feeling for life that underlies the difference of subject and object in the consciousness and thus transcends them in every situation in life. In this respect we should perhaps redefine the relation between spirit and consciousness if the feeling for life expresses the living presence of the Creator Spirit in living creatures. Not the I but the divine Spirit is the ultimate basis for the interrelatedness of that which is distinct in the consciousness, of the interrelatedness also of the I and the things of the world, especially similar living creatures.

Awareness of the infinite as such in its distinction from the finite rests on the fact that we are always "ecstatic" in relation to the other - always apart from the other. We can know the other as such, not merely as our own correlate. We thus learn to distinguish each from the other in its own particularity. Finally, relative to the whole sphere of the finite that is defined and limited by this difference from the other, we form the thought of the infinite. In grasping the finite there is always a nonthematic sense of the infinite as that which is other than the finite. We are aware of the infinite in the religious awareness of a divine power at work in every finite phenomenon. In all knowledge of the world we always see God's eternal power and deity in his works (Rom. 1:20), which is true even though we do not glorify God as God or give him thanks but become foolish and irrational in our religious ideas (v. 21). When this happens we do not distinguish the infinite reality of God (or do so only inadequately) from the medium of creaturely things in whose finitude it may be seen, nor are we aware of our own finitude as beings that, along with the whole world of finite phenomena, owe their existence totally to the one infinite God.

Nevertheless, in a rational distinction of each finite thing from every other, and of all finite things, including ourselves, from the infinite, the divine Logos is at work, who creates and rules all creaturely existence in its individuality. In spite of all the perversion due to sin, of which we must speak later, human intelligence in its perception of the otherness of the other participates in the self-distinction of the eternal Son from the Father by which he is not merely united to the Father but is also the principle of all creaturely existence in its individuality. Human reason, of course, can generate only thoughts and not directly the reality of finite things. But these thoughts do not simply represent finite objects in their distinction from one another. They can also form a basis for the constructs of human technology.

As the Son, in his self-distinction from the Father, is united with him by the Spirit in the unity of the divine life, and as, in his creative activity, he unites what is distinct by the power of the Spirit, so the differentiating activity of human reason needs the Spirit who enables it, by mediating the imagination, to name each thing in its particularity, and in all the distinction to be aware of the unity that holds together what is different. In the process human reason is not of itself filled with the Spirit. In its creatureliness it needs, like every other vital function, to be quickened by the living power of the Spirit if it is to be active, and it also needs the inspiration that lifts it above its own finitude and that in all its limitation makes it aware of the presence of truth and totality in the individual.

The biblical view of the Spirit of God as the creative principle of everything living insofar as it has soul and has life in itself may also be explained in terms of the varied nature of the consciousness and the activity of reason, i.e., those dimensions of the soul that attracted the special attention of Greek philosophy and still form a central sphere of the life of the soul according to our modern understanding. In this respect the view of the soul as the vital principle of the body forces us to inquire into the function of the consciousness for life in general. We best approach this question by recalling the relation of all the phenomena of life to their environment. Environmental reality becomes a theme for living creatures in their perceptive consciousness. By the perception that internalizes what is around us, life also becomes "ecstatic"— that which stands outside of us. The more the life of consciousness develops, the more we move outward in our consciousness, and the more the world around us moves inward and becomes present in us. The same applies to social relations, for our knowing the human self-consciousness forms the highest stage of the relation of outwardness and inwardness. The objectivity of our relation to objects is the condition on which, in terms of the world, we can become objective to ourselves as members of it.

The "ecstasy" of consciousness—that it "stands outside"—means enhanced and more inward life and therefore more intense participation in the Spirit, the creative origin of all life. This participation does not have to involve being snatched out of the world, as in the extreme case of a sense of the antithesis of the infinite to everything finite. Instead, it expands the soul by experience of the world, which the Spirit creatively permeates, and especially by the experience of human fellowship in face of the infinite ground of the world. Only in others do we meet a life that in its feeling for life is permeated in some way by the infinite ground of the world and the associated promise of the totality of life that is common to each and to all. The presence of this dimension characterizes all encounter with others, even though it is in the negative mode of a cramping or corrupting of their spiritual potential. It runs through all social relations, beginning with those of the family. Not least of all it gives personal depth to the encounter of the sexes.

Without the works of the divine Spirit in us there could be no personality in the deeper sense of the term. For personality has to do with the manifestation of the truth and totality of individual life in the moment of its existence. We are not persons simply because we have self-consciousness and can distinguish and maintain our own ego apart from others. We do not cease to be persons where we no longer have this identity in the self-consciousness, nor are we without personality where it is not present. Personality is grounded in the destiny that transcends our empirical reality. It is primarily experienced in the other, the Thou, as the secret of an inwardness that goes beyond all that we perceive outwardly of the other, so that this other meets us as a being that is active not merely of itself but in terms of a ground of existence that we cannot finally see externally.

Although psychological knowledge explains much in the conduct of the other, psychology cannot lay hold of a final origin of its freedom. That which meets me in this way touches me as personal reality. Part of this is that a totality of existence that I cannot control meets me through that which is externally present to the senses, and does so in such a way that I am also claimed with my own life. We can understand this only on the premise that the ground of my own existence meets me in the person of the other. Encounter with the other can thus stimulate inner awareness of my own personality, and it can also be an occasion for critical independence vis-à-vis all intersubjective dependencies.

Although all human life is personal in its individual concretions, it took a long time before the concept of person became a theme of basic anthropological reflection. In the history of Western culture this fact was perhaps related to the further fact that only under the impact of biblical faith was the individual as such—each individual—viewed as a target of the divine address. Materially this was a consequence of the divine likeness. In expression of it the faith of Israel, in virtue of the divine likeness, declared individual life to be sacrosanct (Gen. 9:6). Yet this did not yet imply that each individual human life in its uniqueness has infinite worth for God. The decisive breakthrough to this insight came with the message of Jesus that God reaches out to each of his creatures with eternal love, which we see pointedly in his love for those who have gone astray and are lost. Only in Christian thinking does this characterization of human life then come into relation to the concept of person. The historical starting point for this is christology, with its insistence on the personal unity of Jesus with the divine Logos.

Investigation of the pre-Christian use of *prosopon* in Greek and *persona* in Latin has shown that the concept of personality was linked to the role that the individual embodied on the stage or in social life. As a generalized term for the individual in the rhetorical and legal language of late antiquity, the word had no real content, since no regard was had to the decisive content supplied by social roles. The same applies to the famous definition of Boethius that the person is a rational individual. This simply added to the general definition of a human being as a rational animal, or even more generally as a rational nature, an abstract definition of individuality according to which the concept of person is a matter of indifference compared to all other differences.

The christological use, however, found in "person" a term for the relation to God that was constitutive for the human existence of Jesus. In more general anthropological application this meant that each individual is a person in virtue of the special relation to God, either (like Jesus) in openness to fellowship with him, or in being closed to this destiny. Trinitarian discussion of the term also had an anthropological impact as "person" came to denote what was specific to Father, Son, and Spirit in their mutual relations. If the personhood of Jesus is that of the eternal Son in relation to the Father, all individuals are persons in virtue of the relation to God, which is the basis of their whole existence or in emancipation from this relation, for even in turning from God they are held to their destiny of fellowship with God, though now in the mode of alienation of a life that misses its destiny.

We are all persons in our psychosomatic totality as this finds manifestation at each moment of our existence. Totality and personhood are linked, for as we understand it today, "person" means not an exchangeable role but the human self. Selfhood, however, means identity in all individual life. This is true even over a stretch of time, hence selfhood never achieves definitive manifestation in life. It does not yet appear who we truly are, but we exist now as persons. This is possible only in anticipation of the truth of our existence, which is mediated to us now through the Spirit by means of our feeling for life.

We can attain to the totality of our own lives, notwithstanding its fragmentary form at each moment, only in the relation to our Creator. But we achieve our particularity in our encounter with others. Both types of relation are in their own ways constitutive for our individual personhood. We are all persons in our necessary particularity as husbands and wives; fathers, mothers, and children; friends and foes; teachers and students; commanding and obeying; in work, renunciation, and pleasure. Yet personhood transcends all the singularities and changes of circumstances because it finally draws upon the relation to God as the source of its integrity. Thus in every detailed concretion it can coincide with being human as such, so that encounter with others can be a summons to be a person who accepts the particularity of individual existence. The special circumstances of life and relations to others are no longer, then, external roles that we may exchange at will. In them, however, the definitiveness of the selfhood that is grounded by God takes on its impress in all its individuality.

In the person, then, the integration of the individual moments of life results in an identity of authentic selfhood. In this process the rational consciousness takes the lead, for by recollection and expectation it can hold the moments of life together in the present and reflect on their compatibility. The philosophical and theological tradition discussed the leadership role of the rational consciousness from the standpoint of the governing of the body by the soul. Like all forms of rule, this can take the perverted form of oppression—in this case the oppression of the body and its needs by a tyrannical "I." But this is no argument against the need for this rule as the integration of otherwise opposing elements in life. Without self-rule there can be no unity or integrity of life. Personal unity of life is not, however, the product of self-discipline. We need the unity of selfhood to constitute the identity of an ongoing and constant ego, which for its part can manifest itself as the subject of acts. All action presupposes the identity of those who act, at least to the extent that this identity is needed to bridge the difference in time between the planning and the execution of an act. The longer the period of action, the more constant the identity must be if the goal is to be reached. Those who make a promise that they can only keep many years later, or over a whole life, have to retain their identity if they are to meet the promise. Actions owe their unity to the time-bridging identity of their subjects. Hence the identity must already be constituted if the action is to take place. At the same time, the identity of the person is only in the process of coming to be during our whole life-history, which demands that we evaluate soberly the place of the concept of action. For all our inclination to control our own lives and those of others by action, we do not have here a basic anthropological concept. The possibilities of action and achievement are limited in many ways. Biblical wisdom often tells us how much the success of our plans depends on the overruling of divine providence. The same is still fundamentally true for us today, even though modern science and technology have extended the range of human activity. The unity and integrity of human life are constituted in another sphere that precedes all action.

Questions

1 What is the evidential basis Pannenberg gives for denying "traditional ideas" of the soul's relationship to the body? How would you assess his arguments?

2 What traditional difference between humanity and the rest of living creation does Pannenberg deny? What does he see as the difference and why?

3 How would you characterize Pannenberg's understanding of the relationship between the body and the soul? Can the soul survive separation from the body? What implications might this have for the account one gives of Christ's incarnation, death, and resurrection?

4 How does Pannenberg characterize the traditional account of the unity of subjective experience? What is his alternative account?

5 What are the conditions of personhood according to Pannenberg's anthropology? What implications might this have for understanding who/what counts as human?

TEXT 6: NANCEY C. MURPHY, "NONREDUCTIVE PHYSICALISM: PHILOSOPHICAL ISSUES"[7]

Nancey Murphy (b. 1951) is professor of Christian philosophy at Fuller Seminary, where she has been teaching since 1989. Although she writes on a broad range of issues relevant to Christian theology and philosophy, much of her work has focused on "nonreductive physicalism," a view of human ontology that presents the human person as wholly physical beings but without any corresponding reductionism that might eliminate or even minimize the reality and significance of the spiritual, volitional, moral, and relational aspects of human existence. Her account has been significantly influenced by modern developments in the cognitive neurosciences, which have increasingly emphasized the psychophysical nature of the human person. In this essay, Murphy addresses some of the philosophical issues involved in understanding nonreductive physicalism. Most importantly she discusses what reductionism entails and why she thinks we can reject that view and still affirm a physicalist view of human ontology. She also deals with important concerns about the nature of free will on such an account.

Physicalism and reductionism

Hierarchies

Westerners seem always to have attempted to understand the world in terms of hierarchies. For the ancient Greeks, reality was thought of as a hierarchy of *beings*.[8] A "generic" Greek view would go something like this:

divinities (including heavenly bodies)
humans
animals
plants
inanimate objects

During the modern period (beginning around 1600) a different hierarchical understanding has gradually supplanted the Greek. This is not a hierarchy of beings, but a hierarchy of *complex systems*. This hierarchy can be represented by a correlative hierarchy of the sciences that study reality in its varying levels of organization:

---

[7]Nancey Murphy, "Nonreductive Physicalism: Philosophical Issues," in Warren S. Brown, Nancey Murphy, and H. Newton Malony, eds., *Whatever Happened to the Soul? Scientific and Theological Portraits of Human Nature* (Minneapolis: Fortress, 1998), 127–48.
[8]See Arthur O. Lovejoy, *The Great Chain of Being* (Cambridge, MA: Harvard University Press, 1936).

biology
chemistry
physics

Here physics is at the bottom because it studies the most basic constituents of reality; chemistry studies these "atoms" as they relate to complex structures (molecules)[9]; biology studies a number of levels of structure, from the biochemical through the levels of organelles, cells, tissues, organs, organisms, to colonies of organisms in their environments.

A contentious issue throughout the modern period has been whether psychology and the social sciences could be added in turn to this natural-science hierarchy—psychology being the study of the *behavior* of whole organisms, the social sciences being the study of human behavior in groups.

Another contentious issue has been reductionism. Here we need to distinguish among various sorts of reductionist theses: *Methodological reductionism* is a research strategy of analyzing the thing to be studied into its parts. *Causal reductionism* is the view that the behavior of the parts of a system (ultimately, the parts studied by subatomic physics) is determinative of the behavior of all high–level entities. Thus, this is the thesis that all causation in the hierarchy is "bottom–up." If this thesis is true, it would follow that the laws pertaining to higher sciences in the hierarchy should be reducible to the laws of physics.

Another sort of reductionism is the claim that higher–level entities are "nothing but the sum of their parts." However, this thesis is ambiguous; we need names here for two distinct positions. One is the view that as one goes up the hierarchy of levels, no new kinds of metaphysical "ingredients" need to be added to get living beings from nonliving materials; no immaterial mind or soul is needed to get consciousness; no *Zeitgeist* is needed to form individuals into a society. Let us use the term *ontological reductionism* for this position. There is a stronger claim than the previous one that also sees the higher–level entities as nothing but the sum of their parts, but with the addition that only the entities at the lowest level are *really* real; higher–level entities—molecules, cells, organisms—are only composites of atoms. This thesis we here designative *reductive materialism*. It is important to stress that it is possible to hold ontological reductionism without subscribing to this thesis. Thus, one might want to say that higher–level entities, such as human beings, are real—as real as the entities that compose them—and at the same time reject all sorts of vitalism and dualism.

A variety of philosophers, biologists, and others have taken care to distinguish these latter two theses. For example, "organicists" in biology rejected both vitalism and reductive materialism. The American philosopher Roy Wood Sellars developed a new view of the entire hierarchy of the sciences that he called, variously, "emergent realism," "emergent naturalism," and "evolutionary naturalism." Sellars argued that organizations and wholes are genuinely significant; they are not mere aggregates of elementary particles. Reductive materialism, he believed, overemphasizes the "stuff"

---

[9] Of course this is an oversimplification: physics itself is now many-layered, and atoms as understood by chemists are no longer "atoms" in the philosophical sense of being the most basic constituents of matter.

in contrast to the organization. The levels Sellars countenanced were the inorganic, the organic, the mental or conscious, the social, the ethical, and the religious or spiritual.[10]

So Sellars, and a number of contemporary thinkers as well, accept ontological reductionism but vehemently reject reductive materialism. In addition, they say that while methodological reductionism has been a crucially important strategy in all the sciences it is a limited strategy and needs to be balanced by studies of how entities at one level relate to higher levels—for example, organisms to their environments. They reject causal reductionism—one has to take account of causal influences of the whole on the part, as well as of the part on the whole. This is referred to as "downward causation," "top–down causation," or whole–part causation."

Let us use the term "nonreductive physicalism" to refer to this constellation of positions: the acceptance of ontological reductionism, but the rejection of causal reductionism and reductive materialism. Applied to the specific area of studies of consciousness, it denies the existence of a nonmaterial entity, the mind (or soul) but does not deny the existence of consciousness (a position in philosophy of mind called eliminative materialism) or the significance of conscious states or other mental (note the adjectival form) phenomena. In brief, this is the view that the human nervous system, operating in concert with the rest of the body in its environment, is the seat of consciousness (and also of human spiritual or religious capacities). Consciousness and religious awareness are emergent properties and they have top–down causal influence on the body. This is the view advocated here. As mentioned above, there are a number of philosophical issues that need investigation in order to show that this position is coherent and intelligible. That is, can one consistently say that the neural system performs all of the functions once assigned to mind (and soul), and that this entails no significant loss to our understanding of human life? I believe that this general issue is best considered under the heading of the causal reductionism: is it possible to accept ontological reductionism without causal reductionism? I begin with this issue.

Defeating causal reductionism

The central question to be addressed here is, how can a physicalist account of the person *fail* to be reductive? The question of *causal* reduction seems to be the one that matters for retaining our traditional conceptions of personhood. There are several related issues. First, if mental events can be reduced to brain events, and the brain events are governed by the laws of neurology (and ultimately by the laws of physics), then in what sense can we say that humans have free will? Are not their intendings and willings simply a product of blind physical forces, and thus not their willed actions merely the product of blind forces?

---

[10]*The Philosophy of Physical Realism* (New York: Russell and Russell, 1966), first published in 1932; and *idem, Principles of Emergent Realism: The Philosophical Essays of Roy Wood Sellars*, ed. W. Preston Warren (St. Louis, Mo.: Warren H. Green, Inc., 1970).

Second, if mental events are simply the product of neurological causes, then what sense can we make of *reasons*? That is, we give reasons for judgments in all areas of our intellectual lives—moral, aesthetic, scientific, mathematical. It seems utter nonsense to say that these judgments are merely the results of the "blind forces of nature."

If free will is an illusion and the highest of human intellectual and cultural achievements can (*per impossible*) be counted as the mere outworking of the laws of physics, this is utterly devastating to our ordinary understanding of ourselves, and of course to theological accounts, as well, which depend not only on a concept of responsibility before God, but also on the justification (not merely the causation) of our theories about God and God's will. So, how to avoid this unacceptable outcome of a physicalist account of the mental realm?

Supervenience. I claim that it is only with the assistance of recent conceptual developments that physicalist accounts of the mental can avoid causal reductionism. We saw in chapter 1 that there have been a variety of strategies proposed for understanding the relation of mental events to brain events, and all run into difficulties: for dualists there is the problem of psychophysical interaction; for identity theorists there is the problem that mental events become the result of neurological causes rather than conscious reasons.

To see where the problem lies, let us begin with the vague thesis that every mental event (state, property) is *related* to some brain event. Add to this the assumption of causal connections among the neurological events, and we inevitably get a picture like the following where M_1 through M_3 represent a temporal series of mental events, and the arrows represent causal connections among the brain events:

$$M_1 \qquad M_2 \qquad M_3 \ldots$$
$$| \qquad\quad | \qquad\quad |$$
$$B_1 \quad \rightarrow \quad B_2 \quad \rightarrow \quad B_3 \ldots$$

Until recently only two relations were conceivable between mental events and brain events: identity and causation.[11] So we can make the picture more specific in one of two ways (arrows represent causal relations, ‖ represents an identity relation):

$$M_1 \qquad M_2 \qquad M_3 \ldots$$
$$\uparrow \qquad\quad \uparrow \qquad\quad \uparrow$$
$$B_1 \quad \rightarrow \quad B_2 \quad \rightarrow \quad B_3 \ldots$$

or:

$$M_1 \qquad M_2 \qquad M_3 \ldots$$
$$\| \qquad\quad \| \qquad\quad \|$$
$$B_1 \quad \rightarrow \quad B_2 \quad \rightarrow \quad B_3 \ldots$$

---

[11]Mere correlation is also a possibility, but this runs into all the problems of dualism.

In either case, if we assume causal connections at the physical level, causal reductionism seems inevitable. The mental events appear as mere epiphenomena.

In order to explain how reductionism can be avoided it is advantageous to consider the relation between consciousness and the neural system as but one instance of hierarchical ordering of complex systems because we can see analogies and borrow concepts from less problematic levels. Recall that Sellars included both the conscious and the ethical as level in the hierarchy of complex systems. In 1952, R. M. Hare introduced the term "supervenience" as a technical term to relate evaluative judgments (including ethical judgments) to descriptive judgments. Hare says:

> First, let us take that characteristic of "good" which has been called its supervenience. Suppose that we say, "St. Francis was a good man." It is logically impossible to say this and to maintain at the same time that there might have been another man *placed exactly in the same circumstances* as St. Francis, and who behaved in exactly the same way, but who differed from St. Francis in this respect only, that he was not a good man.[12]

So the higher–level property or description "good" *supervenes* on a collection of descriptions of Francis's character traits and actions. Or, to say the same thing, these character traits and actions constitute Francis's goodness.

In 1970 Donald Davidson introduced the concept of supervenience to describe the relation between mental and physical characteristics. Davidson describes the relation as follows:

> Mental characteristics are in some sense dependent, or supervenient, on physical characteristics. Such supervenience might be taken to mean that there cannot be two events alike in all physical respects but differing in some mental respect, or that an object cannot alter in some mental respect without altering in some physical respect. Dependence or supervenience of this kind does not entail reducibility through law or definition.[13]

The concept of supervenience is now widely used in philosophy of mind, but there is as yet no agreement on its proper definition. Terrence E. Horgan writes:

> The concept of supervenience, as a relation between properties, is essentially this: Properties of type A are supervenient on properties of type B if and only if two objects cannot differ with respect to their A-properties without also differing with respect to their B-properties. Properties that allegedly are supervenient on others are often called consequential properties, especially in ethics; the idea is that if

---

[12]From *The Language of Morals* (1952); quoted by Terence E. Horgan in "Supervenience," in Robert Audi, ed., *The Cambridge Dictionary of Philosophy* (Cambridge: Cambridge University Press, 1995), 778–79. My italics.
[13]*Essays on Actions and Events* (Oxford: Claredon Press, 1980), 214. Reprinted from *Experience and Theory*, ed. Lawrence Foster and J. W. Swanson (Boston: University of Massachusetts Press and Duckworth, 1970).

something instantiates a moral property, then it does so *in virtue of*, i.e., as a (non-causal) *consequence of*, instantiating some lower-level property on which the moral property supervenes.[14]

Notice that there are two distinguishable notions of supervenience in this passage. In the first sentence (substituting 'S' for 'A' for clarity, so that S-properties are *subservient* and B-properties are subvenient or *base* properties):

1   Properties of type S are supervenient on properties of type B if and only if two objects cannot differ with respect to their S-properties without also differing with respect to their B-properties.

But from the last sentence we can construct the following definition:

2   Properties of type S are supervenient on properties of type B if and only if something instantiates S-properties in virtue of (as a noncausal consequence of) its instantiating some B-properties.

These two possible definitions are not equivalent; 1 does not entail 2. The reason can be seen in Hare's original use of the term. Francis's character traits and actions (B–properties) only constitute him (or someone like him) a good person (an S–property) *under certain circumstances*. That is, it is conceivable that identical behavior in different circumstances would *not* constitute goodness. For example, we would evaluate Francis's life much differently if he had been married and the father of children.

The difference between these two accounts of supervenience is absolutely crucial. If mental properties or events are supervenient in the first sense, this ensures the reducibility of the mental to the physical and raises all the problems mentioned above. If mental events or properties are supervenient only in the second sense, then, I claim, reduction is not a necessary consequence. Thus, I offer the following definitions (which I take to be equivalent):

3   Property S is supervenient on property B if and only if something instantiates S in virtue of (as a non–causal consequence of) its instantiating B under circumstance c.

4   Property S is supervenient on property B if and only if something's being B constitutes its being S under circumstance c.

An important feature of the supervenience relation, which has long been recognized, is that supervenient properties are often *multiply realizable*. This is a term from computer science—different configurations of hardware (vacuum tubes versus circuits) can realize, constitute, the same machine considered at the functional level. So if S supervenes on B (given circumstance c), then something's being B entails its being S, but its being S does not entail its being B. For example, goodness is multiply realizable; there are many life patterns different from Francis's that also constitute one a good person. Thus, from the statement "R. M. Hare was a good

---

[14]Horgan, "Supervenience," in *The Cambridge Dictionary of Philosophy*, 778–79.

man" we cannot infer that he lived as St. Francis did. This is one respect in which supervenience relations fail to be identity relations ($S \Leftrightarrow B$) since it is not the case that S entails B ($S \Leftrightarrow B$). (Here arrows represent entailment rather than causation.)

My definition of supervenience recognizes another way in which supervenience relations fall short of identity. The fact that S supervenes on B does not means that B entails S ($B \Leftrightarrow S$) because of the dependence upon circumstances. Under c_1, $B \Leftrightarrow S$, but under c_2 it may be the case that $B \Leftrightarrow$ not $-S$. For example, under the circumstance of having a family to support, giving away all one's money may not constitute a good act.

For the purposes of getting clear about the use of these terms, we need a very simple example, one not complicated by the added perplexities associated with either the mind–brain issue or moral issues. Suppose that I have a light in my window and that I have arranged with a friend to use it as a signal to let her know if I am at home or not: on means yes; off means no. I flip the switch; one state of affairs ensues, with two levels of description.

> *supervenient*: the message is "I'm home"
> *subvenient*: the light is on.

It is important to emphasize that there is one state of affairs, two descriptions. Turning the light on *constitutes* my sending the "at home" message under the circumstances of our having made the appropriate prior arrangement.

The "at home" message is multiply realizable. We could have agreed instead that I'd leave the light off if I were home, or we could have agreed to use some other device altogether, such as leaving the window shade up or down.

We need a term to call our attention to an opposite sort of failure of the two descriptions to be identical. Not only is it the case that a *variety* of subvenient states can *realize* the *same* supervenient state (light on, shade up), but also, *again depending on circumstances*, the same subvenient state can *constitute* a variety of supervenient states. Suppose, for example, that we have agreed that the light's being on means I'm home only on Mondays, but on any other day the light's being on means I'm out. So depending on the circumstances of the day of the week, the same subvenient state constitutes either one message or the other. I suppose we could refer to this as "multiple constitutability."

It is this latter feature of the supervenience relation that I mean to highlight by emphasizing the role of *circumstances*. The variability in circumstances and their role in such cases is what makes for the difference between a supervenience relation and ordinary identity relations, and thus explains why some supervenient descriptions are not reducible to lower level. This is the aspect that Horgan's first definition in the quotation above leaves out of account.

Let us now summarize the factors that distinguish between cases where reduction is and is not possible. The issues that matter are the following: (1) whether there are multiple circumstances such that B constitutes S in circumstance c but it is not the case that B constitutes S in circumstances c^1; and if so (2) whether or not c, c^1 etc. are describable at the subvenient level; (3) whether S is multiply realizable; and if so (4) whether there is a finite disjunctive set of realizands.

Reduction will be possible in the limiting case where B constitutes S under all circumstances and S is not multiply realizable. Reduction will not be possible when:

1   there are multiple circumstances that make a difference to the supervenience relation and these circumstances cannot be defined in terms of the subvenient level; or

2   when S is multiply realizable and there is no finite disjunctive set of realizands.

The example above wherein the light's being on has opposite meanings on Monday and Tuesday is an example of the first type of nonreducibility: days of the week cannot be defined the language of electrical phenomena.

For an example of the second type of nonreducibility we cannot use agreed signals because this will necessarily be a finite list. Instead consider the variety of natural signs or evidence of someone's being home: lights on, television, car in the garage, etc. Here there is no finite list of states of affairs that constitute the supervenient state "evidence of someone's being home"; thus, there can be laws relating the two levels.

I emphasize that my conclusions here depend on using my more complex definition of supervenience, which gives due attention to circumstances. One might wonder why the disagreement over the definition of supervenience. ... It is important to recognize that many of the theorists working in this area are in favor of reductionism. Thus, the matter cannot be left to mere stipulation; we have to pursue the more difficult task of judging which definition better fits the facts: mine, in which circumstances at a higher level of description need to be taken into account, or the more common definition in which they do not.

Many cases will fit the simpler definition of supervenience. However, there will also be a number of cases (perhaps most) where only the more complex definition does justice to the phenomena. A clear case where non–neural *circumstances* are widely recognized to make a difference is the role of *mental set* in perception. Two subjects induced to hold different expectations will often have different perceptual experiences resulting from the same physical stimulus. Mental set is a variable easily describable at the mental level, but in most cases (all cases?) will not be definable in terms of a finite set of neural realizands. For example, consider a well–known experiment in which subjects receive a small electrical shock on the back. Depending on their mental set, they will experience the sensation either as a burn or as ice. So at the subvenient level is a series of physical events including the application of the shock, the transmission of a nerve impulse to the brain, and the set of brain events that realize the sensation of either heat or cold. The mental set will, of course, be realized neurologically, but it is multiply realizable: it could be the realization of a variety of perceptions of the environment (ice–cube tray on the counter, burn ointment), or the result of statements by the experiments, or any one of an unbounded set of other devices resulting in what we can only meaningfully describe at the mental level as the *expectation* of heat or of cold.

Another example: children asked to estimate the size of disks will generally estimate coins to be larger than other disks of the same size. The concept of economic value simply does not translate to the neurological level of discourse.

This last example is important. If we take the hierarchy of levels to include the moral and the social (with its political, economic, legal dimensions) we can see that we will have here a vast array of concepts that most philosophers would agree are not logically reducible to neurological variables. So these higher levels of reality are not in danger of causal reduction to the biological level. This, I claim, is exactly what is needed to protect traditional views of the meaningfulness of human intellectual endeavors. In Warren Brown's terms, there are *emergent levels* as we go from the neurological to the cognitive, to the interpersonal, to the political, economic, and legal, to the moral, and finally to the spiritual. While all human behavior supervenes on the biological (genetic and neurological), little of it is reducible to biology.

Free will

It would be foolhardy to attempt to solve the problem of free will in one short section of one chapter. However, the reflections in the previous subsection are certainly relevant to this issue. Clearly, if I have succeeded in defeating causal reductionism with regard to the mental and the neurobiological, this opens the door to treatments of human freedom that do not depend on denying either physicalism or the law–governed character of neurobiological processes. That is, one of our strongest reasons for denying free will in the modern period has been the supposition that causal determinism applies to the human body. Rebut this supposition and the burden of proof shifts to those who would deny the freedom that seems an obvious fact of human experience.

As Malcolm Jeeves has pointed out, discussions of free will often distinguish between compatibilist and incompatibilist accounts. An incompatibilist view maintains that free will is incompatible with a determinist view of the natural world. A compatibilist view, in contrast, maintains that human freedom means being able to act as one chooses. It is irrelevant whether one's choices themselves can be shown to be a product of prior causes of certain sorts. The important issue, it seems, is whether our choices are determined by the kinds of factors that we believe to be operative, or whether we are self–deceived. For example, is one's choice motivated by the reasons one gives, consistent with one's values, a true reflection of one's character; or is it instead, unbeknown to the actor, a product of genetic predisposition, unconscious drives, or social manipulation?

The argument of the previous subsection is relevant here. In addition to the above list of suspicions, the physicalist has to answer the question whether what appear to us to be reasoned choices are not actually the products of the laws of physics (with the laws of neurophysiology being but special cases). It was the intent of previous argument to show that we can sometimes (and I would actually want to make the stronger claim—*usually*) only make causal sense of a series of human actions by attending to the mental–level description, which includes reasons, judgments, and so on. Yet this is *compatible* with causal determinism at the neurobiological level.

Now, it is one thing to rebut determinist arguments; it is another to give a positive account of how free will is embodied in neurological functioning. My guess is that such an account will come from appreciating the multiple interacting layers of information processing in the brain.

Questions

1 What does Murphy mean by "nonreductive physicalism"? How is it different from reductionism?

2 What is "causal reduction" and how does it relate to this discussion?

3 What is "supervenience" and how does Murphy use the concept to explain nonreductive physicalism?

4 How does Murphy address the problem of free will for nonreductive physicalism? How would you assess her argument?

5 What implications might nonreductive physicalism have for one's theological anthropology?

TEXT 7: ALVIN PLANTINGA,
"AGAINST MATERIALISM"[15]

One of the foremost contemporary philosophers of religion and a key figure in the resurgence of Christian philosophy during the latter part of the twentieth century, Alvin Plantinga (b. 1932) taught for years at Calvin College before moving to the University of Notre Dame. Retiring from that position in 2010, he has returned to Calvin College where he continues to exercise tremendous influence on various discussions in philosophy of religion. In this essay, Plantinga identifies two possible objections to a materialist view of the human person—the possibility of conceiving that my body is distinct from my soul and the question of whether material things can think. Each of these arguments illustrate some of the concerns people have raised about materialism, but the essay as a whole is also a good illustration of how important contemporary analytic philosophy has been for this discussion.

Materialism is the idea that human beings are material objects—brains, perhaps, or some part of the brain—without immaterial selves or souls. I give two arguments against materialism. The first is an argument from possibility: it is possible that I should exist when no part of my body exists, in which case I am not identical with my body or any part of my body. The second is an argument from impossibility. If materialism is true, a belief, for example, the belief that the British lost the American Revolutionary War, would have to be something like an event in one's nervous system. But it is impossible that a material process or event be *about* something; no such process could be about the British or anything else. So either there are no beliefs or materialism is false. But obviously there are beliefs.

I propose to give two arguments against materialism—or, if you think that's too negative, two arguments for substantial dualism. 'Substantial' is to be taken in two senses: first, the dualism in question, the dualism for which I mean to argue, is substantial as opposed to trivial; some versions of property dualism seem to me to be at best wholly insubstantial Second, according to the most popular form of dualism—one embraced by Plato, Augustine, Descartes and a thousand others—a human person is an immaterial substance: a thing, an object, a substance, a suppositum (as my Thomist colleagues would put it), and a thing that isn't material, although, of course, it is intimately connected with a material body. But there is also the view the name 'dualism' suggests: the view according to which a human person is somehow a sort of composite substance S composed of a material substance S* and an immaterial substance S**. We can sensibly include this view under 'dualism'—provided, that is, that having S* as a part is not essential to S. (I add this proviso because my first argument is for the conclusion that possibly, I exist when my body does not.)

---

[15]Alvin Plantinga, "Against Materialism," *Faith and Philosophy* 23, no. 1 (2006): 3–32.

Perhaps a better name for the view I mean to defend is 'immaterialism'; the view that a human person is not a material object. Of course it's far from easy to say just what a material object is. For present purposes let's put it recursively: a material object is either an atom, or is composed of atoms. Thus atoms, molecules, cells, hearts, brains and human bodies are all material objects; we'll leave open the question whether such things as electrons, quarks, protons, fields, and superstrings (if indeed there are such things) are material objects. What I'll argue for, accordingly, is the view that human persons are not material objects. They *are* objects (substances), however; therefore they are immaterial objects. My conclusion, of course, is hardly original (going back at least to Plato); my general style of argument also lacks originality (going back at least to Descartes and possibly Augustine). But the method of true philosophy, unlike that of liberal theology and contemporary French thought, aims less at novelty than at truth.

Three more initial comments: (i) when I speak of possibility and necessity, I mean possibility and necessity in the broadly logical sense—metaphysical possibility and necessity, as it is also called. (ii) I won't be arguing that it is possible that I (or others) can exist disembodied, with no body at all. (iii) I will make no claims about what is or isn't conceivable or imaginable. That is because imaginability isn't strictly relevant to possibility at all; conceivability, on the other hand, is relevant only if 'it's conceivable that p' is to be understood as implying or offering evidence for 'it's possible that p.' (Similarly for 'it's inconceivable that p.') It is therefore simpler and much less conducive to confusion to speak just of possibility. I take it we human beings have the following epistemic capacity: we can consider or envisage a proposition or state of affairs and, at least sometimes, determine its modal status—whether it is necessary, contingent, or impossible—just by thinking, just by an exercise of thought.

I The replacement argument:
An argument from possibility

I begin by assuming that there really is such a thing, substance or suppositum as I, I myself. Of course I'm not unique in that respect; you too are such that there really is such a thing as you, and the same goes for everybody else. We are substances. Now suppose I were a material substance: which material substance would I be? The answer, I should think, is that I would be my body, or some part of my body, such as my brain or part of my brain. Or perhaps I would be something more exotic: an object distinct from my body that is constituted from the same matter as my body and is colocated with it. What I propose to argue is that I am none of those things: I am not my body, or some part of it such as my brain or a hemisphere or other part of the latter, or an object composed of the same matter as my body (or some part of it) and colocated with it. (I'll call these 'eligible' material objects.) For simplicity (and nothing I say will depend on this simplification) I shall talk for the most part just about my body, which I'll name '*B*.' (I was thinking of naming it 'Hercules' or maybe Arnold,' but people insisted that would be unduly self-congratulatory.)

The general strategy of this first argument is as follows. It seems possible that I continue to exist when B, my body, does not. I therefore have the property *possibly exists when B does not.* B, however, clearly lacks that property. By Leibniz's Law, therefore (more specifically, the Diversity of Discernibles), I am not identical with B. But why think it possible that I exist when my body does not? Strictly speaking, the replacement argument is an argument for this premise. Again, I conduct the argument in the first person, but naturally enough the same goes for you (although of course you will have to speak for yourself).

So first, at a macroscopic level. A familiar fact of modern medicine is the possibility and actuality of limb and organ transplants and prostheses. You can get a new heart, liver, lungs; you can also get knee, hip, and ankle replacements; you can get prostheses for hands and feet, arms and legs, and so on. Now it seems possible— possible in that broadly logical sense—that medical science should advance to the point where I remain fully dressed and in my right mind (perhaps reading the *South Bend Tribune*) throughout a process during which each of the macroscopic parts of my body is replaced by other such parts, the original parts being vaporized in a nuclear explosion—or better, annihilated by God. But if this process occurs rapidly— during a period of 1 microsecond, let's say—B will no longer exist. I, however, will continue to exist, having been reading the comic page during the entire process.

But what about my brain, you ask—is it possible that my brain be replaced by another, the brain I now have being destroyed, and I continue to exist? It certainly seems so. Think of it like this. It seems possible (in the broadly logical sense) that one hemisphere of my brain be dormant at any given time, the other hemisphere doing all that a brain ordinarily does. At midnight, we can suppose, all the relevant 'data' and 'information' is 'transferred' via the corpus callosum from one hemisphere—call it 'H_1'—to the other hemisphere—H_2—whereupon H_2 takes over operation of the body and H_1 goes dormant. This seems possible; if it were actual, it would also be possible that the original dormant half, H_2, be replaced by a different dormant half (in the same computational or functional state, if you like) just before that midnight transfer; then the transfer occurs, control switches to the new H_2, and H_1 goes dormant—at which time it is replaced by another hemisphere in the same computational or functional condition. In a period of time as brief as you like, therefore, both hemispheres will have been replaced by others, the original hemispheres and all of their parts annihilated by God. Throughout the whole process I serenely continue to read the comics.

This suffices, I think, to show that it's possible that I exist when neither my body nor any part of it exists. What about material objects distinct from my body and its parts, but colocated with it (or one of them) and constituted by the same matter as they? I doubt very much that there could be any such things. If objects of this kind *are* possible, however, the above argument also shows or at least suggests that possibly, I exist when none of them does. For example, if there is such a thing as *the matter of which B is composed*—if that phrase denotes a thing or object—it too would be destroyed by God's annihilating all the parts of my body.

Of course very many different sorts of object of this kind—object constituted by the matter of my body and colocated with it—have been suggested, and I don't have the space here to deal with them all. However, we can offer a version of the replacement argument that will be relevant to many of them. Turn from macroscopic replacement to microscopic replacement. This could go on at several levels: the levels of atoms, molecules, or cells, for example. Let's think about it at the cellular level. It seems entirely possible that the cells of which my body is composed be rapidly—within a microsecond or two—replaced by other cells of the same kind, the original cells being instantly destroyed. It also seems entirely possible that this process of replacement take place while I remain conscious, thinking about dualism and marveling at some of the appalling arguments against it produced by certain materialists. Then I would exist at a time at which B did not exist.

But is it really true that this process of replacement would result in the destruction of B? After all, according to current science, all the matter in our bodies is replaced over a period of years, without any obvious compromise of bodily integrity or identity. As a matter of fact, so they say, the matter in our brains is completely replaced in a much shorter time. Why should merely accelerating this process make a difference?

Well, as they say, speed kills. When a cell is removed from an organism and replaced by another cell, the new cell doesn't become part of the organism instantaneously; it must be integrated into the organism and assimilated by it. What does this assimilation consist in? A cell in a (properly functioning) body is involved in a network of causal relations; a neuron, for example, emits and responds to electrical signals. A cell receives nourishment from the blood, and cooperates with other cells in various causal activities. All these things take time—maybe not much time, but still a certain period of time. At the instant the new part is inserted into the organism, and until it has begun to play this causal role (both as cause and effect), the new part is not yet a part of the organism, but a foreign body occupying space within the spatial boundaries of the organism. (Clearly not everything, nor even everything organic, within the spatial boundaries of your body is *part* of your body: think of the goldfish you just swallowed, or a tapeworm.) Let's use the phrase 'assimilation time' to denote the time required for the cell to start playing this causal role. The assimilation time is the time required for the cell to become assimilated into the body; before that time has elapsed the cell is not yet part of the body. To be rigorous, we should index this to the part (or kind of part) and the organism in question; different parts may require different periods of time for their assimilation by different organisms. For simplicity, though, let's assume all parts and organisms have the same assimilation time; this simplification won't make any difference to the argument.

That a given part and organism are such that the time of assimilation for the former with respect to the latter is dt, for some specific period of time dt, is, I take it, a contingent fact. One thinks the velocity of light imposes a lower limit here, but the time of assimilation could be much greater. (For example, it could depend on the rate of blood flow, the rate of intracellular transport, and the rate at which information is transmitted through neuron or nerve.) God could presumably slow down this process, or speed it up.

There is also what we might call 'the replacement time': the period of time from the beginning of the replacement of the first part by a new part to the end of the time of the replacement of the last part (the last to be replaced) by a different part. The time of replacement is also, of course, contingent; a replacement can occur rapidly or slowly. Presumably there is no non-zero lower limit here; no matter how rapidly the parts are replaced, it is possible in the broadly logical sense that they be replaced still more rapidly.

What's required by the Replacement Argument, therefore, (or at any rate what's sufficient for it) is

(Replacement) It is possible that: the cells in B are replaced by other cells and the originals instantly annihilated while I continue to exist; and the replacement time for B and those cells is shorter than the assimilation time.

Objections and replies

(1) Doesn't a Star Trek scenario seem possible, one in which you are beamed up from the surface of a planet to an orbiting spacecraft, both you, and in this context more importantly, your body surviving the process? This objection is relevant to the Replacement Argument, however, only if in this scenario your body survives a process in which its matter is replaced by other matter, the original matter being annihilated. But that's not how the Star Trek scenario works: what happens instead is that the matter of which your body is composed is beamed up (perhaps after having been converted to energy), not annihilated. You might think of this case as one of disassembly (and perhaps conversion into energy) and then reassembly. Perhaps your body could survive this sort of treatment; what I claim it *can't* survive is the rapid replacement of the matter in question by other matter, the original matter being annihilated.

(2) I've been assuming that you and I are objects, substances; but that assumption may not be as innocent as it looks. Might I not be an *event*—perhaps an event like a computer's running a certain program? We ordinarily think of an event as one or more objects $O_1 \ldots O_n$, exemplifying a property P or relation R, (where P or R may be complex in various ways and, may of course entail extension over time). Perhaps what I am is an event involving (consisting in) many material objects (organs, limbs, cells, etc.) standing in a complex relation. Then, although I wouldn't be a material object, I *would* be an event involving nothing but material objects—a material event, as we might call it; and why wouldn't that be enough to satisfy the materialist?

Further: suppose I were a material event: why couldn't that event persist through arbitrarily rapid replacement of the objects involved in it? Think of an event such as a battle; clearly there could be a battle in which the combatants were removed and replaced by other combatants with extremely great rapidity. Let's suppose the commanding officer has an unlimited number of troops at his command. He needs 1000 combatants at any given time: eager to spread the risk, he decrees that each combatant will fight for just thirty seconds and then be instantly replaced by another combatant. (Imagine that technology has advanced to the point where the obvious technical problems can be dealt with.) The battle, we may suppose, begins on Monday morning and ends Tuesday night; this one event, although no doubt including many subevents, lasts from Monday morning to Tuesday night—and this despite the constant and rapid replacement of the combatants. Although there are never more than 1000 troops in the field at anyone time, several million are involved in the event, by virtue of those rapid replacements....

Now suppose I were an event. Why couldn't the event which I am persist through arbitrarily rapid replacement of the material objects involved in it? Is there any reason, intuitive or otherwise, to suppose not? Perhaps a material *substance* can't survive the arbitrarily rapid replacement of its parts; is there any reason to think a material *event* suffers from the same limitation?

(3) We can conveniently deal with objection (2) by considering it together with another. According to Peter van Inwagen, human beings are material objects; a material object, furthermore is either an elementary particle or a living being. Living beings comprise the usual suspects: organisms such as horses, flies, and oak trees, but also cells (neurons, for example), which may not rise to the lofty heights of being organisms, but are nonetheless living beings. It is *living* horses, flies etc., that are objects or substances. Indeed, 'living horse' is a pleonasm. On van Inwagen's view, there aren't any dead horses; a 'dead horse,' strictly speaking, is not really a thing at all and *afortiori* not a horse; it is instead a mere heap or pile of organic matter. Once that horse has died, its remains (as we say in the case of human beings) are a mere assemblage of elementary particles related in a certain way; there is no entity or being there in addition to the particles. A living horse, on the other hand, is a thing, a substance, in its own right and has as parts only other living beings (cells, e.g.) and elementary particles. Strictly speaking, therefore, there isn't any such thing as a hand, or arm or leg or head; rather, in the place we think of as where the hand is, there are elementary particles and other living things (cells, e.g.) related in a certain way....

This elegant position certainly has its attractions. It's not wholly clear, of course, that there *are* any elementary particles (perhaps all particles are composed of other particles so that it's composition all the way down, or perhaps what there really is, is 'atomless gunk' configured in various ways); perhaps electrons, etc., aren't particles at all, but perturbances of fields; and it's a bit harsh to be told that there really aren't any such things as tables and chairs, automobiles and television sets. Nevertheless van Inwagen's view is attractive. Now suppose we add (b) to van Inwagen's view; the resulting position suggests an objection to the Replacement Argument (an objection that doesn't have van Inwagen's blessing). For (again) why couldn't the event which is my life persist through arbitrarily rapid replacement of the objects it involves? Is there any intuitive support for the thought that there is a lower limit on the rapidity of replacement through which this event could persist? If not, then even if I couldn't be a material substance, I could be a material event; no doubt the materialist would find this materialism enough.

We can respond to these two objections together. According to objection (2), I can sensibly think of myself as an event: presumably the event that constitutes my life. Now perhaps the objector's (a) is true: for any replacement, no matter how rapid, there will be an event of the sort (a) suggests. But of course nothing follows about the modal properties of any particular event. So suppose I am an event: nothing about my modal properties follows from or is even suggested by (a); and it is my modal properties that are at issue here. In particular, it doesn't follow that if I were my life, then I could have continued to exist (or occur) through the sort of rapid replacement envisaged in the Replacement Argument. Now turn to (3). Suppose for the moment we concede (b): we still have no reason to think my life, that particular event, the event which is in fact my life, could have survived those rapid replacements of the objects involved in it. No doubt for any such replacement event, there is an event of the sort suggested by (a); nothing follows with respect to the modal properties of the event which is in my life. In particular it doesn't follow that it could have persisted through the sort of rapid replacements we've been thinking about.

So (a) is really a red herring. But there is a more decisive response here. Objection (3) endorses (b), the claim that there is an event—my life—such that, necessarily,

I exist just when it does. Objection (2) also (and trivially) entails (b); if I just *am* my life then, naturally enough, (b) is true. Fortunately, however, (b) is false. For (b) entails (c) I and my life are such that necessarily, I exist just when it occurs, and (as I'll now argue) (c) is false.

Why think (c) is false? First, it's far from clear just which properties events have essentially. Some think it essential to any event that it include just those objects that it does in fact include, and also that these objects exemplify just the properties and relations they do in fact exemplify. If that were true, an event involving an object O's having a certain property could not have occurred if O had not had that property. But that seems a bit strong; surely the Civil War, for example, (that very event) could have taken place even if a particular Confederate soldier had not trodden on a blade of grass he did in fact step on. Still, there are serious limits here. Perhaps the Civil War (the event which is the Civil War) would have existed even if that soldier hadn't trampled that blade of grass; but the Civil War (that event) could not have lasted only ten minutes. There is a possible world in which there is a very short war between the states (and it could even be called 'The Civil War'); but there is no possible world in which the war that did in fact take place occurs, and lasts for only ten minutes. Similarly for my life (call it 'L'): if (b) is true, then of course L has existed exactly as long as I have. L, therefore, has by now existed for more than seventy years. Clearly enough, however, *I* could have existed for a much shorter time: for example, I could have been run over by a Mack truck at the age of six months (and not been subsequently sustained in existence by God). L, however, could not have existed or occurred for only those first few months, just as the Civil War could not have existed or occurred for only ten minutes. There is a possible world in which I exist for just those first few months, or even for just a few minutes; there is no possible world in which L exists for that period of time. Of course, if I had existed for, say, just ten minutes, there *would have been* an event which would have been my life, and which would have existed for just ten minutes; that event, however, would not have been L. We can put it like this: in any world in which I exist, there is an event which is my life; but it is not the case that there is an event which is my life, and which is my life in every world in which I exist.

(c), therefore, is false; it is not the case that I and the life of my body are such that necessarily, we exist at all the same times—that is, it is not the case that I and the life of my body are such that I have essentially the property of existing when and only when it does. But if (c) is false, the same goes for (b); since objections (2) and (3) both entail (b), both objections fail.

(4) If, as I say is possible, the replacement time for B and those parts is shorter than the assimilation time, there will be a brief period during which I don't have a body at all. I will no longer have B, because all of B's parts have been replaced (and destroyed) during a time too brief for the new parts to be assimilated into B. I won't have any other body either, however; I won't have a body distinct from B, because there hasn't been time for these new parts to coalesce into a body. I therefore have no body at all during this time; there is no body that is *my* body at this time. How, then, can I continue to be conscious during this time, serenely reading the comics? Isn't it necessary that there be neurological activity supporting my consciousness during this time, if I am to be conscious then?

But is it *logically* necessary that there be neurological or other physical activity supporting my consciousness at any time at which I am conscious? That's a whopping assumption. The most I need for my argument is that it is *logically possible* that I remain conscious during a brief period in which no neurological activity is supporting my consciousness; that's compatible with its being causally required that there be neurological activity when I am conscious. My entire argument has to do with what *could* happen; not with what *would* as a matter of fact happen, if this sort of replacement were to occur. So the most that argument needs is that possibly, I exist and am conscious when no neurological activity is supporting my consciousness. But the fact is it doesn't require even that. For consider a time t after the end of the replacement time but before the assimilation time has ended; let t be as close as you please to the end of the replacement time. At t, the replacing elements, the new parts, haven't yet had time to coalesce into a body. Nonetheless, any one of the new elements could be performing one of the several functions it will be performing when it has been integrated into a functioning human body. It could be playing part of the whole causal role it will be playing when the assimilation time has elapsed. In particular, therefore, the new neurons, before they have become part of a body, could be doing whatever it is they have to do in order to support consciousness. Accordingly, my argument requires that possibly I am conscious when I do not have a body; it does not require that possibly I am conscious when no neuronal or neurological activity is occurring.

II Can a material thing think?
An argument from impossibility

The Replacement Argument is an argument from possibility; as such, it proceeds from an intuition, the intuition that it is possible that my bodily parts, macroscopic or microscopic, be replaced while I remain conscious. But some people distrust modal intuitions. Of course it's impossible to do philosophy (or for that matter physics) without invoking modal intuitions of one sort or another or at any rate making modal declarations of one sort or another. Still, it must be conceded that intuition can sometimes be a bit of a frail reed. True, there is no way to conduct philosophy that isn't a frail reed, but intuition is certainly fallible. Further, some might think modal intuitions particularly fallible—although almost all of the intuitions involved in philosophy have important modal connections. Still further, one might think further that intuitions of *possibility* are especially suspect. That is because it seems easy to confuse *seeing the possibility of p* with *failing to see the impossibility of p*. You can't see why numbers couldn't be sets; it doesn't follow that what you see is that they *could* be sets. Maybe I can't see why water couldn't be composed of something other than H_2O; it doesn't follow that what I see is that water could be something other than H_2O. And perhaps, so the claim might go, one who finds the replacement argument attractive is really confusing seeing the possibility of the replacements in question with failing to see their impossibility. Granted: I can't see that these replacements are impossible; it doesn't follow that what I see is that they are indeed possible.

To be aware of this possible source of error, however, is to be forewarned and thus forearmed. But for those who aren't mollified and continue to distrust possibility intuitions, I have another argument for dualism—one that depends on an intuition, not, this time, of possibility, but of impossibility. One who distrusts possibility intuitions may think more kindly of intuitions of impossibility—perhaps because she thinks that for the latter there isn't any obvious analogue of the possible confusion between failing to see that something is impossible with seeing that it is possible. Or rather, while there is an analogue—it would be confusing failure to see the possibility of p with seeing the impossibility of p—falling into that confusion seems less likely. In any event, the argument I'll now propose is for the conclusion that no material objects can think—i.e., reason and believe, entertain propositions, draw inferences, and the like. But of course I can think; therefore I am not a material object.

A Leibniz's problem

I (and the same goes for you) am a certain kind of thing: a thing that can think. I believe many things; I also hope, fear, expect, anticipate many things. I desire certain states of affairs (desire that certain states of affairs be actual). I am capable of making decisions. I am capable of acting, and capable of acting on the basis of my beliefs and desires. I am conscious; and conscious of a rich, kaleidoscopic constellation of feeling, mental images, beliefs, and ways of being appeared to, some of which I enjoy and some of which I dislike. Naturally enough, therefore, I am not identical with any object that lacks any or all of these properties. What I propose to argue next is that some of these properties are such that no material object can have them. Again, others have offered similar arguments. In particular, many have seen a real problem for materialism in *consciousness*: it is extremely difficult to see how a material object could be conscious, could enjoy that vivid and varied constellation of feelings, mental images and ways of being appeared to. Others have argued that a material object can't make a decision (although of course we properly speak, in the loose and popular sense, of the chess playing computer as deciding which move to make next). These arguments seem to me to be cogent. Here, however, I want to develop another argument of the same sort, another problem for materialism, a problem I believe is equally debilitating, and in fact fatal to materialism. Again, this problem is not a recent invention; you can find it or something like it in Plato. Leibniz, however, offers a famous and particularly forceful statement of it:

> 17. It must be confessed, moreover, that *perception,* and that which depends on it, *are inexplicable by mechanical causes,* that is by figures and motions. And supposing there were a machine so constructed as to think, feel and have perception, we could conceive of it as enlarged and yet preserving the same proportions, so that we might enter it as into a mill. And this granted, we should only find on visiting it, pieces which push one against another, but never anything by which to explain a perception. This must be sought for, therefore, in the simple substance and not in the composite or in the machine.[16]

---

[16]*Monadology* 17. In *Leibniz Selections,* ed. Philip Weiner (New York: Charles Scribner's Sons, 1951), 536.

Now Leibniz uses the word 'perception' here; he's really thinking of mental life generally. His point, in this passage, is that mental life—perception, thought, decision—cannot arise by way of the mechanical interaction of parts. Consider a bicycle; like Leibniz's mill, it does what it does by virtue of the mechanical interaction of its parts. Stepping down on the pedals causes the front sprocket to turn, which causes the chain to move, which causes the rear sprocket to turn, which causes the back wheel to rotate. By virtue of these mechanical interactions, the bicycle does what it does, i.e., transports someone from one place to another. And of course machines generally—jet aircraft, refrigerators, computers, centrifuges—do their things and accomplish their functions in the same way. So Leibniz's claim, here, is that thinking can't arise in this way. A thing can't think by virtue of the mechanical interaction of its parts.

Leibniz is thinking of *mechanical* interactions—interactions involving pushes and pulls, gears and pulleys, chains and sprockets. But I think he would say the same of other interactions studied in physics, for example those involving gravity, electro-magnetism, and the strong and weak nuclear forces. Call these 'physical interactions.' Leibniz's claim is that thinking can't arise by virtue of physical interaction among objects or parts of objects. According to current science, electrons and quarks are simple, without parts. Presumably neither can think—neither can adopt propositional attitudes; neither can believe, doubt, hope, want, or fear. But then a proton composed of quarks won't be able to think either, at least by way of physical relations between its component quarks, and the same will go for an atom composed of protons and electrons, a molecule composed of atoms, a cell composed of molecules, and an organ (e.g., a brain), composed of cells. If electrons and quarks can't think, we won't find anything composed of them that *can* think by way of the physical interaction of its parts.

Leibniz is talking about thinking generally; suppose we narrow our focus to *belief* (*although* the same considerations apply to other propositional attitudes). What, first of all, would a belief *be,* from a materialist perspective? Suppose you are a materialist, and also think, as we ordinarily do, that there are such things as beliefs. For example, you hold the belief that Marcel Proust is more subtle than Louis L'Amour. What kind of a thing is this belief? Well, from a materialist perspective, it looks as if it would have to be something like a long-standing event or structure in your brain or nervous system. Presumably this event will involve many neurons related to each other in subtle and complex ways. There are plenty of neurons to go around: a normal human brain contains some 100 billion. These neurons, furthermore, are connected with other neurons at synapses; a single neuron can be involved in several thousand synapses, and there are some 10^{15} synaptic connections. The total number of possible brain states, then, is absolutely enormous, vastly greater than the 1080 electrons they say the universe contains. And the total number of possible neuronal events, while no doubt vastly smaller, is still enormous. Under certain conditions, groups of neurons involved in such an event fire, producing electrical impulses that can be transmitted (with appropriate modification and input from other structures) down the cables of neurons that constitute effector nerves to muscles or glands, causing, e.g., muscular contraction and thus behavior.

From the materialist's point of view, therefore, a belief will be a neuronal event or structure of this sort. But if this is what beliefs are, they will have two very different sorts of properties. On the one hand there will be *electrochemical* or *neurophysiological* properties ('NP properties,' for short). Among these would be such properties as that of involving *n* neurons and n^* connections between neurons, properties that specify which neurons are connected with which others, what the rates of fire in the various parts of the event are, how these rates of fire change in response to changes in Input, and so on. But if the event in question is really a *belief,* then in addition to those NP properties it will have another property as well: it will have to have a *content.* It will have to be the belief that *p,* for some proposition *p.* If this event is the belief that Proust is a more subtle writer than Louis L'Amour, then its content is the proposition *Proust* is *more subtle than Louis L'Amour.* My belief that naturalism is all the rage these days has as content the proposition *Naturalism* is *all the rage these days.* (That same proposition is the content of the German speaker's belief that naturalism is all the rage these days, even though she expresses this belief by uttering the German sentence 'Der Naturalismus ist dieser Tage ganz gross in Mode'; beliefs, unlike sentences, do not come in different languages.) It is in virtue of having a content, of course, that a belief is true or false: it is true if the proposition which is its content is true, and false otherwise. My belief that all men are mortal is true because the proposition which constitutes its content is true, but Hitler's belief that the Third Reich would last a thousand years was false, because the proposition that constituted its content was false.

And now the difficulty for materialism is this: how does it happen, how can it be, that an assemblage of neurons, a group of material objects firing away *has a content?* How can that happen? More poignantly, *what is it* for such an event to have a content? What is it for this structured group of neurons, or the event of which they are a part, to be related, for example, to the proposition *Cleveland is a beautiful city* in such a way that the latter is its content? A single neuron (or quark, electron, atom or whatever) presumably isn't a belief and doesn't have content; but how can belief, content, arise from physical interaction among such material entities as neurons? As Leibniz suggests, we can examine this neuronal event as carefully as we please; we can measure the number of neurons it contains, their connections, their rates of fire, the strength of the electrical impulses involved, the potential across the synapses—we can measure all this with as much precision as you could possibly desire; we can consider its electro-chemical, neurophysiological properties in the most exquisite detail; but nowhere, here, will we find so much as a hint of content. Indeed, none of this seems even vaguely *relevant* to its having content. None of this so much as slyly suggests that this bunch of neurons firing away is the belief that Proust is more subtle than Louis L'Amour, as opposed, e.g., to the belief that Louis L'Amour is the most widely published author from Jamestown, North Dakota. Indeed, nothing we find here will so much as slyly suggest that it has a content of *any* sort. Nothing here will so much as slyly suggest that it is *about* something, in the way a belief about horses is about horses.

The fact is, we can't see how it *could* have a content. It's not just that we don't know or can't see how it's done. When light strikes photoreceptor cells in the retina, there is an enormously complex cascade of electrical activity, resulting in an electrical signal to the brain. I have no idea how all that works; but of course I know it happens all the time. But the case under consideration is different. Here it's not merely that I don't know how physical interaction among neurons brings it about that an assemblage of them has content and is a belief. No, in this case, it seems upon reflection that such an event could *not* have content. It's a little like trying to understand what it would be for the number seven, e.g., to weigh five pounds, or for an elephant (or the unit set of an elephant) to be a proposition. (Pace the late (and great) David Lewis, according to whom the unit set of an elephant *could* be a proposition; in fact, on his view, there are uncountably many elephants the unit sets of which *are* propositions.) We can't see how that could happen; more exactly, what we can see is that it *couldn't* happen. A number just isn't the sort of thing that can have weight; there is no way in which that number or any other number could weigh anything at all. The unit set of an elephant, let alone the elephant itself, can't be a proposition; it's not the right sort of thing. Similarly, we can see, I think, that physical activity among neurons can't constitute content. There they are, those neurons, clicking away, sending electrical impulses hither and yon. But what has this to do with content? How is content or aboutness supposed to arise from this neuronal activity? How can such a thing possibly be a belief? But then no neuronal event can as such have a content, can be *about* something, in the way in which my belief that the number seven is prime is about the number seven, or my belief that the oak tree in my backyard is without leaves is about that oak tree.

Here we must be very clear about an important distinction. Clearly there is such a thing as *indication* or *indicator meaning*. Deer tracks in my backyard indicate that deer have run through it; smoke indicates fire; the height of the mercury column indicates the ambient temperature; buds on the trees indicate the coming of spring. We could speak here of 'natural signs': smoke is a natural sign of fire and the height of the mercury column is a natural sign of the temperature. When one event indicates or is a natural sign of another, there is ordinarily some sort of causal or nomic connection, or at least regular association, between them by virtue of which the first is reliably correlated with the second. Smoke is caused by fire, which is why it indicates fire; measles cause red spots on your face, which is why red spots on your face indicate measles; there is a causal connection between the height of the mercury column and the temperature, so that the latter indicates the former.

The nervous systems of organisms contain such indicators. A widely discussed example: when a frog sees a fly zooming by, the frog's brain (so it is thought) displays a certain pattern of neural firing; we could call such patterns 'fly detectors.' Another famous example: some anaerobic marine bacteria have magnetosomes, tiny internal magnets. These function like compass needles, indicating magnetic north. The direction to magnetic north is downward; hence these bacteria, which can't flourish in the oxygen-rich surface water, move towards the more oxygen-free water at the bottom of the ocean. Of course there are also indicators in human bodies. There are structures that respond in a regular way to blood temperature; they are part of a complex feedback system that maintains a more or less constant blood temperature by inducing (e.g.) shivering if the temperature is too low and sweating if it is too high. There are structures that monitor the amount of sugar in the blood and its sodium content. There are structures that respond in a regular way to light of a certain pattern striking the retina, to the amount of food in your stomach, to its progress through your digestive system, and so on. Presumably there are structures in the brain that are correlated with features of the environment; it is widely assumed that when you see a tree, there is a distinctive pattern of neural firing (or some other kind of structure) in your brain that is correlated with and caused by it.

Now we can, if we like, speak of 'content' here; it's a free country. We can say that the mercury column, on a given occasion, has a certain content: the state of affairs correlated with its having the height it has on that occasion. We could say, if we like, that those structures in the body that indicate blood pressure or temperature or saline content have a content on a given occasion: whatever it is that the structure indicates on that occasion. We could say, if we like, that the neural structure that is correlated with my looking at a tree has a content: its content, we could say, is what it indicates on that occasion. We can also, if we like, speak of information in these cases: the structure that registers my blood temperature, we can say, carries the information that my blood temperature is thus and so.

What is crucially important to see, however, is that this sort of content or information has nothing as such to do with *belief,* or belief content. There are those who—no doubt in the pursuit of greater generality—gloss over this distinction. Donald T. Cambell, for example, in arguing for the relevance of natural selection to epistemology, claims that *II* evolution—even in its biological aspects—is a knowledge *process.*"[17] Commenting on Cambell's claim, Franz Wuketits explains that

> The claim is based on the idea that any living system is a "knowledge-gaining system." This means that organisms accumulate information about certain properties of their environment. Hence life generally may be described as an information process, or, to put it more precisely, an information-increasing process.[18]

At any rate Wuketits has the grace to put 'knowledge' in scare quotes here. Knowledge requires belief; correlation, causal or otherwise, is not belief; information and content of this sort do not require belief. Neither the thermostat nor any of its components believes that the room temperature is thus and so. When the saline content of my blood is too low, neither I nor the structure correlated with that state of affairs (nor my blood) believes the saline content is less than it should be—or, indeed, anything else about the saline content. Indication, carrying information, is not belief; indicator content is not belief content, and these structures don't have belief content just by virtue of having indicator content. And now the point here: I am not, of course, claiming that material structures can't have indicator content; obviously they can. What I am claiming is that they can't have belief content: no material structure can be a belief.

Here someone might object as follows. "You say we can't see how a neural event can have content; but in fact we understand this perfectly well, and something similar happens all the time. For there is, after all, the computer analogy. A computer, of course, is a material object, an assemblage of wires, switches, relays, and the

---

[17]"Evolutionary Epistemology" in P. A. Schilpp, ed., *The Philosophy of Karl Popper* (LaSalle, IL: Open Court, 1974), 413.
[18]"Evolutionary Epistemology" in *Biology and Philosophy,* vol. 1, No. 2 (1986): 193.

like. Now suppose I am typing in a document. Take any particular sentence in the document: say the sentence 'Naturalism is all the rage these days.' That sentence is represented and stored on the computer's hard disk. We don't have to know in exactly what *way* it's stored (it's plusses and minuses, or a magnetic configuration, or something else; it doesn't matter). Now the sentence 'Naturalism is all the rage these days' *expresses* the proposition *Naturalism is all the rage these days*. That sentence, therefore, has the proposition *Naturalism is all the rage these days* as its content. But then consider the analogue of that sentence on the computer disk: doesn't it, too, express the same proposition as the sentence it represents? That bit of the computer disk with its plusses and minuses, therefore, has propositional content. But of course that bit of the computer disk is also (part of) a material object (as is any inscription of the sentence in question). Contrary to your claim, therefore, a material object can perfectly well have propositional content; indeed, it happens all the time. But if a computer disk or an inscription of a sentence can have a proposition as content, why can't an assemblage of neurons? Just as a magnetic pattern has as content the proposition *Naturalism is all the rage these days*, so too a pattern of neuronal firing can have that proposition as content. Your claim to the contrary is completely bogus and you should be ashamed of yourself." Thus far the objector.

If the sentence or the computer disk really *did* have content, then I guess the assemblage of neurons could too. But the fact is neither does—or rather, neither has the right kind of content: neither has *original* content; each has, at most, *derived* content. For how does it happen that the sentence has content? It's simply by virtue of the fact that we human beings *treat* that sentence in a certain way, *use* the sentence in a certain way, a way such that if a sentence is used in that way, then it expresses the proposition in question. Upon hearing that sentence, I think of, grasp, apprehend the proposition *Naturalism is all the rage these days*. You can get me to grasp, entertain, and perhaps believe that proposition by uttering that sentence. How exactly all this works is complicated and not at all well understood; but the point is that the sentence has content only because of something *we*, we who are *already* thinkers, do with it. We could put this by saying that the sentence has *secondary* or *derived* content; it has content only because we, we creatures whose thoughts and beliefs already have content, treat it in a certain way. The same goes for the magnetic pattern on the computer disk; it represents or expresses that proposition because we assign that proposition to that configuration. But of course that isn't how it goes (given materialism) with that pattern of neural firing. That pattern doesn't get its content by way of being used in a certain way by some other creatures whose thoughts and beliefs already have content. If that pattern has content at all, then, according to materialism, it must have *original* or *primary* content. And what it is hard or impossible to see is how it could be that an assemblage of neurons (or a sentence, or a computer disk) could have original or primary content. To repeat: it isn't just that we can't see how it's done, in the way in which we can't see how the sleight of hand artist gets the pea to wind up under the middle shell. It is rather that we can see, to at least some degree, that it can't be done, just as we can see that an elephant can't be a proposition, and that the number 7 can't weigh seven pounds.

B Parity?

Peter van Inwagen agrees that it is hard indeed to see how physical interaction among material entities can produce thought: "it seems to me that the notion of a physical thing that thinks is a mysterious notion, and that Leibniz's thought-experiment brings out this mystery very effectively."[19]

Now I am taking this fact as a reason to reject materialism and hence as an argument for dualism. But of course it is a successful argument only if there is no similar difficulty for substance dualism itself. Van Inwagen believes there *is* a similar difficulty for dualism:

> For it is thinking itself that is the source of the mystery of a thinking physical thing. The notion of a non-physical thing that thinks is, I would argue, equally mysterious. How any sort of thing could think is a mystery. It is just that it is a bit easier to see that thinking is a mystery when we suppose that the thing that does the thinking is physical, for we can form mental images of the operations of a physical thing and we can see that the physical interactions represented in these images—the only interactions that can be represented in these images—have no connection with thought or sensation, or none we are able to imagine, conceive or articulate. The only reason we do not readily find the notion of a non-physical thing that thinks equally mysterious is that we have no clear procedure for forming mental images of non-physical things. (loc. cit.)

So dualism is no better off than materialism; they both have the same problem. But what precisely *is* this problem, according to van Inwagen? "[W]e can form mental images of the operations of a physical thing and we can see that the physical interactions represented in these images—the only interactions that can be represented in these images—have no connection with thought or sensation or none we are able to imagine, conceive or articulate." As I understand van Inwagen here, he is saying that we can imagine physical interactions or changes in a physical thing; but we can see that the physical interactions represented in those images have no connection with thought. We can imagine neurons in the brain firing; we can imagine electrical impulses or perhaps clouds of electrons moving through parts of neurons, or whole chains of neurons; we can imagine neural structures with rates of fire in certain parts of the structure changing in response to rates of fire elsewhere in or out of that structure: but we can see that these interactions have no connection with thought. Now I'm not quite sure whether or not I can imagine electrons, or their movements, or electrical impulses; but it does seem to me that I can see that electrical impulses and the motions of electrons, if indeed there are any such things, have nothing to do with thought.

Another way to put van Inwagen's point: no change we can imagine in a physical thing could be a mental change, i.e., could constitute thought or sensation, or a change in thought or sensation. But then we can't imagine a physical thing's thinking:

---

[19]*Metaphysics*, second ed. (Boulder, Colorado, 2002), 176.

i.e., we can't form a mental image of a physical thing thinking. And this suggests that the problem for materialism is that we can't form a mental image of a material thing thinking. But the same goes, says van Inwagen, for an immaterial thing: we also can't imagine or form a mental image of an immaterial thing thinking. Indeed, we can't form a mental image of any kind of thinking thing: "My point," he says, "is that nothing could possibly count as a mental image of a thinking thing" (177). Materialism and dualism, therefore, are so far on a par; there is nothing here to incline us to the latter rather than the former.

Thus far van Inwagen. The thought of a physical thing's thinking, he concedes, is mysterious; that is because we can't form a mental image of a physical thing's thinking. But the thought of an immaterial thing's thinking is equally mysterious; for we can't form a mental image of that either. This, however, seems to me to mislocate the problem for materialism. What inclines us to reject the idea of a physical thing's thinking is not just the fact that we can't form a mental image of a physical thing's thinking. There are plenty of things of which we can't form a mental image, where we're not in the least inclined to reject them as impossible. As Descartes pointed out, I can't form a mental image of a chiliagon, a 1000-sided rectilinear plane figure (or at least an image that distinguishes it from a 100-sided rectilinear plane figure); that doesn't even suggest that there can't be any such thing. I can't form a mental image of the number 79's being prime: that doesn't incline me to believe that the number 79 could not be prime; as a matter of fact I know how to prove that it *is* prime. The fact is I can't form a mental image of the number 79 at all—or for that matter of any number; this doesn't incline me to think there aren't any numbers.

Or is all that a mistake? Is it really true that I can't form a mental image of the number 7, for example? Maybe I *can* form an image of the number '7; when I think of the number seven, sometimes there is a mental image present; it's as if one catches a quick glimpse of a sort of partial and fragmented numeral 7; we could say that I'm appeared to numeral-7ly. When I think of the actual world, I am sometimes presented with an image of the Greek letter alpha; when I think of the proposition *All men are mortal* I am sometimes presented with a sort of fleeting, fragmentary, partial image of the corresponding English sentence. Sets are nonphysical, but maybe I can imagine the pair set of Mic and Martha; when I try, it's like I catch a fleeting glimpse of curly brackets, enclosing indistinct images that don't look a whole lot like Mic and Martha. But is that really imagining the number 7, or the actual world, or the pair set of Mic and Martha? Here I'm of two minds. On the one hand, I'm inclined to think that this isn't imagining the number 7 at all, but instead imagining something connected with it, namely the numeral 7 (and the same for the actual world and the set of Mic and Martha). On the other hand I'm a bit favorably disposed to the idea that that's just how you imagine something like the number 7; you do it by imagining the numeral 7. (Just as you state a proposition by uttering a sentence or uttering certain sounds.) So I don't really know what to say. Can I or can't I imagine nonphysical things like numbers, propositions, possible worlds, angels, God? I'm not sure.

What is clear, here, is this: if imagining the numeral 7 is sufficient for imagining the number 7, then imagining, forming mental images of, has nothing to do with possibility. For in this same way I can easily imagine impossibilities. I can imagine the proposition *all men are mortal* being red: first I just imagine the proposition, e.g., by forming a mental image of the sentence 'All men are mortal,' and then I imagine this sentence as red. I think I can even imagine that elephant's being a proposition. David Kaplan once claimed he could imagine his refuting Gödel's Incompleteness Theorem: he the *Los Angeles Times* carrying huge headlines: 'UCLA PROF REFUTES GODEL; ALL REPUTABLE EXPERTS AGREE.' In this loose sense, most anything can be imagined; but then the loose sense has little to do with what is or isn't possible. So really neither the loose nor the strong sense of 'imagining' (neither the weak nor the strong version of imagination) has much to do with possibility. There are many clearly possible things one can't imagine in the strong sense; in the weak sense, one can imagine many things that are clearly impossible.

What is it, then, that inclines me to think a proposition can't be red, or a horse, or an even number? The answer, I think, is that one can just see upon reflection that these things are impossible. I can't form a mental image of a proposition's having members; but that's not why I think no proposition has members; I also can't form a mental image of a set's having members. It's rather that one sees that a set is the sort of thing that (null set aside) has members, and a proposition is the sort of thing that cannot have members. It is the same with a physical thing's thinking. True, one can't imagine it. The reason for rejecting the idea, thinking it impossible, however, is not that one can't imagine it. It's rather that on reflection one can see that a physical object just can't do that sort of thing. I grant that this isn't as clear and obvious, perhaps, as that a proposition can't be red; some impossibilities (necessities) are more clearly impossible (necessary) than others. But one can see it to at least a significant degree. Indeed, van Inwagen might be inclined to endorse this thought; elsewhere he says: "Leibniz's thought experiment shows that when we carefully examine the idea of a material thing having sensuous properties, it seems to be an impossible idea."[20] But (and here is the important point) the same clearly doesn't go for an immaterial thing's thinking; we certainly can't see that no immaterial thing can think. (If we could, we'd have a quick and easy argument against the existence of God: no immaterial thing can think; if there were such a person as God, he would be both immaterial and a thinker; therefore.)

Van Inwagen has a second suggestion:

In general, to attempt to explain how an underlying reality generates some phenomenon is to construct a representation of the working of that underlying reality, a representation that in some sense "shows how" the underlying reality generates the phenomenon. Essentially the same considerations as those that show that we are unable to form a mental image that displays the generation of thought and sensation by the workings of some underlying reality (whether the underlying reality involves one thing or many, and whether the things it involves are physical or non-physical) show that we are unable to form any sort of representation that

---

[20] "Dualism and Materialism: Athens and Jerusalem?", *Faith and Philosophy* 12:4 (October 1995): 478. That is (I take it), it seems to be necessary that material things don't have such properties. Van Inwagen's examples are such properties as *being* ill *pain* and *sensing redly;* the same goes, I say, for properties like *being the belief that p* for a proposition p.

displays the generation of thought and sensation by the workings of an underlying
reality. (*Metaphysics,* pp. 177–78)

The suggestion is that we can't form an image or any other representation displaying
the generation of thought by way of the workings of an underlying reality; hence
we can't see how it can be generated by physical interaction among material objects
such as neurons. This much seems right—at any rate we certainly can't see how
thought could be generated in that way. Van Inwagen goes on to say, however, that
this doesn't favor dualism over materialism, because we also can't see how thought
can be generated by the workings of an underlying *non-physical* reality. And perhaps
this last is also right. But here there is an important dissimilarity between dualism
and materialism. The materialist thinks of thought as generated by the workings
of an underlying reality—i.e., by the physical interaction of such physical things as
neurons; the dualist, however, typically thinks of an immaterial self, a soul, a thing
that thinks, as *simple.* An immaterial self doesn't have any parts; hence, of course,
thought isn't generated by the interaction of its parts. Say that a property P is *basic*
to a thing x if x has P, but x's having P is not generated by the interaction of its parts.
Thought is then a basic property of selves, or better, a basic activity of selves. It's
not that (for example) there are various underlying immaterial parts of a self whose
interaction produces thought. Of course a self stands in causal relation to its body:
retinal stimulation causes a certain sort of brain activity which (so we think) in turn
somehow causes a certain kind of experience in the self. But there isn't any *way* in
which the self produces a thought; it does so immediately. To ask "How does a self
produce thought?" is to ask an improper question. There isn't any how about it.

By way of analogy: consider the lowly electron. According to current science,
electrons are simple, not composed of other things. Now an electron has basic
properties, such as having a negative charge. But the question 'How does an electron
manage to have a charge?' is an improper question. There's no how to it; it doesn't
do something else that results in its having such a charge, and it doesn't have parts
by virtue of whose interaction it has such a charge. Its having a negative charge is
rather a basic and immediate property of the thing (if thing it is). The same is true
of a self and thinking: it's not done by underlying activity or workings; it's a basic
and immediate activity of the self. But then the important difference, here, between
materialism and immaterialism is that if a material thing managed to think, it would
have to be by way of the activity of its parts: and it seems upon reflection that this
can't happen. Not so for an immaterial self. Its activity of thinking is basic and
immediate. And it's not the case that we are inclined upon reflection to think this
can't happen—there's nothing at all against it, just as there is nothing against an
electron's having a negative charge, not by virtue of the interaction of parts, but in
that basic and immediate way. The fact of the matter then is that we can't see how
a material object can think—that is, upon reflection it seems that a material object
can't think. Again, not so for an immaterial self.

True, as van Inwagen says, thought can sometimes seem mysterious and wonderful,
something at which to marvel. (Although from another point of view it is more
familiar than hands and feet.) But there is nothing here to suggest that it can't be
done. I find myself perceiving my computer; there is nothing at all, here, to suggest
impossibility or paradox. Part of the mystery of thought is that it is wholly unlike

what material objects can do: but of course that's not to suggest that it can't be done at all. Propositions are also mysterious and have wonderful properties: they manage to be about things; they are true or false; they can be believed; they stand in logical relations to each other. How do they manage to do those things? Well, certainly not by way of interaction among material parts. Sets manage, somehow, to have member—how do they do a thing like that? And why is it that a given set has just the members it has? How does the unit set of Lance Armstrong manage to have just *him* as a member? What mysterious force, or fence, keeps Leopold out of that set? Well, it's just the nature of sets to be like this. These properties can't be explained by way of physical interactions among material parts, but that's nothing at all against sets. Indeed, these properties can't be explained at all. Of course if you began with the idea that everything has to be a material object, then thought (and propositions and sets) would indeed be mysterious and paradoxical. But why begin with that idea? Thought is seriously mysterious, I think, only when we assume that it would have to be generated in some physical way, by physical interaction among physical objects. That is certainly mysterious; indeed it goes far beyond mystery, all the way to apparent impossibility. But that's not a problem for thought; it's a problem for materialism.

Questions

1 What is Plantinga's "replacement" argument? Do you find it convincing? Why or why not?

2 Why is *consciousness* a problem for materialism? How might a materialist respond to this concern?

3 Why does Plantinga think it's important to realize that material events cannot have "content"? How does he respond to the objection that material objects like computers actually do have content?

4 Why does van Inwagen think that dualists face a problem here as well? How does Plantinga respond?

5 What are "modal intuitions"? What role do they play in arguments like these?

4

Free Will

The puzzle of the freedom of the human will has been and continues to be one of the most perplexing and debated matters in theology and philosophy. In the twentieth century, psychology and neuroscience began to make their own contributions to the debate. On the one side of the equation, the notion of free will seems to be necessary if there is to be any conception of morality. How can individuals be called upon to act in a moral way if they are not in some sense free to do so? How can they be held responsible for their intentions and their actions if they are not made freely? If a person is compelled to act by factors extrinsic to them, then they cannot be held liable for any consequence that results. Moral judgment becomes impossible. Given that, like almost all theological systems, the Christian Bible posits a moral universe in which human beings are agents who are called to act in the light of the divine character and in accordance with the divine judgment, it naturally follows that Christian theologians have been attracted to the notion of human free will and have sought to expound it at great depth. Psychologist N. Rose echoes this tradition of thought when he writes:

> We are not merely "free to choose," but obliged to be free, to understand and enact our lives in terms of choice under conditions that systematically limit the capacities of so many to shape their own destiny.[1]

Human freedom is not simply then a fact in the world but actually something that humans must rise to in opposition to all that threatens it, as a means to human flourishing.

On the other side, there are two kinds of difficulty. One is the rational puzzle caused by the embeddedness of the human person in a world of cause and effect. When the will is shaped so deeply by the forces that swirl around it—genes, parents, culture and even advertising—then in what sense is there any real "freedom" of the will? Indeed, can we even explain the mental processes involved in making decisions in terms of the word "freedom" with any credibility? The brain is itself a complex

---

[1]N. Rose, *Inventing Ourselves: Psychology, Power and Personhood* (Cambridge: Cambridge University Press, 1999), 17.

entanglement of subconscious and conscious thoughts, and it is by no means evident that conscious thought *precedes* or in some way governs the subconscious. In fact, there's good reason to think of the process happening the other way around.

The second problem is theological and moral, and is most vehemently expressed by Martin Luther in his debate with Erasmus. Human beings cannot resist sin, and indeed, there are none that avoid sin. In Pauline terms we are possessed of a fallen *sarx*—"flesh"—by which he means that there is something unavoidable about our lapse into sinful behavior because of something about us. We are imprisoned by our *epithumia,* or "sinful desire." The metaphor of slave-bondage or death, chosen by Paul and revisited by Augustine and later Luther, reflects the profound corruption of the human will to the degree that no simple and unaided decision of the human will can overcome it. This point remains controversial: even in the midst of his controversy with Pelagius, Augustine was loath to reject the term "free will," and wanted rather to say that even though the will is free, men and women freely but inevitably choose to sin. Others would say that humankind was created with free will, but that free will was either lost or restricted because of the fall. That the individual commits sin is still her fault, for which she is still blameworthy. The theological conundrum was lessened because it was refracted through the medieval theology of purgatory. *Original* sin, which doomed the individual to hell, could be absolved by baptism; but individual acts could still be judged on the assumption of a free decision to do them.

The Reformation insistence on grace alone sharpened the contrast once more. For Luther, and for the Reformed, if grace was to be truly alone in soteriology, then the state of human bondage had to be absolute. The human will could not be described as "free," since it was bound and corrupted by its own habitual sinfulness. It is not simply a matter of coaxing the human individual to choose differently; a wholesale renovation of the human person by grace was necessary.

Nevertheless, the issue of human free will is not simply determined on denominational lines. In the seventeenth century, Jacob Arminius, a Dutch theologian who had a lasting impact on Anglican theology and eventually, through John Wesley, on Protestantism in general, restated the older, more optimistic position on human free will. Arminius and Wesley would claim that they could reconcile this with a Protestant soteriology, with its emphasis on divine grace. Eastern Orthodox theology likewise still prefers to speak of a human free will which is not inimical to its dependence on grace.

TEXT 1: GREGORY OF NYSSA "SIXTH SERMON ON THE BEATITUDES"[2]

The younger brother of Basil of Caesarea, Gregory of Nyssa (*c.* 335–95) was instrumental in the defeat of Arianism and the establishment of the orthodoxy of the Nicene definition of the Trinity. The strong influence of Neoplatonism is evident in his writings on the doctrines of humanity and creation. Gregory taught that the atonement was the paying of a ransom to the Satan, who was trapped, since he was unaware that God himself was concealed in Christ's flesh like a fishhook. Despite this strongly objective account of the atonement (whatever its problems), Gregory also taught that the soul could ascend, given the requisite effort, to contemplate the divine. This was because even though man is a material creation, and thus mortal, his immortal soul has the innate capacity to draw nearer to God. Gregory held that, as part of being made in the image of God, human beings have free will. As a corollary, Gregory also strongly opposed slavery, since it is evil to enslave that which God has declared to be free.

Blessed are the pure in heart for they will see God

As I ponder the stirring words of the Lord, it is like I am sitting on the edge of a cliff overlooking the sea. The boundless depths of the water are reminiscent of the depths of the Lord's thoughts that are beyond my ability to describe. As some of you who live along rocky coastal regions know, it is not unusual to come across a jagged peak protruding over the sea whose side has been sheared off by erosion. Now, if you were the adventurous type you might have carefully walked over to the edge and peered over. What would you feel? A little dizzy? Wobbly? Or would you feel fear mixed with exhilaration? In a similar way my spirit also was unsteady when I immersed myself in the words of our Lord, "Blessed are the pure in heart, for they will see God." God is promising to us that God will be seen by those whose heart has been made clean. Yet, isn't this the same God of whom the Gospel writer John asserted, "No one has ever seen God, not so much as a glimpse" (Jn 1:18)? Or as Paul, the highly respected scholar of the apostolic church, affirmed, "He's never been seen by human eyes—human eyes can't take him in!" (1 Tim 6:15).

When these verses are compared with our verse, "blessed are the pure in heart, for they will see God," they appear contradictory. Yet it is a basic Christian belief that all Scripture is Spirit inspired and useful for teaching. As a result, the bits of information and insight that the Bible provides should fit together in such a manner that they are not contradictory. If at first glance scriptural affirmations appear contradictory, it is essential that we dig deeper and look below the surface.

Further, I am reminded of Moses' teaching on the subject: "No one can see me and live" (Ex 33:20). Moses climbed to the top of Mount Sinai only to learn that

---

[2]Gregory of Nyssa, *Sermons on the Beatitudes*, Classics in Spiritual Formation, trans. Michael Glerup (Downers Grove: IVP Books, 2012), 85–97.

it was not possible for him to catch a glimpse of the face of God. So it is with our own reasoning; over time we keep adding facts on top of facts hoping that we may perceive the reality of God, only to find that all our intellectual efforts fall short of our desire.

In another instance we are taught that to see God is eternal life. Yet three of the most trustworthy guides in the Christian life, John, Paul and Moses, tell us that this is impossible. Do you see why I feel woozy as I attempt to comprehend the depths of these words? Our predicament may be stated this way: If God is life, then the person who does not see God does not see life. Yet, the prophets and apostles, who we confess are divinely inspired, all agree that God cannot be seen. Should we then lose hope in the possibility of experiencing Life itself? Not necessarily, because we can trust in the Lord, who supports the weak in faith. It is helpful to recall the Gospel episode in which Peter walked on the water toward Jesus only to become fearful and begin to sink. Jesus reached out and brought him to safety by lifting him up onto the solid surface of the water (see Mt 14:28–31). Likewise, if the hand of the Son of God reaches out to us and lifts us up, we will be able to stand on the solid surface of our muddled thinking. Once in the grasp of the Lord, freed from fear, we receive the gentle guidance of the firm hand of the Word. For the Lord says to us, "Blessed are the pure in heart, for they will see God."

The promise made by Jesus concerning those who should be considered blessed is staggering. In the language of Scripture, seeing means the same as to have or enjoy. In Psalm 128:5, the psalmist writes, "May you see the prosperity of Jerusalem" (NIV); this means the same as "enjoy the good life in Jerusalem." Or as the prophet writes, "Let the wicked be taken away so that he shall not see the glory of God" (see Is 26:10 LXX). In this instance "not see" means "not share in." As a result, whoever has seen God will enjoy the one thing that is all things to us. Let me explain: Scripturally speaking, when it says "we will see the glory of God," it is shorthand for the following: "We will enjoy all the good gifts of God such as eternal life, freedom from the decay of death and the never-ending happiness of the kingdom of God." In addition, we will hear the gentle voice of the Spirit in our hearts and experience constant joy and spiritual clarity. In short, we will experience all the good we long for in the goodness of God.

Yet, how does this knowledge benefit us? For the problem persists: What benefit is it to know how to see God if we do not have the capability to realize this promise?

It would be like someone saying, "It is a great thing to be in heaven because in heaven we enjoy things that cannot be seen in this life." Now if included in this statement was a description of the means of transportation that made it possible to travel to heaven, then this would be delightful news. But as long as this journey remains impossible, what is the use of being told such things? In fact, it would be cruel to describe heaven in such lofty terms and then in the next breath say there is no way for us to make this journey.

Do you think that the Lord would command something beyond our nature and boundaries of human capability? I don't think so. He would never ask us to fly like the birds without providing us wings and feathers or to live under water when he has designed us to live on dry ground. In all other examples, the law matches the capabilities of those to whom it applies and asks nothing beyond one's natural capacities. Therefore, we should be comforted that what is asked in the beatitude is not hopeless. Heroes of the faith—Paul, John, Moses and others like them—did not miss the mark in attaining the blessedness that comes from seeing God. No, for one said, "There is in store for me the crown of righteousness, which the Lord, the righteous Judge, will award to me on that day" (2 Tim 4:8 NIV), and the other leaned on the chest of Jesus, and Moses heard God's voice say, "I know you by name" (Ex 33:17). Now if these men, who tell us that to see God is beyond us, are blessed and this is achieved through purity of heart, then it follows that purity of heart—the way we become blessed—cannot be impossible. How is it then that those like Paul, speaking scriptural truth, say that seeing God is beyond us and at the same time the Lord's promise that God may be seen by the pure in heart not contradict each other?

Before we move forward, I think it would be best to address some issues of methodology by which we might dig deeper into the subject at hand. The divine nature, whatever it might be in and of itself, is beyond human comprehension. God is unapproachable and inaccessible to human speculation. No method has been devised as a means of understanding the things way over our heads. This is why Paul describes God's ways as "beyond tracing out" (Rom 11:33 NIV), which means the way to knowledge of the divine essence is inaccessible to human rationality. The fact is, no one before us has left a trace of understanding of that which is way over our heads. God's nature is above every nature, and as such, the Invisible and Incomprehensible must be seen and known by some other way. There are many means for understanding. It is possible to see God, who has made all things in wisdom (see Ps 104:24), secondarily through the wisdom displayed in the universe. Archaeologists and historians do this when they examine an ancient art work. They make rational inferences about the artist based on the work of art itself. This example is not completely accurate because what is seen is not the nature of the artist but only the artistic skill mirrored in the work.

Similarly, when we study the mechanisms of creation, we form a rational image not of God's essence but of the wisdom of him who made all things wisely. Another means for understanding is to consider why God created us. He did not create us because he had to; rather, he freely created us out of his goodness. We can say, if we think of God in this way, that we understand God according to his goodness, though again, not his essence. In fact, anything you consider that directs your attention to God's goodness is a means for knowing God, since each of these make God seen. Power, integrity, faithfulness, freedom and all such things stamp on our souls the image of a heavenly and awe-inspiring vision. What I have tried to do here is to demonstrate that the Lord speaks truthfully when he promises that God will be seen by the pure in heart. At the same time, Paul does not lie when he affirms that no one has seen God nor can see God. For God is by nature invisible. He becomes visible in his operations because he may be seen in certain aspects he possesses.

The meaning of this beatitude is not limited to the analogy drawn from operations to Operator. If this were so, then even the secular intellectuals would gain knowledge of divine wisdom and power from their study of the intricacies of the universe. Rather, I think the splendor of the beatitude, available to those who accept its counsel, is something else. I'll give a few examples to illustrate what I'm trying to say. A healthy body is considered a good thing in our society, yet happiness is found not in just knowing the principles of healthy living but in living a healthy life. Take, for example, the person who goes on and on about eating healthy, but his kitchen is filled with junk food. And because of his poor eating habits he suffers a vitamin deficiency that then leads to poor health. What good is it to such a person to talk up healthy living when in fact he is suffering poor health because of his choices?

In the same way we should understand the passage under discussion. The Lord does not say it is blessed to know something about God; rather, it is blessed to have God living in your heart. "Blessed are the pure in heart, for they will see the Lord." I'm not convinced that God promises an immediate vision of God to a person whose spiritual eyesight is purified; rather, I think we should understand this passage along the lines of what Jesus said to others: "The kingdom of God is within you" (Lk 17:21). By this I think he means that if a person's heart is purged of any disruptive affections, she will see the image of God in the beauty of her inner being. It seems to me, in this pithy statement, Jesus counsels this: In every person there is a longing to experience the really Real, and when you hear that the divine majesty is way, way above your head, that its glory is incomprehensible, its beauty is beyond words, do not give up hope in seeing what you long to behold. Why? Because it is in your reach! Inside you are the means to see the really Real. God, in the beginning, gifted you with this amazing aptitude. God impressed on your being the splendor of his likeness as though he was fashioning a replica in soft wax. The bad news is that sin obscured, like layers of accumulated grime, the divine image and made its benefits useless to you. The good news is that by practicing a life of faithfulness, you can scrub off the accumulated filth, and the beauty of the really Real will again radiate from your heart.

A good example of this is a rusty tool. With a little elbow grease and steel wool you can remove the rust and restore it to its original shiny condition. And so it is with the inner person, which the Lord calls the heart; when the rust of moral decay is scrubbed off, the heart will recover the likeness of its prototype (Jesus) and be good—for what is like the good is also good. Therefore, if a person who is pure in heart sees within himself what he desires, he becomes blessed because when he gazes on his own purity he sees the reflection of the divine image.

As an example, most people don't stare directly into the sun but observe the sun indirectly through a mirror. The reflection in the mirror is not the sun, though you can see the sun's disc shape just like those who gaze directly at the sun. So the Lord says it is with you. Even though we are too weak to look directly on the divine light, we can see the light indirectly in ourselves if we return to the grace of the image that was formed in us at the beginning of creation. For God is purity, freedom from corrupted desires and separation from all wickedness. It follows that if these good things can be found in you, then indeed God is in you. Therefore, if your mind is not watered down with any evil, free from corrupted desires and steers clear from any stain, then you are blessed because of your laser like vision. For by becoming pure you now can see clearly what is undetectable to those not purified. With the cataract of materialism that blurred the eye of your heart removed, you now see in the radiance of your heart the blessed vision. And what is this vision? It is purity, sanctification, simplicity, and other reflections of the really Real by which God is seen.

Now I fully affirm that what has been said so far is true, but it seems that we still face the same predicament as presented at the beginning of the sermon. We know that if someone sees and enjoys heaven's amazing sights but because the way to these amazing wonders is not possible, we are left knowing that none of these amazing insights are of any value to us. So it is with the happiness that comes from a purified heart. I don't think anyone doubts that a person is blessed if his heart is purified, but for most of us purifying our hearts is equally as mystifying as trying to make our way to heaven. What means of transport is available for that type of trip? Where does one find Jacob's ladder or the fiery chariot that carried Elijah to heaven? Anyone wise in the ways of the heart knows that escaping from the snares of misdirected desire is impossible, or at the least impractical. Our whole life is somehow connected to passions. Our conception is the effect of the consummation of our parents' sexual desires. Our growth into adulthood and later decline into old age is fuelled by desire. Misdirected desires have overwhelmed holy desires since Adam and Eve's disobedience allowed them to take root in our heart. Humans are very similar to animals in this aspect of generation. For animals in each generation inherit the traits of their parents and their parents' parents and so on. So it is with us, we inherit the sinful ways of our parents—sinner from sinner from sinner. As a result, sin—in some sense—latches onto us when we are born and grows with us until our life comes to its end.

By contrast, virtue is difficult to acquire. Even if we make it our life's pursuit, any movement we make is hardly noticeable. The Bible teaches us this fact. We all know that the path to the kingdom is difficult and goes through a narrow opening, but wide and easy is the way (like cruising downhill on a highway) that leads to wickedness and death. At the same time, the Bible, through the lives and achievements of the saints, affirms that the higher life is not beyond our reach. Again, we come back to—the promise of seeing God takes form in two ways. First, understanding the divine nature which surpasses the universe, and second, that which comes from being united with God through purity of life. The former knowledge is clearly not attainable, which is confirmed by the saints, while the latter is promised to us in the Lord's teaching, "Blessed are the pure in heart, for they will see God."

How to become pure in heart is taught throughout the Gospels. You need only to study the principles one by one to discover what it is that makes the heart pure. Wickedness can be separated into two categories: one consisting in works and the other consisting in thoughts. Wrongdoing observable in actions was punished under the law of the Old Testament. Now the Lord extends the law to cover the latter, not so much punishing the evil act but guarding against the evil taking hold in the first place. To liberate the will from evil is much better than making a person's life free from wrongdoing. Since evil can take shape in many ways, the Lord applies his own teachings to come up with the appropriate cure for each forbidden exploit.

Since anger can touch all aspects of life, he begins with a cure for it by first stipulating no anger. "You've learned," he says, "from the old law not to murder; now learn how to keep your soul from anger at your neighbour." He did not completely outlaw anger. He knew that in some instances that anger could be used toward a good end. What he does outlaw is to be angry with your brother for no good reason. This is made clear when he says, "But I say to you that whoever is angry with his brother without a cause" (Mt 5:22 NKJV). The ending clause "without a cause" shows that sometimes anger is timely, particularly when anger is directed toward the rebuke of sinful behavior. This type of anger is confirmed in the word of Scripture in the case of Phineas, when he appeased God's wrath by slaying the transgressors of the law (see Num 25:6–11).

Jesus' next move is to apply the cure to sins committed through pleasure. And by his commandment he frees the heart from the lust for adultery. Similarly, you find the Lord corrects the fault of each, one by one, by setting up in opposition his law to each vice. He prevents physical attacks from flaring up by not even permitting self-defense. He drives out the passion of greed by instructing a robbery victim to go the distance and give up what he has left to his mugger. He repairs cowardice by commanding us to hold death in contempt. Overall, you see that the Lord, by his commandments, gets to the root issues of evil. Like a plough digging into the depths of our heart, his commandments cut off the growth of weeds.

The Lord does us well in two ways: first by promising good things, and second by providing instruction that leads to the goal. If you are the type of person who thinks pursuing the good is annoying, then compare it with the opposite way of life, and you will discover how much more distressing it is, especially if you value the life to come over the present. People who hear references to hell no longer resist sin by effort and hard work, but fear awakened in the mind becomes enough to chastise one's passions. Something that is implicit in our teaching might also arouse in us a more intense desire. If the pure in heart are blessed, then it follows that the opposite is true: those with a corrupted mind are miserable because they stare into the face of our Adversary. Additionally, if the divine image is stamped on the life of virtue, then it is clear that the life of vice takes on the shape and image of the Adversary. Now certain names are used for God to account for different attributes that correspond to the good—light, life, incorruption and similar things. Conversely, everything opposite of the good is attributed to the ringleader of evil—darkness, death, corruption. Knowing the difference between a good life and an evil life suggests that we have the capability by way of our free will to choose either life path. So let us run away from the form of the devil, discarding the mask of evil and putting on again the image of God. Let us become pure in heart, in order that we might become blessed when the image of God is reformed in us through wholesome conduct, in Christ Jesus, our Lord, to whom be glory forever and ever. Amen.

Questions

1 Gregory asks: "What benefit is it to know how to see God if we do not have the capability to realize this promise?" What makes us unable to see God?

2 Does God ask us to do that which is impossible for us?

3 What is the difference between understanding God according to his goodness rather than his essence?

4 "He becomes visible in his operations because he may be seen in certain aspects he possesses." Is this a satisfactory resolution of the conundrum Gregory presents?

5 What obscures the sight of God from the soul? What can remedy it, for Gregory? What is the path to purity of heart?

6 How does Gregory describe the inner desires and thoughts? How can they be restrained?

7 "Knowing the difference between a good life and an evil life suggests that we have the capability by way of our free will to choose either life path." True or False?

TEXT 2: AUGUSTINE,³
ON GRACE AND FREE WILL?

Augustine of Hippo (354–430) was not only one of the most creative and substantial theological thinkers of the church, he was also one of its doughtiest defenders. Nothing quite engaged his mind (and his pen) like controversy. The Pelagian controversy of the first part of the fifth century was no exception. Pelagius was (it is thought) a British monk who was born around 354 AD. He attributed the moral laxity he observed in Christian Rome to the doctrine of grace as preached by Augustine, believing rather that man could avoid sinning. To deny this was fatalism, in his opinion, and offered no path to moral improvement. Augustine's response in defense of the priority of grace was extensive, beginning with works such as *On the Spirit and the Letter* (412 AD). By 426, however, Augustine had been pressed to provide a more comprehensive response to the relationship between grace and free will, since some monks in Adrumetum (Valentinus was their abbot) had fallen into division over the matter. Was Augustine denying free will entirely? In response, he composed *On Grace and Free Will*, to show that both grace *and* free will are to be upheld.

Chap. 1 – The occasion and argument of this work

With reference to those persons who so preach and defend man's free will, as boldly to deny, and endeavor to do away with, the grace of God which calls us to Him, and delivers us from our evil deserts, and by which we obtain the good deserts which lead to everlasting life: we have already said a good deal in discussion, and committed it to writing, so far as the Lord has granted to enable us. But since there are some persons who so defend God's grace as to deny man's free will, or who suppose that free will is denied when grace is defended, I have determined to write somewhat on this point to your Love, my brother Valentinus, and the rest of you, who are serving God together under the impulse of a mutual love. For it has been told me concerning you, brethren, by some members of your brotherhood who have visited us, and are the bearers of this communication of ours to you, that there are dissensions among you on this subject. This, then, being the case, dearly beloved, that you be not disturbed by the obscurity of this question, I counsel you first to thank God for such things as you understand; but as for all which is beyond the reach of your mind, pray for understanding from the Lord, observing, at the same time, peace and love among yourselves; and until He Himself lead you to perceive what at present is beyond your comprehension, walk firmly on the ground of which you are sure. This is the advice of the Apostle Paul, who, after saying that he was not yet perfect, (Phil 3:12) a little later adds, "Let us, therefore, as many as are perfect, be thus

---

³Augustine, *On Nature and Grace*, in P. Schaff ed., *Nicene and Post-Nice Fathers*, vol 5, (Peabody, Mass: Hendrickson, 1994), pp. 443–6

minded," (Phil 3:15)—meaning perfect to a certain extent, but not having attained to a perfection sufficient for us; and then immediately adds, "And if, in anything, ye be otherwise minded, God shall reveal even this unto you. Nevertheless, whereunto we have already attained, let us walk by the same rule" (Phil 3:16). For by walking in what we have attained, we shall be able to advance to what we have not yet attained,—God revealing it to us if in anything we are otherwise minded,—provided we do not give up what He has already revealed.

Chap. 2 – He proves the existence of free will in man from the precepts addressed to him by God

Now He has revealed to us, through His Holy Scriptures, that there is in a man a free choice of will. But how He has revealed this I do not recount in human language, but in divine. There is, to begin with, the fact that God's precepts themselves would be of no use to a man unless he had free choice of will, so that by performing them he might obtain the promised rewards. For they are given that no one might be able to plead the excuse of ignorance, as the Lord says concerning the Jews in the gospel: "If I had not come and spoken unto them, they would not have sin; but now they have no excuse for their sin" (John 15:22). Of what sin does He speak but of that great one which He foreknew, while speaking thus, that they would make their own—that is, the death they were going to inflict upon Him? For they did not have "no sin" before Christ came to them in the flesh. The apostle also says: "The wrath of God is revealed from heaven against all ungodliness and unrighteousness of men who hold back the truth in unrighteousness; because that which may be known of God is manifest in them; for God hath showed it unto them. For the invisible things of Him are from the creation of the world clearly seen being understood by the things that are made—even His eternal power and Godhead, so that they are inexcusable" (Rom 1:18–20). In what sense does he pronounce them to be "inexcusable," except with reference to such excuse as human pride is apt to allege in such words as, "If I had only known, I would have done it; did I not fail to do it because I was ignorant of it?" or, "I would do it if I knew how; but I do not know, therefore I do not do it"? All such excuse is removed from them when the precept is given them, or the knowledge is made manifest to them how to avoid sin.

Chap. 3 – Sinners are convicted when attempting to excuse themselves by blaming god, because they have free will

There are, however, persons who attempt to find excuse for themselves even from God. The Apostle James says to such: "Let no man say when he is tempted, I am tempted of God; for God cannot be tempted with evil, neither tempteth He any man. But every man is tempted when he is drawn away of his own lust, and enticed. Then, when lust hath conceived, it bringeth forth sin: and sin, when it is finished, bringeth forth death" (James 1:13–15). Solomon, too, in his book of Proverbs, has this answer for such as wish to find an excuse for themselves from God Himself: "The folly of a man spoils his ways; but he blames God in his heart" (Prov. 19:3). And in the book of Ecclesiasticus we read: "Say not thou, It is through the Lord that I fell away; for thou oughtest not to do the things that He hateth: nor do thou say, He hath caused me to err; for He hath no need of the sinful man. The Lord hateth all abomination, and they that fear God love it not. He Himself made man from the beginning, and left him in the hand of His counsel. If thou be willing, thou shalt keep His commandments, and perform true fidelity. He hath set fire and water before thee: stretch forth thine hand unto whether thou wilt. Before man is life and death, and whichsoever pleaseth him shall be given to him" (Eccl. 15:11–17). Observe how very plainly is set before our view the free choice of the human will.

Chap. 4 – The divine commands which are most suited to the will itself illustrate its freedom

What is the import of the fact that in so many passages God requires all His commandments to be kept and fulfilled? How does He make this requisition, if there is no free will? What means "the happy man," of whom the Psalmist says that" his will has been the law of the Lord"? (Ps 1:2) Does he not clearly enough show that a man by his own will takes his stand in the law of God? Then again, there are so many commandments which in some way are expressly adapted to the human will; for instance, there is, "Be not overcome of evil," (Rom 7:1) and others of similar import, such as, "Be not like a horse or a mule, which have no understanding;" (Ps 32:9) and, "Reject not the counsels of thy mother;" (Prov. 1:8) and, "Be not wise in thine own conceit;" (Prov. 3:7) and, "Despise not the chastening of the Lord;" (Prov. 3:2) and, "Forget not my law;" (Prov. 3:1) and, "Forbear not to do good to the poor;" (Prov. 3:27) and, "Devise not evil against thy friend;" (Prov. 3:29) and, "Give no heed to a worthless woman;" (Prov. 5:2) and, "He is not inclined to understand how to do good;" (Ps 36:3) and, "They refused to attend to my counsel;" (Prov. 1:30) with numberless other passages of the inspired Scriptures of the Old Testament. And what do they all show us but the free choice of the human will? So, again, in the evangelical and apostolic books of the New Testament what other lesson is taught us? As when it is said, "Lay not up for yourselves treasures upon earth;" (Matt 6:19) and, "Fear not them which kill the body;" (Matt 10:28) and, "If any man will come after me, let him deny himself;" (Matt 26:24) and again, "Peace on earth to men of good will" (Luke 2:14). So also that the Apostle Paul says: "Let him do what he willeth; he sinneth not if he marry. Nevertheless, he that standeth stedfast in his heart, having no necessity, but hath power over his own will, and hath so decreed in his heart that he will keep his virgin, doeth well" (1 Cor 7:36–37). And so again, "If I do this willingly, I have a reward;" (1 Cor 9:17) while in another passage he says, "Be ye sober and righteous, and sin not;" (1 Cor 15:34) and again, "As ye have a readiness to will, so also let there be a prompt performance; " (2 Cor 8:1) then he remarks to Timothy about the younger widows, "When they have begun to wax wanton against Christ, they choose to marry." So in another passage, "All that will to live godly in Christ Jesus shall suffer persecution;" (2 Tim 3:12) while to Timothy himself he says, "Neglect not the gift that is in thee" (1 Tim 4:14). Then to Philemon he addresses this explanation: "That thy benefit should not be as it were of necessity, but of thine own will" (Philemon 14). Servants also he advises to obey their masters "with a good will" (Eph 6:7). In strict accordance with this, James says: "Do not err, my beloved brethren . . . and have not the faith of our Lord Jesus Christ with respect to persons;" (James 1:16, 2:1) and, "Do not speak evil one of another" (James 4:11). So also John in his Epistle writes, "Do not love the world," (1 John 2:15) and other things of the same import, Now wherever it is said, "Do not do this," and "Do not do that," and wherever there is any requirement in the divine admonitions for the work of the will to do anything, or to refrain from doing anything, there is at once a sufficient proof of free will. No man, therefore, when he sins, can in his heart blame God for it, but every man must impute the fault to himself. Nor does it detract at all from a man's own will when he performs any act in accordance with God. Indeed, a work is then to be pronounced a good one when a person does it willingly; then, too, may the reward of a good work be hoped for from Him concerning whom it is written, "He shall reward every man according to his works" (Matt 16:27).

Chap. 5 – He shows that ignorance affords no such excuse as shall free the offender from punishment; but that to sin with knowledge is a graver thing than to sin in ignorance

The excuse such as men are in the habit of alleging from ignorance is taken away from those persons who know God's commandments. But neither will those be without punishment who know not the law of God. "For as many as have sinned without law shall also perish without law; and as many as have sinned in the law shall be judged by the law" (Rom 2:12). Now the apostle does not appear to me to have said this as if he meant that they would have to suffer something worse who in their sins are ignorant of the law than they who know it. [III.] It is seemingly worse, no doubt, "to perish" than "to be judged;" but inasmuch as he was speaking of the Gentiles and of the Jews when he used these words, because the former were without the law, but the latter had received the law, who can venture to say that the Jews who sin in the law will not perish, since they refused to believe in Christ, when it was of them that the apostle said, "They shall be judged by the law"? For without faith in Christ no man can be delivered; and therefore they will be so judged that they perish. If, indeed, the condition of those who are ignorant of the law of God is worse than the condition of those who know it, how can that be true which the Lord says in the gospel: "The servant who knows not his lord's will, and commits things worthy of stripes, shall be beaten with few stripes; whereas the servant who knows his lord's will, and commits things worthy of stripes, shall be beaten with many stripes"? (Luke 7:47–48) Observe how clearly He here shows that it is a graver matter for a man to sin with knowledge than in ignorance. And yet we must not on him this account betake ourselves for refuge to the shades of ignorance, with the view of finding our excuse therein. It is one thing to be ignorant, and another thing to be unwilling to know. For the will is at fault in the case of the man of whom it is said, "He is not inclined to understand, so as to do good" (Ps 36:3). But even the ignorance, which is not theirs who refuse to know, but theirs who are, as it were, simply ignorant, does not so far excuse anyone as to exempt him from the punishment of eternal fire, though his failure to believe has been the result of his not having at all heard what he should believe; but probably only so far as to mitigate his punishment. For it was not said without reason: "Pour out Thy wrath upon the heathen that have not known Thee;" (Ps 79:6) nor again according to what the apostle says: "When He shall come from heaven in a flame of fire to take vengeance on them that know not God" (2 Thess 1:7–8). But yet in order that we may have that knowledge that will prevent our saying, each one of us, "I did not know," "I did not hear," "I did not understand; "the human will is summoned, in such words as these: "Wish not to be as the horse or as the mule, which have no understanding;" (Ps 32:9) although it may show itself even worse, of which it is written, "A stubborn servant will not be reproved by words; for even if he understand, yet he will not obey" (Prov. 29:19). But when a man says, "I cannot do what I am commanded, because I am mastered by my concupiscence," he has no longer any excuse to plead from ignorance, nor reason to blame God in his heart, but he recognizes and laments his own evil in himself; and still to such a one the apostle says: "Be not overcome by evil, but overcome evil with good;" (Rom 7:21) and of course the very fact that the injunction, "Consent not to be overcome," is addressed to him, undoubtedly summons the determination of his will. For to consent and to refuse are functions proper to will.

Chap. 6 – God's grace to be maintained against the Pelagians; the Pelagian heresy not an old one

It is, however, to be feared lest all these and similar testimonies of Holy Scripture (and undoubtedly there are a great many of them), in the maintenance of free will, be understood in such a way as to leave no room for God's assistance and grace in leading a godly life and a good conversation, to which the eternal reward is due; and lest poor wretched man, when he leads a good life and performs good works (or rather thinks that he leads a good life and performs good works), should dare to glory in himself and not in the Lord, and to put his hope of righteous living in himself alone; so as to be followed by the prophet Jeremiah's malediction when he says, "Cursed is the man who has hope in man, and maketh strong the flesh of his arm, and whose heart departeth from the Lord" (Jer. 17:5). Understand, my brethren, I pray you, this passage of the prophet. Because the prophet did not say, "Cursed is the man who has hope in his own self," it might seem to some that the passage, "Cursed is the man who has hope in man," was spoken to prevent man having hope in any other man but himself. In order, therefore, to show that his admonition to man was not to have hope in himself, after saying, "Cursed is the man who has hope in man," he immediately added, "And maketh strong the flesh of his arm." He used the word "arm" to designate power in operation. By the term "flesh," however, must be understood human frailty. And therefore he makes strong the flesh of his arm who supposes that a power which is frail and weak (that is, human) is sufficient for him to perform good works, and therefore puts not his hope in God for help. This is the reason why he added the further clause, "And whose heart departeth from the Lord." Of this character is the Pelagian heresy, which is not an ancient one, but has only lately come into existence. Against this system of error there was first a good deal of discussion; then, as the ultimate resource, it was referred to sundry episcopal councils, the proceedings of which, not, indeed, in every instance, but in some, I have despatched to you for your perusal. In order, then, to our performance of good works, let us not have hope in man, making strong the flesh of our arm; nor let our heart ever depart from the Lord, but let it say to him," Be Thou my helper; forsake me not, nor despise me, O God of my salvation" (Ps 27:9).

Questions

1 What is Augustine's advice about dealing with obscure and difficult theological questions?

2 Augustine argues that the precepts of God to human beings are evidence that there is in us a "free choice of will." Does this argument follow?

3 Why is it vital to uphold free will as far as Augustine is concerned?

4 In what sense are good works not grounds for "hope in man"?

TEXT 3: ANSELM: *ON FREE WILL*[4]

Anselm of Canterbury (*c.* 1033–1109) has some claim to a rank just behind Thomas Aquinas as the most original and influential theologian of the medieval era. He is often termed a founder of scholasticism—that method of critical academic thought which dominated European intellectual life from about 1100 until 1700. Scholasticism emphasized the use of dialectical reasoning as a tool to resolve the thorny problems of thought. Scholastic thinkers characteristically drew carefully nuanced distinctions and analyzed concepts with a focused rigor. Anselm's treatise *On Free Will* is the second in a trilogy of pieces written between 1080 and 1086, the first being *On Truth* and the third *On the Fall of the Devil*. The dialogue format that Anselm uses here has its origins in Classical thought and enables him to clarify his teaching and anticipate objections. Anselm shows that even by the eleventh century, the dilemmas surrounding the human will were well understood. Sin has an impact on our ability to choose the good. But are we then still culpable for our sin? Anselm asserts that freedom and slavery can coexist in human beings without contradiction. Consideration of what angels may or may not be capable of provides an interesting foil for his anthropology.

1 That the power of sinning does not pertain to free will

Student. Since free will seems to be repugnant to grace, predestination and God's foreknowledge, I want to understand freedom of will and know whether we always have it. For if 'to be able to sin and not to sin' is due to free will, as some are accustomed to say, and we always have it, why do we sometimes need grace? But if we do not always have it, why is sin imputed to us when we sin without free will?

Teacher. I do not think free will is the power to sin or not to sin. Indeed if this were its definition, neither God nor the angels, who are unable to sin, would have free will, which it is impious to say.

S. But what if one were to say that the free will of God and the angels is different from ours?

T. Although the free will of men differs from the free will of God and the angels, the definition of freedom expressed by the word ought to be the same. For although one animal differs from another either substantially or accidentally, the definition attached to the word 'animal' is the same for all. That is why we must so define free will that the definition contains neither too little nor too much. Since the divine free will and that of the good angels cannot sin, to be able to sin does not belong in the definition of free will. Furthermore, the power to sin is neither

---

[4]From Anselm, *Anselm of Canterbury: The Major Works*, ed. Brian Davies and G. R. Evans, (New York: Oxford University Press, 1998), 175–92. ("On Free Will" was translated by Ralph McInerny.)

liberty nor a part of liberty. Pay attention to what I am going to say and you will fully understand this.

S. That is why I am here.

T. Which free will seems more free to you, that which so wills that it cannot sin, such that it can in no way be deflected from the rectitude constituted by not sinning, or that which can in some way be deflected to sinning?

S. I do not see why that which is capable of both is not freer.

T. Do you not see that one who is as he ought to be, and as it is expedient for him to be, such that he is unable to lose this state, is freer than one who is such that he can lose it and be led into what is indecent and inexpedient for him?

S. I think there is no doubt that this is so.

T. And would you not say that it is no less doubtful that to sin is always indecent and harmful.

S. No one of healthy mind would think otherwise.

T. Therefore a will that cannot fall from rectitude into sin is more free than one that can desert it.

S. Nothing seems to me more reasonable to say.

T. Therefore, since the capacity to sin when added to will diminishes liberty, and its lack increases it, it is neither liberty nor a part of liberty.

S. Nothing is more obvious.

2 Both the angel and man sinned by this capacity to sin and by free will and, though they could have become slaves of sin, sin did not have the power to dominate them

T. What is extraneous to freedom does not pertain to free will

S. I can contest none of your arguments, but I am not a little swayed by the fact that in the beginning both the angelic nature and ours had the capacity to sin, since without it, they would not have sinned. Wherefore, if by this capacity, which is alien to free will, both natures sinned, how can we say they sinned by free will? But if they did not sin by free will, it seems they sinned necessarily. That is, they sinned either willingly or necessarily. But if they sinned how so if not by free will? And if not by free will, then indeed it seems that they sinned necessarily. And there is something else that strikes me in this ability to sin. One who can sin, can be the slave of sin, since 'he who commits sin, is the slave of sin' [John 8: 34]. But he who can be the slave of sin, can be dominated by sin. How was that nature created free then, and what kind of free will is it that can be dominated by sin?

T. It was through the capacity to sin willingly and freely and not of necessity that ours and the angelic nature first sinned and were able to serve sin, yet they cannot be dominated by sin in such a way that they and their judgment can no longer be called free.

S. You must expand on what you said since it is opaque to me.

T. The apostate angel and the first man sinned through free will, because they sinned through a judgment that is so free that it cannot be coerced to sin by anything else. That is why they are justly reprehended; when they had a free will that could not be coerced by anything else, they willingly and without necessity sinned. They sinned through their own free will, though not insofar as it was free, that is, not through that thanks to which it was free and had the power not to sin or to serve sin, but rather by the power it had of sinning, unaided by its freedom not to sin or to be coerced into the servitude of sin. What seemed to you to follow does not, namely, that if will could be a slave to sin it could be dominated by sin, and therefore neither it nor its judgment are free. But this is not so. For what has it in its power not to serve cannot be forced by another to serve, although it can serve by its own power: for as long as the power uses that which is for serving and not that which is for not serving, nothing can dominate it so that it should serve. For if the rich man is free to make a poor man his servant, as long as he does not do so, he does not lose the name of freedom nor is the poor man said to be able to be dominated or, if this is said, it is said improperly, for this is not in his power but in another's. Therefore nothing prevents either angel or man from being free prior to sin or from having had free will.

3 How free will is had after they have made themselves slaves of sin and what free will is

S. You have satisfied me that nothing certainly prevents this prior to sin, but how can they retain free will after they have made themselves slaves of sin?

T. Although they subjected themselves to sin, they were unable to lose natural free will. But now they cannot use that freedom without a grace other than that which they previously had.

S. I believe that, but I want to understand it.

T. Let us first consider the kind of free will they had before sin when they certainly had free will.

S. I am ready.

T. Why do you think they had free will: to attain what they want or to will what they ought and what is expedient for them to will?

S. The latter.

T. Therefore they had free will for the sake of rectitude of will. As long as they willed what they ought, they had rectitude of will.

S. That is so.

T. Still to say that they had free will for the sake of rectitude of will is open to doubt unless something is added. So I ask: How did they have free will for the sake of rectitude of will? To take it without any giver when they did not yet have it? To receive what they did not have when it was given to them? To abandon what they received and to get it back again after they had let it go? Or to receive it in order to keep it always?

S. I do not think they had the liberty for the sake of rectitude without a giver, since there is nothing they have that they have not received. We should not say that they had liberty to receive from a giver what they previously did not have, because we ought not to think that they were made without right will. Although it should not be denied that they had the freedom to receive this rectitude, if they abandon it it would be restored to them by the original giver. We often see men brought back from injustice to justice by heavenly grace.

T. It is true as you say that they can receive the lost rectitude if it is restored, but we are asking about the freedom they had before they sinned, since without any doubt they had free will then, and not about what no one would need if he had never abandoned the truth.

S. I will now respond to the other things you asked me. It is not true that they had liberty in order to abandon that rectitude, because to abandon the rectitude of the will is to sin, and we showed above that the power to sin is not liberty nor any part of it. They do not receive liberty in order to take on again a rectitude they had abandoned, since such rectitude is given in order that it might never be lost. The power of receiving again what is lost would bring about negligence in retaining what is had. It follows then that freedom of will was given to the rational nature in order that it might retain the rectitude of will it has received.

T. You have responded well to what was asked, but we must still consider for what purpose a rational nature ought to retain that rectitude, whether for the sake of the rectitude itself, or for the sake of something else.

S. If that liberty were not given to such a nature in order that it might preserve rectitude of will for the sake of rectitude, it would not avail for justice. Justice seems to be the retention of rectitude of will for its own sake. But we believe that free will is for the sake of justice. Therefore without a doubt we should assert that the rational nature receives liberty solely to preserve rectitude of will for its own sake.

T. Therefore, since all liberty is a capacity, the liberty of will is the capacity for preserving rectitude of the will for the sake of rectitude itself.

S. It cannot be otherwise.

T. So it is now clear that free judgment is nothing other than a judgment capable of preserving the rectitude of will for the sake of rectitude itself.

S. It is indeed clear. But as long as will has that rectitude it can preserve what it has. But how, after it has lost it, can it preserve what it does not have? In the absence of the rectitude that can be preserved, there is no free will capable of preserving it. For it does not avail for preserving what is not had.

T. But even if the rectitude of will is absent, the rational nature still has undiminished what is proper to it. I think we have no power sufficient unto itself for action, and yet when those things are lacking without which our powers can scarcely be led to act, we are no less said to have them insofar as they are in us. Just as no instrument suffices of itself to act, and yet when the conditions for using the instrument are wanting, it is not false to say that we have the instrument to do something. What you may observe in many things, I will show you in one. No one having sight is said to be incapable of seeing a mountain.

S. Indeed, one who cannot see a mountain, does not have sight.

T. He who has sight has the power and means of seeing a mountain. And yet if the mountain were absent and you said to him, 'Look at the mountain,' he would answer, 'I cannot, because it is not there. If it were there, I could see it.' Again, if the mountain were there and light absent, he would say that he could not see the mountain, meaning that without light he cannot, but he could if there were light. Again, if the mountain and light are present to one with sight but there is something blocking sight, as when one closes his eyes, he would say that he cannot see the mountain, although if nothing blocked sight, he could without any doubt see the mountain.

S. Everyone knows these things.

T. You see, then, that the power of seeing a body is (1) in the one seeing in one sense and (2) in another sense in the thing to be seen, and in yet another sense in the medium, which is neither the seeing nor the thing to be seen; and with respect to what is in the medium, there we must distinguish between (3) what helps and (4) what does not impede, that is, when nothing that can impede does impede.

S. I plainly see.

T. Therefore these powers are four, and if one of them is lacking the other three singly or together cannot bring it off; yet when the others are absent we do not deny either that he who has sight or the means or the power of seeing can see, or that the visible can be seen to be seen, or that light can aid sight.

4 How those who do not have rectitude have the power to preserve it

T The fourth power is improperly so called. That which can impede sight, is said to give the power of seeing only because by being removed it does not impede. The power to see light [properly] consists in only three things because that which is seen and that which aids are the same. Is this not known to all?

S. Indeed it is unknown to none.

T. If then the visible thing is absent, or in the dark, or if those having sight have shut or covered their eyes, so far as we are concerned we have the power to see any visible thing. What then prevents us from having the power to preserve rectitude of will for its own sake, even if that rectitude is absent, so long as reason whereby we can know it and will whereby we can hold it are in us? It is in these-reason and will-that freedom of will consists.

S. You have put my mind at rest that this power of preserving rectitude of will is always in a rational nature, and that this is the power of free will in the first man and the angel, nor could rectitude of will be taken away from them unless they willed it.

5 That no temptation forces one to sin unwillingly

S. But how can the judgment of will be free because of this power, given the fact that often and without willing it a man who has right will is deprived of his own rectitude under the force of temptation?

T. No one is deprived of this rectitude except by his own will. One who acts unwillingly is said to act against what he wills; and no one is deprived of this rectitude against his will. But a man can be bound unwillingly, because he does not wish to be bound, and is tied up unwillingly; he can be killed unwillingly, because he can will not to be killed; but he cannot will unwillingly, because one cannot will to will against his will. Every willing person wills his own willing.

S. How can one be said to lie unwillingly when he lies to avoid being killed, something he only does willingly? For just as he unwillingly lies, so he unwillingly wills to lie. And he who wills unwillingly to lie, is not willing that he wills to lie.

T. Perhaps then he is said to lie unwillingly because he so wills the truth that he will only lie to save his life, and he wills the lie for the sake of life and not for the sake of the lie itself, since he wills the truth; and thus he lies both willingly and unwillingly. For to will something for its own sake, e.g. as we will health for its own sake, is different from willing something for the sake of something else, as when we will to drink absinthe for the sake of health. Perhaps with respect to these two kinds of willing one could be said to lie both willingly and unwillingly. He is said to lie unwillingly because he does not will it in the way he wills the truth, but that does not conflict with my view that no one unwillingly abandons rectitude of will. He wills to abandon it by lying for the sake of his life, according to which he does not unwillingly abandon it but wills to in the sense of will of which we now speak. That is, willing to lie for the sake of his life, not willing to lie for its own sake. Therefore either he certainly lies unwillingly, because he must either be killed or lie unwillingly, that is, he is not willingly in the anguish because either of these will necessarily come about. For although it is necessary that he be either killed or lie, yet it is not necessary that he be killed, because he can escape death if he lies, nor is it necessary for him to lie, because he could not lie and be killed. Neither of these is determinately necessary, because both are in his power. Therefore although he either lies or is killed unwillingly, it does not follow that he lies unwillingly or is killed unwillingly.

There is another argument frequently given to show why someone is said to do something unwillingly, against his grain and necessarily, yet does not want to. What we do not do because we can only do it with difficulty, we say we cannot do and necessarily turn away from. And what we can abandon only with difficulty we say we do unwillingly and necessarily. In this way, one who lies lest he be killed, is said to lie against his will, not willingly, and of necessity, given that he cannot avoid the falsehood without the penalty of death. He who lies in order to save his life is improperly said to lie against his will, because he willingly lies, and he is improperly said to will to lie against his will, because he wills it precisely by willing it. For just as when he lies he wills himself to lie, so when he wills to lie, he wills that willing.

S. I cannot deny what you say.

T. Why then not say that free will is that which another power cannot overcome without its assent?

S. Can we not for a similar reason say that the will of a horse is free because he only serves his appetite willingly?

T. It is not the same. For in the horse there is not the will to subject himself, but naturally, always and of necessity he is the slave of sense appetite, whereas in man, as long as his will is right, he does not serve nor is he subject to what he ought not to do, nor can he be diverted from that rectitude by any other force, unless he willingly consents to what he ought not to do, which consent does not come about naturally or of necessity as in the horse, but is clearly seen to be from itself

S. You have taken care of my objection about the horse; let us go back to where we were.

T. Would you deny that every free being is such that it can only be moved or prevented willingly?

S. I do not see how I could.

T. Tell me how right will prevails and how it is conquered.

S. To will the preservation of rectitude for its own sake is for it to prevail, but to will what it ought not is for it to be conquered.

T. I think that temptation can only stop right will or force it to what it ought not to will willingly, such that it wills the one and not the other.

S. I do not see any way in which that could be false.

T. Who then can say that the will is not free to preserve rectitude, and free from temptation and sin, if no temptation can divert it save willingly from rectitude to sin, that is, to willing what it ought not? Therefore when it is conquered, it is not conquered by another power but by itself

S. That demonstrates what has been said.

T. Do you see that from this it follows that no temptation can conquer right will? For if it could, it would have the power to conquer and would conquer by its own power. But this cannot be, since the will can only be conquered by itself. Wherefore temptation can in no way conquer right will, and it is only improperly said to conquer it. For it only means that the will can subject itself to temptation, just as conversely when the weak is said to be able to be conquered by the strong, he is said to be *able,* not by his own power but by another's, since it only means that the strong has the power to conquer the weak.

6 How our will, although it seems powerless, is powerful against temptations

S. Although you were to make subject to our will all the forces fighting against it and contend that no temptation can dominate it in such a way that I cannot counter your assertions, none the less I cannot agree that there is no impotence in the will, something nearly all experience when they are overcome by violent temptation. Therefore, unless you can reconcile the power that you prove and the impotence that we feel, my mind will not be at rest on this matter.

T. In what does the impotence of which you speak consist?

S. In the fact that I cannot adhere to rectitude with perseverance.

T. If you do not adhere because of impotence, you are turned away from rectitude by an alien force.

S. I admit it.

T. And what is this force?

S. The force of temptation.

T. This force does not turn the will from rectitude unless it wills what the temptation suggests.

S. That is so. But by its very force temptation prompts it to will what it suggests.

T. But how can it force willing? Because it can will only with great trouble or because it can in no way not will?

S. Although I have to admit that sometimes we are so oppressed by temptations that we cannot without difficulty manage not to will what they suggest, still I cannot say that they ever so oppress us that we can in no way not will what they inspire.

T. I do not see how that could be said. For if a man wills to lie in order that he not suffer death and live a little longer, who would say that to will not to lie is impossible for him in order that he might avoid eternal death and live eternally? So you should not doubt that the impotence in preserving rectitude, which you say is in our will when we consent to temptation, is a matter of difficulty rather than impossibility. We often say that we cannot do something, not because it is impossible for us, but because we can do it only with difficulty. This difficulty does not destroy freedom of will. Temptation can fight against a will that does not give in but cannot conquer it against its will. In this way I think we can see how the power of the will as established by true arguments is compatible with the impotence our humanity experiences. For just as difficulty does not in any way destroy the freedom of will, so that impotence, which we assign to will because it can retain its rectitude only with difficulty, does not take away from the power to persevere in rectitude.

7 How it is stronger than temptation even when it succumbs to it

S. I am unable to deny what you prove but at the same time I cannot absolutely say that will is stronger than temptation when it is conquered by it. For if the will to preserve rectitude were stronger than the impetus of temptation, the will in willing what it keeps would be stronger as temptation is more insistent. For I do not otherwise know myself to have a more or less strong will except insofar as I more or less strongly will. Wherefore when I will less strongly than I ought because of the temptation to do what I ought not, I do not see how temptation is not stronger than my will.

T. I see that the equivocation of 'will' misleads you.

S. I would like to know this equivocation.

T. 'Will' is said equivocally much as 'sight' is. For we say that sight is an instrument of seeing, that is, a ray proceeding from the eyes whereby we sense light and the things that are in the light; and we also call sight the work of this instrument when we use it, that is, vision. In the same way the will means both the instrument of willing which is in the soul and our turning will to this or that as we turn sight to see different things. And this use of the will, which is the instrument of willing, is also called will, just as sight means both the use of sight and that which is the instrument of seeing. We have sight which is the instrument of seeing, even when we do not see, but the sight which is its work is only had when we see. So too will, namely the instrument of willing, is always in the soul even when it does not will something, as when it sleeps, but we only have the will that is the work of this instrument when we will something. Therefore what I call the instrument of willing is always one and the same whatever we will; but that which is its work is as many as the many things that we will. In this way sight is always the same whatever we see, or even in the dark or with closed eyes, but the sight which is its work and which is named vision is as numerous as are the things seen.

S. I see clearly and I love this distinction with respect to will, and I can see how I fell into error through deception. But do continue what you began.

T. Now that you see that there are two wills, namely the instrument of willing and its work, in which of the two do you find the strength of willing?

S. In that which is the instrument of willing.

T. If therefore you know a man to be strong, when he is holding a bull that was unable to escape and you saw the same man holding a ram who was able to free itself from his grasp, would you think him less strong in holding the ram than in holding the bull?

S. I would indeed judge him to be equally strong in both but that he did not use his strength equally in the two cases. For he acted more strongly with the bull than with the ram. But he is strong because he has strength and his act is called strong because it comes about strongly.

T. Understand that the will that I am calling the instrument of willing has an inalienable strength that cannot be overcome by any other force, but which it uses sometimes more and sometimes less when it wills. Hence it in no way abandons what it wills more strongly when what it wills less strongly is offered, and when what it wills with greater force offers itself it immediately drops what it does not will equally. And then the will, which we can call the action of this instrument, since it performs its act when it wills something, is said to be more or less strong in its action since it more or less strongly occurs.

S. I must admit that what you have explained is now clear to me.

T. Therefore you see that when a man, under the assault of temptation, abandons the rectitude of will that he has, he is not drawn away from it by any alien force, but he turns himself to that which he more strongly wills.

8 That not even God can take away the rectitude of will

S. Can even God take away rectitude from the will?

T. This cannot happen. God can reduce to nothing the whole substance that he made from nothing, but he cannot separate rectitude from a will that has it.

S. I am eager to have the reason for an assertion I have never before heard.

T. We are speaking of that rectitude of will thanks to which the will is called just, that is, which is preserved for its own sake. But no will is just unless it wills what God wants it to will.

S. One who does not will that is plainly unjust.

T. Therefore to preserve rectitude of will for its own sake is, for everyone who does so, to will what God wants him to will.

S. That must be said.

T. Should God remove this rectitude from anyone's will, he does this either willingly or unwillingly.

S. He could not do so unwillingly.

T. If then he removes this rectitude from someone's will he wills to do what he does.

S. Without any doubt.

T. But then he does not want the one from whom he removes this rectitude to preserve the rectitude of will for its own sake.

S. That follows.

T. But we already said that to preserve in this way the rectitude of will is for one to will what God wants him to will.

S. Even if we had not said it, it is so.

T. Hence if God were to take from something that rectitude of which we have so often spoken, he does not will one to will what he wants him to will.

S. An inevitable and impossible consequence.

T. Therefore nothing is more impossible than that God should take away the rectitude of will. Yet he is said to do this when he does not impede the abandonment of this rectitude. On the other hand, the devil and temptation are said to do this or to conquer the will and to remove from it the rectitude it has when they offer something or threaten to take away something that the will wants more than rectitude, but there is no way they can deprive it of that rectitude as long as the will wants it.

S. What you say is clear to me and I think nothing can be said against it.

9 That nothing is more free than right will

T. You can see that there is nothing freer than a right will since no alien power can take away its rectitude. To be sure, if we say that, when it wills to lie lest it lose life or safety, it is forced by the fear of death or torment to desert the truth, this is not true. It is not forced to will life rather than truth, but since an external force prevents it from preserving both at the same time, it chooses what it wants more–of itself that is and not unwillingly, although it would not of itself and willingly be placed in the necessity of abandoning both. It is not less able to will truth than safety, but it more strongly wills safety. For if it now should see the eternal glory which would immediately follow after preserving the truth, and the torments of hell to which it would be delivered over without delay after lying, without any doubt it would be seen to have a sufficiency for preserving the truth.

S. This is clear since it shows greater strength in willing eternal salvation for its own sake and truth for the sake of reward than for preserving temporal safety.

10 How one who sins is a slave of sin, and that it is a greater miracle when God restores rectitude to one who has abandoned it than when he restores lift to the dead

T. The rational nature always has free will because it always has the power of preserving rectitude of will for the sake of rectitude itself, although sometimes with difficulty. But when free will abandons rectitude because of the difficulty of preserving it, it is afterward the slave of sin because of the impossibility of recovering it by itself. Thus it becomes 'a breath that goes forth and returns not' [Ps. 77: 39], since 'everyone who commits sin is a slave of sin' [John 8: 34]. Just as no will, before it has rectitude, can have it unless God gives it, so when it abandons what it has received, it cannot regain it unless God restores it. And I think it is a greater miracle when God restores rectitude to the will that has abandoned it than when he restores life to a dead man. For a body dying out of necessity does not sin such that it might never receive life, but the will which of itself abandons rectitude deserves that it should always lack it. And if one gave himself over to death voluntarily, he does not take from himself what he was destined never to lose, but he who abandons the rectitude of will casts aside what he has an obligation to preserve always.

S. I do indeed see what you mean by slavery, whereby he who commits sin becomes the slave of sin, and of the impossibility of recovering abandoned rectitude unless it be restored by him who first gave it, and I see that all those to whom it has been given ought to battle ceaselessly to preserve it always.

11 That this slavery does not take away freedom of will

S. But this opinion does much to depress me because I had thought myself to be a man sure to have free will always. So I ask that you explain to me how this slavery is compatible with what we said earlier. For it seems the opposite of liberty. For both freedom and slavery are in the will, thanks to which a man is called free or a slave. But if he is a slave, how can he be free, and if free, how can he be a slave?

T. If you think about it carefully you will see that when the will does not have the rectitude of which we speak, it is without contradiction both slave and free. For it is never within its power to acquire the rectitude it does not have, although it is always in its power to preserve what it once had. Because it cannot return from sin, it is a slave; because it cannot be robbed of rectitude, it is free. But from its sin and slavery it can return only by the help of another, although it can depart from rectitude only by itself. But neither by another or by itself can it be deprived of its freedom. For it is always naturally free to preserve rectitude if it has it, even when it does not have what it might preserve.

S. This suffices to show me that freedom and slavery can be in one and the same man without contradiction.

12 Why a man who does not have rectitude is called free because if he had it no one could take it from him, and yet when he has rectitude he is not called a slave because if he loses it he cannot regain it by himself

S. I very much want to know why one who has not rectitude is called free because when he has it no one can take it from him, and yet when he has rectitude he is not called a slave because he cannot regain it by himself if he lose it. In fact, because he cannot by himself come back from sin, he is a slave; because he cannot be robbed of rectitude he is called free, and just as no one can take it from him if he has it, so he can never himself regain it if he does not have it. Wherefore, just as he always has this freedom, it seems that he should always have this slavery.

T. This slavery is nothing other than the powerlessness not to sin. For whether we say this is powerlessness to return to rectitude or powerlessness of regaining or again having rectitude, man is not the slave of sin for any other reason than that, because he cannot return to rectitude or regain and have it, he cannot not sin. For when he has that same rectitude, he does not lack the power not to sin. Wherefore when he has that rectitude, he is not the slave of sin. He always has the power to preserve rectitude, both when he has rectitude and when he does not, and therefore he is always free. As for your question why he is called free when he does not have rectitude, since it cannot be taken from him by another when he has it, and not called slave when he has rectitude because he cannot regain it by himself when he does not have it, this is as if you were to ask why a man when the sun is absent is said to have the power to see the sun because he can see it when it is present and when the sun is present is said to be powerless to see the sun because when it is absent he cannot make it present. For just as, even when the sun is absent, we have in us the sight whereby we see it when it is present, so too when the rectitude of will is lacking to us, we still have in us the aptitude to understand and will whereby we can preserve it for its own sake when we have it. And just as when nothing is lacking in us for seeing the sun except its presence, we only lack the power to make it present to us, so only when rectitude is lacking to us, do we have that powerlessness which its absence from us brings about.

S. If I ponder carefully what was said above when you distributed the power of seeing into four powers, I cannot doubt this now. So I confess the fault of doubting it.

T. I will pardon you now only if in what follows you have present to mind as needed what we have said before, so that there is no necessity for me to repeat it.

S. I am grateful for your indulgence, but you will not wonder that after having heard only once things of which I am not in the habit of thinking, they are not all always present in my heart to be inspected. .

T. Tell me now if you have any doubt about the definition of free will we have given.

13   That the power of preserving the rectitude of will for its own sake is a perfect definition of free will

S. There is still something that troubles me. For we often have the power of preserving something which yet is not free because it can be impeded by another power. Therefore when you say that freedom of will is the power of preserving rectitude of will for the sake of rectitude itself, consider whether perhaps it should be added that this power is free in such a way that it can be overwhelmed by no other power.

T. If the power of preserving the rectitude of will for the sake of rectitude itself could sometimes be found without that liberty that we have succeeded in seeing clearly, your proposed addition would be fitting. But since the foregoing definition is perfected by genus and difference such that it can contain neither more nor less than what we call freedom, nothing should be added or subtracted from it. For 'power' is the genus of liberty. When 'of preserving' is added it separates it from every power which is not one of preserving, such as the power to laugh or walk. By adding 'rectitude' we separate it from the power of preserving gold and whatever else is not rectitude.

By the addition of 'will' it is separated from the power of preserving the rectitude of other things, such as a stick or an opinion. By saying that it is 'for the sake of rectitude itself' it is distinguished from the power of preserving rectitude for some other reason, for example for money, or just naturally. A dog preserves rectitude of will naturally when it loves its young or the master who cares for it. Therefore since there is nothing in this definition that is not necessary to embrace the free judgment of a rational creature and exclude the rest it sufficiently includes the one and excludes the other, nor is our definition too much or lacking anything. Does it not seem so to you?

S. It seems perfect to me.

T. Tell me then if you wish to know anything else of this freedom which is imputed to one having it whether he uses it well or badly. For our discourse is concerned only with that.

14 The division of this freedom

S. It now remains to divide this freedom. For although this definition is common to every rational nature, there is a good deal of difference between God and rational creatures and many differences among the latter.

T. There is a free will that is from itself, which is neither made nor received from another, which is of God alone; there is another made and received from God, which is found in angels and in men. That which is made or received is different in one having the rectitude which he preserves than in one lacking it. Those having it are on the one hand those who hold it separably and those who hold it inseparably. The former was the case with all the angels before the good were confirmed and the evil fell, and with all men prior to death who have this rectitude. What is held inseparably is true of the chosen angels and men, but of angels after the ruin of the reprobate angels and of men after their death. Those who lack rectitude either lack it irrecoverably or recoverably. He who recover ably lacks it is one of the men in this life who lack it although many of them do not recover it. Those who lack it irrecoverably are reprobate angels and men, angels after their ruin and men after this life.

S. You have satisfied me with God's help on the definition of liberty such that I can think of nothing to ask concerning such matters.

Questions

1 How would you describe Anselm's theological method? What place has Scripture in his style of argumentation?

2 Anselm argues that "a will that cannot fall from rectitude into sin is more free than one who can desert it." Is this a convincing argument in your opinion?

3 How is free will possible in those who have made themselves slaves of sin?

4 What does Anselm mean by arguing that not even God can take away rectitude of the will?

5 What are the four powers, and how does describing them help to clarify what Anselm means by "freedom of the will"?

TEXT 4: DESIDERIUS ERASMUS, "ON THE FREEDOM OF THE WILL," & MARTIN LUTHER ON THE BONDAGE OF THE WILL[5]

The humanist movement in northern Europe in the early sixteenth century had as its leading light Erasmus of Rotterdam (1466–1536). Erasmus was a moral critic and a philologist of note, intent on reform of church abuses. In 1517, his publication of a printed Greek New Testament made possible critical scrutiny of the Latin Vulgate translation, and exposed some of its flaws. The Reformation which began not long after, propelled by Luther and Zwingli, owed a great deal to the determination of Erasmus to return to the sources of the faith, and from that standpoint critique the existing practices and even the theology of the church. However, by 1524, Erasmus had seen what he felt to be a distortion creeping into the position of the Protestant reformers over the matter of human free will. Luther had gone too far in proclaiming that human beings had no free will following the fall, but were in fact completely in chains. Erasmus, typically irenic, sought a correction of Luther's position. Luther returned fire upon Erasmus in his "On the Bondage of the Will"—as vehement a tract as was ever published in the history of theological writing. He took Erasmus to task for being far too mild, and for allowing the possibility that, in the freedom of the will, human agents might in some way claim credit for their own salvation. This for Luther was the whole problem with the medieval system in the first place. Reform of abuses was only the symptom: for Luther, a far too optimistic analysis of human nature was to blame for the theological lapses of the church. This section contains excerpts from both authors (the works are bound together in the *Library of Christian Classics*).

Erasmus: The dangers inherent in Luther's teachings

Let us, therefore, suppose that there is some truth in the doctrine which Wycliffe taught and Luther asserted, that whatever is done by us is done not by free choice but by sheer necessity. What could be more useless than to publish this paradox to the world? Again, suppose for a moment that it were true in a certain sense, as Augustine says somewhere, that "God works in us good and evil, and rewards his own good works in us, and punishes his evil works in us"; what a window to impiety would the public avowal of such an opinion open to countless mortals! Especially in view of the slowness of mind of mortal men, their sloth, their malice, and their

---

[5]Rupp. E.G. (ed.), *Luther and Erasmus: Free Will and Salvation* (London: S.C.M. Press, 1969), 41–2, 89–91, 139–43.

incurable propensity toward all manner of evil. What weakling will be able to bear the endless and wearisome warfare against his flesh? What evildoer will take pains to correct his life? Who will be able to bring himself to love God with all his heart when He created hell seething with eternal torments in order to punish his own misdeeds in his victims as though he took delight in human torments? For that is how most people will interpret them. For the most part, men are by nature dull-witted and sensual, prone to unbelief, inclined to evil, with a bent to blasphemy, so that there is no need to add fuel to the furnace. And so Paul, as a wise dispenser of the Divine Word, often brings charity to bear, and prefers to follow that which is fitting for one's neighbors rather than the letter of the law: and possesses a wisdom that he speaks among the perfect, but among the weak he reckons to know nothing, save Jesus Christ, and him crucified. Holy Scripture has its own language, adapted to our understanding. There God is angry, grieves, is indignant, rages, threatens, hates, and again has mercy, repents, changes his mind, not that such changes take place in the nature of God, but that to speak thus is suited to our infirmity and slowness. The same prudence I consider befits those who undertake the task of interpreting the Divine Word. Some things for this reason are harmful because they are not expedient, as wine for a fevered patient. Similarly, such matters might allowably have been treated in discussion by the learned world, or even in the theological schools, although I should not think even this to be expedient save with restraint; on the other hand, to debate such fables before the gaze of a mixed multitude seems to me to be not merely useless but even pernicious. I should, therefore, prefer men to be persuaded not to waste their time and talents in labyrinths of this kind, but to refute or to affirm the views of Luther. My preface would rightly seem too verbose if it were not almost more relevant to the main issue than the disputation itself.

* * * *

Erasmus: A mediating view, and a parable of Grace and free choice

But this, meanwhile, is to be avoided, that while we are wholly absorbed in extolling faith, we overthrow free choice, for if this is done away with I do not see any way in which the problem of the righteousness and the mercy of God is to be explained. Since the Early Fathers could not extricate themselves from these difficulties, some of them were driven to posit two Gods: one of the Old Testament, whom they represented as just, but not as good; another of the New Testament who was good but not just-whose wicked opinion Tertullian sufficiently exploded. Manichaeus, as we have said, dreamed of two natures in man, one which could not avoid sin, and another which could not avoid doing good. Pelagius, while he feared for the justice of God, ascribed too much to free choice, and those are not so far distant from him who ascribe such power to the human will that by their own natural strength they can merit, through good works, that supreme grace by which we are justified. These seem to me, through showing man a good hope of salvation, to have wished to incite him to more endeavor, just as Cornelius by his prayers and alms deserved to be taught by Peter, and the eunuch by Philip, and as the blessed Augustine when he avidly sought Christ in the letters of Paul deserved to find him. Here we can placate those who cannot bear that man can achieve any good work which he does not owe to God, when we say that it is nevertheless true that the whole work is due to God, without whom we do nothing; that the contribution of free choice is extremely small, and that this itself is part of the divine gift, that we can turn our souls to those things pertaining to salvation, or work together (*synergein*) with grace.

After his battle with Pelagius, Augustine became less just toward free choice than he had been before. Luther, on the other hand, who had previously allowed something to free choice, is now carried so far in the heat of his defense as to destroy it entirely. But I believe it was Lycurgus who was rebuked by the Greeks because, in his hatred of drunkenness, he gave the order for the vines to be cut down, when he should rather, by giving access to the fountains, have excluded drunkenness without destroying the use of wine.

For in my opinion free choice could have been so established as to avoid that confidence in our merits and the other dangers which Luther avoids, without counting those which we have mentioned already, and without losing those benefits that Luther admires. That is to my mind the advantage of the view of those who attribute entirely to grace the first impulse which stirs the soul, yet in the performance allow something to human choice which has not withdrawn itself from the grace of God. For since there are three stages in all things-, beginning, progress, and end-they attribute the first and last to grace, and only in progress say that free choice achieves anything, yet in such wise that in each individual action two causes come together, the grace of God and the will of man: in such a way, however, that grace is the principal cause and the will secondary, which can do nothing apart from the principal cause, since the principal is sufficient in itself. Just as fire burns by its native force, and yet the principal cause is God who acts through the fire, and this cause would of itself be sufficient, without which the fire could do nothing if he withdrew from it.

On this more accommodating view, it is implied that a man owes all his salvation to divine grace, since the power of free choice is exceedingly trivial in this regard and this very thing which it can do is a work of the grace of God who first created free choice and then freed it and healed it. And so we can appease, if they are capable of being appeased, those who cannot bear that man should own anything good which he does not owe to God. He owes Him this indeed but otherwise and under another name, just as an inheritance which legally comes to children is not called a benevolence because this is a common right of all men; but if something is given beyond the bounds of common law, it is called a benevolence, and yet the children's debt to their parents is called inheritance.

Let us try to express our meaning in a parable. A human eye that is quite sound sees nothing in the dark, a blind one sees nothing in the light; thus the will though free can do nothing if grace withdraws from it, and yet when the light is infused, he who has sound eyes can shut off the sight of the object so as not to see, can avert his eyes, so that he ceases to see what he previously saw. When anyone has eyes that once were blinded through some defect, but can now see, he owes even more gratitude. For first he owes it to his Creator, then to the physician. Just as before sin our eye was sound, so now it is vitiated by sin; what can a man who sees boast for himself?

And yet he has some merit to claim if prudently he shuts or averts his eyes. Take another illustration: A father lifts up a child who has fallen and has not yet strength to walk, however much it tries, and shows it an apple which lies over against it; the child longs to run, but on account of the weakness of its limbs it would have fallen had not its father held its hand and steadied its footsteps, so that led by its father it obtains the apple which the father willingly puts in its hand as a reward for running. The child could not have stood up if the father had not lifted it, could not have seen the apple had the father not shown it, could not advance unless the father had all the time assisted its feeble steps, could not grasp the apple had the father not put it into his hand. What, then, can the infant claim for itself? And yet it does something. But it has nothing to glory about in its own powers, for it owes it's very self to its father. Let us apply this analogy to our relation with God. What, then, does the child do here? It relies with all its powers on the one who lifts it, and it accommodates as best it can its feeble steps to him who leads. No doubt the father could have drawn the child against its will, and the child could have resisted by refusing the outstretched apple; the father could have given the apple without the child's having to run to get it, but he preferred to give it in this way, as this was better for the child. I will readily allow that less is due to our industry in following after eternal life than to the boy who runs to his father's hand.

Luther: Divine necessity and the human will

As for the . . . paradox, that whatever is done by us is done not by free choice but of sheer necessity, let us look briefly at this and not permit it to be labeled most pernicious. What I say here is this: When it has been proved that salvation is beyond our own powers and devices, and depends on the work of God alone (as I hope to prove conclusively below in the main body of this disputation), does it not follow that when God is not present and at work in us everything we do is evil and we necessarily do what is of no avail for salvation? For if it is not we, but only God, who works salvation in us, then before he works we can do nothing of saving significance, whether we wish to or not.

Now, by "necessarily" I do not mean "compulsorily," but by the necessity of immutability (as they say) and not of compulsion. That is to say, when a man is without the Spirit of God he does not do evil against his will, as if he were taken by the scruff of the neck and forced to it, like a thief or robber carried off against his will to punishment, but he does it of his own accord and with a ready will. And this readiness or will to act he cannot by his own powers omit, restrain, or change, but he keeps on willing and being ready; and even if he is compelled by external force to do something different, yet the will within him remains averse and he is resentful at whatever compels or resists it. He would not be resentful, however, if it were changed and he willingly submitted to the compulsion. This is what we call the necessity of immutability: It means that the will cannot change itself and turn in a different direction, but is rather the more provoked into willing by being resisted, as its resentment shows. This would not happen if it were free or had free choice. Ask experience how impossible it is to persuade people who have set their heart on anything. If they yield, they yield to force or to the greater attraction of something else; they never yield freely. On the other hand, if they are not set on anything, they simply let things take their course.

By contrast, if God works in us, the will is changed, and being gently breathed upon by the Spirit of God, it again wills and acts from pure willingness and inclination and of its own accord, not from compulsion, so that it cannot be turned another way by any opposition, nor be overcome or compelled even by the gates of hell, but it goes on willing and delighting in and loving the good, just as before it willed and delighted in and loved evil. This again is proved by experience, which shows how invincible and steadfast holy men are, who when force is used to compel them to other things are thereby all the more spurred on to will the good. Just as fire is fanned into flames rather than extinguished by the wind. So not even here is there any free choice, or freedom to turn oneself in another direction or will something different, so long as the Spirit and grace of God remain in a man.

In short, if we are under the god of this world, away from the work and Spirit of the true God, we are held captive to his will, as Paul says to Timothy (II Tim. 2:26), so that we cannot will anything but what he wills. For he is that strong man armed, who guards his own palace in such a way that those whom he possesses are in peace (Luke 11:21), so as to prevent them from stirring up any thought or feeling against him; otherwise, the kingdom of Satan being divided against itself would not stand (Luke 11:18), whereas Christ affirms that it does stand. And this we do readily and willingly, according to the nature of the will, which would not be a will if it were compelled; for compulsion is rather (so to say) "unwill." But if a Stronger One comes who overcomes him and takes us as His spoil, then through his Spirit we are again slaves and captives–though this is royal freedom–so that we readily will and do what he wills. Thus the human will is placed between the two like a beast of burden. If God rides it, it wills and goes where God wills, as the psalm says: "I am become as a beast (before thee) and I am always with thee" (Ps. 73:22 f.). If Satan rides it, it wills and goes where Satan wills; nor can it choose to run to either of the two riders or to seek him out, but the riders themselves contend for the possession and control of it.

What if I can prove from the words you yourself use in asserting freedom of choice that there is no free choice? What if I convict you of unwittingly denying what you seek so carefully to affirm? Frankly, unless I do so, I swear to regard everything I write against you in the entire book as revoked, and everything your Diatribe either asserts or queries against me as confirmed.

You make the power of free choice very slight and of a kind that is entirely ineffective apart from the grace of God. Do you not agree? Now I ask you, if the grace of God is absent or separated from it, what can that very slight power do of itself? It is ineffective, you say, and does nothing good. Then it cannot do what God or his grace wills, at any rate if we suppose the grace of God to be separated from it. But what the grace of God does not do is not good. Hence it follows that free choice without the grace of God is not free at all, but immutably the captive and slave of evil, since it cannot of itself turn to the good. If this is granted, I give you leave to make the power of free choice, instead of something very slight, something angelic, indeed if possible something quite divine; yet if you add this mournful rider, that apart from the grace of God it is ineffective, you at once rob it of all its power. What is ineffective power but simply no power at all?

Therefore, to say that free choice exists and has indeed some power, but that it is an ineffective power, is what the Sophists call *oppositum in adjecto* ("a contradiction in terms"). It is as if you said that there is a free choice which is not free, which is as sensible as calling fire cold and earth hot. For fire may have the power of heat, even infernal heat, but if it does not burn or scorch, but is cold and freezes, let no one tell me it is a fire at all, much less a hot one, unless you mean a painted or imaginary fire. But if the power of free choice were said to mean that by which a man is capable of being taken hold of by the Spirit and imbued with the grace of God, as a being created for eternal life or death, no objection could be taken. For this power or aptitude, or as the Sophists say, this disposing quality or passive aptitude, we also admit; and who does not know that it is not found in trees or animals? For heaven, as the saying is, was not made for geese.

It is settled, then, even on your own testimony, that we do everything by necessity, and nothing by free choice, since the power of free choice is nothing and neither does nor can do good in the absence of grace—unless you wish to give "efficacy" a new meaning and understand it as "perfection," as if free choice might very well make a start and will something, though it could not carry it through. But that I do not believe, and will say more about it later. It follows now that free choice is plainly a divine term, and can be properly applied to none but the Divine Majesty alone; for he alone can do and does (as the psalmist says (Ps. 115:3) whatever he pleases in heaven and on earth. If this is attributed to men, it is no more rightly attributed than if divinity itself also were attributed to them, which would be the greatest possible sacrilege. Theologians therefore ought to have avoided this term when they wished to speak of human ability, leaving it to be applied to God alone. They should, moreover, have removed it from the lips and language of men, treating it as a kind of sacred and venerable name for their God. And if they attributed any power at all to men, they should teach that it must be called by another name than free choice, especially as we know and clearly perceive that the common people are miserably deceived and led astray by that term, since they hear and understand it in a very different sense from that which the theologians mean and discuss.

For the expression "free choice" is too imposing, too wide and full, and the people think it signifies-as the force and nature of the term requires-a power that can turn itself freely in either direction, without being under anyone's influence or control. If they knew that it was not so, but that hardly the tiniest spark of power was meant by this term, and a spark completely ineffectual by itself as a captive and slave of the devil, it would be surprising if they did not stone us as mockers and deceivers who say one thing and mean something quite different, or rather who have not yet decided or agreed on what we do mean. For he who speaks sophistically is hateful, as the Wise Man says (Prov. 6:17), particularly if he does this in matters of piety, where eternal salvation is at stake.

Since, then, we have lost the meaning and content of such a vainglorious term, or rather have never possessed it (as the Pelagians wanted us to, who like you were led astray by the term), why do we so stubbornly hold on to an empty term, deceptive and dangerous as it is for the rank and file of believers? It is as sensible as when kings and princes hold on to or claim for themselves and boast about empty titles of kingdoms and countries, when in fact they are practically paupers and anything but the possessors of those kingdoms and countries. That, however, can be tolerated, since they deceive or mislead no one by it, but simply feed themselves on vanity, quite fruitlessly. But in the present case there is a danger to salvation and a thoroughly injurious illusion.

Who would not think it ridiculous, or rather very objectionable, if some untimely innovator in the use of words attempted to introduce, against all common usage, such a manner of speaking as to call a beggar rich, not because he possessed any riches, but because some king might perhaps give him his, especially if this were done in seeming seriousness and not in a figure of speech, such as antiphrasis or irony. In this way, one who was mortally ill could be said to be perfectly well because some other might give him his own health, and a thoroughly illiterate fellow could be called very learned because someone else might perhaps give him learning. That is just how it sounds here: Man has free choice—if, of course, God would hand over his own to him! By this misuse of language, anyone might boast of anything, as for instance, that man is lord of heaven and earth—if God would grant it to him. But that is not the way for theologians to talk, but for stage players and public informers. Our words ought to be precise, pure, and sober, and as Paul says, sound and beyond censure (Titus 2:8).

But if we are unwilling to let this term go altogether—though that would be the safest and most God-fearing thing to do—let us at least teach men to use it honestly, so that free choice is allowed to man only with respect to what is beneath him and not what is above him. That is to say, a man should know that with regard to his faculties and possessions he has the right to use, to do, or to leave undone, according to his own free choice, though even this is controlled by the free choice of God alone, who acts in whatever way he pleases. On the other hand in relation to God, or in matters pertaining to salvation or damnation, a man has no free choice, but is a captive, subject and slave either of the will of God or the will of Satan.

Such are my comments on the main heads of your Preface, which even in themselves cover practically the whole subject-more almost than the main body of the book that follows. Yet all I have said might have been summed up in this short alternative: Your Preface is complaining either about the words of God or the words of men. If it is about the words of men, it has been written wholly in vain and is no concern of ours. If it is about the words of God, it is wholly impious. It would therefore have been more useful to have a statement as to whether they were God's words or men's about which we are disputing. But perhaps this question will be dealt with in the Introduction which follows, and in the Disputation itself.

The points you raise in the epilogue to your Preface, however, do not impress me. You call our dogmas "fables" and "useless," and suggest that we ought rather to follow Paul's example of preaching Christ crucified and speaking wisdom among the perfect (I Cor. 1:23; 2:2, 6 ff.); and you say that Scripture has a language of its own, variously adapted to the state of the hearers, so you think it must be left to the prudence and charity of the teacher to teach what is expedient for his neighbor. All this is inept and ignorant, for we too teach nothing but Jesus crucified. But Christ crucified brings all these things with him, even including that "wisdom among the perfect"; for there is no other wisdom to be taught among Christians than that which is hidden in a mystery and pertains to the perfect, not to mere children of a Jewish and legal people that glories in works without faith, as Paul shows in I Cor., ch. 2—unless you want the preaching of Christ crucified to mean nothing other than the making of the bare statement, "Christ has been crucified."

As for your saying that "God in Scripture is angry, rages, hates, grieves, has mercy, repents, yet none of these changes takes place in God," here you are looking for a bone to pick for these things do not make Scripture obscure or in need of adaptation to the various hearers, except that some people like to make difficulties where there are none. These are matters of grammar and the figurative use of words, which even schoolboys understand; but we are concerned with dogmas, not grammatical figures, in this discussion.

Questions

1 Why does Erasmus feel that Luther's position opens a "window to impiety"?

2 "For in my opinion free choice could have been so established as to avoid that confidence in our merits and the other dangers which Luther avoids, without counting those which we have mentioned already, and without losing those benefits that Luther admires." How does Erasmus make his case for a more balanced position?

3 How—and why—does Luther distinguish between "necessity" and "compulsion"?

4 Is Luther right in arguing that to describe the will as an "ineffective power" is a contradiction in terms?

5 Will Luther allow any application of the term "freedom of choice" to be applied to human beings?

TEXT 5: WILLIAM GT SHEDD, *DOGMATIC THEOLOGY*[6]

William Greenough Thayer Shedd (1820–1894) was a Presbyterian theologian who served as professor of systematic theology at Union Theological Seminary in New York for more than sixteen years. Shedd is a representative of the flowering of Calvinist theology in the United States, in the middle of the nineteenth century, and writes as an heir to the long and rigorous tradition of Reformed scholasticism, and of Princeton's great philosopher-theologian Jonathan Edwards. He was writing his theology, however, in the midst of a changing world—something which is reflected in his writing. Shedd was a prodigious author, and reflects in his work an astonishing breadth of reading in literature, philosophy and science, as well as a detailed knowledge of the many theological traditions. He was often commended for his literary style. Like Anselm, we observe him struggling to refine his terminology in a philosophically appropriate way. At the same time, he is determined to work toward a synthesis of the teaching of Holy Scripture and to an exposition of it in the contemporary world.

Definition of the will

In discussing the subject of original sin, much depends upon the definition of the will; whether it be taken in a wide or in a narrow sense. The elder psychology divides the powers of the soul into understanding and will; the later psychology divides them into intellect, sensibility, and will. The former includes the moral affections and desires in the will; the latter excludes them from it. For the former, inclination is the principal characteristic of voluntariness; for the latter, volition is the principal characteristic. In classifying the powers of the soul under two modes, it is not meant that there is a division of the soul into two parts. The whole soul as cognizing is the understanding; and the whole soul as inclining is the will...

. . . We regard the elder psychology as correct in including the moral desires and affections in the total action of the will and in making two faculties of the soul, namely, understanding and will.

The understanding is the cognitive faculty or mode of the soul. It comprises the intellect and the conscience. These are percipient and perceptive powers. They are destitute of desire and inclination; and they are not self-determining and executive powers. The intellect perceives what ought to be done, and the conscience commands what ought to be done, but they never do anything themselves. They do not incline to an end. They have no love and desire for what is commanded; and no hatred and aversion toward what is forbidden. The intellect neither loves nor hates, neither

---

[6]From W.G.T. Shedd, *Dogmatic Theology*, 3rd ed. (Phillipsburg: P&R Publishing, 2003), 509–27.

desires nor is averse. The conscience approves and disapproves; but approbation is not love and desire, nor is disapprobation hatred and abhorrence.

The understanding is the fixed and stationary faculty or mode of the soul. It can be vitiated and injured, but not radically changed. The operation of the human intellect cannot be totally reversed and revolutionized, as that of the human will may be. After the apostasy, the understanding of man obeys the same rules of logic as before and possesses the same mathematical and ethical ideas and intuitions. And the same is true of the human conscience, as involving the perception of right and wrong. Its structure and laws are unaltered by apostasy. After the fall, man does not have moral perceptions that are exactly contrary to those he had before it. He does not perceive that the love of God is evil or that the love of sin is good. He does not approve of disobedience of law and disapprove of obedience. The energy with which both intellect and conscience operate after apostasy is, indeed, greatly diminished; but the same general mode of operation continues. The effect of sin upon the cognitive side of the human soul is to darken, dim, and stupefy, but not radically to change. This fixedness of the understanding is in striking contrast, as we shall see, with the mobility and mutability of the will.

The will is that faculty or mode of the soul which self-determines, inclines, desires, and chooses in reference to moral and religious objects and ends. These objects and ends are all centered and summed up in God. We say moral and religious objects and ends because there is a class of propensities and desires that refer to nonmoral and nonreligious objects. They are the natural or instinctive desires, which are involuntary. Speaking generally, the voluntary and moral desires relate to God. They are either inclined or averse to him; they are either love or hatred. The natural and instinctive desires, on the other hand, relate to the creature. Of these latter, there are four kinds: a) physical appetites, (b) family affections, c) social affections, and (d) esthetic feeling. These all relate to some form or phase of the finite and therefore are not in themselves of the nature of virtue or religion, because religion relates to the infinite. They may be sanctified by the moral and religious desires and are so sanctified when the religious desires coexist with them; but they are in themselves neither sinful nor holy. They are constitutional, nonmoral propensities, flowing necessarily from man's physical and structure. Unregenerate men have them, as well as regenerate. They are none of them the object of a divine command or prohibition, like the moral and religious desires. When husbands are commanded to "love their wives" (Col 3:19) and wives to "love their husbands and children" (Titus 2:4), they are commanded to love "in the Lord." The mere instinctive love itself is not commanded. This is provided for in the created relation of husband and wife, of parent and child. The instinctive affection as sanctified by a connection and union with the religious of supreme love of God is what is enjoined. The same is true of the love and obedience of children toward their parents (Col. 3:20), of the love and care of parents toward their children (3:21), of the relation of the citizen to the state (Rom. 13:5; 1 Pet. 2:13–14), of the relation between master and servant (Col 3:22; 1 Tim. 6:1–2), and of the appetites (Rom. 14:6; 1 Cor. 10:31). None of these are commanded merely as natural instinctive desires and affections, but as sanctified instinctive desires and affections.

The instinctive or natural desires and affections are transient. They relate to the temporal, not the eternal. The family and the state are institutions that are confined to earth and time. This fact shows that they are nonmoral in their nature. The moral and religious is eternal. None of the natural and instinctive desires were lost by the fall, though all of them were vitiated and corrupted by it. None of them were converted into their contraries by the apostasy of Adam.

****

The terms *inclination, desire,* and *affection* are interchangeable. The "desire" of the psalmist's heart is one and the same thing with the "inclination" of his will. He often asks God to "incline" his heart. The inclination of the will is its constant self-determination. The affections or desires are the various phases or aspects of the inclination. Love of God is an affection of the heart; but it is also one variety of the disposition or inclination of the Christian. Hatred of sin is the aversion of a good man's will, its disinclination to evil: "To will is nothing other than a certain inclination toward an object of the will, which is universal good" (Aquinas, *Summa* 1.105.4).

****

The will, unlike the understanding, is mutable. It is capable of a radical and total change or revolution. It has met with such a change in the apostasy of Adam. Man now is inclined exactly contrary to what he was by creation. In respect to moral and religious ends and objects, he inclines, desires, loves, and acts directly contrary to what he did when he came from the Creator's hand. This great change is denominated a "fall." It is an overthrow, a catastrophe. It is not a mere difference in the degree or intensity with which the will operates, but it is an entire alteration of the direction of its activity. The fall of the will was a revolution, not an evolution.

****

Moral desires and affections are the self-activity of the will; its inclination and tendency showing itself in the phases of love or hatred of God, of desire or aversion toward goodness. They are commanded or prohibited by the moral law, which proves that they are voluntary. The feelings of supreme love toward God and of equal love toward a fellow creature are not instinctive, but voluntary. Such love and inclination is not, like the *storgē* of the parental relation or the involuntary affection of the citizen for his country, a merely natural and necessary efflux from the human constitution, deserving neither praise nor blame; but it is the free determination of the human will. To have it is meritorious. Not to have it or to have its contrary is guilt requiring atonement and remission. Again, the feeling of aversion toward God or of hatred toward a fellowman is not like the shrinking of animal life from death or the recoil of a child from a viper, an involuntary activity of the soul which stands in no relation to law and justice and is deserving of no punishment. This aversion toward God is called "enmity" (Rom. 8:7), the positive hostility of the inclination, the disinclination of the will in its deepest recesses. This hatred of a fellow creature is the repugnance of the will and is murderous in its quality; for "he that hates his brother is a murderer" (1 John 3:15). Accordingly, in Scripture, holy desire is holy inclination: "My soul thirsts for you, my flesh longs for you" (Ps. 63:1); "so pants my soul after you" (42:1). Such desire is the object of command: "Delight yourself in the Lord" (37:4). The sum of the moral law is a command to love: "You shall love the Lord your God with all your heart." And evil desire is evil inclination: "The desire of the wicked shall perish" (112:20); "grant not, O Lord, the desires of the wicked" (140:8); "the expectation of the wicked shall perish" (Prov. 10:28); "depart from us; for we desire not the knowledge of your ways" (Job 21: 14).

* * * *

Inclination vs. Volition

The distinction between the will's inclination and its volition is of the highest importance in both psychology and theology. The key to the distinction is found in the following discrimination by Descartes *(Passions* 1.18): "Our acts of will are of two kinds. One are the actions of the soul which terminate on the soul itself; as when we will to love God. The other kind are the actions of the soul that terminate on the body; as when from the mere will to take a walk, there follows the movement of our limbs, and we go forward." The first of these acts of will is inclining; the last is the exertion of a volition. The same distinction is referred to by Constant: "I am able to do good and sound deeds, but I cannot find the good means of accomplishing them."

When I say, "I will pick up that stone," this is volition. The action of the will terminates on the body. I am conscious of ability to do it or not. In this instance, there is a power of alternative choice. I can do one as easily as the other. But when I say, "I will love God supremely," this is inclination. The action of the will terminates on the will. I am not conscious of ability to do it or not. In this instance, there is not a power of alternative choice. I cannot do one as easily as the other. And the reason is that I am already loving myself supremely. I am already inclined or self-determined. I am already doing the contrary of loving God supremely. And the existing inclination precludes the other. I can do the one which I am doing, but not the other which I am not doing. But when I said, "I will pick up that stone," I was not already inclined to the contrary act-namely, not to pick it up. In this instance, I was indifferent and undetermined in regard to the act of picking up the stone. Consequently, I could do one thing as easily as the other. In the instance of a proposed change of self-determination or inclination, there is a contrary self-determination or inclination already existing and opposing. In the instance of a change of volition, there is indifference or the absence of inclination or self-determination.

The difference between inclination and volition is seen by considering the moral desires and affections. The desire of human applause or ambition does not rise by a volition. In this sense, it is involuntary, and those who resolve all the action of the will into volition so denominate it. Yet it is free and unforced activity. It rises by spontaneous inclination. In this sense, it is voluntary. The man is willingly proud and ambitious and is punishable for it. His desire for fame is the determination of the self. If it is not self-determination, it must be determination by some cause other than self. But in this case, the sense of guilt which accompanies it is inexplicable.

The same reasoning applies to envy, hatred, malice, and all other sinful desires. They are not volitionary, but they are voluntary; they are the inclination of the will, not its volition.

The following particulars mark the difference between inclination and volition.

Inclination is the central action of the will; volition is the superficial action. The inclination is the source of volitions. "It is," says Edwards *(Original Sin* 2.1.1), "the general notion, not that principles derive their goodness from actions, but that actions derive their goodness from the principles whence they proceed." By "principles" Edwards means, as he teaches in the context, the disposition or inclination; and by "actions" he means particular choices or volitions. That the inclination is more profound action than a volition is proved by the fact that a man cannot incline himself by a volition or resolution. When he is already inclined, no exertion of that volitionary power by which he lifts a hand or applies his mind to a given subject, like geometry, for example, can originate a contrary inclination. He may by volitionary effort fix his thoughts upon God as the being toward whom he ought to incline, but this is as far as he can go, if he is not already inclined. No conceivable amount of resolution, even though it rise to spasm, can start that profound and central action of the will which is its inclination and is identical with its moral affection and disposition. The central action of the will in inclining is better denominated "voluntary," and the superficial action in choosing "volitionary." The voluntary is the spontaneous. Milton speaks of "thoughts that voluntarily (i.e., spontaneously) move harmonious numbers." If the term *voluntary* is made to do double duty and designate both the central and the superficial action of the will, both inclination and volition, it leads to confusion. Some things are predicable of a volition that are not of an inclination. Volitions can be originated at any instant and in any number; an inclination cannot be. If, however, the term *choice* be used to denote the inclination, it should be qualified as the choice of an ultimate end in distinction from the means to it and also as not proceeding from an indifferent state of the will.

The volition has the same moral quality with the inclination. This is taught by Christ in Matt. 7:17: "Every good tree brings forth good fruit; but a corrupt tree brings forth evil fruit." Hence the volition has been denominated "executive volition" and the inclination "immanent volition" by those who do not discriminate technically between inclination and volition.

All the volitionary acts of particular choice are performed in order to gratify the prevailing inclination or determination of the will. A man is inclined to ambition; and he endeavors to attain the ambitious end to which he is self-determined by thousands and tens of thousands of volitions. These are all of them of the same moral quality with the inclination. They are vicious, not virtuous. Self-seeking or selfishness is the generic character of human inclination; pride, envy, malice, covetousness, etc., are varieties of this. These are modes of man's inclination, all of which have the creature not the Creator for the ultimate end. Volitions are exercised in choosing and using means in order to gratify these varieties of inclination. In their moral quality, they are the same as the inclination. A volition exerted to attain an ambitious end and gratify an ambitious inclination is ambitious. A volition exerted to attain a malignant end is malignant. And so through the entire list. Volitions cannot be morally different from the inclination which prompts them. This also is taught by our Lord in Matt.

7:18: "A good tree cannot bring forth evil fruit, neither can a corrupt tree bring forth good fruit."

The volition sometimes seems to run counter to the inclination, but really it does not. A drunkard, from fear or shame, may by a volition reject the cup that is offered to him. He acts contrary, in this particular instance, to his physical appetite for alcohol, but not contrary to the central inclination of his will to self. By the supposition, he is still determined to the creature as the ultimate end, not to the Creator. He still loves himself supremely. The motive, consequently, from which he rejects the intoxicant in the instance supposed is a selfish one: shame, pride, fear of man, or some other merely prudential consideration. He is still controlled by his inclination to self. The volition by which he rejected the cup agrees in its moral quality with the state of his heart. It is not holy, because not prompted by the desire and determination to please and obey God. Had he rejected the intoxicant from regard to the divine command against drunkenness, this would prove him to have obtained a new inclination of the will. But in the case supposed, his volition, though counter to his physical appetite, yet agrees with his moral character and disposition of will. He has carried out his selfish inclination by his volition, only in a different manner from common. His volition in this instance ministered to his pride instead of to his physical appetite.

The inclination of the will is the result of self-determination, not of a volition, because the inclination is the self-determination viewed objectively. Consider the facts. Adam as created was inclined to holiness. This inclination, although created with his will, was at the same time the self-motion of his will. Viewed with reference to its first author and origin, it was the product of his maker; but viewed with reference to his own will, it was the activity of his will and in this secondary sense the product of his will. This holy inclination was both concreated and self-determined; the former, because it was a created voluntariness; the latter, because of the intrinsic nature of voluntariness.

Now it is evident that this holy inclination was not the product of a volition exerted prior to the inclination and when there was no inclination, but it was the simple self-motion of the will. The will of Adam moved spontaneously to God as a supreme end, and this spontaneity of the will was identical with the will's inclination. The will as uninclined did not choose to incline and by this choice made an inclination, but it simply inclined, and this inclining was its inclination.

And the same is true of Adam's evil inclination. This, also, was the result of self-determination, not of a volition. Adam, in the act of apostasy, did not make a choice between two contraries, God and the creature, to neither of which was he yet inclined; but he passed or "lapsed" from one inclination to another, from one self-determination to another. This instant, he is wholly inclined to good; the next instant, he is wholly inclined to evil. Such a fall of the will cannot be accounted for by an antecedent choice from an indifferent state of the will. It is explained by the *possibilitas peccandi*.[7] This is the power of self-determining to evil, implied in the mutable holiness of a creature who is not self-sustaining and omnipotent. When God created Adam's will with a holy inclination, this inclination, because finite, was

---

[7]possibility of sinning.

not immutable. Mutable Adam, unlike his immutable maker, could lose holiness. He was able to persevere in his holy self-determination, and he was able to start a sinful self-determination. God left it to Adam himself to decide whether he would continue in his first created inclination or would begin a second evil inclination. This was his probation. The first sin was the self-determining of the will to evil, which expelled the existing self-determination to good, and not a volition in a state of indifference. It was self-determination to an ultimate end, not a choice of means to an ultimate end. Sinful inclination began in Adam immediately by self-determination and not mediately by a foregoing volition. He did not choose to incline to evil, but he inclined.

In the instance of regeneration, also, a new inclination is begun immediately by the Holy Spirit, not mediately by the exertion of a human volition. The Holy Spirit regenerates the fallen will instantaneously, and the effect is a new inclining or self-determining of the faculty. The will is "powerfully determined," as the Westminster Confession phrases it. The sinner does not choose or resolve to incline to God, but God the Spirit immediately inclines him. The inclination or self-determination of regeneration differs from that of apostasy in that it is the effect of God "working in the will to will." God in this instance determines the will by renewing it, while in the instance of the apostasy Adam determined himself to evil without any immediate operation of God. Yet there is no compulsion of the will in regeneration, because the Holy Spirit operates as spirit upon spirit, that is, in accordance with the nature of a mental and self-moving substance and not as matter operates upon matter. The new inclination of the will is real and true spontaneity or self-determination. But, there are two beings concerned in it, namely, the Holy Spirit the efficient and the human spirit the recipient. In the case of the sinful self-determination in the apostasy, there was only a single being concerned, namely, man.

Consequently, inclination or self-determination may be viewed either subjectively or objectively, as an activity or as a result, as an act or as a fact. Holy inclination, viewed subjectively, is the activity of the will, its voluntary spontaneity: *justitia originans*.[8] Viewed objectively, it is this spontaneity as originally created or subsequently recreated by God: *justitia originata*.[9] Sinful inclination, viewed subjectively, is the activity of the will, its voluntary spontaneity: *peccatum originans*.[10] Viewed objectively, it is this spontaneity considered as an abiding state of the will originated by the will itself in Adam's fall: *peccatum originatum*.[11]

Inclination differs from volition as the end differs from the means. Inclination is self-determination to an ultimate end, God or the world. When Adam apostatized, his will inclined to self and the creature as the supreme end. This was a self-originated self-determination. When this new inclination to self and sin had begun, then began a series of choices or volitions by means of which he might attain the new end of existence which he had set up. And the first of these choices, the first volition that succeeded the origination of the inclination, was the reaching forth of the hand and

[8]originating righteousness.
[9]originated righteousness.
[10]originating sin.
[11]originated sin.

taking the forbidden fruit. This volitionary act was the means of attaining the selfish end he had now assumed. He gratified his new inclination by a choice. For Adam had fallen in his heart and will before he ate the fruit of the tree of knowledge. He was already inclined to self prior to this outward act; and the volition by which he reached forth the hand and took the fruit was executive of his new inclination. It did not originate his inclination, but expressed and exhibited it.

The term *choice,* as has been observed, is applied indiscriminately to the election of the end as well as of the means by those who do not distinguish between voluntary and volitionary action. Adam, they say, chose self as the ultimate end instead of choosing God. But this indiscriminate use of the term is confusing. It is preferable to appropriate each term to its proper act. The will "inclines" to an end and "chooses" a means. Edwards *sometimes* appropriates the term *choice* to volitions and uses the term *disposition* or *affection* to denote inclination. "It is agreeable," he says *(Original Sin* 2.1.1), "to the sense of the minds of men in all nations and ages, not only that the fruit or effect of a good choice is virtuous, but the good choice itself from which that effect proceeds; yea, and not only so, but also the antecedent good disposition, temper, or affection of mind from whence proceeds that good choice is virtuous." In this passage three elements are mentioned: (a) the outward act: "the fruit or effect of a good choice"; (b) the choice or volition that caused the outward act; and (c) the "disposition, temper, or affection" which produced the volition. Edwards's position in regard to each of them is (a) that the outward act is preceded and produced by the volition; (b) that the volition is preceded and produced by the disposition or inclination; and (c) that the disposition or inclination, if holy, is either concreated with the will or else reoriginated in regeneration; if sinful it is originated in Adam's apostasy. But inasmuch as Edwards does not formally and technically appropriate the term *choice* to volitions, but employs it oftentimes to designate the inclination; and still more, because he uses the term *voluntary,* as his Arminian opponents did, to denote alike what is volitionary or "caused by antecedent choice" *(Works* 2.122) and what is bias or inclination, he has exposed himself to the misinterpretation which his views have sometimes met with.

* * * *

Will in man is rational, unnecessitated self-activity toward a moral end. Will in animals is irrational, necessitated activity in choosing means to a physical end necessitated by physical instinct. The former is real self-determination; the latter is not. The animal is forced by the law of his physical nature to the end aimed at in his volitions; the man is not. The brute must attain the end of his creation; the man may or may not. Instinct in the animal is involuntary; inclination in man is voluntary.

Volition is common to man and the animal creation; inclination or self-determination belongs only to man and other rational beings. The movements of the fingers of a pianist are each caused by an act of choice, in distinction from an act of self-determination to an ultimate end. There are thousands of volitions exerted in a few moments. Volition is also seen in insects and is inconceivably rapid in them. Volition here is innervation. Excitement of the nerve results in excitement of the muscle. If the molecular theory of vitality were true, volition in insects would be rightly defined as Haeckel defines will: "the habit of molecular motion." It would be the molecular process in the nervous-muscular system. A gnat, according to a French naturalist, vibrates its wings five hundred times in a second. The vibrations of the wings of the common fly, according to an English naturalist, are as many as six hundred in a second (Pouchet, *Universe,* 112). These are each and every one of them volitionary, not voluntary acts--choice not self-determination-and are the same in kind with those by which the pianist plays a tune or a drummer beats a tattoo. For if the vibrations of the gnat's wing were not caused by volitions, it could not stop flying. The motion would be mechanical and animals would be machines, as Descartes asserted in his curious theory. Naturalists are now distinguishing between vegetable (or passive) life and active (or willful) life. The vegetable puts forth no volitions; the animal does.

But volition in the animal or the insect has something behind it as its ground and cause, as volition in man has. This background and originating source in the animal is instinct. This takes the place of self-determination or inclination in man. All the volitions of an animal or an insect are exerted for the purpose of attaining the end prescribed by animal instinct, just as the volitions of a man are exerted for the purpose of reaching the end prescribed by his moral inclination. Volitionary action in man is responsible because the disposition or inclination prompting it is self-moved. But in the animal, volitionary action is irresponsible because instinct is not self-moved. Instinct is the necessitated motion of physical substance in accordance with physical properties and laws. Inclination is the free motion of mental and spiritual substance, which is not controlled by physical law.

Inclination or self-determination is inherited; volitions or choices are not. The bias of the will is born with the individual. His choices or volitions are not born with him and do not begin until self-consciousness begins. The sinful self-determination began in Adam prior to birth; sinful volitions begin in the individual after birth.

Inclination is free because it is self-determined; volition is necessitated because it is determined in its morality by the inclination of which it is the executive. The selfishly inclined drunkard may drink or not drink in a particular instance and thus seems to be free in regard to volition, but in either case his volition is selfish like his inclination. Apparently and formally it is free, but really it is necessitated. No volition can be holy if it is the executive of a sinful inclination or sinful if it is the executive of a holy inclination. Hence man's freedom must be sought for in his inclination, not in his volitions. Moral necessity can be predicated of volitions, but not of inclination. There is a necessary connection between volitions and the foregoing inclination of which they are the index and executive; but no such necessary connection exists between an inclination and a foregoing inclination or between and inclination and a foregoing volition. It is improper to say that a person must incline in a certain manner, but proper to say that he must choose in a certain manner. If he has an evil inclination, his choices are necessarily evil; but his inclination itself is not necessarily evil. Inclination has no antecedent, but constitutes an absolute beginning *ex nihilo;* but a volition does not.

* * * *

The law of cause and effect or of the antecedent causing the consequent operates in regard to the phenomenal series of volitions in time, but not in regard to the abiding inclination which underlies them and which is referable to no particular moment of time. The inclination is not a series, but a unit. There is only one inclination (*noumenon*), but myriads of volitions. The inclination is not caused either by an antecedent inclination or by a volition, but is self-caused. And the inclination is the real will of the man: the *Ding an sich*.[12] Ritschl states Kant's doctrine as follows: "Freedom denotes the will as unconditioned causality out of time, in distinction from the phenomena of will that run on in time, and are subject to natural necessity. The reason why every recollection of an act committed long ago calls forth sorrow is that reason in all that pertains to our moral existence recognizes no distinctions of time, but asks only if the action was really mine." Edwards teaches the same truth in his doctrine of moral necessity-according to which the volition in its moral quality necessarily follows the inclination.

* * * *

Self-determination is causative and originative of character. It starts a bias or disposition in the will. Volition is unproductive of character and disposition. A volition leaves the man's inclination exactly as it found it. It makes no alteration in the bias of the will. This is seen in the futile attempt of the moralist to change his inclination by volitionary resolutions. Inclination is a positive determination of the will in one direction and toward one final end. Volition or choice is the selection of one out of two or more things, not from any interest in one rather than another, but because it is best adapted to the end in view. A volitionary choice is indifferent toward the thing chosen. If the drunkard could gratify his selfish inclination to physical pleasure better by water than by alcohol, he would choose water.

Inclination is spontaneous; volition is nervous and often spasmodic. Inclination is easy and genial; volition is more or less an effort, whether exerted against the inclination or in accordance with it. When the drunkard by a volition refuses the cup because of his selfish inclination in the form of shame or fear, this volition costs him a great effort. When the drunkard by a volition takes the cup because of his selfish inclination in the form of desire of sensual pleasure, the volition is still an effort, though not a great one. He is, at least, compelled to exert his will sufficiently to move his muscles and limbs. Volition moves the body; and this requires a distinct and separate resolution of the will back of the bodily movement. Inclination moves the will itself; but this does not require a distinct and separate resolution of the will back of the mental and voluntary movement. The inclining is itself the mental activity; the cause and the effect are one and the same thing. But the volition is not itself the muscular bodily action; the cause and the effect are two different things. When a person loves or hates, he does not need to resolve to do it. But when he picks up a pin or applies his mind to a geometrical proposition, he must resolve to do so. Love and hatred are easy because spontaneous; volitions are more or less an effort.

To recapitulate, then, we say that the total action of the will is to be distinguished into voluntary and volitionary action, according as we speak of the central abiding inclination or the superficial momentary choice. "Voluntary" action both originates

---

[12]the thing in itself

and is inclination, according as the action is viewed as subjective or objective, as *originans*[13] or *originata*.[14] It has only three points at which it may begin: (1) the instant of creation, when a holy inclination commenced by being concreated in the will of the specific Adam; (2) the instant of apostasy, when a sinful inclination commenced in the will of the specific Adam by solitary self-determination without divine cooperation; or (3) the instant of regeneration, when a holy inclination is reoriginated in the sinful will of the individual man by the Holy Spirit. The beginning of a self-determined inclination is consequently an epoch in the history of the human will, and epochs are infrequent and rare from the nature of the case. Creation, apostasy, and regeneration are the great epochal points in man's existence. But volitions are beginning continually and are numberless. "Volitionary" action has innumerable points of beginning and in every instance supposes a prior inclination to an ultimate end.

This distinction between "voluntary" and "volitionary" action or between inclination and choice is marked in German by *Wille* and *Willkühr*, in Latin by *voluntas* and *arbitrium,* and in Greek by *thelēma*[15] and *boulē*[16] (cf. Cicero, *Tusculan Disputations* 4.6). The neglect of the distinction results in confusion and misunderstanding. If he who makes this distinction asserts that "original sin is voluntary but not volitionary," he is understood to say that original sin is the inclination of a man and not a successive series of single choices, that it is the constant and central determination of the will to self and sin and not the innumerable outward transgressions that proceed from this. But if one who does not make this distinction between voluntary and volitionary action asserts that "original sin is voluntary," he may be understood to mean that there is no sin but that of volitions, that original sin is the product of a volition and can be removed by a volition.

Theologians who in fact agree with each other appear to disagree in case the distinction is not recognized. Owen, for example, remarks *(Indwelling Sin,* 12) that "the will is the principle, the next seat and cause of obedience and disobedience. Moral actions are unto us, or in us, so far good or evil as they partake of the consent of the will. He spoke truth of old who said: 'Every sin is so voluntary, that if it be not voluntary it is not sin.'" In this statement "will" is employed in the comprehensive sense as antithetic to the understanding, and "voluntary" does not mean "volitionary." Owen would not say that "every sin is so volitionary, that if it be not volitionary it is not sin." Hodge (*Theology* 1.403), on the other hand, asserts that "freedom is more than spontaneity" and that "the affections are spontaneous but not free. Loving and hating, delighting and abhorring do not depend upon the will." This agrees with the modem psychology, not with the elder. For by "will" Hodge here means the volitionary power and by "freedom" the power to the contrary in the exercise of single choices. If this is the true psychology and freedom means the power of contrary choice, then it is correct to say that "the affections are not free" because they are most certainly not the product of volitions. Yet Hodge holds that

---

[13]originating.
[14]originated.
[15]θελημα = will.
[16]βουλη = will.

evil affections are guilty and punishable. But this requires that they be free in the sense of inclination or disposition; that they are not the product of compulsion and necessity. And in saying that "the affections are spontaneous," he implies that they are from the will (*ex sponte*). For spontaneity in a rational being is free will.

Spontaneity in an animal is mere physical instinct; but in man it is rational self-determination. Leibnitz *(Concerning Freedom,* 669) says, "Freedom is the spontaneity of intelligence. Thus, that which is spontaneous in man or another rational substance rises higher than what is spontaneous in a brute or other substance lacking intellect and is called freedom." Instinct in a brute is necessitated because it is grounded wholly in sense and animal nature; inclination in man is free because it is grounded in reason and a spiritual essence. Inclination is the subject of command and prohibition. Man is bidden to have a good inclination and forbidden to have an evil one. The commands to love (Deut. 6:5; Lev. 19:18; Matt. 28:39-40), to "make the tree good" (Matt. 12:33), to love not (1 John 2:15), to lust not (Exod. 20:17) are examples.

The great question in anthropology and in reference to sin and holiness relates to inclination rather than volition is the true subject of inquiry: How does an inclination (either holy or sinful) begin? Had unfallen man power to change his holy inclination? Has fallen man power to change his sinful inclination? That man has power over his volitions is undisputed.

Questions

1   What is the difference between inclination and volition? Why is it theologically crucial for Shedd?

2   What does Shedd mean by "The operation of the human intellect cannot be totally reversed and revolutionized, as that of the human will may be"? How does this relate to the narrative of the fall?

3   "None of the natural and instinctive desires were lost by the fall, though all of them were vitiated and corrupted by it." Would you agree or disagree?

4   Shedd argues that the fall of the will was a "revolution, not an evolution." What does he mean by this?

5   How does Shedd explain the possibility of sinning that lay within Adam?

6   Does Shedd's distinction between the freedom of inclination and the necessity of volition help with the theological conundrum about free will?

TEXT 6: PETER G. H. CLARKE, "DETERMINISM, BRAIN FUNCTION AND FREE WILL"[17]

Among contemporary disciplines, neurobiologists have made a very strong claim to be able to provide a totalizing explanation of the human person at the beginning of the twenty-first century. The theological and philosophical implications for the apparent discovery that human decision-making is, for the most part, subconscious and even determined by a plethora of unseen and unknown factors are, it is claimed, that morality itself vanishes, since the responsibility of human beings for what they actually do is greatly compromised to say the least. Until 2012, neurobiologist Peter Clarke (1946–2015) was an associate professor at the University of Lausanne, Switzerland, researching the mechanisms of neuronal death. His main focus is now on the philosophical implications of neuroscience. He is an associate editor of *Science and Christian Belief* and is a member of the Faraday Institute Advisory Board. In this article, Clarke wants to accept a degree of the neurobiological determinism, and is comfortable to do so as a theologian. He further argues that the appeal by philosophical libertarians to the Heisenberg uncertainty principle is problematic. (NB The paper below is in parts scientifically technical, but that shouldn't discourage a nonspecialist in physics or neuroscience—Clarke's argument is clear enough to a general reader.)

The fact that the laws of nature are deterministic, apart from tiny effects at the quantum level, raises many questions. Was the entire future of the universe determined at the moment of the big bang? Are miracles possible? Can intercessory prayer make any sense in a deterministic universe? Is God on compulsory sabbatical leave as a result of his own impersonal laws? And can free will be real when our brains obey the laws of physics? These are all important questions, but this essay will focus on the last one, that of free will and determinism.

Determinism at different levels

Determinism can be considered at various levels including: physical determinism, resulting from the fact that the laws of physics are (almost) deterministic; social determinism, the thesis that people are trapped in a web of social constraints; psychological determinism; environmental determinism; genetic determinism; and so on. All these levels are important, for both theoretical and practical reasons, but I here focus on physical determinism, because I consider that this is the level where the problem of determinism is most acute. As is argued below, genetic determinism,

[17]Peter G. H. Clarke, "Determinism, Brain Function and Free Will." *Science and Christian Belief* 22.2 (2010): 133–49.

or even the combined determinism of genes and external environment is only partial, whereas physical determinism may be (almost) total.

Genetic determinism of our brains and personalities is only partial

Genetic determinism says that the genotype determines the phenotype. Nobody doubts that many of our physical characteristics, such as height and eye colour, are largely determined genetically. But what about brain development? What about personality?

The complexity of the human brain is far too great for every detail of its interconnections to be specified by the genes. The human genome contains theoretically about 6.2×10^9 bits of information, calculated from the number of nucleotide pairs (3.1×10^9), each worth 2 bits, in both coding and noncoding DNA). The amount of this information that can actually be used is probably several orders of magnitude less. This figure is an absolute upper limit; it cannot be increased by particular devices such as alternate splicing. It follows that there is far too little information in the genome to specify the detailed connections of a person's 10^{11} neurons, each with hundreds or thousands of synaptic contacts.

It is therefore no surprise that the brains and personalities of identical twins differ, as is the case also with lower animals that are genetically identical (see below). Conventionally the differences between genetically identical organisms are attributed to influences from the external environment, but I shall argue that there are additional causes.

Determinism by a combination of genes and environment

By environmental influences, I mean all external influences on the organism, ranging from intrauterine conditions to education. Unlike determinism by genes alone, this combined determinism is often considered to be total, a prison from which we can never escape. I agree that this combined determinism is indeed very considerable, and it is commonplace for students of the determinants of behaviour to assume that the variance in a population (of humans, or mice, or fruit flies. . .) is entirely due to a combination of genetic factors and environmental ones.

But as soon as you get down to understanding the underlying biology, this seems unlikely. As mentioned above, there is nowhere near enough information in the genome to specify all the details of brain connectivity. Environmental influences are certainly not going to provide all the missing information, important though they are. Several authors including myself have drawn attention to the fact that chance events beyond the control of either genes or environment influence many aspects of brain development. As the growing ends of axons and dendrites (called growth cones) advance, they are constantly putting out feelers ('*filopodia*') to recognise molecular guidance molecules along the way. Their growth can be studied, and they can be seen to be constantly making minor changes in direction, as if they are finding their way on a trial and error basis. Most reach more or less the right destination, but the precision is not total. Some (about 1%) make gross mistakes; for example, axons growing from the eye to the brain sometimes turn the wrong way at the optic chiasm, the place where the two optic nerves meet. Some grow to the wrong side of the brain, and others fail even to reach the brain, growing back down the other optic nerve. Far larger numbers (up to 40% in some cases) reach approximately the correct part of the brain, but make more subtle errors (e.g. they may grow to the wrong part of the correct target nucleus). The brain has a well developed signaling system to recognise such errors and eliminate them. If axons fail to obtain a correct signal from appropriate target neurons, the axon degenerates, and in some cases the neuron may die. Thus, our brains develop, not by a rigidly prespecified programme, but by a more approximate process involving imprecision everywhere, gross mistakes occasionally, and elimination of faulty elements at various inspection points along the cellular production line.

The above examples concern events at the cellular level, but it has been argued that there is indeterminacy at the molecular level too. Many molecular processes occurring in cells are currently understood as stochastic events. For example, the binding of a transcription factor (TF) molecule to a particular sequence of DNA (to initiate transcription, i.e. gene copying) involves the apparently random diffusion of many such molecules. One happens to reach the appropriate DNA sequence, whereas many others do not. Typically there may be thousands of TF molecules diffusing in the cell nucleus, but only one of them will reach the appropriate sequence on a particular strand of DNA. The details of which TF molecule will get there, and precisely when, is not specified genetically. When the TF molecules are numerous, the details will not matter, but when they are relatively few in number, it may be a matter of chance whether the TF binding sequence gets bound, and if so when. We still do not know how important such chance factors are for the overall functioning of organisms, but recent attempts at modelling suggest they can be very important. This further underlines that the most extreme forms of genetic determinism are implausible at the cellular level. At every level, genetic specification is only approximate.

Studies of genetically identical animals

This interpretation is supported by studies of isogenic (genetically identical) animals. Even in humans, the brains of monozygotic twins differ morphologically. They differ much less than the brains of dizygotic twins, but they do differ, and so do the intellectual abilities and psychological characteristics of identical twins. Some of these differences are probably due to environmental factors, which act even prenatally; for example, one twin may receive a richer blood supply and therefore be better nourished in the womb. But even when environmental factors are minimised, differences still occur, as has been shown in isogenic animals reared under the same conditions. For example, in isogenic daphniae, even though the position, size and branching pattern of each optic neuron is remarkably constant from animal to animal, there is nevertheless some variability in their connectivity. Similarly, in isogenic grasshoppers, there is variability in the positions of neurons and in the branching patterns of their dendrites—as much, in fact, as in heterogenic clutches. Also, in genetically identical specimens of the tropical fish Poecilia formosa (Amazon Molly), it is almost random whether the optic nerves or the Mauthner cell axons cross left over right or right over left. Even in lowly nematode worms, whose development is considered to be much more tightly controlled genetically than that of more complex species, there are differences between the nervous systems of isogenic worms. Since the environments of these different isogenic animals were essentially identical, the variability probably reflects developmental events below the resolution of genetic control, tiny fluctuations that have been called developmental noise.

In an excellent book, Finch and Kirkwood have reviewed the consequences of this developmental noise in both development and ageing in a wide range of species including humans. They make a strong case that 'chance' events, beyond the combined control of genome and environment, make a major contribution to the differences between individuals.

Physical or 'Laplacian' determinism

What then causes the differences between isogenic insects and fish reared in similar conditions? According to Newtonian physics, everything is determined. What if we could study the behaviour of every atom, every electron, would we not then have to conclude that determinism is total? I shall call this physical determinism; it is sometimes called Laplacian determinism because Laplace was well known for his view that the entire universe works like clockwork. I consider that physical determinism is the most fundamental form of determinism, and it is at this level that I shall focus the rest of this essay, with emphasis on physical determinism of the brain.

Physical determinism has long been considered a problem. When Epicurus (341–271 BC) famously proposed that 'the atoms swerve', it was partly because he considered this was needed for humans to be free. In the seventeenth century, Descartes wrestled with the implications of the new Newtonian philosophy, and realised that its application to the human brain raised major philosophical problems. As a dualist, he was naturally concerned with how the soul could act upon the brain without contravening the deterministic laws of physics. For him, animals were hydraulic machines, in which the driving fluids were 'animal spirits' (from the Latin anima, a soul); despite their name, he envisaged these as being decidedly physical and material. He believed that the nerves constituted the hydraulic system, down which the flow of the animal spirits was controlled by filaments that operated tiny 'valvules' in the nerves and in the ventricles of the brain. He considered that external stimuli moved the skin that in turn pulled on the filaments opening valvules to release the flow. Ultimately this would affect the muscles, producing movement. Descartes' idea was not limited to simple movements. He tried to analyse emotions like fear and love as being due to the way animal spirits were induced to flow as a result of external events. Human reflex actions and emotions were explained on the same mechanical basis as in animals, but human voluntary behaviour required an interaction between the material automaton and the immaterial 'rational soul'. Descartes maintained that this occurred in the pineal gland, where the rational soul redirected small tissue movements so as to regulate the flow of animal spirits. In an attempt to make this compatible with Newtonian laws, he proposed that this redirection involved a change in the direction of motion of the animal spirits but not their speed. We now know that Descartes' attempt is invalid, because momentum is a vector and its conservation applies in every direction.

For this reason, many modern attempts to preserve freedom and humanity against the supposed straightjacket of physical predictability and determinism invoke either chaos theory to undermine predictability even when physical determinism applies, or quantum indeterminism. This essay focuses on the latter and deals with chaos only as applied to quantum effects.

Philosophical approaches to physical determinism and free will

This paper does not attempt to break any new ground philosophically, but it is necessary at least to summarise what the main philosophical positions are. To many people it seems obvious that physical determinism is incompatible with free will. If our brains work mechanistically, then our behaviour must be predetermined, so how can we be free? How can we be responsible for our choices if they were decided before we made them? How can we be responsible for our behaviour if it was determined not by ourselves, but by the impersonal laws of physics and chemistry? This view is called incompatibilism; it is conventionally subdivided into two radically opposed positions: libertarianism, which affirms free will and denies determinism; and hard determinism, which denies free will and affirms determinism. But many philosophers disagree with incompatibilism, adopting the contrary view, which is called compatibilism. Thus we have three classical positions.

1 Compatibilism ('soft determinism'): Determinism is compatible with free will and human responsibility (e.g. Spinoza, Hobbes, Hume, Daniel Dennett).
2 Libertarianism: We do have free will, and this is incompatible with determinism (e.g. Reid, Kant, Robert Kane, Richard Swinburne).
3 Hard determinism: The past completely determines the future, including the future of our own brains. Free will is therefore an illusion (e.g. Holbach, Nietzsche; most modern philosophers reject this label).

This list is not of course exhaustive. For amateurs (like myself) who wish to go into the subject in more detail, libertarian philosopher Robert Kane's recent book gives a very clear and even handed introduction to the different positions, which include the particularly pessimistic one of Galen Strawson, who maintains that both determinism and indeterminism are incompatible with free will.

Problems of defining of free will

One's choice among the above positions is intimately linked to how one defines free will. Some people incorporate their philosophical assumptions into their very definition of free will. For example, the Free Dictionary gives a compatibilist definition: 'The power of making free choices unconstrained by *external* agencies' (italics added). In contrast, the *Handbook of Psychological Terms* gives a blatantly libertarian definition: 'The choices which are said to have no necessary determination from the nervous system or from any other physical cause.'

Many thinkers have commented on the problem of definition. For example, Einstein once wrote:

> Honestly I cannot understand what people mean by free will. I have a feeling, for instance, that I will something or other; but what relation this has with freedom I cannot understand at all. I feel that I will to light my pipe and I do it; but how can I connect this up with the idea of freedom? What is behind the act of willing to light the pipe? Another act of willing?

Philosophers have long been aware of these problems, but the definition of free will is still a subject of debate among them. Some argue that the very term free will is unfortunate, and prefer to speak of freedom of action. All agree that human responsibility is at the heart of the issue.

Free will and ideas of the soul

One's preference for a compatibilist or a libertarian position is likely to be linked to one's beliefs about the brain-mind relationship and the soul. A Cartesian dualist, conceiving the soul as a separate nonphysical entity that interacts with the brain, will require some degree of indeterminism in the brain-machine to provide leeway for the soul to act on the brain. In contrast, a monist, perhaps a dual aspect monist like Malcolm Jeeves, will probably think in terms of a deterministic brain, a machine without loose screws. There are exceptions, however; for example Forster and Marston accept a monist position on biblical grounds but argue for indeterminism.

****

. . . the dualist notion of an eternal nonphysical soul that is so widespread in our society is not considered by most theologians to be the biblical one. It comes from the ancient Greeks, notably from Plato, as is illustrated in the following quotation:

> Does not death mean that the body comes to exist by itself, separated from the soul, and that the soul exists by herself, separated from the body? (Socrates, in Plato's Phaedo.)

This Greek notion of the immortal soul was developed by the neoplatonists and became deeply rooted in Western Society and Christian thinking. But most modern scholars accept that the biblical notion of man is different. In the Old Testament, the word that is most often translated 'soul' is *nephesh*, whose primary meaning is simply life or vitality, with the underlying connotation also of movement. Furthermore, the word translated 'spirit' (*ruah*) in the Old Testament carries the basic idea of air in motion. In many cases it simply means, and is translated, 'wind', but it can also refer to the 'breath of life' that the whole animal creation shares with man (Gen. 6:17). When translated spirit, it usually expresses the vitality of the mind as expressive of the whole personality (Pss. 32:2; 78:8), or it may refer to human inclinations and desires (e.g., Hos. 4:12). Thus, neither *nephesh* nor *ruah* necessarily implies dualism. Admittedly, both are described occasionally as leaving man at death, but never as existing separately from the body. Thus, although there is still some debate on the subject, most scholars consider that the Old Testament sees man as a unity.

In the New Testament, it is more difficult to find out what is meant from the analysis of words, because the original manuscripts were written in Greek, and the available words were all heavily charged with the dualistic overtones of Greek philosophy. There is therefore more debate on this question, but the majority view of theologians is that the New Testament writers also emphasise the unity of the human person, and do not teach the idea of a disembodied soul. Thus, psyche, which is the New Testament equivalent of *nephesh*, carries meanings ranging from life and desire (in St Paul's letters) to the whole personality. Most strikingly, the New Testament doctrine of the resurrection of the body is very far from the Platonic concept of an eternal, immaterial soul with the potential to exist in isolation from the body. This is particularly clear in I Corinthians, chapter 15. Here, St Paul first affirms the physical resurrection of Jesus, and that 'those who belong to Christ' will likewise be raised. He then goes on to analyse the various uses of the word 'body', showing that its meaning can vary, and he explains that after the dead are raised, their body will be a 'spiritual body', very different from the previous 'natural body' (or 'physical body'), but a body nonetheless. His notion of a 'spiritual body' is radically different from the Platonic notion of an eternal, disembodied soul. Indeed, he states that the physical comes first, then the spiritual. Elsewhere he writes: 'God . . . who alone is immortal' (1 Tim. 6:16). Nowhere does the Bible countenance the notion of a disembodied soul or an intrinsically eternal soul.

Admittedly, many great Christian thinkers have been dualists (and neoplatonists) including Origen and Augustine, Luther and Calvin, and Descartes; and dualism, often very different from that of Plato and Descartes, still finds support from modern philosophers and theologians including J. P. Moreland and J.W. Cooper. But in post-Reformation times various scholars have opposed dualism quite explicitly. For example, Joseph Priestley, the British conconformist minister who achieved scientific eminence by isolating 'dephlogisticated air' (oxygen), held essentially the biblical view described above. He maintained that the common dualism between matter and spirit was due to the contamination of biblical Christianity by Greek philosophy. In his *Disquisitions Relating to Matter and Spirit* (1777), he gave sophisticated arguments that the matter-spirit duality should be collapsed and that God worked through causal chains that were neither material nor immaterial in the traditional senses of these words. His arguments were partly scientific, partly philosophical, and partly theological. Among the latter was an objection against the idea of an immortal soul, because it rendered the doctrine of the Resurrection superfluous. More recently, Anglican theologian Austin Farrer wrote in reaction to the dualistic ideas of neurophysiologist John Eccles (see below): 'We will have nothing to do with the fantastic suggestion, that what the supersensitive "reactors" in the cortex react to, is the initiative of a virtually disembodied soul.'[18]

Thus, Christians can be dualists or monists, just as they can be libertarians or compatibilists. But philosophers (Christian or not) who side with dualist/interactionist libertarianism are nowadays usually quantum libertarians.

Quantum libertarianism

The notion that quantum (Heisenbergian) indeterminism might provide a basis for free will was proposed already in the 1930s by the physicists P. Jordan and Eddington, and has continued to be proposed by philosophers and scientists. I shall call this approach quantum libertarianism.

Heisenberg's uncertainty principle

Most readers will be aware that one of the widely accepted consequences of wave mechanics is Heisenberg's Uncertainty Principle, according to which there is a fundamental limit to the precision with which certain pairs of physical quantities can be measured. One such pair is the momentum and position of a particle. If h is Planck's constant, and imprecision is expressed by Δ, then Δmomentum x Δposition $\geq h/4\pi$. There is no limit to the precision with which the momentum alone of the electron, or its position alone, might be measured; but any gain in the precision of measurement of one member of the pair will inevitably be offset by decreased precision for the other member. Another such pair is: $\Delta E.\Delta t \geq h/4\pi$, where E is energy and t is time, and we shall use this below. Since h is very small indeed, Heisenbergian uncertainty is irrelevant to macroscopic objects such as golf balls; but it is very relevant to microscopical entities such as electrons.

Heisenberg's principle was initially proposed as a practical limitation to measurement, but many physicists and philosophers have argued that it goes far deeper than mere practicalities, establishing a fundamental indeterminism in nature. This interpretation has been vigorously disputed by many others including Einstein, who made in this context his famous remark that 'God does not play dice'. The fundamental equation of quantum physics, the Schrödinger equation, is in itself fully deterministic, and the indeterminism arises only in the transition between the quantum level description and the macroscopical one. Nevertheless, many philosophers have seized on Heisenbergian uncertainty as an argument against physical determinism. They treat it as a kind of cloud cover in which small perturbations can occur

---

[18]A. Farrer, *The Freedom of the Will* (London: A & C. Black, 1958).

'unnoticed' by the watchful eye of nature's laws. In the following paragraphs I shall provisionally accept this interpretation to explore its consequences for brain function, but would emphasise that the starting assumption is already controversial.

Quantum libertarians propose that mind-directed changes occur 'hidden' within the cloud cover of Heisenbergian uncertainty. According to standard quantum physics, such hidden effects are assumed to be random, but the unconventional proposal of quantum libertarianism is that they are non-random, directed by the mind (or soul etc.).

Quantum libertarianism at the synapse

Among those who attempted to extend this indeterminism to the brain and free will was Nobel prizewinning neurophysiologist Sir John Eccles, who throughout his long and productive career persistently advocated an essentially Cartesian form of dualism, although he sought more plausible sites of mind-brain liaison than Descartes' proposal of the pineal gland. Eccles invoked Heisenbergian Uncertainty to provide a way for the mind and will to modify brain-function without violating physical laws. His idea was that it provided enough flexibility in the otherwise rigid chain of cause and effect for mental events to be able to influence brain events, and he saw this as necessary for us to be free agents.

To be relevant to conscious decision-making, the mind-brain liaison would need to influence the brain's electrical activity rather directly, and Eccles proposed that this occurs in synapses (junctions between neurons) of the cerebral cortex. He also postulated, rather arbitrarily, that the cortex is divided into open modules (responsive to mental events) and closed modules (unresponsive). There is no experimental evidence for Eccles' propositions, but given the known importance of the cerebral cortex for conscious thought and decision-making, and the critical role played by synapses in neural function, they seem a reasonable starting point for speculation.

In the 1970s and 1980s, Eccles argued that the crucial Heisenbergian uncertainty would be in the position and velocity of synaptic vesicles, tiny membranous bags whose fusion with the cell membrane causes their content of neurotransmitter molecules to be released into the narrow synaptic cleft (space between two neurons). He thought this uncertainty could be sufficient to allow dualistic interactions affecting synaptic fusion with the membrane. This view was criticised by neurophysiologist David Wilson, who argued (correctly in my opinion) that the vesicles were many orders of magnitude too large for this to work.

Eccles then teamed up with physicist Friedrich Beck to present a more sophisticated model of neurotransmitter release in which they argued that quantum indeterminism could be important. I shall not discuss here the biological details of the Beck-Eccles model, some of which are no longer accepted (e.g. the notion that transmitter release involves the transition of a paracrystalline presynaptic grid to a metastable state). Moreover, it has since become clear that the movement of vesicles to the cell membrane and their fusion with it are rigorously controlled; before fusing with the membrane they are 'docked' close to it by a complex of proteins, and the final fusion is only possible when one of these proteins (usually synaptotagmin) changes its conformation as a result of interaction with calcium. As argued by Wilson, it is more plausible (or at least less implausible) to postulate Heisenbergian effects on the control of synaptic calcium concentration rather than on the movement of synaptic vesicles. But the following argument, which is adapted from Wilson, shows that Heisenbergian effects are too small even to affect synaptic calcium.

Quantitative application of Heisenbergian uncertainty to synaptic function

We consider the possibility that Heisenbergian uncertainty might allow a chemical bond to be modified in an ion channel in the synaptic membrane. This could be a calcium channel, influencing synaptic calcium concentration directly, or a sodium channel that influenced it indirectly through changes in electrical potential. According to Heisenberg's principle, there is a limit to the precisions of energy (E) and time (t) given by $\Delta E.\Delta t \geq h/4\pi$ where $h = 6.63 \times 10^{-34}$ J.s. In other words, an energy change ΔE can be 'hidden' for a time Δt providing ΔE is of the order of $h/4\pi\Delta t$. To have even a minimal effect on the synaptic function Δt would need to be at least 10 microseconds, probably much more. Substituting this value gives a ΔE of the order of 5.2×10^{-30} Joules. This is about 200,000 times too small to disrupt even a single Van der Waals interaction, the weakest of all the chemical bonds (E = 1×10^{-24} J). Even if, unrealistically, we took Δt as the time of a single ion to cross the channel (about 10 nanosec.), ΔE is still 200 times too small.

Other possible sites for Heisenbergian effects

The above arguments focus on synaptic ion channels, but apply equally to any solution involving changes in molecular bonds. But what about other loci? Might the calculations come out more favorably for the possibility of Heisenbergian effects if applied to some other cellular structure? We don't know, but currently it seems hard to formulate suitable hypotheses.

One much discussed site for quantum effects (a more general concept that includes Heisenbergian effects) is the microtubules, very fine tubes, about 20 nm in diameter, that run down the insides of axons, and are known to be involved in transporting proteins and other molecules from the cell body to the axon tip or vice versa. The microtubule hypothesis was originally proposed, by Penrose and Hameroff, as part of a theory that the brain works as a quantum computer. They were not concerned with Heisenbergian uncertainty or free will, but some authors have suggested the hypothesis could be adapted to the latter purpose. The scientific and philosophical reasons for proposing microtubules as a site for quantum effects are too complex to be dealt with here. Few neurobiologists take the microtubule hypothesis seriously...

I share the general scepticism about quantum effects in microtubules (whether applied to quantum computation or adapted to Heisenbergian uncertainty and free will), but I admit that more work is required to analyse whether Heisenbergian effects in other cellular events might affect brain activity. Possibilities include: the binding of individual calcium ions to calcium-sensing molecules such as synaptotagmin; local changes in postsynaptic membrane potential that might affect the triggering of an action potential; or events along the axon that might affect the speed of the action potential and its time of arrival at the synapse.

An inadequate counterargument about sensitivity to Heisenbergian effects

The hypothesis that neural functioning could be sensitive to quantum effects is sometimes argued on the grounds that the absorption of a very few photons can affect retinal function. It has indeed been well known, since the 1940s, that the extreme sensitivity of human vision in faint light implies that a single rod photoreceptor can respond to just one or two photons of light. True though this is, it confuses the energy of a photon with the uncertainty of its energy. The ΔE calculated above (5.2×10^{-30} J) is about 10^{-13} times smaller than the energy available in a single photon of (blue-green) light (4×10^{-17} J). Thus, attempts to free the brain from the shackles of deterministic law by means of Heisenbergian uncertainty falter because of the smallness of the uncertainty. An answer to this problem has recently been sought in the fashionable field of chaos theory.

Amplification of Heisenbergian uncertainty by deterministic chaos

There is no universally accepted mathematical definition of chaos, but in rough terms a chaotic system is one that is extremely sensitive to initial conditions or perturbations. As a result of this property, chaotic systems (like the weather) are in practice unpredictable over a long period, even though they are deterministic. The field of chaos research has roots in the work of Poincaré at the end of the nineteenth century, but it took off in the 1960s and has since become a major field. It has been deeply analysed by mathematicians and computational modellers, and chaos has been reported, or predicted to occur, in many different situations in physics, chemistry and biology. Of immediate relevance to our present concerns, it has been claimed to occur in the electric activity of the brain.

Since the 1980s, numerous electrophysiological studies of action potentials in various brain regions have been interpreted as evidence for chaotic processes. It has even been argued that chaotic dynamics can be detected the electroencephalogram recorded from the scalps of awake humans, and that switches between chaos and non-chaos can be diagnostic of normal versus abnormal function. As a note of caution, I should add that it is technically very difficult (perhaps impossible) to prove rigorously from a series of action potentials or waves recorded from the brain that the underlying process is truly chaotic. All that can be said is that there is sufficient evidence to convince many scientists that chaos sometimes occurs in brain activity. The relevance of chaos to quantum libertarianism is that it is sometimes claimed to provide a means of amplifying the tiny indeterminism available from quantum theory.

It is argued that if the mind were to exert even a slight influence (within the limits of Heisenbergian Uncertainty) on brain activity, the small change could be enormously amplified if the brain dynamics were chaotic. Hence, the non-physical mind might act on the physical brain to change conscious experience and/or behaviour. The chaos responsible for the amplification could be in the electrical activity of brain neural networks (as discussed above) or conceivably at an intracellular level, where chaos is likewise claimed to occur.

A major difficulty with this approach is that combining chaos theory with quantum theory is problematic. Quantum chaos has been studied for two decades, but its very existence is debated, because of the mathematically predicted'quantum suppression of chaos'; if the equations of a chaotic system are combined with Schroedinger's equation, the chaos is suppressed. The causes of this seem to be only partly understood, but have been linked to the fractal nature of the behaviour of chaotic systems, to the fact that quantum systems cannot display classical trajectories on a finer scale than that of Planck's constant, and to the fact that Schrödinger's equation gives solutions that are periodic or quasi-periodic and hence incompatible with chaos. Hobbs faced up to the quantum suppression problem and gave provisional arguments that it might be solvable. More recently the pendulum has swung back in favour of quantum chaos, at least in some situations, because of evidence over the last few years that the quantum suppression of chaos can itself be suppressed by another quantum effect, the phenomenon of decoherence caused by interaction between the quantal system and its environment. But I doubt that that quantum chaos, resurrected by decoherence, can provide for fundamental indeterminism in the sense required by quantum libertarianism, because this requires the environment to be considered as an external element outside the quantum-level description. A quantum-level description that included the entire interacting environment would not be subject to decoherence. And there are further problems, as discussed below.

Two further problems with the amplification hypothesis

Quite apart from the problems of quantum chaos, the proposal that soul induced fluctuations might be amplified, whether by chaos or by other means, to provide the changes in brain activity needed for libertarian free will is problematic for three further reasons.

First, as mentioned above, the Schrödinger equation is fully deterministic, and the indeterminism arises only in the transition between the quantum level description and the macroscopical one. The difficulties that this raises for amplification or ultrasensitive quantum detectors in the brain were discussed by Penrose.

Secondly, could the chaos-induced changes be specific enough to provide free will? Even without amplification, the step from indeterminism to free will requires the unconventional interpretation that Heisenbergian indeterminism is not really indeterminism at all, but a kind of cloud cover permitting the soul or mind to determine brain activity unnoticed. Thus, we are asked to accept without evidence that what everybody believed was random is in fact directed and meaningful, and further that the directedness is maintained even after enormous amplification (by chaos or other means). In the current state of knowledge this seems decidedly far-fetched.

Thirdly, brain physiology has (and needs) built-in resistance to small fluctuations. Brain cells live in a warm (310°K), wet environment where they are continually buffeted from within and without by the random movements that all molecules make because of their thermal energy...Thus, the thermal (and hence kinetic) energy of the molecules is 9 orders of magnitude greater than the energy change that can be hidden by Heisenbergian uncertainty. But brain cells (and other cells) have to be resistant to the buffeting due to thermal energy. And if chaos is to amplify tiny mind induced fluctuations, it will presumably amplify also the far greater fluctuations due to thermal energy, as Beck and Eccles recognised. Indeed, despite differences in approach, Beck's quantitative conclusions are similar to mine: that Heisenbergian uncertainty can only be relevant to brain events occurring in the picosecond range or still faster (e.g. electron transfer). The radical difference between us is that Beck thinks that Heisenbergian uncertainty in such rapid events may affect brain functioning, whereas I think this most unlikely. Beck cites evidence for this in the response of photobacteria to light, but there appears to be no evidence in relation to brain function.

A similar resistance to perturbations may exist at the network level as well, because single-pulse microstimulation of a cortical neuron has always been found to affect only neurons receiving direct connections from it without disrupting the overall cortical activity. Libertarian philosopher Robert Kane proposes exactly the opposite, however, for critical moments of decision. Citing theorists such as Henry Stapp and Gordon Globus he writes: '. . . conflicts of will [may] stir up chaos in the brain and make the agent's thought processes more sensitive to undetermined influences. . .'. While several studies have been published on the electrophysiology of decision making, there is no direct evidence about brain activity during conflicts of will. An involvement of chaos cannot currently be excluded, but it seems to me that extreme sensitivity to minor fluctuations at the moment of choice would make the decision making excessively vulnerable to arbitrary factors ranging from irrelevant neural inputs to changes in blood pressure.

Uncertainty about uncertainty

Finally, I would reiterate the warning given above, that the very starting point of this discussion on quantum libertarianism – the use of Heisenbergian uncertainty to obtain ontological indeterminism – is open to debate. A detailed consideration of this much-discussed topic is beyond the scope of this essay, but I would briefly mention that there are at least two kinds of problem. On the one hand, a minority of physicists argue for an interpretation of quantum theory in terms of a fully deterministic theory. On the other hand, even for those who accept fundamental indeterminism in the transition from the quantum-level description to the macroscopical one, the deterministic nature of the Schrödinger equation may still raise problems for ontological interpretation.

Conclusion

Brain determinism by genes plus environment is incomplete, but at the lower level of physical law determinism does seem to be complete apart from the tiny degree of indeterminism that results from Heisenbergian uncertainty. Quantum libertarianism attempts to ground our freedom of action on this scanty foundation, arguing that this quantum-level indeterminism may manifest itself in cerebral functioning. This paper draws attention to quantitative and conceptual problems with this approach.

Questions

1 For Clarke, why is physical determinism the level where the problem of determinism is most acute?

2 How did Descartes attempt to resolve the conundrum of physical determinism?

3 How does the question of the freedom of the will relate to the idea of the soul?

4 What is Heisenberg's Uncertainty Principle, and how is it imagined that it enables some degree of freedom of the will?

5 Why is Clarke unconvinced by the use of chaos theory in the area of indeterminacy?

6 What do you think about Clarke's attempt at an interdisciplinary study? Does it work methodologically? Are his theological assumptions warranted?

7 Does a physical level determinism involve an unsolvable problem for Christian theology?

5

Gender and sexuality

Without a doubt, some of the most difficult questions in theological anthropology surround the nature of gender and sexuality. As commonly used in the literature, "sexuality" refers to biological realities like hormones, genitalia, and brain structure. Gender, on the other hand, typically refers to the ways in which we live out our sexuality in particular contexts. Each of these raises its own set of issues. Is *gender* determined by our biology in any way (gender essentialism) or is it entirely governed by sociocultural norms (gender constructivism)? Either way, are there God-given norms that should guide our understanding of what it means to be male and female in any setting, or are we just given overarching guidelines for being *human* and *Christian* within which we are free to develop diverse expressions of gender within our cultural contexts? More specifically, does God provide gender-specific guidelines for certain offices or rules in the church and home? Regarding *sexuality*, are even the biological conditions of maleness and femaleness entirely fixed, or are the boundaries more fluid and open to refashioning? How should we understand those whose biological structures do not fit neatly into the categories of maleness and femaleness? Are these examples of human nature gone awry, broken bodies that need correction in some way, or are these legitimately diverse ways of expressing the full range of human sexuality? What about those whose sexual identities (i.e., the way they understand themselves) do not align with their biological sexualities? Which should govern how they view themselves and be viewed by others? And of course we cannot neglect the challenging questions surrounding sexual ethics. Regardless of how we answer the above questions, we must still wrestle with the *how* of human sexuality? How should we express our sexualities? What are the appropriate guidelines that should govern sexual behavior? Answering each of these questions receives further complexity from the many disciplines involved in the endeavor: psychology, biology, sociology, philosophy, theology, and more.

Given the complexity of these issues, no single set of readings can possibly hope to address even a partial range of Christian perspectives on these issues.[1] Indeed, each of these questions requires a chapter of its own. So we have decided to focus these readings more specifically on theological reflection about the nature of sexuality. Why did God create us as sexual beings? What purpose does this serve and how should that affect the way that we understand our sexuality today? Answering questions like these provides a theological framework within which to begin addressing other issues in human sexuality. As we will see, early reflections on these questions focused primarily on the nature of marriage and virginity. The modern period has tended to focus more specifically on human sexuality as an object of reflection in its own right, and feminist thinkers challenged and advanced traditional discussions about sexuality in important ways.

---

[1]For additional readings, see Elizabeth Stuart and Adrian Thatcher, *Christian Perspectives on Sexuality and Gender* (Grand Rapids: Eerdmans, 1996); Eugene Rogers, ed., *Theology and Sexuality: Classic and Contemporary Readings* (Oxford: Blackwell, 2002); Maxine Hancock, *Christian Perspectives on Gender, Sexuality, and Community* (Vancouver, BC: Regent College Publishing, 2003); Adrian Thatcher, ed., *The Oxford Handbook of Theology, Sexuality, and Gender* (Oxford: Oxford University Press, 2014).

TEXT 1: GREGORY OF NYSSA,
ON VIRGINITY[2]

Gregory of Nyssa (*c.* 335–84) was one of the famous Cappadocian Fathers, along with his brother Basil the Great and friend Gregory of Nazianzus. Although Gregory would have preferred to live a life of quiet philosophical reflection, he became bishop of Nyssa at his brother's insistence and developed into one of the leading theologians of his day. In this reading, Gregory follows the long-standing tradition of thinking about human sexuality primarily through the rubric of marriage and virginity. From the earliest days of Christian theology, theologians approached sexuality with the presumption that human sexuality was given primarily for the purpose of procreation. Consequently, early writings on sexuality tended to focus on the institution of marriage and guidelines for protecting the sanctity of the marriage bed. At the same time, however, the church valued the importance of virginity and the celibate lifestyle as an expression of complete dedication to God, while also being well aware of how a creational good like sexuality could easily become an occasion for temptation and stumbling. This created somewhat of a tension in theological reflection on sexuality. Although most theologians continued to affirm marriage and sexuality as good aspects of God's created order, they also wanted to emphasize the significance of celibacy and the dangers of sexuality in a fallen world. Gregory reflects this same tension in this selection from his famous work on virginity.

Chapter I

The holy look of virginity is precious indeed in the judgment of all who make purity the test of beauty; but it belongs to those alone whose struggles to gain this object of a noble love are favoured and helped by the grace of God. Its praise is heard at once in the very name which goes with it; "Uncorrupted" is the word commonly said of it, and this shows the kind of purity that is in it; thus we can measure by its equivalent term the height of this gift, seeing that amongst the many results of virtuous endeavour this alone has been honoured with the title of the thing that is uncorrupted. And if we must extol with laudations this gift from the great God, the words of His Apostle are sufficient in its praise; they are few, but they throw into the background all extravagant laudations; he only styles as "holy and without blemish" her who has this grace for her ornament. Now if the achievement of this saintly virtue consists in making one "without blemish and holy," and these epithets are adopted in their first and fullest force to glorify the incorruptible Deity, what greater praise of virginity can there be than thus to be shown in a manner *deifying* those who share in her pure mysteries, so that they become partakers of His glory Who is in actual truth the only Holy and Blameless One; their purity and their incorruptibility being

---

[2]Gregory of Nyssa, *On Virginity*, in *NPNF* 2.5, 343–70.

the means of bringing them into relationship with Him? Many who write lengthy laudations in detailed treatises, with the view of adding something to the wonder of this grace, unconsciously defeat, in my opinion, their own end; the fulsome manner in which they amplify their subject brings its credit into suspicion. Nature's greatnesses have their own way of striking with admiration; they do not need the pleading of words: the sky, for instance, or the sun, or any other wonder of the universe. In the business of this lower world words certainly act as a basement, and the skill of praise does impart a look of magnificence; so much so, that mankind are apt to suspect as the result of mere art the wonder produced by panegyric. So the one sufficient way of praising virginity will be to show that that virtue is above praise, and to evince our admiration of it by our lives rather than by our words. A man who takes this theme for ambitious praise has the appearance of supposing that one drop of his own perspiration will make an appreciable increase of the boundless ocean, if indeed he believes, as he does, that any human words can give more dignity to so rare a grace; he must be ignorant either of his own powers or of that which he attempts to praise.

Chapter II

Deep indeed will be the thought necessary to understand the surpassing excellence of this grace. It is comprehended in the idea of the Father incorrupt; and here at the outset is a paradox, viz. that virginity is found in Him, Who has a Son and yet without passion has begotten Him. It is included too in the nature of this Only-begotten God, Who struck the first note of all this moral innocence; it shines forth equally in His pure and passionless generation. Again a paradox; that the Son should be known to us by virginity. It is seen, too, in the inherent and incorruptible purity of the Holy Spirit; for when you have named the pure and incorruptible you have named virginity. It accompanies the whole supramundane existence; because of its passionlessness it is always present with the powers above; never separated from aught that is Divine, it never touches the opposite of this. All whose instinct and will have found their level in virtue are beautified with this perfect purity of the uncorrupted state; all who are ranked in the opposite class of character are what they are, and are called so, by reason of their fall from purity. What force of expression, then, will be adequate to such a grace? How can there be no cause to fear lest the greatness of its intrinsic value should be impaired by the efforts of any one's eloquence? The estimate of it which he will create will be less than that which his hearers had before. It will be well, then, to omit all laudation in this case; we cannot lift words to the height of our theme. On the contrary, it is possible to be ever mindful of this gift of God; and our lips may always speak of this blessing; that, though it is the property of spiritual existence and of such singular excellence, yet by the love of God it has been bestowed on those who have received their life from the will of the flesh and from blood; that, when human nature has been based by passionate inclinations, it stretches out its offer of purity like a hand to raise it up again and make it look above. This, I think, was the reason why our Master, Jesus Christ Himself, the Fountain of all innocence, did not come into the world by wedlock. It was, to divulge by the manner of His Incarnation this great secret; that purity is the only complete indication of the presence of God and of His coming, and that no one can in reality secure this for himself, unless he has altogether estranged himself from the passions of the flesh. What happened in the stainless Mary when the fulness of the Godhead which was in Christ shone out through her, that happens in every soul that leads by rule the virgin life. No longer indeed does the Master come with bodily presence; "we know Christ no longer according to the flesh"; but, spiritually, He dwells in us and brings His Father with Him, as the Gospel somewhere tells. Seeing, then, that virginity means so much as this, that while it remains in Heaven with the Father of spirits, and moves in the dance of the celestial powers, it nevertheless stretches out hands for man's salvation; that while it is the channel which draws down the Deity to share man's estate, it keeps wings for man's desires to rise to heavenly things, and is a bond of union between the Divine and human, by its mediation bringing into harmony these existences so widely divided—what words could be discovered powerful enough to reach this wondrous height? But still, it is monstrous to seem like creatures without expression and without feeling; and we must choose (if we are silent) one of two things; either to appear never to have felt the special beauty of virginity, or to exhibit ourselves as obstinately blind to all beauty: we have consented therefore to speak briefly about this virtue, according to the wish of him who has assigned us this task, and whom in all things we must obey. But let no one expect from us any display of style; even if we wished it, perhaps we could not produce it, for we are quite unversed in that kind of writing. Even if we possessed such power, we would not prefer the favour of the few to the edification of the many. A writer of sense should have, I take it, for his chiefest object not to be admired above all other writers, but to profit both himself and them, the many.

Chapter III

Would indeed that some profit might come to myself from this effort! I should have undertaken this labour with the greater readiness, if I could have hope of sharing, according to the Scripture, in the fruits of the plough and the threshing-floor; the toil would then have been a pleasure. As it is, this my knowledge of the beauty of virginity is in some sort vain and useless to me, just as the corn is to the muzzled ox that treads the floor, or the water that streams from the precipice to a thirsty man when he cannot reach it. Happy they who have still the power of choosing the better way, and have not debarred themselves from it by engagements of the secular life, as we have, whom a gulf now divides from glorious virginity: no one can climb up to that who has once planted his foot upon the secular life. We are but spectators of others' blessings and witnesses to the happiness of another class. Even if we strike out some fitting thoughts about virginity, we shall not be better than the cooks and scullions who provide sweet luxuries for the tables of the rich, without having any portion themselves in what they prepare. What a blessing if it had been otherwise, if we had not to learn the good by after-regrets! Now *they* are the enviable ones, *they* succeed even beyond their prayers and their desires, who have not put out of their power the enjoyment of these delights. We are like those who have a wealthy society with which to compare their own poverty, and so are all the more vexed and discontented with their present lot. The more exactly we understand the riches of virginity, the more we must bewail the other life; for we realize by this contrast with better things, how poor it is. I do not speak only of the future rewards in store for those who have lived thus excellently, but those rewards also which they have while alive here; for if any one would make up his mind to measure exactly the difference between the two courses, he would find it well-nigh as great as that between heaven and earth. The truth of this statement may be known by looking at actual facts.

But in writing this sad tragedy what will be a fit beginning? How shall we really bring to view the evils common to life? All men know them by experience, but somehow nature has contrived to blind the actual sufferers so that they willingly ignore their condition. Shall we begin with its choicest sweets? Well then, is not the sum total of all that is hoped for in marriage to get delightful companionship? Grant this obtained; let us sketch a marriage in every way most happy; illustrious birth, competent means, suitable ages, the very flower of the prime of life, deep affection, the very best that each can think of the other, that sweet rivalry of each wishing to surpass the other in loving; in addition, popularity, power, wide reputation, and everything else. But observe that even beneath this array of blessings the fire of an inevitable pain is smouldering. I do not speak of the envy that is always springing up against those of distinguished rank, and the liability to attack which hangs over those who seem prosperous, and that natural hatred of superiors shown by those who do not share equally in the good fortune, which make these seemingly favoured ones pass an anxious time more full of pain than pleasure. I omit that from the picture, and will suppose that envy against them is asleep; although it would not be easy to find a single life in which both these blessings were joined, i.e., happiness above the common, and escape from envy. However, let us, if so it is to be, suppose a married life free from all such trials; and let us see if it is possible for those who live with such an amount of good fortune to enjoy it. Why, what kind of vexation is left, you will ask, when even envy of their happiness does not reach them? I affirm that this very thing, this sweetness that surrounds their lives, is the spark which kindles pain. They are human all the time, things weak and perishing; they have to look upon the tombs of their progenitors; and so pain is inseparably bound up with their existence, if they have the least power of reflection. This continued expectancy of death, realized by no sure tokens, but hanging over them the terrible uncertainty of the future, disturbs their present joy, clouding it over with the fear of what is coming. If only, before experience comes, the results of experience could be learnt, or if, when one has entered on this course, it were possible by some other means of conjecture to survey the reality, then what a crowd of deserters would run from marriage into the virgin life; what care and eagerness never to be entangled in that retentive snare, where no one knows for certain how the net galls till they have actually entered it! You would see there, if only you could do it without danger, many contraries uniting; smiles melting into tears, pain mingled with pleasure, death always hanging by expectation over the children that are born, and putting a finger upon each of the sweetest joys. Whenever the husband looks at the beloved face, that moment the fear of separation accompanies the look. If he listens to the sweet voice, the thought comes into his mind that some day he will not hear it. Whenever he is glad with gazing on her beauty, then he shudders most with the presentiment of mourning her loss. When he marks all those charms which to youth are so precious and which the thoughtless seek for, the bright eyes beneath the lids, the arching eyebrows, the cheek with its sweet and dimpling smile, the natural red that blooms upon the lips, the gold-bound hair shining in many-twisted masses on the head, and all that transient grace, then, though he may be little given to reflection, he must have this thought also in his inmost soul that some day all this beauty will melt away and become as nothing, turned after all this show into noisome and unsightly bones, which wear no trace, no memorial, no remnant of that living bloom. Can he live delighted when he thinks of that?

Chapter V

Now we declare that Virginity is man's "fellow-worker" and helper in achieving the aim of this lofty passion. In other sciences men have devised certain practical methods for cultivating the particular subject; and so, I take it, virginity is the practical method in the science of the Divine life, furnishing men with the power of assimilating themselves with spiritual natures. The constant endeavour in such a course is to prevent the nobility of the soul from being lowered by those sensual outbreaks, in which the mind no longer maintains its heavenly thoughts and upward gaze, but sinks down to the emotions belonging to the flesh and blood. How can the soul which is riveted to the pleasures of the flesh and busied with merely human longings turn a disengaged eye upon its kindred intellectual light? This evil, ignorant, and prejudiced bias towards material things will prevent it. The eyes of swine, turning naturally downward, have no glimpse of the wonders of the sky; no more can the soul whose body drags it down look any longer upon the beauty above; it must pore perforce upon things which though natural are low and animal. To look with a free devoted gaze upon heavenly delights, the soul will turn itself from earth; it will not even partake of the recognized indulgences of the secular life; it will transfer all its powers of affection from material objects to the intellectual contemplation of immaterial beauty. Virginity of the body is devised to further such a disposition of the soul; it aims at creating in it a complete forgetfulness of natural emotions; it would prevent the necessity of ever descending to the call of fleshly needs. Once freed from such, the soul runs no risk of becoming, through a growing habit of indulging in that which seems to a certain extent conceded by nature's law, inattentive and ignorant of Divine and undefiled delights. Purity of the heart, that master of our lives, alone can capture them.

Chapter VII

An illustration will make our teaching on this subject clearer. Imagine a stream flowing from a spring and dividing itself off into a number of accidental channels. As long as it proceeds so, it will be useless for any purpose of agriculture, the dissipation of its waters making each particular current small and feeble, and therefore slow. But if one were to mass these wandering and widely dispersed rivulets again into one single channel, he would have a full and collected stream for the supplies which life demands. Just so the human mind (so it seems to me), as long as its current spreads itself in all directions over the pleasures of the sense, has no power that is worth the naming of making its way towards the Real Good; but once call it back and collect it upon itself, so that it may begin to move without scattering and wandering towards the activity which is congenital and natural to it, it will find no obstacle in mounting to higher things, and in grasping realities.

Chapter VIII

Let no one think however that herein we depreciate marriage as an institution. We are well aware that it is not a stranger to God's blessing. But since the common instincts of mankind can plead sufficiently on its behalf, instincts which prompt by a spontaneous bias to take the high road of marriage for the procreation of children, whereas Virginity in a way thwarts this natural impulse, it is a superfluous task to compose formally an Exhortation to marriage. . . . What then, were we saying? That in the cases where it is possible at once to be true to the diviner love, and to embrace wedlock, there is no reason for setting aside this dispensation of nature and misrepresenting as abominable that which is honourable. Let us take again our illustration of the water and the spring. Whenever the husbandman, in order to irrigate a particular spot, is bringing the stream thither, but there is need before it gets there of a small outlet, he will allow only so much to escape into that outlet as is ad- equate to supply the demand, and can then easily be blended again with the main stream. . . . There is no small danger for him lest, cajoled in the valuation of pleasure, he should think that there exists no other good but that which is enjoyed along with some sensual emotion, and, turning altogether from the love of immaterial delights, should become entirely of the flesh, seeking always his pleasure only there, so that his character will be a Pleasure-lover, not a God-lover. It is not every man's gift, owing to weakness of nature, to hit the due proportion in these matters; there is a danger of being carried far beyond it, and "sticking fast in the deep mire," to use the Psalmist's words. It would therefore be for our interest, as our discourse has been suggesting, to pass through life without a trial of these temptations, lest under cover of the excuse of lawful indulgence passion should gain an entrance into the citadel of the soul.

Questions

1   Why does Gregory think that virginity is something to be praised so highly?

2   What does Gregory mean when he says that virginity is also a characteristic of God himself? How does this affect the way he understands virginity?

3   How does Gregory describe married life? What are its challenges and how does he think they should affect the way that we view marriage and virginity?

4   What does Gregory mean when he says that virginity is "the practical method in the science of the Divine life"?

5   What is Gregory's analogy of the stream and how does it help us understand his view of marriage and virginity?

6   Why does Gregory think that his view does not entail any depreciation of marriage? Do you agree?

TEXT 2: AUGUSTINE,
OF THE GOOD OF MARRIAGE[3]

Augustine of Hippo (354–430) wrote this essay on marriage around AD 401, shortly after Gregory of Nyssa completed the above essay on virginity. In this reading, Augustine continues the early tradition of reflecting on human sexuality through the lens of virginity and marriage, and he also exemplifies the tension between emphasizing marriage as a created good and celibacy as a high calling for human persons. Unlike Gregory's essay on virginity, however, Augustine here focuses primarily on the first part of that tension: the value of marriage.

1. Forasmuch as each man is a part of the human race, and human nature is something social, and hath for a great and natural good, the power also of friendship; on this account God willed to create all men out of one, in order that they might be held in their society not only by likeness of kind, but also by bond of kindred. Therefore the first natural bond of human society is man and wife. Nor did God create these each by himself, and join them together as alien by birth: but He created the one out of the other, setting a sign also of the power of the union in the side, whence she was drawn, was formed. For they are joined one to another side by side, who walk together, and look together whither they walk. Then follows the connexion of fellowship in children, which is the one alone worthy fruit, not of the union of male and female, but of the sexual intercourse. For it were possible that there should exist in either sex, even without such intercourse, a certain friendly and true union of the one ruling, and the other obeying.

2. Nor is it now necessary that we enquire, and put forth a definite opinion on that question, whence could exist the progeny of the first men, whom God had blessed, saying, "Increase, and be ye multiplied, and fill the earth;" if they had not sinned, whereas their bodies by sinning deserved the condition of death, and there can be no sexual intercourse save of mortal bodies. For there have existed several and different opinions on this matter; and if we must examine, which of them be rather agreeable to the truth of Divine Scriptures, there is matter for a lengthened discussion. Whether, therefore, without intercourse, in some other way, had they not sinned, they would have had sons, from the gift of the Almighty Creator, Who was able to create themselves also without parents, Who was able to form the Flesh of Christ in a virgin womb, and (to speak even to unbelievers themselves) Who was able to bestow on bees a progeny without sexual intercourse; or whether many things there were spoken by way of mystery and figure, and we are to understand in another sense what is written, "Fill the earth, and rule over it;" that is, that it should come to pass by fullness and perfection of life and power, so that the very increase and multiplication, whereby it is said, "Increase, and be ye multiplied," be understood to be by advance of mind, and abundance of virtue, as it is set in the

---

[3]Augustine, *On the Good of Marriage*, in *NPNF* 1.3, 840–81.

Psalm, "Thou shall multiply me in my soul by virtue;" and that succession of progeny was not given unto man, save after that, by reason of sin, there was to be hereafter departure in death: or whether the body was not made spiritual in the case of these men, but at the first animal, in order that by merit of obedience it might after become spiritual, to lay hold of immortality, not after death, which by the malice of the devil entered into the world, and was made the punishment of sin; but after that change, which the Apostle signifies, when he says, "Then we living, who remain, together with them, shall be caught up in the clouds, to meet Christ, into the air," that we may understand both that those bodies of the first pair were mortal, in the first forming, and yet that they would not have died, had they not sinned, as God had threatened: even as if He should threaten a wound, in that the body was capable of wounds; which yet would not have happened, unless what He had forbidden were done. Thus, therefore, even through sexual intercourse there might take place generations of such bodies, as up to a certain point should have increase, and yet should not pass into old age; or even into old age, and yet not into death; until the earth were filled with that multiplication of the blessing.

3. This we now say, that, according to this condition of being born and dying, which we know, and in which we have been created, the marriage of male and female is some good; the compact whereof divine Scripture so commends, as that neither is it allowed one put away by her husband to marry, so long as her husband lives: nor is it allowed one put away by his wife to marry another, unless she who have separated from him be dead. Therefore, concerning the good of marriage, which the Lord also confirmed in the Gospel, not only in that He forbade to put away a wife, save because of fornication, but also in that He came by invitation to a marriage, there is good ground to inquire for what reason it be a good. And this seems not to me to be merely on account of the begetting of children, but also on account of the natural society itself in a difference of sex. . . . Marriages have this good also, that carnal or youthful incontinence, although it be faulty, is brought unto an honest use in the begetting of children, in order that out of the evil of lust the marriage union may bring to pass some good. Next, in that the lust of the flesh is repressed, and rages in a way more modestly, being tempered by parental affection. For there is interposed a certain gravity of glowing pleasure, when in that wherein husband and wife cleave to one another, they have in mind that they be father and mother.

5. Also the question is wont to be asked, when a male and female, neither the one the husband, nor the other the wife, of any other, come together, not for the begetting of children, but, by reason of incontinence, for the mere sexual intercourse, there being between them this faith, that neither he do it with any other woman, nor she with any other man, whether it is to be called marriage. And perhaps this may, not without reason, be called marriage, if it shall be the resolution of both parties until the death of one, and if the begetting of children, although they came not together for that cause, yet they shun not, so as either to be unwilling to have children born to them, or even by some evil work to use means that they be not born. But, if either both, or one, of these be wanting, I find not how we can call it marriage. . . . Therefore whatever that is immodest, shameless, base, married persons do one with another, is the sin of the persons, not the fault of marriage.

6. Further, in the very case of the more immoderate requirement of the due of the flesh, which the Apostle enjoins not on them by way of command, but allows to them by way of leave, that they have intercourse also beside the cause of begetting children; although evil habits impel them to such intercourse, yet marriage guards them from adultery or fornication. For neither is that committed because of marriage, but is pardoned because of marriage. Therefore married persons owe one another not only the faith of their sexual intercourse itself, for the begetting of children, which is the first fellowship of the human kind in this mortal state; but also, in a way, a mutual service of sustaining one another's weakness, in order to shun unlawful intercourse.

9. Truly we must consider, that God gives us some goods, which are to be sought for their own sake, such as wisdom, health, friendship: but others, which are necessary for the sake of somewhat, such as learning, meat, drink, sleep, marriage, sexual intercourse. For of these certain are necessary for the sake of wisdom, as learning: certain for the sake of health, as meat and drink and sleep: certain for the sake of friendship, as marriage or sexual intercourse: for hence subsists the propagation of the human kind, wherein friendly fellowship is a great good. These goods, therefore, which are necessary for the sake of something else, whoso useth not for this purpose, wherefore they were instituted, sins; in some cases venially, in other cases damnably. But whoso useth them for this purpose, wherefore they were given doeth well. . . . And on this account it is good to marry, because it is good to beget children, to be a mother of a family: but it is better not to marry, because it is better not to stand in need of this work, in order to human fellowship itself.

10. But I am aware of some that murmur: What, say they, if all men should abstain from all sexual intercourse, whence will the human race exist? Would that all would this, only in "charity out of a pure heart, and good conscience, and faith unfeigned;" much more speedily would the City of God be filled, and the end of the world hastened. . . .

18. For what food is unto the conservation of the man, this sexual intercourse is unto the conservation of the race: and both are not without carnal delight: which yet being modified, and by restraint of temperance reduced unto the use after nature, cannot be lust. But what unlawful food is in the supporting of life, this sexual intercourse of fornication or adultery is in the seeking of a family. And what unlawful food is in luxury of belly and throat, this unlawful intercourse is in lust that seeks not a family. And what the excessive appetite of some is in lawful food, this that intercourse that is matter of pardon is in husband and wife. . . .

25. Forsooth continence is a virtue, not of the body, but of the soul. But the virtues of the soul are sometimes shown in work, sometimes lie hid in habit. . . . Thus have perfect souls used earthly goods, that are necessary for something else, through this habit of continence, so as, by it, not to be bound by them, and so as by it, to have power also not to use them, in case there were no need. Nor doth any use them well, save who hath power also not to use them. Many indeed with more ease practise abstinence, so as not to use, than practise temperance, so as to use well. But no one can wisely use them, save who can also continently not use them.

Questions

1 What is the "natural bond of human society" and why does Augustine think that human sexuality is a fundamental aspect of that bond?

2 What does Augustine think about procreation before the fall? Why does he feel it necessary to engage in this kind of speculation?

3 What reasons does Augustine give for thinking that marriage is a good thing?

4 Why does Augustine think it's important to make a distinction between things that are to be sought for their own sake and things that should only be sought for the sake of something else, and how does this distinction inform his view of marriage?

5 What do you think about Augustine's view of marriage?

TEXT 3: THOMAS AQUINAS, *SUMMA THEOLOGIAE*[4]

The reading from Thomas Aquinas (1225–74) takes us in a slightly different direction, focusing specifically on why God created women and what the creation of women suggests about their status vis-à-vis men. Drawing on arguments from "the Philosopher" (Aristotle), in which women were understood to be ontologically inferior in certain ways, as well as Eve's role in the Fall, Aquinas begins by reflecting on the idea that in a perfect creation God would have only created men. Although this sounds like an odd question to modern ears, ancient and medieval thinkers often wrestled with how to understand the differences between men and women and what they implied about their ontological location in the universe. Are such differences really *imperfections* which suggest that women are somehow lower in the hierarchy of being than men? The second selection continues the discussion through the lens of the *Imago Dei*. Some early theologians argued that only men were truly in the image of God, often arguing on the basis of 1 Cor. 11:3 that women were only in the image of men. In these two selections, then, Aquinas considers two reasons for thinking that women are ontologically inferior in some way.[5]

Whether the woman should have been made in the first production of things?

Objection 1: It would seem that the woman should not have been made in the first production of things. For the Philosopher says (*De Gener*. ii, 3), that "the female is a misbegotten male." But nothing misbegotten or defective should have been in the first production of things. Therefore woman should not have been made at that first production.

Objection 2: Further, subjection and limitation were a result of sin, for to the woman was it said after sin (Gn. 3:16): "Thou shalt be under the man's power"; and Gregory says that, "Where there is no sin, there is no inequality." But woman is naturally of less strength and dignity than man; "for the agent is always more honorable than the patient," as Augustine says (*Gen. ad lit*. xii, 16). Therefore woman should not have been made in the first production of things before sin.

---

[4]Thomas Aquinas, *Summa Theologica* Ia. 92–93.

[5]For those not familiar with Aquinas' methodology, it is important to understand the structure of the *Summa*. Each of Thomas' discussions begins with the question he will answer, followed by a series of "objections," each of which provides some reason for rejecting the answer that Aquinas will be giving to that question. These are not necessarily erroneous arguments that need to be rejected, but will often be statements that Aquinas takes as authoritative. After the objections, Thomas gives his "On the contrary" statement, which differs from the objections and creates a tension. How are we to understand the truth of the matter given that we seem to have multiple statements that affirm contrary answers to the initial question. Finally, Thomas provides his answer to the question before concluding with his way of responding to each of the initial objections.

Objection 3: Further, occasions of sin should be cut off. But God foresaw that the woman would be an occasion of sin to man. Therefore He should not have made woman.

On the contrary, It is written (Gn. 2:18): "It is not good for man to be alone; let us make him a helper like to himself."

I answer that, It was necessary for woman to be made, as the Scripture says, as a "helper" to man; not, indeed, as a helpmate in other works, as some say, since man can be more efficiently helped by another man in other works; but as a helper in the work of generation. This can be made clear if we observe the mode of generation carried out in various living things. Some living things do not possess in themselves the power of generation, but are generated by some other specific agent, such as some plants and animals by the influence of the heavenly bodies, from some fitting matter and not from seed: others possess the active and passive generative power together; as we see in plants which are generated from seed; for the noblest vital function in plants is generation. Wherefore we observe that in these the active power of generation invariably accompanies the passive power. Among perfect animals the active power of generation belongs to the male sex, and the passive power to the female. And as among animals there is a vital operation nobler than generation, to which their life is principally directed; therefore the male sex is not found in continual union with the female in perfect animals, but only at the time of coition; so that we may consider that by this means the male and female are one, as in plants they are always united; although in some cases one of them preponderates, and in some the other. But man is yet further ordered to a still nobler vital action, and that is intellectual operation. Therefore there was greater reason for the distinction of these two forces in man; so that the female should be produced separately from the male; although they are carnally united for generation. Therefore directly after the formation of woman, it was said: "And they shall be two in one flesh" (Gn. 2:24).

Reply to Objection 1: As regards the individual nature, woman is defective and misbegotten, for the active force in the male seed tends to the production of a perfect likeness in the masculine sex; while the production of woman comes from defect in the active force or from some material indisposition, or even from some external influence; such as that of a south wind, which is moist, as the Philosopher observes (*De Gener. Animal.* iv, 2). On the other hand, as regards human nature in general, woman is not misbegotten, but is included in nature's intention as directed to the work of generation. Now the general intention of nature depends on God, Who is the universal Author of nature. Therefore, in producing nature, God formed not only the male but also the female.

Reply to Objection 2: Subjection is twofold. One is servile, by virtue of which a superior makes use of a subject for his own benefit; and this kind of subjection began after sin. There is another kind of subjection which is called economic or civil, whereby the superior makes use of his subjects for their own benefit and good; and this kind of subjection existed even before sin. For good order would have been wanting in the human family if some were not governed by others wiser than themselves. So by such a kind of subjection woman is naturally subject to man, because in man the discretion of reason predominates. Nor is inequality among men excluded by the state of innocence, as we shall prove (Q[96], A[3]).

Reply to Objection 3: If God had deprived the world of all those things which proved an occasion of sin, the universe would have been imperfect. Nor was it fitting for the common good to be destroyed in order that individual evil might be avoided; especially as God is so powerful that He can direct any evil to a good end.

Whether the image of God is found in every man?

Objection 1: It would seem that the image of God is not found in every man. For the Apostle says that "man is the image of God, but woman is the image [*Vulg.* glory] of man" (1 Cor. 11:7). Therefore, as woman is an individual of the human species, it is clear that every individual is not an image of God.

Objection 2: Further, the Apostle says (Rom. 8:29): "Whom God foreknew, He also predestined to be made conformable to the image of His Son." But all men are not pre- destined. Therefore all men have not the conformity of image.

Objection 3: Further, likeness belongs to the nature of the image, as above explained. But by sin man becomes unlike God. Therefore he loses the image of God.

On the contrary, It is written (Ps. 38:7): "Surely man passeth as an image."

I answer that, Since man is said to be the image of God by reason of his intellectual nature, he is the most perfectly like God according to that in which he can best imitate God in his intellectual nature. Now the intellectual nature imitates God chiefly in this, that God understands and loves Himself. Wherefore we see that the image of God is in man in three ways. First, inasmuch as man possesses a natural aptitude for understanding and loving God; and this aptitude consists in the very nature of the mind, which is common to all men. Secondly, inasmuch as man actually and habitually knows and loves God, though imperfectly; and this image consists in the conformity of grace. Thirdly, inasmuch as man knows and loves God perfectly; and this image consists in the likeness of glory. Wherefore on the words, "The light of Thy countenance, O Lord, is signed upon us" (Ps. 4:7), the gloss distinguishes a threefold image of "creation," of "re-creation," and of "likeness." The first is found in all men, the second only in the just, the third only in the blessed.

Reply to Objection 1: The image of God, in its principal signification, namely the intellectual nature, is found both in man and in woman. Hence after the words, "To the image of God He created him," it is added, "Male and female He created them" (Gn. 1:27). Moreover it is said "them" in the plural, as Augustine (*Gen. ad lit.* iii, 22) remarks, lest it should be thought that both sexes were united in one individual. But in a secondary sense the image of God is found in man, and not in woman: for man is the beginning and end of woman; as God is the beginning and end of every creature. So when the Apostle had said that "man is the image and glory of God, but woman is the glory of man," he adds his reason for saying this: "For man is not of woman, but woman of man; and man was not created for woman, but woman for man."

Reply OBJ 2 and 3: These reasons refer to the image consisting in the conformity of grace and glory.

Questions

1 The first objection sounds strange to modern ears, but can you think of any ways that people sometimes view women today as "defective men"? How does Aquinas respond to this objection and what do you think about that response?

2 Why does Aquinas think that it was necessary for women to be part of creation? What do you think about his argument that men only need a "helpmate" in one specific area?

3 Aquinas talks about the "active" and "passive" powers in procreation (i.e. planting the seed and receiving the seed), which was a common way of understanding differences between men and women. What implications do you think might come from thinking about men and women in this way?

4 Does Aquinas think that both men and women are created in the image of God? Why?

5 What implications do you think might result from arguing that women are not as fully in the image of God as men?

TEXT 4: MARTIN LUTHER, "THE ESTATE OF MARRIAGE"[6]

From one perspective, this selection from Martin Luther (1483–1546) could be viewed as merely another reflection on human sexuality from the perspective of marriage. And issues of marriage and celibacy remained the predominant emphasis for theologians in this period. Yet in this sermon Luther demonstrates a noticeable shift away from the tension of earlier writings that sought to celebrate both celibacy and marriage as virtues, with a tendency toward a dominant emphasis on the former. Instead, in this reading, we see Luther celebrating marriage without any of the underlying concerns about either the distracting potential of human sexuality or the emphasis on the purity and commitment of celibacy that we saw in the earlier readings. Instead, Luther focuses on the idea that even the most difficult aspects of marriage and parenting should be viewed as good gifts of the Creator.

In this sermon, Luther addresses three distinct issues: which persons should get married, whether divorce is ever permissible, and the value of marriage. This reading will focus on the first part of Luther's response, where he responds to the question of which persons should get married. Here Luther discusses the importance of sexuality for being human and how we should think about those who do not participate in sexual relationships (e.g., those living celibate lives). The third section moves more directly into Luther's understanding of marriage as a created good. Throughout, we will see that Luther thinks that marriage is a normative condition for human persons.

How I dread preaching on the estate of marriage! I am reluctant to do it because I am afraid if I once get really involved in the subject it will make a lot of work for me and for others. The shameful confusion wrought by the accursed papal law has occasioned so much distress, and the lax authority of both the spiritual and the temporal swords has given rise to so many dreadful abuses and false situations, that I would much prefer neither to look into the matter nor to hear of it. But because timidity is no help in an emergency, I must proceed. I must try to instruct poor bewildered consciences, and take up the matter boldly. This sermon is divided into three parts.

In order to proceed aright let us direct our attention to Genesis 1[:27], "So God created man . . . male and female he created them." From this passage we may be assured that God divided humanity into two classes, namely, male and female, or a he and a she. This was so pleasing to him that he himself called it a good creation [Gen. 1:31]. Therefore, each one of us must have the kind of body God has created for us. I cannot make myself a woman, nor can you make yourself a man; we do not have that power. But we are exactly as he created us: I a man and you a woman. Moreover, he wills to have his excellent handiwork honored as his divine creation, and not despised. The man is not to despise or scoff at the woman or her body, nor

---

[6]Martin Luther, "The Estate of Marriage," *LW* 45:11–49.

the woman the man. But each should honor the other's image and body as a divine and good creation that is well-pleasing to God himself.

In the second place, after God had made man and woman he blessed them and said to them, "Be fruitful and multiply" [Gen. 1:28]. From this passage we may be assured that man and woman should and must come together in order to multiply. Now this [ordinance] is just as inflexible as the first, and no more to be despised and made fun of than the other, since God gives it his blessing and does something over and above the act of creation. Hence, as it is not within my power not to be a man, so it is not my prerogative to be without a woman. Again, as it is not in your power not to be a woman, so it is not your prerogative to be without a man. For it is not a matter of free choice or decision but a natural and necessary thing. Whatever is a man must have a woman and whatever is a woman must have a man.

From this word which God speaks, "Be fruitful and multiply," is not a command. It is more than a command, namely a divine ordinance [*wreck*] which it is not our prerogative to hinder or ignore. Rather, it is just as necessary as the fact that I am a man, and more necessary than sleeping and waking, eating and drinking and emptying the bowels and bladder. It is a nature and disposition just as innate as the organs involved in it. Therefore, just as God does not command anyone to be a man or a woman but creates them the way they have to be, so he does not command them to multiply but creates them so that they have to multiply. And wherever men try to resist this, it remains irresistible nonetheless and goes its way through fornication, adultery, and secret sins, for this is a matter of nature and not of choice.

In the third place, from this ordinance of creation God has himself exempted three categories of men, saying in Matthew 19[:12], "There are eunuchs who have been so from birth, and there are eunuchs who have been made eunuchs by men, and there are eunuchs who have made themselves eunuchs for the sake of the kingdom of heaven." Apart from these three groups, let no man presume to be without a spouse. And whoever does not fail within one of these three categories should not consider anything except the estate of marriage. Otherwise it is simply impossible for you to remain righteous. For the Word of God which created you and said, "Be fruitful and multiply," abides and rules within you; you can by no means ignore it, or you will be bound to commit heinous sins without end.

Don't let yourself be fooled on this score, even if you should make ten oaths, vows, covenants, and adamantine or ironclad pledges. For as you cannot solemnly promise that you will not be a man or a woman (and if you should make such a promise it would be foolishness and of no avail since you cannot make yourself something other than what you are), so you cannot promise that you will not produce seed or multiply, unless you belong to one of the three categories mentioned above. And should you make such a promise, it too would be foolishness and of no avail, for to produce seed and to multiply is a matter of God's ordinance [*geschöpffe*], not your power.

From this you can now see the extent of the validity of all cloister vows. No vow of any youth or maiden is valid before God, except that of a person in one of the three categories which God alone has himself excepted. Therefore, priests, monks, and nuns are duty-bound to forsake their vows whenever they find that God's ordinance to produce seed and to multiply is powerful and strong within them. They have no power by any authority, law, command, or vow to hinder that which God has created within them. If they do hinder it, however, you may be sure that they will not remain pure but inevitably besmirch themselves with secret sins or fornication. They are simply incapable of resisting the word and ordinance of God within them. Matters will take their course as God has ordained.

As to the first category, which Christ calls "eunuchs who have been so from birth," these are the ones whom men call impotent, who are by nature not equipped to produce seed and multiply because they are physically frigid or weak or have some other bodily deficiency which makes them unfit for the estate of marriage. Such cases occur among both men and women. These we need not take into account, for God has himself exempted them and so formed them that the blessing of being able to multiply has not come to them. The injunction, "Be fruitful and multiply," does not apply to them; just as when God creates a person crippled or blind, that person is not obligated to walk or see, because he cannot.

I once wrote down some advice concerning such persons for those who hear confession. It related to those cases where a husband or wife comes and wants to learn what he should do: his spouse is unable to fulfill the conjugal duty, yet he cannot get along without it because he finds that God's ordinance to multiply is still in force within him. Here they have accused me of teaching that when a husband is unable to satisfy his wife's sexual desire she should run to somebody else. Let the topsy-turvy liars spread their lies. The words of Christ and his apostles were turned upside down; should they not also turn my words topsy-turvy? To whose detriment it will be they shall surely find out.

What I said was this: if a woman who is fit for marriage has a husband who is not, and she is unable openly to take unto herself another—and unwilling, too, to do anything dishonorable—since the pope in such a case demands without cause abundant testimony and evidence, she should say to her husband, "Look, my dear husband, you are unable to fulfill your conjugal duty toward me; you have cheated me out of my maidenhood and even imperiled my honor and my soul's salvation; in the sight of God there is no real marriage between us. Grant me the privilege of contracting a secret marriage with your brother or closest relative, and you retain the title of husband so that your property will not fall to strangers. Consent to being betrayed voluntarily by me, as you have betrayed me without my consent."

I stated further that the husband is obligated to consent to such an arrangement and thus to provide for her the conjugal duty and children, and that if he refuses to do so she should secretly flee from him to some other country and there contract a marriage. I gave this advice at a time when I was still timid. However, I should like now to give sounder advice in the matter, and take a firmer grip on a man who thus makes a fool of his wife. The same principle would apply if the circumstances were reversed, although this happens less frequently in the case of wives than of husbands. It will not do to lead one's fellow-man around by the nose so wantonly in matters of such great import involving his body, goods, honor, and salvation. He has to be told to make it right. The second category, those who Christ says "have been made eunuchs by men" [Matt. 19:12], the castrates, are an unhappy lot, for though they are not equipped for marriage, they are nevertheless not free from evil desire. They seek the company of women more than before and are quite effeminate. It is with them as the proverb says, "He who cannot sing always insists upon singing." Thus, they are plagued with a desire for women, but are unable to consummate their desire. Let us pass them by also; for they too are set apart from the natural ordinance to be fruitful and multiply, though only by an act of violence.

The third category consists of those spiritually rich and exalted persons, bridled by the grace of God, who are equipped for marriage by nature and physical capacity and nevertheless voluntarily remain celibate. These put it this way, "I could marry if I wish, I am capable of it. But it does not attract me. I would rather work on the kingdom of heaven, i.e., the gospel, and beget spiritual children." Such persons are rare, not one in a thousand, for they are a special miracle of God. No one should venture on such a life unless he be especially called by God, like Jeremiah [16:2], or unless he finds God's grace to be so powerful within him that the divine injunction, "Be fruitful and multiply," has no place in him.

Beyond these three categories, however, the devil working through men has been smarter than God, and found more people whom he has withdrawn from the divine and natural ordinance, namely, those who are enmeshed in a spiderweb of human commands and vows and are then locked up behind a mass of iron bolts and bars. This is a fourth way of resisting nature so that, contrary to God's implanted ordinance and disposition, it does not produce seed and multiply—as if it were within our power and discretion to possess virginity as we do shoes and clothing! If men are really able to resist God's word and creation with iron bars and bolts, I should hope that we would also set up iron bars so thick and massive that women would turn into men or people into sticks and stones. It is the devil who thus perpetrates his monkey-tricks on the poor creature, and so gives vent to his wrath.

* * * * * *

In the third part, in order that we may say something about the estate of marriage which will be conducive toward the soul's salvation, we shall now consider how to live a Christian and godly life in that estate. I will pass over in silence the mater of the conjugal duty, the granting and the withholding of it, since some filth-preachers have been shameless enough in this matter to rouse our disgust. Some of them designate special times for this, and exclude holy nights and women who are pregnant. I will leave this as St. Paul left it when he said in 1 Corinthians 7[:9], "It is better to marry than to burn"; and again [in v. 2], "To avoid immorality, each man should have his own wife, and each woman her own husband." Although Christian married folk should not permit themselves to be governed by their bodies in the passion of lust, as Paul writes to the Thessalonians [1 Thess. 4:5], nevertheless each one must examine himself so that by his abstention he does not expose himself to the danger of fornication and other sins. Neither should he pay any attention to holy days or work days, or other physical considerations.

What we would speak most of is the fact that the estate of marriage has universally fallen into such awful disrepute. There are many pagan books which treat of nothing but the depravity of womankind and the unhappiness of the estate of marriage, such that some have thought that even if Wisdom itself were a woman one should not marry. . . .

So they concluded that woman is a necessary evil, and that no household can be without such an evil. These are the words of blind heathen, who are ignorant of the fact that man and woman are god's creation. They blaspheme his work, as if man and woman just came into being spontaneously! I imagine that if women were to write books they would say exactly the same thing about men. What they have failed to set down in writing, however, they express with their grumbling and complaining whenever they get together.

Every day one encounters parents who forget their former misery because, like the mouse, they have now had their fill. They deter their children from marriage but entice them into priesthood and nunnery, citing the trials and troubles of married life. Thus do they bring their own children home to the devil, as we daily observe; they provide them with ease for the body and hell for the soul.

Since God had to suffer such disdain of his work from the pagans, he therefore also gave them their reward, of which Paul writes in Romans 1[:24–28], and allowed them to fall into immorality and a stream of uncleanness until they henceforth carnally abused not women but boys and dumb beasts. Even their women carnally abused themselves and each other. Because they blasphemed the work of God, he gave them up to a base mind, of which the books of the pagans are full, most shamelessly crammed full.

In order that we may not proceed as blindly, but rather conduct ourselves in a Christian manner, hold fast first of all to this, that man and woman are the work of God. Keep a tight rein on your heart and your lips; do not criticize his work, or call that evil which he himself has called good. He knows better than you yourself what is good and to your benefit, as he says in Genesis 1 [2:18], "It is not good that the man should be alone; I will make him a helper fit for him." There you see that he calls the woman good, a helper. If you deem it otherwise, it is certainly your own fault, you neither understand nor believe God's word and work. See, with this statement of God one stops the mouths of all those who criticize and censure marriage.

For this reason young men should be on their guard when they read pagan books and hear the common complaints about marriage, lest they inhale poison. For the estate of marriage does not set well with the devil, because it is God's good will and work. This is why the devil has contrived to have so much shouted and written in the world against the institution of marriage, to frighten men away from this godly life and entangle them in a web of fornication and secret sins. Indeed, it seems to me that even Solomon, although he amply censures evil women, was speaking against just such blasphemers when he said in Proverbs 18[:22], "He who finds a wife finds a good thing, and obtains favor from the Lord." What is this good thing and this favor? Let us see.

The world says of marriage, "Brief is the joy, lasting the bitterness." Let them say what they please; what God wills and creates is bound to be a laughingstock to them. The kind of joy and pleasure they have outside of wedlock they will be most acutely aware of, I suspect, in their consciences. To recognize the estate of marriage is something quite different from merely being married. He who is married but does not recognize the estate of marriage cannot continue in wedlock without bitterness, drudgery, and anguish; he will inevitably complain and blaspheme like the pagans and blind, irrational men. But he who recognizes the estate of marriage will find therein delight, love, and joy without end; as Solomon says, "He who finds a wife finds a good thing," etc. [Prov. 19:22].

Now the ones who recognize the estate of marriage are those who firmly believe that God himself instituted it, brought husband and wife together, and ordained that they should beget children and care for them. For this they have God's word, Genesis 1[:28], and they can be certain that he does not lie. They can therefore also be certain that the estate of marriage and everything that goes with it in the way of conduct, works, and suffering is pleasing to God. Now tell me, how can the heart have greater good, joy, and delight than in God, when one is certain that his estate, conduct, and work is pleasing to God?

That is what it means to find a wife. Many *have* wives, but few *find* wives. Why? They are blind; they fail to see that their life and conduct with their wives is the work of God and pleasing in his sight. Could they but find that, then no wife would be so hateful, so ill-tempered, so ill-mannered, so poor, so sock that they would fail to find in her their heart's delight and would always be reproaching God for his work, creation, and will. And because they see that it is the good pleasure of their beloved Lord, they would be able to have peace in grief, joy in the midst of bitterness, happiness in the midst of tribulations, as the martyrs have in suffering. We err in that we judge the work of God according to our own feelings, and regard not his will but our own desire. This is why we are unable to recognize his works and persist in making evil that which is good, and regarding as bitter that which is pleasant. Nothing is so bad, not even death itself, but what it becomes sweet and tolerable if only I know and am certain that it is pleasing to God. Then there follows immediately that of which Solomon speaks, "He obtains favor from the Lord" [Prov. 18:22].

Now observe that when that clever harlot, our natural reason (which the pagans followed in trying to be most clever), takes a look at married life, she turns up her nose and says, "Alas, must I rock the baby, wash its diapers, make its bed, smell its stench, stay up nights with it, take care of it when it cries, heal its rashes and sores, and on top of that care for my wife, provide for her, labor at my trade, take care of this and take care of that, do this and do that, endure this and endure that, and whatever else of bitterness and drudgery married life involves? What, should I make such a prisoner of myself? O you poor, wretched fellow, have you taken a wife? Fie, fie upon such wretchedness and bitterness! It is better to remain free and lead a peaceful, carefree life; I will become a priest or a nun and compel my children to do likewise."

What then does Christian faith say to this? It opens its eyes, looks upon all these insignificant, distasteful, and despised duties in the Spirit, and is aware that they are all adorned with divine approval as with the costliest gold and jewels. It says, "O God, because I am certain that thou hast created me as a man and hast from my body begotten this child, I also know for a certainty that it meets with they perfect pleasure. I confess to thee that I am not worthy to rock the little babe or wash its diapers, or to be entrusted with the care of the child and its mother. How is it that I, without any merit, have come to this distinction of being certain that I am serving thy creature and they most precious will? O how gladly will I do so, though the duties should be even more insignificant and despised. Neither frost nor heat, neither drudgery nor labor, will distress or dissuade me, for I am certain that it is thus pleasing in thy sight.

A wife too should regard her duties in the same light, as she suckles the child, rocks and bathes it, and cares for it in other ways; and as she busies herself with other duties and renders help and obedience to her husband. These are truly golden and noble works. . . . Trust joyfully in his will, and let him have his way with you.

Work with all your might to bring forth the child. Should it mean your death, then depart happily, for you will die in a noble deed and in subservience to God. If you were not a woman you should now wish to be one for the sake of this very work alone, that you might thus gloriously suffer and even die in the performance of God's work and will. For here you have the word of God, who so created you and implanted within you this extremity." Tell me, is not this indeed (as Solomon says [Prov. 18:22]) "to obtain favor from the Lord," even in the midst of such extremity?

Now you tell me, when a father goes ahead and washes diapers or performs some other mean task for his child, and someone ridicules him as an effeminate fool—though that father is acting in the spirit just described and in Christian faith—my dear fellow you tell me, which of the two is most keenly ridiculing the other? God, with all his angels and creatures, is smiling—not because that father is washing diapers, but because he is doing so in Christian faith. Those who sneer at him and see only the task but not the faith are ridiculing God with all his creatures, as the biggest fool on earth. Indeed, they are only ridiculing themselves; with all their cleverness they are nothing but devil's fools.

* * * * * *

God's work and ordinance must and will be accepted and borne on the strength of God's word and assurance; otherwise they do damage and become unbearable. . . . No one can have real happiness in marriage who does not recognize in firm faith that this estate together with all its works, however insignificant, is pleasing to God and precious in his sight. These works are indeed insignificant and mean; yet it is from them that we all trace our origin, we have all had need of them. Without them no man would exist. For this reason they are pleasing to God who has so ordained them, and thereby graciously cares for us like a kind and loving mother.

Observe that thus far I have told you nothing of the estate of marriage except that which the world and reason in their blindness shrink from and sneer at as a mean, unhappy, troublesome mode of life. We have seen how all these shortcomings in fact comprise noble virtues and true delight if one but looks at God's word and will, and thereby recognizes its true nature. I will not mention the other advantages and delights implicit in a marriage that goes well—that husband and wife cherish one another, become one, serve one another, and other attendant blessings—lest somebody shut me up by saying that I am speaking about something I have not experienced, and that there is more gall than honey in marriage. I base my remarks on Scripture, which to me is surer than all experience and cannot lie to me. He who finds still other good things in marriage profits all the more, and should give thanks to God. Whatever God calls good must of necessity always been good, unless men do not recognize it or perversely misuse it.

It therefore pass over the good or evil which experience offers, and confine myself to such good as Scripture and truth ascribe to marriage. It is no slight boon that in wedlock fornication and unchastity are checked and eliminated. This in itself is so great a good that it alone should be enough to induce men to marry forthwith, and for many reasons.

* * * * * *

But the greatest good in married life, that which makes all suffering and labor worth while, is that God grants offspring and commands that they be brought up to worship and serve him. In all the world this is the noblest and most precious work, because to God there can be nothing dearer than the salvation of souls. Now since we are all duty bound to suffer death, if need be, that we might bring a single soul to God, you can see how rich the estate of marriage is in good works. God has entrusted to its bosom souls begotten of its own body, on whom it can lavish all manner of Christian works. Most certainly father and mother are apostles, bishops, and priests to their children, for it is they who make them acquainted with the gospel. In short, there is no greater or nobler authority on earth than that of parents over their children, for this authority is both spiritual and temporal.

Questions

1 In the second paragraph, Luther argues from Genesis 1 for the permanence of human sexuality. How should we think about this argument in light of modern medical developments and ongoing discussions about "sex change" surgeries?

2 What does Luther mean with his distinction between a "command" and an "ordinance"? What is the significance of saying that "be fruitful and multiply" is an ordinance? How does this shape his views on marriage?

3 What are the three kinds of people excluded from this ordinance? What do you think about how Luther deals with each of these situations?

4 What does Luther think about vows of celibacy in particular?

5 What do you think about the advice that Luther gave for the situation where one spouse is "unable to fulfill the conjugal duty"? What does this advice tell you about how Luther viewed sex?

6 According to Luther, what is the primary value of marriage? What are some of the other benefits of marriage that he mentions?

7 Why do people often have such a negative view of marriage? How does Luther respond?

TEXT 5: JOHN PAUL II, *MAN AND WOMAN HE CREATED THEM: A THEOLOGY OF THE BODY*[7]

Between 1979 and 1984, John Paul II (1920–2005) presented his understanding of the theological significance of sexuality in a series of catecheses known as the "Theology of the Body." Pushing back on modern views that present the body as a mere instrument that can be used and consumed according to our personal preferences, John Paul II argues instead that the human body, along with its inherent sexuality, is fundamental to understanding the radical gift of the self to another that constitutes true human personhood. This is what John Paul II refers to as the "spousal meaning" of the body. Our embodied sexuality is the basis of the free community in which we most truly experience and manifest God's own relational nature.

A The spousal meaning of the body: Creation as giving

If the account of the creation of man in the two versions, that of Genesis 1 and the Yahwist version in Genesis 2, allows us to establish the original meaning of solitude, unity and nakedness, by this very fact it allows us also to reach the basis of an adequate anthropology, which seeks to understand and interpret man in what is essentially human.

The biblical texts contain the essential elements of such an anthropology, which become clear in the theological context of the "image of God." This concept contains in a hidden way the very root of the truth about man revealed by the "beginning," to which Christ appeals in the dialogue with the Pharisees (see Mt 19:3-9) when he speaks about the creation of man as male and female. One must remember that all the analyses we are carrying out here are connected, at least indirectly, with precisely these words. Man, whom God created "male and female," bears the divine image impressed in the body "from the beginning"; man and woman constitute, so to speak, two diverse ways of "being a body" that are proper to human nature in the unity of this image.

We should now turn anew to those fundamental words that Christ used, that is, to the word "created" and to the subject, "Creator," introducing into the considerations carried out so far *a new dimension, a new criterion of understanding and of interpretation* that we will call *"hermeneutics of the gift."* The dimension of gift is decisive for the essential truth and depth of the meaning of original solitude-unity-

---

[7]John Paul II, *Man and Woman He Created Them: A Theology of the Body*, trans. Michael Waldstein (Boston, MA: Pauline Books & Media, 2006), 178–88.

nakedness. It stands also at the very heart of the mystery of creation, which allows us to build the theology of the body "from the beginning," but at the same time demands that we build it in precisely this way.

On Christ's lips, the word 'created' contains the same truth that we find in Genesis. The first creation account repeats this word several times from Genesis 1:1 . . . to Genesis 1:27. . . . God reveals himself above all as Creator. Christ appeals to this fundamental revelation contained in Genesis. The concept of creation has all its depth, not only a metaphysical, but also a fully theological depth, in Genesis. The Creator is he who "calls to existence from nothing" and who establishes the world in existence and man in the world, *because he "is love"* (1 Jn 4:8). We admittedly do not find this word love (God is love) in the creation account; nevertheless, that account often repeats, "God saw everything that he had made, and indeed, it was very good" (Gen 1:31). Through these words we are led to glimpse in love the divine motive for creation, the source, as it were, from which it springs: *only love, in fact, gives rise to the good and is well pleased with the good* (see 1 Cor 13). As an action of God, creation thus means not only calling from nothing to existence and establishing the world's existence as well as man's existence in the world, but, according to the first account. . . . it also signifies *gift*; a fundamental and 'radical' gift, that is, an act of giving in which the gift comes into being precisely from nothing.

Giving and man

As we reread and analyze the second creation account, that is, the Yahwist text, we must ask ourselves whether the first "man," in his original solitude, "lived" the world truly as a gift, with an attitude that conforms to the actual condition of someone who has received a gift, as one can gather from the account in Genesis 1. The second account, in fact, shows us man in the garden of Eden (see Gen 2:8); but we must observe that, though man existed in this situation of original happiness, the Creator himself (God-Yahweh) and then also the "man" emphasize that the man is "alone," instead of underlining the aspect of the world as a subjectively beatifying gift created for man (see the first narrative and especially Gen 1:26-29). We have already analyzed the meaning of original solitude; now, however, it is necessary to note that for the first time there clearly appears a certain lack of good, "It is not good that the man" (male) "should be alone," God-Yahweh says, "I want to make him a help . . . " (Gen 2:18). The same thing is affirmed by the first "man": he, too, after having become completely conscious of his own solitude among all the living beings on the earth, awaits a "help similar to himself" (see Gen 2:20). None of these beings (*animalia*), in fact, offers man the basic conditions that *make it possible to exist in a relation of reciprocal gift*.

Gift—Mystery of a beatifying beginning

In this way, then, these two expressions, that is, the adjective "alone" and the noun "help," seem truly to be the key for understanding the essence of the gift on the level of man, as the existential content inscribed in the truth of the "image of

God." In fact, the gift reveals, so to speak, *a particular characteristic of personal existence*, or even of the very essence of the person. When God-Yahweh says, "It is not good that the man should be alone" (Gen 2:18), he affirms that, "alone," the man does not completely realize this essence. He realizes it only by existence *"with someone"*—and, put even more deeply and completely by existing *"for someone."* This norm of existing as a person is demonstrated in Genesis as a characteristic of creation precisely by the meaning of these two words, "alone" and "help." They point out how fundamental and constitutive the relationship and the communion of persons is for man. Communion of persons means living in a reciprocal "for," in a relationship of reciprocal gift. And this relationship is precisely the fulfillment of "man's" original solitude.

In its origin, such a fulfillment is beatifying. Undoubtedly, it is implicit in man's original solitude, and precisely constitutes the happiness that belongs to the mystery of creation made by love, that is, it belongs to the very essence of creative giving. When the "male" man, awakened from his Genesis sleep, says, "This time she is flesh from my flesh and bone from my bones" (Gen 2:23), these words in some way express the subjectively beatifying beginning of man's existence in the world. Inasmuch as this [expression of joy] was verified at the "beginning," it confirms the process of man's individuation in the world, and is born, so to speak, from the very depth of his human solitude, which he lives as a person in the face of all other creatures and all living beings (*animalia*). This 'beginning', too, belongs thus to an adequate anthropology and can always be verified based on that anthropology. This purely anthropological verification brings us, at the same time, to the topic of the "person" and to the topic of "body/sex."

This simultaneity is essential. In fact, if we dealt with sex without the person, this would destroy the whole adequacy of the anthropology that we find in Genesis. Moreover, for our theological study, it would veil the essential light of the revelation of the body, which shines through these first statements with such great fullness.

There is a strong link between the mystery of creation, as a gift that springs from Love, and that beatifying "beginning" of man's existence as male and female, in the whole truth of their bodies and of their sexes, which is the simple and pure truth of communion between the persons. When the first man exclaims at the sight of the woman, "she is flesh from my flesh and bone from my bones" (Gen 2:23), he simply affirms the human identity of both. By exclaiming this, he seems to say, *Look, a body that expresses the "person"!* Following an earlier passage of the Yahwist text, one can also say that this "body" reveals the "living soul," which man became when God-Yahweh breathed life into him (see Gen 2:7). His solitude before all other living beings began in virtue of this act. Exactly through the depth of that original solitude, man now emerges in the dimension of reciprocal gift, the expression of which—by that very fact the expression of his existence as a person—is the human body in all the original truth of its masculinity and femininity. The body, which expresses femininity "for" masculinity and, vice versa, masculinity "for" femininity, manifests the reciprocity and the communion of persons. It expresses it through gift as the fundamental characteristic of personal existence. This is *the body: a witness* to creation as a fundamental gift, and therefore a witness *to Love as the source from which this same giving springs*. Masculinity-femininity—namely, sex—is the original sign of a creative donation and at the same time <the sign of a gift that> man, male-female, becomes aware of as a gift lived so to speak in an original way. This is the meaning with which sex enters into the theology of the body.

Discovery of the "Spousal" meaning of the body

This beatifying "beginning" of man's being and existing as male and female is connected with the revelation and the discovery of the meaning of the body that is rightly called "spousal." If we speak of revelation together with discovery, we do so in reference to the specificity of the Yahwist text, in which the theological guiding thread is also anthropological, or better still, appears as a certain reality that is consciously lived by man. We have already observed that after the words expressing the first joy of man's coming into existence as "male and female" (Gen 2:23) there follows the verse that establishes their conjugal unity (Gen 2:24), and then the one that attests the nakedness of both without reciprocal shame (Gen 2:25). That these verses face each other in such a significant way allows us to speak *of revelation together with the discovery of the "spousal" meaning of the body in the mystery of creation*. This meaning (inasmuch as it is revealed and also consciously "lived" by man) completely confirms the fact that creative giving, which springs from Love, has reached man's original consciousness by becoming an experience of reciprocal gift, as one can already see in the archaic text. A testimony to this fact seems also to be—perhaps even in a very specific way—that nakedness of both our first parents, free from shame.

Genesis 2:24 speaks about the ordering of man's masculinity and femininity to an end, in the life of the spouses-parents. Uniting so closely with each other that they become "one flesh," they place their humanity in some way under the blessing of fruitfulness, that is, of "procreation," about which the first account speaks (Gen 1:28). Man enters "into being" with the consciousness that his own masculinity-femininity, that is, his own sexuality, is ordered to an end. At the same time, the words of Genesis 2:25, "Both were naked, the man and his wife, but they did not feel shame," seem to add to this fundamental truth of the meaning of the human body, of its masculinity and femininity, another truth that is not in any way less essential and fundamental. Aware of the procreative power of his own body and of his own sex, man *is at the same time free from the "constraint" of his own body and his own sex*.

The original reciprocal nakedness, which was at the same time not weighed down by shame, expresses such an interior freedom in man. Is this freedom a freedom from "sexual drive"? The concept of "drive" already implies an inner constraint, analogous to the instinct that stimulates fruitfulness and procreation in the whole world of living beings (*animalia*). It seems however, that both Genesis texts, the first and the second account of the creation of man, sufficiently connect the perspective of procreation with the fundamental characteristic of human existence in the personal sense. Consequently, the analogy of the human body and of sex in relation to the world of animals—which we can call analogy "of nature"—is in both accounts (though in each in a different way) also raised in some way to the level of "image of God" and to the level of the person and communion among persons.

To this essential problem, we will have to devote further analyses. For the consciousness of man—also for that of contemporary man—it is important to know that in the biblical texts that speak about man's "beginning" one can find the revelation of the "spousal meaning of the body." However, it is even more important to establish what this meaning properly expresses.

"Freedom of the Gift"—Foundation of the Spousal meaning of the body

. . . . The revelation together with the original discovery of the "spousal" meaning of the body consists in presenting man, male and female, in the whole reality and truth of his body and his sex ("they were naked"), and at the same time in the full freedom from all constraint of the body and of [its] sex. A witness of this seems to be the nakedness of our first parents, interiorly free from shame. One can say that, created by Love, that is, endowed in their being with masculinity and femininity, both are "naked," because they are *free with the very freedom of the gift*. This freedom lies exactly at the basis of the spousal meaning of the body. The human body, with its sex—its masculinity and femininity—seen in the very mystery of creation, is not only a source of fruitfulness and of procreation, as in the whole natural order, but contains "from the beginning" the "spousal" attribute, that is, *the power to express love: precisely that love in which the human person becomes a gift* and—through this gift—fulfills the very meaning of his being and existence. We recall here the text of the most recent Council in which it declares that man is the only creature in the visible world that God willed "for its own sake," adding that this man cannot "fully find himself except through a sincere gift of self" [*Gaudium et Spes*, 24:3].

The root of that original nakedness free from shame, about which Genesis 2:25 speaks, must be sought precisely in the integral truth about man. In the context of their beatifying "beginning," man and woman are free with the very freedom of the gift. In fact, in order to remain in the relation of the "sincere gift of self" and in order to become a gift, each for the other, through their whole humanity made of femininity and masculinity (also in reference to the perspective that Genesis 2:24 speaks about), they must be free in exactly this way. Here we mean freedom above all as *self-mastery* (self-dominion). Under this aspect, self-mastery is indispensable *in order for man to be able to "give himself,"* in order for him to become a gift, in order for him (referring to the words of the Council) to be able to "find himself fully" through "a sincere gift of self" [*Gaudium et Spes*, 24:3]. In this way, the words "they were naked but did not feel shame" can and should be understood as the revelation—together with the discovery—of the freedom that makes possible and qualifies the "spousal" meaning of the body.

The "Spousal Character" of the body and the revelation of the person

Genesis 2:25, however, says even more. In fact, this passage indicates the possibility and the characteristic qualification of such a reciprocal "experience of the body."

Further, it allows us to identify that spousal meaning of the body *in actu*. When we read that 'both were naked, but did not feel shame," we indirectly touch its root, as it were, and directly already its fruits. Interiorly free from the constraint of their bodies and of sex, free with the freedom of the gift, man and woman *were able to enjoy the whole truth, the whole self-evidence of the human being*, just as God-Yahweh had revealed it to them in the mystery of creation. This truth about man, which the Council's text explains with the words quoted above, has two main emphases. The first affirms that man is the only creature in the world that the Creator willed "for its own sake"; the second consists in saying that this same man, willed in this way by the Creator from the "beginning," can only find himself through a disinterested gift of self [*Gaudium et Seps*, 24:3]. Now, this truth about man, which seems in particular to gather within itself the original condition linked with man's very "beginning" in the mystery of creation, can be reread—on the basis of the Council's text—in both directions. Such a rereading helps us to understand even more the spousal meaning of the body, which is evidently inscribed in the original condition of man and woman (according to Gen 2:23-25) and particularly in the meaning of their original nakedness.

If, as we have noted, the interior freedom of the gift—the disinterested gift of self—lies at the root of nakedness, then precisely this gift allows both the man and the woman *to find each other reciprocally*, inasmuch as the Creator willed each of them *"for his own sake"* (see *Gaudium et Spes*, 24:3). In the first beatifying encounter, the man thus finds the woman and she finds him. In this way he welcomes her within himself (and she welcomes him within herself), welcomes her as she is willed "for her own sake" by the Creator, as she is constituted in the mystery of the image of God through her femininity; and, reciprocally, she welcomes him in the same way, as he is willed "for his own sake" by the Creator and constituted by him through his masculinity. In this consists the revelation and the discovery of the "spousal" meaning of the body. The Yahwist narrative, and in particular Genesis 2:25, allows us to deduce that man, as male and female, enters the world precisely with this consciousness of the meaning of his own body, of his masculinity and femininity.

Questions

1   What is the "hermeneutic of gift" and why does John Paul II think that it is of fundamental importance for understanding humanity?

2   In what ways does he think *love* is fundamental to the creation account?

3   Why does Genesis 2:18 play such an important role in his anthropology? How does this inform his definition of the term *person*?

4   Why does he think that *person, body, sex* are inextricably related? What do you think about his argument here?

5   What is the "spousal" meaning of the body and why does he think it is so important for anthropology?

6   How does *procreation* factor into this account? What significance does this have for understanding the status of unmarried people and others who do not participate in procreation?

TEXT 6: ROSEMARY RADFORD RUETHER, "CAN A MALE SAVIOUR SAVE WOMEN?"[8]

One of the leading feminist theologians of the twentieth century, Rosemary Radford Ruether (b. 1936) devoted considerable attention to analyzing a wide variety of Christian doctrines. The following selection is taken from *To Change the World: Christology and Cultural Criticism*, in which Reuther addresses the relationship between our beliefs about Jesus and a wide range of social and theological issues. This selection focuses specifically on the ways in which Christology shapes our vision of human sexuality, specifically our understanding of what it means to be male and female. Along the way, she helpfully discusses a variety of concepts that have become important for theological perspectives on human sexuality today, including the "maleness" of God, women in ministry, and concerns about misogyny and patriarchy.

Christology has been the doctrine of the Christian tradition that has been most frequently used against women. Historically this anti-woman use of christology reached its clearest formulation in the high scholasticism of Thomas Aquinas. Aquinas argued that the male is the normative or generic sex of the human species. Only the male represents the fullness of human potential, whereas woman by nature is defective physically, morally and mentally. Not merely after the Fall, but in the original nature of things, woman's 'defective nature' confined her to a subservient position in the social order. She is by nature under subjugation. Therefore it follows that the incarnation of the Logos of God into the male is not a historical accident, but an ontological necessity. The male represents wholeness of human nature, both in himself and as head of the woman. He is the fullness of the image of God, whereas woman by herself does not represent the image of God and does not possess wholeness of humanity. This view of the male generic character of the *Imago Dei* is also found in St Augustine.

It follows for Aquinas that woman cannot represent headship either in society or in the church. Her inability to be ordained follows from her defective or (as Aquinas put it, following Aristotle's biology) her 'misbegotten' nature. Just as Christ had to be incarnated in the male, so only the male can represent Christ. Mary Daly's succinct judgment in her book, *Beyond God the Father* would seem to be fully vindicated in Aquinas' theology: "When God is male, the male is God."[9]

This male-dominant theology, that relegates woman to inferior status in both creation and redemption, has enjoyed considerable revival in recent years as the keystone of the conservative reaction to the movements for women's ordination. In Roman Catholic, Anglican and Orthodox writings against women's ordination a certain constellation of arguments emerges, centred in the relation of maleness, christology and priesthood. Jesus' historical example is usually cited. Jesus appointed

[8]Rosemary Radford Ruether, *To Change the World* (Crossroad: New York, NY, 1981), 45–56.
[9]Mary Daly, *Beyond God the Father* (Boston: Beacon Press, 1973), 19.

no women disciples; therefore he desired no women to be ordained (without recognition of the historical gaps and anachronisms of this argument).

But the matter is deeper than historical example. This is no issue of passing and relative social forms. No emergence of women as equal to men in society can change the context of the discussion. For these writers, the exclusion of women from church leadership is not based on particular structures of society. Even the traditional doctrine of order of nature is left to the side. Rather, the neoconservatives wish to see in the exclusion of women some unchangeable sacramental 'mystery' that links the maleness of the priest with the maleness of Christ. The bridegroom-bride symbolism is seen as central to this argument. Christ as the head and bridegroom of the church must necessarily be male, and, hence, also his representative, the priest. Obviously only males can be bridegrooms, although, oddly enough, these writers find no difficulty in the idea that males, in the laity, are 'brides'. It is taken for granted that this symbol system of bridegroom over bride, as head over body, male over female, is a revealed truth, rather than itself being simply a projection of a certain male-dominated social order.

Behind this christological argument of the necessary maleness of Christ and his representative, the priest, lies, it seems to me, a theological assumption; namely, the maleness of God. Not just Jesus' historical humanity, but the divine Logos, the disclosure of the 'Father', is necessarily male. In a remarkable forgetfulness of their own traditions of analogy and the *via negativa,* images such as 'Father' and 'Son' for God are not regarded as partial images drawn from limited (male) human experience, but are taken literally. 'Daughter' or 'mother' are not regarded as equally appropriate analogies.

The disclosure of God in history is seen as a disclosure of a fundamentally male reality in such a way as to exclude women from representing this divine redemptive action. They can only represent the passive, the receptive, never the active side of the divine disclosure. The Vatican Declaration against the Ordination of Women in 1976 sums up this new theological materialism when it declares that there must be a "physical resemblance" between the priest and Christ.[10] Since this strange new version of the imitation of Christ does not exclude a Negro, a Chinese or a Dutchman from representing a first-century Jew, or a wealthy prelate from representing a carpenter's son, or sinners from representing the saviour, we must assume this imitation of Christ has now been reduced to one essential element, namely, male sex.

Numerous leading Roman Catholic theologians, including Karl Rähner, have actually condemned this Declaration as 'heretical' at this point. That the Vatican would have unleashed such a document as an authoritative statement seems to me very significant. It reveals the extent of the contradiction between the message of Jesus as redeemer of all humanity 'in which there is neither male nor female' (Gal. 3.28), and the construction of christology through symbols that make it the instrument of patriarchal domination. The question I wish to ask in this chapter is: can christology be liberated from its encapsulation in the structures of patriarchy

---

[10]*Declaration on the Question of the Admission of Women to the Ministerial Priesthood* 27, Vatican City, 15 October 1976.

and really become an expression of liberation of women? Or is it so linked with symbols of male-dominance that it is unredeemable as good news for women?

Certainly many feminists have already concluded that the maleness of Christ is so fundamental to Christianity that women cannot see themselves as liberated through him. Thinkers such as Mary Daly or members of the Women's Spirituality Movement have already declared that women must reject Christ as redeemer for women and seek instead a female divinity and messianic symbol. Thus the question of whether a male saviour can save women is not merely a provocative theoretical question. It is one on which many thousands of women have already voted with their feet by leaving the church and seeking alternative feminist communities.

I will look at three alternative models of christology to see whether there are other resources in the Christ symbol that might disclose different options from those discussed above. These are (a) the imperial Christ; (b) the androgynous Christ; and (c) the prophetic, iconoclastic Christ.

(a) The imperial Christ

The imperial Christ of Nicene theology was constructed by the fusion of two basic symbols from the twin heritages of Christian theology: Hebrew messianism and Greek philosophy. The Messiah symbol was drawn from Hebrew sacral kingship. In the Zechariah prophecy this Messiah is described as a warrior-king who will overthrow enemy empires and install Israel, the oppressed nation, in power. The enemy nations will be reduced to client states who will come up to Jerusalem to pay tribute to the new imperial ruling centre of the world. This vision represents the dream of revenge of the oppressed nation which will, through God's help, turn the tables on the great imperial nations, and itself become the new imperial ruling power.

To this dream of the messianic ruler of the new age, Greek philosophy added the concept of the divine Logos or Nous of God which discloses the mind of God and manifests, in noetic form, the plan of nature. This Nous of God is not only *demiourgos,* or agent of God in creation, but also the means through which the universe is governed. This concept is set in the context of a hierarchical 'chain of Being'. Just as the Nous of God governs nature, so the Greeks must govern barbarians, masters govern slaves and men govern women. The free Greek male is seen as the natural aristocrat, representing mind and headship in nature. Women, slaves and barbarians are the 'body people' who must be governed, who are 'servile by nature'. Greek political thought in the Hellenistic period linked this Logos theology with the universal emperor who must act in the body politic as the representative of the Nous of God governing the universe.

In the christology of Eusebius of Caesarea, adviser to Constantine at the Nicene Council in AD325, these two heritages of Hebrew messianism and Greek Logos philosophy are brought together. Christ becomes the *Pantocrator,* the cosmic governor of a new Christianized universal empire. The Christian emperor, with the Christian bishop at his right hand, becomes the new Vicar of Christ on earth, governing the Christian state of the new redeemed order of history. In this vision, patriarchy, hierarchy, slavery, and Graeco-Roman imperialism have all been taken over and baptized by the Christian church.

Needless to say, elements of this christology might have been constructed in a different way. The victory of the Messiah as vindicator of the oppressed might have been seen as the radical levelling of all hierarchy and subjugation rather than the installation of the New Israel as the centre of a new empire. The Hebrew counterpart of the Logos doctrine identifies God's creative and redeeming Word as Holy Wisdom, represented as a female rather than male symbol. But these options were lost in official Christian development. Instead, imperial christology wins in the fourth century as a sacralized vision of patriarchal, hierarchical and Euro-centred imperial control.

(b) Androgynous christologies

I would like to turn now to a number of alternative christologies that represent Christ as unifying male and female. I mention here gnostic christologies of the early Church, mediaeval Jesus mysticism, especially in Julian of Norwich, women Joachite leaders of the late Middle Ages, nineteenth-century Anglo-American sects, such as the Shakers, and finally Protestant pietism. All of these have been seen as marginal or heretical except pietism, which has actually become the dominant spirituality of much of Western Christianity in the bourgeois era. The root of these christologies lies in the basic Christian affirmation that Christ redeems the whole of human nature, male and female. In Paul's words, in Christ there is 'neither male nor female'.

These ideas are elaborated in the gnostic gospels. The Second Epistle of Clement states: "For the Lord himself being asked by someone when his Kingdom would come, said: When the two shall be one, and the outside as the inside, the male with the female, neither male nor female." Christ is seen as the restored androgene of the original creation, before the separation of female from male. Women are seen as equal participants in this gnostic redeemed humanity, but only by abolishing their roles as sexual persons and mothers. The Gospel of the Egyptians has Jesus declare: "I have come to destroy the works of the female," i.e. sexual desire and procreation (ch. 9.63), while the Gospel of Thomas vindicates the inclusion of women in redemption by having Jesus say, "Lo, I shall lead her, and make her male, so that she too may become a living spirit resembling you males. For every woman who makes herself male will enter the Kingdom of Heaven" (*Logion* 114).

Ancient gnostic androgyny, as well as its modern revivals in mystics, such as Jacob Boehme, is androcentric. Maleness and femaleness are still seen as opposite principles standing for mind and spirit *versus* sense, body and sexuality. The two are brought together in a male-centred concept of the self in which the female is neutralized.

A somewhat different tradition is developed in the Jesus mysticism of Julian of Norwich. Here Jesus is declared to be both mother and father. Like a mother Jesus feeds us with his own body. He nurtures us first with milk, as newborn babes in the faith. The ambiance of these images of the mothering Jesus in mediaeval mysticism is found particularly in eucharistic piety. But since both the human and the divine person of Christ was firmly established in mediaeval thought as male, this means that mothering or female qualities are taken into the male. In Christ the male gains a mode of androgyny, of personhood that is both commanding and nurturing. But it is doubtful that Julian's society would have allowed her to reverse the relation and give to women, through Christ, the right to exercise the male prerogatives.

Perhaps the boldest effort to bring the female into redemption is found in a couple of little-known female leaders of sectarian movements in the tradition of Joachim of Fiore. The Joachimites believed that the Second Age of the Son, represented by the clerical church, would be superseded by a Third Age of the Spirit, which would bring redemption to perfection. This notion allowed many dissatisfied groups in the late mediaeval world to express their disaffiliation with the existing ecclesiastical and feudal hierarchies. Most Joachimites did not see the vindication of the female as a part of their agenda. But one such group gathered around Prous Boneta, founder of a Provençal Beguin sect. They believed she was the incarnation of the Holy Spirit, the new Eve who would bring final salvation to all humanity.

Another group in Milan declared that their leader, Guglielma, was the incarnate Spirit. Just as the second person of the Trinity had appeared as a male, so the new dispensation of the Spirit will appear as a female. The Guglielmites believed that all authority had departed from the corrupt hierarchy. In the new church, built on the foundations of the Spirit, there will be four new spiritual gospels, and women will be spiritual leaders. Such groups were marginal even with the sects, and were regarded by the church as monstrous heresies to be stamped out immediately. Yet here we have the stirring of a much more radical dissatisfaction. Here women do not merely affirm a mothering or female element within a male-centred symbol, but dare to dream of turning the tables on the male-dominated world. Only in recent years, in the feminist Goddess movements, have we seen similar ideas where women announce a 'return of the Goddess', signalling better humanity that will supersede the corrupt religion mediated through the male redeemer.

Although feminist Joachimites were exterminated in the Middle Ages, it is probable that ideas of this kind continued to gestate from various sources in underground currents of European sectarian and mystical thought. Otherwise it is hard to explain the appearance in the late eighteenth century in England of a Quaker sect called the Shakers who also declared their faith in a female Messiah who would supersede and complete the redemption through Jesus.

The Shakers based their belief in a dual Christ, both male and female, on their doctrine of God. God is androgynous, both Father and Mother. So the incarnation of God must take place in both the male and female forms. Redemption has been incomplete so far because it has taken place only in male form. However, in their founder, Mother Ann Lee, the Shakers believed that the long-awaited female Messiah, the manifestation of divine wisdom, had at last appeared, completing the salvation of humanity. This parity of male and female in redeemed humanity must also be expressed in a parity of male and female leaders in the messianic community. However, the Shakers followed the gnostic tradition in defining this messianic community as celibate.

The idea of a need for a new dispensation in female form enjoyed wide currency in the nineteenth century. It is found in such diverse sources as the French utopian socialists, the St Simonians, and the New England Transcendentalists. It is constantly hinted at in Mary Baker Eddy's new Church of Christian Science, who even declared that since the highest meaning of God is Love, the feminine nature is closer to God than the masculine. Eddy rewrote the Lord's Prayer to read: Our Mother-Father God'.

These movements reflect widespread unrest in nineteenth century thought over male and female identities in relation to religion and society. Underlying this unrest are shifting political and economic patterns. The secular liberal revolutions displaced religion from the public political order and located religion instead in the private sphere. At the same time industrialization was depriving women in the home of many of their traditional productive functions. Poor women were being drawn out of the home into the factory. But the normative nature of woman was being redefined in terms of the bourgeois housewife who was primarily seen as a nurturer, rather than a productive labourer in a family business.

This new role of the bourgeois wife coalesced with the privatization of religion to unite the definition of Christianity with the definition of womanliness. This accorded with a pietist tradition that defined religion in terms of affect or feeling rather than reason or dogma. Woman was seen as the more natural bearer of the Christlike virtues of love, altruism and self-sacrifice. Spirituality, piety and self-abnegation were seen as particularly appropriate for women (i.e., 'good' domesticated women).

This idea of women as more Christlike than men allowed very different interpretations that raged on both sides of the battle over women's emancipation in nineteenth-century America. For conservatives, woman's sweetness and goodness was fragile and can be preserved only by the strictest segregation in the home and renunciation of all desires for education influence or leadership. For many feminists, on the other hand, this notion of woman's Christlike nature suggested a messianic meaning to the emergence of woman. If woman represents the higher human qualities of peace, purity, reconciliation and love, then these qualities are too good to keep at home. These are just what the world needs to save it from the various evils that corrupt society. The home, in nineteenth-century female reformism, becomes the launching pad for a crusade into society to redeem it and elevate it to the female standards of goodness.

These traditions of the androgynous Christ reveal an ambivalent heritage. All exhibit a sense that a masculinist Christ is inadequate to express full human redemption, that Christ must in some way represent both male and female. The earlier tradition sees the female as the lower element to be united into the higher male element. But, as we move into the nineteenth century, the valuation shifts. The female comes to be seen as the 'better half', representing redemptive qualities that will uplift and perfect humanity. The emergence of women points to a messianic future that will transform the male world of war, conflict and exploitation into the woman's world of peace and reconciliation.

This heritage still divides the woman's movement today. Women can't decide whether they want to 'get into the man's world', defined as an evil world, but also the 'real world', or hold out for a better but non-existent (utopian) world represented by the still unempowered 'feminine' principles.

(c) The prophetic iconoclastic Christ

Another perspective on christology is being elaborated by liberation theologies. Liberation theologies go back to nineteenth century movements of Christian socialism that began to seek alliances between the gospel and the Left. Liberation theologies base their christologies particularly on the Jesus of the synoptic gospels. Here is a Jesus who does not sacralize existing ruling classes. The messianic prophet proclaims his message as an iconoclastic critique of existing élites, particularly religious élites. The gospel drama is one of prolonged conflict between Christ and those religious authorities who gain their social status from systems of ritualized righteousness. Jesus proclaims an iconoclastic reversal of this system of religious status. The leaders of the religious establishment are blind guides and hypocrites, while the outcasts of the society, socially and morally, prostitutes, publicans, Samaritans, are able to hear the message of the prophet. In Matthew's language, 'Truly the tax collectors and the harlots go into the kingdom of God before you', i.e., the scribes and Pharisees (Matt. 21.31). The gospel turns upside down the present order; the first shall be last and the last first.

This reversal of order is not simply a turning upside down of the present hierarchy, but aims at a new order where hierarchy itself is overcome as a principle of rule. This may have been the source of the messianic struggle between Jesus and his own disciples. It certainly has been the root of misunderstanding of Jesus by the church historically. When the sons of Zebedee ask Jesus if they can sit on his left and right hands when he comes into his Kingdom, he confronts them with his different vision of the way into the messianic future.

You know that the rulers of the Gentiles lord it over them, and their great men exercise authority over them. It shall not be so among you; but whoever would be great among you must be your servant, and whoever would be first among you must be your slave; even as the Son of man came not to be served but to serve and to give his life as a ransom for many. (Matt. 20.25–27)

The meaning of servanthood in this oft-quoted and oft-misused text of Jesus cannot be understood either as a sacralized Christian lordship that calls itself 'servant', but reproduces the same characteristics of domination, or as the romanticizing of servitude. This is why neither existing lords nor existing servants can serve as a model for this servanthood, but only the Christ, the messianic person, who represents a new kind of humanity. The essence of servanthood is that it is possible only for liberated persons, not people in servitude. Also it exercises power and leadership, but in a new way, not to reduce others to dependency, but to empower and liberate others.

This means, in the language of liberation theology, that God as liberator acts in history to liberate all through opting for the poor and the oppressed of the present system. The poor, the downcast, those who hunger and thirst, have a certain priority in God's work of redemption. Part of the signs of the kingdom is that the lame walk, the blind see, the captives are freed, the poor have the gospel preached to them. Christ goes particularly to the outcasts, and they, in turn, have a special affinity for the gospel. But the aim of this partiality is to create a new whole, to elevate the valleys and make the high places low, so that all may come into a new place of God's reign, when God's will is done on earth.

How does the question of the subjugation and emancipation of women fit into such a vision of the iconoclastic prophetic Christ? This world view is not concerned with the dualism of male and female, either as total groups or as representatives of some cosmic principles that need to be related to each other. But women are not ignored in this vision. Indeed, if one can say that Christ comes to the oppressed and the oppressed especially hear him then it is women within these marginal groups who are often seen both as the oppressed of the oppressed and also as those particularly receptive to the gospel. The dialogue at the well takes place not just with a Samaritan. but with a Samaritan woman. Not just a Syro-Phoenician but a Syro-Phoenician woman is the prophetic seeker who forces Jesus to concede redemption to the non-Jews. Among the poor it is widows who are the exemplars of the most destitute; among the moral outcasts it is the prostitutes who represent the bottom of the list. This is not accidental. It means that, in the iconoclastic messianic vision, it is the women of the despised and outcast peoples who are seen as the bottom of the present hierarchy and hence, in a special way, the last who shall be first in the kingdom.

How does this vision of the redemptive work of Christ, that addresses itself particularly to the women among the outcast, differ from those messianic visions of the new age of the 'feminine' which we described earlier? It seems to me that it has some affinities with them, in the sense that Christ is seen as critic rather than vindicator of the present hierarchical social order. The meaning of Christ is located in a new future order still to come that transcends the power structures of historical societies including those erected in the Christian era in 'Christ's name'.

But this biblical vision also differs in important ways from the romantic vision of the advent of the new age of the feminine. These gnostic and romantic traditions abstract the human person as male and female into a dualism of opposite principle, masculinity and femininity. They give different valuations to each side and then try to set up a scheme to unite the two in a new whole This sets up an insoluble problem for human personhood until these qualities labelled masculine and feminine are seen as the product of social power relations rather than 'nature'. 'Woman-as-body-sensuality' and 'woman-as-pure-altruistic-love' are both abstractions of human potential created when one group of people in power is able to define other groups of people over against themselves. To abstract these definitions into eternal essences is to miss the social context in which these definitions arise.

The world of the gospels returns us to concrete social conditions in which maleness and femaleness are elements of a complex web in which humans have defined status superiority and inferiority. The gospel returns us to the world of Pharisees and priests, widows and prostitutes, homeless Jewish prophets and Syro-Phoenician women. Men and women interact with each other within a multiplicity of social definitions: sexual status, but also ethnicity, social class, religious office and law define relations with each other. Jesus as liberator calls for a renunciation and dissolution of this web of status relationships by which societies have defined privilege and unprivilege. He speaks especially to outcast women, not as representatives of the 'feminine', but because they are at the bottom of this network of oppression. His ability to be liberator does not reside in his maleness, but, on the contrary, in the fact that he has renounced this system of domination and seeks to embody in his person the new humanity of service and mutual empowerment.

Together, Jesus and the Syro-Phoenician woman, the widow and the prostitute, not as male and female principles, but as persons responding authentically to each other, point us to that new humanity of the future. This new humanity is described in simple and earthy terms by Jesus as the time when 'all receive their daily bread, when each remits the debts which the others owe to them, when we are not led into temptations (including messianic temptations) but are delivered from evil'.

Questions

1 What does Ruether mean when she says, "Christology has been the doctrine of the Christian tradition that has been most frequently used against women"? How much should this history factor into how we understand the relationship between Christology and anthropology?

2 According to Ruether, both Aquinas and Augustine affirm the "male generic character" of humanity. What is this and why does she think it's a problem?

3 How does all of this relate to questions about the "maleness of God"? To what extent do you think the predominantly masculine nature of the biblical language about God should inform our understanding of either God's essential nature or the nature of human sexuality?

4 What did the Vatican Declaration against the Ordination of Women assert and why does Ruether find that declaration so problematic?

5 What are the three alternative models that Ruether explores for understanding the relationship between Christology and anthropology? What are some potential strengths and weaknesses of each?

6 In light of all this, how will you understand the significance of Christ's "maleness" and how that should/shouldn't inform our understanding of human sexuality?

TEXT 7: SARAH COAKLEY, "THE ESCHATOLOGICAL BODY: GENDER, TRANSFORMATION, AND GOD"[11]

Sarah Coakley (b. 1951) is the Norris-Hulse Professor of Divinity at the University of Cambridge. One of the leading systematic theologians of the last few decades, Coakley has made influential contributions to various issues in Christology, philosophy of religion, patristic studies, and feminist theology, among many others. This essay brings together Coakley's interest in theological perspectives on the body, most clearly evidenced in her *Religion and the Body* and *Powers and Submissions: Spirituality, Philosophy, and Gender*, as well as her research on the theology of Gregory of Nyssa.[12]

I Introduction: bodily obsessions

In this essay I shall attempt to substantiate what may appear to be an initially implausible thesis. I shall be arguing that the obsessive interest in the "body" which has been such a marked feature of late twentieth-century Western culture hides a profound eschatological longing; only a *theological* vision of a particular sort, I shall suggest, can satisfy it. More specifically, I shall test this contention by reference to the work of one leading post-modern secular feminist, Judith Butler, whose work on gender,[13] and the subversion of "gender binaries", is fast achieving the status of dogma in some American women's studies and religious studies circles. Butler, perhaps, we may see as the high-priestess of anti-essentialist feminism, presiding (by means of suitably liturgical *performative* utterance) over the sacrificial death of gender stability. Yet Butler's ingenious attempts to escape the repressive net of sexual stereotypes are—I shall suggest—ironic, if ultimately depressing, secularized counterparts of an *ascetical* programme of gender fluidity into the divine that Christian tradition may hold out to us, especially as we find it in the work of the fourth-century Gregory of Nyssa; and Nyssa's programme works with a necessarily eschatological *telos*. This unlikely pair of interlocutors, then, will form the focus of my analysis: in introducing Judith Butler to Gregory of Nyssa, I shall not merely be inviting a

---

[11]Sarah Coakley, "The Eschatological Body: Gender, Transformation, and God," *Modern Theology* 16.1 (2000): 61–73.

[12]*Religion and the Body* (Cambridge: Cambridge University Press, 1997); *Powers and Submissions: Spirituality, Philosophy and Gender* (Oxford: Blackwell, 2002); and see, for example, Sarah Coakley, ed., *Re-Thinking Gregory of Nyssa* (Oxford: Blackwell, 2003).

[13]Butler's four influential books on gender to date are: *Gender Trouble: Feminism and the Subversion of Identity* (New York, NY: Routledge, 1990); *Bodies that Matter: On the Discursive Limits of "Sex"* (New York, NY: Routledge, 1993); *The Psychic Life of Power: Theories in Subjection* (Stanford, CA: Stanford University Press, 1997); and *Excitable Speech: A Politics of the Performative* (New York, NY: Routledge, 1997).

comparison of a post-modern perspective on "body" and "self" with a pre-modern one (such comparisons have all the dangers of anachronism, but can nonetheless prove theologically instructive); rather, my goal is to reduce a theological answer to a latent—if repressed—eschatological question in our millennial cultural milieu.

But first we need to ask: why do "bodies" "matter" so much? No one can have failed to notice the obsession with the "body" that has gripped the late-twentieth-century popular imagination; yet this very phenomenon bears all the marks of our current deepest *aporias,* fears and longings. The notable explosion of thought and literature on the subject of the "body" in recent decades has, for a start, begged a question of definition which is not so easily grasped, let alone answered. It is as if we are clear about an agreed cultural obsession, but far from assured about its referent. As Judith Butler herself has put it, "I tried to discipline myself to stay on the subject, but found I could not fix bodies as objects of thought...Inevitably, I began to consider that this resistance was essential to the matter in hand."[14] Or, as put from a rather different methodological perspective, by Mary Douglas: "Just as it is true that everything symbolizes the body, so it is equally true that the body symbolizes *everything else.*"[15] It seems that "bodies" are as elusive as they are ubiquitous—curiously hard to get our "hands" around, even as we constantly refer to them as the locus of potential meaning.

The question that seems to press in a post-modern age is this: if we can no longer count on any universal "grand narrative" to bear the burden of religious and philosophical needs for meaning-making, is it perhaps only resistant fleshliness that we can look to as an Archimedean point of stability—a seemingly unambiguous focus for longings, myths and quasi-religious hopes? Yet on closer reflection this too—the post-modern "body"—becomes subject to infinitely variable social constructions. The "body" thus comes to bear huge, and paradoxical, pressure in post-modern thought: just as its Enlightenment partner, the "mind/soul" of Cartesianism, is seen off with almost unexamined vehemence, so, simultaneously, what is left (the "body") becomes infinitely problematized and elusive. It is all that we have, but we seemingly cannot grasp it; nor, more frighteningly, are we sure that we can control the political forces that seek to regiment it. Devoid now of religious meaning or of the capacity for any fluidity into the divine, shorn of any expectation of new life beyond the grave, it has shrunk to the limits of individual fleshliness; hence our only hope seems to reside in keeping it alive, youthful, consuming, sexually active, and jogging on (literally), for as long as possible.

Yet even as we do this (in America, at any rate, with an unexamined neo-ascetical self-righteousness, what from a Christian standpoint we may deem a *sweaty* Pelagianism), the anxious question presses: what is this "body" that I "have"? From what other site of control am "I" pummeling it into submission, beauty or longevity? Herein lie what Daniel Bell has, in another context, called our "cultural contradictions." For in the late twentieth-century affluent West, the "body", to

---

[14]J. Butler, *Bodies that Matter,* ix.
[15]M. Douglas, *Purity and Danger: An Analysis of Concepts of Pollution and Taboo* (London: Routledge & Kegan Paul, 1966), 122, my emphasis.

be sure, is sexually affirmed, but also puritanically punished in matters of diet or exercise; continuously stuffed with consumerist goods, but guiltily denied particular foods in aid of the "salvation" of a longer life; taught that there is nothing *but* it (the "body"), and yet asked to discipline it with an "I" that still refuses complete materialistic reduction. Despite the legion cries for *greater* "embodiment", for a notion of self as body, the spectres of religious and philosophical dualism die hard; the last smile on a Cartesian Cheshire cat still lurks, or is it even a more ancient manifestation of "soul"?

It is, I suggest, precisely these contradictions that should alert us to a latent cultural yearning in the matter of "bodies"—not towards the immediate sexual fulfillment that appears as the ubiquitous cultural palliative (if only in fantasy), but an equally erotic yearning towards a more elusive eschatological goal. From this perspective the bodily obsessions just described—the quest for longevity, beauty, health, sexual performance—bespeak a prevailing denial of death. But as Caroline Bynum remarks, in a penetrating little essay entitled "Why All the Fuss about the Body? A Medievalist's Perspective,"[16] it is also in contemporary "popular" cultural products, such as the film *Truly, Madly, Deeply,* that we encounter an incipient countervailing *acknowledgment* of the facts of death, of a longing for a body beyond death, and of confusion in the face of the changed features of the ghostly body (which, interestingly, will not return without bringing a host of other new "dead" friends with it; the body beyond death, it seems, is intrinsically communal, much to the disgust of the grieving widow in this entrancing and evocative film).

Is, then, the post-modern *intellectual* obsession with "body" as it relates to the theorizing of sexuality and gender an equally subtle subterfuge, another evasive ploy? Is it perhaps fuelling, as well as feeding off, more "popular" manifestations of death-denial, and screening us from political and social horrors that we otherwise cannot face? That, at any rate, is the view of Terry Eagleton, in his pounding assault on the *Illusions of Postmodernism*;[17] and it is a thesis not without point. For Eagleton shows how post-modern loss of faith in "teleology" (what Eagleton terms "holophobia") has undermined the political commitment to classic socialist goals and diverted us from the grinding poverty of the world's dispossessed; yet meanwhile the "power of capital" (a new "grand narrative" if ever there was one) has sneaked up and taken us over whilst we have been comforting ourselves with the more sensuous and narcissistic "new somatics": "The body ... is currently en route to becoming the greatest fetish of all", Eagleton charges, and in this he tars "feminism" undifferentiatedly with the same brush, for he sees much of it as all-too-comfortably compatible with the new global capitalism.[18] Bynum's contention is not dissimilar. For her, "modern treatments of person and body have recently concentrated rather too much on issues of gender and sexuality to the detriment of our awareness of other things" (and here she enumerates death, work, and—elsewhere—"fecundity").[19]

---

[16]C. Bynum, "Why All the Fuss about the Body? A Medievalist's Perspective," *Critical Inquiry* 22.1 (1995): 1–33.
[17]T. Eagleton, *The Illusions of Postmodernism* (Oxford: Blackwell Publishers, 1996).
[18]Ibid., 25.
[19]Bynum, "Why all the Fuss," 33.

But it is here that I shall beg to differ from Bynum's (and Eagleton's) otherwise perceptive and illuminating analyses. By focusing on the feminist theory of Judith Butler, I shall attempt to demonstrate that her radical theory of gender "performativity" leads us inexorably to the questions of eschatological longing that Bynum seeks to retrieve, and thereby—albeit unintentionally—to the horizon of a *divine* "grand narrative". Whilst Butler's own prescriptions relate only to a secular realm and are tinged with a deep pessimism about radical social change, her thematizations of desire, of gender fluidity, and of subversive personal agency all echo older, theistically-oriented traditions of personal transformation within and beyond the "body" of this mortal life. Butler has been accused of "dissolving" the body into "discourse"; I shall argue, on the contrary (and doubtless to Butler's own dismay!), that her theory has the remaining marks of a body longing for transformation into the divine. Like Gregory of Nyssa, with whom I shall compare her, Butler sees the point of "practices" of transformation that start now but have their final goal in the future: they create the future by enacting its possibilities. As Jürgen Moltmann has well said of a falsely-futuristic eschatology, "The person who presses forward to the end of life *misses life itself*."[20] Both Judith Butler and Gregory of Nyssa, as I shall now attempt to demonstrate, know the meaning of that aphorism and present us with visions of bodily (and gendered) transformations that press forward from the present.

II Judith Butler on gender performativity

Butler's impenetrably opaque prose obfuscates as much as it reveals: this is arguably all part of her strategy of linguistic subversion. (It is certainly a challenge to the analytically-trained mind.) At once speculative theorist and practical reformer, Butler invites her reader into a dizzying engagement with (strangely masculinist) forebears as diverse as Nietzsche, Freud, Althusser, Austin, Foucault and Kripke. Not all of these are invoked immediately in her earliest work; but previous feminist theorists of whom she is critical from the start include de Beauvoir, Irigaray, Kristeva and Wittig—all figures whom she regards as veering too closely to gender essentialism. Out of this strange concoction of heroes, detractors and resources, she constructs in *Gender Trouble* (1990) her central theory about the persistent oppressiveness of compulsory heterosexuality. "Gender" is not "natural" but repetitively "performed": "The univocity of sex, the internal coherence of gender, and the binary framework for both sex and gender are ... regulatory fictions that consolidate and naturalize the convergent power regimes of masculine and signification, but ... a set of boundaries, individual and social, politically heterosexist oppression."[21] Thus the "body" is no "ready surface awaiting signified and maintained."[22] Sex is "[n]o longer believable as an interior 'truth' of dispositions and identity", but is rather a "performatively enacted signification . . ., one that, released from its naturalized interiority and surface, can occasion the parodie proliferation and subversive play of gendered

---

[20]J. Moltmann, *The Coming of God: Christian Eschatology* (London: SCM Press, 1996), xi, my emphasis.
[21]*Gender Trouble*, 33.
[22]Ibid.

meanings."[23] Hence Butler, as a lesbian theorist, is out to make "gender trouble," "not through the strategies that figure a *utopian* beyond, but through the mobilization, subversive confusion, and proliferation of precisely those constitutive categories that seek to keep gender in its place by posturing as the foundational illusions of identity."[24]

Butler's theory, we note, assumes both a fluidity of gender and its (re)creation through repeated practice. There is nothing "natural" about it; indeed "de-naturalization" of gender is the point of the whole project. But this is not to say (as Butler is often misunderstood) that gender can be constituted at will, or by mere verbal fiat; that would be to underestimate the "established" nature of the gender binaries that Butler seeks to de-stabilize: "To enter into the repetitive practices of this terrain is not a choice, for the 'I' that might enter is always already inside: there is no possibility of agency or reality outside of the discursive practices that give those terms the intelligibility that they have."[25] Thus: "The task is not whether to repeat, but how to repeat or, indeed, to repeat and, through a radical proliferation of gender, *to displace* the very gender norms that enable the repetition itself."[26] The "performance" of gender is, on this view, *both* a repeated (if unconscious) act in favour of "compulsory heterosexuality" *and* a potentially subversive act of homosexual or lesbian defiance; but the former undeniably has the cultural upper-hand, and provides the resistant backcloth to the latter. Nonetheless, to some undisclosed extent we can at least spoof the social forces of gender that so exercise us.

The spiritual significance of Butler's analysis should at this point give us pause. The "denaturalization" of sex and gender is, as we shall shortly see, a theme shared with an older tradition of ascetical transformation. The possibilities for labile, fluid transformation towards a goal of liberation and personal authenticity is what Butler's vision has in common with this more ancient wisdom. Moreover, it is the yoking of "practice" (Butler's "performance") and theory that also strikes a note of spiritual reminiscence: change cannot occur by mere thought, but is precisely the product of arduous exercise —an exercise *against* the grain of the predominant cultural assumption, the assumption, that is, of heterosexual "marriage and giving in marriage". To the extent that this vision of transformation hangs over Butler's theorizing, then, it begs a question about the possibilities of "grace"; whereas a more cynical reading would suggest that Butler's theory of resistance is merely reinstantiating the conditions of sexual oppression against which she chafes.

Martha Nussbaum, in an intemperate recent review of Butler's corpus,[27] takes the latter interpretative perspective. If "performing" resistance represents the heart of Butler's thesis, she argues, then does it not signal the *necessity* of the remaining conditions of sexual oppression? "For Butler", she charges, "the act of subversion is so riveting, so sexy, that it is a bad dream to think that the world will actually get better. What a bore equality is! No bondage, no delight. In this way [Butler's]

---

[23]Ibid.
[24]Ibid., 34, my emphasis.
[25]Ibid., 148.
[26]Ibid.
[27]Martha C. Nussbaum, "The Professor of Parody," *The New Republic*, February 22, 1999, 37–45.

pessimistic erotic anthropology offers support to an amoral anarchistic politics."[28] Such a critique has its point (since Butler does not explicitly promise us that the world will ever become less "compulsorily heterosexist"); but it fails to engage with the profounder levels of spiritual yearning that I detect in Butler's text.

In other ways, too, Butler's theory of "body" is capable of serious distortion. Bynum is not the only one to charge her with dissolving bodily matter into "discourse". (Were this so, it would be an ironic triumph for feminism, so to elevate the final power of the "word" over body.) But Butler's second major book on gender theory, *Bodies that Matter* (1993), explicitly addresses this question, and wards off the suggestion of the reduction of physical bodiliness to mere forms of verbal instantiation. "Performance", to be sure, as becomes clearer in Butler's new usage here of Austin's *How to Do Things with Words* (1962), effects what it proclaims verbally. But it is gender that is performed, not the material bodies themselves. Language cannot *create* bodies (that would be an odd claim indeed); rather, Butler is insisting that there is no access to bodies that is not already a gendered access: "there is no reference to a pure body which is not at the same time a further formation of that body. . . . In philosophical terms, the constative claim is always to some degree performative."[29] Here we see clearly, then, the distinction in Butler between bodiliness and subjectivity; the one cannot simply be reduced to the other. As one perceptive commentator (Amy Hollywood) has put it, "Butler's most important work in *Bodies That Matter* . . . lies in its assertion that sites of resistance to dominant discourses can be articulated without relying on a concept of materiality that lies untouched by that discourse. Rather than arguing for a transcending idealism of a transcendent materiality, Butler demonstrates the ... possibilities for transcendence that emerge in and through complex bodily experiences."[30] It is the nature of that "transcendence" with which we are especially concerned—an excess of possibility that refuses to limit "desire" to its physical locus of pleasure. "Desire" for Butler always signals a form of "loss", an obscured yearning, an exclusion of possibilities that "compulsory heterosexuality" rules out. Again, we shall have reason to compare this with a more explicitly Christian perception of unending desire (for God) that informs Gregory's "erotic" spirituality.

In Butler's more recent work, it is a post-Foucaultian analysis of "power" that comes to the fore in her analysis, and at points suggests comparison with the "Yahweh" of her Jewish heritage who still lurks at the corners of her discussion. "Power," as one critic has acutely noted, is now the 'God-term' in Butler's text; no wonder, then, that this "power" is inescapable, the only modality in and through which "agency" even becomes possible: "there is no formation of the subject without a passionate attachment to subjection."[31] Yet out of this learned subjection, even out of degradation, come the possibilities of hope and resistance. (Somewhere the myth of cross and resurrection lurks, mediated no doubt through the Hegel who forms the focus of Butler's meditations in *The Psychic Life of Power.*) Less clear now

---

[28]Ibid., 44.
[29]Butler, *Bodies that Matter,* 10–11.
[30]Amy Hollywood, "Transcending Bodies," *Religious Studies Review* 25 (1999), 14.
[31]See the illuminating analysis of Butler's recent work by Michael Levenson, "The Performances of Judith Butler," in *Lingua Franca,* 8 (September 1998), 61–67, cf. 62.

than before is the *optimistic* call to fluid gendered transformation; more clear is her insistence that speech can effect occasional punctures in existing power relations.

Why does Butler's vision exercise such "power" itself? Despite Nussbaum's derisive critique of Butler's "hip defeatism", Butler's work continues to exercise an uncanny degree of influence. Somehow it is the allure of gender liberation (not now sexual liberation, note) that fascinates the late-twentieth-century mind, the prospect of an escape from stereotype, the hope of an elusive personal transformation beyond normal human expectations and restrictions. But to what (eschatological) end? That is a question not answered by Butler herself, although surely her argument begs it. The comparison with an equally fluid Christian spirituality of gender now becomes pressing.

III Gregory of Nyssa (c. 330-c. 395) and the transformations of gender

Nyssa is, as in many other matters, notoriously inconsistent in his theorizing about the resurrection body and our own eschatological end;ever, that his fascinating suggestions in this area should not be considered in abstraction from his equally subtle understandings of gender, which are deeply entangled with them. Bynum, in her recent magisterial volume *The Resurrection of the Body* (1995) gives an illuminating account of Gregory's eschatology but says relatively little about the place of gender in it. We are indebted to Verna Harrison for a first careful consideration of Nyssa's theory of gender, and I draw most gratefully on her pioneering work. However there are points in Nyssa's consideration of gender stereotype (what Butler would call the oppressive "gender binaries") which need deeper consideration than I think has yet been given: Gregory's gender theory, like Butler's, does not claim to *obliterate* the binaries that remain culturally normative, but seeks—also like Butler—to find a transformative way through them. Whereas in Butler, however, this escape is effected by punctiliar subversive acts of "performativity", in Gregory it represents a life-long ascetical programme, a purification and redirection of *eros* towards the divine, a final withdrawal from the whirligig of marriage, child-rearing, the quest for social status and financial security. In Gregory's case this is especially poignant, since we know that he was married as a younger man and he writes of the tragic death of children with enormous insight and grief; but nowhere—and how interestingly contrastive is this with Augustine—does he agonize with guilt or fear about the sexual act itself. Indeed, one might argue on the contrary that his spirituality of progressive ascent and increasing loss of noetic control (as set out in *The Life of Moses*) is figured precisely by analogy with the procreative act; Gregory says as much in the introduction to his *Commentary on the Song of Songs*—that the passage from the physical to the spiritual is not effected by repression of the memory of physical love: "I hope that my commentary will be a guide for the more fleshly-minded, since the wisdom hidden [in the Song of Songs] *leads* to a spiritual state of the soul."[32]

---

[32]Gregory of Nyssa, *Commentary on the Song of Songs,* trans. Casimir McCambley (Brookline, MA: Hellenic College Press, 1987), 35 (my emphasis). For the Greek text, see ed. Werner Jaeger, *Gregorii Nysseni Opera* (Leiden: E. J. Brill, 1960–), (hereafter *GNO*), VI, 4.

As Bynum shows with exemplary clarity, Gregory's eschatological body is an ever-changing one; like Origen, the Syriac writers Ephrem and Aphrahat, and Cyril of Jerusalem before him, he takes Paul's "seed" metaphor in 1 Cor. 15 to heart: the body is labile and changing in this life and is on its way to continuing change into incorruptibility in the next. (This is *unlike* a rival tradition forged in reaction to Origen, which sees the resurrection body as the reassemblage of "bits", or as what Bynum finds in Augustine as a final freezing of "flux.") For Gregory, however, change does not necessarily signal decay, but can on the contrary mark the endless transformations "from glory to glory". Famously re-defining "perfection" as "never arriving"—a daring move for a Platonist—he similarly understands the partaking of Eucharist in this life as an already-anticipated reception of heavenly food. We are on a continuum, then, from this "body" to our "angelic" future "bodies", and death need not be a *dramatic* shift in the case of a holy ascetical body, as we shall see.

Where, then, does gender fit into this picture? As is well known, and Verna Harrison has explicated with especial care, Gregory holds (on the basis of a particular reading of Gen. 1:27, in conjunction with Gal. 3:28) that the original creation was of non-sexed (that is, non-genitalized) beings; his text *On the Making of Man* suggests that it was only *en route*, so to speak, to the Fall, that "man" was distinguished from "woman." times, as he expounds in *On Those who have Fallen Asleep*, we shall expect to be de-genitalized again, and so receive that angelic status that was our lot originally (the contrast with the Augustine of *The City of God* is of course instructive: Augustine becomes sure that we shall be able to recognise each other as men and women in heaven). It is a mistake, however, as Harrison helps illuminate, to read Gregory here as divorcing our development from the exigencies of *gender*, even if our genitalia are finally irrelevant to our "bodily" condition before God, that does not mean that we are released from what Butler would (rather differently) term the "performances" of gender. On the contrary, the whole point of a life of virginity (as Gregory argues in his early work *De Virginitate*, bemusingly enough written at a time when he was probably married), is to become spiritually "fecund." And the continual purgative transformations of the ascetical life involve forms of gender fluidity and reversal (as we shall show) that undercut and subvert what could be expected of someone living according to the late-antique norms of married gender roles.

Three themes in Gregory's eschatologically-oriented theory of gender strike us now as suggestive points of comparison with Butler's more pessimistic secular alternative. First, we must not overlook (as it is tempting to do) the undeniable examples of Gregory's rehearsal of "gender binaries". A particularly revealing example of this phenomenon occurs at the beginning of Book II of *The Life of Moses* (1-8).[33] There Gregory discusses the exegetical meaning to be attached to the fact that "Moses was born at the time Pharaoh issued the decree for *male* offspring to be destroyed": how are we now to "imitate" this, he asks? Surely coming to birth (as a "male") is not something in our power to imitate? However Gregory immediately rehearses here *both* a binary gender stereotype *and* an insistence that gender is fluid and volitional:

---

[33]In what follows, I am using the *CWS* translation, *The Life of Moses*, trans. A. H. Malherbe and E. Ferguson (New York, NY: Paulist Press, 1978), see 55–57 (Bk. II), and 31–32 (Bk. I). For the Greek, see *GNO* VII, 1, 34–37 and 4–6 respectively.

"For the material and passionate disposition to which human nature is carried when it falls is the female form of life . . . The austerity and intensity of virtue is the male birth . . . (2). [But] . . . In mutable nature nothing can be observed which is always the same . . . We are in some manner our own parents [literally, "fathers"], giving birth to ourselves by our own free choice in accordance with whatever we wish to be, whether male or female, moulding ourselves to the teaching of virtue or vice" (3). Is then the stereotype of "female" passion or vice left intact by Gregory? It is a nice point, just as it is a nice point whether Butler's subversive "performativity" of gender needs the gender binaries it seeks to upend. But Gregory adds a further complexification—not found in Butler—when he earlier suggests that such disjunctive gender binaries apply as points of reference primarily for "those who wander outside virtue" (Book I, 11), that is, for mere beginners on the slope of Moses's mystical ascent. Abraham and Sarah (12) are set before such as exemplars, "the men to Abraham and the women to Sarah"; but then, of course, it turns out that they do not represent the "virtue=male" and "passion=female" binary previously named; indeed, with their example we are already well on the way to a set of reversals of such expectation.

Herein lies what I have termed the "eschatologically-oriented" feature of Gregory's complex theory of personal (and gendered) transformation into the divine life, and thus herein too lies our second revealing point of comparison with Butler. As Harrison has tellingly expounded, it is not that either "body" or gender are disposed of in this progressive transformation to a neo-angelic status. Rather, as advances are made in the stages of virtue and contemplation, *eros* finds its truer meaning in God, and gender switches and reversals attend the stages of ascent: the increasingly close relation to Christ marks, in the *Commentary on the Song of Songs,* a shift from active courting of Christ as "Sophia" to passive reception of embraces of Christ as the bridegroom. Does this not, then, at some deeper level merely reinscribe normative gender binaries? This is by no means clear. At this (higher) stage of ascent, one can no longer assume—Jungian importations are distractions here—that the woman ascetic is "primarily" enacting the pole of gender associated at the outset with the "female" and then "adding" "male" virtues to the amalgam. On the contrary, the fascinating banter between Gregory and his older sister Macrina in *On the Soul and the Resurrection* give the lie to such a suggestion. Here, as in the related *Life of Macrina,* Gregory takes the part of the passions and Macrina manifests the stern rational asceticism in which Gregory manifestly fails. As Rowan Williams has put it in a deft analysis of this interaction, its implications for "soul", "body" and gender are subtle ones: "For Gregory . . . we could say, there is no such *thing* as the soul in itself; it is always implicated in contingent matter, and even its final liberation for pilgrimage into God . . . depends . . . upon the deployment and integration of bodiliness and animality . . . the ungenderedness of the soul is never the actual state of a real subject."[34] Part, at least, of this could be applauded by Butler too, we could now suggest. But what she cannot assert unambiguously is that divine referent that forms the final point of meaning in Gregory, what Williams thematizes as "that

---

[34]Rowan Williams, "Macrina's Deathbed Revisited: Gregory of Nyssa on Mind and Passion," in eds. Lionel Wickham and Caroline P. Bammel, *Christian Faith and Greek Philosophy in Late Antiquity* (Leiden: E.J. Brill, 1993), 244.

fundamental *eros* for the endless God that binds the polyphony of our intentionality into some sort of unity."[35]

Our third instructive point of comparison with Butler leads on from here. Butler speaks little of death; yet death, as Gregory well sees, is the most incisive test of a person's life. (Or, as Stanley Hauerwas has put it recently, "Perfection is the art of dying,"[36] an aphorism that fits interestingly in Gregory's case with his assurance that "Perfection is never arriving".) As we have already hinted, death for Gregory is merely a passage into further "bodily" —albeit de-genitalized—life; for his sister Macrina, already so holy that she becomes a "relic" anticipatorily on her death-bed, the continuum between this life and the next is almost complete. Even the little scar on her breast from a miraculous earlier cure of cancer remains, however; as with Christ's scarred risen body, nothing is lost that represents suffering confronted and overcome: "a memorial of the divine intervention, the result and the occasion an aphorism that fits interestingly in Gregory's of perpetual turning toward God through the action of grace".[37] Bynum writes of this touching passage that it is really always Macrina that Gregory has in mind when he tries to speak of the eschatological body: "The resurrected body is both the ascetic who becomes a relic while still alive and the relic that continues after death the changelessness acquired through asceticism."[38] Do we not perhaps detect a yearning for such contemplation in Butler's remorselessly sophisticated and tortured maneuvers?

IV Conclusions: Gender, transformation and God

I have been suggesting in this essay that Judith Butler's profound desire to shift or subvert the weight of "gender binaries" does not grip our late-twentieth-century imaginations for no reason. Much is at stake here; and it is more—frankly—than a debate about politics, speech and homophobia, important though that is. Rather what seems to be being enacted is the gesturing to an eschatological horizon which will give mortal flesh final significance, a horizon in which the restless, fluid post-modern "body" can find some sense of completion without losing its mystery, without succumbing again to "appropriate" or restrictive gender roles. In introducing Judith Butler to Gregory of Nyssa I have courted the dangerous charge of anachronism for the sake of a spiritual challenge of some severity: for it is not, note, the goal of Gregory's vision to enjoy various forms of previously-banned sexual pleasure; or to escape or sneer at a supposedly "repressive" pornography law. Rather, *Gregory's* vision of final "erotic" fulfillment demands an asceticism costing not less than everything; and to a culture fed on bowdlerized Freud and

---

[35]Ibid.

[36]Stanley Hauerwas, "The Sanctified Body Why Perfection Does Not Require a 'Self'," in *Sanctify Them in the Truth Holiness Exemplified* (Nashville, TN Abmgdon Press, 1999), 89.

[37]From the *Life of Macrina*, cited in Bynum, *The Resurrection of the Body*, p 86 For the relevant passage in the Greek edition, see ed. Pierre Maraval, *Grégoire de Nysse Vie de Sainte Macrine*, Sources Chrétiennes 178 (Paris Editions du Cerf, 1971), 242–47.

[38]Bynum, *The Resurrection of the Body*, 86.

equally bowdlerized Foucault—in which erotic "purification" can seemingly only signal "repression"—this is hardly likely to have instant appeal. That Gregory's insights may nonetheless provide us with the clues to some of our profoundest cultural riddles about the "body" it has nonetheless been the burden of this paper to suggest; odd, is it not (or not so odd?), that we needed the anguished insights of a secularized Jewish lesbian feminist to remind us of this deep strand of longing and wisdom.

Questions

1 Who is Judith Butler and why is her work important for understanding gender and sexuality today?

2 What are some of the *aporias* (i.e. contradictions) that attend modern views of the body? Why do you think we struggle with these ideas?

3 What does Butler mean by the "performance" of gender? Does this mean she thinks that we simply *choose* whatever "gender" we want? Why or why not?

4 What are some of the strengths of Butler's view of gender? What criticisms does Coakley offer? What do you think of those criticisms?

5 How does "power" relate to "gender"?

6 In what ways does Coakley think Gregory of Nyssa can contribute to modern perspectives on gender? What do you think about this argument?

7 What role should eschatology play in our understanding of sexuality?

6

Human Personhood

The language of "personhood" or "persons" has a curious and venerable history. In Latin Christianity, the word *persona*, which originally referred to the mask that an actor wore on stage to represent different characters or *personae,* was adapted for use in reference to the three members of the Godhead. Of course, these three *personae* were not *personae*! In fact, the early theologians were adamant that the three "persons" of the Trinity were not masks or guises put on by one single being—that would have been the heresy of modalism—but were three individuated members in unity. In the Greek church, the language of *hypostasis* performed the same function, and has its own background in the philosophy of Aristotle and others. Adapted for use by the Cappadocian Fathers in the fourth century, *hypostasis* came to mean "individual reality." The Father and the Son shared a common nature, or substance, but they were distinct *persons*.

From this shaping of the word "person" as a conceptual tool for theology came its application to anthropology. The human individual, like the divine persons, had a personal identity, and is a some*one* rather than a some*thing*. Like the divine persons, humans express their intentions in words and acts, and respond to the words and actions of others. They are able to think about what they are doing—to feel regret, or nostalgia (which is not what animals do). They are self-reflective agents of communication. This definition immediately shows that we are talking about an individual within a web (or potential web) of relationships.

The concept of "personhood" remains fascinating to theologians as many of the following readings illustrate. But the term has become a complex one, since it has been adapted for use in psychology and related disciplines. What we mean in common parlance by "person" and "personality" is not necessarily what theologians mean when they talk about the divine "persons" or "hypostases." This has led theologians (at least since Karl Barth in his *Church Dogmatics* I/1) to suggest a different terminology—in Barth's case "Modes of Being." Not many critics thought Barth's suggestion workable, but his attempt to find an alternative signaled just how freighted the word "person" had come in common parlance with notions of "personality." The three persons of the Trinity are not three "personalities." Nevertheless, Christian theologians and philosophers of the twentieth and twenty-first centuries continue to deploy the vocabulary of personhood in the context of theological anthropology at least.

TEXT 1 JOHN ZIZIOULAS, "HUMAN CAPACITY AND HUMAN INCAPACITY: A THEOLOGICAL EXPLORATION OF PERSONHOOD"[1]

John Zizioulas (b. 1931), the Eastern Orthodox Metropolitan of Pergamon, is one of the best known Orthodox theologians of the last fifty years. His influence has notably extended westwards, in the sense that he has been read widely by leading Catholic and Protestant theologians, especially Miroslav Volf and Colin Gunton. His early studies were with the leading Russian Orthodox theologian Georges Florovsky. Subsequently, Zizioulas has served professorships in Athens, Edinburgh and Glasgow. His major works, especially the highly regarded *Being as Communion: Studies in Personhood and the Church,* focus on the deeply related themes of ecclesiology and ontology. He has had a rich and ongoing dialogue with existentialist writers such as Camus and Heidegger, with the novels of Dostoevsky, and with patristic authors like Irenaeus and Maximus; and this has given shape to his theology of personhood.

I

Theology, unlike other disciplines dealing with man, is faced with a fundamental methodological problem in its attempt to understand the human being. This problem is due to the Christian view of the Fall. Whatever we may wish to mean by the Fall, the fact remains that there is something which can be called 'sin', and which gives rise to the question: is man that which we know and experience as 'man'? If we answer the question in the affirmative, then we are bound to imply that sin is not an anthropological problem and redemption from sin does not essentially alter our view of man; in fact if we follow up the consequence of this position, we are bound to say that unfallen man or man restored by redemption is not properly speaking 'man' but something of a super-man. If, on the other hand, we do not approach man from the angle of his actual sinful situation, how can we approach him? Is there another angle from which to look at man except from that of what we actually see as man?

This difficulty becomes even clearer when we pose the question of human capacity and human incapacity. For this question stems from man's difficulty to define himself. It is a question that only a human being can ask, precisely because it seems to be a unique characteristic of this sort of being to be unwilling to accept his actual limits and to tend to move beyond them. Thus, even if one looks at the actual man of our experience, one is confronted with the fact that most of man's actions, consciously

---

[1] From Zizioulas, John. "Human Capacity and Human Incapacity: A Theological Exploration of Person-hood." *Scottish Journal of Theology* 28, no. 05 (1975): 401–47.

or unconsciously, go beyond his actual state in a movement of transcendence of the actual human limitations. This is to be seen not only in the impressive history of man's discoveries and conquests over nature, but also in the commonest everyday struggles of man to survive by surpassing all obstacles whether of a natural or of a moral character. Thus the empirical man does not represent the reality of the human being in its fullness even for a purely humanistic approach to man. Whether one speaks, in terms of natural sciences, about the evolution of man or, in terms of social sciences, about the man of the evolving society, it remains true that the empirical man is essentially 'the raw material' for the conception or creation of the real man. Only by setting up the empirical man against a certain vision do we make him a real man. Marxism in our day speaks openly of its aspirations to go beyond the actual, to a better type of man.

It is precisely this peculiarity of the human phenomenon that makes the question of human capacity and incapacity a complex one. At what point exactly can we draw the line of demarcation between capacity and incapacity? At what point does the actual man cease to be actual, or, to put it bluntly, at what point does man cease to be man and become something else–a sub-man or a super-man or God?

In the lines that follow I shall deal with two possible approaches to the problem of human capacity and incapacity as they are reflected in the theological discussion of the relation between God and man. I should like to emphasise that these approaches represent two anthropological methods, decisively different for the study of human capacity and incapacity. The first of these is to be found in man's attempt to answer the question of human capacity and incapacity by an introspective movement and, in general, by looking primarily into man himself. The second method presupposes—and the reasons for this will be argued—that man's capacity and incapacity can be properly discussed only if man is approached as an indefinable being which can be grasped only by being put in the light of his ability to relate to extra-human realities. The whole argument will be finally placed in the light of some strictly theological doctrines, such as Christology and Pneumatology.

****

III

1. Man's personhood should not be understood in terms of 'personality', i.e. of a complex of natural, psychological or moral qualities which are in some sense 'possessed' by or 'contained' in the human *individuum*. On the contrary, being a person is basically different from being an individual or 'personality' in that the person cannot be conceived in itself as a static entity, but only as it relates to. Thus personhood implies the 'openness of being', and even more than that, the *ek-stasis* of being, i.e. a movement towards communion which leads to a transcendence of the boundaries of the 'self' and thus to *freedom*. At the same time, and in contrast to the partiality of the individual which is subject to addition and combination, the person in its ekstatic character reveals its being in a *catholic*, i.e. integral and undivided, way, and thus in its being ekstatic it becomes *hypostatic*, i.e. the bearer of its nature

in its totality. *Ekstasis* and *hypostasis* represent two basic aspects of Personhood, and it is not to be regarded as a mere accident that both of these words have been historically applied to the notion of Person. Thus the idea of Person affirms at once both that being cannot be 'contained' or 'divided', and that the mode of its existence, its *hypostasis*, is absolutely unique and unrepeatable. Without these two conditions being falls into an a-personal reality, defined and described like a mere 'substance', i.e. it becomes an a-personal thing.

The combination of the notion of ekstasis with that of hypostasis in the idea of the person reveals that Personhood is directly related to ontology—it is not a quality added, as it were, to beings, something that beings 'have' or 'have not' but it is *constitutive* of what can be ultimately called a 'being'.

The notion of 'hypostasis' was for a long time identical with that of 'substance'. As such it basically served the same purpose which the term 'substance' served since Aristotle, namely to answer the ultimate ontological question: what is it that makes a particular being be itself and thus be at all? Suddenly, however, in the course of the fourth century A.D. and under the pressure of conditions which are worth studying, the term hypostasis ceased to denote 'substance' and became synonymous with that of 'person'. The implications of this shift in terminology cannot but be of paramount importance for ontology, for it can hardly be conceivable that those who made this shift dissociated 'hypostasis' from ontology entirely. The Greek Fathers were after all Greeks and the Greek mind could not avoid thinking ontologically.

If the notion of hypostasis, no longer in the sense of 'substance' but of 'person', points to that which makes a being be itself, then we are indeed confronted with a revolution with regard to Greek and especially Aristotelian ontology. For the identification of hypostasis not with '*ousia*' but with Personhood means that the ontological question is not answered by pointing to the 'self-existent', to a being as it is determined by its own boundaries, but to a being which in its ekstasis breaks through these boundaries in a movement of communion. That for which an ultimate ontological claim can be made, that which is, is only that which can be itself, which can have a hypostasis of its own. But since 'hypostasis' is identical with Personhood and not with substance, it is not in its 'self- existence' but in communion that this being is itself and thus is at all. Thus communion does not threaten personal particularity; it is constitutive of it.

Ontological identity therefore is to be found ultimately not in every 'substance' as such, but only in a being which is free from the boundaries of the 'self'. Because these boundaries render it subject to individualisation, comprehension, combination, definition, description and use, such a being free from these boundaries is free, not in a moral but in an ontological sense, i.e., in the way it is constituted and realised as a being. Ontological identity requires freedom in this fundamental ontological sense and as such it is ultimately applicable only to personal beings and not to a-personal things – this is what the shift of hypostasis from *ousia* to personhood implies. Ultimately, therefore, a particular being is 'itself'—and not another one—because of its uniqueness which is established in communion and which renders a particular being unrepeatable as it forms part of a relational existence in which it is indispensable and irreplaceable. That which, therefore, makes a particular personal being be itself—and thus be at all—is in the final analysis communion, freedom and love and that should not surprise any Christian who believes that the world exists only because of God's free love and that even God himself is love. For if the notion of God carries with it the ultimate ontological claim 'I am that I am', it is because only God can claim to be a personal being in the genuine sense I have just indicated: he is the only being that is in an ultimate sense 'itself ', i.e., particular, but whose particularity is established in full ontological freedom, i.e., not by virtue of its boundaries (he is 'incomprehensible', 'indivisible' etc.), but by its ekstasis of communion (he is eternally Trinity and love) which makes it unique and indispensable. When we say, therefore, that God is, we do not refer to a being as being but to the Father—a term which denotes being in the sense of hypostasis, i.e. of Person.

It would seem, therefore, that the identification of hypostasis with Person—this historic crossfertilisation between Greek and Biblical thought that took place in the fourth century—has ultimately served to show that the notion of Person is to be found only in God and that human personhood is never satisfied with itself until it becomes in this respect an *Imago Dei*. This is the greatness and tragedy of man's personhood and nothing manifests this more clearly than a consideration of his capacity and incapacity, especially from an ontological point of view. We can see this by considering one of the most important capacities of human personhood, namely *creating*: man is capable of creating, of bringing things into being.

2. When we employ the terms 'creation', 'creating' or 'creativity' in relation to personhood, we must not have in mind the idea of 'manufacturing' with which we usually associate man's ability to be a creator. Admirable as it may be, man's capacity to manufacture and produce useful objects even of the highest quality, such as the machines of our modern technological civilisation, is not to be directly associated with human Personhood. Perhaps on this point the contrast we have been making here between man as a Person on the one hand and man as an individual thinking or acting agent on the other hand, becomes more evident. The 'creation' of a machine requires man's individualisation both in terms of his *seizing, controlling and dominating* reality, i.e. turning beings into things, and also in terms of *combination* of human individuals in a collective effort, i.e. of turning man himself into a thing, an instrument and a means to an end. Hence, it is only natural that the more collectivistic a society, that is the more it sacrifices personhood, the better the products it achieves. But when we say that man is capable of creating *by being a person*, we imply something entirely different, and that has to do with a double possibility which this kind of creation opens up. On the one hand, 'things' or the world around acquire a 'presence' as an integral and relevant part of the totality of existence, and on the other hand man himself becomes 'present' as a unique and unrepeatable hypostasis of being and not as an impersonal number in a combined structure. In other words, in this way of understanding creating, the movement is from thinghood to personhood and not the other way round. This is, for example, what happens in the case of a work of real art as contrasted to a machine. When we look at a painting or listen to music we have in front of us 'the beginning of a world', a 'presence' in which 'things' and substances (cloth, oil, etc.) or qualities (shape, colour, etc.) or sounds become part of a personal presence. And this is entirely the achievement of Personhood, a distinctly unique capacity of man, which, unlike other technological achievements, is not threatened by the emerging intelligent beings of computer science. The term 'creativity' is significantly applied

to Art par excellence, though we seldom appreciate the real implications of this for theology and anthropology.

Now, this possibility of 'presence', which is implied in human personhood, reveals at the same time the tragic incapacity which is intrinsic in this very capacity of personhood. This is to be seen in the paradoxical fact that the presence of being in and through the human person is ultimately revealed as an absence. The implications of this are of decisive importance for what we are trying to say here. If we take again our example from the world of art, the fundamental thing that we must observe with regard to the 'presence' it creates, is that the artist himself is absent. This is not an entirely negative statement. The tragedy lies in the fact that it is at once positive and negative: the artist exists for us only because he is absent. Had we not had his work (which points to his absence), he would not exist for us or for the world around, even if we had heard of him or seen him; *he* is by *not being there* (an incidental actual presence of the artist next to us while we are looking at his work would add nothing to his real presence in and through his work, which remains a pointer to his absence).

This presence which is realised in absence will be ruled out as sheer fantasy or feeling by all empirically inclined thought. For indeed this presence is not graspable empirically and it does not appear to be compelling rationally. At the same time it is not to be understood or explained idealistically either, i.e., as an imposition of the mind upon reality, for the word 'absence' which is *inseparably* attached to 'presence' is to be taken seriously: the 'present' person is *not* there. In what sense then is this presence a presence at all? Where does the ontological content of this presence lie?

The first indication that this presence is not a matter of psychology but of something far more fundamental and *primordial* is to be found in the fact that it does not rest upon conscious reflection but *precedes* it. When—to use an example offered by Sartre for a different purpose—I have an appointment in a cafe with a friend whose existence matters to me, and on my arrival there I discover that this person is not there, the absent person *precisely by not being there* occupies for me the entire space-time context of the cafe. It is only *after* I reflect consciously on the situation that I realise empirically who 'is' and who 'is not' there. But as I do that a significant distinction emerges between the presence of personal and the presence of a-personal beings.

After my conscious reflection on the situation those who 'are' and those who 'are not' there are not *particular* beings in a personal sense: their identities are established not in communion and freedom but by their own boundaries (as a realist would say) or through those imposed by our own minds (as an idealist would prefer to say). Their presence is compelling for our minds and senses but not for our freedom; they can be turned into things, they can lose their uniqueness and finally be dispensed with. (Those who 'are' in the cafe 'are'—from the point of view of personhood—in the same sense that the chairs 'are' there.) The presence, therefore, of a-personal beings is ultimately demonstrable through mind or sense perception (which allows for them being described, conceived, and finally manipulated or even dispensed with), whereas the presence of persons is ultimately demonstrable through love and freedom.

The implications of this distinction for ontology are extremely important and present Philosophy and Theology with a dilemma they can hardly afford to ignore. For there seem to be two possibilities open to ontology. One is to attribute being to being as such, i.e., to the nature of things, in which case being (and its recognition) emerges as compelling ontologically: presence is ultimately attributed to the very being of a being, to its own nature, that is to say, to something one simply *has to* recognise. In this case ontology operates on the assumption that the world is a *given* datum; it does not raise the radical question of the *beginning* of the world in the radical ontological sense of the possibility of the non-being of what is so obviously— i.e., compellingly there. On the other hand there is the presence of personal beings which is not established on the basis of a *given* 'nature' of the being but of love and freedom: persons can neither be particular – and thus be at all—by way of a nature compelling them to 'be' so, nor be present, i.e., recognised as being there, by compelling us to recognise them. In this case ontology cannot take ultimately for granted the being of any being; it cannot attribute the ultimacy of being to a necessity inherent in the nature of a being; it can only attribute it to freedom and love which thus become ontological notions par excellence. Being in this case owes its being to Personhood and becomes ultimately identical with it.

In so far, therefore, as the human person is an entity whose being or particularity is realised by way of a transcendence of its boundaries in an event of communion, its personhood reveals itself as *presence*. But in so far as the human person is a being whose particularity is established also by its boundaries (a body), personhood realises this presence as *absence*. Since both of these have their focus on one and the same entity, they represent a paradox, the two components of which must be maintained *simultaneously*, if justice is to be done to the mystery of human personhood. For taking the first aspect alone would mean that only bodiless beings can be called persons-which would exclude man from being a person. And taking the second aspect alone would mean that only bodily beings are persons, which would imply that the transcendence of the boundaries of the body is not ontologically constitutive of personhood-hence *all* bodies are actually or potentially persons.

The presence-in-absence paradox is, therefore, inevitable in a consideration of man as person, particularly from the point of view of his capacity to be a creator. A consideration now of the reasons which account for the absence aspect in this capacity of man may help us understand this paradox better.

3. I have been speaking of man's capacity for creation as a movement from thinghood to personhood. This is precisely what we find in a genuine work of Art, as contrasted with technological 'creation' which is realised through the reverse movement. But at this point a hypothesis emerges. Suppose that there are no 'things' to begin with but only 'persons', what happens then to creativity as a movement from 'thinghood to personhood'?

This supposition is compelling for anyone who assumes that a personal being ontologically precedes the world, i.e., of anyone with the Biblical view of creation in mind. It is a sup- position that no Greek philosopher would ever raise. For the Greeks 'being', or the 'world', precedes the '*person*'—hence if we say that God creates we cannot but imply that he creates out of some pre-existing matter. To deny this would imply a denial of the ultimacy of 'being *quâ* being' and give ontological priority to personhood. This is why for the Greeks the world constitutes a *given datum* of ontology: it is because it has always been and will always be. 'Creation' or 'creativity' does not have to do in this case with ontology in a primary sense but with the *formation* of pre-existing matter.

Now it is all too easy to admit *on a doctrinal level* that for a Christian things are different because the world was created *ex nihilo*. But I venture to suggest that unless we admit on a philosophical level that personhood is not secondary to being, that the mode of existence of being is not secondary to its 'substance' but itself primary and constitutive of it, it is impossible to make sense of the doctrine of *creatio ex nihilo*. But this is precisely what Christian theologians would not normally do: even the doctrine of God is based normally on the assumption that God is personal because he *first* 'is' and *then* 'relates'—hence the classical treatment of the doctrine of the Trinity and the problems of intelligibility it has never ceased to present.

The priority of 'being' or 'substance' over against the person, which is a basic Greek idea, seems to have extended its roots well and deep into our minds. And yet without the assumption that personhood is identical with being and prior to thinghood not only the doctrine of creation out of nothing collapses, but what is more directly relevant for our subject, it becomes impossible to explain why there is in all creation the paradoxical structure of presence-in-absence to which I have referred.

The fact that presence in and through personhood is revealed to man in the form of absence constitutes the sign *par excellence* of the creaturely limitation of humanity. The idea of *creatio ex nihilo* was employed by the Fathers in order to oppose the Greek view of a creation of the world out of pre-existing matter. At first sight it may not seem quite clear why this idea is so significant for illustrating the difference between being an uncreated creator and being a creator as creature, but it becomes evident that it is so, as soon as we look at it anthropologically rather than simply and primarily cosmologically and theologically. In this particular case, in which as I have argued the mystery of personhood is at stake, creating out of pre-existing matter implies the distance (*diastema*) due to what we call space and time, i.e. categories indicating a relational event by emphasising simultaneously *unity* and *distance*, i.e. absence and presence, or rather presence-in-absence. The characteristic of creatures, as contrasted with God, lies precisely in this distance which accounts for their multiplicity: creatures are not one, but, taking all together, many and diverse because they are divided up in separated places (Athanasius). The limitation of creaturehood lies in this 'distance' which makes the creatures 'comprehensible' and 'containable' (*chōrēta*). Space and time, when viewed from the angle of the *nature* of creaturehood, are two terms which reveal a relationship of separateness (*chōrismos*) and hence of individualisation; only when they are viewed from the angle of personhood do these terms reveal a relationship of unity (*katholou*) and hence of communion. Thus personhood, when applied strictly to creatures, results in a contradiction between the *katholou* and the *kata meros*. And since personhood affirms the integrity and catholicity of being (cf. *hypostasis*) and must of necessity overcome the distance of individualisation (cf. *ekstasis*), being a person implies, existentially speaking, the frustration of the contradiction between presence and absence. This frustration would not have existed had there not been the spatio-temporal roots of creaturehood, i.e., in the last analysis, *beginning*. Thus the fact that the artist is absent through his personal presence in his work is due primarily to the fact that he has used pre-existing matter, because this means that his personal presence is embodied in something that is already part of the space-time structure which makes it something containable (*chōrēton*) and thus present only by being distant from other things. Had God done the same thing, i.e. used preexisting matter, he would be caught in the same predicament and his presence in his creation would be a presence in absence for him-something that would rule out entirely the possibility of a presence without absence.

4. Similar observations apply to man as an *historical being*. Man's *capacity for history* is not determinable by any substantial qualities of his nature; his capacity for memory is not necessarily a unique characteristic of the human being. It is again personhood that makes man historical and this is to be seen in a way similar to that of the presence of being in terms of space through the creation of Art. Just as in the case of Art human personhood creates 'the beginning of a world' (a presence which is not *causally* determined by the given reality) in the same way history means that the already given in terms of events—the 'past'—does not produce an irresistible causality for man, a necessity such as the one we find in the survival of species or the transformation of various substances or the movement of the stars. The 'events' created by man through history bear the seal of the freedom that is inherent in Personhood.

Presence in terms of space or Art and presence in terms of time or history are *two sides of the same coin*: they refer ultimately to being as freedom and communion and not as a compelling presence. It is this that explains why an ontological term par excellence, namely that of *Parousia* (presence) which has been used here as a key term in connection with creativity and Art, has in Christianity become a technical term to denote an event: the coming of Christ. This would have been inconceivable had it not been for the fact that we cannot properly understand history in an un-ontological way (in terms of man's decisions, consciousness, actions etc.) but only in close connection with the question of being as a whole. History is an ontological matter. The time of history is the same time as that in which natural events occur. The 'future' or the 'eschaton' of history is, therefore, identical with the final incorruptibility of the world, as the Greek Fathers insisted with particular force since Ignatius of Antioch and Irenaeus.

But if this is the case, then the presence-in-absence paradox which I discussed with regard to Art must be applied here, too. The future which is offered by history, like the presence offered by Art, is subject to the antinomy of its negation, to the threat of nothingness. It is this antinomy that accounts for man's fear of the future and which finds its resolution only in *hope* as a distinctive characteristic of personhood related inseparably with love and freedom. This antinomy is due to creaturehood and makes man tragically conscious of a past which is present only in the form of absence and of a future threatened by nothingness. The consciousness of *transience* which accompanies man's historical existence is part of this picture. Thus, becoming implies for man *passion* (*pathos*), due to the fact that creaturehood, taken in itself, has its being rooted in beginning and thus under the constant threat of nothingness, as a presence-in-absence, and therefore its becoming in time reveals being in the form of *change* and *decay*, i.e. threatened by death. The ekstasis of personhood implies a certain kind of 'movement', but for the creature this is realised in the form of pathos whereas for God's Personhood whose being is not threatened by decay and death—ekstasis is *impassible* (*apathēs*; the doctrine of the impassibility of God acquires, in this way, a meaning which does not contradict the ekstatic and creative love of God, both within and without space and time). Man's ekstasis of personhood cannot be impassible in itself, but only in God; passibility is part of creaturehood, yet something that personhood tends to find unacceptable through ekstasis.

The presence-in-absence paradox, therefore, shows that personal presence *quâ presence* is something that *cannot be extrapolated from created existence*. It is a presence that seems to come to us from outside this world—which makes the notion of Person, if properly understood, perhaps the only notion that can be applied to God without the danger of anthropomorphism. Man-especially, though not exclusively, through Art and history-creates a 'presence', thus showing that he is a person. The significance of Art (obviously the reference here is made not to those so-called artists who simply copy things or nature in a more or less photographic fashion) lies in that it shows that Man as a person is not content with the presence of beings as they are given to him in the world. In a Godlike fashion he wants to recognise beings not 'according to their own nature', i.e., according to their compelling givenness, but as 'results of his own free will'—as *idia thēlemata*, to recall Maximus the Confessor. In this he succeeds, yet only, as we saw, in the form of the tragic paradox of presence-in-absence. This in itself is very significant. For it means that Personhood prefers to create its presence as absence rather than be contained, comprehended, described and manipulated through the circumscribability and individualization which are inherent in all creaturehood. Personhood thus proves to be *in* this world—through man—but not *of* this world.

All this means that the ekstatic movement towards communion which is part of personhood, remains for man an unfulfilled longing for a presence-without-absence of being as long as there is no way of overcoming the space-time limitations of creaturehood. This situation implies that there is no possibility of a creature developing into something of an 'uncreated' being, and there is nothing that shows this more dramatically than this 'capacity-in-incapacity' which is implied in human personhood. At the same time this reveals that there is a future, an *eschaton* or a *telos*, a final goal in creation, which must resolve the problem created by personhood.

This is not a kind of wishful thinking but an ingredient of personhood as fundamental—indeed as constitutive—as that of presence for the notion of being. For if there is ultimately no personal presence without absence, then there is no personal presence at all. The very use of the word 'presence' becomes then arbitrary and in the end meaningless. Those, therefore, who, like the atheistic existentialists, do not wish to admit any ontology of pure presence, which would force them to go beyond the actual human situation, will have to answer the question of the meaning of the word presence in the presence-in-absence paradox. For it is of course true that in actual human existence the two categories, presence and absence, are inseparably linked when applied to personhood. But unless there is something like an 'outside-the-actual-human-existence' in which both of these words point to something 'real', then they make no sense in this context either—they represent inventions of the most arbitrary kind. For where have we got the category of presence from, when we apply it to personhood? Is it an extrapolation or an analogy from the experience of the presence of objects as they are observed and recognised through our senses or minds? But the presence of which we are talking in the case of personhood is the very opposite of this experience: in terms of this experience presence in this case is, as we have seen, absence. It is, therefore, impossible to regard the experience of the actual world as the source of the category of presence in the paradox presence-in-absence. And if that is the case, then there are only two alternatives before us. Either what we call presence is an arbitrary use of a category which in this case bears no ontological significance whatsoever and which will prove the empiricist right in calling this kind of presence sheer fantasy. Or if we wish to disagree with the empiricist and attach an ontological significance to the presence of the presence-in-absence paradox, we shall have to admit that presence in this case points to an ontology which does not ultimately depend on the experience of this world. Those who accept this paradox as pointing authentically and ontologically to personal existence are not as far as they may think from an implicit assumption of God.

5. This shows that man has a capacity (in incapacity) *for faith*. Thanks to his ekstatic personhood man confronts nothingness not as a sort of an acceptable 'nirvana', but as a *painful absence* which makes him long for presence. The fact that this absence remains unacceptable to man is due to his personhood which drives him towards communion, and this is what makes faith a possibility for him: *he is confident in presence in spite of absence*. Thus, a man who escapes from the open confrontation with the threat of non-existence with the help of various securities (ideals, ethics etc.) is closer to faithlessness than the one who—to remember the Dostoyevskian scene of Christ's confrontation with the Grand Inquisitor—has no objectified security to rely upon. For a person who has become indifferent to the problem of existence has made a decisive step towards thinghood, and things are incapable of faith.

6. All this 'longing for communion' may sound as if it were a matter of psychology rather than ontology. Although what has already been said about the ontological content of the notion of 'presence' ought to be enough to warn the reader against such a misunderstanding, the ontological point will become clearer when we apply the presence-absence scheme to an area in which human incapacity reveals itself in the most tragic manner, namely *death*. Death appears to be the most tragic event of human life only if man is viewed from the angle of his personhood. To a biologist, death may be a form of life, and to an idealist a meaningful sacrifice of the individual for a higher cause, but to Christian theology it remains the worst enemy of man, the most unacceptable of all things. This cry against death, which is so deeply rooted in us, precedes our cognitive activity and even our consciousness in that it constitutes our primary and ultimate fear, expressed or hidden, the condition of all that we do. It is for this reason that the fear of death is not just a matter of psychology but of ontology; it is the threatening of being with non-being, the possibility that Personhood may be turned into thinghood. The absence that death brings is the absence that threatens presence, as we tried to describe it here. Creativity and Art are thus the Person's defence against death and at the same time his taste of death, as this creativity leads to a presence-in-absence.

Now, death has always been associated with matter and body. In a substantialistic approach to man this fact has led to the idea that there is something like a soul or spirit which possesses *in its nature* a capacity for immortality. The difficulties that this view implies hardly need to be mentioned, and it would suffice to underline that this idea of a natural immortality of the soul is not only unbiblical, but it can hardly explain man's fear of death, as we described it a little while ago. Only if we associate being with its 'mode of being', i.e. Person as the bearer of being, can we make any ontological sense out of this unacceptability of death. It is at this point that the association of death with the body becomes evident.

The body of man is not a *part* of his being in the sense of a bipartite or tripartite division of man to which, in various forms, a substantialistic approach to the human phenomenon has led theology (in sharp contrast to the position of modern medicine and psychology). The body is an *inseparable aspect of the human Person* and for this reason it is regarded as partaking of the *Imago Dei* (for example, by the Greek Fathers). The strong belief in the resurrection of *the body* which goes back to the beginnings of Christianity can make sense only in such an approach.

Now, if the body is associated with the person as an organic part of the mode in which the person realises the presence of man in the event of communion, it is evident that the presence—*in-absence* which is part of the predicament of creaturehood should be experienced in the body *par excellence*: the body becomes the existential reminder of our creaturehood in the double sense we observed in the example of Art, i.e. by being the mode by which man is as a *presence* through his ekstasis towards communion (hence the erotic movement of man is also a matter of the body), but at the same time by emphasising the absence of being through death.

All this means that the overcoming of death represents a longing rooted in the personhood of man. It also means that this overcoming is a matter of turning the presence-in-absence of being into presence-without-absence and this is not a matter of inherent capabilities of a 'substantial' character but of *personal communion*. The agony of nothingness which accompanies existence calls basically for communion. Death shows created existence to be suspended in the void because communion which sustains existence seems to be exhausted or rather negated by the limits of creaturehood. Man was not created immortal, but by having his personhood he was made capable of communion with the immortal God. Death came to him not as a punishment in a juridical sense but as an existential consequence of the break of this communion; it came at the moment that man became introverted, and limited the ekstatic movement of his personhood to the created world.

Sin, therefore, entered as *idolatry*, i.e. as an ekstasis of communion with the created world alone. In this way, what sin did was of deep ontological significance: it made the limitation of creaturehood show itself in the existential contrast between being and nothingness. This contrast appeared inevitably as soon as created existence affirmed itself through communion within the created realm. The possibility of communion was thus preserved only in order to make the longing for communion even stronger and to emphasise the absence of Being in every presence, i.e. the absence of God which ultimately means death. The *Imago Dei*, i.e. man's personhood, was both preserved and destroyed: the presence-in-absence structure of human existence testifies to this paradox. Man can pervert his personhood but he cannot eliminate it entirely. This possibility of perversion can be illustrated by some fundamental results of the Fall which have a direct relationship to man's capacity and incapacity as a person, while the inability to eliminate personhood entirely is to be seen in the existence of human freedom. We shall have to devote a few lines to each of these items as they represent basic aspects of our subject.

7. If we try to understand the way in which human person- hood becomes perverted through the Fall, the following points may serve as illustrations:

(a). The ekstasis of personhood becomes in the fallen situation experienced as apo-stasis (distance) between person and nature. As was explained earlier, by being person man was meant to offer to creation the possibility of hypostatic catholicity, i.e. the fulfilment of nature's ultimate reference to Being, a fulfilment which would take place as a unity respecting the integrity and diversity (*diaphora*) of beings. This would allow man the unique honour of being the *priest of creation*, i.e. the one in and through whom creation would be *referred back* (*anaphora*) to the Creator. But the fall of man destroys this possibility precisely because man's ekstatic movement, by being limited to creation does not allow for the catholicity of creation or nature to be ekstatic towards what is external to it in and through the human person, since the latter, by his introversion has lost his true ekstatic movement towards 'outside' creation, i.e. towards the Creator. This not only explains why 'the whole created universe groans in all its parts' (Rom. 8.22) awaiting our salvation, but at the same time it throws light on the actuality of human existence itself. For the inability of human person- hood to be ekstatic towards what is outside creation and thus to unite nature in personhood, leads to the fragmentation of nature and hence to an individualisation of beings: each being acquires its identity not through the hypostatic differentiation which emerges from communion, but through its affirmation in contrast and opposition to the other beings. Difference becomes division1and person becomes individual, i.e. an entity affirmed by way of contrast to rather than of communion with other entities. Thus 'the other' becomes an existential contrast to one's self, 'my hell' and 'my original sin' (Sartre). Human nature becomes through procreation individualised by bringing forth beings as individuals; its ekstatic movement does not produce diversity in unity, but in division. Fragmentation and individualisation is the price that nature pays for man's intro- version. It is also the very basis of death.

(b) A fundamental consequence of this is to be seen in man's capacity for knowledge. As was stressed earlier in this paper, by being person man recognises being as a 'presence' in an event of communion in which things are 'present' in their catholicity and integrity as beings. Knowing emerges in this way only out of loving: love and truth become identical. But this can be possible only if nature and person are not in a relation of opposition, i.e. as long as the division into distanced individual beings has not taken place. But the fallen state of creation with its implication of individuality inevitably results in a distance of contrast between beings (cf. previous paragraph (a)), which makes knowing receive temporal priority over loving: in order to relate in communion (= love) I must first relate by way of contrast, since 'the other' being poses its identity to me only as an individual, i.e. a being defined by its contrast to myself. Knowing, therefore, begins, inevitably, in this situation, with a process of gathering information about the other being, i.e. by subjecting it to my observation which will lead to a description (establishing characteristics) and evaluation (establishing qualities and value) of this being. And since this can only happen by way of relating all this to what I already know through a rational process, my first step towards communion with the other being, takes place in my rational capacity. One can love only what one knows, since love comes from knowledge, we are told by Thomas Aquinas - except that this is our fallen situation and should not become part of our metaphysical anthropology and even more so of our approach to Trinitarian theology, as was the case with Thomas. From all this the step towards understanding man's capacity for knowledge in terms of 'com-prehension', 'conception', etc. of reality is as inevitable as its repercussions for human life, or even for the life of nature as a whole.

This dichotomy between love and knowledge implies a distance not only between person and nature but also between thought and action within the human being itself. Once the possibility of knowledge arises as independent of and prior to the act of communion (love) with the other being, it becomes possible for man to dissociate his thought from his act and thus falsify the event of truth. Thus man can become a hypocrite, and it is indeed only the human being that is capable of hypocrisy.

This cannot be explained except through this perversion of personhood which provides for the distance between thought and action. In the situation of fallen personhood truth no longer appears as we described it earlier, namely as the outcome of an event of communion in which man takes part, but as a possession of the individual thinking agent who disposes of it as he wishes. Needless to say Truth cannot really arise in such a situation; and yet the paradox is that man can, so to say, deep in himself, be aware of what the Truth is, but dissociate it from his act. The distance between thought and action helps hypocrisy to arise, and this is only part of the general state of individualisation to which reference was made under (a) earlier. Since the 'other' becomes a threat to 'myself' (Sartre) in a fallen state of existence in which difference becomes division, 'myself' needs to be protected from the 'intruder' of my individuality. Hypocrisy serves as a perverted way out, when the ekstasis of personhood drives us towards communion as the event of truth.

8. Now all these examples show that personhood may appear to be perverted in a fallen state of existence but not entirely extinguished. The fact that the illustrations just given apply to the human being par excellence, if not exclusively, indicates this, for it is only the human being that possesses this perverted personhood in which the longing for the real and full personal communion is tragically present. But the preservation of personhood in the most paradoxical form of its extreme self-denial is to be seen in human freedom.

Freedom is an essential part of the *Imago Dei*, for without it man could not be in any way like God, since he would have to be governed by necessity (Gregory of Nyssa). In the fallen state of existence which is characterised by the dialectic of good and evil, freedom has come to signify the possibility of choice between two things, and thus it has acquired a rather ethical significance. But the primary and true meaning of freedom is to be found in its ontological content to which I referred in some detail earlier.

That freedom represents such an ultimate existential possibility is to be seen precisely in the fact that one is free not simply to choose between two things—there is nothing existentially ultimate about that—but to refuse his existence: this is the proof of the fact of freedom. Man is thus free to refuse his personhood, i.e. the difference between person and nature: he can choose to become a thing.

That this is the main issue behind the fall of man, is precisely what I have been trying to say in this paper. Man by his fall chooses to sacrifice his personhood by individualising his existence in the manner of the division and fragmentation of thinghood. Yet, in saying this, I have also noted that this individualisation does not eliminate the personal dimension of longing for communion, and a similar thing is to be noted with regard to freedom. Freedom was given to man as a dimension of personhood, in order that the essential or natural difference between God and creation would not become distance and division (*diairesis*), but, on the contrary, a realisation of communion between the two. In creating man as a person God had in mind communion, and freedom was the only way to this. With man's choice to introvert the ekstatic movement of his personhood towards himself and creation, the ontological difference between Creator and creatures was affirmed as a gap, i.e. not as difference, but as division, and man became enslaved to nature. Freedom led to slavery, but paradoxically enough, like the ekstatic tendency of personhood to which I referred earlier, it did not disappear. How does this appear in human existence? This problem lies behind the very essence of the question of human capacity and incapacity, and I have not yet found anyone who grasped this in all its fullness and acuteness better than Dostoevsky. I should like therefore to refer to him rather extensively at this point.

In the writings of Dostoevsky the problem of freedom is presented in the form of two extremes. On the one hand man still, deep in his heart, wants to feel so independent that he wishes to be free not only to create but also to destroy. Reasonableness and harmony are not his ultimate goals in existence; those who assume this are rebuked bluntly by Dostoevsky: 'Where then have all these wiseacres found that man's will should primarily be normal and virtuous? Why have they imagined that man needs a will directed towards reason and his own benefit? All he needs is an independent will, whatever it may cost him, and wherever it may lead him. . . .' (*Letters from the Underworld.*) This is the moral that follows from the words of the hero of these Letters after describing the order which humanity could achieve through its culture and civilisation: 'I should not be surprised if amidst all this order and regularity of the future there should suddenly arise some common-faced or rather cynical and sneering gentleman who, with his arms akimbo, will say to us: "Now then, you fellows, what about smashing all this order to bits, sending their logarithms to the devil and living according to our own silly will?". That might not be much, but the annoying thing is that he would immediately get plenty of followers.'[1] Dostoevsky did not live long enough to see this very thing happen in the two world wars which confirmed so tragically his insight into the human being.

But this is only the one extreme in which freedom survives in man. The other is seen by Dostoevsky to exist in the form of man's deep longing for suffering: 'I am sure that man will never renounce genuine suffering even if it brings him ruin and chaos'. The reason for this is that 'suffering is the one and only source of true knowledge; adversity is the mainspring of self-realisation'. This interpretation of freedom in terms of suffering, on which Dostoevsky insists throughout his works, reveals the mystery of freedom as the capacity of man to embrace fully his incapacity, i.e. as his ability to turn weakness into strength or rather to realise his power in weakness. This paradox is nothing else but what Paul means when he writes in 2 Cor. 12.10 after mentioning his full acceptance of suffering: 'for when I am weak, I am strong'. Human freedom, in its true meaning, abolishes the scheme 'capacity versus incapacity' and replaces it with the paradox of 'capacity in incapacity'. In the light of this, the approach to human capacity and incapacity as concrete endowments and possessions of human nature is shown once more to be wrong. Man in his freedom appears to deny any natural possession, any capacity-only by so doing he proves fully that he is free, and thus shows himself to be capable of something that no impersonal creature has. It is this kind of freedom that the Grand Inquisitor in Dostoevsky's Brothers Karamazov cannot forgive to Christ who stands before him having—and offering men—nothing, no worldly or religious security, but 'freedom'.

Man's capacity willingly to embrace suffering to the utmost point shows that even in the slavery of his fallen state he remains a person, though an unhappy one. Just as by frankly facing absence man becomes capable of faith in presence, in the same way by facing suffering and not turning away from it with the help of various 'securities', man affirms his freedom in a negative way. This is no romanticising of suffering as there is no idealisation of absence and death; these are man's worst enemies. But the important thing in human existence is that the only way to abolish these things, the only way to conquer them, is freedom, and this implies freedom to undergo them. The Cross is the only way to the Resurrection, and this does not take away from the Cross its utter shame and repulsiveness. Now, the most paradoxical thing that lies in the fact of freedom is that man cannot 'free himself' from it—if he wanted to do so—unless he extinguishes himself completely. This makes Sartre's words 'man is condemned to be free' sound quite true. For the alternative which freedom poses for man's existence lies between accepting existence as a whole as some- thing of which man freely partakes, or making existence something which man controls himself. The world as it is given to us tempts man's personhood to disregard or even destroy it and in a God-like fashion create it, as it were, anew. This is inherent in personhood as part of the ontological ultimacy which, as we have seen, is implied in it. Indeed, if personhood is to be regarded as being of this world, it becomes demonic, tending towards the negation of the given world. Hence evil, which in its ultimacy aims at such a destructive negation of the given world cannot but be personal, for only a person, as we described personhood here, can move towards the annihilation of the existent. Art, for example, being a distinctive characteristic of human personhood, by denying or even destroying all forms of the given reality can also do that (as we can observe in many forms of modern art which, not insignificantly, have emerged at a time when personhood and freedom have become predominant notions in our culture). This is genuine, though demonic, personhood. Genuine because, as I said earlier, it is part of personhood to recognise beings not as compelling realities but as *idia thelemata*, and demonic because in fact the world is not man's *idion thelema*—it exists independently of his choice-and therefore human freedom can prove itself ultimately only through the annihilation of what exists. If personhood in all its ontological implications were to be extrapolated from this world as something belonging to it so to say 'naturally' or even 'analogically' then we could be sure that this world, i.e., this given presence of being, would not exist-and man being himself 'given' would not exist either. Personhood, understood in its terrifying ontological ultimacy to which I have tried to point in this paper, leads to God-or to non-existence. To recall the words of Kirilov in Dostoevsky's *The Possessed*, 'Every one who wants to attain complete freedom must be daring enough to kill himself . . . . This is the final limit of freedom, that is all, there is nothing beyond it. Who dares to kill himself becomes God. Everyone can do this and thus cause God to cease to exist, and then nothing will exist at all'. But the world continues to exist in spite of man's ability to opt for nonexistence. Freedom thus is shown to be ultimately not a matter of decision: its ontological content lies beyond the concept of choice, it is indeed incompatible with it. As long, of course, as non-being appears to threaten being or even to condition it, non-existence will appear to be a possibility, a sort of an alternative or choice (man, for example, may reach a point of destroying creation and signs of that are already filling us with horror). As long as death goes on, Evil will tempt us to opt for the demonic, as if it were an ultimate possibility (as long as it is, for example, possible for someone to die the temptation for killing him will be there for us). If, therefore, ontology depends on the observation of this world, if our metaphysics is nothing but 'descriptive', being is ultimately just as much of a possibility as non-being. But will death go on forever? This will depend on whether metaphysics is 'descriptive' or, in terms of what I have been saying here, 'ekstatic'. It will depend on whether being de- pends ultimately on its own nature or on love which is 'as strong as death'. The ontology of personhood is the key to the answer of the question whether being is in any sense ultimate or not. Freedom, therefore, appears to present man with 'two' ultimate possibilities: either to annihilate the 'given' or to accept it as *idion thelema*. But because in fact the world is not man's *thelema*, if he is still to maintain his freedom in accepting the world he can do this only by identifying his own will with that of God. Is that conceivable? Christianity throughout the centuries has tried to conceive this in terms of obedience of man to God. It has failed because it has been unable to maintain freedom in and through this obedience. Man has felt like a slave and rejected the yoke of God. Atheism sprang out of the very heart of the Church and the notion of freedom became prominent again. There is more than 'obedience', or rather something quite different from it, that is needed to bring man to a state of existence in which freedom is not a choice among many possibilities but a movement of love. This state obviously can only be realised from outside human existence. The whole of Christian doctrine ought to be precisely about this.

* * * *

V

If we now try to summarise the views presented in this paper with particular reference to the classical theological debate concerning human capacity and human incapacity, the following points seem to emerge as the most basic ones.

(a) Methodologically, the issue under discussion cannot be decided on the basis of human nature as such. The phenomenon of man escapes all substantialist definitions. The borderline of human capacity and incapacity lies only in God himself. Hence the issue can be decided on the level not of nature but of relationship, i.e. of personhood. Human capacity and incapacity are revealed only in the way man relates to God and the rest of creation.

In speaking of the human nature, therefore, Chalcedonian Christology is not to be understood as implying that human nature per se is an indication of humanity. No, the humanity which is revealed in and through Christ is not a humanity which is ultimately defined in terms of its nature as such; it is true and real humanity only because it is constituted in and through personhood; it is 'hypostatic' in being 'ekstatic', i.e. free from its 'natural' boundaries and united in communion with God.

The anthropology of Chalcedon would be entirely misunderstood if humanity were to be defined a priori, outside the 'hypostatic union', as if the phenomenon of man could be conceived in itself. This misunderstanding has in fact occurred and continues to occur, accounting for the actual problematic of the Christological question. The anthropology of Chalcedon depends entirely on the notion of personhood as I tried to describe it here: man emerges as truly man, as a category distinct both from God and the animals, only in relation to God. For Chalcedon the equation 'man = man' is unacceptable; it is that of 'man = man-in-communion-with-God' that emerges from its Christology. The first equation corresponds to the ontology and the logic of the 'self-existent'; the second one is 'logically' conceivable only if what has been said here about the ontology of personhood is accepted.

(b) The debate whether man is in his nature *capax Dei* (or *infiniti*) or not, in this way becomes irrelevant and extremely misleading. For it stabilises the states of capacity and incapacity on the permanency of naturehood. Instead of this, an approach to man via personhood, with all that this implies, reveals that capacity and incapacity are not to be opposed to each other but to be included in each other. Only the scheme *capacity-in-incapacity* does justice to the mystery of man.

(c) The highest form of capacity for man is to be found in the notion of *Imago Dei*. Yet, if this notion is put in the light of personhood rather than nature, it has to be modified, for what it in fact means is not that man can become God in his 'nature', but can be in communion with God. The word Dei in this expression does not imply a Deistic view of God but a Trinitarian one: man can himself live the event of communion which is realised in divine life and he can do this with and for the entire creation; he is in fact made as *Imago Trinitatis*, and this is possible for him only because of his ability to be a *person*.

(d) Looked upon from the angle of personhood man reveals his creaturehood in a way of *difference* and not *division* from God. Only through personhood, which implies communion as well as the integrity of being, can God and man be clearly distinguished from each other, precisely by affirming their distinct identities in communion. Any *a priori* juxtaposition of divine and human natures is part of the individualisation which results from the Fall and which is overcome in Christ who unites God and man in a communion that poses clearly the identity of each nature.

(e) The division and individualisation of natures, which results from the break of communion and the distortion of personhood in the fall, poses the relation between man and God as one of presence-in-absence. Creaturehood, in this way tragically reveals its natural limitations of space and time in the form of absence, especially through death which signifies human incapacity *par excellence*. Christ as the man, by restoring the communion of natures in and through his *personhood*, turns the created realm into a presence of God. The world acquires thus its ekstatic catholicity as it is lifted up to communion with God through man.

(f) Thus, the overall relationship between God and the world ('two realities or one?') is determined by the distinction, suggested by Maximus the Confessor, between difference and division. This can make sense only through personhood as the *Imago Dei* by means of which God has willed his world to relate to himself in communion. Juxtaposing *a priori* the world to God goes against the very heart of Christology, since Christ realises the unity of God and the world, through man, in communion. The issue of human capacity and incapacity serves as a significant illustration of this when it ceases to represent a dilemma. In communion with God man is capable of everything (Mark 9.23; Phil. 4.13 etc.) though only in the incapacity of creaturehood which poses itself clearly in such a communion. Thus the conclusion brings with it the echo of Paul's words: 'when I am weak I am strong' (2 Cor. 12.10).

Questions

1 What, in Zizioulas' view, is the "fundamental methodological problem" for theology's attempt to understand human being? What hope is there, if any, for a theological anthropology?

2 What does Zizioulas mean by "openness of being," or "*ek-stasis* of being"? How does that make "personhood" distinct from "personality"?

3 What is "freedom in an ontological sense" and why does Zizioulas think it is necessary for ontological identity?

4 Why is the human capacity for creation a "movement from thinghood to personhood"? Do you agree with Zizioulas' reasoning?

5 What is the "presence-in-absence" paradox? How does Zizioulas relate it to personhood?

6 Under what circumstances might personhood decline into thinghood?

7 Can you trace the influence of existential thinkers on Zizioulas' thought?

8 What does Zizioulas mean by conception of personhood, and what is the role of faith in his conception of personhood?

9 How does Zizioulas relate Christology and Pneumatology to personhood in the latter part of his article?

TEXT 2: HARRIET A. HARRIS, "SHOULD WE SAY THAT PERSONHOOD IS RELATIONAL?"[2]

Harriet A. Harris (b. 1968) is currently serving as the University chaplain and head of the Chaplaincy Service at the University of Edinburgh. She is a priest in the Scottish Episcopal Church and convenes the Doctrine Committee of that denomination. Her early work was a critical study of Fundamentalism and Evangelicalism. In this article, Harris challenges the prevailing fashion, led by theologians such as John Zizioulas and Alistair I. McFadyen among others, to consider personhood through the lens of relationality. In particular, she is concerned as a feminist that this consigns women to the prison of the roles set for them by men.

A current emphasis in theological anthropology is that we become persons through our relations to others. Ethically valuable and pastorally illuminating insights that as persons we develop in relation to others have been used wrongly to underpin the claim that personhood is relational - a claim which is logically confused and ethically precarious. Alistair I. McFadyen, whose book *The Call to Personhood* has been influential in this respect, describes personhood as the 'sedimentation' of interpersonal relations.[3] Elaine L. Graham places the stress on cultural interaction as a prerequisite for the development of beings into persons. In her study of gender and personhood, *Making the Difference*, Graham argues that her 'relational' account of gender is 'suggestive of a model of human nature as profoundly relational, requiring the agency of culture to bring our personhood fully into being'.[4] The potential ethical danger behind a view of personhood as relational is apparent from statements made by Vincent Brummer in his volume *The Model of Love*, to the effect that 'both our identity and our value as persons is constituted by our relations of fellowship with others'.[5]

I would like to ask three sets of questions about such statements, and have divided this paper into three parts accordingly.

I. Are they really about personhood? Are they even about personal identity? Or are they about concepts of personhood, a sense of oneself as a person, and self-esteem?

II. If personhood is relational between what are relationships formed out of which persons come into being?

III. Should we prescribe a relational concept of personhood, or will this undermine the personhood of people who cannot form relationships, cannot sustain healthy relationships, or who are not valued in their relationships?

Part I calls for clarity of concepts. Parts II and III ask respectively about the ontological and normative implications of the claim that personhood is relational.

---

[2]Harriet A. Harris, "Should We Say That Personhood Is Relational?" *Scottish Journal of Theology* 51.2 (1998): 214–34.
[3]*The Call to Personhood: A Christian Theory of the Individual in Social Relationships* (Cambridge: CUP, 1990), passim.
[4]*Making the Difference: Gender, Personhood and Theology* (London: Mowbray, 1995), 223.
[5]*'The Model of Love: A Study in Philosophical Theology* (Cambridge: CUP, 1993), 235.

I Should we say that personhood is relational?

****

Current emphases upon our relationality are in part a rejection of assumptions that our personal development is primarily linguistic or 'rational', such that the individual is first established and then becomes liable to influences from outside. Philosophical encouragement to move away from this picture comes partly from existentialist emphases on being-in-the-world and becoming as central aspects of personality, and from Wittgenstein's reminder to us that we are bodily and communal beings. Also, theologians have been grappling with psychological and sociological accounts of how human beings develop an awareness of themselves as persons. Feminist theologians, in particular, bring to theology a critique of excessively linguistic conceptions of our development, and atomistic, asocial, disembodied portrayals of the self.

There are numerous forms of analysis one might use in thinking about personhood, and numerous concepts of personhood are available. One might see the issue in terms of choosing between materialist, idealist or dualist philosophies, as does Richard Swinburne, or one might take instead a 'Personalist' or existentialist approach following Buber or Sartre, or a narrative approach like Paul Ricoeur's, or one might begin elsewhere in social psychology as does McFadyen—to mention options most commonly taken up in recent theology. The purpose of this paper is not so much to promote one approach over another as to draw attention to problems that arise when various philosophical and social scientific influences are combined in such a way that the concepts employed lose their clarity.

McFadyen merges several concepts together: 'persons have to be understood in social terms—if only because they are somehow the product of their relations. Individuality, personhood and selfhood do not refer to some internal and independent source of identity, but to the way one is and has been in relation. If it is the case that our personal identities are moulded through our relationships, then there must be some connection between the quality of those relationships and that of our personhood' (p. 18). Later his argument is about 'the sense of oneself as a subject' which he says is 'not individually but socially acquired' (p. 70). A frequently occurring problem in McFadyen's work and elsewhere is that discussions about personality or about the sense of one's self are treated as discussions about personhood (what it is to be a person) and about personal identity (what it is to be the same person over time). Strange implications follow, such as that personal identity is refashioned whenever personality and self-understanding change, or that personhood is itself vulnerable to change and might in fact fail to be established.

Personal identity

The confusion is most apparent in discussions of personal identity. It is helpful to distinguish two kinds of identity: qualitative identity and numerical identity. Qualitative identity holds between two or more entities or states which are exactly similar, such as DNA molecules which are perfectly replicated within each chromosome in my body cells, or such as my mood now and my mood a split second ago (if my mood has remained wholly constant). Numerical identity picks out that which is one and the same. It is a one-one reflexive relation: this article is identical with itself; I am identical with myself. This article remains numerically identical with itself (it is one and the same article) while I alter it qualitatively by adding words to it and moving its paragraphs around. I remain numerically identical with myself through my various changes of mood. It would make sense to say 'she has not been the same person since finding religion ', because both types of identity are at play in this claim.

She, the (numerically) same person, is not now (qualitatively) the same person. It is usual to talk of a qualitative change in someone as a change in their personality.

Discussions of personal identity are most commonly discussions of numerical identity, where the term identity is properly applied to that which stays the same through time. McFadyen complicates the term. He speaks of 'the determination of personal identity through relation' (p. 17). If personal identity is established through relation to other persons, then identity is not a one-one relation because a factor in my being the same person today as I was yesterday would be how I relate to those around me. Let us try an analogous proposal: a factor in this article being the same today as it was yesterday is how it relates to other articles, for example, whether new articles are written which agree or disagree with it. This proposal is invalid, because clearly an article remains identical with itself regardless of any comeback. It might be said, however, that persons differ from articles in ways which significantly affect the question of identity. This article is not able to bring about changes within itself whereas persons do change within and of themselves in response to appraisal or to new events, even if the changes are subconscious, reflexive reactions. However, this difference between articles and persons is relevant to qualitative rather than to numerical identity. This article will not change qualitatively unless I do more work on it. Persons can change qualitatively within and of themselves, but in changing themselves their numerical identity is unchanged.

McFadyen attempts to incorporate both qualitative and numerical identity within his definition of personal identity. He defines personal identity, partly, as 'the way in which one exists 'in', to, for and with others' (p. 317). The term 'personality' would be more suitable here. 'Personality' refers to certain qualities of a person. If a particular person 's personality changes, for example, in becoming compassionate where he had previously been detached in his relationships, then qualitative identity no longer holds. Changes in personality, however, do not affect the numerical identity of that person. McFadyen also wants to insist on the 'continuity' of 'the same person in different times and places' (p. 317), which is a matter of numerical identity. He cannot have it both ways. If the term personal identity is used to refer to an individual's 'way of. ..relating' (p. 317) it is associated with growth and change. It cannot then also be used to refer to that which remains constant in a person throughout these changes.

The problem is exacerbated by McFadyen's central metaphor for personal identity: 'a compounded sedimentation of a significant history of interaction' (p. 317). Personal identity is depicted as the latest product of a history of relatedness. It must therefore be different at each new stage in that history. This is unfortunate, for personal identity is one thing which is not made sense of by this metaphor. We could describe one's character or personality, and one's sense of oneself (even one's sense of oneself as a person) as sediment from a history of interaction. My present character is shaped by all my experiences and relations up until now. My sense of myself is affected by the affirming and discouraging reactions I have received from others, and may change during the course of twenty-four hours. My sense of myself as a person (my belief that I am a person, and my corresponding view of person hood) is more stable, learned from infancy and through the filter of my culture, and affected by the philosophy, theology and psychology that I have read. My personal identity is affected by none of these things, but is found in that history of interaction or line of continuity. It cannot be, as McFadyen would have it, both 'a dynamic line of continuity' and the way one exists in relation to others (p. 317), for if it is a line of continuity it is that regardless of relations to others, and if it is a way of being for others there is no logical reason why it should be continuous.

****

We would speak most clearly if we reserved the term 'personal identity' for what is involved in the continued existence of a person over time.[22] We need then to ask, 'what is it that is continuous with itself?', or 'what is it that enjoys a history of interaction?'. These questions tend not to be pushed when personhood is described as relational. I suspect such questions are avoided because the answers will bring back those criteria which relational accounts wish to de-emphasise, notably bodily or psychological continuity. We know that relationality is not a condition of bodily or psychological continuity. (That relations aid physical and mental health and longevity is a different matter.) A body and a psyche can have temporal continuity without the being to whom they are attached having personal relations, let alone continuity in their personal relations.

The idea rejected in relational accounts is that everyone is a person simply by virtue of his or her constitution as a human being, although this is probably the safest account we can give of human persons both descriptively and prescriptively! McFadyen argues instead that socially we learn to think of ourselves as persons (pp. 69–70). His mistake lies at the heart of relational accounts here considered. He treats claims that we learn through social interaction to regard ourselves as persons, as statements about personal identity in flux or the relationality of person hood. The claims are really about psychological and social processes that we go through on route to developing an inner, 'personal' integration and to regarding ourselves as separate individuals.

We do not want to say that a different personal identity is established every time one's personality changes or one's sense of self receives affirmation or misrecognition. Theologians must therefore formulate a more sophisticated view of personal identity and perhaps not follow sociologists whom, Ralph Ruddock argued in the 1970s, have 'much too simple a view of the identity problem – the view that one changes one's identity, as one might change one's clothes, with every change of role'. Without continuity of personal identity how can I make sense of 'my feeling uncomfortable with myself' or 'disappointed with myself'? I hope that I remain the same person while my understanding and assessment of myself fluctuate. And I hope to benefit from new relationships rather than be replaced by some newly constituted person.

More seriously, morally we want to affirm the possibility of personal development and moral growth. We therefore need persons to remain continuous throughout these changes. This is also necessary theologically if we are to have a concept of redemption, especially if redemption is achieved through transformed relations. McFadyen describes redemption as 'the re-creation and reconstitution of the same person as a person (i.e. free and responsible subject)' (p. 72). But what is it that stays the same if personhood and personal identity are relational and if redemption occurs through transformed relations?

The underlying problem in all of the relational accounts considered here is failure to attend to how notions of personal development which have been informed by social science should relate to notions of personhood which are intended to be normative or ontological. Psychologists and sociologists are not in the business of providing normative concepts to inform moral reasoning, nor are they so concerned with finding an ontological basis for their concepts as are theologians and ethicists. If we fail to realise this then we are in danger of collapsing a psychological or even a moral judgement about someone's self-development into an assessment of their ontological status as a person, as though it would make sense to attribute only a limited degree of personhood to someone who has not been properly nurtured in community or who has difficulty in relating to others.

II Should we say that personhood is relational?

If, as McFadyen proposes, 'God uses the relational processes through which we are formed as persons for our redemptive reconstitution' (p. 71), it must be the case in a culturally transcendent way that there is something about personhood which flourishes through healthy relations. Indeed, McFadyen speaks of an 'ontological structure of human being as relational and responsible' which he calls the vertical divine image (p. 22). We are created as being-in-relation. This is our ontological nature and we cannot change it, though we can chose how we respond to God (and to others) (p. 22). McFadyen grants ontological status to human being which (although he does not explicitly say so) is irrespective of the actual relations humans form. Human being is created as relational by God, created in the divine image as 'a being-in-partnership with God, a being addressed as Thou by God's I' (p. 19). This means that all human beings are created as relational, but that they might be inauthentic persons if their relations are distorted. Thus it would seem that all human beings are relational as a matter of ontological fact, and that judgements about their authenticity as persons are normative rather than ontological. We are spared the conclusion that some people have less personhood than others depending on the nature of their relations, and instead can categorise judgments of authenticity as prescriptive judgements pointing towards an ideal of personal achievement.

Between what are relationships formed?

This problem averted, we are landed instead with a logical problem of positing relations between relational entities, and so perhaps a never-ending regress of relations. It might be claimed that the regress finds its starting-point in God, where God is the unrelated relator -a sort of relational form of the cosmological argument. However, where God's triune nature provides the model by which we conceive the relational nature of personhood, such a cosmological argument is hard to sustain.

McFadyen describes the persons of the Trinity as 'Persons in relation and Persons only through relation' (p. 27). 'The Father', he writes, 'is a sedimentation of His significant history of relations. The effects of a significant history of relation 'fall out', settle and then accumulate around distinct personal centres gradually building up specific personal identities' (p. 41). How then can God fulfil the role of unrelated relater, unless God has existence apart from the three persons of the Trinity? God is no longer the uncaused cause. The triune God is explained as coming into being in a way wholly analogous to the development human persons.

Perhaps the greatest puzzle is the nature of these 'personal centres' or whatever the entities are between which relationships form. How do they come in to being and what are they like prior to the build-up of sedimentation from interpersonal relations? The question of the nature of presedimentary beings is less puzzling in the case of human being because in McFadyen's account human being is created with metaphysical status as that which is personally related to God. Human beings are created as relational and therefore can grow into persons. Divine persons, however, had to develop from some sort of relational web in which relations preceded the existence of any person.

This difficulty may have been apparent to readers from the outset. We are urged to view persons as relational, yet do not relations need to be understood as personal if they are to be the sort of relations from which persons arise? Indeed McFadyen speaks of persons being developed through interpersonal relations and as the sedimentation of relationships. It is instructive to contrast the sedimentation metaphor with John Macmurray's analysis of the mother-child relationship as the basic form of human existence.[6] The thrust of Macmurray's account is not that a being becomes a person through relations, but that humans are persons because relationality is central to human life. It is not that relations precede persons so much as that personal existence is created as relational, or 'personal relation ...is constitutive of personal existence' (p. 12). This we can accept if we are careful, and we might add that nature and nurture are constitutive of personal existence but are not part of the definition of personhood. Macmurray reasons that 'the infant is born a person and not an animal' because, lacking in animal instinct for survival, 'the impulse to communication is his sole adaptation to the world into which he is born' (p. 60). The infant is dependent upon and adapts to the framework of personal mutuality. All of the infant's subsequent experience, the habits he forms and the skills he acquires fall within this framework, and are fitted to it (pp. 60- 61). That human infants are born needing to communicate with others locates them already in the realm of the personal. McFadyen, by contrast, has persons emerging from relations. On the one hand he seems to imply that a human being can fail to

---

[6]*Persons in Relation* (London: Faber and Faber, 1961), esp. 60–1.

become a person. On the other hand he regards human beings as created with the metaphysical status of being personally related to God. Yet, since he argues that the persons of the Godhead also grew out of relations it remains a mystery how personal relations ever began.

By way of drawing these first two sections to a close I will distinguish four claims:

1   that our account of person hood is relative and culturally conditioned;
2   that all sorts of relationalities and relativities are involved in being a person, i.e. that to describe life as a person you do have to mention all sorts of other things including the social order, psychological development etc, and these other things manifest the relationality involved in being a person;
3   that from infancy we develop our awareness of ourselves as persons through our relation to others;
4   that personhood is relational.

(1), (2) and (3) may be readily granted but they do not imply or warrant (4). (4) is about the concept personhood or the entities that are persons. We cannot jump from recognizing the relationality involved in being a person to affirming that persons are relational entities. Persons are ontologically prior to relations. It is one thing to say that human beings develop characteristics which we regard as personal through having persons relate to them. This idea is contained in (2) and (3) above and is illustrated most clearly in the case of nurturing infants. It is quite another to suggest that relations precede persons as in (4). (4) cannot follow from (2) and (3), because (2) and (3) presuppose interpersonal relations (it takes persons to make persons) , and persons must precede anything interpersonal. (4) also raises ethical problems, reopening the possibility of withholding the label 'person ' from those who appear to us to be relationally underdeveloped.

III Should we say that personhood is relational?

Theologians who do not want ontological grounding for their anthropology are rare, but Elaine Graham is such a one. Graham would not follow McFadyen in positing an unchangeable ontological human nature. In particular her 'relational' account of gender clashes with McFadyen's view of 'male- female relatedness [as] a structural paradigm of human life in the image' (McFadyen, p.36). Graham proposes that ' 'Truth' [about human nature] ...be understood as realised within and through human practices and material transformation'. She regards any claims to realist truth as oppressive.[7] She shares with many feminist ethicists a suspicion of ontology because of the universal claims which accompany realist accounts of human nature and which are predominantly 'masculine, white and Western ' in their outlook. '[W]hatever human nature may be', Graham writes,

---

[7] Elaine L. Graham "Gender, Personhood and Theology," *Scottish Journal of Theology*, 48/3 (1995): 341–58.

'even if there are universal common elements, they remain inaccessible to our understanding beyond the medium of our own culture and interpretation'. Yet she is a universalist of sorts, hoping that 'ethical and political value-commitments' can be 'founded on some enduring notion of the person that does not collapse into metaphysics or essentialism'.[8] So she asks 'what might be the possibilities and grounds for an emancipatory knowledge and action based on some notion of ultimate good (teleology)'. As with other feminists concerned with how society is best able to promote the human good she faces the problem of articulating an appropriate universalism, to use Susan Parson's phrase. So Graham would like to find a satisfactory normative, non-ontological notion of personhood. It is not inconsistent to look only for a normative concept of person hood to guide our ethical prescriptions without insisting on ontological grounding for that concept. However, the task is more possible for those with liberal leanings, such as Martha C. Nussbaum. Nussbaum grounds universal claims about the nature of personhood in our experience of continuities and similarities that exist among people of different cultures and times. She undertakes an evaluative and ethical enquiry, asking which components of life we regard as so important that we would not call a life human without them.[9] She notes that the label 'person' has 'frequently been withheld from women without substantial argument' (p. 75), and hopes that an empirical account which looks at what is most central to human life will make it difficult to withhold the title 'person' from certain beings in an arbitrary way. Her account includes factors which relate to our bodiliness such as hunger, thirst, the need for shelter, sexual desire, and the capacity for pleasure and pain; and factors which relate to our cognitive capability, such as perceiving, imagining and thinking. She also includes both our affiliation with other human beings, and our 'separateness' in that 'However much we live with and for others, we are, each of us, 'one in number'. Each person is separate and able to feel only his or her pain, and dies without logically entailing the death of another (p. 79). That many of these capabilities are not unique to humans does not frustrate our purpose, which is to see whether it is possible to posit factors important to personhood which transcend culture and which can undergird a social ethic. Although these items are to some extent differently constructed by different societies, Nussbaum is optimistic that we are not merely projecting local preferences. She proposes that there is sufficient overlap and continuity to ground a working political consensus (p. 74).

While Graham grounds her observations on the formation of gender empirically in anthropological, biological and psychoanalytical study, she feels that such studies highlight the cultural specificity of our conceptions of human nature. The normative concept she does put forward is that which I mentioned at the beginning, that human nature is 'profoundly relational, requiring the agency of culture to bring our person hood fully in to being'. As a normative concept this does not invite all the logical problems we encountered above. When Graham speaks of our person hood coming

---

[8]"Gender, Personhood and Theology, 354–55.
[9]"Human Capabilities, Female Human Beings," in Martha C. Nussbaum and Jonathan Glover eds., *Women, Culture, and Development: A Study of Human Capabilities* (Oxford: Clarendon, 1995), 61–104.

fully in to being, we shall read her as prescribing how we ought to develop and to what sort of wellrounded development we ought to attach the term person. However, new dangers arise: personhood becomes a matter of degree dependent on the quality of relationships formed.

To accept Graham's talk of personhood as provisional is by implication to put some beings in to categories of lesser, inauthentic or non-persons. This is not helpful. We need to affirm the personhood of those who have been relationally impoverished. A promising solution is to argue that however undervalued some people have been in human society, everyone has a relationship with God, and society will be judged by its failure to treat people accordingly. However, such an appeal to the person hood of those who are overlooked would need ontological backing, which Graham is not prepared to give.

The problem continues to lie in the claim that person hood is relational – claim 4 above. Accepting claims 1, 2 and 3 above does have advantages for a social ethic and for pastoral theology. An ethic which appreciates relationships as essential to our development affords promising insights and paradigms, such as the model of the family, for reforming social structures and practices. Such an ethic takes as its starting point our actual relations with actual persons. Women philosophers have criticised the lack of reality in moralities which focus on 'Cool, distanced relations between more or less free and equal adult strangers'. However, such an ethic does not require that personhood be relational. So in this section I will argue two points. First, an ethic which seriously considers our relational development could be conducive to human well-being, but must be formulated with caution. I will mention two anxieties about what I call in shorthand a 'relational ethic'. Second, the claim that personhood is relational is ethically dangerous.

Relational ethics

One advantage for ethics of the emphasis on the relational aspect of personal development is that it enables a social critique of structures and attitudes which foster distorted relations and so inhibit healthy personal development. In particular, feminist critiques highlight 'latent aspects of domination and exclusion', which otherwise are ploughed back into moral, legal and political thought. Feminist morality which emphasises our embedded and embodied nature and our emotional involvement with particular, actual persons, offers significant insights to theologians whose task is to describe a redemptive community which is best able to nurture healthy persons.

* * * *

Most feminists agree that the family, and maternal love in particular, is a good paradigm for other social relations—even as they believe that existing family structures and practices need to be morally scrutinised.

I will assume familiarity with such ethical theories and move on to register two worries about 'relational ethics'. First, if not carefully formulated such an ethic may lay itself open to the charge of relational determinism. An emphasis on our relationality encourages us to take seriously our responsibility for our role in shaping persons, but it may also undermine our responsibility for the development of our moral selves. While it is true that we cannot establish our moral orientation independently of our social relations, it is morally important that we have the ability to assess and make changes within it, and to question the identity that our relationships bestow upon us. This is particularly important where relations are oppressive or not entirely healthy, which brings me to my second concern.

Most of us find ourselves in non-ideal relational situations much of the time. We need to make theoretical sense of our ability as individuals to challenge our present standing and to evaluate the influence of past relationships on our self-development and self-image. Relationships frequently work in ways which undermine the standing of certain individuals, and this can happen most insidiously in families where patterns of behaviour are so ingrained. An ethic which puts personal relations at its centre must be able to cater for individual persons whose interests are not represented or protected in their relations, otherwise the situations will be exacerbated.

Therefore we need an ethic which distinguishes the identity of individual persons from the sum of their relationships.

Might I not count as a person?

My further point is that in order to reap the benefits of an ethic concerned to promote healthy relations, it is not necessary to claim that personhood is relational. In fact I regard this claim as ethically dangerous.

If personhood is relational, persons can be adequately defined by their relations. I can be defined as my father's daughter and my husband's wife—haven't we been here before? Admittedly I can also be defined as my student's tutor which would not have been possible a hundred years ago. To this one might respond that these are only partial definitions. They do not reflect the full range of my relationships and therefore the fullness of my personhood. An adequate account of me would consist in a thorough account of all my relationships, including how they have contributed to my development and my self-understanding. But what if my relationships are judged not to be authentically or fully personal? Do they then yield a definition of me as an inauthentic person? To push this further, if we can be adequately defined by our relations, we might also be defined as nonpersons if we are deemed to have no socially significant relations, as were slaves in ancient Rome, and as perhaps were the 100 or so million women whom Armatya Sen has discovered are 'missing' around the world.

If personhood is relational it then becomes a matter of degree dependent on relations formed. To use Graham's terminology, personhood is provisional. If judgements about unformed or distorted relations and impoverished personal development get blurred in to judgments about lack of personhood, we would have an unsafe foundation for our ethical thinking—one in which, for example, the oppressed become lesser or non-persons. A quotation from Vincent Brümmer will help to demonstrate the problem: 'your love bestows value on me which I would otherwise not have. It does not merely recognise a value which I already have apart from this recognition' (p. 235). I cannot imagine that Brümmer's meaning here is that people who are unloved have no value, but that is the logical implication of his statement. Do we not want to say that all people have value and that we will be judged in our failure to recognise value in others? We talk of damaged or inauthentic persons, but we mean by this something about their personal or self-development. We do not mean that they are any less members of the class of persons than are well-adjusted beings. We have insights these days in to the injury done to persons through breakdown in relationships, but there must be clarity that the damaged person, for example, the person who has severed relational ties or who has known only abusive relations, is still a person. Moreover, her ability to be so damaged is evidence of her personhood.

Recognition that we develop as selves and that we gain self-awareness through relations does not justify either ontological or normative claims that personhood is relational—claims which I regard as logically and ethically problematic. Nor is personal identity, or continuity if you prefer, relational except insofar as it describes a relationship which one holds with oneself. Theologians and ethicists require constancy in personal identity for ideas of moral development and of redemptive transformation. We should therefore not take ideas about the relationality of self-development to imply that either personhood or personal identity are themselves in constant flux or development. A normative concept of personhood should recognise that relations are crucial to self-development, and inform our ethics accordingly. But it has to include more than that, otherwise a person's value is dependent on the richness of her relations. Ontological accounts need include less because they are not directly undergirding ethical prescriptions. An ontological account has to make sense of what we feel is fundamental to being a person and to being the same person over time.

Here is a suggestion, Aristotelian in flavour and so by no means novel. Persons are beings with the capacity to acquire certain skills, notably understanding, will and decision-making. Can the skills be realised only through relationships? I suspect we do not know. However, the capacity to acquire them is not dependent on relationships. (An animal born in the dark and kept in the dark still has the capacity to see.) A being with the relevant capacities is a person whether or not the skills have been successfully nurtured in any particular instance. Capacity precedes relationships even if development does not. Relations between persons are of greater ethical import than relations between a person and a cat, or a computer, because of the capacity that persons have to develop in particular ways and to be damaged. Continuity of personal identity involves (at least) psychological continuity through whatever processes of development persons undergo. The burden of this article has been to uncover flaws in relational accounts of personhood, rather than to posit an alternative account. Nevertheless an alternative is required and this claim provides a sounder starting-point: that to be a person is to have certain capacities whether or not these are realised. This is not to deny that relationality is in fact part of living our lives as persons (any more than it is to deny that choosing our fundamental goals is part of personal life). However, it is to deny that persons exist because relationships exist, and it puts paid to that strange metaphysical picture of relations hanging around waiting for persons to happen.

Questions

1 In what sense is the "claim that personhood is relational" "logically confused and ethically precarious," in Harris' mind? What is the substance of her critique of McFadyen's work?

2 Harris writes: "A body and a psyche can have temporal continuity without the being to whom they are attached having personal relations, let alone continuity in their personal relations." Is this a telling blow against the idea that persons are constituted by relations? How so?

3 Why is the nature of "personal centres" the "greatest puzzle" in Harris' mind?

4 "Persons are ontologically prior to relations." True or false?

5 What is Harris' alternative to relationship as a basis for personhood? Is it successful?

6 Having read Zizioulas and Harris, who do you think has the better of the argument? Does Harris convincingly outflank a Zizioulasian conception of personhood?

TEXT 3: ROBERT SPAEMANN, *PERSONS: THE DIFFERENCE BETWEEN "SOMEONE" AND "SOMETHING"*[10]

Robert Spaemann (b. 1927) is a Roman Catholic philosopher who has been emeritus professor at the University of Munich since 1992. His two most important works are *Happiness and Benevolence* (1989) and *Persons: The Difference between "Someone" and "Something."* Spaemann's work has been widely influential, and noted in particular by Pope Benedict XVI. He is a highly original thinker, while still maintaining a conservative outlook informed by Roman Catholic orthodoxy. Spaemann's particular interest has been in the question of human personhood, personal identity and dignity, which he seeks to expound in the terms presented by the Christian tradition. For Spaemann, that tradition enables a retrieval of the concept of personhood from the terrible reductionism encountered in modernity. This excerpt from his major work, Persons, finds its place as piece of philosophy among theological writing because Spaemann so obviously makes use of a theological frame of reference in his work; and sees his work as providing a complement for more explicitly theological thought.

I

The meaning of the word 'person' is exceptionally dependent upon its context. For the most part we speak of persons to denote human beings, referring, for example, to 'eight persons at table'. In such a phrase the word 'person' is not emphatic, but rather the opposite. 'Eight human beings at table' would be more forceful and strike a somewhat more solemn note. 'Eight persons' is abstract and impersonal, simply a way of counting. It would seem rather pretentious to speak of a human-to human, instead of a person-to-person, telephone call. And the phrase 'this person' is especially impersonal–either bureaucratic or deliberately dismissive.

In other contexts, however, the contrary is true, and especially when the word 'person' functions as a predicate, *i.e.* when it is said that some specified subject 'is a person'. The recent proposal to replace the expression 'human rights' with 'personal rights' illustrates a use of language in which 'persons' are those human beings, and only those, who are distinguished by certain qualities. And the reply that *all* human beings are persons, treats the term 'person' as a *nomen dignitatis* in just the same way. To ascribe 'personal existence' is to recognize that someone can claim a certain kind of treatment from anyone who encounters him.

Traces of an older and different use of the term may be found in the heading of a list of characters in a play: *dramatis personae*. 'Persons' in this context are precisely

---

[10]Spaemann, Robert. "Why we speak of persons" in *Persons : The Difference between "Someone" and "Something"*. Tr. O. O'Donovan (Oxford: Oxford University Press, 2006), 5–15

not persons, i.e. human beings. They are roles, distinct from the actors who present them. We see something like the same use in St Paul's remark that 'God does not look upon the person.'[11] If we ask what God *does* look upon, the answer must be that he looks precisely on 'the person' in the modern sense. Finally, and not only for the sake of completeness, we must remember the grammatical expressions, 'first person', 'second person', 'third person', which have come to assume a decisive importance in our contemporary use of 'person'.

The discussion that follows will principally have to do with the sense of the word 'person' used as a predicate, when we say that this or that subject 'is a person'. This sense sheds some light, however, on the secondary use, when we employ it impersonally for the purposes of numerical identification.

'Person' is not a classificatory term, on the one hand, identifying a particular *this* as *such* a thing. 'X is a person' does not answer the question 'What is X?', as do 'X is a human being' or 'X is a lampstand'. In order to know whether X is a person, we must first know whether X is a human being or a lampstand. The term 'person' does not identify an X as a such-and-such; it says something further about an X already specified as a such-and-such. On the other hand, it does not ascribe some further property to X, for there is no 'property' of personal existence. On the contrary, it is on the basis of certain definite identifiable properties that we are licensed say of some Xs that they are persons.

What are these properties? And when we have established them, what does the predication of personal existence add? We begin with a preliminary and unsystematic collection of pointers.

We need some preconception to help us embark upon our exploration, an idea of what we are searching for. And this lies to hand in the phenomenon that we have already noticed, that the word 'person' is applied in a peculiar way. On the one hand, it ascribes a special value, on the other serves for numerical indexing, ignoring distinguishing features. On the one hand, it is not a classificatory term, identifying any X as belonging to some class of thing; on the other, it is not a property, but denotes the bearer of certain properties. If we refrain from dismissing these two patterns of use as simple equivocations and pay attention to what connects them, we have our first pointer in the right direction. A person must be someone who is what he is in a *different way* from that in which other things, or other animals, are what they are.

What do we mean by 'a different way'? Perhaps a line from *The Magic Flute* can help us. Sarastro's well-known aria commending philanthropy, 'Within this hallowed dwelling is heard no rage or strife', ends with a sentence that sounds odd, but which everyone will understand: 'Whoe'er these truths will not maintain, doth not deserve to be a man.'[12] 'Being a man' is here represented as a privilege, something one can forfeit. We understand readily enough what it might mean that a man did not deserve to be a prince; but who is there that could deserve, or not deserve, to be a man? 'Man' is a classificatory term that specifies *a limine* who is in a position to deserve or not deserve things. It is a substance-term, in Aristotle's language, distinguished by

---

[11]Galatians 2:6 [where Paul's Greek has πρόσωπον the Latin Vulgate *personam*. 'God does not recognise these personal distinctions' NEB.]

[12]E. Schickaneder and W. A. Mozart, *The Magic Flute* no. 15.

not being a predicate of any other thing but identifying things that may then be the subject of predicates.

We can clarify the point by thinking of a dog, who is sometimes a barking animal and sometimes a not-barking animal. When not barking he continues to exist; but the moment he stops being a dog, we say that 'he' is no more. To this paradigm one might object: he has simply stopped being a *dog*, just as when he is not barking he has stopped being a *barker*. In ceasing to be a dog he has not vanished into thin air, but has changed into something else, a corpse initially and compost later. There is an underlying material substrate of which one can predicate dogginess at first and decomposition afterwards. But this line of thought is successfully rebutted by Aristotle's distinction between two kinds of change, coming-to-be and ceasing-to-be on the one hand, alteration on the other. When a human being dies, we do not say that something, a piece of spatio-temporally localized matter, has altered its condition; we say that someone, a human being, has ceased to exist. The classificatory term is what gives primary a *limine* specification to any X of which we propose to say anything. The stuff of which X is composed is referred to simply as 'the stuff of X'. It is not the true subject of our predication.

So when Sarastro says, 'Whoe'er these truths will not maintain, doth not deserve to be a man' he does not mean that some piece of matter defined by space-time coordinates has forfeited manhood as a man may forfeit princedom. A piece of matter has nothing to do with deserving or forfeiting. Only a man can deserve or forfeit manhood, which is what makes Sarastro's saying paradoxical. To be able to deserve or forfeit, one must be a man already. Yet we have an intuitive grasp of Sarastro's meaning, and that is because we do not think about a man's relation to manhood in the same way that we think of a dog's relation to dogginess. We think in terms of a mental self-differentiation, something we never conceive of in the relation of other individual members to their kinds. A man is obviously not a man in the same way that a dog is a dog, i.e. simply and solely by being an instance of the species.

This becomes dearer when we consider the application of the term 'human'. In one sense anything that human beings do is human, even those peculiar atrocities of which animals are incapable. But we do not use the word like that. We use it as a normative term to differentiate kinds of conduct of which we approve from others of which we disapprove. Sometimes this rule of speech is interestingly reversed, as when we call some kinds of conduct 'human' which we disapprove of to a degree, but wish to excuse: 'to err is human'. But such excusable conduct is always a breach of the norm through weakness. We do not use the word 'human' of malicious breach, though malice, too, is characteristic of human beings. On the contrary, we call the most perversely malicious kinds of behaviour 'inhuman'. Inhumanity, it is dear, is a trait specifically restricted to the human race.

II

These paradoxes, then, provide us with a first pointer to something that makes us designate instances of *homo sapiens* not only with the species-name, 'man', but as 'persons'.

As a rule we make a distinction between men and animals. But 'man' is first and foremost a zoological species-term, and ancient and medieval philosophy treated 'man' as one among the animal species, *animal rationale*. The fact that for us the word 'animal' (*Tier*), like bestia in Latin, carries the connotation of 'non-human', makes us prefer the formal expression 'living creature' (*Lebewesen*) when we want a category embracing both men and animals. This again reveals how a man instantiates the human species in a different way from that in which individual members of other species instantiate theirs. This peculiarity can be clarified by the way we refer to ourselves with the personal-pronoun 'I'. 'I' is an ostensive term. When we say 'I', we are not referring to '*an* Ego'-a pure invention of the philosophers!- but to a particular living creature, a particular human being identified by other speakers with the use of a personal name. But when this particular human being identifies the selfsame person that he or she actually is, the term 'I' is used. And the account to be given of this 'I' is anomalous in two respects.

In the first place, nobody can doubt that 'I' refers to something real. The same cannot be said about 'he', 'she', 'it', 'this', 'that', or even 'you', which may all on occasion refer to imaginary objects. But anyone who says 'I', exists. That is the truth behind Descartes's celebrated *Cogito ergo sum*.

But what do we mean, 'exists'? Who is it that says 'I' and exists, and what is he? One can imagine someone saying 'I' and not knowing the answer to this, or getting it wrong. And that is the second anomaly with this personal pronoun. To identify a thing, as we have observed, means to identify it qualitatively as a such-and-such, to situate it as a member of a kind by the use of a classificatory term. But that is not true of identification with the personal pronoun 'I'. Someone may be mistaken about who and what he is, ignorant of his position in time and space; robbed by an accident of memory and sight, he may ask, 'Who am I?' 'Where am I?', even forgetting that he is a human being.

Yet there is no unclarity about who 'I' refers to. 'I' simply picks out an item regardless of its qualitative features; it refers to the speaker, irrespective of what the speaker may be besides.

We should not make the mistake of thinking that 'I' refers to a purely mental *res cogitans*, or to a bare existent without a nature, which must, as it were, first realize itself *ex nihilo* as something with some nature. That is to misunderstand the phenomenon. It is not insignificant that when the victim of amnesia asks, 'Who am I? Where am I?', he presumes he is *someone*, with characteristics of *some* kind, situated *somewhere* in the wide world. He does not think of himself as 'an Ego'. If he is conscious at all, he is aware that he is more than consciousness. Yet the knowledge of who and where he is has not kept up with the knowledge *that* he is. He cannot identify himself by qualitative distinguishing features. I know that I have a nature of a certain kind and with certain characteristics; but this nature is not simply what I am. When I say 'I am', I have not said enough to plot my coordinates in time and space; but I aspire to plot them.

The human being, then, is not what he is in the same way as everything else we encounter is what it is. Our talk of 'persons' has to do with this phenomenon. Pointing in the same direction is the universally attested idea of metamorphosis. In Kafka's *novella* 'Metamorphosis' a man is transformed into a giant insect. Such transformations crowd the pages of folk-tale and myth-we may think of 'The Frog

King' or 'Brother and Sister'. Ovid collected a series of transformation-myths in his *Metamorphoses*, and from more recent literature we should mention Guimaraes Rosa's short story 'My Uncle the Jaguar', a monologue in which the reader accompanies the narrator through his transformation into a jaguar. What is going on in these stories?

It is not what Aristotle calls 'substantial change'. Substantial change consists in the ceasing-to-be of one thing, and the coming- to-be of another out of the material substrate of the first. The one thing is finished with; the other has taken its place. The material continuum between the two is what Aristotle calls *hylē*, 'matter', and the matter of which the two successive substances are composed is the only continuous element. In nature we experience such changes constantly. An organism disintegrates and turns to loam, and this in tum provides material for a new organism. But that is not the stuff of nightmares, myths, or literary fantasies.

The distinctive feature of metamorphosis is that the subject himself, not only a material substrate, survives the transformation. The subject exists at first as a human being who says 'I', and subsequently exists as an insect, frog, hind, jaguar or even, in Ovid, a tree. The interesting thing is that only human beings undergo metamorphosis of species with their identities intact, and they may on occasion be changed back, or 'set free'. We do not find animals transformed into men unless they were men before. Abstract individual identity is a feature of dreams, too, where we encounter someone whom we know to be so-and-so, though he has no resemblance to the person in question at all. We simply know that it is this person. But what is it that we know? What does it mean to say, it is this person, whose name we know but with whom the image in our dream very dearly has nothing in common? This is another case of abstracting individual identity from qualitative similarities. It does not matter that all these examples are fictive. The point is simply that though the abstraction is possible only because human beings have qualitative attributes, qualitative attributes do not define personal identity. *Who* we are is not simply interchangeable with *what* we are.

Generally speaking the same conception of metamorphosis is at work in ideas of reincarnation—most strongly, naturally, in those where men are reborn as animals. In Western doctrines a human being comes back only as another human being, but with such new characteristics as prompt us to distinguish his individual identity from an identity of quality. In Indian doctrines, on the other hand, Sarastro's line is taken literally: someone 'does not deserve to be a man' next time, and so comes back as something else, yet without ceasing to be the selfsame someone.

III

There is a third angle, finally, from which I would like to approach the phenomenon of inner difference between the human subject and himself.

Any entity in nature displays what it is by what it does, by its manner of expressing itself. As the scholastic adage had it: *agere sequitur esse*. But this applies in the strictest sense only to the objects of physics. Even plants and animals display what we call 'deviation from type Even animals are not simply 'what they are: To a certain extent they may fail to realize what they are, for what they are is not accounted for wholly in terms of how they display themselves. No, essentially the animal is an 'inside', something that 'goes out for' (*Aussein-auf*), or pursues things. Only when we treat it as such do we take it seriously as a *living* creature. Normally we speak of the pursuit of living things as 'drive' for self-and species-preservation. Not as though this purpose was actually present to the animal as an idea; the ideas that are present to animals are food, mate, prey, peril; it is only we, the observers, for whom these drives function as a system explained by the theory of evolution. But be this explanation as it may, wherever there is teleological destination, the pursuit of something, there is the possibility of failure.

In physics there is no such thing as failure. In the physicist's realm only the physicist fails, nature never. To fail in anything, a thing must pursue it. A three-legged hare is a 'malformed' hare or an 'unlucky' hare, because three-leggedness is more than simple deviance from a statistical norm; it means the hare is less well adapted to its ecological niche than a four-legged hare, less well in itself, with slimmer chances of survival. To 'go for', to 'fare well', to 'fare ill': all these expressions point to the same inner difference between what a living creature *properly* is, and what it *actually* is. Human beings are living creatures, too, and so participate in this difference that Aristotle says is characteristic of all higher life-forms, the difference between *zēn* and *eu zēn*, living and living well.

Human beings are apparently unique in being conscious of this difference. In speaking about animals we are forced back upon one of two possible analogies: an analogy with our own human experience, or an analogy with machines, which are systems that appear such only to our view. That is to say, the phenomenon of pursuit, the specific difference introduced by 'drive', is discernible only to the kind of being that rises above this difference and relates to the form of its own animal life at a higher level. In pain, for example, human beings can see something beyond the sheer impairment of their vitality. Defence or evasion are not their only reactions. They can expose themselves to pain deliberately; they can take a negative view of life as the condition of pain; or else, in a kind of selective self-negation, they can distance themselves from this or that property, wish or drive, regretting that they are as they are, and wishing they were different. When we say that someone must learn to 'accept himself', we are not recommending the closing-up of this inner difference, a return to blind self-assertion, the response of defiance when criticized for some inconsiderateness: 'That's just the kind of person I am!' 'The kind of person I am' is only the other side of 'the kind of bastard he is!', which is how we nail someone pitilessly to the character revealed in his behaviour and deny him the possibility, which forgiveness could facilitate, of appearing in a different light. No one is simply and solely what he is. Self-acceptance is a process that presumes non-identity with self, and must be seen as the conscious appropriation of the non-identical-in Jung's term, 'integration:

Harry Frankfurt has developed a similar line of thought in speaking of 'secondary volitions'. This is the phenomenon of taking a position on our own desires and acts of will. We can desire to have, or not to have, certain desires. We evaluate not only the objects of our desires, but our desires themselves. When we succeed in bringing our desires into line with our evaluation, we feel free; when we do not, we experience impotence, like addicts and compulsive offenders who have wills that run counter to their own wills. One can even desire to desire something without the will to gratify the desire, merely willing to experience it. When Odysseus wanted to hear the Sirens and experience the longing that their song aroused, he took careful precautions not to fall victim to that longing: he had his companions chain him to the mast of the ship, their ears stopped up, his unstopped, Plato in the *Laws* suggests that where possible young people should be administered anxiety-producing drugs, to train them in the cool-headedness to do what they see to be good and right in the teeth of anxieties. Secondary volitions are not simply stronger resolutions that prevail within the parallelogram of motives. In fact, they do not always prevail, in which case we may try to manipulate the parallelogram itself, by organizing a system of rewards and penalties for ourselves to reinforce desirable but weak first-order resolutions, when the crunch comes, with another first-order resolution. The damage smoking does to one's health may often not be a sufficient motive to overcome the desire to smoke; but one may compensate by a device that rewards abstinence, so that the anticipated reward is enough to enable one to give up smoking. In secondary volitions we treat ourselves as we would another person whose behaviour we seek to control. In this, however, we come up against an unbreachable boundary. It lies beyond our control to alter the fundamental direction in which we influence ourselves. If it were not so, we would face the problem of an infinite series of willings-to-will.

At this stage of our initial exploration we cannot go into the nature of this primary, spontaneous movement that is distinct from all its objective indications. The point to grasp is simply how it demonstrates the self-differentiation of a human subject from everything that may be true about him. This, it seems, is fundamental to our talk about persons. We are familiar with this selfdifference from discussions of 'reflection'. But reflection is only one of its manifestations. Our existence is marked by interior difference even when we are not reflecting; it makes reflection possible, but does not depend on it. Reflection is turning in on oneself, but we can also describe difference as coming out of oneself, as the 'de-centred position', in Helmut Plessner's term. Here the decisive factor is not the use of 'I' in speaking of oneself, but the use of the third person. Small children regularly speak of themselves in this way, which is more remarkable in some respects even than the use of 'I'. To speak of oneself in the third person is to step out of the central position that all living things in nature occupy in relation to their environments, and to see oneself with other people's eyes as something 'out there'. For this one must adopt a point of view from outside one's own organic centre. Morality is possible only with this capacity for self-objectification and selfrelativization; only on these terms, too, is speech possible. Speech differs from the cries of living things in nature, in that it anticipates the standpoint of the one who is to hear what is spoken. When someone says 'I am in pain', that statement is not merely a cry by other means. The immediate expression of pain must be suppressed, in order to form a communication about the pain as an event in the world and to make that communication intelligible to another. To this end, far from merely 'expressing ourselves', we must submit to a prescribed system of rules that makes understanding possible. Correspondingly, the system of speech itself prompts the emergence of selfdifference, the distance from ourselves that gives rise to our talk of 'persons'.

As human beings we are aware of another's gaze fixed on us. We are aware of the gaze of *all* others, the gaze of all *possible* others, the 'view from nowhere'. That we experience this gaze and know about it, or believe we do, makes it impossible to understand ourselves as mere organic systems that constitute their own environment, where every encounter has meaning only in relation to the system's requirements. Stepping out of our organic centre, we stand in a dimension where there is no 'natural' decision about what has significance, and what the significance is. The medium of understanding itself is not given in nature, for there is no natural human speech. But neither is speech an invention. It is a presupposition of our entering the communicative event in which we realize ourselves as what we are, as persons.

Questions

1 What might a change of language from "human rights" to "personal rights" achieve?
2 What identifiable properties licence us to say of some Xs that they are "persons"?
3 "A man is obviously not a man in the same way that a dog is a dog." What does Spaemann mean here?
4 What is going on in stories of metamorphosis that adds a perspective to the discussion of personhood?
5 How can there be an inner difference between the human subject and himself? What does Spaemann mean by the "self-differentiation of a human subject from everything that may be true about him"? Why is that fundamental to our talk about persons?
6 Does Spaemann's account give any help to an attempt to ground talk of persons theologically?

TEXT 4: ROBERT JENSON,
SYSTEMATIC THEOLOGY[13]

Robert Jenson (1930-2017) is one of the most influential and widely read U.S. theologians of the last forty years. A Lutheran, Jenson underwent a large part of his postgraduate studies in Germany and Switzerland, immersing himself in the philosophy of Kant, Hegel, and Heidegger and the theology of Karl Barth in particular. He read deeply in patristic thought, but also published a groundbreaking study of the eighteenth-century preacher and theologian Jonathan Edwards. His book *The Triune Identity* was published at the dawn of the revival of Trinitarian theology at the beginning of the 1980s. Jenson's writing is densely philosophical, but also richly versed in the broad stream of the tradition of Christian orthodoxy. Jenson's two-volume *Systematic Theology* was published in 1997–9.

I

Humanity's uniqueness is the specific relation God takes up with us. This relation is not itself a resemblance. The "image of God," if we are to use this phrase comprehensively for humanity's distinctiveness, is simply that we are related to God as his conversational counterpart.

With these propositions in place, however, we are free to recognize what may indeed be called a human resemblance to God, and at the very place where the tradition located it. Because God speaks with us, we know he is personal. As we answer him, we too are personal.

It is often and convincingly claimed that personhood first became a metaphysically deep concept within the Christian doctrine of God, and especially within the thinking of the Eastern fathers and their Byzantine appropriators; this was important from a different angle in the first volume of this work. Pagan antiquity of course knew that some entities were personal and some were not but understood being a human person as simply one characteristic of being a human being and being a divine person as one characteristic of being a divine being. For pagan antiquity's theology, being is the embracing category, and personhood is secondary.

Christian theology was compelled to drastic revision: in the Cappadocian and Neo-Chalcedonian doctrine of Trinity, personhood is not an aspect of God's being but is rather correlated to the three *who live* deity, also when we speak of the Trinity himself as personal. That the three are God is a characteristic of the specific personalities they are; it is divine personhood, not divine being, that is metaphysically primary.

The contest between the concepts of personhood and being would of course be moot if the first volume's revision of the latter concept were followed. In order to

---

[13]Robert Jenson, *Systematic Theology*, II (Oxford: Oxford University Press, 2001), 95–111.

recognize Orthodoxy's point without constant circumlocution, the preceding and following few paragraphs prescind from that proposal.

It is a chief truth of Eastern insistence on the Father's "monarchy": it is not God's divinity—not his being—that is the origin of the triune life but the Father as person. God is not first divine and thereupon triune. He is first triune and thereupon divine. The Father's love, an exclusively personal reality, is the origin of the Son, and the Father's personal intent to be free in order to love is the origin of the Spirit. It is, moreover, the Father with the Son in the Spirit who are the one God. "If God exists, he exists because the Father exists."[14]

Since with God personhood is prior to being, it must be so absolutely. Within thinking enabled by the Cappadocian achievement, it is the fact of personhood that "enables entities to be entities" and not vice versa. Also things that are themselves impersonal belong to a creation that results from the Creator as a personal freedom beyond it; this contradicts all pagan antiquity's theology, for which even divine personhood and freedom, if affirmed at all, are phenomena within the itself impersonal whole.

But are there other persons than the divine three? Can there be created persons? If the ground of God's personhood and freedom were his divinity, if personhood were a predicate of beings of a certain sort, then such freedom would surely be an exclusive predicate of divine beings. But since it is the other way around, since God's free personhood is the ground of his nature, the triune communion is not bound even to the purity of its own deity and can open to others than the three if God so wills it; and then as respondents in that communion these others will also be personal. We have arrived again at a central position of this work, and one to which we have come from several starting points.

It will be the task of this chapter to analyze human personhood as it is created by God's triune personal life. A decisive caution must stand at the beginning: we must not be guided by any general principle of likeness, so as to trace the structure of human personhood from that of divine personhood. We could thereby easily violate Thomas Aquinas's principle, which we have regularly invoked: that essence and existence are distinguished in creatures and not distinguished in God. We have described a triune person as an existent with no other reason than his own existence and that of other persons who are the same being he is; we must not so describe created personhood.

In the first volume, we analyzed personhood around three poles: transcendental unity of apperception, Ego, and freedom. The previous paragraphs suggest continuing in these terms; it is not thereby proposed that they provide the only terms in which the analysis might be conducted. This is also the place to warn that discourse about the "I" or Ego is easily misunderstood, since throughout the modern period the word has been used for different things in different theories. This chapter will speak of the Ego in a relatively commonsensical way: it is the entity we denote with the subject term of such first-person descriptive or hortatory sentences as "I painted that house" or "I ought to be more energetic."

[14]John Zizioulas, *Being as Communion* (Crestwood: St. Vladimir's Seminary Press, 1985), 41.

II

The phenomenon Immanuel Kant called "the transcendental unity of apperception" surely obtains.

We would not call an entity personal that was not conscious, that did not in Kant's peculiar language "apperceive"; nor would we call a consciousness personal that was not focused at a viewpoint. A personal consciousness is precisely "transcendental," that is, a perspectival focus that is not itself within the field there focused.

It is perhaps just possible to conceive a consciousness that was from no viewpoint. The modern sciences in their first flowering drew a picture of the universe that if perfected would have been "a view from nowhere." And Aristotle conceived a consciousness whose whole content might be such a picture: his God is a universal consciousness without perspective, the consciousness perhaps of an omniscient and passionless classical physicist.

But Aristotle's God is not, and therefore the metaphysical situation his reality would establish not only does not obtain but could not have obtained. God is Father, Son, and Spirit. Each is other than the other two, and each is a person; and since a divine person *is* a subsisting relation to the other divine persons, each of Father, Son, and Spirit is precisely a perspective. Moreover, since there are created persons only as enabled within the triune community of persons, the proposition is universal: all consciousness is perspectival. It will be seen that these arguments reproduce arguments of the first volume, the other way around.

Thus Kant's phenomenological observation is not theologically neutral, whatever Kant may have supposed. Indeed, however far Kant may have departed from specific Christianity, the insight he followed was enabled only within the history of Christian theology. The pioneer of "the first-person standpoint" as an epistemic attitude seems to have been Augustine himself.

Augustine's reflexive identification with his own subjectivity was undoubtedly shaped by his Neoplatonism, with its cosmological and psychological pyramid stemming from "the One" through "Mind." But he would hardly have come to it had he not also been a worshiper of the Christian God. The Creator was the supreme goal of Augustine's consciousness, and unlike Greek deity the Creator is too intimate to his creatures to appear in our knowing only as something we know, however encompassing and dominant; he must be apprehended as "the ... underlying principle of our knowing activity" itself.[15] Just in this reflection Augustine drew attention to our consciousness in its own depth, and made "us aware of this in a first-person perspective."[16]

God's consciousness is focused and so is ours; and of both facts we can give some account. As Augustine perhaps did not quite say, divine consciousness is focused because each of the persons God is has *dramatic location* in and by community with the others. And human consciousness is focused by its accommodation in this same mutuality.

---

[15]Charles Taylor, *Sources of the Self: The Making of the Modern Identity* (Cambridge: Harvard University Press, 1989), 129.
[16]Ibid., 136.

Thus transcendental unity of apperception, wherever it occurs, is enabled by the triune life. And the unity of consciousness is therefore always a *narrative* unity. It has the integrity of a location within a story and is unitary because the story is coherent. Just so it occurs in and by virtue *of community,* foundationally by virtue of the triune community.

Here an error is to be avoided. The Kantian notion of a transcendental unity of apperception is individualistic as he uses it. The rest of the world provides raw data, which are then pulled together into an experienced world from the inalienably private focus of my consciousness. The intent of this chapter would be radically perverted were its appropriation of Kant's notion to carry this supposition with it. There *are no* raw data of experience; the world that I receive and unify in my experience is always already the world interpreted in the discourse of a community, first the community of the Trinity and then the human communities I thereupon inhabit. And I experience reality from a perspectival point precisely because I am located in those same communities.

The triune narrative and the triune community are in contingent fact God's history with a human community actual in that history. We humans belong to the triune history and community only by virtue of this contingency; none of us nor all of us together are one of the Trinity. We belong as those whom the Son brings with himself, whose whole life and intention are the others to whom he is sent and for whom he died. Thus we created persons have each our perspectival integrity as we are simultaneously located within divine history and community and within human history and the human community. This is true both of the human person Jesus and of the rest of us, but differently.

According to our christological conclusions, the identity of the eternal Son is the human person Jesus. Thus the viewpoint from which this man grasps reality is identically that of *the one whose* place in the human narrative and community is that of a Palestinian Jew, Mary's child, an unordained rabbi, one of Rome's victims, and so on, and that of *the one whose* place in the triune narrative and community is that of the Son of the Father and the defining beneficiary of the Spirit.

With each of the rest of us the viewpoint from which consciousness stems is that of one of those *for whom* this Jew and prophet and victim lived and died, and who is *some particular one of* them as, for example, a lay deacon, a professor of physics, Susannah's child, and so on. Just and only so it is also that of one of those who appear with the Son before the Father in the Spirit. It is apparent that those who do not acknowledge the Son must be in constant danger of mislocating the viewpoint from which they are conscious, and so of losing perspective on their world: they do in fact grasp the world only from a position within the Christological story but do not know that they do this.

What brings my experience, in Kant's sense, together to be my experience is nothing I am by myself, Kant and his successors to the contrary. It is the coherence of the narrative in which I belong and it is the justice of the community of that narrative. Or we may say it is the grammar of the language of that community, in which it tells its narrative. Both as I narrate my life and as I live in community, I must be competent in a language I do not invent: the givenness of a specific language and my induction into it are, in Kant's proper sense, a transcendental condition of unified consciousness.

The transcendental viewpoint of those whose community is finally the church and only in the meantime other "public things" and that of those whose community is the latter only have the same abstract structure. To avoid God, modernity and its precursors posited a focus of consciousness that was itself this abstraction, the same for all by virtue of its pure formality. No such thing subsists. My life has originating focus either within the community of the church and the communities of the *libido dominandi* or within the latter communities only.

I can, to be sure, pretend I am self-existent, the condition of my own hypostasis. And I can try actually to live by that pretense, in violation of the conditions by which I subsist to pretend things. Sin, which is always itself the same old thing, has many faces; one is acting as if my essence and existence were not distinct. Augustine was led to the transcendental unity of his own consciousness by his passion for God. Within the reflection he inaugurated, to seek only myself at the focus of my consciousness is to mistake myself for God. A great deal of Western epistemology is simply Eve's and Adam's error . . .

III

In the foregoing, a step was elided. The transcendental unity of a hypothetical human consciousness was described as "that of one of those for whom this Jew and child and prophet and victim lived and died, and who is some particular one of them as, for example," an American, a professor of physics, and so on. But this use of identifying descriptions anticipated its justification. A focus of consciousness simply in and of itself, even if that focus is a place in a community and narrative, would not be that of a describable someone. And so it would not be personal.

That I from the focus of my consciousness identify that of which I am conscious as included in my experience, in such fashion that "my" has descriptive content, depends on my identifying myself as, continuing the hypothetical case, one of those for whom Jesus died and among them as an American, a professor of physics, and so on. It depends, that is, on finding myself as a describable object. The "I" in "That so-and-so is I" remains to be discussed. The "I" in "I did that" seems on face value to have the same function as "John" in "John did that." The point of my saying to you, for example, "I painted the house" is to point out an entity within the experience of us both that is claimed to be the agent of the house's new appearance; the claim moreover is arguable between us.

If this face value is accepted, my Ego is something within the field of my consciousness, there/or me as it is for you, and in the presently relevant respects there for me just as John or Mary is there for me. At face value, it belongs to my personhood that I recognize myself in a figure presented to my consciousness by the narrative and community in which I am located, so that this Ego is not itself located at the perspectival point from which I recognize it. It belongs to the face value of our self-referential language that there is a structure of deferral built into personhood, that the two personal pronouns in "I recognize that I did that" do not initially point in the same direction, but must catch up with each other.

* * * *

Christian theology . . . knows that something outside the individual focus of consciousness grants and guarantees its precision and steadiness, the coherence of God's life and the person's relation to it, and is therefore not surprised that introspection fails to discover the person's coherence. It knows also that there is not a sheer plurality of social identities presented to my consciousness, because not individuals but the one human community, constituted a unity by Jesus' life and death for all, presents me with my identification. And it knows that the "material" identity, the body, and this social identity are not really different things.

The man Jesus identifies himself as a Palestinian Jew, Mary's child, who died for his sisters and brothers, and as Son of the Father and resting place of the Spirit. Each of the rest of us may identify her- or himself as one of those for whom this one lived and died and lives, and who is particular within this community as the self seen and offered by this community and by others that "recognize" him or her. Thus the structures of the communities within which individuals have their transcendental focus and from which they receive their Egos shape the structure of their personhood. There is a personhood proper to a representative democracy and a different personhood proper to a popular tyranny and so on. Moreover, the voices of others are constitutive within the individual's life: I am who and what I am precisely in conversation with those who offer me myself.

The soteriological significance of these last points can hardly be overestimated. So long as it is supposed that the individual human person inhabits a sort of shell from within which he or she deals with others outside the shell, the key soteriological propositions of Scripture are unintelligible. For example, "It is not I who live but Christ who lives in me" can at most be taken as overheated rhetoric.

Finally, because theology knows these things it can rest content with the one thing with which modernity could not be content, deferral of the subject's identification between itself as transcendental viewpoint and itself as Ego. Indeed, it calls this deferral freedom and regards the freedom of the supposed autonomously self-contained individual as the most barren of slaveries. I am not bound within my own self-equivalence; it is not so that I intractably am what I am what I am what.

IV

The interpretation of created freedom is perennially controverted in the Western church—and this is surely one point where aloofness from such broils has not been for the good of the Eastern churches. There are several notable places where we could join the argument; Martin Luther's reply to Erasmus, *On the Bondage of the Will*, commends itself by unique willingness to state and argue the issues without shielding equivocation.

The phrase "the free will" has generated many cross-purposes. Those who affirm "free will" often affirm different things, usually without noticing; and those who deny "free will" often deny different things, regularly mistaking the opponent against whom they direct the denial.

Thus Augustine explicitly teaches that the existence of human free will, *liberum arbitrium* in his fateful phrase, is an essential truth of Scripture and reason. Yet in modernity his doctrine of predestination is customarily cited as the paradigmatic denial of free will; as is his reiterated more general teaching that all human wills "are so absolutely in God's power that he makes them incline to whatever he wills whenever he wills it." Vice versa, in the course of Luther's savage assault on "free will," he offhandedly affirms anthropological features that some would say are all they ever meant by the phrase.

We will not here try to straighten out the historical confusions of language and analysis. We will simply follow Luther's treatise, noting the phenomena adduced in it and following the arguments he attaches to them; perhaps we may avoid some ambiguities by thus following the track of one interlocutor.

Luther agrees with his opponents that human creatures have a dispositional property of being apt for willing action. We may put it so: the question "Was Jones willing to go to Chicago or was he coerced?" is a meaningful question, whereas the question "Was that rock willing to fall or was it coerced?" is not. Indeed, Luther considers human possession of the property a triviality too obvious for discussion.

Moreover, when someone possessed of this aptitude makes a choice and is permitted by the circumstances to do what he or she has chosen, Luther says the action is done "freely." Such action displays *voluntas faciendi*, or "willingness," the contingent unity of choosing and doing.

But if the great denier of free will affirms all the foregoing, what then is it he thinks we do not have? All Luther's arguments are directed against forms of the same supposition: that our wills are antecedent to themselves, that we not only choose but choose what to choose. This supposition, Luther argues, is absurd.

It is, to begin, absurd to claim a power to alter the choices by which all our powers are marshalled in the first place. If contingent circumstances permit us to act upon courses we have chosen, our action is willing and free; and that is all that can or need be said.

The claim that we can choose what to choose supposes that there occurs in us "a sort of absolute willing," a will that does not yet will anything. This, Luther argues in very modern fashion, is a "dialectician's figment" that results from "ignoring realities and attending to words," from the metaphysician's besetting fallacy of supposing that because we need a word for certain purposes, in this case the word "will" to speak of our determinate choices, the word must therefore denote something merely by itself. Whether a word denotes by itself is settled only by experience; and if in this case we consult the facts of experience we will find only our determinate choices and the circumstances that do or do not allow us to act on them.

But why is Luther so urgent that we not make this claim, however foolish it may be analytically? The concern is soteriological. The claim supposes that the dispositional property of being apt for willing action is itself a sort of occult power actually so to act, is itself the sufficient condition of its own actualization. On the contrary, says Luther, if I am actually to act with voluntas faciendi, I must be "seized" (or "rapt") into willingness by another than myself; and moreover such rapture is always determinate. Willing action, the making and carrying out of personal choices, is enabled only in community, only by the provocation of an antecedent and determinate other will; it is not enabled within me as a closed system.

There are, moreover, only two by whom we are or can be thus seized: God and Satan. We are in fact seized by Satan, and so are unfree for God; this is the occasion of God's saving action. God's act is to seize us for himself and so make us unfree for

Satan. Within either rapture we often act "willingly": the usual choices of human life, to marry or not, to obey some civil law or not, to order steak instead of fish, and so on, are made and sometimes can terminate in action.

Luther has withheld the great word *libertas* both from the dispositional property and from "willing" action simply as such; he withholds it also and vehemently from the rapture worked by Satan. But then Luther does finally let the word fall, for the rapture by God. Indeed he crowns it as "royal freedom," regia libertas:God "seizes us for his booty, by his Spirit he makes us his slaves and captives—which is not bondage but royal freedom—that we willingly may choose and do what he chooses." It is God's appearance to seize us which qualifies resultant "willingness" of action as—at last—freedom.

We may ask why it must be God who seizes us for freedom. Why cannot your promises or importunities seize me for freedom; or for that matter why is not Satan's rapture freedom? The answer is plain, though not explicit in any one set of texts: rapture to freedom is not causative but participatory. Were you to be the ground of my freedom it would have to be because you shared freedom with me, which you cannot do because you no more have freedom in yourself than do I. As for Satan, he is an empty parody of freedom, a sort of personification of his own bondage, so that although he can indeed seize me into a *voluntas faciendi*, this can only be that of those who consent to share his slavery. *Liberum arbitrium* belongs to God and to those with whom he shares it.

But if, as Luther has argued, it is absurd to say that any will is antecedent to itself, how is it then meaningful to say it of God's will? How does a "dialectical figment" suddenly become a deep truth when it is predicated of God? And how is it now meaningful to speak of our sharing in this capacity? The clue is in the last feature to be noted from Luther's teaching: when God is on the scene to snatch us into freedom, it is always "by his Spirit."

It is not absurd to say that the triune God freely chooses his own determinate choices, for the Spirit is God and is precisely the freedom of the Father over against the Son, as whom the Father has what he chooses and in whom the Father knows what he chooses. Of a monadic will it is indeed absurd to assert that it chooses what to choose, but such a will is precisely what God is not. It would also be absurd to say that human persons as individuals have or can share God's triune free will. But as members of the community whose uniting and animating spirit is God the Spirit and who therefore stand with the Son before the Father, we share the liberation that the Spirit brings the Father and the Son.

True human freedom—or anyway the sort that Luther is willing to dignify with the name—is an ecclesial reality. All this is true of the man Jesus and of his sisters and brothers in the church, only differently. The risen Jesus, as present to and in the church, is at once liberated by the Spirit and giver of the liberating Spirit, so that it can even be said, "the Lord is the Spirit." And "where the Spirit of the Lord is, there is freedom." It cannot be said of us, individually or together, that we are the Spirit or that where we are there is freedom. But with the risen Jesus, as the totus Christus, we other members of the church are free as he is. Individually, we are being freed, as we live into the free community.

As for those who do not yet belong to the church, they act "willingly" within the communities whose uniting principle is the *libido dominandi*. They are creatures of the triune God and do not escape God's choice that their human choices occur freely; nor is the Spirit who evokes all created spontaneity other than the Spirit who enlivens the church. There is of course an inherent contradiction: that Satan's rapture is a sphere of the Creator Spirit's presence. It is the same contradiction we have encountered whenever the word "sin" has fallen.

V

So far, this work has used the word "soul" only to quote Socrates; this may be surprising, since the word has traditionally provided the overall rubric of theological anthropology. Do we, a la Socrates, "have souls"? It depends on what one means by "soul." For it might be said that these three chapters have all along discussed nothing else than the fact and nature of the human soul.

In the Hebrew Old Testament, the word translated "soul," nephesh, is a word for the human person as such, insofar as he or she is living and active and effective within community. A key passage of the second creation-narrative, so far omitted from our account, tells that God, having "formed the man from the dust of the ground," then "breathed into his nostrils the breath of life" so that "the man became a living soul ." It is not soul itself that is breathed into the not-yet living man; and what comes of God's breathing is not that the man acquires a soul but that he becomes one. Implicitly, our whole discussion of human personhood has had this passage as its guide.

The Greek of the New Testament displays no similarly consistent anthropological terminology. Comparing with the Old Testament, we may note that the word sometimes translated "soul," psyche, shows a certain shift away from denoting the living person to denoting the life of the living person. Thus in Jesus' saying, "Those who want to save their life will lose it, and those who lose their life for my sake . . . will save it," the word translated "life" is psyche. When psyche then appears paired with "body" (soma), the difference is between life and that which might not live or no longer lives; thus "the destroyer" can kill the body but not "the life" itself. Here it may appear that "soul" and body can be independently dealt with; it is by way of such language that a different sense of "soul" will enter Christian thinking.

"Soul" as mostly encountered in Scripture is what anthropologists have called body-soul, a representation of the difference between the living person and the corpse. Socrates' "soul," very differently, is what has been called an escape-soul, a representation of the person's seemingly possible liberation from his or her own body, as in dreams or shamanistic practice. It is "soul" of this second sort of which Socrates could say that death is "nothing other than the release of the soul from the body," and that the good person practices and longs for just this separation, in which human personhood first achieves its true nature. This is the "soul" that Platonism located decisively on the upward side of a metaphysical distinction between "spirit" and "matter." And this is the "soul" that became ambiguously fateful for Christian thinking.

Christianity adopted the Socratic notion of the soul not so much for its anthropologically interpretive power, which is in fact nil or close to it, as for its apparent eschatological service. What of the dead who have died in the Lord? Their bodies are in the earth; is that where they are? They are to rise in the body; but what of the meantime? Thus the one New Testament appearance of "souls" actually separated from their bodies is in the Revelation: "I saw under the altar the souls of those who had been slaughtered for the Word of God," where they are waiting for the final redemption.

The very thing that makes the Socratic notion of soul seem useful for eschatology is what creates the difficulty in our present context. Christianity attributes to embodiment a worth Socrates did not: the body is constitutive for the identity of the person. For Socrates, the soul that departs its body is the person perfected; whereas the Christian creeds locate the perfecting of the person not in the survival of the soul but in the resurrection of the body.

Thus the adopted Socratic notion of soul has through theological history been a fruitful source of puzzlement. In the Aristotelian language which Western scholasticism adapted to state the difficulties, the Socratic soul is a substance," that is, it does not require any other created reality to exist. But the human embodied person is also a substance. Given their creation, the soul and the besouled body both subsist in themselves. The question then has been: How are these two substances related? It was understood that they could not be regarded as two substances who merely happen for a time to be associated; theology was never quite so alienated from Scripture as to suppose such a thing.

After centuries of convoluted discussion, Thomas Aquinas devised a solution that is satisfactory if one accepts certain other scholastic positions. The soul, according to Thomas, is the "form" of the body, that is, the principle of that liveliness that distinguishes a body from a corpse—in this relation, we may say, Thomas's soul is a body-soul. Nevertheless, the soul must also be a substance other than the body, for its defining activity, consciousness, is in principle independent of bodily mediation, even though contingently it is in this life so mediated—in this relation, Thomas's soul is an escape-soul. Finally, this independent substantiality of the soul can be conceived because, although the soul is not matter instantiated by form, being itself the form of the body, it is nevertheless form instantiated by the act of existence.

Only one—but of course one is fatal—of the propositions on which Thomas relies is unacceptable within this work: that our creaturely consciousness is in principle a disembodied act. Sheer cognition may just possibly be conceivable as such an act, by abstracting the notion of "sight" as did the chief Greek thinkers. But our actual created consciousness is not so pure; it is compound of hearing and seeing as sensuous acts, and of smelling, tasting, and feeling as well, all apprehensions of external reality not readily attributable to a disembodied spirit.

This is a convenient place to make explicit what has been assumed through this volume: the personal body, as the person's availability to others and thereupon to him or herself, is just so constituted first in those modes of presence that resist dissolution into subjectivity...One might even say that "my body" is a way of referring to the logical product of "I see," "I taste," "I smell," "I touch," and so on. The discourse of systematic theology—as that of "philosophy"—too easily elides the sensuousness of human being. Let this paragraph at least recognize the temptation.

Nor has theology generally, popular or scholarly, been up to the subtlety of Thomas's solution. It may safely be said that nearly all Christians, once habituated to think of themselves as "having" a soul, have tended to revert to Socrates' pagan simplicity and conceive the soul as the real person hidden somehow "in" the body, until we "die and our souls go to heaven." But such devaluation of embodiment cannot cohere with the gospel, and must be repudiated no matter how embedded in piety.

If we must speak of souls, it will perhaps be best to discipline ourselves to the sense that predominates in Scripture: the soul is simply the person in his or her liveliness and communal uniqueness. And the person—the soul, if we will—does not have the body as something else than itself; the body is the very same person insofar as he or she is available to others and so to him or herself. We will have to deal with the eschatological problems without much help from Socrates.

Questions

1 "Personhood is not an aspect of God's being but is rather correlated to the three *who live* deity." What does this mean?

2 Is the link between speech and personhood made in any other of the readings here? Where, and in what way?

3 What is the problem Jenson identified with Aristotle's God? How does Jenson argue that even the divine persons have a perspectival consciousness?

4 What does it mean to say that consciousness is "focused"?

5 How does Jenson relate soteriology to his consideration of personal identity?

6 Jenson argues that true human freedom is an ecclesial reality. What does he mean by this, and do you agree?

7 What is Thomas' solution to the body-soul dilemma? Should we continue to speak of "souls"? How do bodies relate to human personhood?

TEXT 5: DAVID H. KELSEY,
ECCENTRIC EXISTENCE: A THEOLOGICAL ANTHROPOLOGY[17]

David Kelsey (b. 1932) taught at Yale Divinity School from 1965 until 2005, when he retired. During that time, he formed part of the so-called "Yale School" with his colleagues Hans Frei and George Lindbeck. Influenced by Karl Barth, the Yale writers—often also called "postliberal"—emphasized the centrality of the narratives of Scripture as the basis and measure of systematic theology. The philosophy of Ludwig Wittgenstein relating to "language games" also has a strong influence on postliberal theology, which is reacting against the focus on the autonomous individual. Kelsey's most influential work on this theme was *The Uses of Scripture in Recent Theology*. His interests more latterly turned to theological anthropology, and he published his two-volume magnum opus *Eccentric Existence: A Theological Anthropology* to wide acclaim in 2009.

CHAPTER 9B

Doxological Gratitude: Who We Are and How We Are to Be as Faithful Creatures

Thus far, our exploration of anthropological implications of the basic Christian claim that the triune God relates creatively to all that is not God has yielded remarks in response to the "What?" question. The full complexity of what we are as creatures, I suggested, is best conveyed by telling two different but inseparable stories about our being created in our being born: one a story about our being created as living human bodies, and the other about our being created in being loaned a living human body for whose orientation toward, and practices in, its proximate contexts it is accountable. I promoted the phrase "personal bodies" as a placeholder for the entire set of remarks about what we are in virtue of God's double way of relating to us creatively, at once directly and indirectly. It follows from those remarks, I urged, that personal bodies are the glory of God *both* insofar as they simply are living human bodies *and* insofar as they orient themselves in their proximate contexts in ways that are appropriate responses to the peculiar way in which God has already related to them creatively. In regard to the former, I proposed, lies their flourishing in the sense of "blossoming," whether in health or unhealth, simply as the living bodies they are. In regard to the latter–that is, in orientations and practices that are shaped as appropriate responses to the way in which God relates to them, I proposed, lies

[17]From David Kelsey, *Eccentric Existence: A Theological Anthropology* (Louisville: Westminster, 2009), 357–402.

their creaturely flourishing in the sense of "thriving," having themselves in hand. And the fitting name for the fundamental attitude comprising such orientations and practices, I suggested, is faith…

* * * *

"Personal Identities" vs. "Identities of Persons"

It is no part of this project to defend a claim about what the English word "person" really means in theological contexts or otherwise. Indeed, chapter 7 urged that, for the purposes of Christian theological anthropology, it is wise to avoid altogether the use of the substantives "person" and "self," and more abstract related terms such as "the person," "the self," "personhood," and "selfhood," to name the subject matter of theological anthropology—as in the remark, "Christian theological anthropology elaborates 'the Christian concept of the human person,' or 'the Christian understanding of human personhood,'" Used in that way, "person" and related terms are used to name members of a distinctive class of actual concrete entities. Instead, chapter 7 proposed, it will be less misleading to use the adjectival form "personal" to characterize the task of theological anthropology as the elaboration of a Christian understanding of what makes human creatures "personal creatures." Used in that way, the term "human creature" is used to name members of a distinctive class of concrete entities, and "personal" is used to characterize those entities in a certain way. Part of the task of this chapter is to develop more fully some reasons for adopting these proposals. What is to be noted here is that, given adoption of these proposals, the phrase "personal identities" does not mean "the identities of entities called 'persons.'" Rather, "personal" qualifies "identities" in a certain way, without specifying which entities it is whose identities are thus qualified.

One of the reasons for urging that the proposals made in theological anthropology not be framed as proposals about an entity called "person" is that in both theological and nontheological contexts, the word "person" has a variety of intelligible meanings. The meanings vary with how the word is used in different discursive contexts and subject to different interests. Each of them is a valid meaning of the term in its context. It is not possible to show that some one of them is what the word "person" *really* means.

In Christian theological contexts, for example, different ways of using the word "person" have developed that are governed by theological interests specific to different theological *loci*:

> – In the context of the traditional Christian doctrine of the Trinity, as developed by the fourth-century Cappadocians, God is one substance in three "persons" who are distinguished from each other solely by certain "incommunicable" or unshareable properties—namely, the unique way in which each is related to the other two. It is not clear that this concept of person can be generalized to cover human beings. Strictly speaking, it is a concept of person appropriate only in the context of the doctrine of God because only God is capable of having the eternal generative relations ("begetting," "begotten," "proceeding") that differentiate

the three divine "persons." These are relations in being. Furthermore, the eternity of these relations is conceptually inseparable from their nonmateriality. God has no body. Human beings, on the other hand, live in time and have material bodies. Moreover, since the three relations that constitute the divine "persons" in their differentiation from one another are profoundly different from one another, and each is unique to the "person" it differentiates, the word "person" may be ambiguous in this context. The concept of person may be different in each case. If this sense of "person" is to be generalized to cover human creatures as well, it would seem to be possible only by an analogical (or controlled equivocation) use of the term that blurs its equivocal character and is so extended that its illuminating power would be very dim.

– Arguably, Richard of St. Victor retrieves key insights in this Cappadocian analysis in his twelfth-century definition of "person" (in the context of Trinitarian discourse) as "an incommunicable existence of divine nature." For him the "incommunicable existence" of each divine person consists of (1) the fact that it has its existence in itself and not in anything else, and (2) its originating relation– that is, where it has its being from, as understood specifically in terms of Richard's analysis of God's eternally self-giving love. Because neither of these can be shared or communicated with any other, they constitute a distinct divine person. Arguably, this marks a significant distinction between the Cappadocians' concept of person and Richard's. Both may result in controlled equivocations ("analogies") in their uses of "person." For the Cappadocians, the differences in relations of origin that distinguish the divine persons from one another are differences in ways in which the richness of divine being inherently spills over or gives itself as another who is nonetheless divine. Because divine "being" is (in the modern sense of the term) an "impersonal" category and inherently unknowable to finite minds, human beings have no analogues in their own experience or knowledge of themselves that can be used to control the equivocations in this Trinitarian use of the term "person." For Richard, on the other hand, divine being is understood in terms of divine "love" which (in the modern sense of the term) is a "personal" category that has analogues in human experience and self-knowledge. Perhaps on that basis, Richard is able persuasively to sort out similarities and differences among types of divine love that can serve to control equivocal use of "person" in reference to the divine Trinity. If Richard's concept of "divine person" can be generalized to cover human beings, it can only be done by abstracting the defining characteristics of a human person from God's nontemporality and nonphysicality so that they reduce to a human being's personal identity (it has its existence in itself and not in anything else) and its constitution through the "other's" love of them.

– A different theological concept of "person" was explicitly developed in the fifth century by Boethius in the context of traditional christological (rather than Trinitarian) doctrine interested in clarifying the way the Incarnate Son of God is one "person": A person is "an individual substance of a rational nature." In such a concept, a person is not constituted through its relationships to any "other," but only by its individual subsistence as a concrete instance of a particular kind of being–a "rational" kind. While it may clarify questions in Christology by addressing christological conceptual interests, this concept of person would not be adequate in the context of the doctrine of the triunity of the one God. God's (one) nature is itself "individual substance of a rational nature." To define the three divine persons in the same way would yield doctrinal incoherence and polytheism. On the other hand, because it disregards relations as constitutive of persons, this concept does not raise any conceptual issues about the differences between divine and human individuals and may easily be generalized from the Incarnate One to cover creaturely persons such as bodied human beings and nonbodied angels. Perhaps for that reason, it was dominant in much medieval theology and philosophy. Insofar as "rational" (in "rational substance") is understood to be not only the capacity to know truth, but also the capacity for free action, this is a sense of the word "person" that is conceptually open to the claim that human persons are above all centers of agency capable of exercising their distinctive array of powers freely and intentionally in public space. Insofar as the "substance" (as in "rational substance") that is specifically human is understood as "formed matter," this is a sense of the word "person" that is conceptually open to the claim that bodiliness is in some way essential to being a human person. That claim, of course, has been the subject of much metaphysical debate in Christian history. What is Significant about this concept of person is that it makes that debate possible.

In the quite different context of legal discourse, "person" is used in yet another way, governed by core legal interests:

– In U.S. law, for example, "person" is used to refer to any member of the class of parties that have standing in the law and have relevant legal rights in relation to a given case, a class that equally includes individual human beings and legally chartered retail corporations like Wal-Mart, financial corporations like Citibank, or manufacturing corporations like Boeing. Conceived in this way, persons are not constituted by their relations, nor are they constituted through the "other." Moreover, while in certain cases human beings may lose their legal status as persons if they can be shown not to be of sound mind, it is not evident that rationality is definitive of corporations' legal standing as persons. It is striking that, insofar as legal standing is the ground of a variety of types of social, economic, and political power, this is a sense of the term that defines "person" in terms of possession of power in the public realm.

Undoubtedly the most influential meaning of the word "person" in the discursive contexts of modern Western cultures has been governed by the Enlightenment's interests in human liberation from arbitrary, unjust, and oppressive authority– that is, from heteronomous, political, social, moral, and religious authorities... Anthropology arose as an independent theological locus in the eighteenth century and was from the beginning framed in terms provided by a distinctively "modern" concept of person:

– This is the concept of person that comes with the Enlightenment's celebrated "turn to the subject": A person is a morally perfectible, autonomous center of self-aware consciousness, in contradistinction to non-self-aware, nonconscious "things" that are subject to physical determinism. A person is a "subject" in contrast to an "object." Insofar as "consciousness" may be–indeed, must be–analyzed in relational terms, this concept of person is open to elaboration in the thesis that persons are constituted through the "other." It is less clear how a concept of person as center of consciousness can be used to develop an account of human persons that systematically includes scientific knowledge about persons as bodied, how and why their living bodies function, and how consciousness is related to their bodies. It is also less clear how a concept of person as center of consciousness can be used to develop an account of human persons, not only as subjects of experiences of personal and nonpersonal others and imaginers of possible actions in the privacy of their subjective interiorities, but as active agents in a public world.

These uses of "person" overlap in many ways and arguably exhibit numerous family resemblances. No doubt there are additional uses of the term. However, it would be wrongheaded to postulate some one core, basic, or essential meaning underlying or shared by all of these senses of "person." There is no basis on which to argue that one or another of these meanings of "person" is the real or true meaning of the term, of which the rest are at best partial distortions or one-sided uses.

It is commonplace, for example, to explain the meaning of the word "person" by observing that the word has its historical roots in the classical Greek *prosopon*, "face," and the Latin *persona*, "mask," which were used to refer to the mask through which an actor speaks or to the role an actor plays.

However, it cannot be argued that the real or fundamental meaning of the word "person" is the social role a human being plays, or the more or less stylized self-presentation through which a human being expresses herself or himself to others, on the historical grounds that the origins of the English word "person" are the Greek *prosopon* and Latin *persona*. While it is sometimes illuminating, the etymology of a word does not determine its meaning.

Nor can such a thesis be argued on cultural-anthropological or sociological grounds. There is a highly influential narrative of the development of the modern "category of the person" that grows out of "the work of the French school of sociology," influenced especially by Emile Durkheim, and summarized in a celebrated 1938 essay by Marcel Mauss, "A Category of the Human Mind: The Notion of Person; The Notion of Self" (1985, 1–25). The narrative outlines "the succession of forms that this concept [of "self," *moi*] has taken in the life of men in different societies, according to their systems of law, religion, customs, social structures and mentality".

1. On the basis of the reports of anthropological field studies of the Pueblo of Zuni, American North-West Indians, and Australian traditional cultures, Mauss generalizes that "a whole immense group of societies" construe their common life as a sacred drama and that an individual's name identifies which of the limited number of roles *(personages)* in that drama is his or hers, identifies his or her status in the society, and identifies his or her kinship relations with ancestors who filled the same role, all of which is expressed by the mask the individual wears in social rituals.

2. The next stage is the rise of awareness of "the individual, of his consciousness–may I say, of the 'self' *(moi)*" (13). Mauss thinks there is evidence that this concept

first emerged in India, and then in China, but in both cases the "self" was considered to be composite and dissoluble.

Rome's is the most important culture to "have made of the human person a complete entity, independent of all others save God" (14). The context of this development is the evolution of Roman law. "'[P]erson' *(personne)* is more than an organizational fact, more than a name or a right to assume a role and a ritual mask. It is a basic fact of law. In law, according to the legal experts, there are only *personne, res,* and *actiones...*" (14). The fundamental "independence" of human persons from one another (i.e., their individuation) is rooted in the fact that their rights and responsibilities before the law are independent of anything anyone else is or does.

3. This development is reinforced and enriched by the Latin and Greek moralists (200 BC–AD 400) who add to the juridical meaning of *persona* a moral one, "a sense of being conscious, independent, autonomous, free and responsible".

4. Christianity introduces the next step by making a sacred "metaphysical entity of the 'moral person'". Mauss holds that Christianity's stress on the indissoluble "one," first in regard to the divine persons, but then also regarding the church, led to its stress on the irreducible metaphysical oneness of the human person: "The person is a rational substance, indivisible and individual" (20). Moreover, for Mauss, this Christian concept grounds the unity of the human person in its sacred, although created, soul.

5. The final step to the "category of the 'self'" *(moi)* involves a shift from the person as a metaphysical and sacred being to the person as a "psychological" being. It is a shift from conceiving of the person in metaphysical terms related to "substance" to conceiving it in terms related to "consciousness." In such figures of the early Enlightenment as Descartes, Spinoza, and Leibnitz, the person was still conceived in metaphysical categories, although the definitive function of the metaphysical soul was discursive, clear, and deductive thought. Mauss holds that it was the sectarian religious movements of the seventeenth and eighteenth centuries rather than the early.

Enlightenment philosophers who provided "the basis on which is established the notion: the 'person' *(personne)* equals the 'self' *(moi)* equals consciousness, *and* is *its primordial category*". Although it embraces current understanding of "the psychological" as the dynamics of the affections, broadly construed, Mauss intends "psychological" to cover more. Kant, the Pietist, "made of the individual consciousness, the sacred character of the human person, the condition for Practical Reason." He posed, "but did not resolve," the question "whether the 'self' *(moi), das Ich,* is a category". "It was Fichte," Mauss contends, "who made of it [individual consciousness] as well the *category of the 'self' (moi)*, the condition of consciousness and of science, of Pure Reason" and of all action. As the phrases I have underscored emphasize, Mauss seems to be arguing that the distinctively modern "psychological" understanding of the person that arises at the last moment of his narrative not only construes· "person" in terms of consciousness, rather than metaphysically in terms of a concept of "substantial soul," but construes consciousness as a "category," presumably in contradistinction to a mere "concept." As he puts it at the end of a one-sentence summary of his narrative, the last moment of the narrative is a move from "person" as "sacred being" to "person" as "a fundamental form of thought and action', perhaps a "transcendental" category that provides the framework that defines the range of application and meaning of all possible statements about the nature of human beings.

Mauss is clear and emphatic that his intent in telling this narrative is to impress on his readers that the concept of "person" has changed profoundly several times across human history. The modern notion of the person may function as a (transcendental?) category for those who are formed by modern cultures, but it is not universal or innate in human consciousness. There are many other possible ways of understanding the person. The modern category of the person is historically very recent. It has developed out of earlier concepts, but Mauss is not, apparently, arguing for any type of logical necessity to that development.

The irony of Mauss's narrative, however, is that it is told in a way that is open to being read as an argument for the superiority and, in some not very clear way, the inevitability of the modern category of the person. This possibility is a function, I think, of the narrative being cast as a retrospective story of a teleological process. It is made a single, continuous process by its *telos,* which is already known at the beginning of the story. That *telos* is the modern psychological category of the person. The story is told retrospectively from the perspective of the realization of its *telos* That unavoidably gives the impression either that the moments in the process that came before the *telos's* realization inevitably lead to that realization because they are all organic to the process of the *telos's* unfolding, or that the narrative is misleading and unpersuasive because the moments have been preselected from a much larger array of data, cherry-picked because they seem most clearly to anticipate or prefigure the distinctively modern understanding. The first impression is reinforced by Mauss's opening observation that "the notion [person; self *(moi)*] has assumed" different "forms" at "various times and in various places", and by his concluding observation that this type of "social anthropology, sociology and history…all teach us to perceive how human thought 'moves on". Is there some one notion that undergoes a process of metamorphosis over time, perhaps unfolding according to its inner logic? People think, and change what they think. But what does the moving when thought moves on—perhaps reason itself, according to its inner logic? Either way, the essay's narrative reads as though haunted by Hegel's ghost. Mauss's explicit intent for the essay rules out its narrative as the ground for declaring the modern psychological meaning of "person' to be the word's real meaning; the reading the essay too easily invites, however, offers nothing but a bad argument for the same thesis.

One reason for adopting chapter 7's proposal that theological anthropology not be framed as a discussion of the properly Christian concept of person is the variety of valid senses of the word "person" already at work in theological and nontheological contexts, and the impossibility of showing that one of them is the basic or correct meaning of the term. Granted that proposal, the phrase "personal identities" does not mean that the topic for discussion is the nature of the identities of entities called "persons." Rather, as chapter 7 urged, "personal" in the phrase "personal identities" should be understood to qualify in a theocentric way the identities of entities not specified by the phrase itself (but specified in chapter 6 as "actual living human creaturely bodies").

But, it might be asked, why should not a project in Christian anthropology stipulate a technical theological concept of "person"? It need not be claimed to be the real meaning of the word that is fundamental to all other valid uses of the term.

It need only be claimed to be the correct way of using "person" in the practice of Christian secondary theology addressing the locus of anthropology.

Excursus: The power and inadequacy of the modern concept of person

The major problem with framing a Christian anthropology as a theological concept of person lies in the inherent power and current cultural dominance of the modern concept of person. A theological anthropology will have theological reasons for affirming some of the features of the modern concept that make it powerful. However, in other respects the modern concept of person is finally insufficient to articulate its own Enlightenment interests, and is in any case inadequate to central Christian theological interests. Consequently, a theological anthropology that is framed in terms provided by the modern concept in order to acknowledge and affirm theologically some part of what makes it a powerful concept would also need to modify the concept radically, and in some respects to distance itself from it. The difficulty is that the cultural dominance of the modern concept of person is so strong that it is next to impossible in the context of modern culture to employ its central terms, especially the term "person," in a way that does not also implicate the very features of the modern concept of person that need to be revised or rejected for theological reasons.

Readers of, or listeners to, theological anthropological discourse that is framed in terms provided by the modern concept of person will inevitably associate it with, and infer from it, the key assumptions about what it is to be a person that are conventionally ready at hand in modern culture, including theologically problematic assumptions, no matter how skillful the theologian's conceptual strategies may be to set limits to the modern concept so that one goes only so far with it and no further. Analyses by Michael Welker, Hans Frei, and Christoph Schwoebel show ways in which the modern concept of person is powerful and ways in which it is at the same time insufficient to explicate the most important Enlightenment interests it was created to serve and is inadequate to explicate core Christian theological anthropological interests.

* * * *

Although they do not explicitly argue for the thesis that it should not be adopted, Michael Welker and Christoph Schwoebel give strong reasons not to adopt the modern concept of person in Christian theological anthropology. The tropes of the mask, self-expression, and relational being help bring to focus a number of features of the modern concept of person that have made it a powerful concept in modern Western cultures and, for that reason, very attractive to modern theological anthropology as a way in which to explicate Christian anthropological convictions in a fashion that is both intelligible and persuasive within the context of modern culture. However, not adopting the modern concept of person is not so easy to do by Christians who gave grown up in, now live in, and whose consciousness is thereby deeply formed by modern cultures and their reigning concept of the person. As Peter Berger and his associates write, "Modern consciousness is rather hard to get rid of". Culturally speaking, "Demodernization in advanced industrial societies has limits that may be shifting but are nonetheless quite firm. ...These limits are grounded in the necessity of maintaining the fundamental technological and bureaucratic machinery of the society. This means that demodernization, and the social constellations created by it" (including "modern consciousness") "will be parasitical upon the structures of modernity".

Nor can the modern concept of person be eliminated from theological anthropology simply by providing an alternative theological concept of person. So dominant is the modern concept in modern culture, and such is its power that, it seems to me, it is virtually impossible to use the English word "person," however much it is qualified, without leading the listener or reader to absorb what is said or written into this already-well-known concept of person. The very use of the word "person" to name the subject of the discussion would invite confusion of the received modern concept of person with what is proposed as a theological alternative, regardless of how explicit, dearly different, and intellectually powerful the theological formulation of the alternative concept might be. The systematic irony of every polemical strategy that might be employed to distance a proposed theological concept of person from the unacceptable modern concept of person is that the more one compares and contrasts the preferable concept to the unacceptable one, the more the preferable concept is defined in terms of the inadequate concept. Even if it is only defined by negation of the unacceptable concept, the preferable concept ends up sounding like a new, improved version of the unacceptable one. To turn an unacceptable concept on its head simply leaves one with an unacceptable upside-down concept.

Because there are strong theological reasons not to adopt the modern concept of person, I suggest—going beyond anything either Welker or Schwoebel suggests— simply setting aside completely the word "person" as the name for the subject of theological anthropology. In chapter 7, I concurred that theological anthropology requires a logically primitive concept of human being that is not derived from or defined through any other concept. I think Schwoebel is correct that such a concept functions as a "category" (in his sense of the term) in theological anthropology. That is, among other things, this primitive concept determines the meaning and range of application of all possible theological statements about a human person and provides the framework in which statements about what human persons are can be made. For example, as I urged in chapter 7, theological anthropology's primitive concept determines that claims about human being employ a theocentric conceptual scheme that is simultaneously classificatory and evaluative. One could use the English word "person" to express this concept, calling it the "Christian theological concept of person." After all, one is free to stipulate technical meanings of words as one chooses. However, for the reasons reviewed above, I urge that that would be misleading and that it would be wise to retire the word "person" from this role in theological anthropology, at least temporarily. In place of "person," I have urged in this part of this work that anthropology's primitive categorical concept be expressed by the phrase "human creature," and that "personal" be used to underscore the conjointly classificatory and evaluative character of properly formulated theological claims about human creatures.

Questions

1   What are "personal bodies"? How does faith help them to flourish?

2   Why is Kelsey cautious about the language of "person"? Is the caution warranted, in the light of the other readings? What is his alternative? Does it work in your opinion?

3   What are some of the different theological uses of the term "person"?

4   What is Mauss' narrative of the use of the word "person"? How does Kelsey critique Mauss?

5   What might Spaemann say in rejoinder to Kelsey?

7

Worship and Desire

The study of the human being as a religious creature has taken some fascinating turns in the history of human thought. It is a general axiom of anthropology that where we have human beings, we also observe religion. We search in vain into the deep past to find a pre-religious human culture. Even the Neanderthals, it seems, had religious practices. That ancient peoples observed this Godwards orientation in human hearts is suggested in the Hebrew Scriptures: *He has made everything beautiful in its time. He has also set eternity in the human heart; yet no one can fathom what God has done from beginning to end* (Eccl. 3:11). It would seem obvious that if there is a God, he would make human beings with the capacity to engage with him and with the yearning to seek him out.

But how is this longing to be analyzed? And, if there is a movement within human beings toward the divine, why does it result in so much diversity? Why among human beings does this impulse result in a cacophony of religious and spiritual outcomes, rather than a unity? John Calvin and others pick up the strain in the Old Testament which is extremely critical of false worship. Like everything else about humankind, the impulse to worship is infected and corrupted by sin. The human heart contains an immortal longing, but is too easily satisfied with God substitutes rather than the real thing. Perhaps the desire within us is a false trail, and indeed we ought to wait for divine revelation, rather than pursue it, such is the risk.

That has not been the majority finding in Christian theology, however. Mostly, Christian theologians have agreed that the religious impulse in us, though prone to distortion and corruption, corresponds to the reality that it points toward. The human individual hungers for God because God is indeed there to be encountered.

Since the nineteenth century, however, there has been a renewed interest in the universal anthropological datum. Religious experience across times and places can be compared, and contrasted. Is it perhaps that there is a common core of experience that is really the essential thing—as opposed to the dogma of churches and temples? Is there in fact a way in which a unifying field of religious thought and practice could be developed? This was the thought that drove William James in his Gifford lectures to collect and classify a huge range of religious testimony.

But this line of inquiry took a new turn with the development of neuroscience in the latter part of the twentieth century. What neuroscience has promised is the possibility of examining religious experience not simply via the first person and subjective testimony of individuals undergoing religious experiences, but via the objective frame of neuro-imaging. Could it be that there is, observable in the brain patterns of the test subjects, some structure or feature that "makes" us religious? Is there a way to explain, at the level of neurobiology, this persistent religiosity in the human creature? For some atheists, this meant a way of reducing religious experience to brain waves, rendering them illusory, and neutralizing the argument for God from subjective experience. This seems to be an over-claim, however. A Bernard of Clairvaux would, one feels, not at all be surprised to discover that the human brain was shaped so as to crave experience of the divine.

TEXT 1 BERNARD OF CLAIRVAUX, *ON LOVING GOD*[1]

Bernard of Clairvaux (1090–1153) was the most influential churchman and theologian in the European church of his era. Born of noble parents, Bernard entered the Cistercian order at the Abbey of Citeaux at the age of twenty-one. Only three years later he was assigned the task of leading the new monastery at Clairvaux, where he proved a strong and capable leader. Bernard was a visible figure in many ecclesiastical debates of the twelfth century, a role that was enhanced when one of his monks became Pope Eugenius III in 1145. Eugenius commissioned Bernard to preach in support of the Second Crusade, which he did so with extraordinary fervor and masterly rhetoric.

As a theologian, Bernard successfully opposed the teachings of Peter Abelard to the point that Abelard was condemned by the Council of Sens in 1140. He wrote a number of treatises, including *On Grace and Free Choice*, and was a prolific preacher and letter writer. His most famous work is *On Loving God*, a spiritual as much as a theological work. It had a great influence on John Calvin among others, probably because both Calvin and Bernard shared an Augustinian cast of mind. In this work he answers the perennial questions of how God can and ought to be loved by fallen and limited human beings.

Chapter I

Why we should love God and the measure of that love

You want me to tell you why God is to be loved and how much. I answer, the reason for loving God is God Himself; and the measure of love due to Him is immeasurable love. Is this plain? Doubtless, to a thoughtful man; but I am debtor to the unwise also. A word to the wise is sufficient; but I must consider simple folk too. Therefore I set myself joyfully to explain more in detail what is meant above.

We are to love God for Himself, because of a twofold reason; nothing is more reasonable, nothing more profitable. When one asks, Why should I love God? he may mean, What is lovely in God? or What shall I gain by loving God? In either case, the same sufficient cause of love exists, namely, God Himself.

And first, of His title to our love. Could any title be greater than this, that He gave Himself for us unworthy wretches? And being God, what better gift could He offer than Himself? Hence, if one seeks for God's claim upon our love here is the chiefest: Because He first loved us (1 John 4.19).

---

[1]Bernard of Clairvaux, *Saint Bernard on Loving God*, (Grand Rapids: Christian Classics Ethereal Library) https://www.ccel.org/ccel/bernard/loving_god.txt

Ought He not to be loved in return, when we think who loved, whom He loved, and how much He loved? For who is He that loved? The same of whom every spirit testifies: Thou art my God: my goods are nothing unto Thee' (Ps. 16.2, *Vulg.*). And is not His love that wonderful charity which seeketh not her own'? (I Cor. 13.5). But for whom was such unutterable love made manifest? The apostle tells us: When we were enemies, we were reconciled to God by the death of His Son' (Rom. 5.10). So it was God who loved us, loved us freely, and loved us while yet we were enemies. And how great was this love of His? St. John answers: God so loved the world that He gave His only-begotten Son, that whosoever believeth in Him should not perish, but have everlasting life' (John 3.16). St. Paul adds: He spared not His own Son, but delivered Him up for us all' (Rom. 8.32); and the Son says of Himself, Greater love hath no man than this, that a man lay down his life for his friends' (John 15.13).

This is the claim which God the holy, the supreme, the omnipotent, has upon men, defiled and base and weak. Some one may urge that this is true of mankind, but not of angels. True, since for angels it was not needful. He who succored men in their time of need, preserved angels from such need; and even as His love for sinful men wrought wondrously in them so that they should not remain sinful, so that same love which in equal measure He poured out upon angels kept them altogether free from sin.

****

Chapter VI

A brief summary

Admit that God deserves to be loved very much, yea, boundlessly, because He loved us first, He infinite and we nothing, loved us, miserable sinners, with a love so great and so free. This is why I said at the beginning that the measure of our love to God is to love immeasurably. For since our love is toward God, who is infinite and immeasurable, how can we bound or limit the love we owe Him? Besides, our love is not a gift but a debt. And since it is the Godhead who loves us, Himself boundless, eternal, supreme love, of whose greatness there is no end, yea, and His wisdom is infinite, whose peace passeth all understanding; since it is He who loves us, I say, can we think of repaying Him grudgingly? I will love Thee, O Lord, my strength. The Lord is my rock and my fortress and my deliverer, my God, my strength, in whom I will trust' (Ps. 18.1f). He is all that I need, all that I long for. My God and my help, I will love Thee for Thy great goodness; not so much as I might, surely, but as much as I can. I cannot love Thee as Thou deservest to be loved, for I cannot love Thee more than my own feebleness permits. I will love Thee more when Thou deemest me worthy to receive greater capacity for loving; yet never so perfectly as Thou hast deserved of me. Thine eyes did see my substance, yet being unperfect; and in Thy book all my members were written' (PS. 139.16). Yet Thou recordest in that book all who do what they can, even though they cannot do what they ought. Surely I have said enough to show how God should be loved and why. But who has felt, who can know, who express, how much we should love him.

Chapter VII

Of love toward God not without reward: and how the hunger of man's heart cannot be satisfied with earthly things

And now let us consider what profit we shall have from loving God. Even though our knowledge of this is imperfect, still that is better than to ignore it altogether. I have already said (when it was a question of wherefore and in what manner God should be loved) that there was a double reason constraining us: His right and our advantage. Having written as best I can, though unworthily, of God's right to be loved. I have still to treat of the recompense which that love brings. For although God would be loved without respect of reward, yet He wills not to leave love unrewarded. True charity cannot be left destitute, even though she is unselfish and seeketh not her own (1 Cor. 13.5). Love is an affection of the soul, not a contract: it cannot rise from a mere agreement, nor is it so to be gained. It is spontaneous in its origin and impulse; and true love is its own satisfaction. It has its reward; but that reward is the object beloved. For whatever you seem to love, if it is on account of something else, what you do really love is that something else, not the apparent object of desire. St. Paul did not preach the Gospel that he might earn his bread; he ate that he might be strengthened for his ministry. What he loved was not bread, but the Gospel. True love does not demand a reward, but it deserves one. Surely no one offers to pay for love; yet some recompense is due to one who loves, and if his love endures he will doubtless receive it.

On a lower plane of action, it is the reluctant, not the eager, whom we urge by promises of reward. Who would think of paying a man to do what he was yearning to do already? For instance no one would hire a hungry man to eat, or a thirsty man to drink, or a mother to nurse her own child. Who would think of bribing a farmer to dress his own vineyard, or to dig about his orchard, or to rebuild his house? So, all the more, one who loves God truly asks no other recompense than God Himself; for if he should demand anything else it would be the prize that he loved and not God.

It is natural for a man to desire what he reckons better than that which he has already, and be satisfied with nothing which lacks that special quality which he misses. Thus, if it is for her beauty that he loves his wife, he will cast longing eyes after a fairer woman. If he is clad in a rich garment, he will covet a costlier one; and no matter how rich he may be he will envy a man richer than himself. Do we not see people every day, endowed with vast estates, who keep on joining field to field, dreaming of wider boundaries for their lands? Those who dwell in palaces are ever adding house to house, continually building up and tearing down, remodeling and changing. Men in high places are driven by insatiable ambition to clutch at still greater prizes. And nowhere is there any final satisfaction, because nothing there can be defined as absolutely the best or highest. But it is natural that nothing should content a man's desires but the very best, as he reckons it. Is it not, then, mad folly always to be craving for things which can never quiet our longings, much less satisfy them? No matter how many such things one has, he is always lusting after what he has not; never at peace, he sighs for new possessions. Discontented, he spends himself in fruitless toil, and finds only weariness in the evanescent and unreal pleasures of the world. In his greediness, he counts all that he has clutched as nothing in comparison with what is beyond his grasp, and loses all pleasure in his actual possessions by longing after what he has not, yet covets. No man can ever hope to own all things. Even the little one does possess is got only with toil and is held in fear; since each is certain to lose what he hath when God's day, appointed though unrevealed, shall come. But the perverted will struggles towards the ultimate good by devious ways, yearning after satisfaction, yet led astray by vanity and deceived by wickedness. Ah, if you wish to attain to the consummation of all desire, so that nothing unfulfilled will be left, why weary yourself with fruitless efforts, running hither and thither, only to die long before the goal is reached?

It is so that these impious ones wander in a circle, longing after something to gratify their yearnings, yet madly rejecting that which alone can bring them to their desired end, not by exhaustion but by attainment. They wear themselves out in vain travail, without reaching their blessed consummation, because they delight in creatures, not in the Creator. They want to traverse creation, trying all things one by one, rather than think of coming to Him who is Lord of all. And if their utmost longing were realized, so that they should have all the world for their own, yet without possessing Him who is the Author of all being, then the same law of their desires would make them contemn what they had and restlessly seek Him whom they still lacked, that is, God Himself. Rest is in Him alone. Man knows no peace in the world; but he has no disturbance when he is with God. And so the soul says with confidence, Whom have I in heaven but Thee; and there is none upon earth that I desire in comparison of Thee. God is the strength of my heart, and my portion for ever. It is good for me to hold me fast by God, to put my trust in the Lord God' (Ps. 73.25ff). Even by this way one would eventually come to God, if only he might have time to test all lesser goods in turn.

But life is too short, strength too feeble, and competitors too many, for that course to be practicable. One could never reach the end, though he were to weary himself with the long effort and fruitless toil of testing everything that might seem desirable. It would be far easier and better to make the assay in imagination rather than in experiment. For the mind is swifter in operation and keener in discrimination than the bodily senses, to this very purpose that it may go before the sensuous affections so that they may cleave to nothing which the mind has found worthless. And so it is written, Prove all things: hold fast that which is good' (1 Thess. 5.21). Which is to say that right judgment should prepare the way for the heart. Otherwise we may not ascend into the hill of the Lord nor rise up in His holy place (Ps. 24.3). We should have no profit in possessing a rational mind if we were to follow the impulse of the senses, like brute beasts, with no regard at all to reason. Those whom reason does not guide in their course may indeed run, but not in the appointed race-track, neglecting the apostolic counsel, So run that ye may obtain'. For how could they obtain the prize who put that last of all in their endeavor and run round after everything else first?

But as for the righteous man, it is not so with him. He remembers the condemnation pronounced on the multitude who wander after vanity, who travel the broad way that leads to death (Matt. 7.13); and he chooses the King's highway, turning aside neither to the right hand nor to the left (Num. 20.17), even as the prophet saith, The way of the just is uprightness (Isa. 26.7). Warned by wholesome counsel he shuns the perilous road, and heeds the direction that shortens the search, forbidding covetousness and commanding that he sell all that he hath and give to the poor (Matt. 19.21). Blessed, truly, are the poor, for theirs is the Kingdom of Heaven (Matt. 5.3). They which run in a race, run all, but distinction is made among the racers. The Lord knoweth the way of the righteous: and the way of the ungodly shall perish' (Ps. 1.6). A small thing that the righteous hath is better than great riches of the ungodly' (Ps. 37.16). Even as the Preacher saith, and the fool discovereth, He that loveth silver shall not be satisfied with silver' (Eccles. 5.10). But Christ saith, Blessed are they which do hunger and thirst after righteousness, for they shall be filled' (Matt. 5.6). Righteousness is the natural and essential food of the soul, which can no more be satisfied by earthly treasures than the hunger of the body can be satisfied by air. If you should see a starving man standing with mouth open to the wind, inhaling draughts of air as if in hope of gratifying his hunger, you would think him lunatic. But it is no less foolish to imagine that the soul can be satisfied with worldly things which only inflate it without feeding it. What have spiritual gifts to do with carnal appetites, or carnal with spiritual? Praise the Lord, O my soul: who satisfieth thy mouth with good things (Ps. 103.1ff). He bestows bounty immeasurable; He provokes thee to good, He preserves thee in goodness; He prevents, He sustains, He fills thee. He moves thee to longing, and it is He for whom thou longest.

I have said already that the motive for loving God is God Himself. And I spoke truly, for He is as well the efficient cause as the final object of our love. He gives the occasion for love, He creates the affection, He brings the desire to good effect. He is such that love to Him is a natural due; and so hope in Him is natural, since our present love would be vain did we not hope to love Him perfectly some day. Our love is prepared and rewarded by His. He loves us first, out of His great tenderness; then we are bound to repay Him with love; and we are permitted to cherish exultant hopes in Him. He is rich unto all that call upon Him' (Rom. 10.12), yet He has no gift for them better than Himself. He gives Himself as prize and reward: He is the refreshment of holy soul, the ransom of those in captivity. The Lord is good unto them that wait for Him' (Lam. 3.25). What will He be then to those who gain His presence? But here is a paradox, that no one can seek the Lord who has not already found Him. It is Thy will, O God, to be found that Thou mayest be sought, to be sought that Thou mayest the more truly be found. But though Thou canst be sought and found, Thou canst not be forestalled. For if we say, Early shall my prayer come before Thee' (Ps. 88.13), yet doubtless all prayer would be lukewarm unless it was animated by Thine inspiration.

Questions

1 Bernard asks why and how God ought to be loved, and gives a simple answer: "the cause of loving God is God himself." What does he mean by this? Is it a satisfactory answer? What other answers to the question could be proposed?

2 What does God do to deserve human love?

3 How would you outline Bernard's anthropology? What does he mean by "dignity"?

4 How does consideration of human nature lead to consideration of the divine nature, in Bernard's construal?

5 What is, for Bernard, at the root of human sin?

6 How does Bernard make use of the erotic imagery of the Song of Songs in the excerpt?

7 How does the faithful soul increase its love for God?

TEXT 2: JOHN CALVIN, *INSTITUTES OF THE CHRISTIAN RELIGION*[2]

John Calvin (1509–1564) thought of his *Institutes* as part of a package to go with his commentary work. He attempted in his commentaries to be brief, and made use of the format of the *Institutes* to make more extensive theological reflections. The work itself evolved over more than two decades and became eventually one of the classics of Western literature. Calvin deploys his humanist and legal training with skill, choosing apt similes and collating texts with remarkable insight.

Along with the other reformers, Calvin was adamant that idolatry was among humankind's greatest sins. No doubt this was because of the prevalence of statues and images among the Roman Catholic churches from which Calvin wished to distinguish himself. He depicted God the Father as the invisible, speaking God. Human beings cannot gaze upon him, though their longing for him means that they construct many an idol in an attempt to visualize him. What they must do, rather, is *listen*.

8. In regard to the origin of idols, the statement contained in the Book of Wisdom has been received with almost universal consent—viz. that they originated with those who bestowed this honour on the dead, from a superstitious regard to their memory. I admit that this perverse practice is of very high antiquity, and I deny not that it was a kind of torch by which the infatuated proneness of mankind to idolatry was kindled into a greater blaze. I do not, however, admit that it was the first origin of the practice. That idols were in use before the prevalence of that ambitious consecration of the images of the dead, frequently adverted to by profane writers, is evident from the words of Moses (Gen. 31:19). When he relates that Rachel stole her father's images, he speaks of the use of idols as a common vice. Hence we may infer, that the human mind is, so to speak, a perpetual forge of idols. There was a kind of renewal of the world at the deluge, but before many years elapse, men are forging gods at will. There is reason to believe, that in the holy Patriarch's lifetime his grandchildren were given to idolatry: so that he must with his own eyes, not without the deepest grief, have seen the earth polluted with idols—that earth whose iniquities God had lately purged with so fearful a Judgment. For Joshua testifies (Josh. 24:2), that Torah and Nachor, even before the birth of Abraham, were the worshipers of false gods. The progeny of Shem having so speedily revolted, what are we to think of the posterity of Ham, who had been cursed long before in their father? Thus, indeed, it is. The human mind, stuffed as it is with presumptuous rashness, dares to imagine a god suited to its own capacity; as it labours under dullness, nay, is sunk in the grossest ignorance, it substitutes vanity and an empty phantom in the place of God. To these evils another is added. The god whom man has thus conceived inwardly he attempts to embody outwardly. The mind, in this way, conceives the idol, and the hand gives it

---

[2]Jean Calvin, *Institutes of the Christian Religion*, trans. H. Beveridge (London: James Clarke, 1953), I.ix.8

birth. That idolatry has its origin in the idea which men have, that God is not present with them unless his presence is carnally exhibited, appears from the example of the Israelites: "Up," said they, "make us gods, which shall go before us; for as for this Moses, the man that brought us up out of the land of Egypt, we wet not what is become of him," (Exod. 22:1). They knew, indeed, that there was a God whose mighty power they had experienced in so many miracles, but they had no confidence of his being near to them, if they did not with their eyes behold a corporeal symbol of his presence, as an attestation to his actual government. They desired, therefore, to be assured by the image which went before them, that they were journeying under Divine guidance. And daily experience shows, that the flesh is always restless until it has obtained some figment like itself, with which it may vainly solace itself as a representation of God. In consequence of this blind passion men have, almost in all ages since the world began, set up signs on which they imagined that God was visibly depicted to their eyes.

Questions

1. What according to Calvin is the source of idolatry?

2. What does he mean by calling "man's nature" a "perpetual factory of idols"? In your view, is this analysis regarding the immortal longings of the human heart too pessimistic? Evaluate this claim theologically.

3. Why is the physical absence of God such a wellspring for idol-making?

4. Calvin writes: "Flesh is always uneasy until it has obtained some figment like itself in which it may fondly find solace as in an image of God." What does he mean by this? And what is his evidence for making this claim?

5. Why is the desire that Calvin describes a "blind desire"?

TEXT 3 WILLIAM JAMES *THE VARIETIES OF RELIGIOUS EXPERIENCE*[3]

William James (1842–1910), the great Harvard psychologist and philosopher, was asked to deliver the Gifford Lectures in Scotland in 1901 and 1902. This was a conspicuous honor. If they were to fulfill the charter left behind in Lord Gifford's will, James's lectures would "promote and diffuse the study of natural theology in the widest sense of the term—in other words, the knowledge of God." James had long been interested in the phenomena of religious experiences, and collected a filing cabinet full of testimonies from across the world, and from several religions— although mostly from Christianity. James was not interested in dogma as such, but rather in the experiences behind dogmatic claims. Likewise, religious institutions were really the product of religious genius, which should thus be the real topic of interest in the study of religion. In addition, it was the whether or not religious experiences and beliefs made a positive difference to the lives of people that made them valuable or not. James was not an orthodox Christian by any means, and would be more accurately described as a pantheist. His attempt to account for and classify the religious yearning within the human soul remains a classic. The following excerpt is from his final, summative lecture, in the book *The Varieties of Religious Experience.*

Lecture XX

The material of our study of human nature is now spread before us; and in this parting hour, set free from the duty of description, we can draw our theoretical and practical conclusions. In my first lecture, defending the empirical method, I foretold that whatever conclusions we might come to could be reached by spiritual judgments only, appreciations of the significance for life of religion, taken 'on the whole.' Our conclusions cannot be as sharp as dogmatic conclusions would be, but I will formulate them, when the time comes, as sharply as I can.

Summing up in the broadest possible way the characteristics of the religious life, as we have found them, it includes the following beliefs:

1   That the visible world is part of a more spiritual universe from which it draws its chief significance;

2   That union or harmonious relation with that higher universe is our true end;

3   That prayer or inner communion with the spirit thereof—be that spirit 'God' or 'law',—is a process wherein work is really done, and spiritual energy flows in and produces effects, psychological or material, within the phenomenal world.

---

[3]William James, *Varieties of Religious Experience: A Study in Human Nature* (London: Penguin, 1985), 485–519.

382 T&T CLARK READER IN THEOLOGICAL ANTHROPOLOGY

4 Religion includes also the following psychological characteristics:

5 A new zest which adds itself like a gift to life, and takes the form either of lyrical enchantment or of appeal to earnestness and heroism.

6 An assurance of safety and a temper of peace, and, in relation to others, a preponderance of loving affections. In illustrating these characteristics by documents, we have been literally bathed in sentiment. In re-reading my manuscript, I am almost appalled at the amount of emotionality which I find in it. After so much of this, we can afford to be dryer and less sympathetic in the rest of the work that lies before us.

The sentimentality of many of my documents is a consequence of the fact that I sought them among the extravagances of the subject. If any of you are enemies of what our ancestors used to brand as enthusiasm, and are, nevertheless, still listening to me now, you have probably felt my selection to have been sometimes almost perverse, and have wished I might have stuck to soberer examples. I reply that I took these extremer examples as yielding the profounder information. To learn the secrets of any science, we go to expert specialists, even though they may be eccentric persons, and not to commonplace pupils. We combine what they tell us with the rest of our wisdom, and form our final judgment independently. Even so with religion. We who have pursued such radical expressions of it may now be sure that we know its secrets as authentically as anyone can know them who learns them from another; and we have next to answer, each of us for himself, the practical question: what are the dangers in this element of life? and in what proportion may it need to be restrained by other elements, to give the proper balance?

But this question suggests another one which I will answer immediately and get it out of the way, for it has more than once already vexed us. Ought it to be assumed that in all men the mixture of religion with other elements should be identical? Ought it, indeed, to be assumed that the lives of all men should show identical religious elements? In other words, is the existence of so many religious types and sects and creeds regrettable?

To these questions I answer 'No' emphatically. And my reason is that I do not see how it is possible that creatures in such different positions and with such different powers as human individuals are, should have exactly the same functions and the same duties. No two of us have identical difficulties, nor should we be expected to work out identical solutions. Each, from his peculiar angle of observation, takes in a certain sphere of fact and trouble, which each must deal with in a unique manner. One of us must soften himself, another must harden himself; one must yield a point, another must stand firm,—in order the better to defend the position assigned him. If an Emerson were forced to be a Wesley, or a Moody forced to be a Whitman, the total human consciousness of the divine would suffer. The divine can mean no single quality, it must mean a group of qualities, by being champions of which in alternation, different men may all find worthy missions. Each attitude being a syllable in human nature's total message, it takes the whole of us to spell the meaning out completely. So a 'god of battles' must be allowed to be the god for one kind of person, a god of peace and heaven and home, the god for another. We must frankly recognize the fact that we live in partial systems, and that parts are not interchangeable in the spiritual life. If we are peevish and jealous, destruction of the self must be an element of our religion; why need it be one if we are good and sympathetic from the outset? If we are sick souls, we require a religion of deliverance; but why think so much of deliverance, if we are healthy-minded? Unquestionably, some men have the completer experience and the higher vocation, here just as in the social world; but for each man to stay in his own experience, whate'er it be, and for others to tolerate him there, is surely best.

Let us agree; then, that Religion, occupying herself with personal destinies and keeping thus in contact with the only absolute realities which we know, must necessarily play an eternal part in human history. The next thing to decide is what she reveals about those destinies, or whether indeed she reveals anything distinct enough to be considered a general message to mankind. We have done as you see, with our preliminaries, and our final summing up can now begin.

I am well aware that after all the palpitating documents which I have quoted, and all the perspectives of emotion-inspiring institution and belief that my previous lectures have opened, the dry analysis to which I now advance may appear to many of you like an anticlimax, a tapering-off and flattening out of the subject, instead of a crescendo of interest and result. I said a while ago that the religious attitude of Protestants appears poverty-stricken to the Catholic imagination. Still more poverty-stricken, I fear, may my final summing up of the subject appear at first to some of you. On which account I pray you now to bear this point in mind, that in the present part of it I am expressly trying to reduce religion to its lowest admissible terms, to that minimum, free from individualistic excrescences, which all religions contain as their nucleus, and on which it may be hoped that all religious persons may agree. That established, we should have a result which might be small, but would at least be solid; and on it and round it the ruddier additional beliefs on which the different individuals make their venture might be grafted, and flourish as richly as you please. I shall add my own over-belief (which will be, I confess, of a somewhat pallid kind, as befits a Critical philosopher), and you will, I hope, also add your over-beliefs, and we shall soon be in the varied world of concrete religious constructions once more. For the moment, let me dryly pursue the analytic part of the task.

Both thought and feeling are determinants of conduct, and the same conduct may be determined either by feeling or by thought. When we survey the whole field of religion, we find a great variety in the thoughts that have prevailed there; but the feelings on the one hand and the conduct on the other are almost always the same, for Stoic, Christian, and Buddhist saints are practically indistinguishable in their lives. The theories which Religion generates, being thus variable, are secondary; and if you wish to grasp her essence, you must look to the feelings and the conduct as being the more constant elements. It is between these two elements that the short circuit exists on which she carries on her principal business, while the ideas and symbols and other institutions form loop-lines which may be perfections and improvements, and may even some day all be united into one harmonious system, but which are not to be regarded as organs with an indispensable function, necessary at all times for religious life to go on. This seems to me the first conclusion which we are entitled to draw from the phenomena we have passed in review.

The next step is to characterize the feelings. To what psychological order do they belong?

The resultant outcome of them is in any case what Kant calls a 'sthenic' affection, an excitement of the 'cheerful, expansive, 'dynamogenic' order which, like any tonic, freshens our vital powers. In almost every lecture, but especially in the lectures on Conversion and on Saintliness, we have seen how this emotion overcomes temperamental melancholy and imparts endurance to the Subject, or a zest, or a meaning, or an enchantment and glory to the common objects of life. The name of 'faith state,' by which Professor Leuba designates it, is a good one. It is a biological as well as a psychological condition, and Tolstoy is absolutely accurate in classing faith among the forces *by which men live*. The total absence of it, anhedonia, means collapse.

The faith-state may hold a very minimum of intellectual content. We saw examples of this in those sudden raptures of the divine presence, or in such mystical seizures as Dr. Bucke described. It may be a mere vague enthusiasm, half spiritual, half vital, a courage, and a feeling that great and wondrous things are in the air.

When, however, a positive intellectual content is associated with a faith-state, it gets invincibly stamped in upon belief, and this explains the passionate loyalty of religious persons everywhere to the minutest details of their so widely differing creeds. Taking creeds and faith-state together, as forming 'religions,' and treating these as purely subjective phenomena, without regard to the question of their 'truth,' we are obliged, on account of their extraordinary influence upon action and endurance, to class them amongst the most important biological functions of mankind. Their stimulant and anesthetic effect is so great that Professor Leuba, in a recent article, goes so far as to say that so long as men can use their God, they care very little who he is, or even whether he is at all. "The truth of the matter can be put," says Leuba, "in this way: God is not known, he is not understood; he is used – sometimes as meat-purveyor, sometimes as moral support, sometimes as friend, sometimes as an object of love. If he proves himself useful, the religious consciousness asks for no more than that. Does God really exist? How does he exist? What is he? are so many irrelevant questions. Not God, but life, more life, a larger, richer, more satisfying life, is, in the last analysis, the end of religion. The love of life, at any and every level of development, is the religious impulse."

At this purely subjective rating, therefore, Religion must be considered vindicated in a certain way from the attacks of her critics. It would seem that she cannot be a mere anachronism and survival, but must exert a permanent function, whether she be with or without intellectual content, and whether, if she have any, it be true or false.

We must next pass beyond the point of view of merely subjective utility, and make inquiry into the intellectual content itself.

First, is there, under all the discrepancies of the creeds, a common nucleus to which they bear their testimony unanimously?

And second, ought we to consider the testimony true? I will take up the first question first, and answer it immediately in the affirmative. The warring gods and formulas of the various religions do indeed cancel each other, but there is a certain uniform deliverance in which religions all appear to meet. It consists of two parts: -

1   An uneasiness; and
2   Its solution.

1   The uneasiness, reduced to its simplest terms, is a sense that there is something wrong about us as we naturally stand.
2   The solution is a sense that we are saved from the wrongness by making proper connection with the higher powers.

In those more developed minds which alone we are studying, the wrongness takes a moral character, and the salvation takes a mystical tinge. I think we shall keep well within the limits of what is common to all such minds if we formulate the essence of their religious experience in terms like these:-

The individual, so far as he suffers from his wrongness and criticises it, is to that extent consciously beyond it, and in at least possible touch with something higher, if anything higher exist. Along with the wrong part there is thus a better part of him, even though it may be but a most helpless germ. With which part he should identify his real being is by no means obvious at this stage; but when stage 2 (the stage of solution or salvation) arrives, the man identifies his real being with the germinal higher part of himself; and does so in the following way. *He becomes conscious that this higher part is conterminous and continuous with a MORE of the same quality, which is operative in the universe outside of him, and which he can keep in working touch with, and in a fashion get on board of and save himself when all his lower being has gone to pieces in the wreck.*

It seems to me that all the phenomena are accurately describable in these very simple general terms. They allow for the divided self and the struggle; they involve the change of personal centre and the surrender of the lower self; they express the appearance of exteriority of the helping power and yet account for our sense of union with it; and they fully justify our feelings of security and joy. There is probably no autobiographic document, among all those which I have quoted, to which the description will not well apply. One need only add such specific details as will adapt it to various theologies and various personal temperaments, and one will then have the various experiences reconstructed in their individual forms.

So far, however, as this analysis goes, the experiences are only psychological phenomena. They possess, it is true, enormous biological worth. Spiritual strength really increases in the subject when he has them, a new life opens for him, and they seem to him a place of conflux where the forces of two universes meet; and yet this may be nothing but his subjective way of feeling things, a mood of his own fancy, in spite of the effects produced. I now turn to my second question: What is the objective 'truth' of their content?

The part of the content concerning which the question of truth most pertinently arises is that 'MORE of the same quality' with which our own higher self appears in the experience to come into harmonious working relation. Is such a 'more' merely our own notion, or does it really exist? If so, in what shape does it exist? Does it act, as well as exist? And in what form should we conceive of that 'union' with it of which religious geniuses are so convinced?

It is in answering these questions that the various theologies perform their theoretic work, and that their divergencies most come to light. They all agree that the 'more' really exists; though some of them hold it to exist in the shape of a personal god or gods, while others are satisfied to conceive it as a stream of ideal tendency embedded in the eternal structure of the world. They all agree, moreover, that it acts as well as exists, and that something really is effected for the better when you throw your life into its hands. It is when they treat of the experience of 'union' with it that their speculative differences appear most clearly. Over this point pantheism and theism, nature and second birth, works and grace and karma, immortality and reincarnation, rationalism and mysticism, carry on inveterate disputes.

At the end of my lecture on Philosophy I held out the notion that an impartial science of religions might sift out from the midst of their discrepancies a common body of doctrine which she might also formulate in terms to which physical science need not object. This, I said, she might adopt as her own reconciling hypothesis, and recommend it for general belief. I also said that in my last lecture I should have to try my own hand at framing such an hypothesis.

The time has now come for this attempt. Who says 'hypothesis' renounces the ambition to be coercive in his arguments. The most I can do is, accordingly, to offer something that may fit the facts so easily that your scientific logic will find no plausible pretext for vetoing your impulse to welcome it as true.

The 'more,' as we called it, and the meaning of our 'union' with it, form the nucleus of our inquiry. Into what definite description can these words be translated, and for what definite facts do they stand? It would never do for us to place ourselves off hand at the position of a particular theology, the Christian theology, for example, and proceed immediately to define the 'more' as Jehovah, and the 'union' as his imputation to us of the righteousness of Christ. That would be unfair to other religions, and, from our present standpoint at least,—would be an over-belief.

We must begin by using less particularized terms; and, since one of the duties of the science of religions is to keep religion in connection with the rest of science, we shall do well to seek first of all a way of describing the 'more,' which psychologists may also recognize as real. The subconscious self is nowadays a well-accredited psychological entity; and I believe that in it we have exactly the mediating term required. Apart from all religious considerations, there is actually and literally more life in our total soul than we are at tiny time aware of. The exploration of the transmarginal field has hardly yet been seriously undertaken, but what Mr. Myers said in 1892 in his essay on the Subliminal Consciousness is as true as when it was first written: "Each of us is in reality an abiding psychical entity far more extensive than he knows—an individuality which can never express itself completely through any corporeal manifestation. The Self manifests through the organism; but there is always some part of the Self unmanifested; and always, as it seems, some power of organic expression in abeyance or reserve." Much of the content of this larger background against which our conscious being stands out in relief is insignificant. Imperfect memories, silly jingles, inhibitive timidities, 'dissolutive' phenomena of various sorts, as Myers calls them, enter into it for a large part. But in it many of the performances of genius seem also to have their origin; and in our study of conversion, of mystical experiences, and of prayer, we have seen how striking a part invasions from this region play in the religious life.

Let me then propose, as an hypothesis, that whatever it may be on its farther side, the 'more' with which in religious experience we feel ourselves connected is on its hither side the subconscious continuation of our conscious life. Starting thus with a recognized psychological fact as our basis, we seem to preserve a contact with 'science' which the ordinary theologian lacks. At the same time the theologian's contention, that the religious man is moved by an external power is vindicated, for it is one of the peculiarities of invasions from the subconscious region to take on objective appearances, and to suggest to the Subject an external control. In the religious life the control is felt as 'higher'; but since on our hypothesis it is primarily the higher faculties of our own hidden mind which are controlling, the sense of union with the power beyond us is a sense of something, not merely apparently, but literally true.

This doorway into the subject seems to me the best one for a science of religions, for it mediates between a number of different points of view. Yet it is only a doorway, and difficulties present themselves as soon as we step through it, and ask how far our transmarginal consciousness carries us if we follow it on its remoter side. Here the over-beliefs begin: here mysticism and the conversion-rapture and Vedantism and transcendental idealism bring in their monistic interpretations and tell us that the finite self rejoins the absolute self, for it was always one with God and identical with the soul of the world. Here the prophets of all the different religions come with their visions, voices, raptures, and other openings, supposed by each to authenticate his own peculiar faith.

Those of us who are not personally favored with such specific revelations must stand outside of them altogether and, for the present at least, decide that, since they corroborate incompatible theological doctrines, they neutralize one another and leave no fixed result. If we follow any one of them, or if we follow philosophical theory and embrace monistic pantheism on non-mystical grounds, we do so in the exercise of our individual freedom, and build our religion in the way most congruous with our personal susceptibilities. Among these susceptibilities intellectual ones play a decisive part. Although the religious question is primarily a question of life, of living or not living in the higher union which opens itself to us as a gift, yet the spiritual excitement in which the gift appears a real one will often fail to be aroused in an individual until certain particular intellectual beliefs or ideas which, as we say, come home to him, are touched. These ideas will thus be essential to that individual's religion; —which is as much as to say that over-beliefs in various directions are absolutely indispensable, and that we should treat them with tenderness and tolerance so long as they are not intolerant themselves. As I have elsewhere written, the most interesting and valuable things about a man are usually his over-beliefs.

Disregarding the over-beliefs, and confining ourselves to what is common and generic, we have in *the fact that the conscious person is continuous with a wider self through which saving experiences come*, a positive content of religious experience which, it seems to me, is literally and objectively true as far as it goes. If I now proceed to state my own hypothesis about the farther limits of this extension of our personality, I shall be offering my own over-belief—though I know it will appear a sorry under-belief to some of you—for which I can only bespeak the same indulgence which in a converse case I should accord to yours.

The further limits of our being plunge, it seems to me, into an altogether other dimension of existence from the sensible and merely 'understandable' world. Name it the mystical region, or the supernatural region, whichever you choose. So far as our ideal impulses originate in this region (and most of them do originate in it, for we find them possessing us in a way for which we cannot articulately account), we belong to it in a more intimate sense than that in which we belong to the visible world, for we belong in the most intimate sense wherever our ideals belong. Yet the unseen region in question is not merely ideal, for it produces effects in this world. When we commune with it, work is actually done upon our finite personality, for we are turned into new men, and consequences in the way of conduct follow in the natural world upon our regenerative change. But that which produces effects within another reality must be termed a reality itself, so I feel as if we had no philosophic excuse for calling the unseen or mystical world unreal.

God is the natural appellation, for us Christians at least, for the supreme reality, so I will call this higher part of the universe by the name of God. We and God have business with each other; and in opening ourselves to his influence our deepest destiny is fulfilled. The universe, at those parts of it which our personal being constitutes, takes a turn genuinely for the worse or for the better in proportion as each one of us fulfills or evades God's demands. As far as this goes I probably have you with me, for I only translate into schematic language what I may call the instinctive belief of mankind: God is real since he produces real effects.

The real effects in question, so far as I have as yet admitted them, are exerted on the personal centres of energy of the various subjects, but the spontaneous faith of most of the subjects is that they embrace a wider sphere than this. Most religious men believe (or 'know,' if they be mystical) that not only they themselves, but the whole universe of beings to whom the God is present, are secure in his parental hands. There is a sense, a dimension, they are sure, in which we are all saved, in spite of the gates of hell and all adverse terrestrial appearances. God's existence is the guarantee of an ideal order that shall be permanently preserved. This world may indeed, as science assures us, someday burn up or freeze; but if it is part of his order, the old ideals are sure to be brought elsewhere to fruition, so that where God is, tragedy is only provisional and partial, and shipwreck and dissolution are not the absolutely final things. Only when this farther step of faith concerning God is taken, and remote objective consequences are predicted, does religion, as it seems to me, get wholly free from the first immediate subjective experience, and bring a *real hypothesis* into play. A good hypothesis in science must have other properties than those of the phenomenon it is immediately invoked to explain, otherwise it is not prolific enough. God, meaning only what enters into the religious man's experience of union, falls short of being an hypothesis of this more useful order. He needs to enter into wider cosmic relations in order to justify the subject's absolute confidence and peace.

That the God with whom, starting from the hither side of our own extra-marginal self, we come at its remoter margin into commerce should be the absolute world-ruler, is of course a very considerable over-belief. Over-belief as it is, though, it is an article of almost every one's religion. Most of us pretend in some way to prop it upon our philosophy, but the philosophy itself is really propped upon this faith. What is this but to say that Religion, in her fullest exercise of function, is not a mere illumination of facts already elsewhere given, not a mere passion, like love, which views things in a rosier light. It is indeed that, as we have seen abundantly. But it is something more, namely, a postulator of new facts as well. The world interpreted religiously is not the materialistic world over again, with an altered expression; it must have, over and above the altered expression, a natural constitution different at some point from that which a materialistic world would have. It must be such that different events can be expected in it, different conduct must be required.

This thoroughly 'pragmatic' view of religion has usually been taken as a matter of course by common men. They have interpolated divine miracles into the field of nature, they have built a heaven out beyond the grave. It is only transcendentalist metaphysicians who think that, without adding any concrete details to Nature, or subtracting any, but by simply calling it the expression of absolute spirit, you make it more divine just as it stands. I believe the pragmatic way of taking religion to be the deeper way. It gives it body as well as soul, it makes it claim, as everything real must claim, some characteristic realm of fact as its very own. What the more characteristically divine facts are, apart from the actual inflow of energy in the faith-state and the prayer-state, I know not. But the over-belief on which I am ready to make my personal venture is that they exist. The whole drift of my education goes to persuade me that the world of our present consciousness is only one out of many worlds of consciousness that exist, and that those other worlds must contain experiences which have a meaning for our life also; and that although in the main their experiences and those of this world keep discrete, yet the two become continuous at certain points, and higher energies filter in. By being faithful in my poor measure to this over-belief, I seem to myself to keep more sane and true. I can, of course, put myself into the sectarian scientist's attitude, and imagine vividly that the world of sensations and of scientific laws and objects may be all. But whenever I do this, I hear that inward monitor of which W. K. Clifford once wrote, whispering the word 'bosh!' Humbug is humbug, even though it bear the scientific name, and the total expression of human experience, as I view it objectively, invincibly urges me beyond the narrow 'scientific' bounds. Assuredly, the real world is of a different temperament,—more intricately built than physical science allows. So my objective and my subjective conscience both hold me to the over-belief which I express. Who knows whether the faithfulness of individuals here below to their own poor over-beliefs may not actually help God in turn to be more effectively faithful to his own greater tasks?

Questions

1 What do you think James means by saying that in prayer or inner communion "work is really done"?

2 How does he defend his selection of materials for his study?

3 Is the existence of so many religious types and sects and creeds regrettable? Why not?

4 Critically evaluate James' method for studying the phenomena of religious experience.

5 "The theories which Religion generates, being thus variable, are secondary; and if you wish to grasp her essence, you must look to the feelings and the conduct as being the more constant elements." Do you agree or disagree?

6 How does James explain the passionate commitment people have to their religious systems? How does James think that religion is "vindicated from her critics"?

7 What does he mean by the "uneasiness" and the "solution" that lie under religious systems?

8 Does James think that there is an objective truth behind religious experiences? Why/why not?

9 What is the "pragmatic" view of religion?

TEXT 4: FERGUS KERR,
IMMORTAL LONGINGS[4]

Fergus Kerr (b. 1931) is a Dominican priest and scholar who taught at Oxford University for more than twenty years, and has also had a long association with the University of Edinburgh. His work *Theology After Wittgenstein* (1986) was extremely well-received, and he is noted as a scholar of Thomas Aquinas. He is the editor of *New Blackfriars,* the theological and philosophical review of the English Dominicans. His book *Immortal Longings—Versions of Transcending Humanity* (1997), from which this excerpt is taken, is a survey and analysis of the various ways in which philosophers and theologians have accounted for the desire for the transcendent that lies within the human breast.

Seven versions of transcending humanity

Martha Craven Nussbaum's work includes a variety of ways of dealing with the desire to transcend humanity that has long seemed natural at least in Western metaphysics and culture. She rejects Diotima's recipe, in Plato's *Symposium,* for concentrating desire on the abstract non-human good, and favours a fairly low-key transfiguration of the everyday world; she prefers the guilt-free playfulness of the birds and the bees to the sex-hating and body-loathing effects of a certain (mis) conception of the doctrine of original sin; she favours a secularization of the same doctrine, quite differently understood, in an endlessly deepening knowledge of one's tragically flawed existence; she entertains the possibility of a god who might accept the conditions of human life, suffering and mortality; and throughout she fears any project of transcending humanity which translates us into the life of any sort of non-human being. Within Nussbaum's writing, perhaps we may say, the pull of the absolute is ubiquitous, and she has incommensurable ways of dealing with it.

That need not be an objection. On the contrary, a self-consistent monolithic way of dealing with our immortal longings might be exactly what is not the most satisfactory solution. Martin Heidegger's project might be exactly the kind of thing that Nussbaum most fears (she only mentions his name once or twice). His way of dealing with the solitary soul's desire to ascend to unmediated communion with the absolute is to immerse the self—disperse the self, we might even say—in the mirror-game, das *Spiegel-Spiel,* by which the non-human realities of sky, earth, death and the sacred, joined in a kind of round dance, open the space for the human being to be both finite and transcendent, both situated and decentred, at one and the same time. To Nussbaum, this radical decentring of the self would surely seem as humanly alienating and destructive as Diotima's project. In either case the human being as conceived in the Cartesian/Kantian picture of the self-directing agent disappears,

---

[4]Fergus Kerr, *Immortal Longings: Versions of Transcending Humanity* (London: SPCK, 1997), 159–84.

either into the impersonal absolute or into something that lies in the gift of a quartet of non-human realities.

On the other hand, Iris Murdoch's project, with her emphasis on the human being as prey to egoistic fantasy, sees the Platonic project of liberation by perpetual submission to the always greater ideals of the good, the true and the beautiful, as the only hope for human beings to become fully and properly human. Far from feeling threatened by Diotima's project (as Nussbaum understands it), we need precisely that metaphysical ascent to discover and maintain any sort of humanly congenial and worthy moral life. By gradually stripping away our selfish and prejudiced subjectivity we may at last gain the freedom of obedience to something objective. In contrast, according to Luce Irigaray, Diotima's project, largely misunderstood by Socrates, offers a glimpse of *eros* as the divine intermediary, as the coincidence of bodiliness and spirituality in the finite transcendence, the ecstatic immanence, of the encounter between sexually different beings. In effect, the event of a meeting between man and woman—woman at last enabled to be herself and not a man's mirror image -would itself be divine.

If Heidegger invites us to find our true selves by participating in the dance of the quaternity, and if Murdoch directs us to disciplined subjection to the sovereignty of the form of the good, the true and the beautiful, then Irigaray invokes sexual difference as the suprahuman 'given', with respect to which human beings may at last come into their own in practical acknowledgement of their otherness.

Heidegger, Murdoch and Irigaray, with the quaternity, the form of the good and *la différence sexuelle* respectively, offer variations on Diotima's ascent of love which, contrasted with Nussbaum's explorations, all seem extremely, even frighteningly, monolithic.

Stanley Cavell's resting with 'a yearning at once unappeasable and unsatisfiable' and Charles Taylor's retrieval of 'sources of the self' bring us back into a conversation in which the voices are, like Nussbaum's, a good deal more tentative and self-doubting. Cavell seems vulnerable to the attractions of the liberal-existentialist self; he cannot take religion seriously as a possibility for intelligent people; and yet his insistence on the 'truth' of scepticism as the endless interrogation of ultimate values is, in its way, an unstoppable oscillation between immanence and transcendence. Taylor, by contrast, makes no bones about his Catholic beliefs, though, on present evidence, his theology seems rather thin compared with his neo-Romantic ecological consciousness.

Karl Barth comes in between Nussbaum and Heidegger. If Nussbaum displays a range of ways of dealing with aspirations to transcend humanity, settling for none and leaving a good deal of unresolved tension, Heidegger offers a very coherent and single-minded project for securing the insertion of humanity in the finitude of the self-transcending fourfold. Barth too has a monolithic solution to Diotima's dream, but far from being a descent into the confines of the world remythologized as the mirror-game of the quaternity, as in Heidegger, he invites us to remember that the only absolute there is has become one of us and opened the way, in an unexacted and unanticipatable dispensation of grace, for us to become more fully human than ever in communion with the only truly human being there has ever been. The historical event of the incarnation, death and resurrection of Jesus Christ, the one whose human nature is united hypostatically - really and ontologically, not just psychologically and morally—with the divine nature, seizes the ancient quest for the absolute and turns it on its head.

Plainly, it is impossible to reconcile these different versions of transcending humanity. But should we expect to be able to do so—even to grade them according to some scale of plausibility or proximity to the truth? Any attempt would have to be measured against the traditional Christian recognition of the powerlessness of finite mortal life to fulfil our natural desire for transcendence in a way that respects our humanity without grace.

Christianity or nothing?

According to Hans Urs von Balthasar, in one of his moods, Christianity has been so successful in our culture that the religious experience of the world that people used to have, and that people outside post-Christian cultures still have, has been devalued and marginalized. Three or four centuries have been needed, he thinks, but the diffuse sense of the sacred, once taken for granted, has all but faded away, leaving us with nothing but the choice between the story of Christ crucified and raised from the dead and, on the other hand, the tabula rasa of an empty universe upon which we simply have to impose what values we can conceive.

This has no doubt sharpened our sense of the uniqueness of the gift—of the Christian dispensation of grace; but it leaves that gift - that grace -completely isolated. The God of natural religion, once found in one form or another everywhere, has become definitively and uniquely located in Jesus Christ in such a way that the alternative now is nothing but 'the great void'. 'Finite human freedom, with its superhuman aspirations, has been treated as absolute.' The alternative to acceptance of the Christian economy of grace, it would appear, is simply idolatry of human will — liberal- existentialist voluntarism, we may say.

It is always a good question to ask what a philosopher fears. Von Balthasar's highly implausible claim that the success of Christianity has wiped out all other forms of religion and metaphysics is tied up with his suspicions of Karl Rahner's theology. He fears that the deity of natural religion is 'the kind of God whom now, in the post-Christian age, modern transcendental theology would like to reinstate'. The metaphysical perspective, inherited from Stoicism and Neoplatonism, has been 'rolled up and set to one side'.

This state of affairs has a good as well as a bad side. For example, it explains why the cosmological arguments for God's existence remain valid but have become unconvincing for people for whom nature is no longer manifestly ordered and sacred. It means, on the other hand, that, since we no longer regard our natural environment with reverence, we treat it as raw material for technological exploitation. This desacralization of nature, however, affords new opportunities for Christian faith. Finding ourselves alone in this demythologized universe, we discover that we human beings are the only sources of ultimate value. When we regard another human being as of such unique and intrinsic worth, we begin to suspect that this becomes visible only in the illuminating perspective of the Christian tradition. The collapse of religion clears the stage for the appearance of Christianity in all its specificity. Indeed, previously, the biblical world itself was 'almost like an episode, clarifying and symbolizing the deep embrace of infinite and finite freedom', seldom or never allowed to stand out in its historical particularity.

The religious world picture is irretrievably lost. What angers von Balthasar about 'today's transcendental theologians' is that they 'would like to interpret Christ as the "highest, unsurpassable instance" of a self-disclosure to man on God's part that is coterminous with creation as such'. But these theologians—Karl Rahner, above all - come too late on the scene: 'the stage's background has already been cleared'. With perceptible glee, von Balthasar concludes that Rahner's theology 'still thinks in terms of a fundamental religious instinct in man'—an instinct 'that may already be defunct'.

This is a pretty wild story. Rahner's transcendental argument about the a priori conditions of our subjectivity does not result in anything that might fairly be called a religious 'instinct'. Von Balthasar, we may note in passing, is equally dismissive of the other major projects in recent Catholic theology. In particular, he denounces liberation theology, which 'builds the gospel (in which cross and resurrection have become superfluous) into the temple of humanity it is trying to erect', as well as what is evidently the work of Edward Schillebeeckx: 'a soteriology backed up by exegesis' that 'shifts the accents in the picture of Jesus to his "solidarity" with the oppressed and the marginalized, to such an extent that today the Cross . . . is nothing more than the logical expression of this solidarity'. These two projects, at least as he characterizes them, depend on his view of modem man's desacralized world. They are wrong headed because they water down Christian revelation; but at least they are not grounded, like Rahner's theology, on an appeal to 'a fundamental religious instinct in man'.

What has surely emerged from our study of a half-dozen recent philosophers is how important theological motifs and considerations are in the development and articulation of their projects. Besides that, they are all engaged, in no doubt very different ways, in recreating, rediscovering, something like the religio-meta-physical conception of human life into which Christianity erupted. Also, they all believe, and argue, that as moral agents, as subjects, we are indebted to something other than ourselves. In one way or another, they believe that human life as a moral and spiritual enterprise is essentially *responsive*. However tentative, provisional, off centre and misguided they may be, their projects cannot be dismissed as posturings against the void. But that is not the main point. Von Balthasar's refusal to acknowledge the continuing existence and validity of religious and metaphysical views is dictated by his determination to discredit Karl Rahner's theology.

The nature/grace controversy

Hatred among theologians is legendary—*odium theologicum*! The bitterest dispute in Roman Catholic theology this century has been over the proper way to characterize the relationship between nature and grace. In its most acute form, it is the question of what we are to say, in a theological perspective, about the longings that human beings naturally seem to have for some sort of transcendence of finitude.

In neo-Scholastic jargon it is the question of the point of insertion of supernatural life into human nature. In the Reformed tradition, in Karl Barth's attack on the notion of the *Anknüpfungspunkt*, the point of contact between the Christian gospel and human nature, we have an equally vigorous debate. (How far the partisans of the two debates were aware of one another's work is hard to say from the published evidence.)

For Barth, there could be nothing already existing in our nature to which the gospel might appeal. On the contrary, conversion to Christ 'consists in a miracle performed upon man, in a miracle which makes it not a phrase but literal truth to say that he has become a new man, a new creature'. He quotes St Paul: 'there is a new creation whenever a man comes to be in Christ' (2 Corinthians 5.17). While accepting the traditional doctrine that human beings are created 'in the image and likeness of God', he holds that this image has been so radically defaced by the fall as to leave nothing behind. We remain human, 'even as a sinner man is man and not a tortoise', Barth quaintly says. But we are no more receptive than a tortoise to the call of God until, through the gift of faith in Christ, the image of God is created in us *de novo* . . .

Questions

1 What is Nussbaum's method for dealing with "the desire to transcend humanity"?

2 What is Nussbaum's critique of Heidegger's response to the same problem?

3 For Iris Murdoch, what is "Diotima's project", and why does she favor it?

4 What is Luce Irigaray's account? Is it in anyway similar to the others that Kerr has outlined?

5 Why is he (who is the antecedent of this pronoun?) concerned about these accounts being "monolithic"?

6 Describe the accounts of Cavell, Taylor, and Barth.

7 "The traditional Christian recognition of the powerlessness of finite mortal life to fulfil our natural desire for transcendence in a way that respects our humanity without grace." What do you think of Kerr's suggestion that these different versions of transcending humanity could be evaluated against this yardstick?

8 Kerr gives an account of the debate between Balthasar and Rahner within Roman Catholic theology in the latter part of the twentieth century. What are the features of this debate as a response to the problem of "immortal longings"? What are the different theological accounts of nature and grace?

9 "However tentative, provisional, off centre and misguided they may be, their projects cannot be dismissed as posturings against the void." Evaluate this assessment, by Kerr, of the thinkers he has introduced.

TEXT 5: UFFE SCHJOEDT, "THE RELIGIOUS BRAIN: A GENERAL INTRODUCTION TO THE EXPERIMENTAL NEUROSCIENCE OF RELIGION"[5]

The discussion of the yearning within human beings to connect with the transcendent in some way would be incomplete without an introduction to the neuroscientific research that has been conducted in the area. Uffe Schjoedt (b. 1978) is a Danish scholar from the University of Aarhus working in the field of religion, but whose interest lies in the attempt to study by empirical means, the human phenomena of prayer and mystical experience. The essay included here offers an introduction and overview of latest developments in the field. While much—too much—is probably claimed for neuroscience, the important questions for theologians remain: What is to be made of evidence that is gleaned from such a study? Does it have any value as a theological datum? What should we expect, given Christian theological claims, to discover in our brains? What if it isn't there, or something else is?

I Introduction

Brain science has become increasingly popular in the humanities. A few decades ago, experimental neuroscience was almost exclusively used in the study of basic biological and psychological processes. Now, the wide distribution and availability of modern brain scanners invites the humanities to investigate the neural processes that underlie even more complex cultural phenomena. These advanced technologies enable researchers to design and test causal hypotheses of religious behaviour by using the insights on brain function as a point of departure. Classic theories on the emotional and cognitive aspects of religious experience now appear to be experimentally testable. Not surprisingly, such prospects have resulted in incredibly high expectations to this new approach. The prospects for eventually being able to answer age-old questions that have been under considerable debate among scholars of religion are tantalizing. Experiments demonstrating whether religious behaviour is dominated by emotion or reason, or whether religious experience is a unique mental phenomenon or simply a by-product of human thought, are almost too good to be true. This is also the reason why neuroscience has unwittingly become an effective tool for myth creation and wild speculations about religious brain processes and God modules. However, one could ask: does it makes sense to ask such categorical questions at all in the context of the modern study of religion? This article is an

---

[5]Uffe Schjoedt, "The Religious Brain: A General Introduction to the Experimental Neuroscience of Religion." *Method & Theory in the Study of Religion* 21, no. 3 (2009): 310–39. For ease of reading, the extensive references in Schjoedt's article have been removed.

introduction to the experimental neuroscience approach, intended for scholars of religion who have an interest in the neurobiological and cognitive aspects of religion, but who do not have the necessary background knowledge to evaluate this exciting field's limitations and potential.

At present, only a small number of studies exist on the relation between neural activity and religious behaviour, and the majority of these have focused on how religiously inspired techniques of meditation modulate practitioners' states of consciousness… However, meditation does not necessarily include references to supernatural beings, so treating religious practice and meditation under the same category is not without its problems. Religious practice and experience is in itself a problematic category, although it has played a major role in the experimental neuroscience of religion. Most studies have used monks, nuns or meditation experts from widely different cultures under the assumption that different forms of praying and techniques of meditation fundamentally express the same category of human experience.

The behavioural diversity observed in anthropological, psychological and sociological records, however, demonstrates an enormous variability of religious practice: (a) within individuals over time and context; (b) among individuals with different personalities and social status; and (c) among cultures with different climatic, demographic, historical and socio-economic properties.

****

Religious behaviour encompasses widely different thoughts and practices and must be assumed, like other forms of mental practice, to differ widely in both cognitive content and corresponding neural correlates.

This article reviews six lines of research that use experimental neuroscience to study religious behaviour. They each represent a specific approach to the field, and some of them have had significant impact in the media. These six projects, to my knowledge, cover all published experiments using imaging technology on religious practices other than meditation. Each project will be critically evaluated with a strong focus on issues of ecological validity, the use of contrast conditions, and theoretical grounding.

****

I will not pursue an in-depth analysis of each study but focus instead on their scientific strengths and weaknesses.

The first project tests the hypothesis that religious experience corresponds to a specific altered state of consciousness. The second project is a clinical approach to examine the hypothesized health promoting effects of religious practices. The third project is a particularly controversial study, where the mystical experience of a "felt" presence is associated with specific electrical impulses in the brain. The fourth project uses imaging technology to answer the question whether religious behaviour is dominated by cognition or emotion. The fifth project is a relatively new study that investigates the neural substrates of Christian mystical experience. Finally, the sixth project is the University of Aarhus project, where we investigate what happens in the brain when religious subjects converse with God in different forms of praying.

The article concludes with a few comments on the future status of experimental neuroscience in the study of religion.

****

I argue that in order to understand the complexity of religious practices and experiences in terms of cognitive processes and brain function at least two important issues need to be addressed. First, rather than developing new controversial claims on brain processes unique to religious experience, experimental neuroscience should rely on conventional theories of brain function. Second, experimental neuroscience must appreciate the diversity of religious thought and behaviour analyzed by the comparative study of religion for more than 150 years. However, I will begin this introduction by introducing some of the general methods and procedures in experimental neuroscience and sketch some of the technical and methodological challenges in this promising field.

II Methods and procedures

Most of the experiments reviewed in this article measure the brain's blood flow by using imaging technologies such as SPECT (Single Photon Emission Computed Tomography), PET (Positron Emission Tomography) or fMRI (functional Magnetic Resonance Imaging) which are all stationary scanning technologies, usually located at a hospital research unit. In most of these studies, participants arrive at the hospital and receive instructions about the scanning procedures and safety regulations before being placed in the scanner, which typically covers the participant's head and torso (fMRI). In PET and SPECT studies, participants are injected with a radioactive tracer prior to the examination which traces the blood flow in the brain by emission of radiation. In studies using MR-technology, participants will experience noise (app. 110db) from the magnets measuring the blood flow from changes in the blood's magnetic properties. Participants are instructed not to move, and often the head is fixed to avoid potential movement traces in the data. While lying in the scanner, participants often receive stimuli and instructions through headphones or on a screen.

In order to measure which brain areas are active in a particular condition, it is necessary to contrast the target condition with one or more contrast conditions. Contrast conditions typically include a "rest" condition, in which subjects can think about whatever they want, and a mental task, which is similar to the target condition in all aspects except for the aspect of interest. For example, the recital of a religious text can be contrasted to the recital of a non-religious text if it is the aim of the analysis to filter out the effect of recitation. Target and contrast conditions are typically repeated several times during sessions to increase the statistical power of the analysis. The raw data from the scanner are pre-processed before analysis. This usually consists of a series of complex procedures that transforms the data from each subject to fit onto a template brain which is then used for group analysis. Finally, a range of advanced statistical analyses are applied to the pre-processed data to reach the results that most people know from newspapers and journal articles, where probability maps show the regional differences of blood flow as plots with graded colour intensities on a brain image.

This brief description is crude and generic, but it illustrates some of the most common methodological and technological issues in imaging studies. First, there is the issue of ecological validity. Ecological validity refers to the authenticity of the subjects' behaviour. There are several factors in the scanning procedure that potentially compromise this authenticity. For some people, being in a hospital is enough to generate anxiety, while others experience severe claustrophobia when their heads are fixed and their bodies enter the scanner. The injection in PET studies can be associated with discomfort, and the noise from the MR scanner can make it difficult for the participants to concentrate. Poor instructions, dubious stimuli and problematic contrast conditions can ruin the experimental paradigm, causing the task of interest to be executed in ways other than experimenters expect. The contrast conditions are problematic if they resemble the target conditions too much so that the signals of interest disappear in the contrast, or if the contrasts are too different so that the signals of interest are flooded by too many irrelevant brain activations. If the recital of a religious text (verbal/active) is contrasted with listening to music (auditory/passive), the results will show massive brain activations because the two conditions are widely different cognitive processes. But these activations do not say anything about the religious aspects of the recital and are thus irrelevant for the study of religion. If, on the other hand, the contrast condition resembles the target condition too much, there is a risk of activating the same areas in the brain causing potentially interesting activations to remain hidden in the analysis or even to come out as deactivations relative to the contrast condition. Unfortunately, the brain does not offer a default baseline condition which could work as a universal contrast in imaging studies. For example, in so-called baseline conditions where the participant is instructed to rest, it is difficult for the experimenter to control what the participant is actually doing; he or she could be practicing the task of interest! This is why brain scientists and scholars of religion have to critically consider the contrasts of choice in any study reported on religious practice and its neural correlates.

Pre-processing the imaging data is another story, and I will not discuss the technical details here. It is important, however, to be aware that the raw data from the scanner undergo massive transformations before being used in the statistical analyses. Critical assumptions about the neural processes and functional neuroanatomy together with a wide range of manipulations and transformations of the raw data render the connection between the processed data and the hypothesized blood flow in the individual brain indirect. The activation patterns presented in journal articles are not analogue brain signals but statistical maps of the probability of true signals.

The number of participants in imaging studies is important for the statistical power of the results. Depending on number (the studies reviewed use between 3–15 participants), results sometimes only inform us on the neural activity of the persons participating in the study rather than the wider population from which the sample is taken. Furthermore, the data analysis is dependent on the questions addressed by the researcher which means that the results reported in journals, at best, mirror a set of prior hypotheses advanced by the experimenter and therefore should not be taken as objective descriptions of the data. This problem is not trivial in the scientific study of religion because external funding from special-interest organizations like The John Templeton Foundation, who promote collaboration between science and religion, may influence which hypotheses get examined and how the results are interpreted.

III Altered states of consciousness

The work of Eugene G. d'Aquili and Andrew B. Newberg on religious experience and brain activity is almost classic, and their methods and theories are prototypical examples of how research is being conducted in this field. D'Aquili and Newberg develop a surprisingly detailed account of mystical experience on the basis of both novel claims of brain mechanisms and conventional neuroscience.

According to d'Aquili and Newberg's theory, religious experience in rituals and meditation is caused by an overload of the limbic structures involved in emotions and homeostatic regulations, e.g., the hypothalamus and the amygdala. This overload of stimuli blocks perceptual input which in turn causes a deafferentation of the associative areas and eventually leads to an altered state of consciousness. A prominent example of this mechanism is the blocking of input to posterior superior parietal cortex (PSPL) which according to d'Aquili and Newberg induces an experience of absolute unitary being with the world or higher order of reality. PSPL is supposedly the brain region that constantly processes representations of the spatial dichotomy between self and others but when it gets blocked from perceptual input from the sensory apparatus, this process runs amok which suspends the dichotomy. This regional isolation occurs through two different processes characteristic of religious practice. One process floods the brain by sympathetic or parasympathetic activities during rhythmic practices and rich sensations as seen in ritual ceremonies causing a direct blocking of PSPL. Another process, which is associated with focused attention in meditation, activates the sympathetic processes of the autonomous nervous system through the hippocampus and amygdala. Via feedback, this process increases activity in the prefrontal cortex, causing a total blocking of PSPL.

Newberg and d'Aquili have tested their theory using functional brain imaging (SPECT). In one study with eight Tibetan Buddhist meditators results did show increased activity in the dorsolateral prefrontal areas and decreased activity in the superior parietal cortex (SPL). According to Newberg and d'Aquili this suggests that the meditators experienced a suspension of the self-other dichotomy. A surprising aspect of this study is the lack of qualitative data in support of their claims. The participants were not interviewed about their subjective experience in the scanner even though such data are clearly important to Newberg and d'Aquili's interpretation.

In another study (SPECT), five volunteers from the Pentecostal movement were scanned during glossolalia. This study reported decreased activity in the prefrontal cortex but increased activity in the SPL, the opposite pattern of the Tibetan meditation study. The decrease of prefrontal activity is interpreted as a result of the lack of control during glossolalia which is contrary to the focused attention of meditation. The increased activity in SPL is not discussed in the report, but, according to Newberg et al., the reason why SPL activity did not decrease is that glossolalia does not necessarily dissolve the self-other dichotomy. In a third study (SPECT), Newberg et al. investigated the neural correlates of prayer recitation by three Franciscan nuns.

In this study, they did find a negative correlation between prefrontal activity and SPL activations relative to the contrast condition which corresponds to the results from the Tibetan meditation study.

The significant differences observed in glossolalia and meditation suggest that spiritual practices like other forms of mental practice differ widely in both cognitive content and corresponding neural correlates. Yet it is unclear whether Newberg and d'Aquili's mixed findings challenge their own basic assumption that religious experience is defined by universal neural mechanisms.

Newberg and d'Aquili's theory contains several controversial claims about brain function and the neural correlates of conscious experience. For instance, we do not know if the brain's associative areas, as argued by Newberg and d'Aquili, are divided into dedicated inference systems which process specific higher order cognitive functions ...We also lack concrete evidence that such a system exists in the PSPL region, and that its cognitive function correlates with the subjective experience of the self-other dichotomy. Furthermore, there is no concrete evidence that the brain can isolate areas of the association cortex without inhibiting its activation and it is difficult to give a natural and evolutionarily viable explanation for such cognitive mechanisms in normal healthy individuals. The standard assumption in experimental neuroscience is that increased or decreased blood flow corresponds to the level of function in a particular area, not its level of isolation.

Furthermore, Newberg and d'Aquili's experiments are generally subject to the methodological issues common to imaging studies. Results in functional imaging studies refer to the contrast between two conditions. This means that, for example, reduced activity in the prefrontal areas could potentially be caused by a relatively higher prefrontal activity in the contrast condition and thus not by a task-specific decrease in the target condition. This can be illustrated by the glossolalia study where the contrast condition was a religious song which is a relatively demanding verbal task containing melody and rhythm. The decreased activity of the prefrontal cortex observed in glossolalia may be a product of the relatively higher load on the prefrontal "concentration" in this condition rather than a significant lack of concentration during glossolalia. Anecdotally, I recently analyzed imaging data in Aarhus from one case of glossolalia relative to personal praying. In this contrast, glossolalia showed strong prefrontal activations mainly in regions involved with linguistic processing, e.g., supplementary motor cortex and Broca's area. It would have been helpful if Newberg and d'Aquili had considered the consequences of task-difficulty and different attention loads between conditions in their discussion of the results because the areas of interest in their hypothesis are sensitive to these factors.

In conclusion, Newberg and d'Aquili's project is a good example of how this field of research is able to design experiments and test hypotheses. However, several controversial notions of brain organization and neural processes make their theory problematical, e.g., the existence of specific cognitive systems that get blocked in certain situations causing a specific subjective experience (the idea that blocking input to PSPL equals a subjective experience of spatial unity). These assumptions are still largely unsupported, but they should not, of course, be ruled out automatically. The experimental design, however, would require further refinement. One way to examine their ideas would be to use transcranial magnetic stimulation (TMS) on the brain regions of interest (e.g., PSPL) and see if the experience of absolute unitary being can be induced.

Another possibility is to investigate the relation between mystical experience and PSPL activity in patients with haemorrhages, infarcts, or focal epilepsy in that particular area. This approach has already been used to study hemispheric religiosity traits in split-brain patients and temporal lobe religiosity in patients with epilepsy.

Newberg and d'Aquili describe their research project as "neurotheology" which is characterized by the assumption that religious experience as a broader category is subserved by universal brain mechanisms. Such mechanisms, however, remain to be discovered.

IV The relaxation response

A large portion of the money spent on research on the relation between physiological processes and religious strategies goes to clinical studies on the health promoting effects of religion. And there are good reasons for this according to a 1993 study concluding that Americans made an estimated 425 million visits to providers of unconventional therapy compared to 388 million visits to primary care physicians. In the broader category of unconventional therapies the most common practices were by far religious ones like personal and intercessory prayers (67% of alternative treatments in the U.S.). Several books have been published recently on the relation between religion and health, many of which were significantly supported by the John Templeton Foundation. Dr. Herbert Benson, who is head of the Mind-Body Medical Institute at Harvard Medical School, has over the last decades conducted several studies investigating the physiological effects of self-regulatory mental strategies such as prayer and meditation. In a recent and fascinating studysponsored by The John Templeton Foundation, Benson analyzed the possible clinical effects of remote intercessory prayer. In this study, which is the largest of its kind (n=1800), Benson et al. compared the complications following by-pass surgery in three groups of patients. Two groups were uncertain whether they received prayer or not, while the third group was certain they were prayed for. Results showed no positive effects of receiving remote intercessory prayer. Curiously, the group who knew they were prayed for experienced more complications following the surgery compared to the two groups who did not know whether they received prayer (one group did not receive intercessory prayer; the other group did not know they were actually prayed for). The negative result was interpreted as a harmful stress-related effect of knowing about the study. This study may perhaps be the last of its kind because of ethical issues if participation is associated with a higher health risk.

Herbert Benson's main interest, however, lies in the so-called relaxation response which includes a range of physiological processes associated with relaxation (e.g., decreased metabolism, reduced oxygen uptake, and heart rate, etc.). According to Benson such parasympathetic processes can be achieved through frequent repetition of simple thoughts and behaviours similar to those observed in religious practice like recitation of prayers, practicing daily rituals, and meditation. In addition to the habitual aspect of such repetitive strategies, religious practice often presupposes a belief in a higher truth or supernatural being which is capable of reciprocating the religious effort by answering prayers or rewarding ritual performances. According to Benson this belief contributes to an extra effect similar to that of placebo in medical trials. This extra effect, Benson argues, is caused by a boosting of the relaxation response in practicing individuals. Benson therefore argues that religious strategies ought to be implemented in medical treatments as a supplement to conventional medical therapy for those who already believe.

Benson and his colleagues have examined the relation between the relaxation response and brain activity using EEG (Electroencephalography). In an experiment with three experienced Tibetan monks, Buddhist meditation was shown to correlate with a general decrease in metabolic rate and a hemispheric asymmetry of brain activity with a global increase of beta-activity which may be associated with concentration and focused attention. In other words, the participants did not seem to reach a calm state similar to that of sleep, but instead increased their attention during meditation. This description of meditation as a focused state of attention rather than mental rest is supported by other studies of meditation reporting increases of brain activity in regions associated with concentration and focused attention, e.g., the dorsolateral prefrontal areas.

In order to map the neural correlates of the relaxation response, Benson et al. used fMRI-technology to scan the brains of five experienced Kundalini yoga practitioners performing a specific technique characterized by focus on breathing and recitation of different mantras. As contrast condition the participants were instructed to breathe freely and to list a number of random animals. Meditation was practiced for 12 minutes while the contrast task lasted 6 minutes. Epochs of these lengths are normally discouraged in fMRI studies because the magnets of MR-scanners are vulnerable to drifting which significantly reduces signal-to-noise ratio. Unfortunately, epochs of this length can be necessary in order for practitioners to reach a meditative state. Results showed activity in the dorsolateral prefrontal areas which Benson and colleagues attribute to the focused attention on breathing and recitation of mantras in the Kundalini practice. At the same time, though reluctantly, Benson and colleagues report activities in several subcortical areas like amygdala and the hypothalamus, structures that are important in regulating the autonomic and endocrine processes of the body. This is interpreted in favour of the hypothesis that meditation is capable of influencing the physiological activities involved in the relaxation response.

Like most functional imaging studies, this study investigated the difference between two conditions, a target condition and a contrast condition, in this case a formalized recitation with controlled breathing (Kundalini-practice) relative to an improvised recital with free breathing. The results thus indicate the neural correlates of the aspects of recitation and controlled breathing in Kundalini practice. They do not, however, tell us anything about other meditation techniques that do not involve formalized recitation and controlled breathing. Other techniques are expected to activate the brain regions that correspond to their particular cognitive properties. On the other hand, several meditation studies have reported dorsolateral prefrontal activity. Thus, regardless of particular techniques, meditation in general seems to correlate with this region as well as the subjective experience of focused attention.

Whether this imaging study supports the hypothesis of the relaxation response is uncertain. Imaging studies need a well-defined neural correlate of physiological relaxation induced by cognitive processes before conclusive evidence can be found. Potential activations of relevant brain stem nuclei are difficult to measure with today's technologies because the image resolutions are still too low. Thus, a clear connection between cognitive processing of religious belief and activation of the relaxation response remains to be discovered by future studies.

V The God helmet

The Canadian psychologist Michael A. Persinger claims that by stimulating specific patterns of brain activity, it is possible to induce the experience of a "felt" presence in normal healthy subjects. This neural phenomenon, he argues, generates beliefs about supernatural beings and may explain how religious systems originated in the first place. Persinger's work—which counts almost two hundred articles in the journal of Perceptual and Motor Skills on various exotic topics, such as the relation between earthquakes and UFO reports and "haunt" experiences in electronically dense buildings (http://ejournals.ammonsscientific.com)—is extremely popular with the media. It also represents a controversial scientific approach with important methodological and theoretical issues. In his theory, Persinger builds on the hypothesis that religious and spiritual experiences are related to transient electrical impulses in the temporal lobe. The phenomenon is best known in studies of patients with temporal lobe epilepsy which report frequent or strong spiritual experiences in patients both during and between seizures.

The general idea is that transient electrical charges in the temporal lobe stimulate the region that underlies the subjective experience of a felt presence. Persinger expands on this hypothesis by arguing that the "felt" presence may be caused by transient neural impulses in the right-hemispheric equivalent to the left-hemispheric processing of self. According to Persinger it is the left hemisphere that represents the self because representations of self are closely linked to linguistic processing which is predominantly located in the left hemisphere. When the right-hemispheric homologue of sense of self is allowed into the left hemispheric awareness via seizure-like impulses, subjects experience a "felt" presence of another being.

In an early experiment (EEG) Persinger observed electrical changes in the temporal lobe in persons practicing transcendental meditation and glossolalia, which evidently supported his theory. However, to confirm his hypothesis, Persinger has devised a helmet capable of stimulating the brain through the skull using TMS (Transcranial Magnetic Stimulation) to see if religious experiences can be induced in normal healthy persons. Participants in Persinger's experiments do not know when the TMS device is active, and sometimes they are instructed to push a button if they experience a felt presence. The participants are subsequently asked to describe their experience and complete questionnaires. Persinger's results suggest that the so-called God Helmet works on 80% of the general population, so it is no surprise that his project has attracted massive media coverage by major TV channels such as CNN, BBC and the Discovery Channel. The popularity peaked when consciousness researcher Susan Blackmore tested the helmet and wrote about her unique spiritual experience during stimulation. Other prominent persons have tried Persinger's God helmet with ambiguous results. The famous biologist Richard Dawkins, who is an avid atheist, underwent the same treatment without experiencing anything.

Persinger still runs experiments using the God Helmet, and he has recently investigated the relation between different types of mystical experience and specific magnetic pulses. He now claims that he can map specific mystical experiences to specific patterns of magnetic stimulus.

Persinger's scientific data are controversial. Granqvist et al. replicated the experiment in a double-blind, randomized study and did not find comparable TMS effects in their subjects. They concluded that the remarkable experiences in Persinger's subjects must be a product of suggestion which is supported by their own study showing that high scores on a suggestibility scale predict the chance of participants having a mystical experience. Another serious concern with Persinger's work is its theoretical background for using TMS. The fact that Persinger uses extremely weak magnetic fields to induce the mental state is problematic. While clinical TMS research usually involves fields on the order of 1-2 Tesla to excite the brain's neurons, Persinger uses magnetic fields measured in nano and microTesla which approximate the Earth's geomagnetic properties. It is unknown whether such values are capable of affecting neurons through the skull enough to modulate our subjective experience. One could ask whether, from an evolutionary perspective, it makes sense to have brains that are susceptible to such weak magnetic fields. Persinger needs to provide a persuasive neurobiological explanation as to how the helmet activates the neural processes behind mystical experiences. One possible way of further exploring Persinger's hypothesis would be to use supplemental technologies with a higher spatial resolution like fMRI, PET, and MEG. Persinger himself doubts the benefits of fMRI and PET because they lack the temporal resolution of the subtle characteristics of the electrical impulses, but MEG with its high temporal and spatial resolution may prove ideal for testing Persinger's hypothesis in the future.

VI Cognition or Emotion?

Psychologist Nina P. Azari and colleagues have tried to answer the question of whether religious experience can be characterized mainly by cognitive or emotional processes. Similar to the studies of Persinger and Newberg, Azari assumes that religious experience is subserved by a common set of neural processes. However, she disagrees with their hypothesis that religious experience is mainly a precognitive, primitive, and emotional phenomenon. Grounded in the attribution theories of psychology represented by Wayne Proudfoot's work, Azari argues that religion develops in a cultural system and that meaning and interpretation are central features in both spiritual experiences and religious feelings.

This discussion is central in the scientific study of religion. Many scholars follow the pattern of William James, Carl G. Jung, Rudolph Otto, and Mircea Eliade by favouring the notion of a sui generis religious experience. In contrast, social constructivists continue to draw inspiration from Èmile Durkheim, George Herbert Mead, Peter L. Berger, and Clifford Geertz by claiming that even basic feelings and common sense notions are products of society. Azari and colleagues join this discussion by analyzing imaging data of the same experiment from different angles. The study measured the brain activity (PET) of six Christian fundamentalists and six non-religious participants under six conditions: reading and reciting the Bible (Psalm 23), reading and reciting a nursery rhyme (non-melodic), reading a neutral text, and simply resting (baseline). Results showed that religious participants activated dorsolateral prefrontal regions in the psalm recital relative to both contrast conditions and control group which is interpreted as the correlate of the participant's recollection of relevant knowledge about religious texts (memory retrieval). Relative to "rest" and "rhyme" the psalm recital also activated the dorsomedial frontal cortex and precuneus. The areas precuneus and dorsomedial frontal cortex have anatomical connections to the prefrontal regions, which supports the hypothesis that a specific distributed neural network which is controlled by higher order cognitive areas, underlies religious experience. According to Azari the observation of cortical activities together with the lack of activity in the limbic system, which is normally associated with emotional processing, suggest that religious experience is first and foremost a cognitive phenomenon.

In a recent article, Azari and colleagues returned to the data to investigate potential networks separating the rhyme recital from the religious recital by using Principal Component Analysis. In accordance with their prior analysis they found prefrontal activations to correlate with Bible recitation. The prefrontal cortex has been associated with social cognition and interpersonal interaction, and Azari and colleagues use this evidence to argue that this region may subserve the personal experience of God.

The results support Azari's general hypothesis that religious experience is essentially a cultural phenomenon. The finding that Bible recitation activated the prefrontal cortex rather than subcortical regions, Azari argues, suggests that religious experience may take on different expressions in different cultural systems. Interestingly, Azari finds support for this claim in Newberg and d'Aquili's study on Tibetan meditation. According to Azari and colleagues the prefrontal activity reported in their study as well as in Newberg and d'Aquili's meditation study, serves the same function in these two fundamentally different religious experiences. One is within the Christian world view where the personal relation to God plays a major role. The other one is within a Buddhist world view where unitary experience is central. This interpretation, however, radically separates itself from Newberg and d'Aquili's own explanation of prefrontal activity in meditation. They interpret it as a function of focused attention while it is the isolation of the posterior superior parietal lobe (PSPL) that causes the experience of unity. Azari argues that the particular relation between PSPL and prefrontal cortex in Newberg and d'Aquili's study is merely an indication of the complex nature of meditation. On the contrary, Newberg and d'Aquili argue that the blocking of input to PSPL is caused by a well-defined interaction in the fronto-parietal networks which originates in the brain's limbic structures, e.g., the hypothalamus and the amygdala. To Newberg and d'Aquili the experience of unity is caused by a precognitive altered state of consciousness. This discrepancy shows that there really is no clear solution to this classic debate over the nature of religious experience.

A few methodological and theoretical issues are also relevant to Azari's study. Like most studies in this field, Azari and colleagues use a very limited number of participants. An analysis of six persons in each group (target and control) is not ideal for generating claims about other than the participants of the study. Increasing the number to fifteen or twenty participants in each group would strengthen their conclusions about the wider population of German Christian Protestant fundamentalists. Another issue worth mentioning is the statistical treatment of the data. Results from the analysis were not corrected for multiple comparisons ($p < 0.001$), and some of the p-values were thresholded higher than is normally considered significant even for uncorrected results ($p < 0.01$). Uncorrected results of whole brain analyses are usually interpreted as trends in explorative data rather than robust results.

Although Azari et al. stress the cultural aspects of religious experience rather than precognitive sensory mechanisms, they do agree with the general assumption that religious experience is a neurologically consistent phenomenon. Azari et al. suggest, however, that "religious experience" may turn out to be divided into a variety of subprocesses comparable to recent models of memory. Thus, neural activity in one particular religious practice (psalm recitation) may enlighten us on the universal processes of a broader category of religious experience. An example of this neurophenomenological overlap can be found, Azari argues, in the prefrontal activity observed in Newberg and d'Aquili's meditation study which may serve the same function as in the prefrontal activity during psalm recitation. In other words, Azari argues that the prefrontal activity may point to a cross-cultural invariance of religious experience which subserves an "essential relational cognitivity". However, this "invariance" of prefrontal activity in psalm recitation and meditation may well be more broadly associated with attention and executive processing. This finding, then, may not add anything particular to our understanding of religion as focus and complex processing underlie most complex cultural phenomena that include semantic and linguistic processing, social cognitive inferences, and focused attention. In this perspective the claim of invariance is a neurofunctional pendant to claiming that religious texts are dependent on human hands and that verbally transmitted myths and rituals are partly due to vocal anatomy.

Regardless of these issues, this project represents a new direction which integrates well-supported insights on the neural substrates of executive function, memory, and social cognition to give a plausible account of the observed brain activity in religious practice. Rather than hypothesizing new neural mechanisms subserving the mystical aspects of religion Azari and colleagues rely on better grounded insights on brain function. Whether Azari and her colleagues have found an invariant pattern of neural activity that subserves religious experience across cultures remains an open question.

VII Mystical experiences

In a recent study sponsored by special interest organizations, The John Templeton Foundation and The Metanexus Institute, Mario Beauregard and Vincent Paquette explored the neural substrates of mystical experience in Carmelite nuns.

In the study fifteen nuns who described a mystical experience as a feeling of unconditional love and oneness with God were instructed to re-experience a past mystical experience in the scanner. Results, which were not corrected for multiple comparisons (thresholded at $p<0.001$), showed that a mystical experience relative to rest and a non-religious contrast condition (to think of a past happy experience with a human being) activated several brain regions (e.g., the orbitofrontal cortex, temporal cortex, anterior cingulate cortex, superior and inferior parietal cortex, caudate nucleus, insula, medial prefrontal cortex, and brain stem).

Beauregard and Paquette interpret these regional activations separately by reference to, among others, Persinger, Newberg and d'Aquili. In accordance with Persinger's hypothesis and previous research on temporal lobe epilepsy, the activations in the temporal lobe are associated with a felt presence of a spiritual reality. Activations in the parietal cortex are associated with a subjective experience of unity along the lines of Newberg and d'Aquili's theory of fronto-parietal networks in religious experience. The orbitofrontal activation is associated with a pleasant feeling during the mystical experience, while the anatomical structures insula and caudate nucleus are interpreted as the neural correlates of unconditional love and feeling of happiness which, according to the Carmelite nuns' self-reports, is characteristic of mystical experience.

Unfortunately, the study suffers from both methodological and analytical problems. Beauregard and Paquette did not measure on actual mystical experience. Instead they measured the recall of a mystical experience because the Carmelite nuns considered it impossible to reach a true mystical experience since "God can't be summoned at will". Thus, it is unclear what the results actually showed. The theoretical premise of the study is that the participants are able to simulate or re-experience this unique state in the scanner. What that means exactly is neurophenomenologically uncertain. This premise makes it difficult to claim ecological validity in spite of post-scan questionnaires suggesting a certain extent of experiential authenticity.

Furthermore, the length of recall was five minutes which is difficult to control experimentally especially because the target condition in this study lacks precise instructions and support from external stimuli (e.g., visual screen or headphones). It is uncertain whether participants were able to stay focused on the task throughout the entire epoch. Perhaps the multitude of activations in Beauregard and Paquette's study suffer from the noise of irrelevant thoughts and might therefore not relate to the target condition, namely, the simulation of mystical experience.

In their discussion Beauregard and Paquette mostly refer to literature on complex cultural phenomena rather than basic research on cognitive functions. The observed activity in the caudate nucleus, for example, is interpreted as the neural correlate of unconditional love by reference to an earlier study of love. However, the underlying function of the caudate nucleus (dorsal striatum) in love presumably has to do with reward learning and forming habits in social interaction. When Beauregard and Paquette refer to studies of complex cultural phenomena rather than basic brain function, the uninformed reader may come to believe that these brain regions are specifically involved in that particular phenomenon. Caudate activity in love (Bartels & Zeki), temporal lobe activity in a "felt" presence of supernatural beings (Persinger), and parietal deactivations in a transcendental unitary experience (Newberg and d'Aquili), probably subserve these phenomena as basic components, e.g., reward processing, linguistic processing, semantic or episodic processing, visuo-spatial processing, somato-sensory processing, etc. In this light, Beauregard and Paquette's interpretations may be overly ambitious.

Their conclusion that mystical experience is a complex phenomenon which recruits many brain regions and processes seems reasonable. This hypothesis separates itself from other studies reviewed in this article which work with the hypothesis that specific systems or processes underlie a uniform category of religious experience. However, instead of analyzing the mental composition of mystical experience in Carmelite nuns by reference to basic cognitive processing, Beauregard and Paquette refer to studies on complex experiences like love, sense of a felt presence, and dissolution of the self/other dichotomy. This weakness in their interpretation together with the problematic premise of recalled mystical experience leaves Beauregard and Paquette's findings in the midst of unanswered questions. Although the study is explorative and therefore not confined by strict hypotheses, the methodological and analytical issues make Beauregard and Paquette's results inconclusive and in great need of further testing.

VIII Formalized and improvised prayers

The last line of research presented is our project at the University of Aarhus which uses fMRI to investigate the neural changes in response to different forms of praying, e.g., personal prayer, formalized prayer, and intercessory prayer.

This project takes its point of departure in the general assumption in the comparative study of religion that religious practice and experience encompass an enormous variety of diverse thoughts and behaviour. This has been demonstrated by psychologists, sociologists, anthropologists, and scholars of religion who have produced numerous typologies on different forms of religious expression. As demonstrated, the assumption that religion varies substantially within and between individuals and cultures is rarely entertained in the experimental neuroscience literature. The various lines of research reviewed above have mainly held the hypothesis that religious experience is fundamentally a uniform category of human experience.

Even though each of the projects proposes different hypotheses on the neural substrates of religious experience, they generally agree on the uniformity of this broad phenomenon. Persinger thus claims that the felt presence of a supernatural being, and perhaps even the origin of religion, is caused by a specific pattern of transient electrical impulses in the temporal lobe, and d'Aquili and Newberg hypothesize that the transcendental experience of absolute unitary being is caused by specific neural processes in the fronto-parietal networks.

In our study we generally interpret religious thoughts and actions in accordance with the broader theoretical framework of the brain's functional organisation. Akin to the idea that cognitive processing relies on the same regions as perception and action, we assume that complex cultural phenomena such as religious practices are subserved by the basic processing of our biologically evolved dispositions, e.g., sensory-motor activities, reward processing, and social cognition. Thus, our aim is not to map the neural correlates of the mystical or transcendental in religious experience but to describe the basic neural processing employed by religious subjects in various religious practices.

In our experimental design, we implemented a particularly strong typology that categorizes religious behaviour in two different domains containing either formalized or improvised forms of expression. Although this dual typology is reductionist in scope, it has survived scientific scrutiny for more than a century and is still being employed by top researchers in the field of cognitive anthropology and the cognitive science of religion. We do not argue that formalized and improvised forms of religion are essential categories with distinct and uniform neural correlates, but we do agree that this distinction is observable in the ethnographic and psychological data and therefore worthy of investigation. According to this general typology religious practice can be divided into two different categories depending on their structure:

(a) a highly formalized mode of religion which consists of rigidly performed rituals and prayers and (b) an improvised mode consisting of non-institutionalized and low-structured practices.

We used functional magnetic resonance imaging (fMRI) to investigate how the performance of formalized and improvised forms of praying changed the evoked BOLD response in a group of twenty young Christians belonging to the Inner Mission, a fraction of the Danish Lutheran Church known for its orthodox views. We used the Lord's Prayer as a highly formalized prayer and Personal Prayer as an improvised prayer. Praying comprises multiple subgenres and varies tremendously in form and content within and between cultures (Geertz 2008). We therefore expect that praying, like other forms of mental practice, differs widely in both cognitive content and corresponding neural correlates. Specifically, we hypothesized that social cognition and its neural substrates are particularly active in improvised prayers where religious subjects converse with a god believed to be real and capable of reciprocating personal requests (Schjoedt et al. 2009). We used a well-known rhyme of own choice to control for the effects of formalization and wishes to Santa Claus to control for the effect of improvisation. We then contrasted the four conditions in a two-by-two design and further introduced a linguistic, non-semantic base line (counting backwards from 100).

EXPERIMENTAL DESIGN DOMAIN
SPEECH ACT

	Religious	Secular
Formalized	The Lord's Prayer	Nursery Rhyme
Improvized	Personal Praying	Making wishes to Santa Claus

IX Social cognition

The contrasts between the individual conditions revealed a specific pattern of neural activity in personal praying relative to making wishes to Santa Claus as well as to the Lord's Prayer, which consisted of the anterior medial prefrontal cortex (MPFC), the temporoparietal junction, and the temporopolar region. These regions together are sometimes called the classic "theory of mind" areas in social cognition which refers to the regions' involvement in thinking about other persons' intentions, beliefs, and desires. Studies have shown that subjects playing reciprocity games against computers or abstract entities and humans recruit the anterior MPFC and the temporoparietal junction specifically for "human" interaction.

We argue that this pattern of activation in Personal Praying suggests that talking to God who is considered "real" rather than "fictitious" like Santa Claus is comparable to normal interpersonal interaction. This finding is not only interesting for the social cognitive and affective neuroscience and the cognitive science of religion. It also offers important insights to the study of theology in which Christian doctrine on God's nature includes abstract concepts like God's omnipresence, omniscience, and omnipotence. Interestingly, in terms of brain function, our results suggest that the IM participants mainly think of God as a person rather than as an abstract entity. This observation supports previous cognitive studies which have demonstrated that religious subjects are generally incapable of keeping a strict doctrinal representation of God in online cognitive processing. Christian subjects for example generally seem to answer questions about God's nature as if God is constrained by time and space like normal persons are.

X Habit forming and reward processing

Another important aspect of praying is the considerable time and energy that religious subjects spend on their prayers, e.g., devoted Muslims prostrate five times a day in prayer. The actual practice seems to be central to religious behaviour and cannot be separated from its other putative functions, e.g., dealing with epistemological questions or coping with challenges. Because of this we assumed an effect of praying in the dorsal striatum which is the dopaminergic system involved in motivating repeated behaviours. This function has been extended to the social domain in recent studies showing a relation between reward behaviours dependent on social trust in reciprocity games and activity in this system.

Based on this prior hypothesis we made a region of interest analysis of the caudate nucleus, which is involved with instrumental reinforcement. The regional analysis revealed a significant main effect of religious praying in the right caudate nucleus. This activation supports the hypothesis that religious prayer is capable of stimulating the dopaminergic system of the striatum in practicing individuals.

In King-Casas et al.'s study learning to trust partners in economic exchange games was predicted and mirrored by caudate activation. Our results suggest that intrinsic belief in God and a high confidence that God reacts to one's prayers may have similar effects on the dorsal striatum in praying subjects. This finding may provide valuable insight on how praying is reinforced at a neuronal level, and it could be a significant step towards understanding why devoted believers succeed in motivating a range of repeated behaviours. Habitual praying, however, might divert from social reinforcement learning as reported by King-Casas et al. because subject-God reciprocity exclusively relies on the anticipation of future outcomes and interpretation of past events rather than on concrete monetary rewards. Praying offers no immediate feedback, and trusting God does not depend on trivial trial and error learning.

A relevant approach to further examine the relation between the dorsal striatum and religious practice would be to study patients with infarcts or haemorrhages in this region. However, this approach requires a detailed battery of religiosity measures to separate habitual behaviours from socially dependant practices. To my knowledge, this has not yet been attempted. Another interesting approach is the study of religiosity in patients with Parkinson's disease (PD) which targets this region in order to examine how decreased dopamine levels affect religious practice. A pioneering study on this particular relation reported a significant difference between PD patients and a matched control group revealing a decrease in frequency of private practices like praying and meditation. This finding supports our hypothesis that the motivational systems of the dorsal striatum may play an important role in motivating frequently repeated religious behaviours.

XI Methodological remarks

Compared to previous studies in the field we increased the number of participants in our study, and we tried to attain maximum ecological validity by studying a religious practice which did not have to be re-experienced or induced by external stimuli. The two prayers were largely context-independent conditions because the participants were used to practicing both forms of praying in widely different contexts, e.g., at bedtime or while riding a bike. Furthermore, our results are relatively robust (thresholded at $p<0.05$ corrected for multiple comparisons), and our interpretations rely on conventional theories of brain function rather than on new claims about specific neural mechanisms or on results from other studies of complex cultural phenomena. Finally, we examined two different forms of praying rather than solely contrast religious conditions relative to non-religious conditions. This is crucial for examining differences and commonalities in various religious practices.

Our results suggest that for young Danish Christians of the Inner Mission, personal praying to God is fundamentally an intersubjective experience comparable to that of normal interpersonal interaction. In addition to this finding both forms of praying seem to be motivated by the dopaminergic reinforcement systems associated with habit forming and reward evaluation. However, praying which lies at the centre of all religions, is a complex phenomenon including acts of individual prayer, collective prayer, intercessory prayer, ritual incantation, and meditative prayer, each of them having multiple subgenres (e.g., petition, hymns, worship, thanksgiving, confession, chanting) and demonstrating significant variance across cultural contexts. Further studies of other religious groups and other forms of praying are needed to grasp the differences and commonalities of this broad category of religious practice. One example of such study is our recently completed experiment on intercessory prayer where participants listened to prayers performed by persons with differing religious status. This study explores how assumptions about the praying speaker change the brain activity in secular and Christian participants who receive intercessory prayer. The hypothesis is that religious authority, especially charismatic authority, depends on the participants' recognition of the authority as endowed with special powers. Participants who believe in healing miracles through intercessory prayer should therefore respond differently to persons who they believe have healing powers compared to persons who they believe are "ordinary" practitioners. In this study we use the participants' post-scan reports in the analysis of the brain data to correlate their subjective experience with specific brain processes. The intriguing results from this experiment are currently in preparation. Note that this study takes a context-based approach which uses the participants' expectations in interpersonal interaction as a central factor in the experimental design. This approach aims at understanding how perceived religious categories affect neural systems rather than how neural systems affect religious categories. The study exemplifies a new direction in the social cognitive neurosciences which stands in strong contrast to the standard cognitive science of religion which has mainly focused on mapping the cognitive and neural systems behind various religious behaviours and explaining religious phenomena as a function of specific cognitive mechanisms.

XII Concluding remarks

The aim of this article has been to give scholars of religion a sense of this field's limitations and potential. I have briefly introduced some of the standard procedures in cognitive experimental neuroscience, and I reviewed six lines of pioneering research on the relation between brain activity and religion which use modern imaging technologies as the tool of choice. These are not the only projects investigating the neurobiological underpinnings of religion. There exists a large number of studies using EEG and neuroimaging on religiously inspired meditation techniques, and a few studies which use clinical evidence from patients with various brain lesions. In fact there are several papers and articles on the relation between religion and brain function, but the vast majority of these only includes theoretical considerations and indirect evidence on potentially relevant brain regions and functional systems. The list of actual experiments is surprisingly short, and no one has yet examined the relation in a systematic way.

There is little doubt that the experimental neuroscience of religion holds great potential, but it is clear from the studies reviewed that it also faces serious methodological and theoretical challenges. Some of these challenges are problems general to the experimental neurosciences. Issues with the data acquisition, data analysis, and critical assumptions on brain anatomy and brain function are problems common to most studies which use imaging technology. It is reasonable to assume, however, that in time these issues will be reduced as developments in theory and methodology continue to improve. Such improvements need to be implemented in the experimental design and interpretation of the data in order to optimize future studies on religion.

Other issues that need to be addressed which are more specific to the study of religion have been reviewed in a recent article by Wildman & McNamara (2008). These include the relation between participants' subjective experience and underlying brain processes and the challenges of diversity and complexity of its subject matter. With regard to the former, future studies need to implement participants' behavioural data and subjective reports in their analysis of the brain data in order to make sure that the hypothesized relation between conscious experience and brain activity is significant. This is already being done in many social cognitive and affective imaging studies demonstrating rather convincing results as a consequence. With regard to the latter, religious practice and experience pervade the lives of billions but in many cultures there are no phenomenological equivalents to the Western concept of religious experience or the Eastern concept of meditation. Nevertheless, the majority of the studies reviewed in this article has investigated either of these two as religious experiences per se. This idea that religious and mystical experiences are uniform and well-defined categories is no longer viable in the comparative study of religion. The fact that studies still use such concepts may be due to religious agendas or cross-cultural ignorance. Unfortunately, such studies have been the ones attracting the most attention in the media. The universal aspects of transcendental and mystical experience are more appealing to the general population than the diverse and basic processes employed by different forms of less striking practices, e.g., the daily recitation of the Lord's Prayer.

If the field wishes to obtain a proper scientific dialogue with the broader disciplines of neuroscience and the general study of religion, I believe two issues stand out as critical. First, it will be necessary for future studies to use well-established theories of brain function for interpretation rather than developing new controversial hypotheses on mechanisms supposedly unique to religious experience. Expert researchers of cognitive neuroscience today offer significant insights on the neural underpinnings of both basic and complex social behaviours. Experimental researchers of religion who often approach the study with mixed educational backgrounds should use these insights as a framework for interpretation rather than trying to expand on these by making new claims about neural mechanisms specific to religion. Second, experimental neuroscience must take the diversity of religious thought and behaviour into account in order to understand the complexity of religion and to give a realistic account of distinct religious practices and experiences. Beyond the fact that religious experience and practice across cultures all recruit various forms of "normal" cognitive processing (e.g., emotions, perceptions and actions), the only common feature that religious experiences and practices seem to share is an associated link to a supernatural instance. The cognitive underpinnings of this link are difficult to define because it varies from practice to practice, from person to person, and from culture to culture. The link is sometimes made implicit and sometimes explicit; it is sometimes concrete and sometimes abstract. It is uncertain whether we will ever find a common neural substrate of such diverse association. I therefore suggest that instead of spending enormous amounts of resources to pinpoint the neural substrate of a universal link to a supernatural instance, as exemplified by Newberg and d'Aquili's and Persinger's theories, the major challenge of the experimental neuroscience of religion should be to investigate how specific cultural traditions modulate the "normal" cognitive processes of the brain. This will undoubtedly lead to less exciting theories and less spectacular results, but it will also contribute to a more sober discussion which in turn will make it more useful for the academic study of religion.

By implementing new research paradigms from the social cognitive and affective neurosciences, and using the latest methods and theories in conventional brain science, researchers should soon be able to reach a new milestone in the neuroscience of religion, where the results offer robust and credible evidence on the neural substrates of various religious phenomena. The evidence that I have introduced and reviewed in this article may pose too many issues for scholars of religion who already feel uncomfortable with the recent turn toward cognitive science in the study religion. From this perspective, the neuroscience project may be considered another attempt to reduce complex cultural phenomena to simple products of human biology. Indeed the experimental neuroscience of religion as it stands is marred by reductionist theories and unsatisfactory accounts of supposedly universal religious phenomena. However, the suggested shift of focus to how diverse cultural traditions and practices modulate the already known cognitive systems of the brain may represent a compromise, a sweet spot for future research, where comparative scholars and cognitive scientists alike could benefit from experimental neuro-science. This approach may contribute to the comparative study of religion with important insights regarding how culture-specific beliefs influence religious behavior, and on the differences of how believers with diverse cultural backgrounds react to traditional and charismatic authorities in religious interactions. With our project in Aarhus we attempt to move the field in this direction by investigating the basic neural processes employed in various forms of religious practice, and to examine how different cultural backgrounds change the brain response to various religious practices.

Questions

1 What are some of the "age-old" questions that neuroscience promises to answer or test?
2 What are the methods of analyzing the brain that are deployed? What are the dangers or pitfalls? Do you perceive any limitations in such research?
3 What does Schjoedt mean by "ecological authenticity"?
4 Outline each of the six studies that Schjoedt references.
5 What is the "God Helmet," and why is Schjoedt skeptical about it?
6 What are Azari's grounds for claiming that religious experience is cognitive rather than emotional?
7 What limitations and potential is there in the field of neuroscientific research into religious experience?
8 Why should the diversity of religious practices be taken into account by researchers in this field?
9 "The neuroscience project may be considered another attempt to reduce complex cultural phenomena to simple products of human biology. Indeed the experimental neuroscience of religion as it stands is marred by reductionist theories and unsatisfactory accounts of supposedly universal religious phenomena." Does Schjoedt consider this problem to be unsolvable? Why/why not?

AUTHOR INDEX

Althusser 303
Alvarez, Robert 66
Anselm 213, 225, 234
Aquinas, Thomas 74, 80–90, 101, 108, 130, 145–9, 159, 163, 180, 213, 236, 273, 276, 291, 299, 323, 351, 359, 390
Arce, Carlos 67
Aristotle 80, 132, 135, 145, 146, 147, 148, 159, 163, 273, 291, 311, 314, 343, 344, 346, 347, 352, 360
Arminius, Jacob 200
Athanasius 31
Athenagoras 158
Augustine 2, 31, 53, 74, 75–9, 80, 81, 82, 83, 84, 85, 86, 87, 88, 90, 107, 108, 117, 145, 147, 148, 161, 162, 163, 180, 181, 200, 207, 212, 226, 228, 252, 269, 272, 273, 275, 291, 299, 306, 307, 352, 354, 355
Azari, Nina P. 404, 405, 406, 414

Baily, Derrick Sherwin 113
Barth, Karl 33–49, 74, 93–9, 107, 108, 109, 113, 114, 118, 119, 311, 350, 361, 391, 393, 394
Basil of Caesarea 75, 107, 138–44, 201, 263
Beauregard, Mario 406
Beck, Friedrich 254
Bell, Daniel 301
Benson, Herbert 401
Berger, Peter L. 404
Bernal, Guillenno 68
Bernard of Clairvaux 372, 373, 378
Bird, Phyllis 122
Boethius 81, 82, 167
Boneta, Prous 295
Brown, Warren 178
Brümmer, Vincent 330, 339, 406

Bultmann 20
Burns, J. Patout 8, 25–32
Butler, Judith 300, 301, 303, 304, 305, 306, 307, 308, 309, 310
Bynum, Caroline 302, 303, 305, 306, 307, 309

Calvin, John 90–2, 101, 103, 104, 105, 122–3
Cambell, Donald T. 192
Cavell, Stanley 391
Chysostom, John 75, 90
Clarke, Peter G. H. 246, 259
Clement of Alexandria 159, 294
Clifford, W. K. 389
Coakley, Sarah 300, 310
Coleridge, Samuel Taylor 110–13

d'Aquili, Eugene G. 399, 400, 401, 405, 406, 407, 408, 413
Daly, Mary 291, 293
Davidson, Donald 174
de Gruchy, John 104, 105
Descartes 107–8, 117, 180, 181, 194, 237, 242, 249, 250, 252, 254, 259, 345, 366
Dionysius 81, 82
Dodds, E. R. 109
Dostoevsky 312, 325, 326
Durkheim, Emile 365

Eagleton, Terry 302, 303
Eccles, John 253, 254, 258, 295, 312, 357, 360, 373, 377
Eddy, Mary Baker 295
Edwards, Jonathan 234, 238, 241, 243, 250, 350
Einstein, Albert 251, 253
Eliade, Mircea 404

Erasmus   200, 226, 227, 233, 355
Eusebius of Caesaria   293

Farrer, Austin   253
Fichte   164
Foucault, Michel   118, 303, 305, 310
Frankfurt, Harry   347
Freud, Sigmund   303, 309
Fulkerson, Mary McClintock   100–6

Geertz, Clifford   404
Globus, Gordon   258
Graham, Elaine   330, 336, 337, 338, 339
Gregory of Nazianzus   263
Gregory of Nyssa   30, 31, 74, 83, 130,
    138–44, 161, 201, 206, 263, 268, 269,
    273, 300, 303, 305, 306, 307, 308, 309,
    310, 324
Grenz, Stanley   121
Gunton, Colin   107–16, 312
Gutierrez, Gustavo   64

Hardy, Daniel   112
Hare, R. M.   174, 175
Harris, Harriet A.   330, 341
Harrison, Verna   306, 307
Hauerwas, Stanley   309
Hegel, George Wilhelm   164
Heidegger, Martin   350, 390, 391, 394
Herbert, George   404
Hilary of Pontiers   80, 81, 84
Hodge, Charles   244
Holbach   250
Horgan, Terrence E.   174
Horton, Michael S.   117–28
Hume, David   117

Inwagen, Peter van   185, 194–7
Irenaeus   26, 57, 74, 158, 312, 319
Isasi-Diaz, Ada Maria   61–71

James, William   371, 379, 381, 404
Jeeves, Malcolm   178
Jenson, Robert   350, 360
Jerome   31
Joachim of Fiore   295
John of Damascus   83, 108
John Paul II   285, 290
Jordan, P.   253
Julian of Norwich   294
Jung, Carl G.   404

Kafka   345
Kane, Robert   250, 258
Kant, Immanuel   117, 243, 250, 350, 352,
    353, 366, 383, 390
Kelsey, David H.   361, 370
Kerr, Fergus   390, 394
Kline, Meredith   122, 126
Kümmel, Werner George   20–4

Lactantius   75
Lee, Mary Ann   295
Leibnitz, Gottfried   188–90, 194, 196,
    245, 366
Levine, Daniel   63, 65
Lewis, David   191
Lindbeck, George   361
Linzey, Andrew   114
Locke, John   117
Lombard, Peter   87
Ludemann, H.   20
Luther, Martin   161–2, 200, 226, 227,
    228, 229, 233, 252, 277, 284, 350, 355,
    357, 409
Lycurgus   228

Maduro, Mott   63
Martyr, Justin   28, 158
Mauss, Marcel   365
Maximus the Confessor   312, 320, 328
McFadyen, Alistair I.   330, 331, 332, 333,
    334, 335, 336, 341
Moltmann, Jurgen   120, 123
Murdoch, Iris   391, 394
Murphy, Nancey   170–9

Newberg, Andrew B.   399, 400, 401, 404,
    405, 406, 407, 408, 413
Nicholas of Cusa   163
Niebuhr, H. Richard   59
Niebuhr, Reinhold   103
Nietzsche, Friedrich   250, 303
Nussbaum, Martha   304

O'Donovan, Oliver   123
Origen   28–9, 31, 75, 159
Otto, Rudolph   404
Owen, John   244

Pannenberg, Wolfhart   157–69
Paquette, Vincent   406
Pelagius   1, 2, 31, 200, 207, 227, 228

Persinger, Michael A.   403, 404, 407, 408, 413
Philo   161
Plantinga, Alvin   130, 180–98
Plato   109
Poincaré   256
Pope Benedict XVI   342
Pope Eugenius III   373
Pouchet   242
Proudfoot, Wayne   404

Rähner, Karl   292, 392, 393, 394
Ramirez, Oscar   67
Richard of St. Victor   363
Ricouer, Paul   124–5
Ritschl, Albert   243
Rose, N.   199
Ruddock, Ralph   333
Ruether, Rosemary Radford   291, 299

Sartre, Jean Paul   316, 323, 324, 326, 331
Schjoedt, Uffe   395, 409, 414
Schlatter, A.   23
Schrödinger, Erwin   253, 257, 258
Schwoebel, Christoph   369
Sellars, Roy Wood   171, 172, 174
Shedd, William G. T.   234, 245
Socrates   148

Solomon   208, 281, 282, 283
Spaemann, Robert   342, 349, 370
Spinoza, Baruch   110, 118, 250, 366
Stapp, Henry   258

Tanner, Kathryn   50–60
Taylor, Charles   117
Tertullian   130, 131–7, 158, 227
Thiselton, Anthony   125
Tolstoy, Leo   384

Valentinus   207
Volf, Miroslav   312
Vos, Geerhardus   119

Welker, Michael   368, 369
Wesley, John   200
Westermann, Claus   9–19
Whitehead, A. N.   121
Williams, Rowan   308
Wolff, Hans Walter   130, 150–6
Wuketits, Franz   192
Wycliffe, John   226

Yu, Carver   110

Zizioulas, John   111, 115, 312, 329, 330, 341, 351

SUBJECT INDEX

Adam   19, 23, 27, 91, 101, 115, 118–19,
    120–6, 134, 159–62, 205, 236,
    239–42, 244–45, 278, 311, 354, 379
affection   69, 91, 141, 204, 235–8, 241,
    244–5, 266, 270, 366, 375–7,
    382–3
androgyny   294
Angel   26, 48, 124, 126, 195–6, 209,
    213–15, 217, 225, 230, 283, 303,
    307–9, 330, 364, 374
anthropology   1, 3–9, 20–1, 25–6, 28,
    30–1, 33–4, 37, 42–4, 48, 50, 52, 58,
    61–2, 64–7, 70, 73, 90, 101, 103,
    107–10, 113–15, 117, 119, 121, 129,
    150, 157–9, 161, 213, 245, 285, 287,
    299, 311, 329, 361, 362, 367, 369,
    371, 409
Apostasy   235–6, 239–41, 244
Arianism   91, 201, 250, 253–4, 256–9
Aristotelianism   80, 130, 132, 135, 145,
    159, 165, 273, 291, 311, 314, 343–4,
    347, 352, 360
art   203, 264, 309, 315–17, 319, 320–2,
    326, 374
authority 12, 36, 63, 65, 75, 80, 91, 96,
    102, 109, 110, 123, 133, 141, 277–8,
    295, 297, 364, 411

beauty   53, 54, 104, 122, 138, 204, 263,
    265, 267, 301–2, 375
biology   1, 3, 7, 36, 171, 178, 192, 247,
    256, 261, 291, 372, 414
birth   9, 12, 23, 30, 71, 86, 121, 124, 132,
    135, 159, 242, 266, 269, 278–9,
    307–8, 379, 380, 385
body   1, 2, 4, 21, 29, 48, 55, 70, 74, 78,
    85–7, 91, 107, 109, 110, 116, 119–
    21, 129–31, 133–42, 144–51, 157–9,
    163–4, 166, 168–9, 178, 180, 181–4,

    186–7, 192, 197, 203, 209, 217, 222,
    229, 232, 237, 243, 247, 251–2, 255,
    257, 267, 270–1, 277–9, 281–94,
    298, 300–3, 305–10, 317, 321–33,
    341, 345, 355, 360, 361, 363, 377,
    379, 386, 389–90, 401, 402
bondage   53, 200, 226, 304, 355, 357
brain   141, 157, 172, 173, 176–7, 179–83,
    189–92, 194, 197, 199, 246, 247,
    248, 249, 250, 251, 254–9, 261, 372,
    395–408, 396, 410–14

capacity   25, 27–9, 56, 62, 65, 66, 73–4,
    82, 93, 100, 108, 133, 162, 181,
    201, 214, 216, 280, 301, 312, 313,
    315–17, 319–29, 337, 340, 348, 357,
    364, 371, 374, 379
celibacy   263, 269, 277, 284.
Chalcedon   1, 327, 328, 350
chemistry   7, 171, 250, 256
choice   3, 26–8, 30, 43, 114, 153, 178,
    199, 204, 208, 209, 212, 226–33,
    237–44, 250, 251, 258, 266, 278,
    304, 323, 326, 327, 356–8, 392, 398,
    409, 412
church   1, 14, 17, 26, 27, 31, 34, 45,
    48–9, 50–1, 65, 74, 99, 101–5, 107,
    124–6, 129, 134, 159, 207, 226,
    261, 263, 291–3, 295, 311, 312,
    327, 330, 354–8, 366, 371, 373,
    379, 409
communion   48, 55, 113, 114, 143,
    287, 288, 312–15, 327–9, 351,
    381, 389–91
community   9, 12, 14–17, 28, 53–5, 61,
    65, 68–70, 98, 99, 106, 114–16, 142,
    262, 285, 295, 334, 338, 352–8
compatibilism   250
compulsion   229, 230, 233, 240, 245

conscience   13, 17, 43, 55, 65, 88, 103,
    104, 106, 115, 130, 157–8, 163–7,
    171–4, 183, 186–8, 234, 235, 271,
    277, 281, 389
corporeality   21, 85–7, 90, 110, 133, 140,
    142, 144–7, 158, 164
covenant   38, 39, 44, 45, 46, 48, 49, 54,
    56, 57, 93–9, 117–27, 154, 278
creation   2, 5, 9, 10–13, 18, 21, 25–6, 29,
    30, 37, 38, 44–7, 50, 51, 53, 55, 60,
    73, 74, 76, 83, 90, 91, 93–9, 101–6,
    108, 111, 113–16, 118–21, 123,
    124–7, 129, 150, 156, 158–9, 161–2,
    201–4, 208, 236, 241, 244, 252, 263,
    268, 272–3, 275, 277, 278, 280, 282,
    285–91, 293, 294, 304, 307, 313,
    315, 317–20, 323, 325, 327–9, 334,
    351, 358–9, 376, 393–5
    Creatio ex nihilo   112, 121, 242,
        318, 345
    living creation   52, 74, 82, 91, 94, 125,
        132, 134, 136, 138, 140, 145–6, 150,
        153–6, 159, 160–5, 185, 286–8, 358
    non-living creation   171
    re-creation   83, 124, 240, 393
creator   2, 9, 10, 21, 38, 39, 40, 44–9, 54,
    56, 79, 94, 96–8, 101, 111, 114–16,
    125, 133, 141, 156, 158, 160–3, 168
culture   6, 7, 10, 25, 27, 31, 50, 61, 66–9,
    105, 117, 157, 158, 167, 199, 267,
    300, 309, 325, 330, 333, 337, 364,
    365, 367–9, 371, 390, 390, 392, 396,
    406, 408, 409, 413, 414

death 9, 12–13, 15, 16, 18, 22–3, 26–30,
    39, 45, 53, 54, 57, 96, 110, 120,
    123–4, 129, 130, 134, 136, 145,
    151, 154, 155, 157, 158, 160, 200,
    202, 205, 206, 208, 209, 218, 220,
    222, 223, 225, 231, 236, 246, 251,
    252, 266, 269, 270, 282–4, 300, 302,
    306–9, 319, 321–3, 326, 327, 328,
    337, 355, 358, 374, 377, 390, 391
    mortality   56, 99, 110, 158, 160, 190,
        196, 270, 321, 385, 390
    immortality   26, 110, 120, 129, 132,
        136, 138, 158, 270, 321, 385
desire   22, 26, 29, 30, 65, 103, 109, 152–3,
    159, 188, 190, 200, 202, 205, 206,
    234–7, 239, 243, 245, 252, 265, 279,
    280, 282, 294, 296, 303, 305, 309,

    337, 348, 371, 375–7, 389, 390, 392,
    394, 410
determinism   110, 178, 246–51, 253, 254,
    256–9, 338, 365
devil   135, 206, 213, 222, 231, 270, 280,
    281, 283, 325
divine nature   84, 141, 203, 205, 363,
    378, 392
dominion   29, 74, 90–2, 95, 96, 97, 99,
    120–3, 139, 162, 289
dualism   21, 107–8, 109–10, 115, 119, 120
    mind/body dualism   120, 130
    substance   130, 131, 157–8, 180, 183,
        188, 196–8
    Thomism   130, 145–49

Ekstasis   314, 315, 318, 319, 320, 322,
    323, 324
Enlightenment   117, 162–3, 301, 364,
    366, 368
Epithumia (sinful desire)   22, 200
eschatology   26, 115, 117, 118, 119–21,
    124–7, 161, 303, 306, 310, 359
eternal life   158, 202, 229, 231
ethics   73, 80, 104, 119, 122, 125, 127,
    172, 174, 261, 321, 338, 340
evil   23, 26–8, 47, 57, 62, 91, 102, 109,
    134–5, 144, 160, 201, 204–10, 211,
    225–7, 229, 230, 235–40, 242, 244,
    245, 267, 270–1, 275, 279–83, 296,
    298, 324, 326–7
Eve   115, 118, 120, 121, 124–5, 205, 273,
    295, 354
environment   27–8, 96, 166, 171–2, 177,
    192, 246–9, 258–9, 348–9, 392

faith   9, 12, 16, 22, 23, 30, 38, 39, 42, 44,
    47, 63, 123, 125, 132, 133, 153, 167,
    202, 203, 210, 226, 227, 232, 270,
    271, 282–4, 295, 302, 308, 321, 326,
    329, 361, 362, 370, 378, 384, 387,
    388, 389, 392, 394
faculty   87, 121, 135, 140, 142, 162, 234,
    235, 240
fear   67, 70, 112, 188, 189, 201, 202, 206,
    209, 211, 222, 227, 232, 239, 243,
    249, 264, 266, 301, 306, 319, 321–2,
    376, 379, 383, 390, 392
feminist   50, 61, 93, 100–6, 262,
    291, 293–6, 300, 303, 310, 330,
    331, 336–8

flesh   4, 21–3, 26, 29, 30, 54, 57, 58, 102,
        119, 129, 134, 140, 142–4, 148, 154,
        60, 200, 201, 208, 211–12, 227, 236,
        264, 267–71, 274, 287, 288, 301,
        306, 309, 380
   Basar   128
   Sarx   20–3, 129
   Soma   20, 22
freedom   1, 2, 5, 27, 28, 40–2, 44–7, 110,
        112, 113, 115, 163, 167, 178, 199,
        202, 203, 204, 209, 213–17, 220,
        223–6, 230, 233, 242, 243, 244, 245,
        250, 251, 253, 259, 288–90, 313–17,
        319, 322, 324, 325, 326, 327, 329,
        351, 355, 357, 360, 387, 391–3
free will   1, 3, 5, 83, 130, 170, 172–3,
        178, 199, 200, 201, 206–18, 222–6,
        245, 246, 250, 251, 253–5, 257, 320,
        355–7, 373

gender   1, 61, 63, 93, 103, 106, 261–2,
        300, 302, 303, 305–10, 330, 336–7
gender constructivism   261
gender essentialism   261, 303
gender performativity   303
God   1,2, 5, 6, 9–13, 15–24, 25–30,
        33–41, 43–9, 50–60, 62, 73–9,
        80–92, 93–9, 100–16, 118–28, 129,
        132, 134–6, 140–3, 150, 153, 156,
        156, 159–63, 165–8, 173, 182–3,
        186, 195–6, 201–13, 221–2, 225–41,
        246, 252, 253, 261–5, 268–71, 273,
        274, 276, 277, 278, 279, 280, 281,
        282, 283, 284, 285, 286, 287, 288,
        289, 290, 291, 292, 293, 294, 295,
        297, 299, 300, 303, 305, 307, 308,
        309, 311, 313, 315, 317, 318, 319,
        320, 321, 322, 324, 325, 326, 327,
        328, 329, 334, 335, 336, 338, 343,
        350, 351, 352, 353, 354, 355, 356,
        357, 358, 359, 360, 361, 362, 363,
        364, 366, 371, 372, 373, 376, 377,
        378, 379, 380, 381, 382, 384, 385,
        387, 388, 389, 390, 392, 394, 395,
        397, 403, 404, 405, 406, 407, 409,
        410, 411, 414
gift   13, 30, 45, 52–54, 56, 57, 58, 96, 104,
        123, 162, 202, 204, 209, 228, 263,
        264, 268, 269, 277, 285, 286–90,
        373, 374, 377, 382, 387, 391,
        392, 394

glory   11, 33, 41, 45, 54, 57, 77, 82–3,
        103, 116, 121, 123, 124–7, 202, 204,
        206, 211, 222, 229, 263, 275, 307,
        361, 384
goodness   5, 26, 27, 29, 30, 40, 53, 55, 81,
        82, 83, 91, 101, 102, 105, 106, 115,
        122, 143, 174, 175, 202, 203, 206,
        236, 238, 296, 374, 377
grace   28, 30, 39–46, 48–9, 53, 54, 56, 57,
        59, 77, 83, 94–7, 118, 119, 123, 124,
        140, 192, 200, 204, 207, 211, 213,
        215, 216, 227, 228, 230, 231, 263,
        264, 267, 275, 280, 304, 309, 373,
        385, 391–4
Gnosticism   5, 25–6, 158, 161, 256, 294,
        295, 298
guilt   19, 23, 39, 106, 236, 237, 245, 302,
        306, 390

happiness   26, 27, 53, 202, 203, 205,
        265, 266, 280, 282, 283, 286, 287,
        342, 407
hatred   228, 234, 235, 236, 238, 243,
        266, 393.
health   11, 53, 57, 59, 155, 203–4, 218,
        232, 271, 302, 333, 348, 361,
        396, 401
heart   18, 30, 41, 45, 56, 69, 91, 100, 140,
        162, 181, 201–12, 224, 227, 229,
        236, 237, 239, 241, 251, 267, 271,
        281, 282, 286, 307, 325, 327, 328,
        333, 371, 375, 376, 380, 401
heaven   26, 56, 57, 76, 78, 86, 94, 100,
        110–11, 115, 125, 126, 136, 139,
        202–5, 208, 211, 216, 231, 232,
        265–7, 274, 278, 280, 294, 307, 360,
        376, 377, 382, 388
Heisenberg uncertainty principle   246,
        253–5, 257–9
hell   57, 133, 200, 206, 222, 227, 230,
        281, 323, 388
heterosexuality   303–5
hope   18, 19, 43, 45, 51, 57–8, 62, 98–9,
        126, 151, 158, 189, 202, 203, 204,
        211, 212, 227, 265, 301, 305, 306,
        319, 329, 377, 391
Holy Spirit   23, 45, 54, 57, 75, 92, 113,
        114, 119, 123, 124, 125, 126, 127,
        158–68, 202, 229, 230, 231, 240,
        244, 264, 282, 295, 351–3, 355, 357,
        358

humanity   1–3, 5, 7–9, 11, 13, 18–20, 25,
    26, 28–30, 33, 39, 43–56, 58, 59, 63,
    64, 66, 70, 71, 74, 75, 93, 99, 101,
    102, 104, 105, 108, 109, 114–16,
    118–20, 122, 127, 138, 157, 159,
    169, 201, 220, 250, 277, 288–91,
    294–9, 318, 325, 327, 328, 344,
    350, 390–4
hypostasis   148, 149, 311, 314, 315, 318,
    354

identity   58, 66, 70, 105, 119, 120, 125,
    133–4, 167–9, 176, 183, 287, 300,
    303, 304, 311, 314, 323, 328, 329,
    330, 331, 332, 333, 334, 339, 340,
    342, 346, 347, 350, 352, 353, 355,
    359, 360, 363
Image of God (*Imago Dei*)   2, 5, 9, 28,
    29, 30, 55, 59, 73–4, 75–9, 80–9,
    91–9, 100–9, 112–17, 120–8, 133,
    138, 141, 161, 201, 204, 206, 273,
    275, 276, 278, 285, 286, 288, 290–2,
    294, 308, 334, 336, 350, 378–80,
    394, 403
immateriality   5, 129, 130, 150, 250, 252,
    267, 268
immortality   120, 136, 138, 158, 171, 180,
    181, 195–97, 270, 321, 385.
immutability   229
incompatibilism   178, 250, 257, 327, 387
inclination   54, 91, 169, 230, 234, 236–45,
    252, 264

Jesus Christ   22–3, 26, 28–9, 31, 40–2, 47,
    53, 54, 56, 74, 91, 99, 101, 114, 132,
    141, 202, 203, 204, 205, 206, 209,
    210, 227, 232, 252, 264, 291, 292,
    294, 295, 297, 298, 353, 354, 355,
    357, 358, 391, 392, 393
    Christological anthropology   25–31,
        33–9, 43–9, 168
    incarnation   30, 47, 54, 57, 122,
        126, 162
    Logos   74, 162, 166, 167, 291–4
    Messiah   293–5
    Preincarnate Son   126
    Second Adam   118, 119
    Son of God   39, 44, 46, 121–4,
        202, 363
    Word of God   33, 34, 35, 36–42, 45,
        47, 76, 95, 97, 99

judgment   22, 199, 214–17, 225, 263, 291,
    334, 339, 376, 379, 381–2
justice   50, 122, 154, 216, 227, 236, 317,
    328, 353

Kingdom of God   44, 202, 204, 297
knowledge   1, 11, 13, 26, 29, 30, 33, 34,
    36, 39–40, 42, 47–8, 51–2, 76, 78,
    84, 85, 87, 88, 101, 111, 134, 135,
    141, 145, 146–7, 157, 161–3, 165,
    167, 192, 202, 203, 205, 208, 210,
    211, 213, 234, 237, 241, 258, 265,
    323–5, 337, 345, 353, 363, 365, 368,
    375, 381, 390, 391, 393, 396, 405,
    411

language   90, 106, 117, 118, 122, 167,
    177, 190, 208, 227, 231, 232, 297,
    299, 305, 311, 342, 343, 349, 352–4,
    356, 358, 359, 361, 370, 388
Libertarianism   250, 253, 254, 256–9
liberty   29, 30, 214–16, 223–5
life   5, 10, 12–13, 16–18, 22–4, 26–31, 43,
    45, 45, 50–5, 58, 59, 62, 63 ,66–7,
    77, 82, 85, 91–7, 99,   103, 112–13,
    115, 118, 120–1, 123–5, 129–30,
    133, 134, 136, 138–40, 143–6, 150,
    152, 69, 172, 175, 185, 186, 192,
    202, 203, 204, 205, 206, 207, 209,
    211, 213, 218, 222, 223, 225, 226,
    227, 229, 231, 236, 242, 252, 263,
    264, 265, 266, 267, 268, 269, 271,
    274, 280, 281, 282, 283, 284, 287,
    288, 297, 300, 301, 302, 303, 304,
    305, 306, 307, 308, 309, 321, 324,
    328, 335, 336, 337, 340, 347, 351,
    353, 354, 355, 357, 358, 359, 365,
    374, 376, 379, 381, 382, 383, 384,
    385, 386, 387, 389, 390, 391, 392,
    393, 394
likeness   48, 73, 75, 76, 81–4, 86, 90–4,
    96–101, 105, 108, 116, 120–6, 138,
    141, 142, 144–6, 158, 162, 167, 204,
    269, 274, 275, 351, 394
law   27, 12, 17, 21, 22, 28, 31, 48, 104,
    105, 118, 136, 139, 140, 155, 171,
    173, 174, 177, 178, 202, 205, 206,
    209, 210, 226–8, 235, 236, 237, 241,
    242, 246, 249, 250, 254, 256, 267,
    268, 271, 277–8, 298, 309, 340, 348,
    357, 364–6, 376, 381, 389–90

Liberation theology   297, 393
love   24, 26, 29, 30, 40, 41, 46, 54, 56, 83,
         85–8, 111, 114, 130, 140, 153, 154,
         167, 207, 209, 210, 220, 225, 227,
         230, 234–7, 239, 243, 245, 249, 263,
         268, 275, 281, 282, 286–90, 295, 296,
         298, 306, 314–17, 319, 320, 323, 324,
         327, 330, 337–40, 351, 363, 373–5,
         377, 378, 384, 388, 391, 406–8
lust   151, 205, 208, 245, 270, 271, 280

marriage   2, 12, 31, 262, 263, 266,
         268–72, 277, 278–84, 304, 306
memory   11, 64, 87, 88, 158, 306, 319,
         345, 379, 405, 406
mind   14, 21–2, 24, 51, 74, 76, 77, 81–3,
         85–8, 91, 107, 108, 110–12, 115–17,
         120, 123, 131, 133, 135, 137, 140–2,
         151, 153, 171, 172, 174, 176, 182,
         204, 206, 207, 214, 217, 219, 224,
         226–8, 238, 241, 243, 251, 252, 254,
         257–8, 266, 267, 269, 270, 275, 281,
         293, 294, 303, 306, 309, 314–17,
         325, 341, 352, 364, 365, 373, 376,
         379, 383, 386, 401, 410
   intellect   66, 76, 81, 82, 83, 85–7, 92,
         95, 107, 108, 115, 140–2, 147–9,
         160, 162, 163, 173, 178, 202, 203,
         213, 234–5, 245, 248, 267, 274–5,
         302, 369, 384, 387
   rationality   29, 73, 74, 76, 77, 81, 85,
         88, 101, 107–8, 121, 139–40, 144,
         161, 163, 166–8
   reason   28, 76–8, 80, 84–6, 88, 93, 105,
         107–10, 113, 115, 120–1, 130, 139–
         40, 144, 147, 161, 166, 178, 188
morality   5, 199, 242, 246, 280, 281,
         338, 348
mystery   45, 96, 99, 134, 194, 197, 198,
         232, 269, 286–90, 292, 309, 317,
         318, 325, 328, 336

nature   202, 203, 205, 214, 216, 217, 222,
         225–7, 230, 231, 235–6, 239–41,
         244–6, 253, 254, 257, 258, 261, 262,
         264, 266–9, 271, 274, 275, 278, 279,
         280, 283, 285, 288, 291–6, 298, 299,
         304, 305, 308, 311, 313, 317–28,
         330, 334–8, 341, 345–9, 351, 358,
         363, 364, 367, 378, 380–2, 385, 388,
         391–4, 405, 410

naturalism   171, 190, 193
necessity   3, 47, 84, 142–4, 146, 181, 209,
         214, 215, 218, 222, 224, 226, 229,
         231, 233, 242, 243, 245, 267, 283,
         291, 304, 317–19, 324, 367, 369
neoplatonism   75, 201, 352, 392
Nephesh   129, 130, 150, 159, 162,
         252, 358
neuroscience   199, 246, 371, 395–7, 399,
         400, 408, 410, 412–14

obedience   27, 30, 37, 41, 91, 119, 205,
         235, 244, 270, 282, 327, 391.
ontology   74, 107–10, 114, 116, 119,
         129–98, 312, 314, 316–17, 320, 321,
         327, 328, 336.
ordination   105, 291, 292, 299
original sin   200, 234, 238, 241, 244,
         323, 390

peace   9, 43–5, 53, 98, 207, 209, 230, 282,
         296, 374, 376, 382, 388
Pelagian Controversy   2 07, 211, 212,
         231, 301
perfection   25, 26, 40, 78, 91, 120,
         140, 231, 269, 273, 295, 307,
         309, 383
person   1–7, 9–12, 16–18, 20, 25, 26–30,
         32, 42, 44, 46, 48, 67, 70, 77, 80,
         84, 86, 107–22, 129–30, 136–8,
         144, 145, 148–52, 155–8, 160,
         162, 167–72, 180–2, 196, 199, 200,
         202–5, 206, 210, 217, 242–3, 246,
         247, 252, 278, 279, 287, 288–90,
         294, 295, 297, 298, 302, 303, 309,
         311–18, 320–6, 328, 330–40, 342,
         343, 345–8, 350–3, 355, 358–71,
         382, 387, 410, 413
personality   110, 112, 167, 247, 252, 311,
         313, 329, 331–3, 387
personhood   6, 115–17, 120, 121, 168,
         169, 172, 199, 285, 294, 298, 311–31,
         333–40, 342–3, 345, 347, 349, 351,
         353–5, 357–63, 365, 367, 369
physicalism   5, 130, 157, 170–9
Platonism   27, 28–29, 75, 158, 358
pleasure   27, 29, 44, 48, 62, 69, 78, 110,
         163, 168, 205, 243, 265–8, 270, 281,
         282, 305, 309, 337, 376
pneuma   20, 21, 22, 129, 160–1, 313, 329
pneumatology   124, 313, 329

power   11–13, 18, 21–2, 26–7, 29, 30,
    31, 44–7, 52, 56, 64–6, 72, 87, 96,
    99, 103, 104, 123–5, 138–40, 142,
    146, 155, 160, 163, 165–6, 199, 203,
    209, 211, 213–20, 222–5, 227, 228,
    230–1, 233, 237–9, 244, 245, 251,
    266, 267, 269, 271, 273, 274, 277,
    278, 280, 288–9, 293, 297–8, 300,
    302–7, 310, 325, 356, 358, 363–4,
    368–9, 380, 385–7, 397–8
prayer   17, 18, 29–31, 50, 63, 227, 246,
    265, 295, 377, 381, 386, 389, 395,
    399, 401, 402, 408–11, 413
procreation   69, 97, 263, 268, 272, 276,
    288–90, 294, 323
promise   15, 45, 48, 96–9, 107, 119, 126,
    167, 169, 202–6, 208, 246, 278, 305,
    357, 371, 375, 398, 414
psyche   129, 150, 153, 156, 252, 333, 341,
    358
psychology   1, 7, 36, 51–2, 67, 131, 167,
    171, 199, 234, 237, 244, 261, 311,
    316, 321, 322, 331, 333, 404
punishment   16, 18, 23, 27, 96, 133, 210,
    211, 229, 236, 270, 322
purity   30, 44, 45, 48, 203–6, 263–5, 267,
    277, 296, 301, 351

race   3, 18, 23, 99, 102–3, 106, 109, 269,
    271, 344, 377
rationality   29, 74, 96, 101, 108, 144,
    330–3, 335, 336, 338, 340
rectitude 119, 214–25
reductive materialism   171–2, 180, 185,
    188, 190, 193, 195, 197
resurrection   5, 28, 30, 39, 45, 54, 116,
    123, 126, 127, 129, 158, 169, 252,
    253, 305–9, 322, 326, 359, 391, 393
righteousness   90, 120, 122, 127, 138,
    203, 208, 227, 240, 297, 301, 377,
    386

salvation   1, 2, 20, 22, 24, 26, 27, 29, 30,
    31, 50, 57, 96, 98, 101, 118, 212,
    222, 227–9, 231, 232, 265, 279, 280,
    284, 295, 302, 323, 385
satan   201, 230, 232, 356, 357, 358
scholasticism   80, 102, 123, 159, 161, 163,
    213, 234, 291, 359
science   34, 35, 36, 37, 38, 52, 130, 131,
    137, 157, 169, 171, 175, 182, 183,

    189, 197, 199, 234, 235, 246, 267,
    268, 271, 277, 281, 295, 313, 315,
    334, 352, 366, 371, 382, 386, 387,
    388, 389, 395, 396, 397, 399, 400,
    408, 409, 410, 412, 413, 414
Ssrvant   10, 45, 121, 122, 123, 125, 210,
    211, 215, 235, 297
sex   97, 69, 77, 86, 95, 269–70, 274, 284,
    287–92, 300, 303, 304, 390
sexuality   1, 3, 5, 6, 69, 70, 106, 261–3,
    269, 272, 277, 284–5, 288, 291, 294,
    299, 302, 304, 310
simplicity   204, 359
sin   2, 5, 18, 20–4, 26–7, 29, 31, 33, 39–
    44, 46–9, 53, 54, 57, 76, 78, 79, 83,
    91, 99, 101–3, 105–6, 114, 118–20,
    125, 129, 144, 166, 200, 205, 204,
    205, 206, 208, 210, 213, 214, 215,
    219, 222, 223, 224, 225, 227, 228,
    235, 236, 240, 244, 245, 270, 273,
    274, 275, 278, 279, 280, 312, 322,
    354, 358, 371, 374, 378, 379
slave   17, 21, 22, 44, 200, 214, 215, 218,
    222–4, 230–2, 297, 327
slavery   21, 201, 213, 223, 224, 293, 325,
    326, 357
socialism   296
society   7, 9, 14, 15, 17, 27, 59, 66, 67, 71,
    90, 92, 100, 104, 143, 171, 203, 251,
    252, 265, 269, 270, 272, 291, 294,
    296, 297, 313, 315, 337, 338, 365,
    369, 404
sociology   1, 3, 7, 36, 52, 261, 365, 367
Socrates   135, 148, 251, 358–60, 391
soteriology   119, 127, 200, 360, 393
soul   21, 76, 81, 86–8, 91, 101, 104,
    107–11, 117, 119, 121, 129–30,
    131–6, 138, 140, 142, 144, 145–50,
    153, 157–60, 162–4, 171–2, 180,
    201, 203, 205, 206, 220, 228, 234–7,
    249–54, 257, 259, 265, 267, 268,
    270, 271, 279–81, 284, 287, 301,
    302, 306, 308, 321, 358–60, 366,
    375–8, 381, 383, 386–7, 389–90
  Nephesh   129, 130, 150, 159, 162,
    252, 358
  Psuche   20, 21
spirit   5, 21–2, 26, 29–30, 31, 35, 54, 55,
    70, 76–7, 85, 87, 90, 102, 107, 115,
    124, 129, 131, 133–5, 140, 150,
    155, 159–60, 162, 164, 165, 172,

178, 201–2, 207, 229–31, 240, 242,
244–5, 249, 250, 252, 265, 282–3,
294, 295, 321, 351–3, 355, 357–9,
374, 381, 388
pneuma　20, 21, 161
Ruach　129, 150

temptation　27, 46–7, 102, 217, 219–22,
263, 268, 298, 327, 359
transmigration　143, 158
Trinity　31, 50, 74, 75, 85–8, 108–9,
111–12, 201, 295, 311, 315, 318,
335, 350, 353, 362–3
truth　33–5, 37–9, 41, 44, 47, 49, 77,
99, 111, 122, 123, 132, 133, 144,
157, 162–4, 166, 167, 168, 181,
203, 208, 213, 216, 218, 222, 226,
243, 244, 263, 266, 269, 273, 283,
285, 286–92, 303, 309, 323–4, 336,
343–5, 351, 355, 357, 364, 384–5,
389, 391–2, 394, 401

Universe　1, 28–9, 50, 58, 79, 81–2, 100,
107, 111, 116, 119, 135, 142–3, 189,

199, 203, 205, 242, 246, 249, 264,
273, 275, 293, 323, 352, 381, 385,
388, 392

virgin　209, 262–9, 280, 307
virginity 27, 31, 262–9, 280, 307
virtue　26, 27, 37–8, 44–5, 47–8, 55, 81,
97, 104, 107–8, 114, 120, 123, 134,
138, 142–4, 167–8, 175, 184, 205–6,
235, 263–5, 269–71, 274, 277, 283,
287, 296, 308, 315, 333, 353–4, 361
volition　130, 170, 234, 237–45, 307, 347–8

will　1–5, 22, 23, 26, 59, 83, 86, 87, 88,
91, 93, 103, 112, 123, 130, 138,
141, 143, 158, 170, 172, 173, 178–9,
199–245, 356, 357, 377, 392
wisdom　12, 14, 26, 32, 41, 42, 52–3, 74,
76, 82, 132, 139, 154, 155, 161–2,
169, 203, 227, 232, 271, 280, 294–5,
304, 306, 310, 374, 379, 382
worship　6, 10, 106, 154, 161, 284, 352,
371, 379, 411
wrath　19, 41, 98–9, 205, 208, 211, 280